POVERTY REDUCTION AND GROWTH:
VIRTUOUS AND VICIOUS CIRCLES

THE PRINCIPAL AUTHORS OF THIS BOOK ARE AS FOLLOWS:

Chapter 1:   Guillermo E. Perry, J. Humberto López, and William F. Maloney
Chapter 2:   William F. Maloney
Chapter 3:   J. Humberto López
Chapter 4:   J. Humberto López
Chapter 5:   J. Humberto López
Chapter 6:   J. Humberto López
Chapter 7:   William F. Maloney
Chapter 8:   Omar S. Arias
Chapter 9:   Omar S. Arias

POVERTY REDUCTION AND GROWTH: VIRTUOUS AND VICIOUS CIRCLES

Guillermo E. Perry
Omar S. Arias
J. Humberto López
William F. Maloney
Luis Servén

THE WORLD BANK
Washington, D.C.

© 2006 The International Bank for Reconstruction and Development / The World Bank
1818 H Street NW
Washington DC 20433
Telephone: 202-473-1000
Internet: www.worldbank.org
E-mail: feedback@worldbank.org

All rights reserved

1 2 3 4 5 09 08 07 06

This volume is a product of the staff of the International Bank for Reconstruction and Development / The World Bank. The findings, interpretations, and conclusions expressed in this volume do not necessarily reflect the views of the Executive Directors of The World Bank or the governments they represent.

The World Bank does not guarantee the accuracy of the data included in this work. The boundaries, colors, denominations, and other information shown on any map in this work do not imply any judgement on the part of The World Bank concerning the legal status of any territory or the endorsement or acceptance of such boundaries.

Rights and Permissions

The material in this publication is copyrighted. Copying and/or transmitting portions or all of this work without permission may be a violation of applicable law. The International Bank for Reconstruction and Development / The World Bank encourages dissemination of its work and will normally grant permission to reproduce portions of the work promptly.

For permission to photocopy or reprint any part of this work, please send a request with complete information to the Copyright Clearance Center Inc., 222 Rosewood Drive, Danvers, MA 01923, USA; telephone: 978-750-8400; fax: 978-750-4470; Internet: www.copyright.com.

All other queries on rights and licenses, including subsidiary rights, should be addressed to the Office of the Publisher, The World Bank, 1818 H Street NW, Washington, DC 20433, USA; fax: 202-522-2422; e-mail: pubrights@worldbank.org.

ISBN-10: 0-8213-6511-8
ISBN-13: 978-0-8213-6511-3
eISBN-10: 0-8213-6512-6
eISBN-13: 0-8213-6512-0
DOI: 10.1596/978-0-8213-6511-3

Library of Congress Cataloging-in-Publication Data

Poverty reduction and growth : virtuous and vicious circles / Guillermo E. Perry ... [et al.].
    p. cm - (World Bank Latin American and Caribbean studies)
  Includes bibliographical references and index.
  ISBN-13: 978-0-8213-6511-3
  ISBN-10: 0-8213-6511-8
    1. Poverty-Latin America. 2. Latin America—Economic conditions—1945– 3. Poverty—Government policy—Latin America. 4. Latin America—Economic policy. I. Perry, Guillermo. II. World Bank. III. Series.

HC130.P6P72 2006
339.4'6098—dc22

2005057764

Cover art: Remedios Varo, "Spiral Transit" © 2005 Artists Rights Society (ARS), New York / VEGAP, Madrid.

For more information on publications from the World Bank's Latin America and the Caribbean Region, please visit www.worldbank.org/lacpublications (o en Español: www.bancomundial.org/publicaciones).

Contents

Foreword xi

Acknowledgments xiii

Acronyms and Abbreviations xv

Chapter 1: From Vicious to Virtuous Circles 1
    Poverty as a multidimensional and dynamic concept 1
    The twin disappointments: Destiny or choice? 2
    The link from growth and development to income-poverty reduction 4
    Closing the virtuous circle: The link from poverty to growth 5
    Global convergence clubs 6
    Does poverty matter for growth? 7
    Regional convergence clubs 8
    Household-level poverty traps 9
    Implications of the report 11
    Pro-growth poverty reduction 15
    Notes 19

Chapter 2: Dimensions of Well-Being, Channels to Growth 21
    Income poverty 21
    Beyond income and consumption 27
    Why not just ask them? 29
    Snapshots vs. movies: Life-cycle welfare, mobility, and risk 31
    Intergenerational mobility 37
    Conclusion 40
    Annex 2A: Estimating the monetary value of mortality changes 41
    Annex 2B: A tractable welfare measure that captures income, mobility, and risk 42
    Annex 2C: Intergenerational mobility in Latin America: Country comparison 42
    Notes 42

Chapter 3: How Did We Get Here? 45
    Per capita income in Latin America: A long-run comparative perspective 46
    Long-run inequality 53
    Notes 56

Chapter 4: The Relative Roles of Growth and Inequality for Poverty Reduction 57
    The relative roles of growth and income distribution for poverty reduction 59
    Growth and inequality: Bringing country specificity into the picture 63
    Concluding remarks 70
    Annex 4A: Testing for lognormality of income 71
    Notes 72

CONTENTS

Chapter 5: Pro-Poor Growth in Latin America **75**
   Are all pro-growth policies equally pro-poor? 76
   Does the composition of growth matter? 89
   The role of taxes and transfers in reducing income inequality 92
   Concluding remarks 100
   Annex 5A: Simulating the impact of pro-growth policies on poverty 101
   Notes 102

Chapter 6: Does Poverty Matter for Growth? **103**
   A poverty-traps view of the development process 104
   Empirical evidence on poverty traps 108
   What is the empirical evidence on poverty's impact on growth? 115
   Transmissions channels from poverty to growth? 118
   Concluding remarks 123
   Annex 6A 124
   Notes 126

Chapter 7: Subnational Dimensions of Growth and Poverty **129**
   What is spatial inequality, how is it measured, and what are the regional trends? 129
   Identifying spatial concentration 130
   Why do we observe regional convergence clubs? 135
   Does migration work as an equilibrating mechanism? 138
   The link back to growth and policy issues 139
   Conclusions 143
   Notes 143

Chapter 8: Microdeterminants of Incomes: Labor Markets, Poverty, and Traps? **145**
   The distribution of earnings: The role of worker endowments and labor markets 146
   Microdrivers of changes in the income distribution 151
   Determinants of income dynamics: Lessons from rural El Salvador 152
   Implications for policies 159
   Annex 8A: Data and methodological details 160
   Notes 162

Chapter 9: Breaking the Cycle of Underinvestment in Human Capital in Latin America **165**
   The educational transition in the region: Slow and unbalanced progress 166
   Poverty and human capital: A two-way relationship 167
   Human capital formation: Sources of underinvestment traps 169
   The educational ladder in Latin America: A persisting educational divide 171
   Liquidity constraints, family factors, and educational investments: A sneak preview 178
   The private value of schooling: How much does it pay? To whom? 181
   Short-term or long-term poverty: Which is more pressing for schooling investments? 190
   Implications for human capital formation policies 194
   Investing now: The demographic window of opportunity 196
   Annex 9A: Data and methodological details 197
   Notes 199

Bibliography **203**

Index **217**

Boxes

Chapter 2
   2.1   Income poverty lines 23
   2.2   National accounts and household surveys-based growth: How different are they? 25
   2.3   Inflation inequality: What really happened to LAC poverty and inequality 26
   2.4   Mobility and poverty traps 32
   2.5   Is it inequality or risk? Maybe Latin America has less inequality than we thought 34
   2.6   . . . Or maybe more: Inequality and demographics 35

Chapter 4
4.1 Decomposing poverty into growth and income distribution effects ... 60
4.2 The size distribution of income ... 64
4.3 Total growth elasticities of poverty and the efficiency of growth ... 65

Chapter 5
5.1 Trade policy and income risk ... 82
5.2 Taxes, transfers, and inequality ... 96
5.3 Conditional cash transfers in Colombia ... 98

Chapter 6
6.1 Education and technology ... 107
6.2 Is Latin America different? ... 117

Chapter 7
7.1 Tools to detect spatial association ... 131
7.2 Will trade liberalization increase regional disparities? NAFTA and Mexico ... 136
7.3 Trade-offs in regional policy: The Spanish experience ... 140
7.4 Rural roads and poverty reduction in El Salvador ... 142

Figures

Chapter 1
1.1 Per capita income relative to the OECD, 1870–2000 ... 2
1.2 Gini coefficient for Latin America, 1950–2000 ... 2
1.3 Poverty rates in Latin America, 1950–2000 ... 2
1.4 Low educational traps persist across generations among the poor and excluded ... 3
1.5 Although they stand to gain the most from education, poor people actually have low returns ... 3
1.6 Gini coefficients for market and disposable incomes ... 5
1.7 Indicators for poor and rich countries ... 7
1.8 Convergence clubs in life expectancy throughout the world ... 8
1.9 Poverty and investment throughout the world ... 8
1.10 Regional income dynamics in Brazil: The persistence of two convergence clubs ... 9
1.11 The sharp educational divide between the poor and the rich in Latin America ... 10
1.12 Total tax revenue versus per capita income, throughout the world ... 18

Chapter 2
2.1 Poverty in selected Latin American countries ... 22
2.2 The evolution of Latin American poverty during the 1990s ... 24
2.3 Gini coefficient for Latin America, 1950–2000 ... 25
2.4 Income poverty profile for Bolivia: Self-rated by head of household versus data driven ... 30
2.5 Elasticity of son's income relative to father's income ... 38
2.6 Mobility indicators ... 39

Chapter 3
3.1 Per capita GDP for eight major Latin American countries, 1850–2000 ... 48
3.2 Per capita growth and initial income levels in eight major Latin American countries ... 48
3.3 Cross-country dispersion of per capita GDP in Latin America, 1870–2000 ... 49
3.4 Aggregate per capita income in Latin America, 1850–2000 ... 49
3.5 Per capita income of five groups relative to the United States, 1850–2000 ... 51
3.6 Incomes in Spain and peripheral Europe relative to OECD countries ... 51
3.7 GDP per capita in Latin America relative to several country groupings, 1850–2000 ... 52
3.8 Latin American per capita GDP relative to Western Europe, 1500–2001 ... 53
3.9 Income inequality in the United States and Spain, 1910–90 ... 55
3.10 Income inequality in the United Kingdom and France, 1910–90 ... 55

Chapter 4
- 4.1 Growth, inequality, and poverty reduction throughout the world ... 58
- 4.2 Decomposition of poverty into growth and distribution effect ... 60
- 4.3 Share of changes in poverty explained by growth and inequality ... 62
- 4.4 Share of changes in Latin American poverty explained by growth and inequality ... 63
- 4.5 Empirical and theoretical quintiles ... 67
- 4.6 Iso-poverty curves for headcount poverty ... 68
- 4.7 Mapping Latin American countries in the income inequality space ... 69

Chapter 5
- 5.1 Policies, growth, distributional change, and poverty reduction ... 76
- 5.2 Incidence of public spending in Latin America ... 84
- 5.3 Enrollment rates for secondary education relative to per capita GDP, for selected Latin American countries ... 88
- 5.4 Institutions and per capita income levels ... 88
- 5.5 Rural and urban headcount poverty rates ... 89
- 5.6 Potential spillovers between rural and nonrural GDP ... 90
- 5.7 Relative labor intensity per sector ... 91
- 5.8 Poverty changes and labor-intensive growth throughout the world ... 91
- 5.9 The impact of public transfers on income inequality ... 92
- 5.10 Gini coefficient in selected countries before and after taxes and transfers ... 94
- 5.11 Total tax revenue versus per capita income, throughout the world ... 95
- 5.12 Social protection spending mix in Latin America ... 99
- 5.13 Impact of social insurance and social assistance programs on inequality ... 99
- 5.14 Incremental tax rate needed to halve poverty in 10 years ... 100

Chapter 6
- 6.1 Traditional view of the growth-poverty relationship ... 105
- 6.2 Poverty-traps view of the growth-poverty relationship ... 105
- 6.3 Multiple equilibriums in the presence of increasing returns to scale ... 105
- 6.4 Interest rate spreads in Latin America, 2003 ... 106
- 6.5 Growth in developed (OECD) and developing countries, 1963–2000 ... 108
- 6.6 Income in Latin America relative to the OECD countries, 1960–2002 ... 108
- 6.7 Histograms for per capita income, 1960s versus the 1990s ... 110
- 6.8 Histograms for per capita income in Latin America, 1960s versus the 1990s ... 112
- 6.9 Twin peaks ... 112
- 6.10 Equilibrium and distribution in 1999 ... 113
- 6.11 Latin American states: One peak? ... 113
- 6.12 Convergence clubs in life expectancy ... 114
- 6.13 Income, poverty and investment ... 118

Chapter 7
- 7.1 Variation in regional poverty rates in Latin America ... 130
- 7.2 Income dynamics and space in Brazil ... 132
- 7.3 Income dynamics and space in Brazil at the municipal level ... 133
- 7.4 Income dynamics and space in Chile ... 134
- 7.5 Income dynamics and space in Mexico ... 134
- 7.6 The distribution of municipal incomes and life expectancy in Brazilian municipalities ... 135
- 7.7 Social indicators in Mexico, by period ... 135
- 7.8 Poverty rates versus poverty densities in Brazil ... 141

Chapter 8
- 8.1 Productivity and wages go hand in hand ... 147
- 8.2 Earnings gap between the formal and informal sectors in Bolivia, 2002 ... 149
- 8.3 Transitions between the formal and informal sectors, and between salaried employment and self-employment in Mexico, 1987–2001 ... 151
- 8.4 Complementarities in the income generation process in rural El Salvador ... 156
- 8.5 Sources of persistent poverty and low incomes in rural El Salvador ... 158
- 8A.1 Differences in returns to education ... 161
- 8A.2 Changes in returns over time ... 161

Chapter 9
9.1 Latin America is in a slow educational transition 166
9.2 Most Latin American countries show deficits in secondary and tertiary enrollments .167
9.3 Poverty is higher in families in which parents have little education 168
9.4 Children and youth in poor families have low educational attainment 168
9.5 Educational attainment of working age population, by country 172
9.6 Educational attainment for the poorest 30 percent and the richest 30 percent in Argentina,
 Mexico, Brazil, and El Salvador 174
9.7 Educational attainment for urban and rural areas in Nicaragua, El Salvador, Brazil, and Bolivia 175
9.8 Educational attainment for three age groups in Argentina, Colombia, Mexico, and El Salvador 176
9.9 Low educational attainment is reinforced in current cohorts 177
9.10 Poor children and youth stay out of school because of high costs and low benefits 179
9.11 Opportunity costs and schooling gaps get larger for secondary to post-secondary school-age children 180
9.12 Low education continues for generations, especially among the poor 181
9.13 Average rates of return for education increase at the tertiary level 182
9.14 The returns to education differ for urban and rural labor markets 184
9.15 Differences in returns to education in Brazil largely reflect unequal human capital
 and a secondary effect of skin color 185
9.16 Returns to each level of education for the three tiers of the earnings distribution 187
9.17 Correlation between returns to each level of education and poverty 188
9.18 Returns to education are generally lower for workers at the bottom of the earnings scale 189
9.19 Education quality differences lead to differential returns to education in Brazil 191
9.20 Factors that have an impact on moving up the educational ladder 192
9.21 The demographic transition and human capital accumulation—an opportunity that should not be missed 197
9A.1 Labor force by educational level 197

Tables

Chapter 1
1.1 Growth rates needed to compensate for a 1-percentage-point increase in inequality 4

Chapter 2
2.1 Poverty in Latin America 22
2.2 Economic growth in Latin America 24
2.3 Welfare gains from increased longevity 29
2.4 Welfare comparisons: Argentina and Mexico 36
2.5 Intergenerational transition matrix for Colombia, 1997 38

Chapter 3
3.1 Economic growth in eight major Latin American countries 47
3.2 Aggregate per capita growth in Latin America 49
3.3 Economic growth in several reference groups 50
3.4 Inequality in Latin America 1950–2000, as measured by Gini coefficients 54

Chapter 4
4.1 Poverty, growth, and redistribution in Latin America 61
4.2 Growth and inequality elasticity of poverty 66
4.3 Impact on poverty of different growth scenarios 68
4.4 Growth rates needed to compensate for a 1 percent increase in inequality 69

Chapter 5
5.1 Economic policies and growth: Review of the evidence 77
5.2 Economic policies and income inequality: Review of the evidence 79
5.3 Growth and inequality regressions 85
5.4 Net growth elasticities of poverty to selected policies 86
5.5 Institutional quality in Latin America 89
5.6 Poverty reduction and sectoral growth 91
5.7 How much is Latin America undercollecting? 96
5.8 Results of simulations of income-neutral growth rate and incremental tax rate 100

Chapter 6
6.1	Median income in Latin America and the Caribbean relative to the industrial countries	109
6.2	Median income of convergence clubs	111
6.3	Does financial sector development play a role in the poverty-investment interaction?	119
6.4	Does poverty lead to lower secondary education?	120
6.5	The impact of risk on growth	123

Chapter 7
7.1	Typology of appropriate actions according to poverty rate and density	141
7.2	Public investment effects in Mexico, 1970–2000	142

Chapter 8
8.1	Decompositions of poverty and inequality changes in Argentina, 1992–2001	152
8.2	Decompositions of poverty and inequality changes in Peru, 1997–2002	152
8.3	Determinants of rural individual wages, El Salvador	153
8.4	Determinants of rural per capita family incomes, El Salvador	154
8.5	Permanent and transitory poverty in rural El Salvador, 1995–2001	157

Chapter 9
9.1	Average years of schooling in the "1–12" educational system and excess years spent in school, 6–18 age range, circa 2000	178

Foreword

LATIN AMERICA'S DEVELOPMENT IN THE PAST few decades has been characterized by two disappointments: lagging growth and persistent poverty and inequality. Set against the performance of other regions, notably China and India, and the East Asian miracles before them, Latin America's average annual growth of 4.2 percent in 2005 is at best modest, and at worst, inadequate to tackle poverty quickly. And the region's poverty remains acute, with one quarter of Latin Americans with incomes of under $2 a day, and the highest measures of inequality in the world.

Over the past decade, the World Bank, through the flagship publications of the Latin American and Caribbean Region, has sought to understand these issues individually. In the area of growth, we have looked at the impact of structural reforms, at the promise and constraints of natural resource abundance, and at the burden of educational and technological shortfalls. On the issue of poverty and inequality, we have examined the root causes and impacts of poverty and inequality, and the social implications of income insecurity.

This, our eighth flagship, takes a fresh look at how growth and poverty are interlinked, and makes new recommendations on how to boost growth and reduce poverty at the same time. The report revisits how growth can reduce poverty and how much emphasis should be placed on growth relative to distribution, given a country's income and inequality levels. It also reopens the question of how much policy can influence how "pro poor" the growth process is. Latin America's inequality is undeniably partly due to the results of inherited economic structures and resource endowments, but it is also the case that the United Kingdom and Sweden have distributions of market incomes close to Latin America. Their achievement of more egalitarian social outcomes is good news: Even without fundamental shifts in economic structure, policies targeting the poor can go a long way towards ameliorating social injustice.

That such investments in the poor are good business for society as whole is a central theme of the report. Poverty itself hampers the achievement of high and sustained growth rates, completing a variety of vicious circles. For instance, poor students, faced with substandard schools and volatile returns to their human capital, underinvest in education. Poor entrepreneurs, excluded from capital markets, underinvest in good projects. Poor regions, lacking infrastructure, fail to attract investment, and have fewer citizens able to adopt, manage, and generate new technologies. Poor countries, unable to moderate income disparities, find ethnic or racial tensions exacerbated that, in turn, thwart the establishment of a healthy business climate.

To move to a virtuous circle of growth and poverty reduction will take action on many poverty fronts and an approach that not only considers how the poor can benefit from growth, but also how they can contribute to it. Key among these is investment in human capital. Here the report emphasizes that an integrated strategy, taking into account barriers to getting education and the entire lifecycle of students, is essential. For example, educating rural children will pay greater dividends if improved infrastructure attracts firms who can employ their enhanced skills. Social safety nets that mitigate labor market risk increase the perceived return to education. Improved access to financing for college, where the returns to education are highest, gives impetus to finishing secondary school. At the national, regional, and household levels, and on the health, trade, and financial sector fronts, policies that build on these interrelationships have been shown to be more effective in fighting poverty. These and many other findings and recommendations throughout the report are grounded in detailed analysis and examples and should provide additional insights to policy makers and development practitioners in the different countries of the region.

We believe this year's flagship, *Poverty Reduction and Growth: Virtuous and Vicious Circles* to be a valuable contribution to the intense current regional debate on poverty and growth. As a development institution, we at the World Bank are committed to enriching, supporting, and learning from this debate, a debate that is critical to the design of policies conducive to enhancing welfare in all its dimensions among the poor of Latin America and the Caribbean.

Pamela Cox
Vice President for Latin America and the Caribbean
The World Bank

Acknowledgments

POVERTY REDUCTION AND GROWTH: VIRTUOUS AND VICIOUS CIRCLES IS THE PRODUCT OF A collaborative effort by a number of professionals from within and outside the Bank. The report was prepared under the guidance and direction of Guillermo Perry by a core team comprising Humberto López, William Maloney, Omar Arias, and Luis Servén. Other significant contributors to the drafting of the report included Mariano Bosch (LSE), Cesar Calderón (World Bank), Anna Fruttero (World Bank), and Edwin Goñi (World Bank). Background papers were prepared by Patricio Aroca (Universidad Católica del Norte, Chile), Monserrat Bustelo (World Bank), Ana María Diaz Escobar (World Bank), Maurizio Bussolo (World Bank), Maria Victoria Fazio (World Bank), Leonardo Gaspariani (CEDLAS and Universidad Nacional de la Plata), Federico Gutierrez (CEDLAS and Universidad Nacional de la Plata), Tom Krebs (Syracuse University), Pravin Krishna (Johns Hopkins University), Norman Loayza (World Bank), Alex Mariana Marchionni (Universidad de la Plata), Denis Medvedev (World Bank), Leandro Prados de la Escoura (Universidad Carlos III), Claudio Raddatz (World Bank), Lucas Siga (University of California, San Diego), Walter Sosa (Universidad de San Andres), and Leonardo Tornarolli (CEDLAS and Universidad Nacional de la Plata). Emmanuel Skoufias (World Bank), Kathy Lindert (World Bank), and Joseph Shapiro (World Bank) also shared with us many of the results of the regional study *Redistributing Income to the Poor; Public Transfers in Latin America and the Caribbean*. Patricia Macchi (Boston University), and Guillermo Beylis (World Bank) provided excellent research assistance at different times during the project. The report has also benefited from comments by Nancy Birdsall (Institute for International Economics), Nora Lustig (Universidad de las Américas), Nohra Rey de Marulanda (Inter-American Development Bank), and John Williamson (Institute for International Economics), and by our two principal advisers: Francisco Ferreira and Roberto Zagha. Finally, Elena Serrano and Catherine Russell coordinated the report's publication and dissemination activities, working closely with Dana Vorisek and Susan Graham in the World Bank's Office of the Publisher.

Acronyms and Abbreviations

CCT	conditional cash transfers	IV	instrumental variable
CPI	consumer price index	LAC	Latin America and the Caribbean
ECLAC	Economic Commission for Latin America and the Caribbean	LISA	local indicators of spatial associations
		NAFTA	North American Free Trade Agreement
FUSADES	Fundación Salvadoreña para el Desarrollo Económico y Social	OECD	Organisation for Economic Co-operation and Development
GATT	General Agreement on Tariffs and Trade	PPP	purchasing power parity
		PWT	Penn World Tables
GDP	gross domestic product	RER	real exchange rate
GIS	Geographical Information Systems	SA	social assistance
GMM	Generalized Methods of Movement	SEDLAC	Socio Economic Database for Latin America and the Caribbean
i.i.d.	independent and identically distributed		
IPEA	Instituto de Pesquisa Economica Aplicada (Brazil)	SI	social insurance

Note: All dollar amounts are U.S. dollars unless otherwise indicated.

CHAPTER 1

From Vicious to Virtuous Circles

That raising income levels alleviates poverty, and that economic growth can be more or less effective in doing so, is well known and has received renewed attention in the search for pro-poor growth. Less well explored is the reverse channel: that poverty may, in fact, be part of the reason for a country's poor growth performance. This more elaborated view of the development process opens the door to the existence of vicious circles in which low growth results in high poverty and high poverty in turn results in low growth. This report is about the existence of those vicious circles in Latin America and about the ways and means to convert them into virtuous circles in which poverty reduction and high growth reinforce each other.

LATIN AMERICA'S TWIN DISAPPOINTMENTS OF relatively weak economic growth and persistent poverty and inequality are longstanding and intimately related. That raising income levels alleviates poverty, and that economic growth can be more or less effective in doing so, is well known and has received significant attention in the search for pro-poor growth. Less well explored is the reverse channel—poverty may, in fact, be part of the reason for a region's poor growth performance, creating vicious circles where low growth results in high poverty and high poverty in turn results in low growth. This report is about finding ways of converting this negative cycle into a virtuous circle of poverty reduction, in which broad-based attacks on poverty feed back into higher growth that in turn reduces poverty.

Latin America's economic performance in the last 50 years has been disappointing. Growth lagged behind core countries of the OECD (Organisation for Economic Co-operation and Development), at a time when East Asia and Spain, the *madre patria* on the periphery of Europe, were quickly catching up (figure 1.1). Income inequality has remained very high in Latin America over the past 50 years (figure 1.2), posing a double impediment to poverty reduction. First, had growth been accompanied by reduced inequality, it would have been more pro-poor. Second, even when inequality remains unchanged, economic growth is less effective in reducing poverty in countries with less equal distributions of income: To attain the same reduction of poverty, unequal countries must grow more than more equal ones. Given the region's acute growth divergence during the lost decade of the 1980s and the slowdown from 1998 to 2003, as well as lack of progress on the inequality front, it is not surprising that income poverty has been so persistent since 1980 (figure 1.3). Though the report discusses important caveats in traditional comparisons across countries and across time, it remains true that, with the exception of Chile, there has been little poverty reduction beyond the gains of the 1950–80 period, and in many countries growth has not been especially pro-poor.

Poverty as a multidimensional and dynamic concept

These conclusions broadly hold when a broader view of poverty and welfare is taken (chapter 2). As the literature increasingly stresses, poverty is a concept that spans a range of dimensions, such as health, mortality, and security, that may be uncorrelated with conventional measures of income poverty. Further, a complete concept of well-being needs to

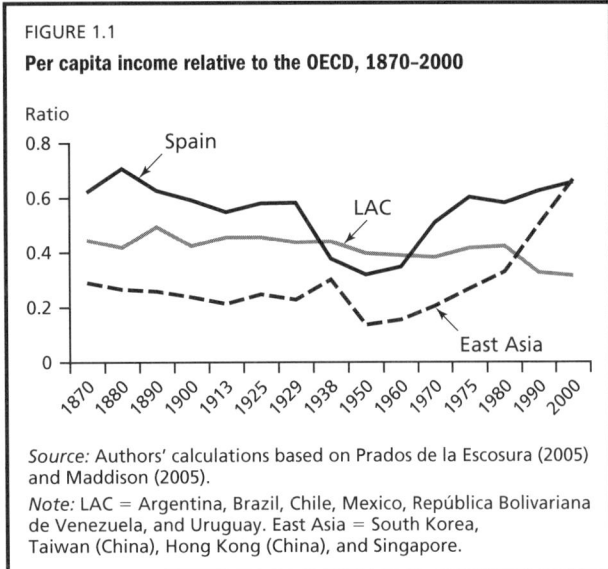

FIGURE 1.1
Per capita income relative to the OECD, 1870–2000

Source: Authors' calculations based on Prados de la Escosura (2005) and Maddison (2005).
Note: LAC = Argentina, Brazil, Chile, Mexico, República Bolivariana de Venezuela, and Uruguay. East Asia = South Korea, Taiwan (China), Hong Kong (China), and Singapore.

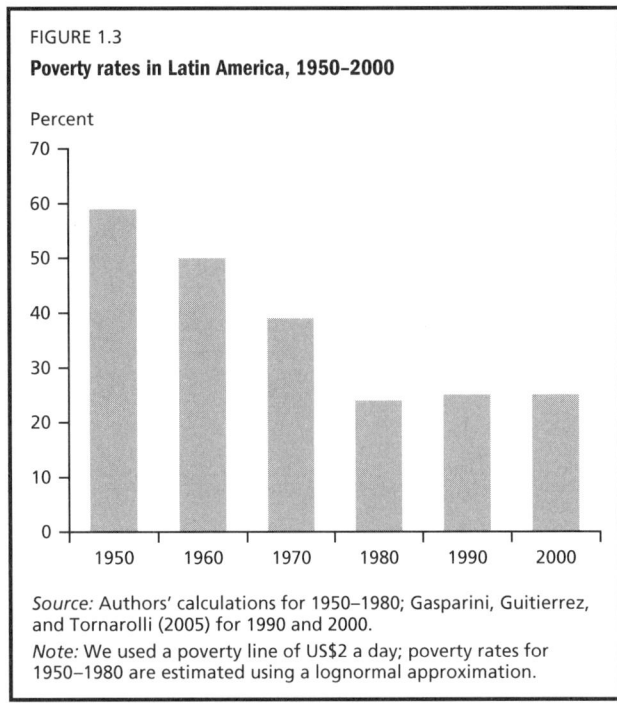

FIGURE 1.3
Poverty rates in Latin America, 1950–2000

Source: Authors' calculations for 1950–1980; Gasparini, Guitierrez, and Tornarolli (2005) for 1990 and 2000.
Note: We used a poverty line of US$2 a day; poverty rates for 1950–1980 are estimated using a lognormal approximation.

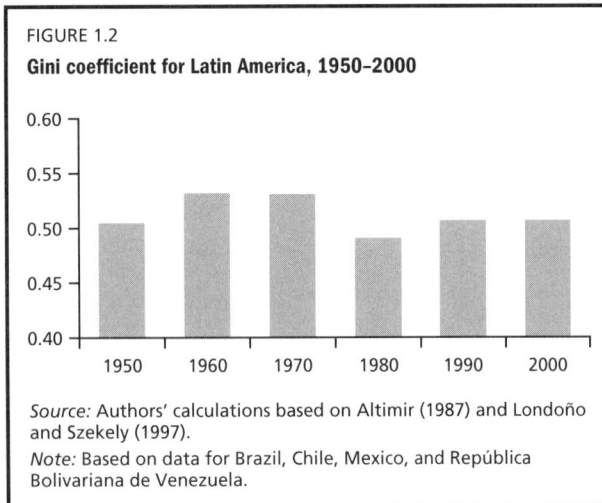

FIGURE 1.2
Gini coefficient for Latin America, 1950–2000

Source: Authors' calculations based on Altimir (1987) and Londoño and Szekely (1997).
Note: Based on data for Brazil, Chile, Mexico, and República Bolivariana de Venezuela.

incorporate income movements across lifetimes or even generations, which means that issues of risk and mobility through the income distribution must be examined. Ignoring these considerations leads to large distortions in the concepts of poverty and inequality.

Although the limited existing data on these aspects of poverty do not permit the kind of global comparisons that measures of income inequality and headcount poverty numbers do, the picture they sketch is only somewhat more optimistic. It is true that mortality rates have fallen far more than income levels would predict and account for large improvements in welfare in those countries with little growth. However, intergenerational mobility remains lower in Latin America and the Caribbean than in the worst of the OECD countries. Recent evidence indicates that the children of poor families and of parents with low education face a relatively high probability of achieving low educational levels, obtaining lower returns for their education, and remaining poor (figures 1.4 and 1.5). The fact that Chile is one of the most mobile societies in the region suggests that the modernization of the country across the last decades has offered more opportunities to the less well-off. Finally, as documented in the World Bank's Latin American region flagship *Securing Our Future in a Global Economy* (de Ferranti and others 2000), the high economic volatility in the region implies that the poor are subject to higher risks than the poor in other regions. Although macroeconomic volatility was reduced in the 1990s after peaking in the 1980s, it still remains exceptionally high, and labor market volatility remains substantially higher than it is in the United States, for example.

As later chapters show, all these dimensions not only provide a more complete view of poverty, they also constitute channels back to growth.

The twin disappointments: Destiny or choice?

Is there something intrinsic to the region that has left it with relatively low growth and high levels of inequality

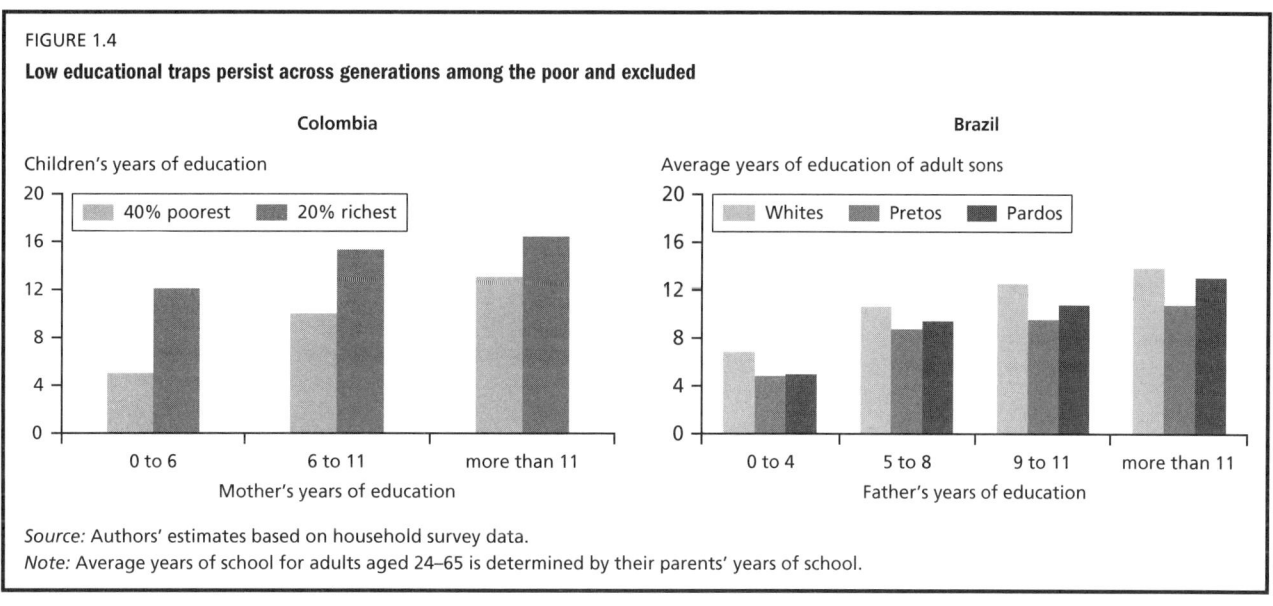

FIGURE 1.4
Low educational traps persist across generations among the poor and excluded

Source: Authors' estimates based on household survey data.
Note: Average years of school for adults aged 24–65 is determined by their parents' years of school.

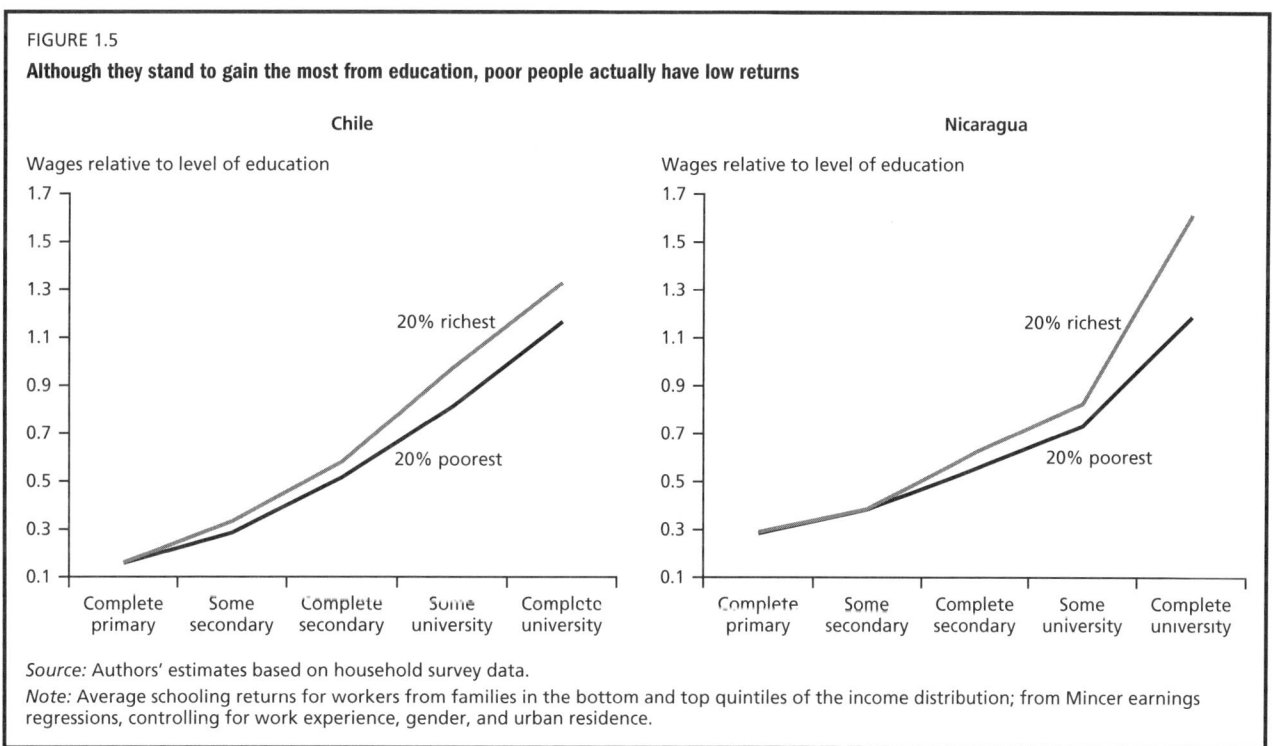

FIGURE 1.5
Although they stand to gain the most from education, poor people actually have low returns

Source: Authors' estimates based on household survey data.
Note: Average schooling returns for workers from families in the bottom and top quintiles of the income distribution; from Mincer earnings regressions, controlling for work experience, gender, and urban residence.

and poverty? The World Bank's Latin American region flagship *Inequality in Latin America: Breaking with History?* (de Ferranti and others 2004) argued that exclusionary institutions set up during the European conquest to exploit existing mineral wealth and indigenous populations, and the particular crops suited to the region's climate (such as sugar plantations based on a slave workforce), led to highly unequal access to land, education, and political power at least until the late 1800s and thus had adverse consequences for growth and inequality for a long time.

In chapter 3, we show that indeed Latin America was well behind the advanced economies in the mid-1800s, when the region's per capita income levels represented about 60 percent of the U.S. levels and 55 percent of those in the broader OECD group. More important, we also show that a significant part of the current development gap in the region dates from the middle of the 20th century, when other regions took more advantage of the rapid pace of global expansion. Latin America's relative retardation in this period was in all likelihood related to the extreme inward-looking policies instituted then and to the lack of macroeconomic prudence that led to the devastating debt crisis of the 1980s. Although policies are importantly conditioned by historical context, more promising roads were not taken.

The same appears true in the realm of income distribution. The report shows that as the 20th century began, France, Spain, the United Kingdom, and the United States all had high levels of income inequality. Yet they managed to lower income inequality dramatically during the century and over relatively short periods of time (two to three decades). Such achievements appear related to the universal provision of basic education and health services and the establishment of highly redistributive welfare states.

Both Latin America's loss in relative income position in the last 50 years and the OECD's ability to sharply reduce inequality are, perhaps counterintuitively, good news: our history is not our destiny—choices of policies and institutions can lead to major improvements along both dimensions. Breaking with history is indeed difficult, but it is by no means impossible.

The link from growth and development to income-poverty reduction

Chapter 4 of the report concentrates on the effect of growth and changes in inequality on income-poverty reduction in countries with different characteristics. It shows that achieving the greatest reduction in poverty may imply placing differing relative emphasis on growth versus redistribution depending on the individual country's initial conditions: poor countries (such as Bolivia, Haiti, and Honduras) and relatively equal countries that, bluntly put, have little to distribute, need first and foremost high and sustained growth, even at the expense of some increases in inequality; this might be called the China model. In contrast, relatively richer and more unequal countries—most of Latin America, and especially Argentina, Brazil, Colombia, and Mexico—need both higher growth and significant redistribution if they want to make a fast and significant dent in poverty reduction (table 1.1).

Chapter 5 examines how different policies and different sectoral patterns of growth affect income-poverty reduction. It finds that sectoral composition matters: different

TABLE 1.1

Growth rates needed to compensate for a 1-percentage-point increase in inequality

Country	Compensatory growth rate	Country	Compensatory growth rate
Argentina	2.5	Peru	1.6
Chile	2.4	St. Lucia	1.5
Brazil	2.3	Guatemala	1.5
Mexico	2.1	Paraguay	1.5
Costa Rica	2.1	El Salvador	1.4
Colombia	2.1	Venezuela, R.B. de	1.2
Trinidad and Tobago	2.0		
Dominican Republic	1.9	Ecuador	1.1
Panama	1.9	Nicaragua	1.1
Belize	1.8	Guyana	1.1
Uruguay	1.8	Bolivia	1.0
Jamaica	1.7	Honduras	0.8

Source: Authors' calculations.
Note: The table reports the growth rates that would leave poverty unchanged when the Gini coefficient increases by 1 percent. Higher values indicate that inequality plays a more important role in poverty reduction.

industries show large differences in labor intensity (agriculture and construction are generally more labor intensive than manufacturing and services, and the latter are more labor intensive than mining and utilities); and poverty reduction is stronger when growth has a labor-intensive inclination. The chapter also finds that policies such as increased access to education and infrastructure have had direct positive impacts on growth, inequality, and poverty reduction, while others, such as trade opening, have had positive effects on growth but have tended to increase inequality and even poverty in the short run. In the long run, however, all pro-growth policies tend to reduce income poverty.

Chapter 5 also discusses the importance of transfers as a means of sharing the fruits of growth by investing in the poor. Bringing the historical discussion above into the present, the chapter shows that roughly half of the stark difference in income inequality between Latin America and contemporary OECD countries results from differences in returns to factors of production—the result of the unequal distribution of human and other capital in Latin America. But the other half results from the generally unprogressive nature of Latin America's system of transfers. The core OECD countries use transfers from the rich to the poor, and extensive pension schemes that distribute income from the those working today to those retired tomorrow, to lower

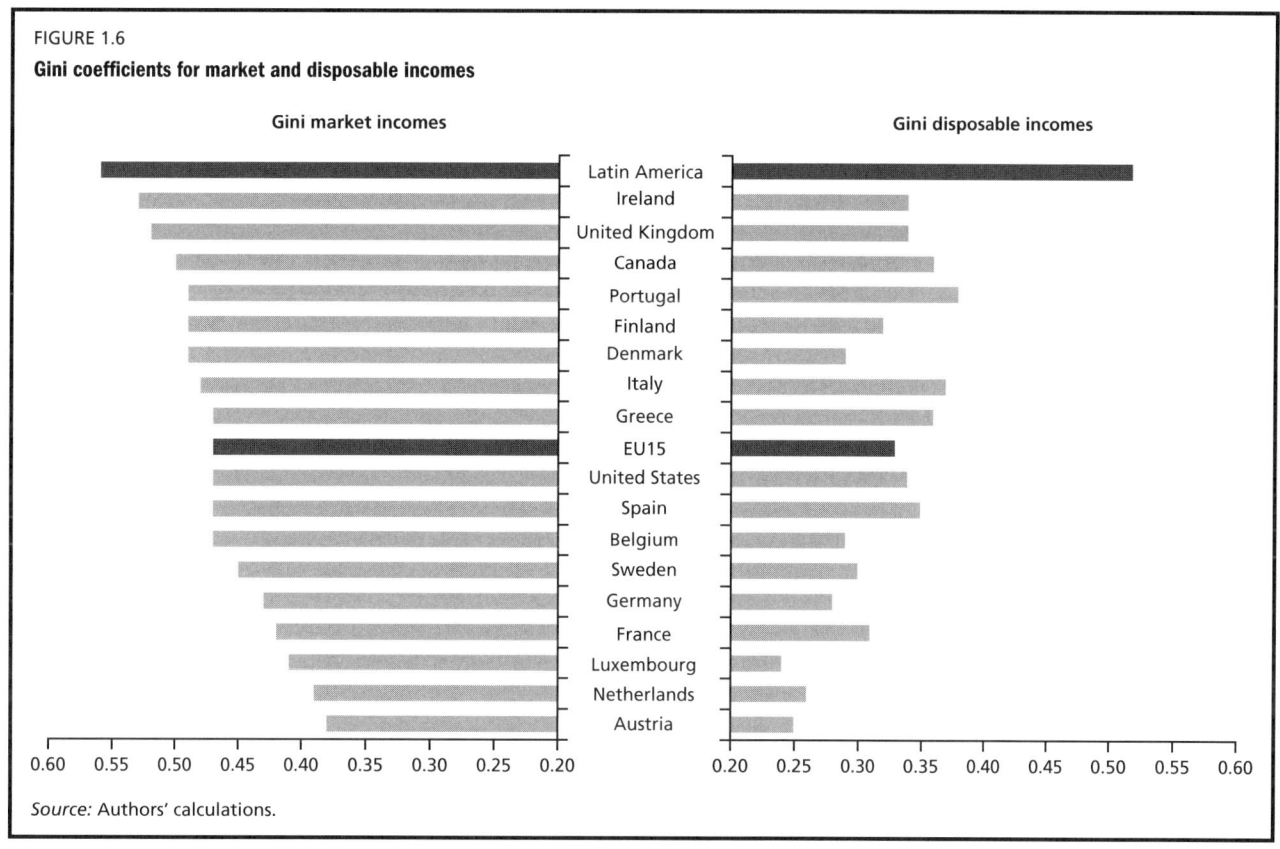

FIGURE 1.6
Gini coefficients for market and disposable incomes

Source: Authors' calculations.

the Gini (the standard measure of inequality) by about 15 percentage points (from, for instance, 0.53 in the United Kingdom to 0.35).[1] Transfers in a typical Latin American country, in contrast, alter the Gini by 2 percentage points or less, although there are a few exceptions such as Chile, which managed to reduce the Gini by twice as much (figure 1.6).

Whether the pure transfers of the magnitudes discussed above for Europe have been optimal from a growth point of view is debatable, as is their wisdom or political feasibility in Latin America. Arguably, for a variety of reasons, and in particular to be consistent with growth objectives, redistributive policy probably should focus on equalizing opportunities through more equal access to assets, such as human capital, rather than on equalizing outcomes measured as incomes per se. What is clear, however, is that Latin America has not made the efforts to mobilize the resources to attack poverty that it could. First, the region's tax collections are below those in similar countries (when benchmarked by income per capita), with a few exceptions such as Brazil and Nicaragua, and collections for progressive taxes, such as personal income and property taxes, are especially low. More important, although Latin American public expenditures underwrite large, progressive items (basic education and health), they also fund large regressive items (subsidies to pensions, tertiary education, and energy), which offset the progressive spending. An encouraging recent development is the introduction of successful policies such as *Progresa/Oportunidades* in Mexico, *Familias en Acción* in Colombia, and *Bolsa Escola* in Brazil, that combine fiscal transfers to the poor with incentives for them to build human capital through both health and education investments from early childhood.

Closing the virtuous circle: The link from poverty to growth

The more novel thesis of the report is that Latin America's persistent poverty may itself be impeding the achievement of higher growth rates—that there are reinforcing vicious circles that keep families, regions, and countries poor and unable to contribute to national growth. The now-expansive literature on poverty traps has elaborated a large number of channels that may perpetuate poverty. The emphasis we place on the multidimensionality of poverty and on lifetime and intergenerational considerations in welfare measurement further enriches the universe of channels through which poverty impedes growth. To list just a few we discuss:

- Poor people often have limited access to financial markets or other necessary complements to private investment (such as property rights and infrastructure) essential to the accumulation of physical and knowledge capital and participation in the growth process.
- Poor people are often in poor health, which reduces their productivity and impedes their ability to manage and generate knowledge.
- Poor people attend low-quality schools and the low and late returns to education and diminished prospects for mobility deter the accumulation of human capital essential for growth. Education enhances earnings potential, expands labor mobility, promotes the health of parents and children, and reduces fertility and child mortality.
- Poor people may face more labor market risk, or may be less able to hedge against it, and thus find returns to investing in human capital adjusted for risk to be less attractive. Further, the inability to diversify risk prevents specialization in agriculture or movements to off-farm activities, for example, that would lead to greater productivity. Since the poor are typically more risk averse than the rich because losses hurt them more severely, in the absence of well-functioning insurance and credit markets, the poor skip profitable investment opportunities that they deem too risky. Once again, societies with high poverty rates show a tendency to underinvest.
- Poor regions and countries have fewer individuals capable of adopting, managing, and generating new technologies that would contribute to productivity.
- Poor regions may lack the infrastructure or human capital that would make them attractive to extraregional investment or the resources to develop them and that would facilitate sectoral and territorial labor mobility in search of higher income opportunities.
- Poor countries with poor regions may find ethnic or racial tensions exacerbated by income disparities leading to interregional tensions that make both regions and the country as a whole riskier to invest in.

In each case, poverty in itself prevents taking actions that would facilitate the exit from poverty and results in lower aggregate growth. Such vicious circles can lead to "convergence clubs"—richer and poorer countries, regions, or households tend to converge to different income or welfare levels even in the long run. Whether these are, in fact, poverty traps that cannot be escaped without intervention, or whether it simply takes much longer to transition to higher-income states, is to us a distinction of secondary importance, particularly when political economy issues are considered. What we do argue is that smart investments in the poor can lead to virtuous circles and that the issue of "pro-growth poverty reduction" should perhaps be as important a policy concern as traditional concerns with "pro-poor growth." In other words, investing in the poor is good business for society as a whole, not just for the poor.

Tracing these reinforcing circles implies necessarily moving away from static concepts of poverty and studying the *dynamics* of poverty at every level, and this report aspires to break new ground in this area. It provides evidence on the existence of convergence clubs at the household, regional, and international level and in several cases shows that these appear to reveal the evidence of poverty-trap dynamics.

Global convergence clubs

Do poorer countries grow less than richer countries? The evidence presented in chapter 6 suggests that, with a few notable exceptions, they do. Panel a of figure 1.7 suggests that, apart from two short periods (one in the second half of the 1970s and another in the early 2000s), the typical developing country (and Latin America is not an exception here) has always experienced lower growth rates than the typical rich country. Over the 1963–2003 period, median per capita growth in industrial countries outpaced median growth in developing countries by an average of more than 1 percent per year.

The difference in per capita growth rates between the developed and developing countries has led to an expanding gap between rich and poor countries over time (figure 1.7, panel b). In the early 1960s the median Latin American country had an income level that was slightly less than one-third the income of the median developed country; today that gap is less than 20 percent. Globally speaking, the typical developing country had an income level about 12 percent that of the richer countries in 1960; and today it is closer to 5 percent. There is little to support the convergence hypothesis that poorer countries will tend to catch up with the richer ones. Rather, as panel c of the figure

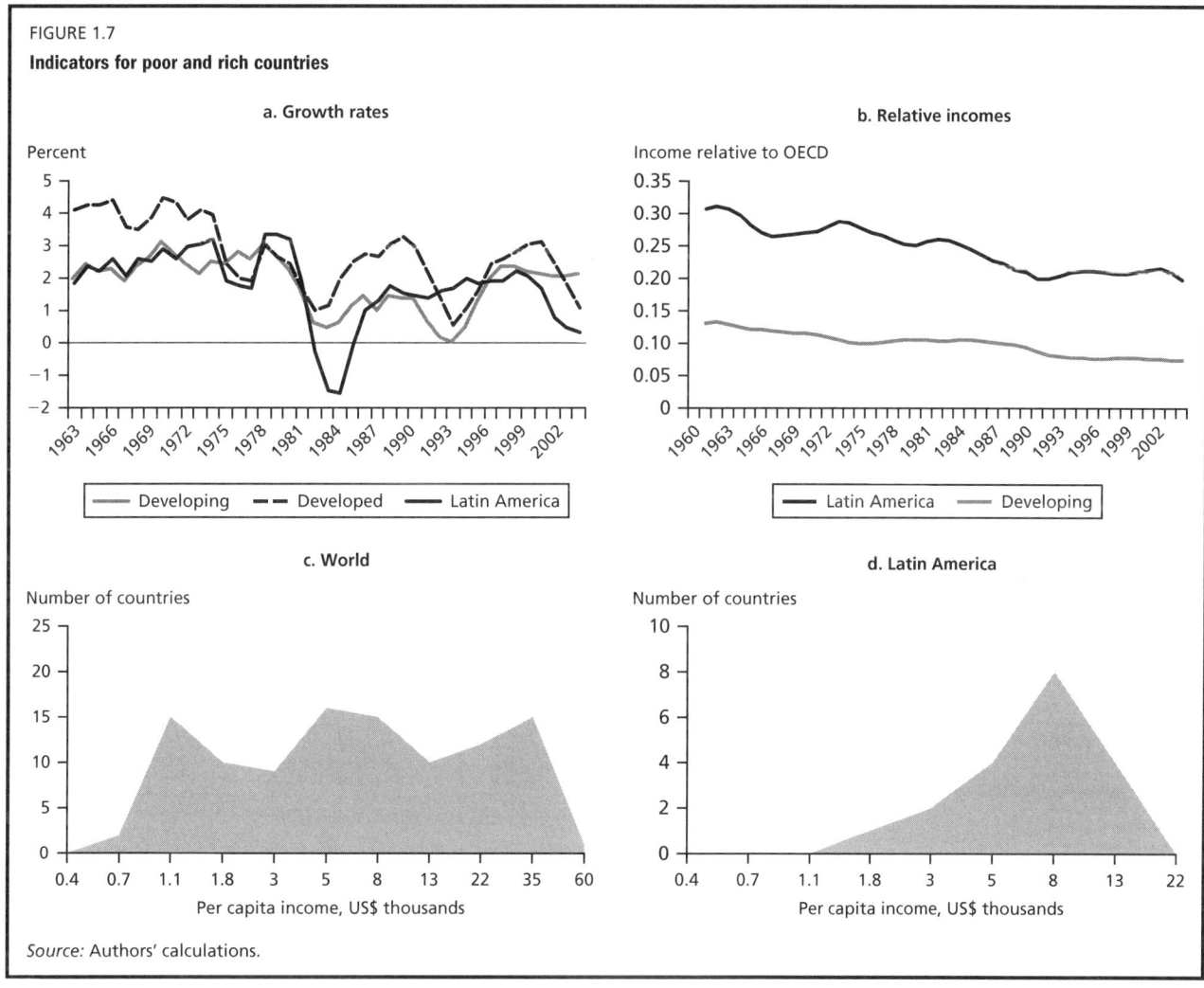

FIGURE 1.7
Indicators for poor and rich countries

Source: Authors' calculations.

suggests, the poor stay poor, while the rich get richer. The histogram for the world in 1999 suggests a trimodal distribution, with a low peak at $1,100; a second at between $5,000 and $8,000, and a third peak around $35,000 forming poor, middle-income, and rich convergence clubs. (Chapter 7 shows that since 1960 there has been convergence within these clubs but divergence among them.) Panel d shows that Latin America as a region is unimodal with its single peak at about $8,000 and belongs to the middle cluster that is slowly separating both from the very poor and, distressingly, from the very rich.

Convergence clubs at the cross-national level are also evident, though much less so, when nonincome dimensions of welfare are considered. For example, figure 1.8 presents the cross-national life expectancy histograms for 1960 and 2002. These histograms indicate the presence of a two-peaked pattern in both periods, but it is also evident that the mass of the low peak declines between 1960 and 2002, whereas the mass of the high peak increases (worldwide life expectancy has increased and is slowly converging).

Does poverty matter for growth?

Are high poverty levels to blame for the disappointing growth performance of poorer countries? A bimodal distribution in income or life expectancy levels does not, in itself, prove that poverty is a brake on growth, and chapter 6 finds only mixed evidence for the extreme case of poverty traps. However, the chapter does identify several self-reinforcing mechanisms that may retard growth and cause poverty to persist, and these may be more relevant from a policy point of view. Looking across countries, poverty does appear to deter growth and investment (figure 1.9), especially when the degree of financial development is limited. More specifically, we estimate in chapter 6 that, for the average country, a 10-percentage-point increase in income poverty lowers the growth rate by about

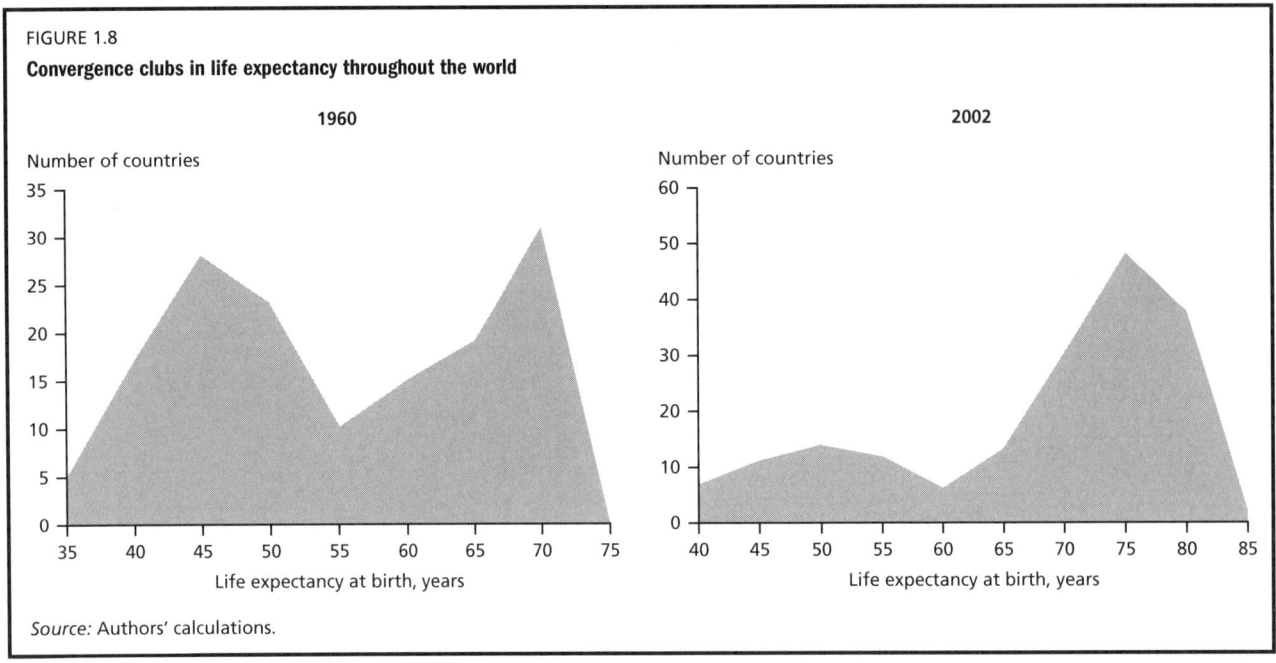

FIGURE 1.8
Convergence clubs in life expectancy throughout the world

Source: Authors' calculations.

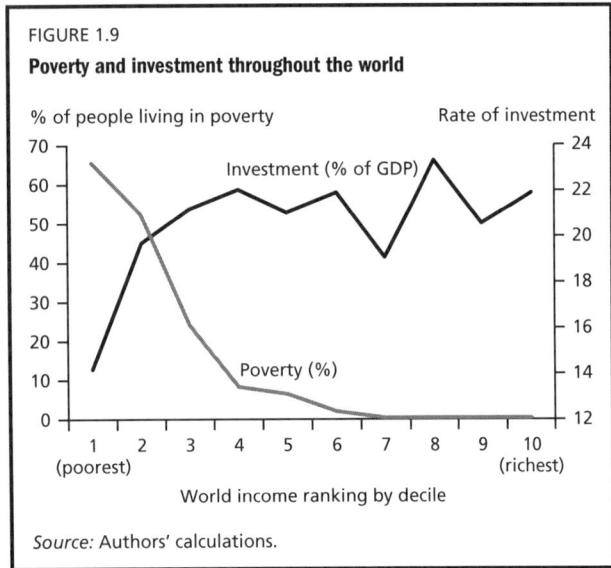

FIGURE 1.9
Poverty and investment throughout the world

Source: Authors' calculations.

1 percent, holding other determinants of growth constant. Further, we estimate that a 10-percentage-point increase in income poverty reduces investment by 6–8 percentage points of gross domestic product (GDP) in countries with underdeveloped financial systems. These results validate the predictions of theory: that poverty may limit growth when financial sectors are imperfect because the poor, who lack access to credit and insurance, will not undertake many socially profitable investments, thus depressing the aggregate level of investment and growth. The report also finds evidence that poverty limits the level of innovation (as measured by research and development expenditures) and the accumulation of human capital (see below), both of which are additional channels through which poverty influences aggregate growth.

Regional convergence clubs

Chapter 7 finds an unusual combination of converging income among subnational units, but increased spatial concentration within countries. Modern spatial econometric tools show that within Brazil, Chile, and Mexico, there are clear convergence clubs of rich and poor regions, that appear to be drifting increasingly apart (figure 1.10). This finding is consistent with the New Economic Geography literature that has focused on how larger, already established regions enjoy scale economies while lagging regions are less productive and hence less attractive to factors of production.

These dynamics, and those discussed for national poverty traps in chapter 6, apply to national or subnational units equally. Two considerations are particular to the latter, however. The first is that within countries, labor can legally move freely. In practice it does not, leaving large wage gaps of often 50 percent among regions. Evidence from Chile and Mexico suggests that this phenomenon is partly the result of another poverty-trap dynamic—the poor cannot muster the savings or liquidity to migrate and hence cannot leave. But other evidence suggests that this story may be incomplete. Nonincome measures of poverty, such as mortality, show convergence within countries, much the

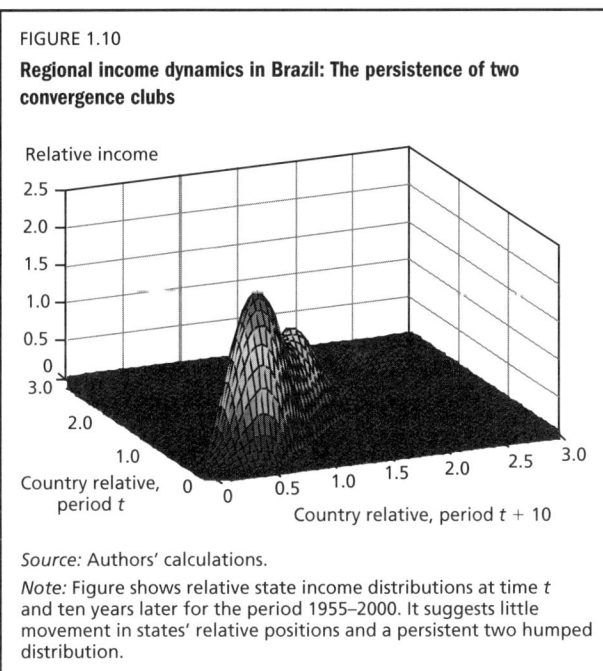

FIGURE 1.10
Regional income dynamics in Brazil: The persistence of two convergence clubs

Source: Authors' calculations.
Note: Figure shows relative state income distributions at time t and ten years later for the period 1955–2000. It suggests little movement in states' relative positions and a persistent two humped distribution.

way they do internationally, suggesting that the welfare gap broadly considered may be less dramatic. Further, simply asking people how poor they feel reveals some provocative anomalies. The poorest group in the Bolivian altiplano (largely indigenous) self-rates as the least poor in Bolivia, while inhabitants of the rich province of Buenos Aires rate themselves as the poorest in Argentina. These findings suggest that "congestion externalities"—the negative aspects of living in concentrated urban areas—may be important, that relative income disparities may be more brutally apparent in urban contexts, or simply that researchers are missing key dimensions of well-being that are uncorrelated with income.

Second, laggard regions in general have low levels of education and infrastructure that require special efforts to bring them toward the country average. However, to the degree that agglomeration externalities—the economies of scale that may arise from concentrating economic activity—dictate that poor regions have lower growth potential and lower returns to investment, governments may be confronted eventually with a trade-off between aggregate growth and geographical equity.

Household-level poverty traps

The fundamental building block underlying the international and regional analyses discussed above is the household. Addressing persistent poverty requires an understanding of the factors preventing poor families from moving out of low-productivity economic activities. The poverty-traps literature emphasizes insufficient asset holdings (including human capital), thresholds in the returns to those assets, fixed costs of productive transitions, and limited access to credit or insurance among the poor as main determinants of their inability to take advantage of growth opportunities. Of particular importance is the ability of the poor to use their labor (their most abundant asset) in wage jobs, self-employment, or their own microenterprises. Labor earnings often account for more than two-thirds of total household income of the Latin American poor. The pricing of labor reflects productivity differentials across workers and jobs, sector and regional supply-demand imbalances, and non-market factors. Low-earnings traps can arise from deficiencies in the endowments that enhance the productivity (quality) of labor assets (such as human capital and infrastructure) and from earnings differentials unrelated to skills (such as ethnic discrimination and location) that arise from barriers to mobility in the labor market.

Chapter 8 examines some of the mechanisms that may prevent the Latin American poor from participating in the growth process and lead to persistent poverty. Unfortunately, the limited long-span panel data prevent in-depth analyses of the duration of poverty and its main determinants throughout Latin America. The chapter draws on the limited, though highly consistent, evidence available on these issues and reaches two main conclusions. First, low levels of productivity, rather than labor market segmentation, is the overwhelming driver of low earnings. Most poverty is thus not generated directly by labor market failures but by deficiencies in workers' productive endowments, especially education, combined with the low levels of overall productivity of their local economy. This effect is exacerbated by high volatility and the inability to insure against shocks, much more so than in developed countries. Second, detailed analyses of rural El Salvador and consistent evidence from other countries suggest that poverty traps surrounding the accumulation of these productive assets are a phenomenon of practical relevance in the region.

Chapter 9 then takes on one of the central channels that can support a two-way causality between poverty and economic growth: the accumulation of human capital. Human capital, proxied by education or health levels, is generally believed to be one of the key determinants of long-term growth, while cross-country empirical evidence suggests that poverty may affect education levels (see chapter 8). Chapter 9 investigates the micromechanisms that could support this double causality, so that specific actions to increase the educational attainment of the poor could ignite a virtuous circle of faster growth and poverty reduction in the region.

The chapter begins with a well-known fact: families with little education (specifically those with less than secondary schooling) tend to be poor, and in turn they tend not to invest enough in their and their children's education to escape poverty. The chapter documents several pieces of evidence on self-reinforcing mechanisms driving this vicious circle.

First, despite the region's recent progress toward universal primary enrollment, there is a clear and persistent educational divide in educational attainment. The population sorts into two groups: individuals with low-education attainments (typically less than secondary education) and individuals with secondary education and above (figure 1.11). Rural residents and the poorest families, including disadvantaged ethnic groups, are predominantly trapped in the low educational group. This divide continues replicating itself among the current cohort of students in high rates of repetition and dropout of these same groups. The smooth decline in enrollments during the secondary cycle in most countries suggests that lack of school facilities is not the main driving factor, although in some countries physical access constraints remain a problem.

Second, returns to schooling tend to increase with the level of education, a finding consistent with a skill bias in labor demand caused by technological change in the region, as detailed in the World Bank's Latin American region flagship *Closing the Gap in Education and Technology* (de Ferranti and others 2003). Schooling returns are flat during the basic and secondary cycles and increase after completion of secondary education; in some cases, the full return materializes only after completion of tertiary education. That is, schooling returns become attractive just as the opportunity cost, in terms of wages forgone by the student, becomes most acute for poor families. In addition, the chapter strikingly shows that in most countries poor families face below-average returns to tertiary (and sometimes secondary) education, plausibly due to low-quality schools as well as disadvantages arising from family background and attitudes toward education (see figure 1.4). Poor families have to juggle current subsistence needs against schooling investments with a remote, uncertain, and less-attractive

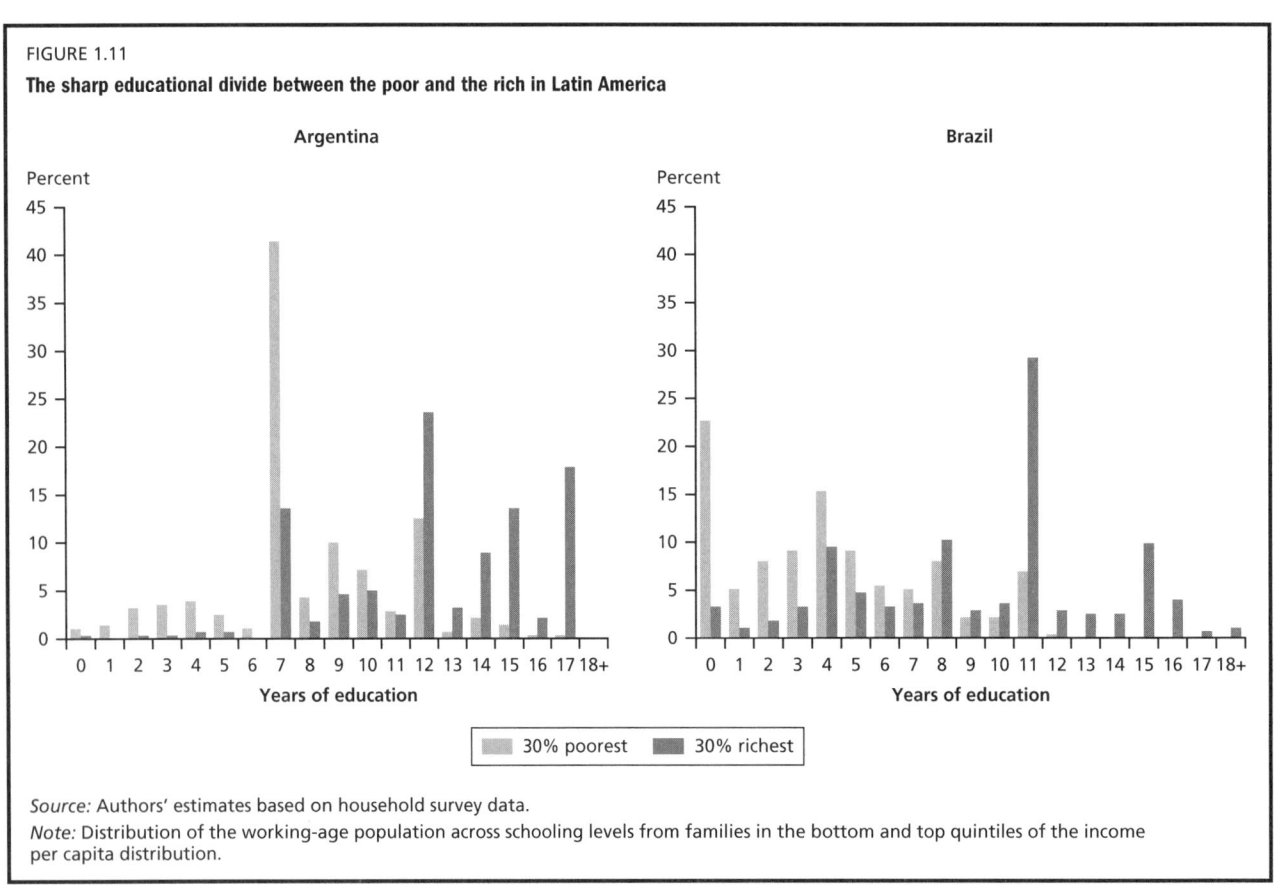

FIGURE 1.11

The sharp educational divide between the poor and the rich in Latin America

Source: Authors' estimates based on household survey data.
Note: Distribution of the working-age population across schooling levels from families in the bottom and top quintiles of the income per capita distribution.

payoff. The statistical evidence describing the low incentives and barriers to accumulating human capital is corroborated by the responses that poor children and youth give for dropping out of school: high opportunity costs at older ages, perceived low benefits in the 1–12 grade schooling cycle, and physical access constraints.

In sum, the completion of a secondary education necessary for poor families to move out of poverty remains out of reach and children's education remains strongly correlated with that of their parents. The educational divide is self-reinforcing across generations and is a critical underlying driver of the vicious circles of poverty observed at the household, regional, and national levels.

Implications of the report

A number of implications emerge from the analyses described above. We discuss them along two main dimensions: strategic and policy levels.

Strategic implications

The report uncovers several lessons that have implications for the way we view poverty reduction.

1. *Pro-poor growth and pro-growth poverty reduction.* The existence of virtuous circles between growth and poverty reduction enriches the debate on optimal poverty reduction strategies in several ways.
   - First, the debate about whether strategies should emphasize pro-growth or pro-poor policies now appears somewhat less germane. Strategies that do not focus on growth forswear perhaps the most potent weapon for improving human well-being at our disposal, especially in light of the likely limits of explicitly pro-poor policies discussed above. Yet failing to take account of the constraints facing the poor in participating in and contributing to growth undermines its generation. For example, liquidity constraints, risk, and indivisibilities or lumpiness in human capital investments appear to prevent the poor from acquiring the education that would move them out of poverty and fuel growth. Redressing these constraints gives rise to an underexamined dimension of policy analysis that might be called pro-growth poverty reduction.
   - Second, the bidirectional relationship between growth and poverty reduction suggests that ideally consideration of policies should take into account their direct and indirect effects on growth and poverty reduction. This awareness introduces new but necessary levels of complexity in the evaluation of policy options on both agendas. As a simple but important example, conditional cash transfer programs have an impact on poverty that goes beyond the increased incomes for poor households provided by straight transfer policies. Conditional transfer programs also relieve credit constraints on and provide a further incentive to the accumulation of human capital that raises income both at the household and, eventually, at the economywide level.
   - Third, pro-growth policies that have short-run adverse impacts on distribution and poverty, as appears to be the case with trade opening, may actually create a drag on growth creation (see chapter 5). However, when combined with complementary policies such as improved access to education and infrastructure, the short-run adverse poverty effect can be mitigated, enhancing both the direct and indirect effects on growth. Further, compensatory actions to offset some of these effects (for example, support to small farmers in noncompetitive sectors during trade opening) gain a new rationale in increasing the efficiency of reform policies in addition to those justifications related to social protection.
   - Finally, transfer programs should always seek to directly stimulate the accumulation of assets that will advance the growth process, as programs like *Oportunidades* in Mexico, *Bolsa Escola* in Brazil, and *Familias en Acción* in Colombia do.
2. *Pro-poor growth vs. pro-poor government policy.* The finding that at most half of the difference in inequality between Latin America and OECD countries arises from differences in the distribution of market incomes implies two things. First, while efforts need to be made to improve both the endowments of the poor and the returns to them offered by the market, there appear to be limits to what can be done. For example, Sweden, a country well known for its concerns with equity and human capital formation, has a market distribution that is very similar to that of many countries in Latin America, suggesting that even states that put equity high on their policy agenda may end up with high levels of inequality in

market incomes. Second, much of the heavy lifting of equalizing incomes in the OECD countries appears to have been done by their expansive transfer systems that dwarf anything found in the Latin American region to date, although the report suggests that, here too, there are limits posed by political economy and efficiency. In short, policies designed to obtain equal opportunities for development of human capital, and hence more equal market incomes, need to be complemented with redistribution through taxes and transfers.

3. *Multiple dimensions of poverty, multiple channels to growth.* The narrowness of the traditional focus on income poverty becomes increasingly unsatisfactory in the context of tracing feedbacks to growth. As examples:

- The strong gains in longevity in the region are only weakly correlated with income growth. In some countries where incomes have remained stagnant, welfare has risen substantially because of improvements in health care and disease prevention. As noted above, health is linked to productivity growth, and policies dedicated to redressing this dimension of poverty are thus both pro-poor and pro-growth.
- The prospect of moving out of poverty or upward in the income distribution is a major motivation for the accumulation of human capital. However, the lower, late, and uncertain rates of return to education of the poor, for the reasons discussed above, foreclose such mobility and discourage individuals and their children from accumulating this capital. Clearly, one lesson is that redressing these disincentives both improves social indicators that more completely measure poverty and stimulates growth. But a second lesson is that antipoverty policy must take a life-cycle view, with policies that look at the barriers to mobility in a comprehensive way.
- The risk associated with unanticipated mobility—high volatility in wages, for example—is also a disincentive to long-term investments in human capital. Clearly, reducing the high macroeconomic volatility of the region, as well as designing mechanisms to mitigate the various types of risk—health or income, for example—reduces poverty in all its dimensions and has pro-growth impacts.

In short, policy makers need to consider more comprehensive measures of poverty and inequality not only to get a more accurate view of the evolution of societal well-being but to better understand and take advantage of the channels back to growth.

4. *Nonlinear thinking: Humps and black holes, agglomeration externalities, and complementarities.* One critical insight of the poverty-traps literature is that the response to policy is nonlinear: it may vary depending upon the magnitude and comprehensiveness of the effort.

- There are thresholds (or humps) below which effort may have no impact; in such cases policy makers are effectively throwing resources down a black hole. For example, the fact that the returns to secondary education often materialize only upon completion—or, worse, upon completion of tertiary education—implies that it is not worth it for households to invest beyond primary school. Programs that seek to create incentives to invest in education may have a greater impact on poverty if they are designed to get the student "over the hump"—through the end of secondary school and not just to the next grade level.
- The literature suggests that the returns to assets, such as human capital, depend greatly on other public assets that are complements, such as roads, communications systems, and credit markets. Major investment in education, for example, may have limited payoff if individuals cannot commute to a job that uses the higher level of skills. In the same way, a pro-growth policy of building roads in a region may have a greater impact if the population has the human capital to work in emerging industries than if they are sick, illiterate, or constrained by language.
- Policies toward lagging regions may be complicated by the fact that concentrations (agglomerations) of economic activity are self reinforcing—that is, they are more economically dense. Richer areas may have intrinsic dynamism and yield higher returns to capital and labor than poorer areas where there is no natural equilibrating tendency toward geographical equality over the long run. There seems to be ample scope for policies that would facilitate growth and labor mobility in

regions whose citizens have had particularly low levels of access to markets, education, and infrastructure. Yet, as discussed in the World Bank's Latin American region flagship *Beyond the City: The Rural Contribution to Development* (de Ferranti and others 2005), investing excessive state resources in some of these areas could lower overall aggregate growth, and thus governments may eventually face a growth-equity dilemma. Even in such cases, however, a smart combination of conditional cash transfers for the poor and payments for environmental services can enhance both poverty reduction and long-term growth.

Policy implications

These considerations have important implications for specific policies. The report does not offer universal recipes to break the vicious circle between low growth and poverty. For one thing, different countries will likely have different policy priorities; policy makers in poorer and more equal countries should focus mainly on growth, whereas those in richer and more unequal countries should try to balance growth-enhancing objectives with policies to reduce inequality. Nonetheless, the following examples emerge from the report as illustrative.

Making growth more pro-poor

There is no doubt that economic growth has to be at the center of the development strategies, and numerous studies conducted by the Latin American Region of the World Bank have explored constraints on growth that the region faces. For example, both the 2002 and 2003 World Bank's Latin American region flagships (de Ferranti and others, 2002, 2003) stressed the need to address the gaps in education (particularly secondary schooling) and innovation to get the most out of its existing endowments and to develop dynamic new areas of comparative advantage. Similarly, the World Bank's Latin American regional study *The Limits of Stabilization: Infrastructure, Public Deficits, and Growth in Latin America* (Easterly and Servén 2003) stressed how the region's wide gaps in infrastructure implied significant lost opportunities in growth and welfare.

This report offers suggestive evidence that investments in these areas have, in fact, been highly efficient in both promoting growth and allowing the poor to connect with that process over the last 40 years, providing a classical "win-win" situation (see chapter 5). As *Inequality in Latin America: Breaking with History?* (de Ferranti and others 2004) showed, the poor were the primary beneficiaries of efforts within the region in the 1990s to provide universal basic education and health services and to expand some public services, such as access to safe water and electricity (that were already provided to rich and middle-income groups). Going forward, care must be taken to guarantee that the poor continue to benefit from efforts to expand coverage of secondary and tertiary education (which up to now have benefited more middle- and high-income groups) and to improve educational quality. In the same vein, future investments in infrastructure must benefit laggard regions and increase the poor's access to those services where past expansions primarily benefited rich and middle-income groups (telecommunications and access to the Internet, for example).

In addition, under a broad definition of poverty, two other areas have the complementary potential to reduce poverty and promote growth. First, improvements in health have important impacts on welfare and demonstrated positive effects on growth. Second, the report provides conceptual grounds for treating the income, health, and other risks that households face as a critical dimension of poverty. The macroeconomic instability arising from unsound policy therefore has a direct impact on the well-being of the poor and a documented adverse impact on growth.

There are, however, other pro-growth areas where Latin America needs to make progress but where there may be potential trade-offs with inequality and even with poverty reduction goals in the short run, according to the results discussed in chapter 5. Indeed, several previous studies have found that trade openness (an area of particular relevance given potential liberalization efforts) may lead to higher inequality through greater divergence of wage incomes.[2] This result appears to be related to the very desirable adoption of technologies that tend to be skill biased and thus enhance the returns and the demand for education. This phenomenon, found globally, nonetheless leaves the poor, and often poor regions, behind in the short run. Chapter 5 argues that governments may need to take complementary policies behind the border—facilitating access to education, expanding infrastructure to lagging areas with potential to tap into the benefits of liberalization, and providing conditional transfers for poor peasants who may lose out in the transition. Such policies permit a country to take full advantage of the opportunities brought about by trade opening, and thus significantly mitigate the inequality effects and considerably enhance the growth effects of trade liberalization. A parallel argument could be made based on concerns that greater trade openness will increase the risk that workers face. To date, little evidence has emerged to suggest that this is true, but were it the case, income support programs could mitigate the impact on poverty and the disincentive effects on human capital accumulation.

Although chapter 5 suggests that financial deepening over the past 40 years appears to have had adverse impacts on inequality and even on poverty in the short term, chapter 6 finds that it is precisely in countries with low access to financial services where poverty may become more of a drag for investment and growth. Chapters 8 and 9 reinforce this conclusion at the household level. Thus, even if past limited advances in financial deepening in the region may have left most of the poor behind, it is essential that future efforts guarantee that the poor gain access to both credit and insurance markets. Now that Latin America has apparently succeeded in achieving more resilient financial sectors to avoid the costly crises of the past, extending access to credit and insurance markets appears as a key policy agenda to strengthen the virtuous circles between poverty reduction and growth.

Another strand of the literature has explored the impact on poverty of the structure of growth. In particular this literature argues that the higher the representation of sectors that use unskilled labor, the more the favorable effect on poverty. Findings reported in chapter 5 give support to this view. The potential conceptual conflict is that policies that induce a sectoral bias in growth may conflict in the long run with pursuit of a country's natural comparative advantage, leading to growth-impeding inefficiencies. While this report does not delve deeply into the complex (country-specific) issues surrounding the sources of growth and interlinkages across sectors or into the political economy of government intervention, the evidence provided here and in de Ferranti and others (2005) suggests that interventions to induce strong sectoral biases are probably ill advised. A different matter is to ensure that policy biases and inefficiencies against rural development, for example, are lifted and that growth opportunities are enhanced by the efficient provision of public goods and national and sectoral "innovation" policies. Incomes of the poor, including those from agriculture and off-farm activities, thrive with higher trade openness, when public rural expenditures focus on the provision of public goods (such as rural roads, health and education, research and development, and extension services) and when policy biases against labor mobility (such as fiscal generosity for capital-intensive activities and stiff labor markets) are removed.

Nor does this report delve into policies to stimulate more "labor intensity" within all sectors, apart from making sure that potential biases against labor use are removed. However, the previous discussion suggests that one would have to carefully weigh the potential adverse effects on efficiency and growth of more "active" policies in this regard against potential short-term gains in poverty reduction. Given the potential short-term adverse effects of trade opening on poverty and the negative effects of poverty on growth, an area of future research regards the desirability of attempting to keep undervalued exchange rates in the early phases of trade opening, as long as inflationary pressures are kept at bay, as Chile did after 1984 and China is currently practicing.

Pro-poor government policy

In the end, the relatively young literature on pro-poor growth has not given us a feel for how much it is possible to engineer growth in order to promote income distribution. That the differences in the distributions of market incomes between Latin American and OECD countries explain at most only 50 percent of differences in disposable incomes suggests the important complementary role of taxes and public expenditures to ensure that the fruits of growth are broadly distributed. Chapter 5 argues that Latin America has made relatively modest use of these tools. Although recent trends toward universal basic education and health and the introduction of targeted conditional transfers (among others) are likely to have had a progressive impact on the distribution of income, many big-ticket items continue to be highly regressive: the high subsidies to pensions do not benefit the poor since they are seldom covered; since the poor seldom finish secondary education, they do not benefit from subsidized universities; gasoline, electricity, and other goods and services subsidized by the state are mostly consumed by the well-to-do.

Achieving a more redistributive and efficient pattern of public expenditures similar to the OECD patterns would greatly reduce poverty and inequality. However, given the centrality of growth to the goal of poverty reduction, policy makers may wish to ensure that state efforts of such magnitude have favorable effects on growth. Vehicles that condition cash transfers on the acquisition of human capital could be substantially expanded. The forthcoming World Bank's Latin American regional study *The Redistributive Impact of Transfers in Latin America and the Caribbean* finds that conditional cash transfers tend to be well targeted and make a strong marginal contribution to social welfare, outranking not only social insurance schemes but also most of the existing social assistance programs. However, the central thesis of this report is that, in addition to conditional cash transfers, there are numerous other areas where interventions to aid the poor would also be pro-growth. Some of these interventions are reviewed in the next sections.

First, we should emphasize once more that the relative weight of different instruments depends on initial conditions in individual countries. As mentioned above, poor (and more equal) countries should concentrate on achieving increased growth, even at the expense of some increases in inequality, while middle-income countries with high inequality should aim for policies that achieve a better balance of pro-growth and pro-poor effects (including redistribution through conditional transfers).

Pro-growth poverty reduction

The report presents some of the first empirical evidence that poverty adversely affects growth at economywide levels. As noted above, a central channel appears to work through underdeveloped financial sectors—more specifically, through the poor's lack of access to credit. This lack may arise from institutional failures that make contract enforcement difficult and do not address the problems of information asymmetries and the poor's lack of collateralizable wealth. The search for efficient means and innovations to overcome information asymmetries (including credit bureaus) and enforcement constraints and to convert the scarce wealth of the poor into collateralizable assets are key priorities for policy and further research.

Addressing spatial concerns

All the concerns that could potentially lead to lower economic growth at the national level hold for low growth in subnational regions as well, and a case can be made for policies analogous to those discussed above. Further, regional inequalities correlated to ethnic, linguistic, or religious divisions provide fertile ground for internal conflict that can undermine economywide growth. Yet in the world of the New Economic Geography, the case for major reorientation of resources to disadvantaged zones becomes less clear, and the literature to date has been very circumspect on policy prescriptions. Fundamentally, if the existing agglomeration externalities imply that those regions that are already most advanced are also those with the highest potential for growth, concentrating all types of costly infrastructure investments on poor regions may decrease national growth. Unfortunately, the literature offers little guidance on whether the externalities relative to agglomeration or those leading to dispersion of activity are more important, so we cannot know whether existing agglomerations are too big or too small. However, as indicated in *Beyond the City: The Rural Contribution to Development* (de Ferranti and others 2005), some policies targeted to rural areas, such as improved rural education and access to communications, are clearly win-win solutions: they would increase productivity in agriculture and other rural activities and at the same time increase labor mobility toward more productive activities and toward richer areas with higher growth potential.

A more subtle use of geographic information can attenuate the potential trade-offs to some extent. In many countries—the report looks specifically at Bolivia and Brazil—lagging regions frequently have the highest poverty rates, but larger urban areas actually contain the most poor people. Therefore, the theoretical trade-offs, providing existing agglomerations are not too large already, may be less important than initially thought: a large chunk of the poor are, in fact, in areas with potentially higher growth. In addition to those advanced regions with no poverty, three different spatial categories emerge that imply distinct policies, some of which allow investment in potential high-growth areas with large numbers of poor people.

- Areas with *high poverty rates but low poverty density* lack economies of scale arising from agglomeration externalities and are unlikely to develop substantial economic dynamism. Policies thus need to focus more on direct poverty alleviation and on programs that will impart skills useful in other more dynamic regions. Conditional cash transfer programs or other education and health initiatives, agricultural research and development, and payments for environmental services would be most appropriate in these circumstances (see de Ferranti and others 2005).

- In areas with *low poverty rates but high poverty density*, often urban or relatively dense rural areas where agglomeration forces have already taken place, policies aimed at fostering growth have a good chance of reaching the poor and translating into important poverty reductions. The major problem is to ensure that wealthy groups do not capture the flow of resources. For this reason, self-targeting mechanisms, such as those envisaged in the Argentine and Colombian workfare programs, are particularly appropriate. That said, conditional cash transfer schemes, such as those in Colombia and Mexico where targeting is quite good, perform well in this type of situation.
- Areas with *high poverty rates and high poverty density* have the potential to take advantage of projects with economies of scale with low levels of leakage of resources to the nonpoor. Infrastructure investments such as rural roads may be a good example of the type of projects for these kinds of areas.

From a practical point of view, the increasing use of detailed poverty maps to identify poor groups and target poverty policies may yield high dividends.

History suggests, however, that policy makers often either judge that current agglomerations are too big or allow other considerations to lead them to resist abandoning entire regions to low levels of economic activity and extensive conditional cash transfer programs. In fact, as several recent World Bank reports have noted, Latin America has substantial experience with ambitious regional development programs that have met with mixed success. The now vast OECD literature on the effects of public investment policies generally finds a positive impact on growth and sometimes inequality, although, as the Spanish case suggests, they do not necessarily maximize national growth. The evidence for Latin America is thinner but generally concurs.

What should be emphasized, however, is that traditional regional policy has not focused enough on the complementary roles of human capital, knowledge transmission, innovation, and improved economic environments, all of which consistently emerge as correlated with differences in regional income.

Addressing household concerns

Coordinated policies are needed to reverse the vicious cycles of poverty and low asset accumulation in the region. One of the findings of the report in this area is that public investments and policies in one area may have different impacts depending on the existing level of assets and other initial conditions affecting the poor. Ensuring that poor households have access to minimum bundles of assets (such as education, health, or access to infrastructure) is essential for their capacity to exploit growth opportunities.

On the human capital front, demographic forces offer many countries in the region a unique opportunity to translate the human capital accumulation of young cohorts into a more productive labor force and faster reduction in poverty. There is a need for integrated, long-term strategies for skills development that go beyond narrow educational policies and exploit the synergies in the life-cycle human capital accumulation process in which both families and schools play a central role. This calls for actions to correct deficiencies in early-childhood development of poor children, strengthen degree completion and schooling transitions, upgrade education quality for the poor, and improve the fluidity of labor markets. The main specific implications for human capital formation policies are:

- *Leveling the initial playing field for children at risk.* The unequalizing impact of deficiencies in early-childhood development and deficient parenting on poor children's educational attainment and returns to education as adults needs to be addressed. Almost half of the countries in the region are off track on meeting the UN Millennium Development Goal of halving malnutrition by 2015. Early-childhood interventions and other policies that strengthen the capacities of families to create early human capital should be given more attention. For example, conditional cash transfer programs should systematically incorporate health and nutritional components for mothers and infants. The experience with the Head Start program in the United States and similar interventions elsewhere in the world may merit consideration for replication in the region.
- *Strengthening the full option value of education for the poor.* Education policies should aim to strengthen transitions to secondary school and enable opportunities for tertiary education for the poor. While spending and reform priorities must be set according to binding constraints, acting at all levels of the education system, even on a small scale, is crucial to signal

low-income families that their educational investments have better chances of maturing in higher grades. Where returns are high and basic infrastructure is deficient, the construction and upgrading of schools and roads are of paramount importance. The development of multigrade schools, learning from best practices such as the Colombian *Escuela Nueva* and the Chilean MECE Rural, can address supply constraints cost-effectively; when appropriate, public-private partnerships and other modalities such as distance education should be considered. Schemes to use conditional cash transfers to the poor for encouraging completion of full courses of education (basic or lower secondary) may hold promise to reduce dropouts especially of children from poor families and parents with little education. Also needed are policies to promote the development of the tertiary education market, including student loan programs and well-designed (means-tested and merit-based) university scholarships.

- *Making education count for the poor.* Increasing or leveling the returns to educational investments of the poor is key to encourage them to move up the education ladder. Well-informed actions to improve the scholastic performance of poor children are needed. These may include removing automatic promotion policies in early grades, offering special programs to address learning deficiencies resulting from a poor learning environment at home, and addressing failures in the instruction process such as inadequate teaching and large class sizes. Effective interventions include decentralizing school management to get parents more involved in their children's school progress, offering incentives to encourage qualified teachers to work in disadvantaged schools, adapting innovations to improve learning environments in disadvantaged schools and communities, upgrading textbooks and school aids, providing teacher training, expanding computer education in secondary schools, and consistently using international standardized tests to assess performance progress. Some targeted and performance-based increases in public expenditures, particularly at the secondary level, might be needed in some countries.

Finally, chapter 9 shows that the higher levels of labor market risk found in the region have strong disincentive effects on the accumulation of human capital that, in turn, slow down growth. Income security policies, such as unemployment insurance, workfare programs, or conditional cash transfers as used in Colombia, therefore become both pro-poor and pro-growth. Policies to improve access to jobs may be needed that include enacting and enforcing antidiscrimination laws and establishing labor market intermediation services that help well-educated ethnic and racial populations gain greater access to better-quality jobs.

Some of the best policies from a social cost-benefit calculation, such as early-childhood interventions and overhauls of the educational system, may be complex to implement for reasons of political economy. However, considering the positive spillovers on technology adoption, productivity, and growth from a labor force with a minimum level of education, it is hard to overstate the critical importance of overcoming political failures that prevent pushing "education for all" (see de Ferranti and others 2003). This is critical to the region's long-term human capital accumulation and prospects for sustained growth. In many countries, the demographic window of opportunity is closing; the time to invest is now.

Bridging the gaps in both the quantity and quality of education and other productive characteristics of workers can go a long way toward reducing the wide earnings disparities in the region, but it will not be enough to reduce poverty significantly. In most countries, low levels of labor productivity are a chief constraint to earnings potential. Policies that promote an economic and institutional environment conducive to productivity growth are thus important to reduce the incidence of low-paid jobs and in turn make investments in skills more attractive.

For example, rural investments seem to correlate positively with rural household characteristics, indicating a need to increase access to markets through expansion of basic infrastructure while simultaneously strengthening the capacity of households to ensure a minimum level of wealth and education skills.

Rural development could be made more inclusive with some minimum coordination of rural investments and programs—such as education, the construction of roads to markets, the establishment of microcredit schemes, and the provision of agricultural extension—to ensure that all the potential returns to these investments are realized and the conditions of the rural poor improved. A minimum coordination of public interventions in poor areas can help exploit synergies and overcome the associated potential poverty traps that may affect households with a bundling of unfavorable characteristics.

How are we going to pay for these interventions?

This report offers a relatively large number of areas that may require additional attention if the vicious circle between growth and poverty is to be converted into a virtuous circle. For example, it urges that the levels of human capital and public infrastructure in the region be expanded, in particular by increasing the poor's access to quality education and infrastructure. Similarly, it argues that an expansion of conditional cash transfer programs (especially in richer countries) would likely have a sustained impact on poverty reduction and growth. But what are the real possibilities the region has for financing these interventions, which in some cases can be quite expensive?

It is crucial that policy makers step up efforts toward improving the efficiency of the system and achieving better targeting before they increase public spending. For example, as noted in chapter 5, a number of big-ticket items such as tertiary education are highly regressive. Moreover, many public transfer programs such as pensions or unemployment insurance are typically poorly targeted and do not reach many of the poor. Policy makers are likely to face a trade-off between targeting and coverage: the greater the number of poor covered by a program, the more difficult it is to avoid leakages. A careful review of existing social programs, however, can result in significant savings that may be redirected to priority areas. Even more important, although they would require politically difficult reforms, highly regressive subsidies—of pensions for the well-to-do, of university students from wealthy families or who pay back educational credits, and of the consumption of energy by the middle class and the rich—offer huge opportunities to reallocate expenditures.

Once these potential gains have been tapped, and once efforts to curtail tax evasion have been stepped up, policy makers can consider increasing tax rates. In this regard, chapter 5 argues that most countries in the region (with a few exceptions such as Brazil and Nicaragua) have tax collections that are below what would be expected from their per capita income (figure 1.12). This, too, is a window of opportunity because bringing Latin America in line with the international experience in tax collections would allow some extra space to finance part of the expenditure priorities of the region. One related issue discussed in chapter 5 is that countries aiming at increasing tax collections should avoid, to the extent that it is possible, tax structures with

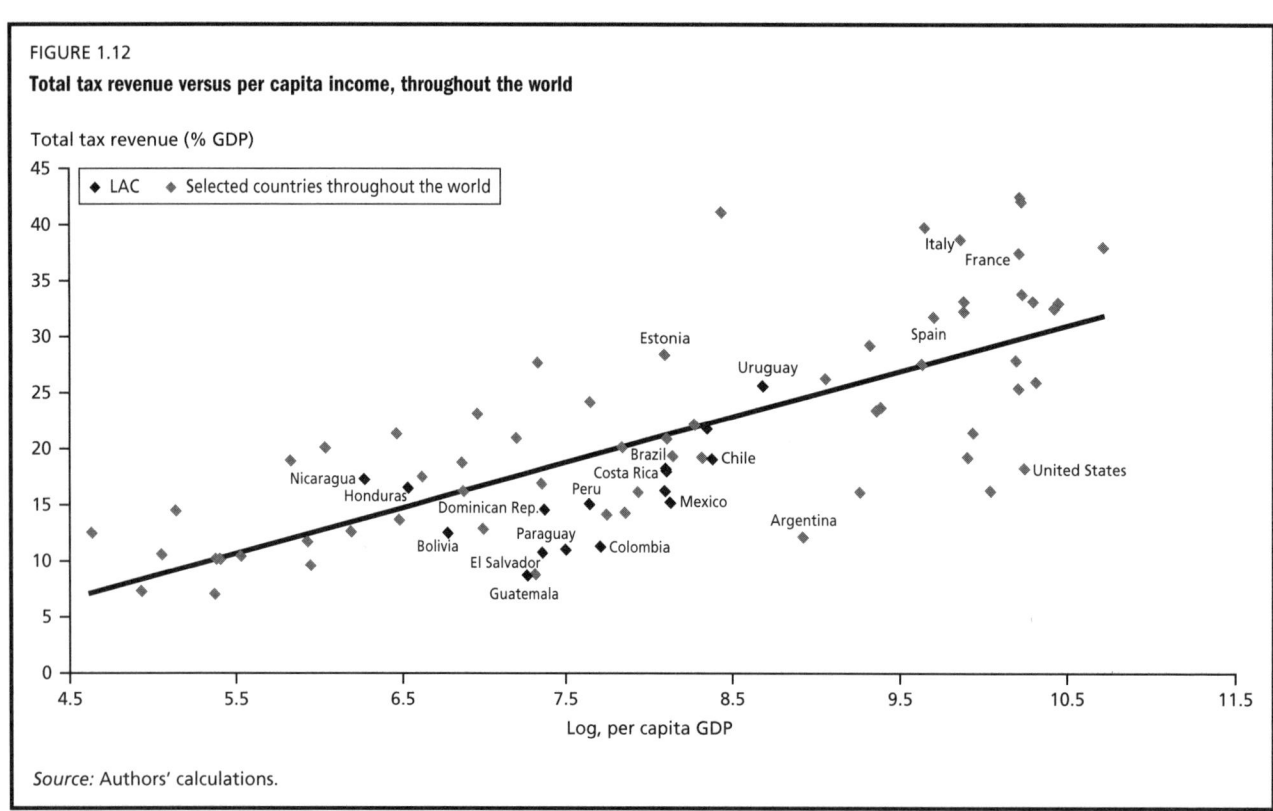

FIGURE 1.12
Total tax revenue versus per capita income, throughout the world

Source: Authors' calculations.

high efficiency costs. Latin American countries tend to have especially low levels of collections from personal income and property taxes—the very taxes that may have some redistributive effect without large costs to economic growth. Thus well-designed systems could increase tax collections while keeping the impact on growth low. Also, the region's value added and income tax productivity is significantly lower than it is in the OECD countries, and most Latin American countries maintain a large set of exemptions that significantly reduce the tax base. Thus the elimination of exemptions combined with additional efforts to enforce compliance would likely increase collections.

Converting the state into an agent that promotes equality of opportunities and practices efficient redistribution is, perhaps, the most critical challenge Latin America faces in implementing better policies that simultaneously stimulate growth and reduce inequality and poverty.

Notes

1. The Gini coefficient is a standard measure of inequality that ranges between 0 and 1. A value of 0 would indicate a perfectly equal distribution. As inequality increases, the Gini coefficient also tends to increase.

2. See, for example, de Ferranti and others (2003); Lederman, Maloney, and Servén (2005); and World Bank (2005c).

CHAPTER 2

Dimensions of Well-Being, Channels to Growth

This chapter reviews recent trends in poverty and inequality in Latin America and the Caribbean, along with the well-known concerns about the implications of static measures of poverty and inequality. The review shows that such concerns are not merely conceptual curiosities—incorporating them in the analysis can and does lead to very different conclusions about the evolution of welfare in the region and complicates inferences about the effect of growth on the welfare of the poor. As important, however, these more complete measures of welfare open several additional channels through which poverty or inequality can affect growth.

THE PERSISTENCE OF HIGH LEVELS OF poverty remains the central disappointment of the last 20 years in Latin America. This chapter begins by presenting the standard indicators of income poverty and inequality for the region—the share of the population living below $2 a day and Gini coefficients—their recent evolution, and some caveats surrounding the conclusions we draw from them.

However, it has long been acknowledged that such indicators are very imperfect measures of well-being, both of the poor and of the society as a whole.[1] Many of the points made in this chapter were foreshadowed in Kuznets's seminal "Economic Growth and Income Inequality," published in 1955; others were made by Sen (1985). Yet in the context of understanding the reinforcing relationship between growth and poverty reduction, these points gain renewed importance. First, to understand how growth may affect the poor, we need to understand the channels through which different characteristics of growth affect the quality of life of individuals across dimensions of well-being, across their lives, and across generations.

Second, excessive narrowness in understanding poverty can lead to overlooking important channels through which the reverse causality may occur and thus prevents the fullest understanding possible of the virtuous circles between poverty reduction and growth. As is generally the case with these reports, we aim not to provide the final word, but rather to contribute some new ideas or, in this case, some new evidence on old ideas, to the debate.

Income poverty

Table 2.1 suggests that the rate of income poverty in Latin America is 24.6 percent, based on a poverty line of $2 a day in purchasing power parity (PPP) weighted by population and using the latest available surveys.[2] It is somewhat higher in Central America and Mexico (30 percent) and the Andean Community (31 percent) and lower in the countries of the Southern Cone (around 19 percent), which nonetheless have a larger number of the poor by virtue of their larger populations. The sample does not have comparable measures for the Caribbean as a whole, but the two most populous countries (excluding Cuba) have poverty rates of 16.4 percent (Dominican Republic) and 44.1 percent (Jamaica). Very similar patterns emerge when working with unweighted averages, which are more relevant when the analysis requires taking the country as the unit of analysis rather than the individual.[3]

TABLE 2.1

Poverty in Latin America (US$2 a day headcount poverty)

Region	Early 1990s (i)	Early 2000s (ii)	Last survey (iii)	Change (iii) –(i)
A. Southern Cone				
Poverty (weighted) (%)	23.6	19.0	18.8	–4.9
Poverty (unweighted) (%)	18.1	16.2	17.1	–1.1
Population (million)	204.4	244.4	246.4	42.1
Number of poor (million)	48.3	46.5	46.2	–2.1
B. Andean community				
Poverty (weighted) (%)	24.8	34.9	31.4	6.6
Poverty (unweighted) (%)	30.6	37.2	34.0	3.4
Population (million)	94.4	118.3	118.0	23.6
Number of poor (million)	23.4	41.3	37.1	13.7
C. Central America and Mexico				
Poverty (weighted) (%)	30.5	29.2	29.2	–1.3
Poverty (unweighted) (%)	36.5	30.0	30.1	–6.4
Population (million)	112.7	140.4	139.6	26.8
Number of poor (million)	34.4	41.0	40.8	6.4
Latin America (A+B+C)				
Poverty (weighted) (%)	25.8	25.6	24.6	–1.2
Poverty (unweighted) (%)	29.3	28.1	27.4	–1.9
Population (million)	411.5	503.1	504.0	92.6
Number of poor (million)	106.1	128.8	124.1	18.0

Source: Gasparini, Gutierrez, and Tornarolli (2005).
Note: Weighted refers to population-weighted averages.

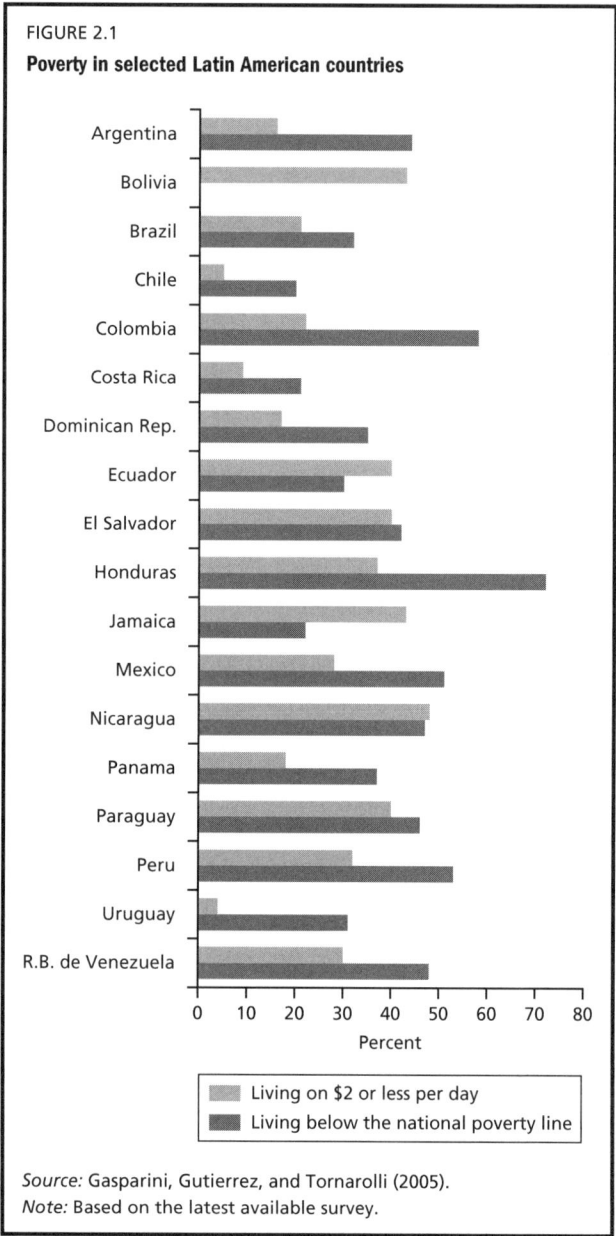

FIGURE 2.1

Poverty in selected Latin American countries

Source: Gasparini, Gutierrez, and Tornarolli (2005).
Note: Based on the latest available survey.

Figure 2.1 offers a closer examination of the great variety of poverty levels across countries. Chile and Uruguay have the lowest poverty rates (about 5 percent) followed very closely by Costa Rica (9 percent). At the other extreme, despite the significant progress made over the past few years, poverty in Nicaragua remains at levels of 50 percent. Although comparable numbers for Haiti are not available, other sources show it to have the most extreme poverty, at between 73 percent and 83 percent.[4] These are followed by several countries with poverty levels around 40 percent (including Bolivia, Ecuador, El Salvador, Guatemala, Honduras, and Jamaica). Among the most populated countries, poverty rates are slightly above 30 percent in Mexico, Peru, and República Bolivariana de Venezuela; about 20 percent in Brazil and Colombia; and about 16 percent in Argentina.

Nationally defined poverty tends to be higher than the measure of $2 a day in most of the countries, although the differences between these two measures are not uniform across countries (box 2.1).

Table 2.1 also suggests that the region has made relatively little progress in reducing poverty over the past 15 years. The weighted average poverty rate declined by only 1.2 percentage points between the early 1990s and the last available survey, and of this decline a significant component was probably related to the recent recovery of the regional economy in 2003 and 2004.[5] Again, there are substantial regional differences. Poverty fell slightly in Central America (from 30 to 29 percent), increased in the Andean Community (from 25 to 31 percent, with a peak of 35 percent in the early 2000s), and declined in the Southern Cone area (from 24 to 19 percent).[6] In the Caribbean, Jamaica experienced a decline in poverty of 15 percentage points between the early 1990s and early 2000s, while the

BOX 2.1
Income poverty lines

Income poverty is defined as the inability to achieve a certain minimum income level, known as the poverty line. Even this limited definition can be contentious because there are neither normative nor objectively clear arguments for setting the line at a particular value below which everybody is poor and above which everyone is nonpoor (Deaton 1997). Despite this central conceptual ambiguity, reducing poverty is still a deliberate policy objective for governments around the world and has been embraced as a Millennium Development Goal by the international community.

Because of the fundamental arbitrariness in defining poverty, different authors and agencies use different poverty lines. The international poverty line is set at $1 a day per person at purchasing power parity (PPP) prices. That measure is meant to define an international norm to gauge the inability to pay for food needs. The $1-a-day line was formally proposed in Ravallion, Datt, and van de Walle (1991) and is generally used in the World Bank's 1990 *World Development Report*. It is a value measured in 1985 international prices and adjusted to local currency using purchasing power parities to take local prices into account. The $1 standard was chosen as being representative of the national poverty lines found among low-income countries. The line has been recalculated in 1993 PPP terms at $1.0763 a day (Chen and Ravallion 2001). This value is multiplied by 30.42 to get a monthly poverty line. Although the $1-a-day line has been criticized, its simplicity and the lack of reasonable and easy-to-implement alternatives has made it the standard for international poverty comparisons. It is, for example, the basis of the United Nations' Millennium Development Goal 1, which calls for eradicating extreme poverty and hunger by halving between 1990 and 2015 the proportion of people whose income is less than $1 a day. A $2-a-day line is also extensively used in comparisons across middle-income countries and is periodically presented in the World Bank's *World Development Indicators*.

Most Latin American countries calculate two poverty lines: national extreme poverty, which is based primarily on the cost of a basic food bundle, and moderate poverty, computed from the extreme lines using the Engel/Orshansky ratio of food expenditures. This methodology is also used by ECLAC (Economic Commission for Latin America and the Caribbean), which in some cases helps governments to calculate the national poverty lines. Despite some similarities, methodologies for estimating national poverty levels differ substantially across nations so they are not comparable. Some countries, such as Mexico, use expenditures; others, such as Argentina, use incomes; and still others, such as Bolivia, use a mix of income and expenditures.

Both international and national measures of poverty are useful. Measurements that use national poverty lines take into consideration the different criteria societies use to identify the poor, while international poverty lines are indispensable instruments for comparing absolute poverty levels and trends across countries and providing regional and world poverty counts.

Nationally defined poverty tends to be higher than $2 a day in most of the countries in Latin America, although the differences are not uniform across countries. Moreover, in three countries—Jamaica, Ecuador, and Nicaragua—the national poverty lines are lower than the internationally defined poverty line. As a result, the poverty ranking in the LAC region changes significantly when one focuses on national poverty lines. Based on national poverty lines, poverty is highest in Honduras (above 70 percent), Colombia and Peru (about 55 percent), and Mexico (51 percent) and lowest in Chile, Costa Rica, and Jamaica (around 20 percent).

Comparison of the comparable international and national poverty figures indicates that in some countries like Argentina, Colombia, Honduras, and Mexico, the national definition of poverty is quite generous (people are being classified as poor in these countries who might not be considered poor in other countries of the region). In contrast, Chile, Costa Rica, El Salvador, and Paraguay appear to use poverty concepts that are very exclusive (people who are not considered poor in these countries might qualify as poor in others). It is worth noting that in some cases the deviations from the regression line are quite important. For example, in Honduras the national poverty rate is 35 percentage points above the internationally comparable poverty rate, whereas in Jamaica it is 21 percentage points below.

Source: Gasparini, Gutierrez, and Tornarolli (2005).

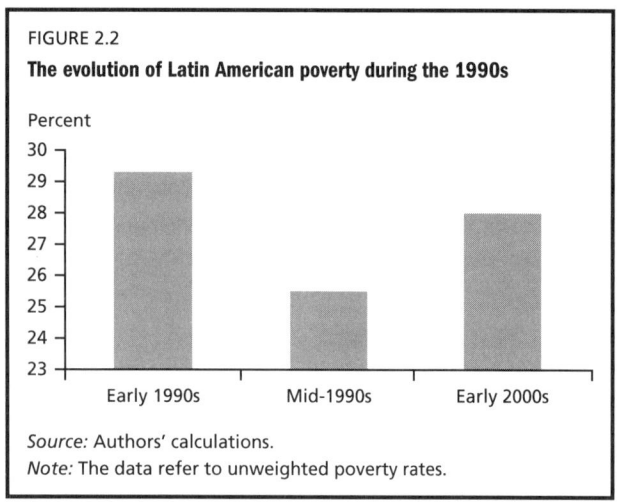

FIGURE 2.2
The evolution of Latin American poverty during the 1990s

Source: Authors' calculations.
Note: The data refer to unweighted poverty rates.

Dominican Republic sustained an 8-percentage-point increase over the same period.

Figure 2.2 suggests that the decadal averages, in fact, obscure important dynamics.[7] The regional poverty rate may have fallen by almost 4 percentage points between the early and mid-1990s, a period of expansion, and increased by almost 3 percentage points between the mid-1990s and early 2000s following the financial crises of East Asia in 1997 and Russia in 1998.

The lack of progress on the poverty front since 1980 is caused both by low average economic growth rates during the period (table 2.2) and by the high and generally stagnant levels of income inequality in the region. Despite some success stories such as Chile (which managed to grow at annual rates above 4 percent per capita over the 1990–2003 period), growth in Latin America during the 1990s was low. Per capita growth for the region as a whole averaged about 1 percent between 1990 and 2003 (see box 2.2 for a discussion of differences in the measures of growth). At this growth rate, per capita GDP doubles every 65 years. That implies that on a continuous trend, the region would need about 150 years to reach the per capita income level of the United States today. The median growth rate for the region during the 1990–2003 period was also around 1 percent, indicating that the poor performance is not the result of a few of the most populated countries displaying low economic growth. In fact, only half of the countries in the region managed to grow at rates above 1 percent. Similarly, fewer than one in four countries averaged per capita growth above 2 percent.

Inequality trends were dealt with in great detail in our flagship report *Inequality in Latin America and the Caribbean, Breaking with History?* (de Ferranti and others 2004); here we offer only a historical view of the evolution of the regionwide Gini coefficients since 1950 (figure 2.3). After some progress in the 1960s and 1970s, inequality levels rose during the lost decade of the 1980s; this increase was not reversed during the 1990s and may, in fact, have continued. As chapter 4 discusses in detail, the level of inequality is an important factor in how "pro-poor" growth is.

As box 2.3 suggests, however, this picture of inequality may be overly pessimistic. Poverty lines need to be adjusted for inflation across time, and Goñi, Lopez, and

TABLE 2.2
Economic growth in Latin America

Region	1990–93	1993–97	1997–2000	2000–03	1990–2003
A. Southern Cone					
Growth (weighted)	2.27	2.85	0.32	−0.52	1.35
Median	3.22	3.16	−0.55	−1.38	0.99
B. Andean community					
Growth (weighted)	0.95	1.84	−1.79	−0.40	0.27
Median	0.58	1.83	−0.55	0.87	0.52
C. Central America and Mexico					
Growth (weighted)	1.41	0.76	3.21	−0.95	1.07
Median	3.30	1.14	2.47	−0.37	1.38
Latin America					
Growth (weighted)	1.78	2.08	0.77	−0.61	1.08
Median	2.08	1.76	0.37	0.46	1.04

Source: Authors' calculations.

DIMENSIONS OF WELL-BEING, CHANNELS TO GROWTH

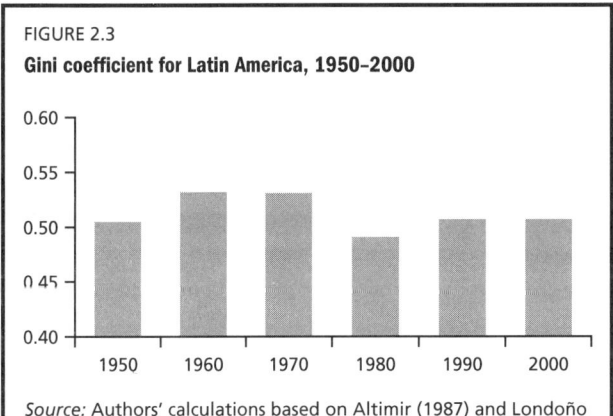

FIGURE 2.3
Gini coefficient for Latin America, 1950–2000

Source: Authors' calculations based on Altimir (1987) and Londoño and Szekely (2000).
Note: Based on data for Brazil, Chile, Mexico, and República Bolivariana de Venezuela.

Servén (2005) show that standard inflation numbers correspond to the consumption basket of the very well-off and greatly overstate the level of inflation relevant to the poor. Hence, deflating poverty lines, or each income share comprising the Gini, by the common consumer price index (CPI) imparts a strongly antipoor bias to the summary statistics during this period.

The implications of these findings are far reaching. To begin, Latin America is doing better than was initially thought on the poverty and distribution fronts, and hence concerns about the negative distributional impacts of reforms have probably been overstated. Second, real figures obtained using incorrect deflators may potentially confuse the relationship between different types of growth strategies

---

BOX 2.2
National accounts and household surveys–based growth: How different are they?

In a joint analysis of poverty and growth, one issue that must be considered is the source of the data used to compute the growth rates. The Latin American growth trends reviewed here are based on the evolution of national accounts (NA) data, whereas poverty rates are computed on the basis of household surveys. If the implied growth rates of the NA and the surveys were the same, then using survey-based poverty rates and national accounts growth rates to analyze the evolution of poverty and growth over time would not be misleading. In practice, however, surveys and NA tend to generate different growth rates, with national accounts data usually producing higher estimates than household surveys (see Deaton 2005 for a discussion).

The figure plots the growth rates based on surveys against those based on the national accounts. Two large outliers are apparent in this figure, one in the southwest quadrant (PRY, or Paraguay) and the other in the southeast quadrant (DOM, or Dominican Republic). The regression line in this chart has an associated slope of 0.97 and an intercept of about −0.9. While the estimated slope suggests an almost one-to-one relationship between the growth rates derived from the two sources, the negative intercept indicates that national accounts growth rates tend to be much higher (almost 1 percentage point) than survey-based estimates.

What does this difference imply in practice? First, since changes in poverty are related to changes in household survey–based income growth, it could be perfectly possible that an increase in poverty associated with a national accounts–based growth episode would be observed (especially at low growth levels). Instead of reflecting an antipoor growth episode, the increase in poverty would just capture the existing statistical discrepancy between two different data sources. Second, if the difference between national accounts and household survey–based data results from a bias in the survey data, then the poverty statistics will be biased upward.

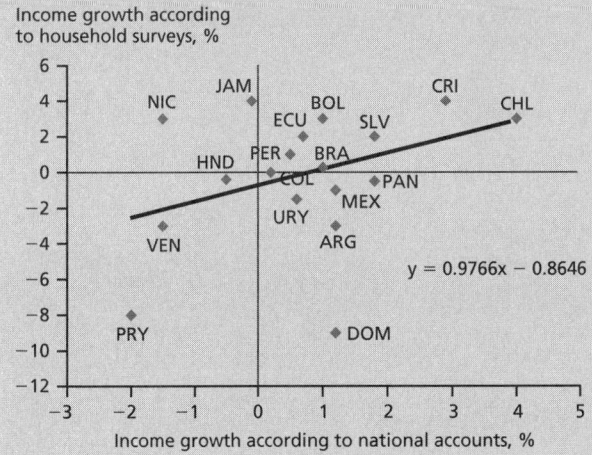

Survey-based income growth versus national accounts–based income growth

BOX 2.3

Inflation inequality: What really happened to LAC poverty and inequality

Rich and poor families consume different baskets of goods, and the inflation rates of these baskets can differ greatly. Goñi, Lopez, and Servén (2005) show that using the aggregate CPI can greatly mislead policy. For one thing, tax brackets, pensions, social transfers, and minimum wages are often indexed to the CPI, and using an inappropriate aggregate index can lead to real transfers among income classes that were not intended. In addition, the picture of the evolution of poverty and inequality can be sharply distorted by assuming that deflators are similar across income classes, either by working with undeflated nominal baskets of goods, or by using aggregate deflators, and contaminating inference about the relationship between these variables and growth or policy.

In Latin America and the Caribbean, as in the OECD, most officially reported inflation rates correspond to the inflation rates of the very rich—defined as those with income between the 80th and 90th percentiles; for the very rich, inflation is relatively high, as the figure for Peru shows. In Brazil (1988–96) the inflation differential between the highest and lowest viniventiles (5 percentile intervals) is 7 percentage points *a year* and in Colombia (1997–2003), Mexico (1996–2002), and Peru (2001–3), the difference is a lower but still noticeable 0.5–0.7 per-

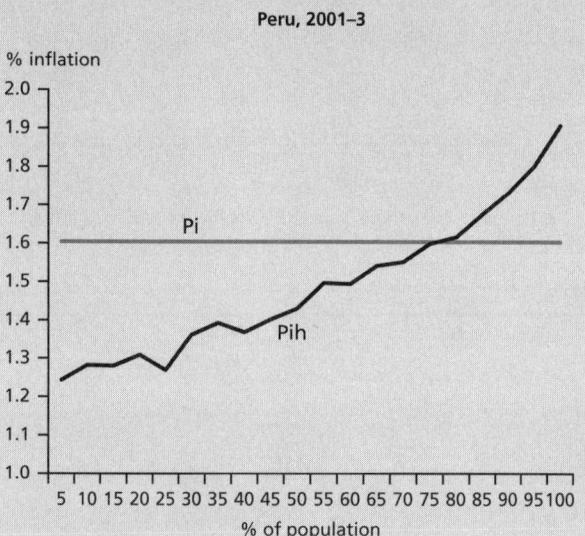

Individual inflation by decile and average annual inflation by viniventiles

Peru, 2001–3

centage points a year. These patterns persist even after adjusting for quality change bias and after recomputing Paasche indexes to control for potential substitution effects.

Since most inequality indexes are calculated using nominal expenditures, such inflation differentials lead to apparent movements in *nominal* inequality without any

Distribution effects of inflation

Period	Inequality t1 (Gini)	Inequality t2 (Gini)	Change (%)	Price change	Quantity change
Brazil					
1988–96	0.54	0.55	1.60	2.17	−0.58
Colombia					
1997–2003	0.53	0.50	−5.49	1.92	−7.41
Mexico					
1984–89	0.50	0.50	−0.20	2.77	−2.97
1989–94	0.50	0.49	−1.85	1.38	−3.23
1994–96	0.49	0.46	−6.88	−1.30	−5.57
1996–2002	0.46	0.49	6.32	1.42	4.90
Peru					
1995–99	0.46	0.50	9.91	1.28	8.63
1999–2001	0.50	0.49	−2.72	1.05	−3.78
2001–03	0.49	0.48	−1.21	0.47	−1.67

real movement, much the way nominal growth rates may rise even if there is no real growth. To measure the magnitude of these distortions, we first recalculate the expenditure of each household in the first period with prices of the second period to get the "real" changes in inequality. Analogously, the difference in the inequality index caused by revaluing the first-period bundle using second-period prices gives us "nominal" changes in inequality.

The table shows the distribution effects of inflation and suggests that these distortions are very important. First, in only one of the nine time spans do prices exert a negative contribution on nominal inequality (Mexico, 1994–96): during the tequila crisis, inflation was antipoor and led to a lower reduction in real inequality than suggested by the standard inequality figures. However, in all the other cases, the changes in the standard inequality measures overstated the changes in real inequality and importantly so. In six of the eight cases (Brazil 1988–96, Colombia 1997–2003, Mexico 1984–89 and 1989–94, and Peru 1999–2001 and 2001–3), the change in prices offset the effect of changes in quantities. In Brazil (1988–96) the real distribution of income improved despite an apparent increase in the Gini. Similarly, in Mexico (1984–89) the Gini showed a small improvement in inequality (−0.2), whereas the real decline was much larger (−2.97). Finally, there are two cases (Mexico 1996–2002 and Peru 1995–99) where price and quantity effects reinforced each other to exaggerate worsening inequality, with prices contributing 23 percent and 12 percent, respectively, of the total variation in nominal inequality.

Source: Based on Goñi, Lopez, and Servén (2005).

and their impact on poverty. For instance, liberalizations and devaluations, *by their design*, have the goal of changing relative prices of goods within the economy. When assessing the impact of trade liberalization on the poor, for example, one needs to ask not only what the impact is on the production side—labor income—but also on the specific basket of goods consumed by the poor. Liberalization of trade in corn in Mexico under NAFTA (the North American Free Trade Agreement) could have led to lower prices that reduced the income of poor corn producers. But one must also take into account the decline in the cost of maize, a key element in the consumption basket of the poor. As a result, the CPI of the poor falls relative to that of the well-off, which is what the national CPI measures. The poor, both urban and rural, are in fact better off than the national CPI would suggest. In a symmetrical way, an increase in the price of cars caused by new export opportunities would affect the bundle of the rich far more than that of the poor who consume them less.

The striking fact is that, in both cases, if the price changes do not lead to major substitutions away from these goods, the Ginis will move in unexpected directions even if calculated correctly. If the poor save the money gained from buying maize more cheaply, their nominal consumption will appear to fall, and if the rich borrow to buy the more expensive car, the value of their consumption will appear to rise. Since the consumption share of the poor is falling and that of the rich is rising, the Gini will appear to worsen even though, in real terms across the course of their lives, distribution has without question improved. The example highlights both the desirability of working in real terms and the need to introduce the intertemporal considerations discussed below.

Beyond income and consumption

It has long been acknowledged that measures of income or consumption poverty and distribution capture well-being only very imperfectly. Sen's celebrated "capacities" approach to poverty analysis stresses the centrality of often overlooked dimensions of deprivation. In his book *Development as Freedom,* for example, Sen (1999) argues that Europe's favorable measures of income inequality relative to those in the United States are offset to an important degree by high unemployment rates in Europe that inhibit participation in the labor market and associated social networks. In another example, he notes that despite their relatively high money incomes, African American men have lower average life spans than Chinese, Costa Ricans, or Jamaicans. Deaton and Paxton (2001) and Becker, Philipson, and Soares (2005) document this fact more rigorously:

clearly there is a component of the health dimension of well-being that is uncorrelated with income and thus needs to be somehow integrated separately into comparisons of welfare. Since the Millennium Development Goals focus attention on deprivation in multiple dimensions, this agenda is extraordinarily relevant.

However, it is far from trivial to operationalize.[8] Markets for some proposed attributes of poverty—longevity, the provision of public goods, security, even freedom and literacy—are imperfect or do not exist and thus provide little guidance on their relative values to the poor.[9] As Atkinson and Bourguignon (1982) show, adding just one dimension (in their case, adding mortality to income) raises the complexity of welfare comparisons significantly: the conclusions about how much and in which direction welfare changed for 61 countries between 1960 and 1970 depend heavily on what particular form of the social welfare function is used to combine the two dimensions. The same indeterminacy emerged in rural Brazil when Bourguignon and Chakravarty (2003) sought to combine income poverty and "educational poverty" measures, which moved in opposite directions.[10] Recent ferment in this literature has generated numerous techniques for multidimensional comparisons, and a careful discussion is beyond the scope of this report.[11] What is clear, however, is a consensus that researchers need to look beyond traditional income measures and that nonincome dimensions of poverty are of important magnitudes and can radically change the view of the evolution of well-being.

One approach to quantifying these magnitudes is offered by Becker, Philipson, and Soares (2005), who convert life span into monetary values to calculate a measure of total welfare gain by calculating how much people would pay for an additional year of life (annex 2A). Globally, convergence in life expectancy has been impressive compared with convergence of incomes, with the "longevity Gini" halving from 0.13 to 0.07 even as the income per capita Gini decreased only slightly. Looking at Latin America and the Caribbean more specifically, Soares (2004) argues that longevity and hence welfare have increased substantially despite continued political instability and almost permanent crisis over the last 25 years. Between 1960 and 2000, average per capita income in the region doubled, from $3,419 to $6,865 (in 1996 international prices). At the same time, average life expectancy at birth increased by 13 years, from 57 to 70 years, an increase that translates into an average monetary gain of roughly $1,365 per capita, or roughly half the monetary gain (table 2.3). But as important, progress in income and longevity has not always been highly correlated, and in some countries—Bolivia, El Salvador, Honduras, and Peru—the greater part of the welfare gains has been in longevity, with life expectancy increasing 20 years while incomes remained relatively stagnant.

Improvements in life expectancy during this period took place across different age groups and causes of death, but most were concentrated at early and old ages and were driven by reductions in mortality from infectious diseases, respiratory and digestive diseases, congenital anomalies and perinatal period conditions, and heart and circulatory diseases. These in turn appear to be driven by improvements in health infrastructure and large-scale immunizations that increased substantially across the period. Soares (2005) finds similar patterns looking across Brazilian municipalities. Life expectancy gains were largely independent of income, but represented between 22 and 35 percent of welfare gains across municipalities. More than half of these gains, 51 percent, can be explained by improved access to water and sanitation and greater literacy.

Soares (2004) also looks at how an environment of insecurity and violence affects welfare. He calculates that, globally, reducing violence rates to zero would add an average of one-third of a year in life expectancy at birth that would have a lifetime value of approximately 15 percent of GDP. For Colombia, Soares calculates that violence reduces life expectancy by 2.2 years, representing a welfare loss on the order of 100 percent of current GDP; for Brazil, the welfare loss is 38 percent.

Although these calculations depend on assumptions that may be debated, at a minimum they suggest that these dimensions of well-being are not well captured by income and are of sufficient magnitudes that they cannot be omitted from the picture of the well-being of the poor. And both longevity and violence potentially have important impacts on growth. The issues related to health are discussed in chapter 7. Those related to violence have been reviewed by Bourguignon (2001) and Londoño and Guerrero (2000) and will not be developed further here.[12] In sum, not only are direct impacts on welfare obtained from a focus on a broader measure of poverty, but these then can feed back into growth.

TABLE 2.3
Welfare gains from increased longevity

Region/country	Income per capita (US$)		Life expectancy at birth (years)		Value of life expectancy gains (US$)	Health share of welfare gain (%)
	1960	2000	1960	2000	1960–2000	1950–2000
Europe and Central Asia	6,813	13,864	68	73	1,454	17
East Asia and Pacific	1,319	5,667	47	70	2,600	37
Middle East and North Africa	1,911	4,898	48	68	1,719	37
North America	12,378	31,761	70	77	2,804	13
South Asia	888	2,269	44	62	635	31
Sub-Saharan Africa	1,442	1,583	41	47	73	34
Latin America and the Caribbean	3,419	6,865	57	70	1,365	28
Argentina	7,386	11,201	65	74	1,071	22
Barbados	6,007	15,850	65	75	2,174	18
Bolivia	2,152	2,701	43	63	881	62
Brazil	2,514	6,989	55	68	1,380	24
Chile	3,919	9,591	58	76	2,383	30
Colombia	2,481	5,393	57	71	951	25
Costa Rica	3,514	5,597	62	78	850	29
Dominican Republic	1,698	4,967	53	67	1,157	26
Ecuador	2,100	3,413	54	70	668	34
El Salvador	3,411	4,339	52	70	1,130	55
Guatemala	2,613	4,005	46	65	1,288	48
Honduras	1,682	2,082	47	66	468	54
Jamaica	2,301	3,286	65	75	283	22
Mexico	3,976	8,391	58	73	1,941	31
Nicaragua	3,204	1,672	48	69	399	−35
Panama	2,453	6,134	61	75	926	20
Paraguay	2,053	4,545	64	70	277	10
Peru	3,179	4,479	49	69	1,482	53
Trinidad and Tobago	3,922	10,557	64	73	1,394	17
Uruguay	5,835	9,919	68	74	624	13
Venezuela, R.B. de	4,480	6,279	60	73	1,062	37

Source: Becker, Philipson, and Soares (2005) calculations.

Why not just ask them?

Given the difficulties in combining nonmonetary measures, a reasonable question might be: "Why not just ask people whether they regard themselves as poor?" This has recently been done in Argentina (Lucchetti 2005), Bolivia (Arias and Sosa-Escudero 2004), and the Dominican Republic (World Bank 2005b), generating some striking conclusions. First, the subjective surveys and income measures generate similar numbers of households in poverty, with roughly 65 percent of the households falling under the poverty line also reporting that they are poor. Second, in all cases, many and varied household characteristics carry a very high statistical significance as determinants of subjective poverty. This finding suggests both that subjective responses contain real content and that a wide variety of factors go into the consideration of being poor, consistent with a multidimensional poverty approach. Third, probit analyses by Arias and Sosa-Excudero for Bolivia suggest that these characteristics appear to be highly similar in their influence on both subjective and objective measures (figure 2.4).

Finally, there are some notable exceptions to these generalizations; we offer four examples:

First, in Argentina, being unemployed has an effect on self-rated poverty that is four times higher than would be predicted by the objective poverty line. This is consistent with Sen's idea that being effectively excluded from the workforce has impacts on well-being extending beyond

POVERTY REDUCTION AND GROWTH: VIRTUOUS AND VICIOUS CIRCLES

FIGURE 2.4

Income poverty profile for Bolivia: self-rated by head of household versus data driven

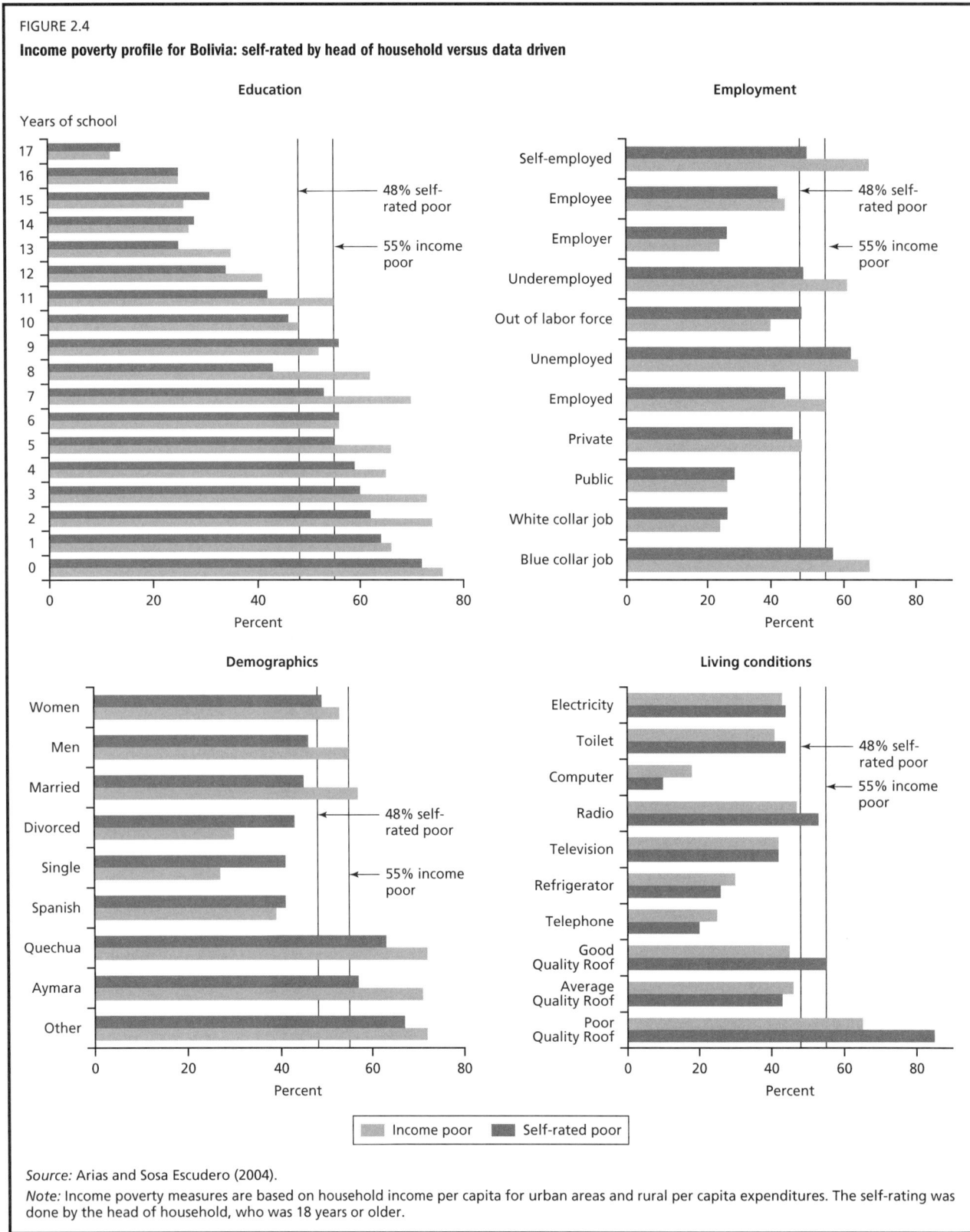

Source: Arias and Sosa Escudero (2004).
Note: Income poverty measures are based on household income per capita for urban areas and rural per capita expenditures. The self-rating was done by the head of household, who was 18 years or older.

immediate income. In Bolivia indigenous groups are twice as likely as the average Bolivian to rate themselves as poor if they are unemployed.

Second, in Bolivia, informal, self-employed workers feel less poor than their incomes would predict, indicating, perhaps, that there is a premium on flexibility or on being one's own boss as some of the recent literature on informality suggests (Maloney 2003). In the Dominican Republic there is no difference between self-employed and other workers, suggesting that the self-employed feel no special vulnerability relative to salaried workers, while in Argentina, where high rates of unemployment may have increased the share of involuntarily self-employed, the reverse is the case—the self-employed do feel more vulnerable.

Third, some of the largest discrepancies are among regional and ethnic groups. Bolivian Quechuas tend to rate themselves as poorer than suggested by income poverty profiles, while the converse is true for Bolivian Aymaras. Even though Gran Buenos Aires is the second richest region in Argentina, its inhabitants feel especially poor, perhaps reflecting larger observable income differentials among households, or congestion externalities in a larger city.

As a final example, Velez and Nunez (2005) attempt to explain the apparent increase in reported subjective well-being in Colombia where the share of the poor ranking their living conditions as "good," the top of the scale, rose by 16 percent from 1997 to 2003. Given the deep recession across the period, income is not driving the ranking. Calculations using eight different techniques to measure two-dimensional poverty indicators capturing income plus security and income plus home crowding still showed worsening poverty. Income plus educational gains did show declining poverty for many techniques, although the results were again very ambiguous when these two factors were combined with security in a three-dimensional poverty indicator. In the end, Velez and Nunez speculate that their indicators may be missing expectations of a much improved security situation in light of the dramatic changes in policy since 2002 and perhaps redistributive programs that doubled as a percent of GDP across the 1990s.

Snapshots vs. movies: life-cycle welfare, mobility, and risk

As the literature has also frequently noted, together, per capita income and measures of distribution or poverty in a single moment in time offer an incomplete vision of well-being. As economic theory suggests, and more fundamentally human behavior attests, individuals are concerned with their welfare across their entire life span, not just at any instant. Yet the scarcity of longitudinal (panel) data sets in developing countries has made a life-cycle perspective difficult to introduce into welfare measures. This absence severely distorts our picture of poverty and inequality. As an extreme example, imagine a country where every young person begins earning wages that place them below the poverty line, but where the returns to each additional year of experience (accumulated human capital) are so large that everyone dies a millionaire. Despite the fact that everyone has equal lifetime welfare, the staggered distribution of ages in the population will reveal substantial poverty and inequality in a single cross-section.[13] Ignoring this mobility renders static measures of poverty and distribution deeply suspect, as Kuznets (1955, 2) bluntly argued:

> To say, for example, that the "lower" income classes gained or lost during the last twenty years in that their share of total income increased or decreased *has meaning only* if the units have been classified as members of the "lower" classes throughout those 20 years—and for those who have moved into or out of those classes recently, such a statement has no significance (italics added).

The appropriate focus on welfare across the life cycle introduces two new elements into discussions of distribution and poverty and their link to growth: mobility and risk.

Mobility

The link between the snapshot Gini we see and true long-term income inequality is *mobility* through the income distribution. This need not be unidirectional, as in the example above. Atkinson and Bourguignon (1982) and Shorrocks (1993) stress that reversals of position—a poor person becoming a millionaire and vice versa—make lifetime incomes more equal and hence can be seen as improving social welfare. But beyond this income equalization angle, mobility is seen as reflecting the equalization of *opportunities*, a conception that links to Sen's concern with capabilities for individual progress and to Roemer's (1998) concern with the leveling of "circumstances" lying beyond the control of the individual but critically affecting the outcome of his or her efforts. Benabou and Ok (2001) argue that these greater opportunities engender a greater tolerance for inequality, in some sense formalizing Hirschman's (1981) famous tunnel allegory where stalled motorists sit patiently watching the next lane of traffic advance, only because they see that as a sign that sooner or later they too will move. Even earlier, Friedman (1962) argued that a lack of mobility in the United States was probably a greater cause for concern than was adverse distribution. These considerations of equality of opportunity underlie the 2006 *World Development Report: Equity and Development.*

The possible structural *absence* of mobility also lies behind the now-established literature on poverty traps or vicious circles, where individuals, communities, or even nations are found to be unable to escape poverty or a low level of development because they lack human, physical, or social assets.[14] This topic is taken up at length beginning in chapter 6 and is only sketched out here.

A large literature (see Fields and Ok 1996 for a review of some) has studied indexes of mobility and, increasingly, general patterns of income dynamics including poverty traps (box 2.4). The need to gather long-term panel data has meant that studying mobility is a reasonably new endeavor for Latin America. As an example, Fields and

---

BOX 2.4
Mobility and poverty traps

Two possible dynamics can lead to poverty traps, as suggested by the figure, taken loosely from Lokshin and Ravallion (2004). In the left panel, there are increasing returns to scale up to Y_u and decreasing returns to scale thereafter. Households below Y_u earn less and less, propelled toward zero while households above Y_u are pushed away from it toward Y_s. Y_u is therefore an unstable equilibrium, and households below it or falling below it are stuck in a poverty trap. Lumpy investment opportunities also pose a trap, as shown in the right panel. For a household earning Y_1, any change that raises income will propel the household toward higher levels of income, and any negative shock could push the family below, into a poverty trap.[a]

Myriad varieties of poverty traps have been discussed in the literature. The efficiency wage hypothesis of Mirrlees (1975) and Stiglitz (1976) stresses that below a certain level of consumption, individuals are too undernourished to work and hence find themselves further malnourished. Lokshin and Ravallion (2004) also postulate that a minimum level of expenditure may be needed to participate in society, for instance, getting a job, having a fixed address, or having adequate clothing. They argue that consuming below this point creates "social exclusion." Mehlum, Moene, and Torvik (2005) posit the existence of a poverty trap based on violence.

a. Paraphrased from Antman and McKenzie (2005), written for this report.

Poverty traps

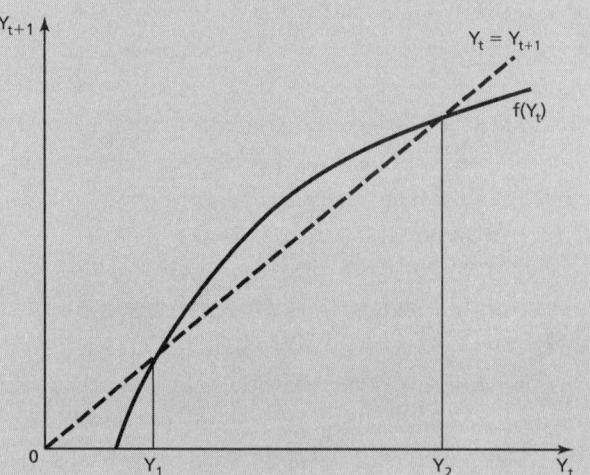

others (2005), looking at panel data for Argentina, Mexico, and República Bolivariana de Venezuela, examine changes in individual earnings during positive and negative growth periods. They find limited evidence in Mexico and none in the other countries for what they term "divergent mobility"—that those starting in the best economic position to begin with experience the largest earnings gains or smallest losses; this finding would suggest overall convergence and perhaps little evidence of poverty traps. However, a problem plaguing the use of these data is their design as short-term labor market surveys spanning no more than two years (Argentina) rather than the longer term. This means that they disproportionately capture measurement error or short-term movements in incomes.[15] Lokshin and Ravallion (2004) examine income dynamics in Hungary and Russia using six-year and four-year panels respectively and propose a simple way of identifying poverty traps.[16] They find no evidence of poverty traps for these two countries, although Rodriguez-Mesa and Gonzalez-Vega (2004), using a similar methodology, find some evidence for poverty traps in El Salvador.

Numerous authors have recently explored techniques for extracting longer-term movements from short series such as the ones in Latin America (see Glewwe 2004; Luttmer 2002; and Krebs, Krishna, and Maloney 2004). One approach proposed by Antman and McKenzie (2005) for this report was to create pseudo panels that effectively average out transitory shocks across an entire cohort. These cohorts are then tracked over repeated cross-sectional surveys where the average of the cohort approximates a type of individual moving across time (see Deaton 1985 for a complete discussion). Comparing the raw transitions to the pseudo panels, they find that correcting for measurement error significantly reduces measured mobility, but in neither case do they find substantial evidence of poverty traps.

The issue of mobility and poverty traps recurs throughout the chapters of this report—first in the mobility of countries in the international distribution (chapter 6), then of regions within countries (chapter 7), and finally of families and individuals (chapters 8 and 9).

Risk

Although on the surface, mobility would seem to be good, whether it is in fact good or not depends to an important degree on the predictability of the movements. If an income reversal occurs randomly, it would still mitigate life-cycle inequality, but it also makes incomes more unpredictable and risky, and with the exception of gamblers, people tend to dislike risk. Generally speaking, people would rather take a smaller income with certainty than a larger average one where they might receive much more or might earn less and fall into poverty.

Risk has moved center stage in discussions of welfare and poverty. The importance of risk to welfare was a central argument of Rodrik's (1997) discussion about whether globalization had gone too far; and concerns about the high economic volatility of Latin America and the Caribbean and the means to reduce it and mitigate its effects were the subject of the 2000 World Bank Latin American regional flagship *Securing Our Future in a Global Economy* (de Ferranti and others 2000). The *World Development Report: Attacking Poverty* (World Bank 2001b) specifically included "security," meaning low risk, as a central dimension of poverty. The expanding literature on "vulnerability" goes beyond the concern with a family's current position to the likelihood (risk) that they may find themselves in a worse position, perhaps falling into poverty.[17]

Risk also can affect measures of inequality (box 2.5). First, income distribution measures are contaminated by risk: one cannot tell if the Gini is showing the distribution of differing incomes that are constant across time, or, at the other extreme, whether everyone, on average, earns the same income over time but with those incomes varying greatly around that average. Either way, a cross-section shows that inequality and higher measured inequality could reflect either an increase in true inequality or increased volatility: for example, the increase in inequality in the United States over the last decades is evenly divided between real increased inequality and increased volatility. Kuznets may have been the first to link measures of inequality with risk when he asked if the apparently declining inequality in the advanced countries might not result in part from workers moving into jobs with fewer "transient disturbances."[18] A related issue, as Deaton and Paxton (1994) note, is that the observed cross-sectional measures of inequality are in fact combinations of the distributions of successive age cohorts, which, given that random life events cause incomes to diverge, should show increasing dispersion with age. That is the case in Costa Rica, as box 2.6 shows.

Relating mobility and risk

That mobility and risk are, to an important degree, two sides of the same coin was recognized by Hart (1981, 11), who

BOX 2.5
Is it inequality or risk? Maybe Latin America has less inequality than we thought . . .

There is a long-established concern that inequality measures are not measuring true inequality in lifetime incomes or opportunities and that instead they may largely be picking up short-term fluctuations in income. For example, consider the following equation $\log y_{ibt} = \alpha_{ib} + \beta(t - b) + \varepsilon_{ibt}$, where y captures the real annual earning in year t of individual i born in year b; α captures more or less permanent characteristics of the individual such as intelligence, motivation, and interpersonal skills; β is the growth rate of wages across the life cycle after reflecting, for instance, the accumulation of experience; and ε represents transitory deviations of measured earnings from the life-cycle earnings trajectory including both short-term fluctuations and measurement error. If one assumes that the three components of income are independent and that transitory shocks are uncorrelated across time, then the observed variance of incomes in the sample can be expressed as $Var(\log y_{ibt}) = \sigma_\alpha^2 + \sigma_b^2 \beta^2 + \sigma_\varepsilon^2$.

From this one sees that if earnings inequality is measured for the entire labor force, part of that inequality simply arises from the second terms and reflects the intercohort variation in stage of the life cycle at any year t. As Paglin (1975), and implicitly Kuznets (1955), note, this variation need not imply inequality in any meaningful sense. Across the life cycle, all are equal. Second, transitory shocks, while important if not smoothable, have the same impact on measured inequality as those shocks arising from true ability or opportunities captured by the first term, which is, in fact, the term we care most about. As Solon (2002) shows, however, if one were measuring the distribution of true discounted lifetime earnings, the transitory variations would nearly completely vanish. Hence, measured cross-sectional inequality of current incomes is distorted by almost the entire value of the transitory component (Lillard 1977; Shorrocks 1981). As Krebs, Krishna, and Maloney (2004) show, the transitory component of variance across time using panels is roughly two-thirds of the total variance, suggesting that these distortions can be large.

These distortions can be important. The table shows that measured inequality among the self-employed in various Latin American countries is roughly double that of salaried workers, much of it attributable to the intrinsically higher risk of the sector. Since the share of self-employment decreases with level of development, the number of self-employed may be of some importance (Maloney 2000). Were Bolivia to have U.S. levels of self-employment, that is, 10 percent instead of 56 percent, the level of inequality as measured by the Theil index for all workers would fall almost 30 percent.

Source: This discussion draws heavily on Solon (2002).

Earning inequality decomposition for salaried and self-employed workers

	Argentina	Bolivia	Chile	Colombia	Uruguay	Venezuela, R.B. de
Self-employed share (%)	26	56	29	33	26	37
Theil Index:						
All workers	0.362	0.642	0.735	0.667	0.398	0.34
Self-employed	0.484	0.819	0.867	0.972	0.499	0.47
Salaried	0.295	0.43	0.411	0.433	0.35	0.264
Within and between group inequality, with groups defined by type of employment						
Within group	0.355	0.642	0.639	0.653	0.395	0.34
Between group	0.007	0.001	0.096	0.013	0.004	0

Source: Maloney and Wodon (1999). Analysis for all workers with incomes above zero in 1995.

BOX 2.6
... Or maybe more: Inequality and demographics

How do demographics affect measures of inequality? As Deaton and Paxton (1994) note, the observed cross-sectional measures of inequality are in fact averages of the distributions in successive age cohorts, which, if the permanent income hypothesis is correct, should show very different distributions of income and consumption. The reason is that the accumulation of positive and negative shocks to income as individuals age leads the incomes of age cohorts to diverge. Deaton and Paxton demonstrate that in Taiwan (China), the United Kingdom, and the United States, any changes in aggregate inequality are many times smaller than the changes in age-cohort inequality. This appears to be the case in Costa Rica as well (see left panel of the figure). Thus, it is possible for substantial changes in the distribution of aggregate income to be driven purely by demographic changes.

Again, Kuznets (1955) foreshadowed this finding in arguing that inequality comparisons should take a cross-section of units at the prime earning phase of the life cycle and avoid the phases of youth or retirement.

Preliminary regressions of Ginis on measures of the age of population suggest that these effects are not small in the aggregate. The right panel of the figure graphs the cross-national partial correlation between the share of people below age 14 and the Gini, and its negative and statistically significant trend line. Were Latin America to have aging Europe's demographic structure as a benchmark, its Ginis might be 4 percentage points higher; Ginis in comparatively youthful Bolivia, Guatemala, Honduras, and Nicaragua could be up to 7 percentage points higher.

Inequality and age of population

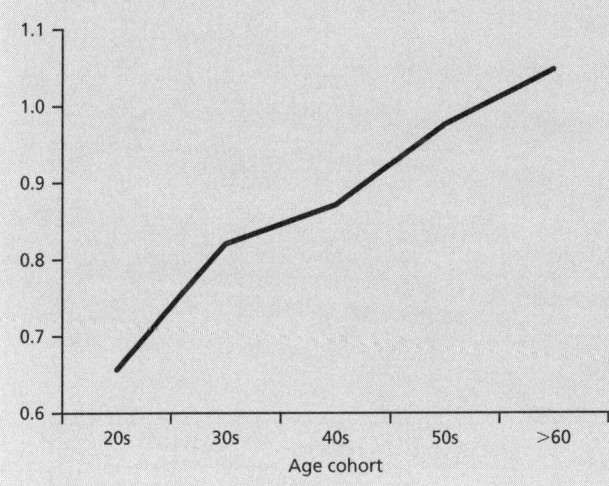

Standard deviation of incomes by age cohort, 2004, Costa Rica

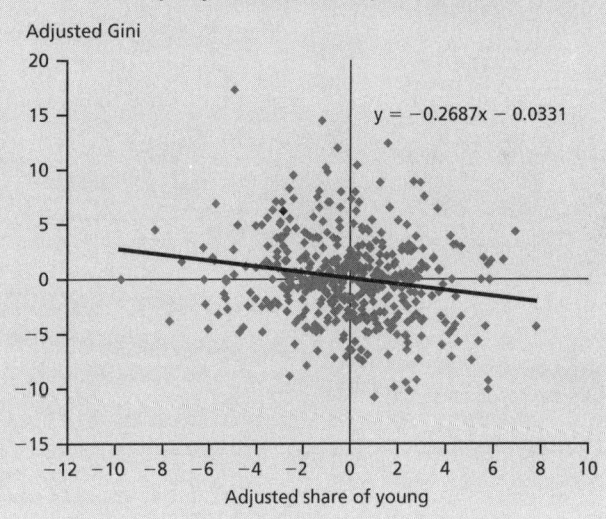

Inequality measures versus age of population, world

argued that "a society with zero correlation [in income levels across time] and very high mobility would be too unstable for most people so there is an optimal level of correlation somewhere between zero and one." The link is also implicit in recent discussions of the new opportunities and increased insecurity arising in economies transitioning to a more market-based economic system (Birdsall and Graham 1998). However, a more rigorous discussion of the relationship between mobility and risk has emerged only recently (see Gottshalk and Spolaore 2002). The complications involved can be suggested by asking what happens if the unexpected shocks to income occur symmetrically: that is, what happens if, on average, an individual experiencing an unexpected income shock has as much chance of moving up as down. In this case, there can be lots of apparent mobility, but on average, and on expectation across the life cycle, everybody stays in the same place. There is no narrowing of expected lifetime income differentials but only more risk, and society is necessarily worse off. In this view, only the predictable elements of mobility can positively affect welfare.

Krebs, Krishna, and Maloney (2005a) offer one possible way of calculating welfare that captures the various elements that are discussed above and dealt with in subsequent chapters. They argue that the welfare measure of the distribution of expected lifetime consumption adjusted for risk needs to incorporate measures of:

- *Initial income position of the individual or group.* If this initial income were considered the permanent and unvarying status of an individual or group, then it would be more or less captured by traditional measures of poverty and inequality. Welfare can clearly be altered by transfers among these individuals or groups, and the feasibility of engineering significant changes through this mechanism is addressed in chapter 5.
- *Predictable mobility.* These measures encompass predictable movements of individuals or groups from their initial income position both absolutely and relative to others. Perhaps the most discussed driver of such mobility is the accumulation of human capital, which in turn is central to growth. Chapters 8 and 9 show that investment in education for the poor yields relatively low rates of return in Latin America and hence the poor do not make the push to complete secondary schooling. Failure to complete secondary school typically prevents the poor from escaping the cycle of poverty.
- *Unpredicatable mobility (risk).* Like mobility, risk also has potentially strong feedbacks to growth. As an example, using cross-country data, Flug, Spilimbergo, and Wachtenheim (1998) find that income volatility adversely affects educational attainment. As later chapters tell in greater detail, simulations suggest that were Mexicans to face the same level of income risk as workers in the United States, they would increase their investment in human capital (health, education, on-the-job training) by roughly 2.5 percent of GDP. Further, the poor appear to face more income volatility than the middle class (Krebs, Krishna, and Maloney 2005b, 2005c).

Annex 2B offers a tractable method for combining all these elements in one measure of welfare, and the results for Argentina and Mexico are presented in table 2.4. Although income distribution statistics are generally calculated using data divided into quintiles or deciles, the need to estimate a measure of the permanent component of risk (the part that cannot be easily smoothed) limits us to three education categories, with "primary" proxying broadly for the poor.

The first line of table 2.4 tabulates the share of the population found in each education category. The second, third, and fourth rows in the table capture the components of expected lifetime utility for each. The fifth calculates this level of utility (increasing as it becomes less negative), and the sixth combines the three different levels of utility into one measure of social welfare. Unsurprisingly, in both countries the poor show lower levels of welfare, and Argentina, with both higher levels of initial income and

TABLE 2.4
Welfare comparisons: Argentina and Mexico

	Argentina education categories			Mexico education categories		
	Primary	Secondary	Tertiary	Primary	Secondary	Tertiary
Share in population (π)	0.352	0.405	0.243	0.606	0.207	0.187
Predictable income growth (μ)	0.010	0.017	0.026	0.009	0.012	0.023
Initial income level [c(i, 0)]	428	595	904	279	348	546
Income risk (σ^2)	0.056	0.045	0.052	0.064	0.046	0.075
Utility	−2.780	−1.966	−1.525	−3.871	−2.734	−2.544
Welfare	−2.059594892			−3.301187884		
Difference			0.389245076			

Source: Krebs, Krishna, and Maloney (2005a).
Note: Difference is measured in the equivalent difference in first period consumption.

lower levels of risk (although slightly lower levels of growth), shows a higher level of total social welfare.

Looking at predictable income growth of the primary-educated group relative to the other subgroups suggests that in neither country are the poor catching up; there is little predictable upward mobility of this class in the distribution. It is straightforward to calculate (not shown) that were the poor to share the same rate of growth as the rich, perhaps from an increased investment in education or a higher return to schooling for the poor, the poor in both countries would gain 32 percent in utility measured in initial consumption, and society as a whole would gain 13 percent in Mexico and 21 percent in Argentina. To determine relative mobility, one could ask what would happen if the growth rate of the poor were raised 1 percent at the expense of the growth rate of the two other groups so that overall growth were unchanged. Making growth more pro-poor in this way would increase total welfare by 1.6 percent in Argentina and 9 percent in Mexico.

Changes in risk also yield large, although opposite, changes in overall welfare. Mexico appears to have a higher level of income risk for every income group than does Argentina, and its aggregate risk measure is 0.073 compared with 0.048 for Argentina and 0.023 for the United States (see Krebs, Krishna, and Maloney 2005a for Argentina and Mexico; Meghir and Pistaferri 2004 for the United States). Were Mexico to lower its aggregate risk to Argentine levels, it would improve its aggregate welfare in an amount equal to an increase in the income growth rate of roughly 0.6 percent or a 15 percent rise in average consumption levels. In both countries, the poor are additionally hit because they have higher risk than the middle class. If the poor had the same risk levels as the middle class, the utility gain for the poor in Mexico would be equivalent to an increase of 0.7 percent in the income growth rate and 19 percent in consumption; for Argentina the figures are 1.3 percent for income growth and close to 30 percent for consumption. While these calculations suggest that measures of poverty and welfare would indeed change greatly by introducing a measure of risk, they are in the realm of those calculated in the mainstream literature for the United States.

Intergenerational mobility

The welfare measure captures the distribution of individual welfare across his or her life span. But again, the omniscient Kuznets (1955, 2) argued that, in fact, mobility across generations is a central issue, both for understanding welfare and for growth.

> Further, if one may add a final touch to what is beginning to look like a statistical economist's pipe dream, we should be able to trace secular income levels not only through a single generation but at least through two—connecting the incomes of a given generation with those of its immediate descendants. . . . If living members of society—as producers, consumers, savers, decision-makers on secular problems—react to long-term changes in income levels and shares, data on such an income structure are essential.[19]

The last decade has generated substantial new research on measuring intergenerational mobility for Latin America and the Caribbean and, to a lesser degree, identifying its correlates and causes. Again, the question is whether people can move out of poverty or whether there may be intergenerational poverty traps where the poor, or some particular groups of poor, simply replicate their parents' status ad infinitum.

The most common strategy for measuring the degree of intergenerational mobility is similar to that for intragenerational mobility: studying the correlation of a generation's well-being with that of its progeny, generally measured as the elasticity of children's earnings or education level relative to that of their fathers.[20] This elasticity is expected to increase with the strength of intrinsic qualities such as genetics or social connectedness of families and decrease with the progressivity of government investment in children's human capital that would allow children to overcome their families' position in the social structure.[21] Numerous studies have postulated, for example, that the lower elasticities in Canada and Sweden arise from their greater efforts in public education.[22] Conceptually, it is not hard to integrate credit constraints as barriers to accumulating the desired level of children's education and the expected volatility of the children's income as being important to these investment decisions.

Comparisons across countries are difficult because of differences in methodology, data sets, and units of comparison, but a fairly consistent picture is emerging. Grawe (2002) attempts a very consistent classification of elasticities for a sample that includes two Latin American countries (figure 2.5). The United Kingdom and the United States,

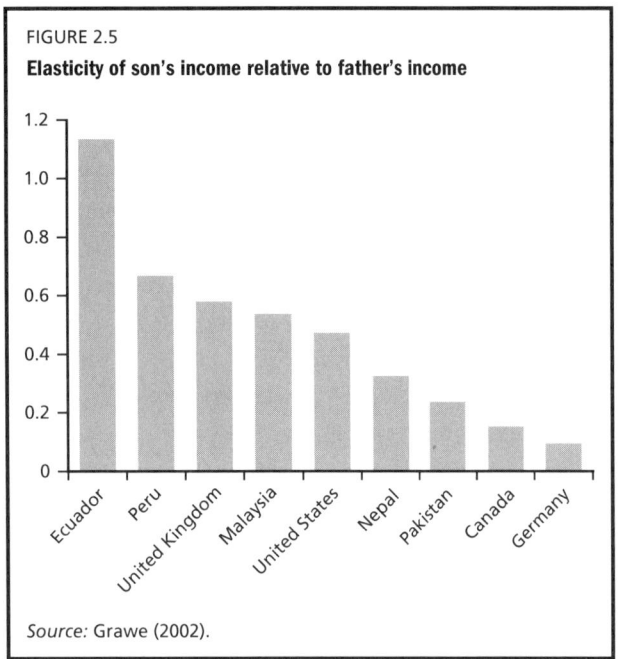

FIGURE 2.5
Elasticity of son's income relative to father's income

Source: Grawe (2002).

with values between 0.5 and 0.6, show little intergenerational mobility relative to Canada and Germany, but Peru at 0.67 is substantially worse and Ecuador at slightly above 1.0 winds up being the country with the least mobility. Although studies conflict, the literature seems to be converging on the United States as being among the least mobile advanced countries, and it is this reference point that the available comprehensive studies of Latin American and Caribbean countries benchmark against (see figure 2.6 and annex 2C).[23]

In general, the focus of studies on specific Latin American countries has been on education because of both the greater reliability of the measure and the apparent consensus, consistent with the framework above, that educaton is the critical driver of intergenerational mobility. Behrman, Birdsall, and Székely (1999) tabulate the correlation between parents' and children's schooling and find that Brazil, Colombia, Mexico, and Peru all do worse than the United States, with a coefficient above .4, as is common in the literature. The finding holds both in urban areas and overall, with correlation coefficients for Brazil and Colombia above 0.6. Andersen (2001) calculates a social mobility index that uses a measure of the schooling gap—what is attained versus what is expected for an individual of a certain age—and finds a similar ranking, with the exception of Peru, whose ranking improves somewhat. Behrman, Gaviria, and Székely (2001) and Dahan and Gaviria (1999) use another measure of parental influence—the correlation of sibling educational attainment: if parental characteristics have no impact, there should be no correlation, and if determinant, then children should have identical attainment. In some cases, the rankings do shift importantly. Mexico goes from high mobility to relatively poor mobility, El Salvador from mid-level to bottom; Argentina from top to middle; Costa Rica from middle to top. Despite this shifting around, a general pattern emerges: Latin America is consistently less mobile than the United States and, therefore, most of the advanced countries. And within the region, Chile, Paraguay, and Uruguay show relatively high mobility; Brazil, Guatemala, and Nicaragua are generally very low.[24]

As is always the case in measuring mobility, such simple indicators also hide important information, in particular about differing patterns across units. For this reason, in looking at mobility of countries, subnational units, and individuals, it is common to report transition matrices showing transitions among a limited number of categories or kernel density plots, using continuous variables as their analogue. The transition matrix for Colombia, given in table 2.5, shows, for example, that the probability that a child of parents with primary education (generally the poor) will obtain tertiary education is 10.5 percent; the probability of that child even finishing secondary school is only 14 percent. Only 61 percent of those children whose parents had some secondary education completed secondary school. These findings are suggestive of a low-education poverty trap that perpetuates a family's poverty across time. Constructing earnings matrices for Brazil, Guimarães and Veloso (2003) find sharp differences by regions, races, and cohorts, and in all cases, mobility is lower for sons of low-wage fathers than for sons of middle-wage fathers.

TABLE 2.5

Intergenerational transition matrix for Colombia, 1997

Education of parents	Education of children			
	Primary or less	Some secondary	Secondary	Some higher
Primary or less	51.2	24.2	14.1	10.5
Some secondary	12.6	26.2	25.4	35.9
Secondary	9.1	17.3	25.4	48.2
Higher education	2.2	6.5	14.2	77.1
Total	41.7	23.2	16.2	18.8

Source: Behrman, Gaviria, and Székely (2001).

FIGURE 2.6
Mobility Indicators

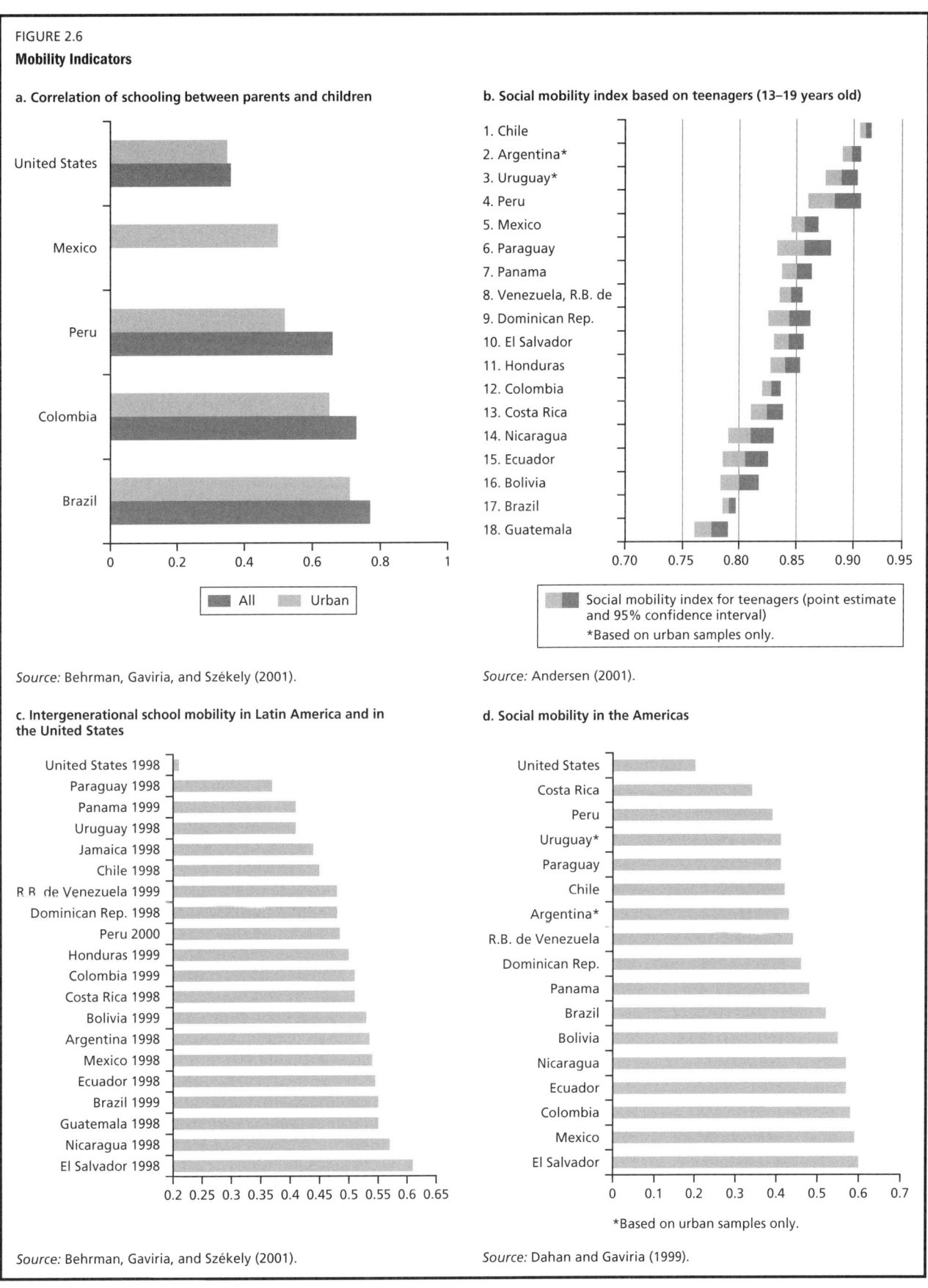

a. Correlation of schooling between parents and children

Source: Behrman, Gaviria, and Székely (2001).

b. Social mobility index based on teenagers (13–19 years old)

Source: Andersen (2001).

c. Intergenerational school mobility in Latin America and in the United States

Source: Behrman, Gaviria, and Székely (2001).

d. Social mobility in the Americas

Source: Dahan and Gaviria (1999).

Theory predicts that borrowing constraints, discrimination, spatial segregation, and marital sorting—all typically mechanisms of exclusion—are among the principal factors that inhibit mobility. Although the thin empirical literature broadly supports this hypothesis, most studies also suggest that greater educational expenditures improve mobility. Behrman, Birdsall, and Székely (1999) argue that for a typical country doubling the share of public expenditures on education as a share of GDP would increase mobility by 25 percent. They also find that higher spending per school-age child on primary education and better quality primary and secondary schooling are positively associated with intergenerational mobility, while relatively greater public spending on tertiary education may actually reinforce the impact of family background and reduce intergenerational mobility. Consistent with these findings, Andrade and others (2003) find evidence that credit constraints increase the persistence of immobility found among poor groups. At the aggregate level, results offer less clarity. Andersen (2001) finds a positive correlation between his measure of social mobility and urbanization and level of development (GDP) and none with measured inequality. Behrman, Gaviria, and Székely (2001) find no correlation with GDP or trade openness, leaving the question about whether mobility and economic growth are related somewhat up in the air. Behrman, Birdsall, and Székely (1999) find that macroeconomic conditions—in particular those related to the extent of internal market development—significantly shape intergenerational mobility by loosening the strong link between parents' background and children's education.

As with the intragenerational mobility discussed in the previous section, the message is that measures to encourage human capital accumulation—certainly in education and in all likelihood across several dimensions—are critical to redressing poverty and improving social welfare in a dynamic context, as are measures to reduce impediments to accumulation of human capital, such as risk and liquidity constraints.

Conclusion

This chapter has elaborated on Kuznets's "economic statisticians pipe dream," reaffirming his now 50-year-old doubts about how well the common measures of poverty and inequality really capture welfare and extending the laundry list of considerations that need to go into a comprehensive welfare measure. We have shown that these considerations are not merely conceptual curiosities—incorporating them can and does lead to very different conclusions about the evolution of welfare in a region and about the relationship of poverty and inequality to growth.

So far, the data remain limited for generating comprehensive indicators of well-being that are comparable across countries in Latin America. The good news is that progress is being made in the region on these fronts. Looking even at simple static measures, better techniques for deflating poverty and distribution series are available, and the literature on multidimensional and subjective poverty measures is ballooning. Since Kuznets wrote in 1955, the macroeconomics literature has erected elegant architecture for analyzing income dynamics and thinking through life-cycle welfare issues. The increased availability of panel data in recent years and the development of techniques for eliminating measurement error and transitory income fluctuations have made feasible serious, if still limited, mappings of mobility, testing for poverty traps, and calculations of the variance measures necessary for dynamic welfare measures. Numerous papers have sought to evaluate the magnitudes and determinants of intergenerational mobility. From these efforts, several findings appear.

- Measurements that use the correct deflators show that for the majority of episodes studied, Latin America and the Caribbean have reduced poverty and inequality more than conventional indicators suggest.
- Health, longevity, and other indicators of welfare have improved much more than the incomes of the poor would suggest. Some countries saw substantial improvements in welfare despite stagnation in incomes.
- At the same time, mobility, measured as the ability to move out of poverty across generations, seems much lower and income risk much higher than they are in advanced countries, suggesting that in relative welfare terms, Latin America and the Caribbean are doing substantially worse than standard poverty indicators may suggest.

A stronger data effort across the region in all these dimensions will further enrich our picture of poverty in the region.

A broader conception of poverty also enriches the discussion surrounding pro-poor growth and, in turn, what might be called pro-growth poverty reduction. At the most elementary level, correctly deflating welfare statistics is, in principle, essential for understanding their links to growth and policy reforms that, by their design, alter relative prices. More profoundly, an expanded concept of poverty also forces policy makers to take a broader look at the channels running in each direction. Progress in health, security, education, and risk reduction is correlated with income growth, but not so tightly as to obviate the need for important antipoverty efforts independent of those promoting income growth per se.

These dimensions of poverty form the reverse channel of a virtuous circle, as chapter 6 shows, and thus affect income growth. Education and, to a lesser degree, health make regular appearances in the ubiquitous growth regressions, while labor market risk affects the accumulation of human capital and hence offers a separate channel to growth. People's prospects for mobility and for the advancement of their children also offer incentives to accumulate human capital. From a growth point of view, poverty reduction in these dimensions is good business.

To some degree, however, we can only sketch a longer-term research agenda. In the short run, global databases of poverty and inequality statistics are not ideally deflated, multidimensional analysis is available for only a few countries, calculation of income risk is data-intensive, and panel data coverage is similarly extremely limited. Yet subjective poverty indicators suggest that income—even when the data are incomplete—is not a *poor* proxy for well-being, meaning that many pending questions in pro-poor growth and antipoverty policy can be fruitfully approached with the data on hand. The next three chapters do this, largely at the macroeconomic and regional levels.

Annex 2A

Estimating the monetary value of mortality changes

Becker, Philipson, and Soares (2005) convert life span into monetary values to calculate a measure of total welfare gain by calculating how much people would pay for an additional year of life:

Assume the existence of a perfect capital market and consider the indirect utility function $V(Y, T)$ of an individual living in a municipality with life expectancy T and lifetime income Y:

$$(A2.1) \quad V(Y, T) = \max_{\{c(t)\}} \int_0^T e^{-\rho t} u(c(t)) \, dt \quad \text{subject to}$$

$$Y = \int_0^T e^{-rt} y(t) \, dt = \int_0^T e^{-rt} c(t) \, dt,$$

where $y(t)$ and $c(t)$ are the income and consumption at t, r is the interest rate, and ρ is the subjective discount factor. Consider a given individual at two points in time (′ denotes the second period). The inframarginal income $W(T, T')$ that would give this person the same utility level observed in the second period but with the life expectancy observed in the first is defined by $V(Y' + W(T, T'), T) = V(Y', T')$.

Consider a *hypothetical life-cycle individual* who receives the municipality's income per capita in all years of life and lives to the age corresponding to the municipality's life expectancy at birth. Assume that $\rho = r$, so that optimal consumption is constant and equal to the constant income flow $[c(t) = c = y]$. In this case, the indirect utility function can be expressed in terms of the yearly income y as in: $V(y, S) = u(y)A(T)$, where $A(T) = (1 - e^{-rT})/r$. Define $w(T, T')$ as the yearly income. Therefore, w satisfies $u[y' + w(T, T')]A(T) = u(y')A(T')$.

The monetary value of the total gains in welfare observed in the period, when measured by yearly income, can be denoted as $(y' - y) + w$. The lifetime value of these changes is the present discounted value of this annual flow. The contribution of health to the total gain in welfare is the fraction $w/[(y' - y) + w]$. Inverting the instantaneous utility function $u(.)$, w turns out to be

$$(A2.2) \quad w = u^{-1}\left[\frac{u(y')A(S')}{A(S)}\right] - y'(*).$$

Two dimensions of $u(.)$ affect the willingness to pay for extensions in life expectancy: the substitutability of consumption in different periods of life (that is, the intertemporal elasticity of substitution), and the value of being alive relative to being dead. To capture both, a particular definition of $u(c)$ is calibrated, $u(c) = \frac{c^{1-1/\gamma}}{1 - 1/\gamma} + \alpha$, where α determines the level of annual consumption at which the individual would be indifferent between being alive or dead, arising from the normalization of the utility of death to zero. If the intertemporal elasticity of substitution γ is larger than 1, then α is negative. With expression (*) and this functional form, a closed form solution for w is obtained.[25]

Annex 2B

A tractable welfare measure that captures income, mobility, and risk

Krebs, Krishna, and Maloney (2005a) assume that incomes evolve over time according to $\log y_{it} = \alpha_t + \psi_t x_{it} + u_{it}$. Income is driven by time-changing shifts in levels, α_t, and returns to human capital (x), ψ. The parameter u captures individual income changes that are caused by changes in observable worker characteristics. In turn, u is composed of a permanent shock, ω, that follows a random walk, and a transitory component η that captures both temporary income shocks and measurement error. It is straightforward to show that the greater the variance of the permanent shocks to income, σ^2, the lower the covariance of the unpredictable component of incomes, that is, the greater the unpredictable component of mobility. This component of mobility is pure risk and hence negatively affects welfare. Krebs (2002) shows that given a one-period utility function given by $u(c) = \frac{c^{1-\lambda}}{1-\lambda}$, $\lambda \neq 1$, the expected lifetime utility of an individual or subgroup facing the above income process is

$$(B2.1) \quad U_i = \frac{c_i^{1-\gamma}}{(1-\gamma)(1-\beta(1+\mu)^{1-\gamma}\exp(.5\gamma(\gamma-1)\sigma^2))},$$

where c_i is initial consumption levels; μ is the *predictable* part of income growth, perhaps arising from accumulated human capital; γ is the coefficient of risk aversion; and β is the discount factor. A Generalized Methods of Moments (GMM) technique is used to separate permanent from temporary shocks.[26]

To capture the fact that societies dislike inequality and hence weight the utility of the poor more than those of the rich, the individual expected utilities are combined into an overall welfare function:

$$(B2.2) \quad W = \left[\sum_j U_j^{1-\theta} \cdot \pi_j\right]^{\frac{1}{1-\theta}},$$

where π is the share of the subgroup in the total population, and θ is the social aversion to inequality. For the discussion in the text, $\theta = \gamma = 1.5$ and $\beta = 0.95$.

Annex 2C

Intergenerational mobility in Latin America: Country comparison

Two sets of rankings comparing intergenerational mobility different from those proposed by Solon (2002) are reported in figure 2.6. Panel A shows the correlation of schooling between parents and children captured by β in the following first-order Markov model: $S_{it} = \alpha + \beta S_{it-1} + w_t$, where S is schooling, i indexes each family, t is the generation of the sons, $t-1$ is the generation of the parents, and w is a stochastic term. Panel B shows Andersen's (2001) social mobility index, which is defined as $SMI = 1 -$ factor inequality weights of the family background variables of the following specification: *Schooling Gap* $= \alpha + \beta_1 \text{Max}(S_f, S_m) + \beta_2 Y_h + \Sigma \gamma_i CON_i + e$, where the gap is the disparity between actual years of education and the potential; S_f, S_m represents the schooling variable for father and mother, respectively; Y_h measures the household income and CON_i are control variables; $\text{Max}(S_f, S_m)$ and Y_h are the family background variables, and the factor inequality weight is the product of the coefficient estimate for each variable, the standard deviation for the same variable, and the correlation between the same variable and the dependent one. These factors are necessary inputs to perform the Fields variance decomposition.

Panels C and D report results based on sibling correlations: $\rho_g = \frac{\sum_{f=1}^{F} B_f(\bar{g}_f - \bar{g})^2}{B\bar{g}(1-\bar{g})}$, where $\bar{g}_f$ is the average value of g_{sf} in family f, B_f is the number of teenage siblings in family f, $\bar{g}$ s is the average value of g in the entire sample, B is the number of individuals, and F is the number of families. This index corresponds to the R^2 obtained by regressing g_{sf} (defined as a dummy variable capturing whether individual s of family f has more years of schooling than the median individual of his or her cohort), on a set of dummy variables for all families in the sample. Since ρ_g could yield positive values even if family background is inconsequential, as is the case, for instance, when children are assigned to families randomly, a modified version of the previous index is used: $\rho_a = 1 - (1 - \rho_g)\frac{B-1}{B-F}$ (the index ρ_a yields positive values only if the previous index ρ_g is greater than would be expected purely by chance). Differences among results on both panels (C and D) emerge more from the more recent data used by Behrman, Gaviria, and Székely (2001) than from the measures per se.

Notes

1. Poverty and inequality analysis has, for the most part, focused on capturing changes in income or consumption measured as a basket of goods. The poverty line itself is generally defined in terms of a basket of goods satisfying minimum caloric intake requirements. This definition, as Thorbecke (2005) highlights, is in itself not trivial, as it immediately raises the problem of what should be in that basket: should that same common basket be used across all countries and subnational regions, as suggested by Ravallion and Bidani (1994) and Ravallion (1998), or should the basket be tailored to each country's tastes, preferences, and relative prices.

2. Unless otherwise noted, the poverty figures refer to the headcount index and a poverty line set at $2 per capita purchasing power

parity. The poverty figures reviewed in this chapter come from a background paper for this report by Gasparini, Gutierrez, and Tornarolli (2005). The calculations are based on the results of processing 57 household surveys for 18 Latin American countries (which represent around 92 percent of the region's population) covering the 1990s and early 2000s.

3. Population-weighted averages are more useful to assess poverty rates when the region is treated as a single entity and hence when individuals in different countries are given the same relevance. To a large extent, population-weighted average poverty rates are driven by the poverty rates of the most populated countries. For example, Brazil's weight would be about 0.35 whereas Jamaica's would be only 0.005. Unweighted averages, in contrast, are more useful to assess poverty when interest centers on countries rather than individuals (that is, when the country is the unit of analysis). Proportionately, poor individuals living in smaller countries are given more relevance in this second measure.

4. See Egset and Sletten (2004) for the former, and *World Development Indicators* (2005f) for the latter.

5. In fact, between the early 1990s and the early 2000s, the change was a mere 0.2 percentage point, as a consequence of the regional slowdown after the Russian crisis. The evolution of headcount poverty based on a $1 a day poverty line would show an even lower decline, from 11.2 percent in the early 1990s to 10.8 percent now.

6. These results are reversed for Central America and the Southern Cone area when looking at the unweighted means, which suggests that poverty would have dramatically declined in Central America (by 6 percentage points) and remained basically constant (−1 percentage point) in the Southern Cone area. To a large extent, this is just a reflection of Brazilian trends (the most populated country of the region), where poverty declined significantly, and Mexican trends (the largest country in the Central America region), where poverty remained unchanged.

7. Figure 2.2 presents estimates of the (unweighted average) regional poverty rate in the mid-1990s, together with those already discussed above for the early 1990s and early 2000s. The period from the early 1990s to the mid-1990s corresponds to an economic expansion, whereas the period from the mid-1990s to the early 2000s represented a mix of expansion and recession. It must be noted that the different country coverage of the samples raises some comparability issues between the different periods.

8. Generally, as Sen (1972) shows, it is hard to squeeze many dimensions of social well-being such as freedom or the ability to get a job into conventional social welfare function analysis.

9. See Thorbecke (2005) for a discussion of these issues.

10. These were, in particular, the relative weights on each measure of poverty and the substitution assumed between them.

11. Several excellent papers covering the topic were included in a recent conference sponsored by the U.K. Department for International Development, Instituto de Pesquisa Economica Aplicada (IPEA) in Brazil, the International Poverty Center, and the United Nations Development Programme. See Anderson, Crawford, and Liecester (2005); Deutsch and Silber (2005); Duclos, Sahn, and Younger (2005); and Thorbecke (2005).

12. *The Economist* estimates that the region pays a cost of 13–15 percent in security; see "The Backlash in Latin America: Gestures against Reform," *Economist,* Nov. 30, 1996, p. 19.

13. In fact, if capital markets were perfect, then individuals could perfectly smooth consumption across their lives, and consumption might be completely equalized across individuals at any period in time.

14. See, for example, Rosenstein-Rodin (1943), Nurkse (1953), Nelson (1956), and Basu (1997). Our thanks to Gary Fields for pointing out these references.

15. On the first point, Lokshin and Ravallion (2004) caution that measurement error is likely to cause spurious negative correlation between income changes and initial income levels. On the second point, short-term variation—for instance, the variation that arises from universally volatile self-employment—is not very interesting from a life-cycle point of view while it is hard to identify whether households really do bounce back from shocks given the likely longer duration of the recovery process. See, for instance, Fajnzylber, Maloney, and Montes (2005) and Bosch and Maloney (2005) on short-term variation.

16. They estimate the degree to which the relationship between income today and yesterday involves a cubic function in income, the empirical structure that would generate a pattern such as seen in the figure in box 2.4.

17. See Ligon and Schecter (2002) and Gamanou and Morduch (2002) for a review of the literature. For applications to specific countries, see Maloney, Cunningham, and Bosch (2004) for Mexico; Glewwe and Hall (1998) for Peru; and Contreras, Cooper, and Heman (2004) for Chile. The disconnect between discussions of risk and mobility is exemplified by the fact that the Maloney, Cunningham, and Bosch paper uses the same Mexican panels for studying income shocks as Fields and others (2005) use to study mobility, yet neither work mentions the other concept.

18. "Do the distributions by annual incomes properly reflect trends in distribution by secular incomes? As technology and economic performance rise to higher levels, incomes are less subject to transient disturbances. If in the earlier years the economic fortunes of units were subject to greater vicissitudes—poor crops for some farmers, natural calamity losses for some nonfarm business units—if the overall proportion of individual entrepreneurs whose incomes were subject to such calamities was larger in earlier decades, these earlier distributions of income would be more affected by transient disturbances." Kuznets (1955, 6)

19. Kuznets continues: "An economic society can then be judged by the secular level of the income share that it provides for a given generation and for its children. The important corollary is that the study of long-term changes in the income distribution must distinguish between changes in the shares of resident groups—resident within either one or two generation—and changes in the income shares of groups that, judged by their secular level, migrate upward or downward. . . ."

20. This is generally taken as the coefficient in an OLS (ordinary least square) regression of a log linear regression of a son's earning (or education) on a father's earning, with age controls for both generations. Solon (2004), extending the canonical framework by Becker

and Tomes (1979), argues that such a specification can be theoretically motivated in a framework that shares a close kinship with the standard permanent income hypothesis used for analyzing intragenerational mobility. Parents are assumed to divide their income between investing in their children and their own consumption, maximizing welfare across generations so that there are increases both in today's consumption and in children's income. Children effectively receive endowments that are determined by genetics, the reputation and connectedness of their families, correlates of race, values placed on learning and the like, which are then augmented by educational expenditure.

21. Roemer (2005) argues that "equality of opportunity" in some circumstances does not necessarily imply zero correlation across generations—innate abilities and inherited values imply correlated outcomes.

22. This approach also offers insights into cross-sectional inequality. The variance of log earnings depends not only on the same factors, with the same sign as mobility, but also on the variance of the innovations to the process of inheritability of endowments. Hence, two countries with the same intergenerational elasticity might differ in inequality if they had differing degrees of heterogeneity of ability or endowments.

23. Checchi and Dardanoni (2002), using a wide variety of indexes on both job quality and education for many OECD countries and a few developing countries, consistently found the United States and the United Kingdom to be the most mobile, and Brazil the least mobile. However, Solon (2002), using other studies in an attempt to make careful transitive comparisons, concludes that the United States and the United Kingdom are substantially less mobile than, say, Canada, Finland, and Sweden.

24. Brazil's low mobility is confirmed by Dunn (2003), Ferreira and Veloso (2003), and Bourguignon, Ferreira, and Menendez (2003).

25. The set of parameters (α, γ, r) needed to compute w can be calibrated from other parameters more commonly estimated in the "value of life" and consumption literatures. More precisely: $\alpha = c^{1-1/\gamma}\left(\frac{1}{\varepsilon} - \frac{1}{1-1/\gamma}\right)$, where $\varepsilon = \frac{u'(c)c}{u(c)}$ is the elasticity of the instantaneous utility function. In particular, U.S. parameters are employed as the ones for Brazil are not available. Murphy and Topel (2003, 23) estimate that $\varepsilon = 0.346$, and Browning, Hansen, and Heckman (1999, 614) suggest that γ is slightly above unity. Using $\gamma = 1.250$, $\varepsilon = 0.346$, and $c = \$26,365$, the value of α is calculated to equal -16.2. (The value of consumption is the value of U.S. per capita income in 1990 in the Penn World Tables 6.1 data set, matching the year in which Murphy and Topel 2003 estimate ε.)

26. Numerous authors (Glewwe 2004; Luttmer 2002) have stressed the need to deal with the problem of separating income risk from measurement error, that is, the need to extract the correct component of risk from the sample. Krebs, Krishna, and Maloney (2004) have discussed the problems of extracting the correct measure of risk from the noisy panel data that are available. We are less interested in the transitory shocks, which even relatively poor households can smooth over, than in permanent shocks, which the poor cannot smooth out.

CHAPTER 3

How Did We Get Here?

The existing differences in development between Latin America and the advanced economies of the world did not appear overnight. In fact, they are likely the result of historical processes that in some cases trace back to the colonial period. That opens the door to several interesting questions: How much has the region grown economically since its independence from colonial rule? How much did Latin America lag behind the more advanced economies in the 19th century? Has that gap widened steadily over time? How has inequality in Latin America evolved historically and how has it evolved elsewhere in the world? Is today's high inequality a permanent feature of modern Latin America? In short, how did we get here?

MOST OF THE COUNTRIES IN THE Latin American region are middle-income countries, and some of the richer ones have per capita income levels that are close to those of the poorer industrial countries and were even higher in the past. For example, in 2003 Argentina's per capita GDP was about two-thirds of Portugal's, but in 1930 Argentina boasted the seventh largest economy in the world, with per capita income higher than that in Canada or France, and nearly as high as that in the United States. Yet the region as a whole still has a long way to go before achieving the living standards of the advanced economies. Today the per capita income of Latin America is about 30 percent of the per capita income of the developed world, on the basis of population-weighted averages, and about 25 percent of U.S. levels. Even if Latin America manages to double the growth rates it experienced during the 1990–2003 period, the region as a whole would still need about 70 years to reach the current levels of development of its northern neighbor.

Differences in income distribution are also dramatic. Levels of inequality in the region are well above those of the developed countries. As noted in the World Bank's Latin American Region 2004 flagship, *Inequality in Latin America and the Caribbean: Breaking with History?* (de Ferranti and others 2004), the Gini coefficient for the region is about 0.55, compared with 0.37 for the developed countries, and is the highest in the world together with that for Sub-Saharan Africa.[1] The negative impact that this higher inequality has on the observed income poverty levels is significant: if Latin America had the level of inequality of the developed world, its income poverty levels would be closer to 5 percent than to the actual rate of 25 percent estimated in chapter 2.[2]

Clearly, the existing differences in development between the region and the developed world did not appear overnight. In fact, they are likely the result of historical processes that in some cases go back to the colonial period. For example, de Ferranti and others (2004) argued that to understand the region's contemporary situation, one needs to recognize the role played by the colonial inheritance (characterized by the extremely high inequality that

---

This chapter relies heavily on a background paper for this report, "Growth and Poverty in Latin America: A Historical View," by Leandro Prados de la Escosura.

emerged soon after the Europeans began to colonize) and the institutional framework put in place at the time (which allowed a small group of elites to protect the large rents they were enjoying and excluded most of the population from access to land, education, and political power). That report also noted that both the initial inequality and the institutions that appeared were shaped more by the factor endowments, found by the colonial powers, that favored the establishment of large plantations and extractive activities relying on forced labor rather than by the nature of the colonial powers themselves.

This type of argument is put forward by, among others, Engerman and Sokoloff (2006), who argue that the impact of the colonial inheritance can be observed not only in the current high levels of income inequality but also in the persistent poverty. This is so because institutional arrangements that place the economic opportunities created in the development process beyond the reach of broad segments of society are likely to result in reduced growth rates, as modern economies require broad participation in entrepreneurship and innovation.[3] Thus Engerman and Sokoloff note that the gap in per capita incomes between Latin America and the richer countries began in the 18th and 19th centuries.

Haber (1997), for example, finds that from 1800 to the early 1900s, per capita GDP grew one and one-half times in Mexico and not at all in Brazil. Over the same period, per capita income in the United States grew sixfold. Put another way, whereas U.S. per capita income in 1800 was not quite twice that in Mexico and roughly the same as in Brazil, in the early 1900s it was about four times that of Mexico and seven times that of Brazil. Similarly, Coatsworth (1998) suggests that Latin America fell into relative backwardness between roughly 1700 and 1900. At the beginning of that period, the Latin American economies (which still were Iberian colonies) were roughly as productive as those of British origin. For most of the subsequent 200 years, however, the Latin American economies stagnated whereas those of North America achieved sustained increases in income levels.

According to the evidence presented in this chapter, in the early 1900s Latin America had per capita income levels that were about 35 percent of the U.S. level and between 40 and 50 percent of the level of a broader group of developed countries. Thus even a century ago, the gap between Latin America and the rich countries was already quite significant.

While those initial conditions help explain the magnitude of the region's current development gap, authors such as Prados de la Escosura (2005) have also stressed the role played by developments during the second half of the 20th century, when Latin America seems to have lost significant ground relative to most of the reference groups that one might consider, including the United States, the developed nations in the OECD, East Asia, peripheral Europe (Greece, Ireland, Portugal, and Spain), and Spain itself. In fact, the Latin American development gap relative to the developed countries may have opened by between 15 and 20 percentage points since 1950.

In this chapter, we review how and when the Latin American development gap appeared and pose some basic questions. How much has Latin America grown economically since its independence from colonial rule? How much did it lag behind advanced economies in the 19th century? Has that gap widened steadily over time? How has inequality in Latin America evolved historically, and how has it evolved elsewhere in the world? Is today's high inequality a permanent feature of modern Latin America? In short, how did we get here?

Clearly, accurate answers to these questions depend largely on data; hence to set the debate, one needs to try to measure the evolution of living standards (per capita income or production and its distribution across the different households or individuals). This chapter is foremost a contribution to that effort in that it presents, discusses, and compares with other countries and regions the long-run trends (1850–2000) of Latin American per capita income and inequality.

Per capita income in Latin America: A long-run comparative perspective

There are two main steps in assessing the evolution of Latin America's income levels over time. The first is assembling historical time-series data on which to base the debate. The second is acknowledging that the exercise of assessing the evolution of the region is comparative in nature and therefore that it requires deciding which country or region to use as the benchmark. We address these two issues in turn.

Historical per capita GDP estimates for Latin America

Research in the quantitative economic history of Latin America still has a long way to go, and we lack complete sets of homogeneously constructed GDP estimates that would

TABLE 3.1

**Economic growth in eight major Latin American countries
(percent on an annual basis)**

Time span	Argentina	Brazil	Chile	Colombia	Mexico	Peru	Uruguay	Venezuela, R.B. de
1850–70	—	0.2	1.7	—	0	—	—	−1.2
1870–90	3.3	0.2	2	—	2	—	0.4	2.6
1890–1900	−0.8	−0.9	1.2	—	1.5	—	0.8	−1.5
1900–13	2.5	2.2	2.3	1.8	1.9	1.4	3.1	2.6
1913–29	0.9	1.4	0.9	3.9	0.4	3.6	0.9	6.8
1929–38	−0.8	1	−0.8	1.4	0.4	0.1	0.1	0.5
1938–50	1.7	1.6	1.3	1.5	3.5	1.2	1.5	4.3
1950–60	1.1	3.7	1.5	1.6	2.3	2.9	0.6	3.4
1960–70	3.9	3.1	1.9	2.2	3.4	2.3	0.8	2.4
1970–80	2.1	5.8	0.9	2.9	2.5	1.7	2.1	0.1
1980–90	−2.4	−0.2	1.2	1.1	−0.1	−3.3	−0.2	−1.9
1990–97	5.0	1.5	6.1	1.3	1.0	3.0	3.2	1.1
1997–2000	−1.2	0.0	0.9	0.6	−0.5	0.8	−2.0	−3.2
1870–29	1.8	0.8	1.6	1.5	1.5	1.3	1.2	3.0
1938–80	2.9	4.5	1.8	2.7	3.9	2.6	1.7	3.5
1980–2000	0.4	0.4	2.9	1.1	0.2	−0.5	0.7	−1.0
1870–1980	1.7	1.8	1.3	2.0	1.9	1.8	1.1	2.7
1870–2000	1.5	1.6	1.6	1.9	1.7	1.4	1.1	2.1

Source: Prados de la Escosura (2005).

allow international comparisons across time. Recent independent attempts to build GDP series for Argentina, Chile, Colombia, and Uruguay ease the problem of assessing Latin America's performance quantitatively over time.[4] Yet for most Latin American countries, product or income data are not available before 1900 and, to the best of our knowledge, no Latin American country has reliable comparable data before 1850 (that is, direct comparisons with the first half of the 1800s are not possible).[5]

Considering these limitations, table 3.1 compares the per capita growth rates of eight major Latin American countries with a combined population that represents almost 90 percent of the whole region's population in 2003. These growth rates are presented at roughly decadal benchmarks for the period 1850–2000 (although admittedly for four of the countries we do not have access to reliable growth rates for the 1850–70 period). The estimates come from Prados de la Escosura (2005), who in a background paper for this report, constructs comparable historical income and inequality series for a number of Latin American countries.

Table 3.1 indicates that over the 1870–2000 period, República Bolivariana de Venezuela had the highest per capita growth rate (2.1 percent a year), followed closely by Colombia (1.9 percent) and Mexico (1.7 percent). Of the eight countries, Uruguay had the lowest per capita growth rate (1.1 percent), followed by Peru (1.4 percent) and Argentina (1.5 percent). Brazil and Chile were intermediate cases, both with an estimated per capita growth rate of 1.6 percent per year. At this growth rate, per capita GDP doubles roughly every 45 years, so today per capita GDP for these countries would be about eight times the observed level in the late 1800s. One interesting issue that emerges from the table regards the low variance of the average growth rates over the 1870–2000 period. In fact, excluding Uruguay and República Bolivariana de Venezuela, the growth rates of the remaining countries ranged within half a percentage point, from 1.4 percent to 1.9 percent.

As for the evolution of per capita growth over time, table 3.1 suggests that for most of the countries, the 1938–80 period was the most productive. This was especially true for Brazil and Mexico, where per capita growth for the period is estimated at 4.5 and 3.9 percent, respectively. The exception is Chile, where average per capita growth over 1938–80 was 1.8 percent, compared with 2.9 percent over 1980–2000.

Except for Chile, however, the last two decades of the 20th century were not very positive (Peru and República Bolivariana de Venezuela actually experienced negative per capita growth rates) due to two negative episodes. The first is the lost decade of 1980s following the Latin American debt crisis. The second is the period following the Asian financial crisis of 1997 and the Russian financial crisis in 1998. Had it not been for the positive performance of the region during 1990–97, when all eight countries under consideration enjoyed substantial positive growth (and half of them enjoyed per capita growth rates that more than doubled their historical trends), the last part of the 20th century would have been much more dramatic than it actually was.[6]

The growth rates in table 3.1, when combined with recent estimates of the level of per capita GDP, can be used to assemble historical trends in per capita GDP. Estimates of the per capita incomes levels circa 1900 for the eight countries covered in table 3.1 show that Uruguay was the richest with a per capita GDP of $1,645 (in 1980 Geari-Khamis PPP $). It was followed by Argentina ($1,375), Chile ($1,209), Mexico, ($1,141), Peru ($491), Brazil ($444), Colombia ($427), and República Bolivariana de Venezuela ($407).

Figure 3.1 plots the per capita GDP trends for the eight Latin American countries in question (in Geari-Khamis PPP 1980 $).[7] Although the figure shows some dispersion in the GDP levels (especially toward the end of the sample), the parallelism in the evolution of the income levels of the different countries is remarkable.

Income convergence in Latin America

One interesting question regards whether the evidence that emerges from the estimated long-run trends supports the

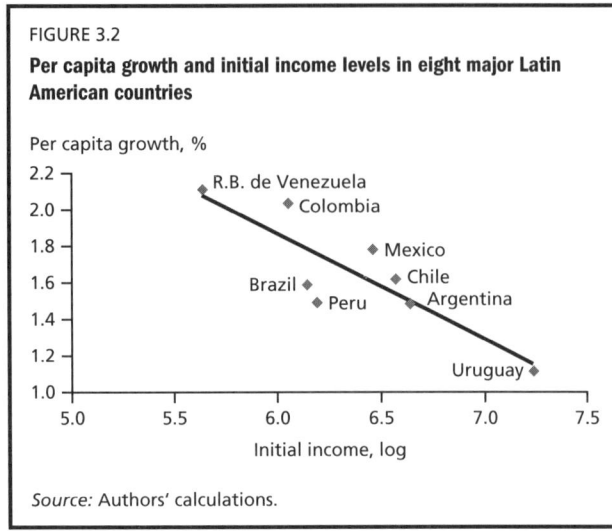

FIGURE 3.2
Per capita growth and initial income levels in eight major Latin American countries

Source: Authors' calculations.

FIGURE 3.1
Per capita GDP for eight major Latin American countries, 1850–2000

Source: Prados de la Escosura (2005).

convergence hypothesis of income levels between the Latin American countries. That is, over the past century or so, have countries that were initially poorer managed to grow faster than those that were initially richer? To explore the empirical evidence on this issue, figure 3.2 compares the average annual growth rates experienced by the different countries between 1870 (or the earliest date available) and 2000 with their corresponding (logged) initial per capita income level in 1870. The figure clearly shows a negative correlation between these two variables. The estimated slope of the regression line is −1.3, and it has an associated standard error of 0.30. Although one has to be careful extrapolating results based on only eight countries, the evidence presented here would indicate that initially poorer countries in the late 1800s grew faster over the ensuing 130 years than the initially richer countries. This, in turn, would lend some support to the hypothesis of convergence of incomes across the Latin American countries during this period.

Figure 3.3 changes the focus of the analysis somewhat and plots the cross-country standard deviation of logged per capita income. This is a measure of income dispersion that can be understood as an alternative way to explore the possibility of convergence.[8] This figure suggests that dispersion of cross-country per capita income increased during the first epoch of globalization (1870–1913) and then decreased during the deglobalization of the interwar years, whereas between the late 1930s and 1970, the dispersion of cross-country per capita income increased once more before falling in 1980 to its historical low. Overall, figure 3.3 suggests a convergence in per capita income levels over the 1870–2000 period, albeit with a number of ups and downs suggesting periodic increases in cross-country inequality.

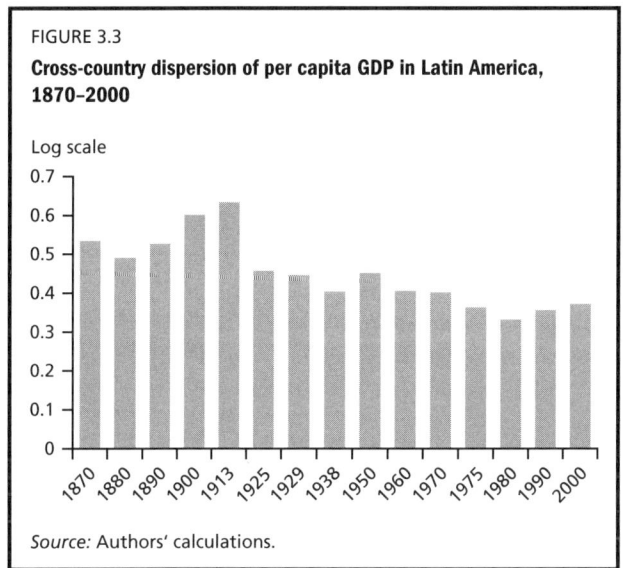

FIGURE 3.3
Cross-country dispersion of per capita GDP in Latin America, 1870–2000

Source: Authors' calculations.

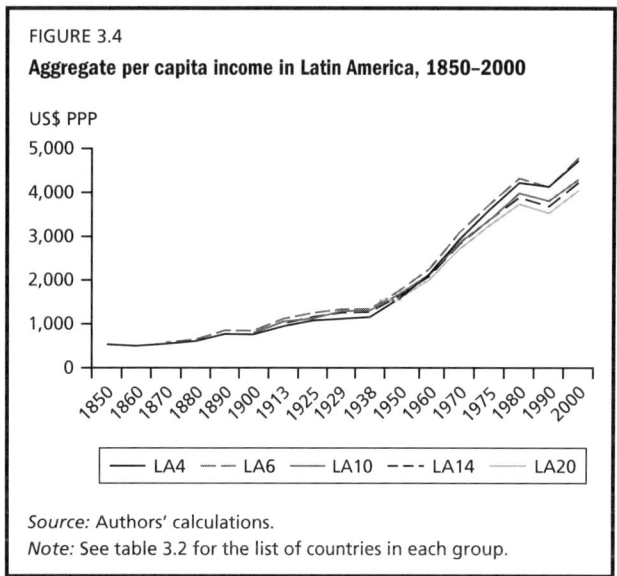

FIGURE 3.4
Aggregate per capita income in Latin America, 1850–2000

Source: Authors' calculations.
Note: See table 3.2 for the list of countries in each group.

Long-run per capita GDP trends in Latin America

Having reviewed the evidence for several individual countries, we now move to analyze the evolution of per capita income at the regional level. The results are shown in table 3.2 and in figure 3.4, which report population-weighted measures of regional real per capita GDP growth (table 3.2) and regional real GDP income levels (figure 3.4) over the past 150 years. In addition to the eight major countries discussed above, we now introduce several other Latin American economies in the time periods for which historical data are available. Clearly, the lengthier the coverage, the lower the number of countries covered.

A number of features can be pointed out regarding the aggregate performance of Latin America. First, the picture of Latin America's performance seems quite robust (this is in part a result of the low variance of growth rates across countries). After a slow start in the mid-1800s when per capita income growth was probably well below 1 percent, growth in Latin America appears to have risen significantly during the 1870s and 1880s, slowed during the 1890s, and accelerated in the early 1900s. It then slowed again because of World War I and came to a halt during the Great Depression.

From the late 1930s up to 1980, however, Latin America began displaying robust growth. Over this period, depending on the sample under consideration, growth appears to have hovered around 2.5–3.0 percent (with this growth, per capita income doubles every 25 years or so). The 1980s, however, saw a reversal of fortunes with per capita income declining by 0.5 percent a year on average (a cumulative decline of 5 percent in per capita income levels). Finally, one can also clearly observe the recovery that took place during the 1990s, which as mentioned previously extended to the end of the decade.

TABLE 3.2
Aggregate per capita growth in Latin America
(percent)

Time span	LA20	LA15	LA10	LA6	LA4
1850–70					0.2
1870–90				1.7	1.4
1890–1900				0.4	0.5
1900–13			2.3	2.2	1.8
1913–29		1.2	1.2	1.0	0.9
1929–38		0.1	0.2	0.1	0.4
1938–50		2.1	2.1	2.3	2.6
1950–60	2.3	2.3	2.3	2.4	3.0
1960–70	2.9	2.9	3.0	3.2	3.2
1970–80	3.3	3.3	3.3	3.4	3.7
1980–90	–0.5	–0.5	–0.4	–0.5	–0.2
1990–2000	1.3	1.3	1.3	1.5	1.3
1870–1929				1.4	1.2
1938–80	2.9	2.6	2.6	2.7	3
1980–2000	0.4	0.4	0.4	0.5	0.6
1870–1980				1.8	1.9
1870–2000				1.6	1.7

Source: Authors' calculations.
Note: LA20 = population-weighted average of Latin American countries; LA15 = population-weighted average of LA10 + Costa Rica, El Salvador, Guatemala, Honduras, and Panama; LA10 = population-weighted average of LA6 + Colombia, Cuba, Ecuador and Peru; LA6 = population-weighted average of LA4 + Argentina and Uruguay; LA4 = population-weighted average of Brazil, Chile, Mexico, and Venezuela.

On the whole, Latin American per capita income levels are now between eight and nine times the observed level in 1850, about six times the level in 1900, and about two and a half times the level in 1950. With this information in hand, we are now in a position to compare the relative evolution of GDP in the region against different reference groups.

Comparative perspective

How does Latin America's per capita GDP perform in comparison with other countries and regions of the world? Typically, historical comparisons of Latin America have taken the United States as reference. Over the 19th century, however, even in western European economies, per capita GDP lagged behind the United States. That suggests comparing Latin America with only the United States may bias the assessment in that the United States was the leading performer during this period and hence serves as a very narrow reference. To try to control for this possibility, we take a broader view and consider the performance of several different groups. These include the group of developed countries that today are part of the OECD; Spain, a country with which Latin America shares some institutional background; peripheral Europe, which includes countries known for quickly catching up with European Union levels; and East Asia (covering Hong Kong, China; the Republic of Korea; Singapore; and Taiwan, China) to take account of the "Asian miracle." Table 3.3 reports the growth rates these reference groups have experienced since 1850.

This table indicates that during the second half of the 19th century, the United States was the fastest-growing economy, with per capita GDP growth of almost 2 percent on an average annual basis (reaching 2.2 percent over 1850–70). OECD's advanced economies grew at 1.5 percent, and Spain and the peripheral Europe group each grew at about half the U.S. rate (1 percent in both cases).[9] Although we do not report data for the four East Asian economies until 1870, the existing estimates suggest that this group also was growing at a much slower pace than the United States (the estimates for the Asian economies in table 3.3 over the 1870–1900 period would suggest an average per capita growth rate of less than 1 percent a year). Thus, as already noted, the United States performed significantly better than all other regions under consideration during this period.

Starting in the 1960s, however, East Asia became the fastest-growing group, with per capita growth rates in the 6–7 percent range until the 1980s. Moreover, while not at

TABLE 3.3

Economic growth in several reference groups (percent)

Time span	United States	Spain	OECD	PE	EA
1850–70	2.2	0.5	1.5	0.8	
1870–90	1.6	1.5	1.4	1.2	0.8
1890–1900	1.8	0.9	1.5	0.9	0.7
1900–13	1.9	1.0	1.6	0.9	0.7
1913–29	1.6	1.7	1.3	1.6	1.9
1929–38	–0.5	–4.8	0	–1.7	2.4
1938–50	4.7	1.8	3.2	0.6	–4.4
1950–60	1.7	3.6	2.7	3.3	3.6
1960–70	2.9	7.4	3.4	6.3	5.6
1970–80	2.1	3.7	2.4	3.9	7.0
1980–90	2.1	2.9	2.1	2.4	5.7
1990–2000	1.9	2.4	1.9	2.7	4.8
1850–1900	1.9	1.0	1.5	1.0	
1870–1929	1.7	1.3	1.4	1.2	1.0
1938–80	2.9	3.9	2.9	3.4	2.5
1980–2000	2.0	2.6	2.0	2.5	5.2
1870–1980	2.0	1.8	1.9	1.8	1.7
1870–2000	2.0	1.9	1.9	1.9	2.3

Source: Authors' calculations based on Maddison (2005).
Note: Peripheral Europe (PE) includes Greece, Ireland, Portugal, and Spain. East Asia (EA) consists of Hong Kong (China), Republic of Korea, Singapore, and Taiwan (China).

the same level as East Asia, both Spain and peripheral Europe also outperformed the United States and the OECD group. Even the OECD group seems to have performed relatively better than the United States over the second half of the 20th century. Thus whether the Latin American experience over this period is considered a success depends to a large extent on the countries and regions being considered as a reference group.

Figure 3.5 graphically illustrates the evolution of income trends (relative to the United States) for a group of four Latin American countries (Brazil, Chile, Mexico, and República Bolivariana de Venezuela) and for the other four groups under analysis. Several messages emerge from the figure. First, in 1850 Latin America's per capita GDP was already about 60 percent of the U.S. level, whereas Spain's was about 80 percent, and peripheral Europe's was 75 percent. The OECD group as a whole was richer than the United States (107 percent). For East Asia the first available estimates correspond to 1870. Then it was the poorest among those considered here with per capita income levels representing only 25 percent of the U.S. levels.

Interestingly, 110 years later, in 1980, the situation continued to be very similar, the result of all the groups under

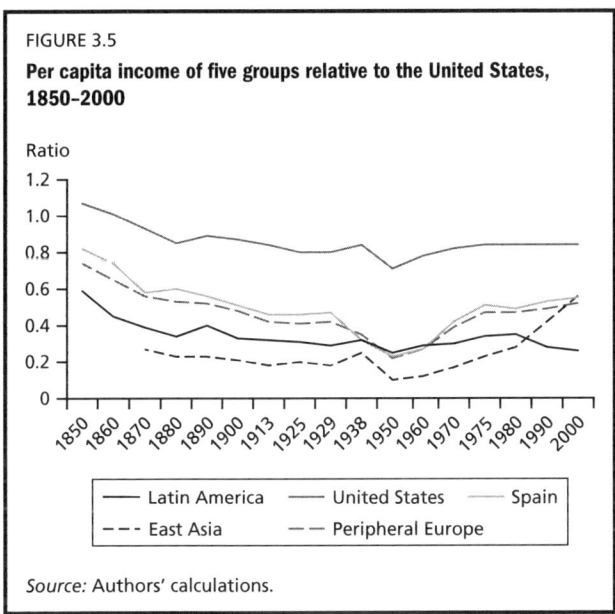

FIGURE 3.5
Per capita income of five groups relative to the United States, 1850–2000

Source: Authors' calculations.

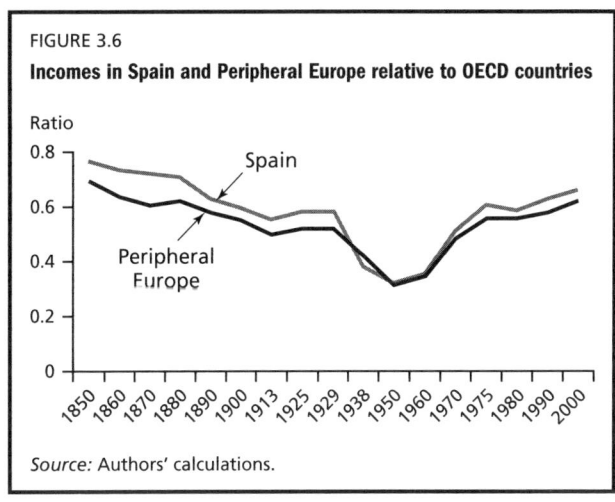

FIGURE 3.6
Incomes in Spain and Peripheral Europe relative to OECD countries

Source: Authors' calculations.

consideration sharing some trends relative to the United States. First, they all lost *significant* ground in the second half of the 19th century, Second, they all lost *some* ground in the first half of the 20th century. And third, they all regained some of the lost ground in the 1950–80 period. In fact, in 1980 the OECD group was still leading our four comparison groups, although its relative income levels had fallen to about 80 percent of those of the United States. Per capita income levels in Spain and peripheral Europe were 50 percent of those in the United States, while in Latin America they were 30 percent, and in East Asia they were close to but still below 30 percent. Thus, over the 1850–1980 period, mobility was quite limited in our country groupings. In relative terms, those groups that started poor compared with the United States remained poor and those that started rich (also compared with the United States) remained rich.

Does this lack of mobility mean that countries cannot break with history and therefore that states of development are given and immutable? Well, the answer is that countries and regions can indeed break with history—as a series of developments since 1980 confirm. East Asia more than doubled its relative income during the last two decades of the 20th century, moving from 27 percent of U.S. levels in 1980 to 55 percent in 2000 (see figure 3.5). Put another way, in just 20 years, the four East Asian economies moved from last in our relative classification to levels comparable with those observed for Spain and peripheral Europe. This achievement is even more remarkable when one considers

Spain and peripheral Europe were also moving up toward U.S. levels, and more significantly toward OECD levels (figure 3.6).

Admittedly, the trends observed in Spain, peripheral Europe, and East Asia during the 1980s and 1990s were to a large extent a continuation of those observed since 1950. This is shown in figure 3.7, which presents the evolution of population-weighted average per capita income levels for Latin America relative to the different reference groups.

Looking first at panel a, which compares Latin America with the OECD, the picture indicates that the region was losing ground during the last part of the 19th century. However, panel a also indicates that Latin America experienced a significant decline over the second half of the 20th century. For example, Latin America's per capita income levels fell from about 45–50 percent of OECD's levels in 1950 to about 30 percent in 2000. Thus Latin America may have experienced the paradox of fast growth (recall that 1950–80 was the fastest-growing experience of the region with per capita growth rates in the 3 percent range) while losing ground relative to the advanced economies.

When the region is compared with Spain (panel b), the picture is somewhat different. Over the 1850–1930 period, Latin America's per capita income remained basically constant relative to Spain, and if anything it increased. The central years of the 20th century, resulting from Spain's civil war and autarkic aftermath, witnessed a dramatic recession in Spain (Latin American income levels were in this period about 20 percent higher than Spain's). However, as Spain reengaged in the world economy in the 1950s, the country began regaining lost ground. Spain

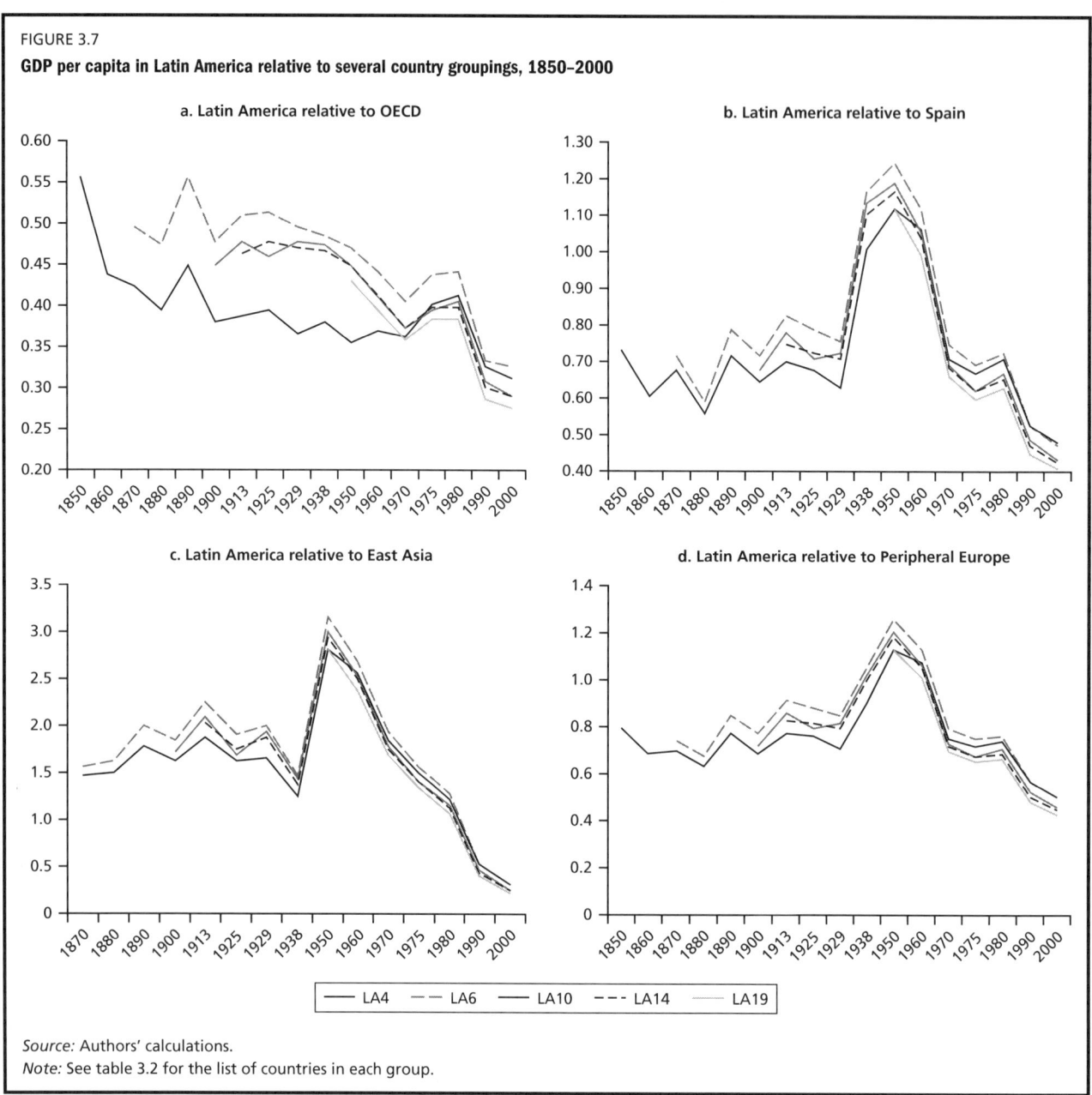

FIGURE 3.7
GDP per capita in Latin America relative to several country groupings, 1850–2000

Source: Authors' calculations.
Note: See table 3.2 for the list of countries in each group.

grew faster in the 1950s than Latin America did and experienced exceptional growth in the 1960s and early 1970s.[10] Moreover, despite near stagnation during the "transition to democracy" (1975–85), Spain's growth was above the OECD average during the last two decades of the 20th century. By the 1980s incomes in Latin America were at about the same levels relative to Spain as they had been 100 years earlier.

In a similar fashion, putting Latin America side by side with peripheral Europe (panel c) and East Asia (panel d), one would also conclude that Latin America performed well between 1850 and 1950. From 1950 onward, however, things changed, and Latin America's performance declined sharply over the next five decades relative to those groups.

The relevance of the second half of the 20th century for understanding the magnitude of Latin America's current development gap relative to several country groupings is also apparent from figure 3.8. This figure is based on the regional estimates of per capita income levels in Maddison (2005), which go back in some cases to 1500. According to figure 3.8, between 1820 and 1870, Latin America

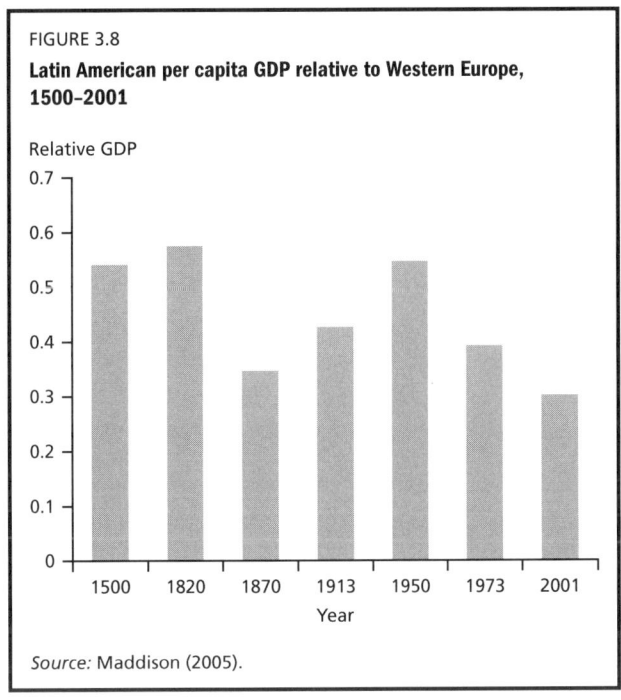

FIGURE 3.8
Latin American per capita GDP relative to Western Europe, 1500–2001

Source: Maddison (2005).

Factor endowments, technology, and relative scarcity of resources have had important implications for the initial inequality levels. For example, in Latin America the characteristics of the colonies favored the establishment of large plantations (such as sugar) and mining activities that employed forced labor. As a result, a social structure emerged where a privileged few were in control of most of the profitable activities and where, most importantly, most of the population was excluded from access to land, education, and political power. In contrast, the colonial powers in North America soon learned that there was no gold, few indigenous peoples to exploit, and soils and climates that would not support the production of crops based on large slave plantations. In fact, unlike in the South, in the North land was cheap and labor scarce. In addition, fewer health problems affected European settlements in North America. Such circumstances led to open competition among the earlier colonies to attract migrants by providing favorable working conditions, something that in turn fostered a remarkable degree of equality.[11]

lost significant ground relative to Western Europe. Latin America's situation then improved markedly vis-à-vis Western Europe in the first half of the 20th century. By 1950 Latin America's position was similar to the one it held in 1820. After 1950, however, the region experienced a dramatic decline, with relative income falling from about 55 percent of that in Western Europe to about 30 percent.

On the whole, Latin America thus appears to have lost ground since the mid-1800s relative to several other country groupings, and the downward slide seems to have been particularly fast in the last half of the 1900s. Breaking with this historic pattern will not be easy, but as East Asia, Spain, and peripheral Europe have demonstrated, it can be done, and countries can put themselves on an upward path.

Long-run inequality

Together with Sub-Saharan Africa, Latin America has long been known as the region with the highest inequality in the world, with a Gini coefficient above 0.50 since the 1960s. What explains this high level of inequality? Various alternative interpretations have been offered, but to a large extent they all follow the colonial inheritance argument coupled with the persistence of the initial institutions.

Inequality in Latin America and the Caribbean: Breaking with History? (de Ferranti and others 2004) stressed the joint role played by factor endowments and institutions.

The issue of what created an initial level of high inequality is clearly different from the issue of why inequality persisted over time. *Inequality in Latin America and the Caribbean: Breaking with History?* argues that the persistence of inequality during the colonial and early independence period occurred because the initial nexus of institutions survived, as did the rationale for these institutions. Given the disparities in resources that resulted from the colonial period, the Creole elite who had benefited from those disparities during colonial times were able to quickly gain effective control of the independent countries and determine the general structure of the institutions in ways that favored their interest.

Explaining the persistence of inequality over the 20th century is more problematic because significant social, economic, and political changes occurred during the 1900s. Moreover, the increase in urbanization rates should have somewhat mitigated the relevance of the highly inegalitarian pattern of land ownership and its impact on income inequality. In addition, modernization moved most of the Latin American countries in the direction of more open and democratic societies. *Inequality in Latin America and the Caribbean: Breaking with History?* offers a number of conjectures in this regard, including slow increases in coverage and low quality of education, a development strategy based on import substitution and isolation from world markets, and imperfect financial markets that may have prevented those at the bottom of the income distribution from exploiting economic opportunities by restricting their access to credit.

Unfortunately, no quantitative assessment of long-run inequality validating these arguments has been carried out for Latin America. A good example is provided by the Bourguignon and Morrisson (2002) investigation of the historical trends in world income inequality. Conventional wisdom and lack of empirical evidence led them to assume that no changes in income distribution had taken place in Latin America from independence to the mid-20th century.

Can we quantify trends in income inequality in modern Latin America? It is possible to infer the evolution of inequality since 1950 on the basis of direct income distribution observations. For example, in table 3.4 we report Gini coefficients for several Latin American countries as well as a population weighted regional average. This table indicates that inequality remained basically constant from 1950 to 2000 at between 0.51 and 0.55 on the Gini index.

Admittedly there is significant country heterogeneity. For example, the Gini index markedly increased in Argentina, from 0.40 to 0.48 between 1950 and 1990, but it may have declined in República Bolivariana de Venezuela from a high of 0.61 in the mid-20th century to about 0.45 four decades later. Similarly, El Salvador may have experienced a significant worsening in inequality over the 1950–90 period, while Honduras saw some improvements.

For the pre-1950 period, data availability prevents direct inequality comparisons. However, one can still explore empirically the evolution of income inequality using indirect indicators and a handful of country studies that follow that approach. One such study is the path-breaking work by Bértola (2005) for Uruguay, which provides crude estimates of income distribution and Gini coefficients that go back to the late 1800s. Also notable is the work by Williamson (1999), who explored the consequences for inequality of the early phase of globalization (1870–1914). On the basis of the wage–land rental ratio, he showed an increase of within-country inequality for Argentina and Uruguay over that period. Bértola and Williamson (2003) follow up on that line of research and argue that inequality trends reversed in the interwar period, when the observed steep decline in the wage-rental ratio stopped, and then increased somewhat after the 1930s. Calvo, Torre, and Szwarcberg (2002) suggest that the extent of inequality changed little during the century in Argentina, whereas Londoño (1995) argues that the inequality levels observed in Colombia during the 1990s were probably similar to those observed in 1938.

In a background paper for this report, Prados de la Escosura (2005) builds on Williamson (2002) to explore the historical evolution of the ratio of GDP per worker to the unskilled wage between 1850 and 1950 (or earliest possible date) for Argentina, Brazil, Chile, Mexico, and Uruguay. The rationale for this choice is that such a ratio compares the returns to unskilled labor with the returns to all production factors, that is, GDP. Since unskilled labor is the more evenly distributed factor of production in developing countries, an increase in the ratio suggests that inequality is rising. On that basis Prados de la Escosura (2005) concludes that in Argentina, Chile, and Uruguay income inequality does not seem to have changed much over the period whereas Brazil and Mexico may have experienced some deterioration in the distribution of income.

On the whole, all the evidence that emerges from these studies indicates that, on average, Latin America entered the 20th century with a very high level of inequality, which persisted for the rest of the century, despite significant variations by country in different periods.

How do these trends compare to those observed in the advanced economies? Spain experienced a significant decline

TABLE 3.4

Inequality in Latin America 1950–2000, as measured by Gini coefficients (percent)

	1950	1960	1970	1980	1990
Argentina	39.6	41.4	41.2	47.2	47.7
Bolivia			53	53.4	54.5
Brazil		57	57.1	57.1	57.3
Chile		48.2	47.4	53.1	54.7
Colombia	51	54	57.3	48.8	50.3
Costa Rica		50	44.5	48.5	46
Dominican Republic			45.5	42.1	48.1
El Salvador		42.4	46.5	48.4	50.5
Honduras			61.8	54.9	57
Mexico	55	60.6	57.9	50.9	53.1
Panama		50	58.4	47.5	56.3
Paraguay				45.1	57
Peru		61	48.5	43	46.4
Uruguay		37	42.8	43.6	40.6
Venezuela, R.B. de	61.3	46.2	48	44.7	45.9
LAC4	50.5	53.2	53.1	49.1	50.7
LAC6		54.8	54.8	53.2	54.2
LAC15			53.9	51.9	53.2
Spain			45.7	36.3	34.7

Source: Altimir (1987); Londoño and Székely (2000).
Note: See table 3.2 for LAC4, LAC6, LAC15 group definitions.

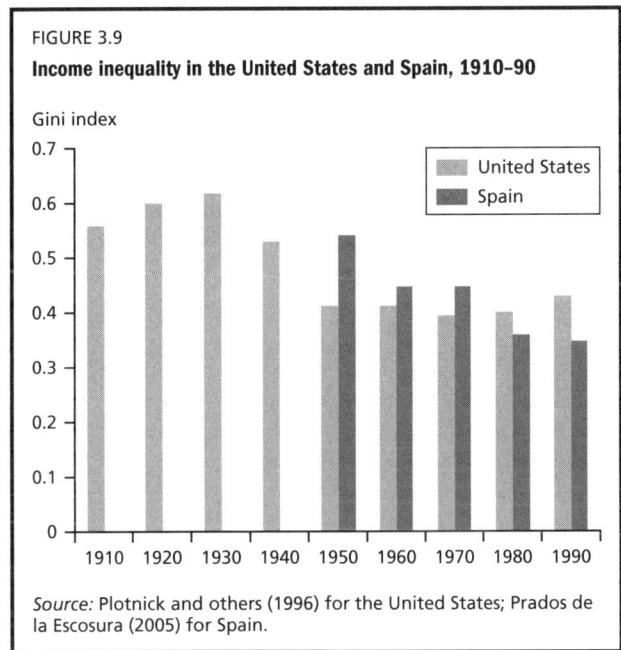

FIGURE 3.9
Income inequality in the United States and Spain, 1910–90

Source: Plotnick and others (1996) for the United States; Prados de la Escosura (2005) for Spain.

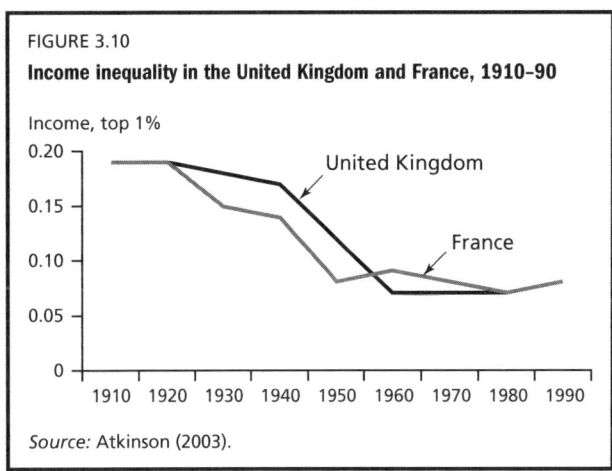

FIGURE 3.10
Income inequality in the United Kingdom and France, 1910–90

Source: Atkinson (2003).

in income inequality between the 1970s and the 1990s, when the Gini coefficient fell by more than 10 percentage points (see the bottom row of table 3.4). Unfortunately, there are no direct estimates of the Gini coefficient for Spain before 1970. However, existing indirect indicators (Prados de la Escosura 2005) suggest that income inequality has been declining in Spain since the 1950s, when Spain may have had inequality levels comparable to (if not higher than) those observed in Latin America. For 1950 Prados de la Escosura (2005) estimates a Gini coefficient for Spain above 0.50. Thus Spain appears to have lowered the Gini coefficient by almost 15 percentage points between 1950 and 1980 and by around 20 percentage points between 1950 and 1990 (figure 3.9).

The estimates of the Gini index for the United States (see figure 3.9) indicate that from the turn of the century until about 1930, inequality remained constant with a high Gini of 0.60 (Plotnick and others 1996). This relative stability was interrupted by World War I, which seems to have had a brief equalizing effect, but starting about 1920 inequality began to rise once more, reaching its pre–World War II high in 1929. From 1929 to 1951, income inequality fell dramatically from the prevailing Gini of 0.60 to about 0.40.

The United Kingdom experienced a similar pattern. Acemoglu and Robinson (2002) present evidence indicating that the Gini coefficient for the United Kingdom could have been around 0.55 in the 1890s. Then, for most of the 20th century, inequality seems to have declined, although to a large extent most of the decline took place between 1940 and the late 1970s. Atkinson (2003) relies on income tax statistics to construct estimates of the income shares of the wealthiest percentile in the United Kingdom. The estimates show that in the early 1900s the richest 1 percent in the United Kingdom shared almost 20 percent of total personal income; in 1940 they had 17 percent; and in the late 1970s, when the declining trend in inequality was reversed, they held a mere 6 percent (figure 3.10).

The results in Atkinson (2003) also indicate that income inequality in France evolved in about the same way as it did in the United Kingdom (at least until the 1980s). In the early 1900s, the share of income of the richest percentile in France was also about 20 percent, whereas in the 1980s it was roughly 7 percent. The main difference between these two countries is that most of the decline in French income inequality took place between the 1920s and 1950. It is notable that Atkinson's estimates of the top percentile's income share for both France and the United Kingdom are consistent with very high inequality levels at the beginning of the century. In fact, if one were to assume that income approximately follows a lognormal distribution (see chapter 4), income inequality in the two countries in 1900 might have been around 0.60.

Thus the empirical evidence reported in this section confirms to a large extent the finding of *Inequality in Latin America and the Caribbean: Breaking with History?* that inequality in Latin America has been persistent and stable over the last century. It also confirms that inequality in Europe and the United States seems to have declined significantly over the 20th century. In addition, the discussion notes that the levels of inequality in Latin America in the early to mid-1900s may not have been so much different from those observed in France, Spain, the United Kingdom, and the United States, but while these countries significantly reduced their inequality at different moments in time, Latin America has yet to do so. The question remains: If other countries have managed to break with their histories on both the growth and income per capita fronts, then why cannot Latin America also break with its history?

Notes

1. See table A19 of the report. The figures refer to the mid-1990s, so the current levels may be different.

2. The inference is based on the results that emerge from using a lognormal approximation for the distribution of income. See chapter 4 of this report for a discussion of that particular assumption.

3. See also chapter 6 of this report for a discussion of how social exclusion from the development process can result in lower GDP growth rates.

4. See Cortés Conde (1994, 1997) and Della Paolera, Taylor, and Bózolli (2003) for Argentina; GRECO (2002) for Colombia; Díaz, Lüders, and Wagner (1998) for Chile; and Bértola (1998) for Uruguay.

5. This is not to say, however, that there is no *estimated* data for the pre-1850 period. In fact, Maddison (2005) presents data going back to 1500.

6. See Loayza, Fajnzylber, and Calderon (2005) for an analysis of the recent Latin American growth experience and the positive impact of the liberalization process of the 1990s on the growth performance of the different countries.

7. Note that the data in figure 3.1 are in constant 1980 PPP dollars, so the per capita GDP ranking of the countries does not necessarily coincide with rankings given in other parts of this report that use constant 1996 PPP dollars (when the source of data is the Penn World Tables (PWT6.1)) or constant 2000 PPP dollars (when the source of data is the *World Development Indicators*).

8. Although now it would be σ-convergence rather than β-convergence. See Barro and Sala-i-Martin (1995) for a discussion of the different concepts of convergence.

9. The OECD group used here consists of Australia, Austria, Belgium, Canada, Denmark, Finland, France, Germany, Netherlands, Norway, Portugal, Spain, Sweden, Switzerland, the United Kingdom, and the United States.

10. In Spain, the year 1938 represents a trough in economic performance.

11. What mattered for the initial inequality level was not the identity of the colonizing power but rather the characteristics of the colonies. The British colonies of British Honduras, Guyana, and Jamaica resulted in levels of inequality similar to most of those in Latin America. In contrast, in Argentina, Costa Rica, and Uruguay, where there were few Native Americans, the social structure was not so unequal.

CHAPTER 4

The Relative Roles of Growth and Inequality for Poverty Reduction

Growth is good for the poor, and growth that is accompanied by progressive distributional change is even better. But are the same type of policies appropriate for all countries that want to reduce poverty quickly? For example, should Chile and Nicaragua—two countries with similar levels of inequality but dramatically different income levels—try to strike a similar balance between growth-promoting and inequality-reducing policies? Similarly, should Uruguay and Brazil—which have similar levels of per capita income but are the least and most unequal countries in the region, respectively—follow similar policies in their attempts to reduce poverty?

THE LAST DECADE HAS WITNESSED A booming literature on the links among growth, inequality, and poverty reduction. As a result of this debate, a more or less broad consensus has emerged on a few findings.

First, nobody seems to doubt the importance of growth for poverty reduction. Countries that have historically experienced the greatest reduction in poverty are those that have experienced prolonged periods of sustained economic growth (panel a of figure 4.1). For example, over the 1981–2000 period, China's poverty rate fell from more than 50 percent to about 8 percent, thanks to an impressive per capita growth rate of almost 8.5 percent a year. Similarly, between 1993 and 2002 Vietnam cut its poverty rate in half, from about 58 percent to about 29 percent, by growing at almost 6 percent a year.

Second, progressive distributional changes are good for poverty reduction (see figure 4.1, panel b). While it is difficult to argue that poverty reduction can be achieved through redistributive policies in the absence of economic growth, growth associated with progressive distributional changes will reduce poverty more than growth that leaves the distribution unchanged. There are two main reasons for this. One is that, in general, for a fixed level of income, progressive distributional change will shift resources from the richer to the poorer and thus lead to poverty reduction.[1] The other reason is that poverty is more responsive to growth the more equal the income distribution. This point is illustrated in panel c of figure 4.1, which plots the total elasticity of poverty against the logged Gini index for a selected number of countries. The upward slope of the regression line in this picture indicates that as inequality increases (that is, as one moves to the right of the horizontal axis), the growth elasticity of poverty becomes less negative. Thus progressive distributional change will have, in addition to the one-shot instant impact on poverty derived from the pure redistribution effect, a long-run effect derived from an increase in the sensitivity of poverty to growth.

The third finding is that there is no strong empirical evidence suggesting a general tendency for growth as such to make income distribution more or less equal (figure 1, panel d). For example, Dollar and Kraay (2002) find that, on average, the income of the poorest fifth of society rises

This chapter is based on the background paper for this report "A Normal Relationship? Poverty, Growth and Inequality" by H. Lopez and L. Servén (2005a).

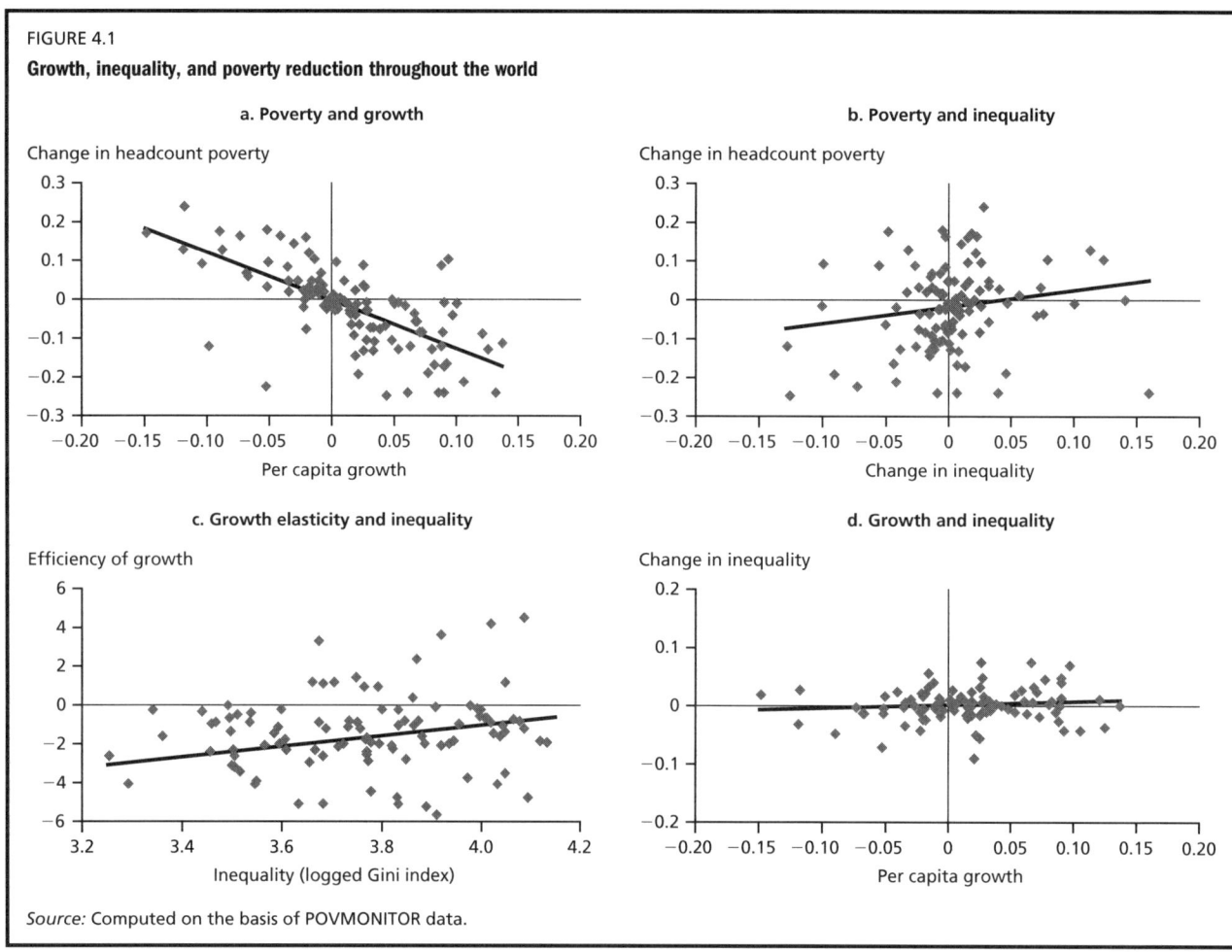

FIGURE 4.1
Growth, inequality, and poverty reduction throughout the world

Source: Computed on the basis of POVMONITOR data.

proportionately with average incomes. Other studies concluding that changes in income and changes in inequality are unrelated include Deininger and Squire (1996), Chen and Ravallion (1997), and Easterly (1999).

The Latin American countries analyzed in chapter 2 also fit this pattern: the linear correlations between changes in a given inequality index and income growth rates are always insignificant regardless of the inequality index and the income variable (either survey-based or national accounts-based). For example, the correlation between the changes in the Gini for the distribution of household income and growth rates in that variable is just −0.02. Growth would thus be good for the poor, or at least as good as for everybody else in society.[2]

On the whole, the previous discussion suggests that a sensible development strategy should focus both on the *quantity* of growth (that is, on the achievement of a high growth rate) and on the *quality* of growth (that is, on who benefits from that growth). Unfortunately, this general advice is not very useful for policy purposes. For one thing, the achievements of both growth and a more equal income distribution are policy outcomes that are a challenge in themselves. But beyond that, the discussion leaves unanswered a number of questions of extreme relevance for policy making. For example, how much emphasis should policy makers place on achieving a high growth rate and how much on achieving a balanced pattern of growth? What is more advisable from a poverty perspective: a high growth rate that has an associated increase in inequality, or a lower growth rate that maintains inequality at a constant level? Are there any conditions under which policy makers can accept a trade-off between growth and a deterioration in the distribution of income?

The answers to those questions are critical to strike the right balance between growth-enhancing and inequality-reducing policies in a particular country. For example, if growth is the main force behind poverty reduction in all circumstances, then poverty reduction strategies should focus on growth, and policy makers should think twice before implementing policies that, in the name of a better income distribution, lead to a deceleration in growth. If, however, trends in relative incomes are found to account for the lion's share of poverty changes, then development strategies should also emphasize the pattern of growth, and policy makers might be willing to accept a trade-off between fast growth and rapid poverty reduction.[3] Clearly, between these two extreme cases, one can expect to find a continuum of possibilities where both growth and changes in inequality will be important, to varying degrees, for poverty reduction and where specific knowledge about the relative importance of each component can prove useful for policy purposes.

This chapter explores the types of questions posed above in two complementary ways. First, it applies standard poverty decomposition techniques to identify the growth and distribution components corresponding to the observed poverty changes for 18 Latin American countries. That is, for each particular country episode, the change in poverty that can be attributed to growth is separated from the change in poverty that can be attributed to changes in income distribution. Then these variance decompositions are used to summarize the relative importance of the different sources of poverty changes.

This type of exercise has been performed in a recent paper by Kraay (2005), who finds that in a global sample of developing countries, growth in average incomes *matters a great deal* for poverty reduction. More specifically, Kraay estimates that over the short run, growth accounts for about 70 percent of the variation in poverty (as measured by a $1-a-day poverty line). As the time horizon lengthens, that proportion increases to above 95 percent. In other words, changes in poverty reduction are almost uniquely driven by growth in mean income. This finding would probably justify development strategies that rely almost exclusively on growth as a tool for poverty reduction.

The analysis in this report adds to this debate in two main dimensions. First, it allows for a comparison between the Latin American countries and the global context. This comparison is interesting because, given the high levels of inequality in the region, one might expect that Latin American development strategies would have to incorporate both growth and inequality concerns. In addition, the chapter also explores (within the Latin American context) whether the results are sensitive to the choice of the poverty line. This issue is important because a country can set its poverty line very high, so that large numbers of individuals qualify as poor, or very low, so that the focus is on the poorest of the poor. Where a poverty line is set could thus determine whether policy makers should focus on growth or poverty reduction when targeting different segments of the population.

The second way in which this chapter addresses the issue of the relative importance of growth and redistribution is through the use of a particular functional approximation for the empirical income distribution. More specifically, we rely on a lognormal function to simulate how growth and changes in inequality affect changes in poverty under different scenarios and, more specifically, under different initial levels of inequality and development. One of the virtues of this type of analysis is that the lognormal function can easily be calibrated with observed values from actual countries so that the discussion can move from some basic generalizations to a country-specific assessment.

The report makes two contributions on this front. First, even though parametric techniques have become very popular in poverty analysis (see, among others, Bourguignon 2004, and Kakwani and Son 2003), little effort has been spent to verify how well the approximations being used fit the actual data. In this regard, we present new (and encouraging) results regarding the goodness of a fit of the lognormal specification. The second contribution is a typology of Latin American countries—grounded on the theoretical analysis—that can be used as a guide to discriminate somewhat between growth and inequality priorities at the country level.

The relative roles of growth and income distribution for poverty reduction

Changes in poverty can be related to two main sources: changes in mean income, and changes in relative incomes. Following Bourguignon (2004), figure 4.2 graphically illustrates this point for a particular measure of poverty, the headcount index (see box 4.1 for a more formal discussion). In the figure, poverty is simply the area under the density function to the left of the poverty line, which in this case is fixed at $1 a day.

When mean income or relative incomes, or both, change from an "initial distribution" to a "new distribution," figure 4.2 shows how the change in poverty can be decomposed using an intermediate step. First, one can simulate the impact of moving from the initial distribution to a

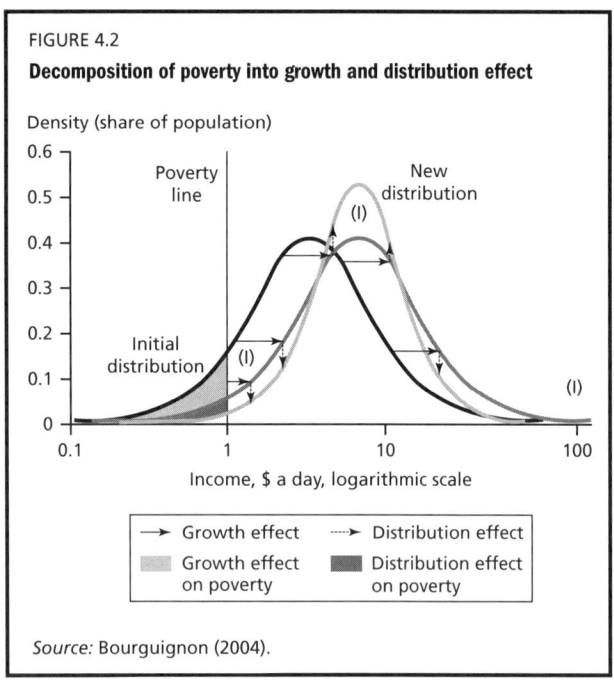

FIGURE 4.2
Decomposition of poverty into growth and distribution effect

Source: Bourguignon (2004).

virtual distribution given by the horizontal translation of the original density. The movement to this intermediate density involves no change in relative incomes and hence can be used to assess the impact of growth on poverty reduction (light gray in the figure). Notice that this is equivalent to asking about the change in poverty that would have taken place if growth had been as observed but the distribution of income remained constant. The second movement simulates the impact of moving from the virtual density to the actual new distribution. It does not involve a change in mean income and hence it captures only the impact of changes in relative incomes on poverty (dark gray in the figure). This is now equivalent to asking about the impact of redistribution had per capita income levels remained fixed. This simple decomposition provides a basic statistical framework that can be used to analyze empirically the relative contribution of growth and changes in income distribution for poverty reduction on the basis of two household surveys.

BOX 4.1

Decomposing poverty into growth and income distribution effects

There is an identity linking poverty to mean income and the distribution of that income across the different individuals or households. It is possible to formally write $P = P[y,L(p)]$, where P is a poverty measure (which for simplicity can be assumed to belong to the Foster-Greer-Thorbecke (FGT) 1984 class, such as headcount poverty, the poverty gap, or the squared poverty gap), y is per capita income, and $L(p)$ is the Lorenz curve measuring the relative income distribution. $L(p)$ is the percentage of income enjoyed by the bottom $100 \times p$ percent of the population. Changes in poverty between period 0 and 1 can then be expressed as $\Delta P_{0,1} = P[y_1,L_1(p)] - P[y_0,L_0(p)]$.

Adding and subtracting to the right-hand side of the previous expression the poverty rate that would have resulted had income increased to the final level y_1, but the Lorenz curve had remained constant at $L_0(p)$—that $P[y_1,L_0(p)]$—it is possible to write:

$$(4.1) \quad \Delta P_{0,1} = P[y_1,L_1(p)] - P[y_0,L_0(p)]$$
$$= P[y_1,L_0(p)] - P[y_0,L_0(p)]$$
$$+ P[y_1,L_1(p)] - P[y_1,L_0(p)].$$

The first term of the right-hand side of equation 4.1— $[P(y_1,L_0(p)] - P[y_0,L_0(p)]$—measures the changes in poverty resulting from changes in mean income (the growth component). The second term—$P[y_1,L_1(p)] - P[y_1,L_0(p)]$—captures the changes in poverty attributable to changes in the Lorenz curve when income levels remain unchanged (distribution component).

Note that this decomposition is not unique (although in principle the empirical differences between alternatives are not likely to be large). The changes of poverty can be rewritten using as reference the poverty rate that would have occurred had income remained constant at y_0, but the Lorenz had shifted to $L_1(p)$:

$$(4.2) \quad \Delta P_{0,1} = P[y_1,L_1(p)] - P[y_0,L_0(p)]$$
$$= P[y_1,L_1(p)] - P[y_0,L_1(p)]$$
$$+ P[y_0,L_1(p)] - P[y_0,L_0(p)].$$

In this alternative decomposition, the growth component is captured by $P[y_1,L_0(p)] - P[y_0,L_0(p)]$, and the distribution component by $P[y_1,L_1(p)] - P[y_1,L_0(p)]$; in principle, these two components do not necessarily have to coincide with $P[y_1,L_0(p)] - P[y_0,L_0(p)]$ and $P[y_1,L_1(p)] - P[y_1,L_0(p)]$.

TABLE 4.1

Poverty, growth, and redistribution in Latin America

Country	Time span	US$1-a-day poverty line			US$2-a-day poverty line		
		Total (ii)	Growth (iii)	Redistribution	Total (ii)	Growth (iii)	Redistribution
Argentina	1992–98	1.8	0.0	1.8	4.1	−0.1	4.2
	1998–2002	6.4	3.2	3.3	15.3	10.9	4.4
	2002–4	−3.8	−2.7	−1.0	−8.6	5.0	−3.5
	1992–2004	4.7	1.0	3.7	11.9	4.3	7.6
Bolivia (urban)	1993–97	−6.2	−5.1	−1.1	−13.4	−12.6	−0.7
	1997–2002	2.8	1.0	1.8	4.4	1.8	2.6
	1993–2002	−3.4	−4.4	1.1	−9.0	−10.7	1.7
Bolivia (national)	1997–2002	5.5	3.3	2.2	6.9	5.4	1.5
Brazil	1990–95	−3.9	−1.9	−1.9	−8.5	−3.7	−4.8
	1995–2003	0.2	0.4	−0.2	−0.1	0.9	−1.0
	1990–2003	−3.6	−1.3	−2.3	−8.6	−2.6	−6.0
Chile	1990–96	−1.8	−1.3	−0.5	−7.6	−7.3	−0.3
	1996–2003	−0.1	−0.2	0.1	−1.6	−1.4	−0.3
	1990–2003	−1.9	−1.6	−0.4	−9.3	−8.4	−0.8
Colombia (urban)	1992–2000	5.2	−0.1	5.3	7.6	−0.9	8.5
Colombia (urban)	2000–4	1.9	3.1	−1.1	4.2	11.2	−7.0
Costa Rica	1992–97	−2.0	−0.8	−1.2	−4.3	−3.1	−1.2
	1997–2003	0.6	−0.6	1.2	0.2	−1.8	2.0
	1992–2003	−1.4	−1.6	0.2	−4.1	−5.3	1.2
Dominican Republic	2000–4	1.4	3.6	−2.1	7.6	8.5	−0.8
Ecuador	1994–98	2.7	−1.4	4.2	3.0	−3.3	6.3
El Salvador	1991–2003	−5.9	−5.0	−0.9	−10.6	−8.6	−2.0
Honduras	1997–2003	2.3	1.1	1.2	3.6	1.6	2.0
Jamaica	1990–99	−21.1	−9.2	−11.9	−25.8	−17.5	−8.3
	1990–2002	−7.9	−8.0	0.1	−14.8	−15.3	0.5
Mexico	1992–96	5.0	4.0	0.9	10.5	9.7	0.8
	1996–2002	−2.6	−3.1	0.5	−9.3	−7.3	−2.0
	1992–2002	2.4	0.9	1.4	1.1	1.9	−0.7
Nicaragua	1993–98	−11.6	−5.9	−5.7	−9.4	−6.6	−2.8
	1998–2001	−4.6	−2.1	−2.5	−3.9	−3.3	−0.6
	1993–2001	−16.1	−7.9	−8.2	−13.3	−10.0	−3.3
Panama	1995–2002	−6.0	0.2	−6.2	−2.9	0.6	−3.4
Paraguay	1997–2002	4.4	6.2	−1.8	9.9	10.8	−0.9
Peru	1997–2002	−1.0	0.0	−1.0	−0.1	0.0	−0.1
Uruguay	1989–98	0.5	−0.1	0.7	0.2	−1.3	1.5
	1998–2003	−0.2	0.7	−0.9	1.6	3.8	-2.2
	1989–2003	0.3	0.3	0.0	1.8	1.8	0.0
Venezuela, R.B. de	1989–95	3.7	1.0	2.7	11.4	3.1	8.3
	1995–2000	0.8	3.9	−3.1	0.9	7.5	−6.6
	2000–3	4.5	3.1	1.4	12.3	9.6	2.6
	1989–2003	13.2	7.5	5.7	26.0	20.2	5.8

Source: Gasparini, Gutierrez, and Tornarolli (2005).

Table 4.1 reports the results of decomposing headcount poverty changes for two poverty lines ($1 a day and $2 a day) in 18 Latin American countries. For example, poverty (as measured by the $2-a-day poverty line) increased 11.9 points in Argentina between 1992 and 2004. We estimate, however, that if the distribution of relative incomes had remained constant, then the poverty headcount ratio would have increased by only 4.3 points. The remaining (7.6 points) was driven by changes in the shape of the income distribution, which in the Argentine case, were unequalizing over the 1992–2004 period. Admittedly, distributional shifts affected poverty in a different way before and after 2002. In fact, the income distribution deteriorated during the 1992–98 and 1998–2002 periods (and contributed to an increase in poverty), but it improved over the 2002–4 period.

There are other countries where the distribution of income has also worked against the poor over the long run (taking the long run as the period between the first and last survey regardless of the number of years spanned by the spell). One is República Bolivariana de Venezuela (1989–2003), where about 6 percentage points of the 26 percent increase in poverty was attributable to a deterioration of income inequality. Urban Bolivia also experienced a deterioration in income inequality over the 1993–2002 period, although it was accompanied by a dramatic decline in poverty (9 percent) as a result of a significant growth component (−11 percent). Similarly, poverty declined in Costa Rica (1992–2003) and in Jamaica (1990–2002), but it could have fallen even more if income distribution had not changed for the worse. In contrast, in Honduras (1997–2003) and Ecuador (1994–1998) the deterioration in income distribution was accompanied by increased poverty. The case of Ecuador is noteworthy because the contribution of the distributional component (6.3 percent) was enough to tilt the balance from a decline in poverty of 3.3 percent to an increase of 3.0 percent.

In other countries the distributional component helped to accelerate poverty reduction. For example, had income distribution income remained constant in Brazil over the 1990–2003 period, poverty would have fallen by only 2.6 percent rather than the observed 8.6 points. Other countries where income distribution tended to favor the poor over the long run are Chile, the Dominican Republic, El Salvador, Mexico, Nicaragua, Panama, Paraguay, and Peru. Among this group, the only country where distributional changes were relatively important is Panama, which experienced a 6 percent decline in poverty, as measured by US$1 a day. Had the distribution of income remained constant, poverty would have increased slightly (0.2 percent).

These results indicate significant country heterogeneity in the Latin American sample. In some countries, such as Argentina, Ecuador, and Panama, the distributional component has been very important. In others, such as Bolivia, El Salvador, and Jamaica, the growth component has clearly predominated. In between are cases such as Brazil and Nicaragua, where both components had similar effects. Given the results of just this single exercise, reaching general conclusions that apply to most countries seems quite daring.

As an alternative, one can try to summarize the cross-country information using variance decomposition techniques as in Kraay (2005). If the changes in poverty (ΔP) are expressed as a growth component (ΔY) and a distributional component (ΔD), then $\Delta P = \Delta Y + \Delta D$. Then the expression for the variance of the changes in poverty can be written: Variance (ΔP) = Variance(ΔY) + Variance(ΔD) + 2 × Covariance($\Delta Y, \Delta D$). This expression can now be used to define the proportion of poverty changes explained by growth as Variance(ΔY) + Covariance($\Delta Y, \Delta D$)/Variance (ΔP).

What then are the relative roles played by growth and changes in relative incomes in the Latin American region? Well, the results of this exercise suggest that the distributional component is likely to be a much more important factor than the global data would suggest. In fact, the share of variance of changes in poverty (now based on a $1 a day poverty line to ensure comparability with Kraay 2005) attributable to growth would be about 50 percent in both the short and the long run (figure 4.3).[4] Thus these results, if taken at

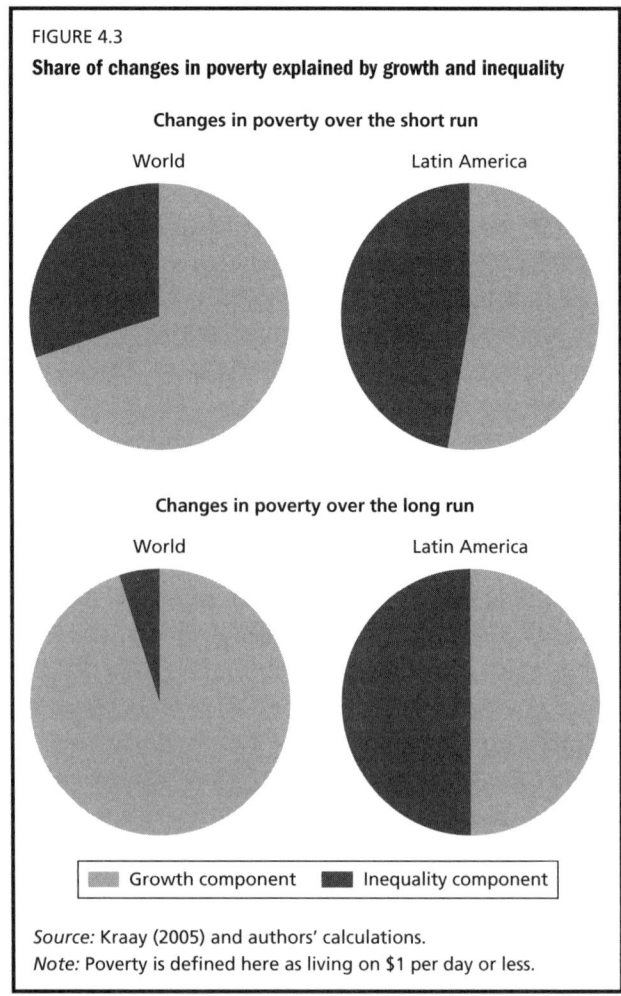

FIGURE 4.3
Share of changes in poverty explained by growth and inequality

Source: Kraay (2005) and authors' calculations.
Note: Poverty is defined here as living on $1 per day or less.

face value, would suggest the need to focus on both growth-enhancing and inequality-reducing policies simultaneously.

Given the prevailing high inequality levels of the Latin American region, our finding may not be surprising.[5] Before jumping to the conclusion that growth and income distribution are equally important in the region, however, notice that these results are extremely sensitive to the choice of the poverty line used to compute the poverty figures. In fact, the relevance of growth for poverty reduction dramatically increases as one moves from a $1-a-day to a $2-a-day poverty line (that is, as the poverty concept becomes more inclusive). The relevance of growth also increases when one shifts from using international poverty lines to using national poverty lines, most likely because countries tend to use more generous poverty lines (see figure 4.4, which focuses only on short-run changes).

On the whole, the results reported here would underscore the importance of both growth and changes in the distribution of income for the evolution of Latin American poverty. Regardless of the poverty line used, the distributional component tends to account for a minimum of 25 percent of the variation of poverty changes and for as much as 50 percent. This is significantly higher than what is found in the sample of developing countries analyzed in Kraay (2005) and is probably related to the high inequality levels that prevail in the region. It must be noted, however, that the choice of poverty lines is important. Typically, in countries with more inclusive poverty lines ($2-a-day or a national moderate line), growth appears to weigh more than changes in income distribution; in those countries with more selective poverty lines ($1-a-day or a national extreme line), redistribution appears to play a bigger role in reducing poverty. Reaching different segments of the population will thus require different policies.

Growth and inequality: Bringing country specificity into the picture

The variance decomposition approach reviewed in the previous section has highlighted some important elements regarding the relative roles played by growth and the distribution of income for poverty reduction. However, those results are probably less useful when interest centers on the relative importance of each component at the individual country level and on the characteristics that determine that importance. For example, should Chile and Nicaragua—two countries with similar levels of inequality but dramatically different income levels—try to strike a similar balance between growth-promoting and inequality-reducing policies? Similarly, should Uruguay and Brazil—which have similar levels of per capita income but are the least and most unequal countries in the region, respectively—follow similar policies in their attempts to reduce poverty? Or for any particular country, should policy makers implement the same type of policies when they focus on the whole universe of poor than when they focus on a particular group, say, the poorest among the poor? Is the same strategy likely to have the same effect on everybody under the poverty line?

To answer these questions, we have to rely on tools that go beyond statistical decomposition techniques and try to relate observed outcomes to some country characteristics that can be useful in discerning which type of policies might be appropriate in each country. One possible tool is a parametric analysis that approximates the actual distribution of income with a more or less tractable functional form (that is, a mathematical model that can be related to some economic variables to approximate the empirical distribution of

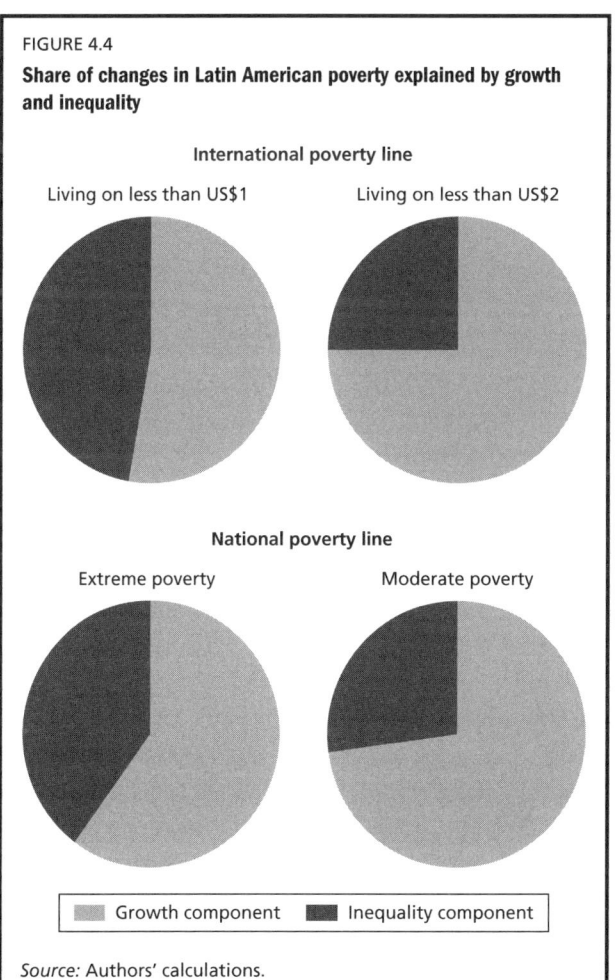

FIGURE 4.4
Share of changes in Latin American poverty explained by growth and inequality

Source: Authors' calculations.

income). This functional form is then used to assess the role of country-specific conditions for the poverty-reducing effects of growth and distributional change (that is, to see how changes in country conditions affect the impact on poverty of growth and changes in relative incomes predicted by the model). To a large extent this is a theoretical exercise that can be fully controlled and with which one can experiment.

Clearly, the usefulness of this approach depends on two critical elements. The first is the tractability of the used approximation. If the selected functional form cannot be related to country characteristics that are easily observable and can be used to discriminate among countries (or poverty concepts), then this approach loses part of its appeal. The second element is the degree to which the chosen parameterization fits the data. Even if the selected functional form is tractable and provides an excellent theoretical framework to deal with the problem at hand, it could provide a very poor approximation to the actual data and hence be empirically irrelevant.

For our purposes, there is a functional form that appears to be a natural choice to approximate the size distribution of income: the lognormal distribution. This is probably the most standard approximation of empirical income distributions in the applied literature and seems to fulfill the two criteria required for this approach to be useful (see box 4.2

BOX 4.2

The size distribution of income

An abundant literature spanning more than a century—from Pareto (1897) to Gibrat (1931), Kalecki (1945), Rutherford (1955), Metcalf (1969), Singh and Maddala (1976), and more recently to Bourguignon (2003) and Kakwani and Son (2003)—has attempted to approximate the distribution of income. They have used a variety of functional forms: Beta, Gamma, Pareto, Champernowne, Dagum, Singh-Maddala, displaced lognormal, and lognormal. Among these, however, the most commonly used in applied research is the lognormal function. Its use in the context of income was pioneered by Gibrat (1931), who noted that it offered a good empirical fit to the observed data and also provided a first theoretical justification based on a model in which individuals' incomes are subject to random proportionate changes. In his original explanation of why the logarithm of income could behave approximately as a lognormal distribution, Gibrat (1931) described three conditions that must be present if the observed distribution is to approximate the lognormal form. First, the distribution of income at any give time must be derived from that of the previous period by assuming that the variable corresponding to each member of the distribution is affected by a small proportionate change. Second, the proportions must differ for different members of the distribution. And third, these differences must be determined in a random manner from a given frequency distribution. Moreover, Gibrat observed that whatever the distribution of income at the initial period, income would approach normality more and more as time passed.

Gibrat's work was followed by a large literature extending his basic framework and offering additional empirical evidence. Kalecki (1945) extended Gibrat's original setup by making negative income changes less likely at low-income levels than at high ones and in that way accounted for the fact that the variance of log income remained relatively constant over time. Rutherford (1955) expanded Gibrat's model to introduce birth and death considerations. He also presented empirical experiments based on the comparison of theoretical and observed quantiles of the distribution of income, searching for a functional form that would improve upon the lognormal. The figure below illustrates how a lognormal distribution might look for different Gini coefficients.

The *look* of the lognormal distribution for different Gini coefficients

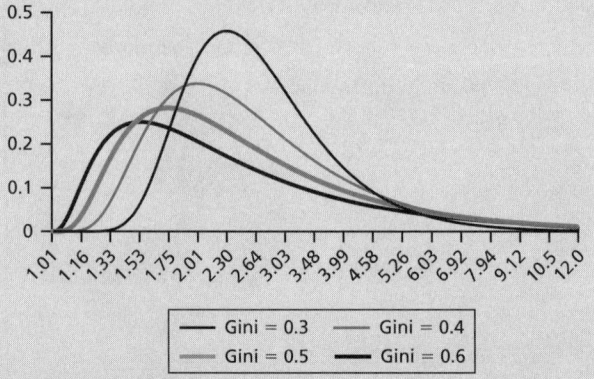

Source: López and Servén (2005a).

for some historical perspective and for some brief background that can theoretically justify its use in practice).

Regarding tractability, one of the appeals of the lognormal distribution is its simplicity, since it can be written as a function of mean income and the Gini coefficient. Given per capita GDP and the Gini coefficient of an economy, one can picture the probability of an individual having a particular level of income. This in turn is all that is needed not only for a static assessment of the poverty situation for different poverty lines but also for the analysis of how poverty evolves when the parameters describing the distribution change:

$$\text{Change in Poverty (\%)} = \eta_v^\alpha \times \text{Income Growth (\%)} + \eta_G^\alpha \times \text{Change in Gini (\%)},$$

where η_v^α and η_G^α are, respectively, the partial growth elasticity of poverty (that is, the impact on poverty of a 1 percent increase in income levels, holding inequality constant) and the partial inequality elasticity of poverty (that is, the impact on poverty of a 1 percent deterioration in income inequality, holding income levels constant).

Thus, for given values of η_v^α and η_G^α, one can map the impact of growth and changes in inequality into poverty. Moreover, under log normality the partial elasticities η_v^α and η_G^α can be shown to depend on just three familiar elements: the level of per capita income, the poverty line, and the Gini coefficient (Lopez and Servén 2005a). Table 4.2 reports the growth and inequality elasticities of headcount poverty that result for various combinations of the Gini coefficient and the ratio of per capita income v to the poverty line z.

Inspection of this table confirms the well-known result (see, for example, Ravallion 1997, 2004; Bourguignon 2003) that the growth elasticity is smaller (in absolute

---

BOX 4.3
Total growth elasticities of poverty and the efficiency of growth

The total growth elasticity of poverty is commonly reported in the development literature as a measure of the poverty efficiency of growth. This is defined as the percentage change in poverty for a given growth rate. Formally, denoting this elasticity by η, growth by g, and the log of poverty by P, η can be expressed as $\eta = \Delta P/g$. Thus a higher η would indicate more effective poverty-reducing growth. Intuitively poverty reduction performance could be improved through two routes: by achieving high growth rates for a given elasticity; or by achieving a higher value (in absolute value) of η for a given growth rate.

However, one has to be careful interpreting these figures. If one assumes that income follows a lognormal distribution, we can express:

(1) $\Delta P = \eta_v g + \eta_G \Delta G.$ $\eta_v < 0, \eta_G > 0$

Thus poverty changes will be determined by the growth component $\eta_v g$ and by the distribution component $\eta_G \Delta G$.

It then follows immediately that the gross growth elasticity of poverty η can be rewritten as a function of the partial growth and inequality elasticities of poverty and of the observed growth and observed changes in inequality: $\eta = \Delta P/g = \eta_v + \eta_G \Delta G/g$. This expression can now be used to analyze how η changes with ΔG and g.

Consider, for example, the case of two economies (countries, states, or regions) that are identical (that is, the countries have similar values of η_v and η_G so that differences in η will result from differences in ΔG and g. Assume also that over a given period of time, inequality changes in the same fashion in both places but that the two economies have different growth rates ($g_1 > g_2 > 0$).

It is clear that if $\Delta G > 0$, the total growth elasticity η of the economy with the highest growth rate will be smaller (higher in absolute value). Thus one would be tempted to interpret this as one state being more progrowth and more pro-poor, when the only thing that is different in these economies is the growth rate. Similarly, if $\Delta G < 0$ in both economies (that is, inequality is falling), the total growth elasticity η will be higher in absolute value in the economy with lower growth. Again, one could be tempted to interpret this as a difference between the pro-poorness of the growth strategies: one economy experiences faster growth but at the apparent cost of a lower growth elasticity of poverty whereas the other economy experiences lower growth, but with a faster growth elasticity.

These somewhat extreme examples should highlight the dangers of reading too much into a simple elasticity.

TABLE 4.2
Growth and inequality elasticity of poverty (headcount index)

	Growth elasticity (Gini coefficient)					Inequality elasticity (Gini coefficient)			
v/z	0.30	0.40	0.50	0.60	v/z	0.30	0.40	0.50	0.60
6	−6.05	−3.25	−1.95	−1.22	6	12.34	7.38	5.10	3.89
3	−3.94	−2.18	−1.33	−0.86	3	5.17	3.28	2.42	1.97
2	−2.80	−1.60	−1.01	−0.66	2	2.48	1.70	1.35	1.18
1.5	−2.06	−1.23	−0.80	−0.54	1.5	1.20	0.92	0.81	0.77
1	−1.16	−0.78	−0.55	−0.39	1	0.18	0.24	0.29	0.35

Source: López and Servén (2005a).

value) the higher the level of inequality. For example, consider the case of a country whose per capita income levels are about three times the poverty line (the row in table 4.2 corresponding to $v/z = 3$). In this country, if inequality levels are low (say, a Gini of 0.3), a 1 percent growth rate would lead to almost a 4 percent decline in poverty. In contrast, if inequality is high (say a Gini of 0.6), the same growth rate would lead to a more modest decline in poverty (about 0.9 percent). Thus, inequality hampers the poverty-reducing effect of growth, as stressed in the literature, and, in highly unequal countries, justifies making a more balanced income distribution an important policy priority. Clearly, an improvement in the distribution of income has a double poverty-reducing effect. On the one hand, it has a pure positive redistribution effect. On the other, it increases (in absolute value) the growth elasticity of poverty and hence makes future growth more effective in reducing poverty.

Table 4.2, however, also indicates that poverty itself (as measured by low per capita income) is a barrier to poverty reduction: for a given Gini coefficient, the growth elasticity of poverty declines rapidly (in absolute value) as average income declines in relation to the poverty line. For example, when the Gini is 0.4, for a country with per capita income equal to six times the poverty line, the growth elasticity of poverty is about 3.25 percent, whereas for a country with per capita income equal to the poverty line, it would be about 0.8 percent. This suggests that economic growth also has a double poverty-reducing effect: first, the direct effect of income growth on the average level of income; and second, the indirect effect that arises from the higher average income via the correspondingly higher growth elasticity of poverty.

Similar results are obtained when one examines the way that income and inequality levels affect the inequality elasticity of poverty. Under most scenarios, higher inequality (lower income) also lessens the impact of progressive distributional change itself on poverty. As illustrated in table 4.2, the inequality elasticity falls as inequality rises (income declines) for a given value of average income relative to the poverty line (for a given Gini index). Note, however, that this relationship is highly nonlinear, and its sign is reversed at very low levels of development (captured in the table by values of v/z close to 1), so that a higher Gini coefficient is associated with a higher inequality elasticity (see the last line of table 4.2).

Clearly, before proceeding with this type of analysis, we have to acknowledge that skeptical readers may question whether the selected functional form provides a reasonable approximation to the real world, particularly because the existing empirical evidence in this regard is quite limited and usually based on individual country studies.

To narrow the existing gap between the empirical popularity of the lognormal distribution and the empirical support for that distribution, Lopez and Servén (2005a) compare the empirical distribution quintiles for almost 800 country-year observations with those obtained theoretically using the lognormal approximation. They reason that if the lognormal distribution provides a reasonable approximation, then any differences between the empirical and the theoretical distributions should not be dramatic. In contrast, if the lognormal distribution provides a poor approximation, then one would expect to find large differences between theoretical and empirical distributions.

Figure 4.5 presents the scatter plots of the empirical (vertical axis) and theoretical quintiles (horizontal axis) for

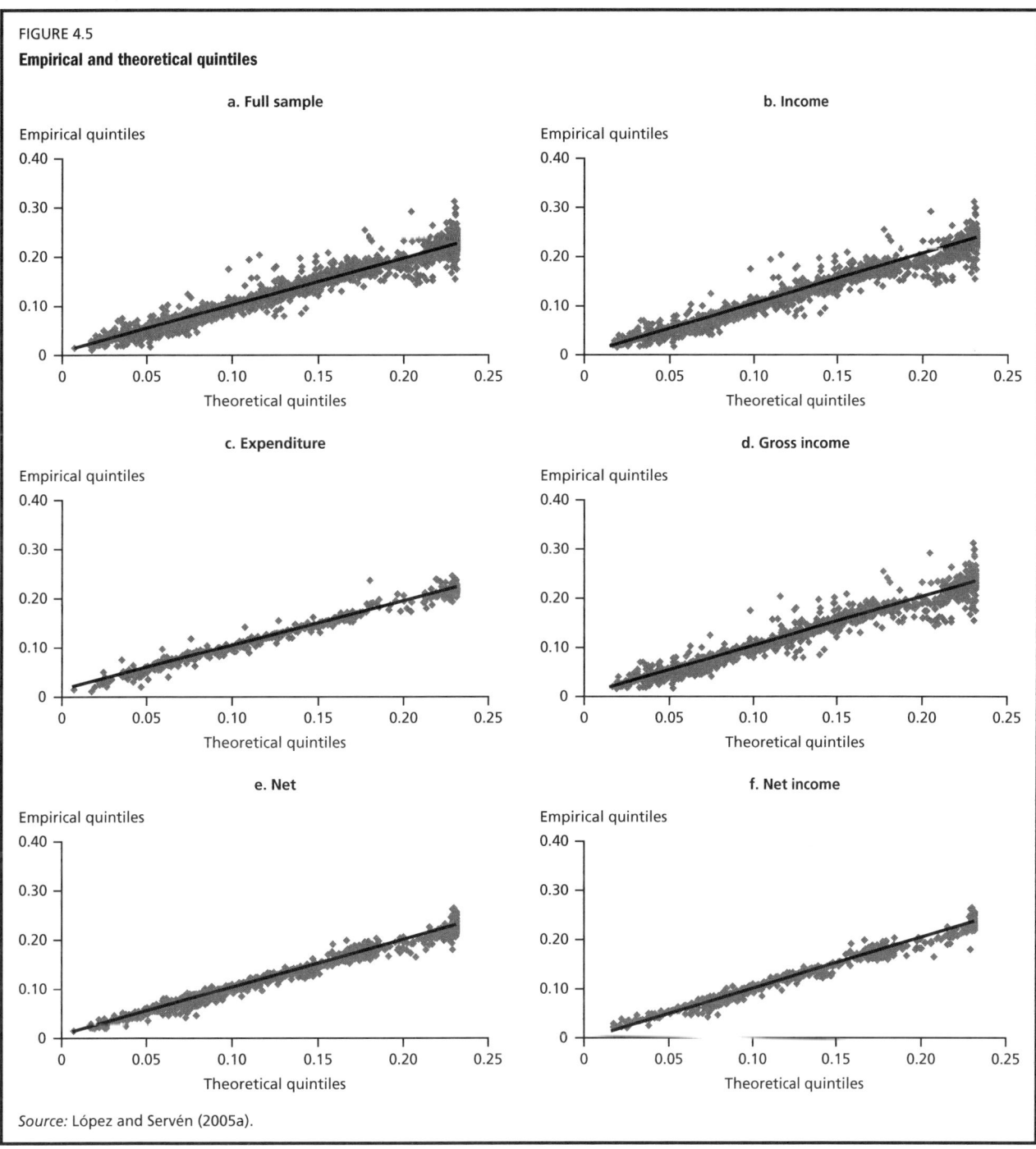

FIGURE 4.5
Empirical and theoretical quintiles

Source: López and Servén (2005a).

a number of samples depending on whether the original data are income (net/gross), or consumption. The different panels also present the 45-degree line (where all the observations should be placed under the null). The figure suggests that the lognormal distribution generally provides a reasonable approximation to the actual data. More formally, Lopez and Servén (2005a) perform several statistical tests on the data and find that the data cannot reject the null hypothesis of lognormality when the test is implemented on the distribution of per capita income, regardless of whether income is measured in gross terms (before taxes and transfers) or net terms (after taxes and transfers). Admittedly, even though the lognormal also seems to approximate the consumption data quite well, the same null hypothesis is unambiguously rejected when applied to per capita consumption data (see annex 4A for details). On

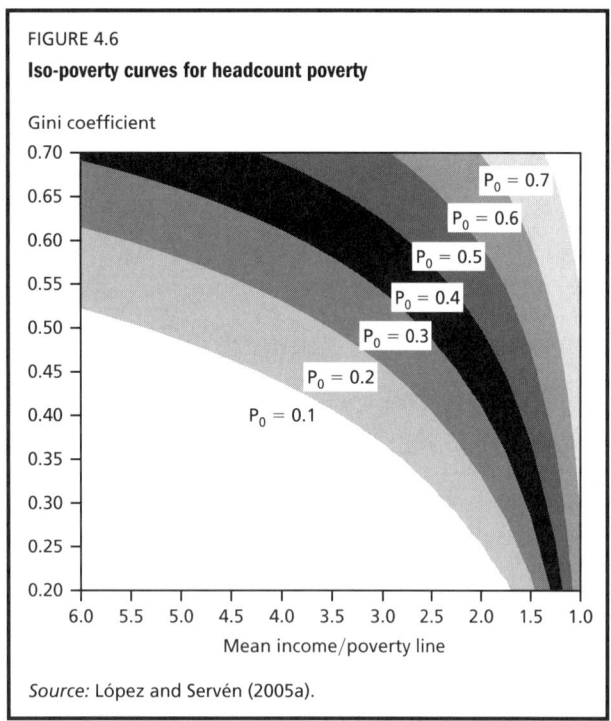

FIGURE 4.6
Iso-poverty curves for headcount poverty

Source: López and Servén (2005a).

headcount. Curves to the northeast of the graph correspond to higher levels of the poverty rate. The slope of these curves depicts the changing trade-off between growth and redistribution. The steeper the slope, the bigger the decline in the Gini coefficient required to keep poverty constant in the face of a given decline in the ratio of mean income to the poverty line. The curves become increasingly steep, and closer to each other, as one moves downward along them. In other words, the more equal and the poorer the economy (as reflected, respectively, by a lower Gini coefficient and a lower mean income/poverty line ratio), the bigger the change in the Gini coefficient required to offset a given change in mean income relative to the poverty line—that is, the more effective growth will be relative to redistribution in attacking poverty. As the economy becomes richer and more unequal (the northwest segment of the figure), the curves become less steep, and therefore a smaller change in the Gini coefficient is now needed to offset a given change in mean income relative to the poverty line. In other words, distributional change now plays a relatively larger role in poverty changes.

the whole, the authors conclude that their results are encouraging for the use of parametric analysis based on the lognormal distribution for the analysis of poverty.

On the basis of the previous discussion, we now perform two different exercises to illustrate how the parametric approach can be used to help gauge the relative priority of pro-growth and pro-redistribution policies when their common objective is poverty reduction. First, consider figure 4.6, which plots a set of isometric poverty curves drawn under the hypothesis of lognormality for different values of the poverty headcount P_0. Each of these curves depicts combinations of Gini coefficients and mean per capita income/poverty line ratios that yield a constant poverty

An alternative analysis would exploit table 4.2 to directly simulate the impact of alternative growth scenarios. These results are reported in table 4.3. The left panel of the table reports the poverty impact of 1 percent growth with no associated changes in inequality, whereas the right panel simulates the impact of 2 percent growth with an associated increase in inequality of 1 percent.

The shaded (no-shaded) cells in the right panel indicate that the poverty outcome of that panel is superior (inferior) to the poverty outcome in the left panel. The simulations presented here clearly indicate that different countries may require different types of policies. The scenario with higher growth and an associated increase in inequality tends to be

TABLE 4.3
Impact on poverty of different growth scenarios

	Panel A. Neutral growth (Gini coefficient)					Panel B. Growth with inequality (Gini coefficient)			
y/z	0.30	0.40	0.50	0.60	y/z	0.30	0.40	0.50	0.60
6	−6.05	−3.25	−1.95	−1.22	6	0.24	0.88	1.20	1.45
3	−3.94	−2.18	−1.33	−0.86	3	−2.71	−1.08	−0.24	0.25
2	−2.80	−1.60	−1.01	−0.66	2	−3.12	−1.50	−0.67	−0.14
1.5	−2.06	−1.23	−0.80	−0.54	1.5	−2.92	−1.54	−0.79	−0.31
1	−1.16	−0.78	−0.55	−0.39	1	−2.14	−1.32	−0.81	−0.43

Source: Authors' calculations.

THE RELATIVE ROLES OF GROWTH AND INEQUALITY FOR POVERTY REDUCTION

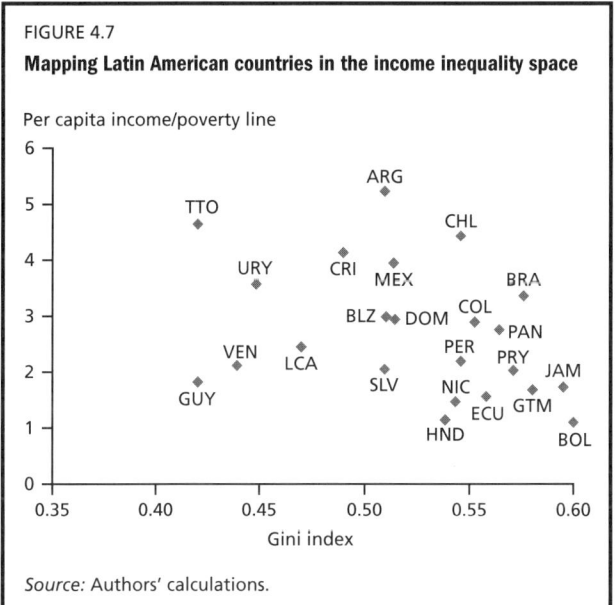

FIGURE 4.7
Mapping Latin American countries in the income inequality space

Source: Authors' calculations.

superior in poorer and more equal countries. In contrast, in richer and more unequal countries, policies that stimulate lower growth with no associated deterioration in income would be a superior alternative. Moreover, as the unshaded portion of the right panel shows, the increase in inequality under this alternative scenario tends to dominate the growth effect, and in several rich or highly unequal countries, the final impact suggests an increase in poverty. Hence richer and very unequal countries will have to pay significant attention to distributional concerns.

Figure 4.7 illustrates how the previous discussion can be used to highlight country policy priorities (whether these are growth-enhancing or inequality-reducing policies) on the basis of different initial conditions. In this regard, it is useful to start mapping the Latin American countries into an income-inequality space comparable to the one used in tables 4.2 and 4.3.[6] Given that this is a static exercise, we expand the sample of 18 countries in table 4.1 to add 5 additional countries (Belize, Guatemala, Guyana, St. Lucia, and Trinidad and Tobago) for which we have at least one measure of income distribution.[7]

As expected, this mapping shows a clustering of countries toward the high-inequality side of the figure (Gini larger than 0.5). This clustering is even more marked for the lower-income countries.[8] The only countries that appear to depart from this norm of high-inequality levels are Uruguay and República Bolivariana de Venezuela and three of the newly added countries (all three in the Caribbean: Guyana, St. Lucia, and Trinidad and Tobago),

which report Gini indexes close to but still above the international norm.

To what extent is it possible to create a typology of countries for the Latin American region, based on their growth and inequality-reducing priorities for reducing poverty? Given the difficulties of clustering countries in a two-dimensional space, we first reduce figure 4.7 to a single dimension by computing the growth rate that each of these countries would need to achieve to compensate for a 1 percent increase in the Gini coefficient and leave poverty unchanged (this statistic could be considered the marginal rate of substitution between growth and changes in inequality). A higher estimate for this compensatory growth rate would indicate that inequality changes are very relevant for poverty reduction in the country in question (given an increase in inequality, poverty will decline only when growth is very high). In contrast, a low value for this compensatory growth rate would indicate the relevance of growth (growth even if accompanied by a deterioration of income distribution may lead to lower poverty). Note that the inverse of this statistic can also be interpreted as the maximum deterioration in the income distribution that could occur for poverty to decline when growth is 1 percent.

Table 4.4 reports these statistics. The table indicates that in a country such as Argentina, a 1 percent deterioration in the Gini coefficient would require a compensatory growth rate of 2.5 percent to maintain poverty at a constant level. Similarly, in Brazil, Chile, Colombia, Costa Rica, and Mexico, growth would have to be above 2 percent

TABLE 4.4

Growth rates needed to compensate for a 1 percent increase in inequality (percent)

Country	Compensatory growth rate	Country	Compensatory growth rate
Argentina	2.5	Peru	1.6
Chile	2.4	St. Lucia	1.5
Brazil	2.3	Guatemala	1.5
Mexico	2.1	Paraguay	1.5
Costa Rica	2.1	El Salvador	1.4
Colombia	2.1	Venezuela, R.B. de	1.2
Trinidad and Tobago	2.0		
Dominican Republic	1.9	Ecuador	1.1
Panama	1.9	Nicaragua	1.1
Belize	1.8	Guyana	1.1
Uruguay	1.8	Bolivia	1.0
Jamaica	1.7	Honduras	0.8

Source: Authors' calculations.

to compensate for a hypothetical deterioration in the income distribution. Note that these countries are all located in the northeast portion of figure 4.7 (that is, they are all relatively rich and unequal). Note also that although Brazil is more unequal than either Argentina or Chile, it would need a lower growth rate to compensate for a 1 percent increase in the Gini index. In all these countries, growth strategies that are accompanied by increases in inequality would probably lead to disappointing results on the poverty front unless the deterioration in inequality is extremely modest or the growth rate very high.

At the other extreme of the table are Honduras and Bolivia, where growth of 0.8 percent and 1 percent, respectively, would be enough to compensate for a 1 percent deterioration in income inequality. Ecuador, Guyana, and Nicaragua are close behind, each needing an estimated compensatory growth rate of 1.1 percent. These low growth rates should highlight the importance of growth for poverty reduction in these countries, where (political economy issues apart) poverty reduction seems to be mainly driven by growth, and where growth even if accompanied by moderate increases in inequality will succeed in reducing poverty.

Between the two extremes is a continuum of values without apparent jumps, something that would indicate that there may not be well-defined clusters of countries with between-group differences and within-group similarities. In any case, Belize, the Dominican Republic, Panama, Trinidad and Tobago, and Uruguay seem to be closer to the group led by Argentina where reducing inequality is quite important for poverty reduction, whereas El Salvador, Guatemala, Paraguay, Peru, St. Lucia, and República Bolivariano de Venezuela seem closer to the group of countries where growth appears as the main priority for poverty reduction.

One final issue we address in this section regards the interpretation given to the ratio of mean income to the poverty line. So far we have implicitly viewed alternative values of the mean income/poverty line ratio as reflecting different levels of average per capita income with a given poverty line. This is probably the natural interpretation when comparing the impact of growth and income distribution on poverty reduction across the different Latin American countries.

However, this ratio could also be interpreted the other way around, namely, as reflecting alternative poverty lines with a given level of average per capita income. For example, as noted in chapter 2, it is standard for countries to rely on poverty figures computed according to at least two poverty lines: a higher poverty line that measures moderate poverty, and a lower poverty line that measures extreme poverty (the international counterparts of these concepts could be the $2-a-day and $1-a-day purchasing power parity poverty lines).

Our analysis can be twisted to explore how the appropriate focus of the development strategy of any given country varies with the concept of poverty used. Given per capita income levels, low poverty lines will result in a high mean income/poverty line ratio (that is, low poverty lines will move a country toward the top of tables 4.2 and 4.3 and figure 4.7). Thus the analysis above of the relevance of growth and distribution in relatively richer countries would apply here. In contrast, a high poverty line will result in a low mean income/poverty line ratio (that is, a high poverty line will push a country toward the bottom of tables 4.2 and 4.3 and figure 4.7). Hence as the poverty line increases, the relative importance of growth for reducing poverty goes up as well, and other things equal, offers a rationale for shifting poverty reduction priorities toward growth-oriented policies and against redistributive policies.

In essence, two main messages emerge from this analysis. First, in any given country, the elements that underlie a poverty reduction strategy should be highly dependent on the definition of poverty used. Given that national poverty definitions deviate notably from the international norm across countries, this analysis means that two countries that rely on different poverty lines but that are otherwise identical are justified in implementing different poverty reduction strategies. Second, and probably more relevant for policy purposes, reaching different groups of poor people requires different sets of interventions that recognize their idiosyncrasies. In particular, this analysis indicates that the extreme poor (those below a relatively low poverty line) probably require targeted interventions, whereas the moderate poor (those below a relatively higher poverty line) require broader interventions that aim at raising incomes for all individuals in society.

Concluding remarks

This chapter started by posing several questions related to the elements that should be at the center of any sensible poverty-reducing strategy. Should such a strategy have a growth bias or instead concentrate mainly on reducing income inequality? Does a country's level of development matter for the chosen poverty reduction strategy? Which strategy is better for poverty reduction: a high growth rate that has an associated increase in inequality, or a lower growth rate that maintains inequality constant? Are there any conditions under which policy makers can accept a trade-off between growth and a deterioration in the distribution of income?

We find the answers to these questions depend on the initial conditions in the individual country and on its concept of poverty. In countries with low per capita income levels and relatively equal distribution, growth in mean income will be relatively more effective in reducing poverty than changes in the income distribution. In contrast, richer and more unequal countries will have to carefully balance the growth and income distribution objectives, because in those cases even small increases in inequality may have a dramatic negative impact on poverty.

As for the relevance of the concept of poverty that each country uses, the chapter has argued that different poverty concepts may require different strategies. In any given country, if poverty is defined in a very inclusive way (that is, if a country relies on a very high poverty line where most of the population qualifies as poor), then strategies that rely on growth will be more appropriate for poverty reduction than strategies that stress redistribution. As the concept of poverty becomes more restrictive (that is, as the poverty line declines and fewer people qualify as poor), the relevance of redistribution as a tool for poverty reduction rises and the relevance of growth declines.

On the whole, the main message that emerges from our analysis is that given the high income inequality levels prevailing in Latin America, it would seem appropriate to focus on both growth and income distribution, although the ideal balance between the two will differ from country to country.

Annex 4A

Testing for lognormality of income

To test the lognormality hypothesis of income, Lopez and Servén (2005a) exploit the one-to-one mapping that arises under lognormality between the Gini coefficient and the Lorenz curve $L(p)$. Letting G and σ respectively denote the Gini coefficient and the standard deviation of log income,

Aitchison and Brown (1966, ch. 11) show that lognormality implies

$$(4A.1) \quad \sigma = \sqrt{2}\, \Phi^{-1}\left(\frac{1+G}{2}\right),$$

and

$$(4A.2) \quad L(p) = \Phi(\Phi^{-1}(p) - \sigma),$$

where $\Phi(.)$ denotes the cumulative normal distribution. Hence a change in the Gini coefficient, and thus in σ, must be reflected in a matching change in the Lorenz curve.

On a cross-country basis, what is usually available to the researcher is some summary information on the shape of the Lorenz curve. One such summary is provided by the income shares of the different quintiles of the population:

$$(4A.3) \quad Q_{20j} = L(0.2j) - L(0.2(j-1)) \quad \text{for } j = 1,2,3,4.$$

Given the one-to-one mapping between the Gini coefficient and the Lorenz curve that follows from equations 4A.1 and 4A.2, under lognormality there must also be a one-to-one mapping between the Gini coefficient and the quintile shares (equation 4A.3). Thus, a test of the null hypothesis of lognormality can be based on the comparison of the empirical quintiles, say E_{20j}, with their Gini-based theoretical counterparts Q_{20j}. Following this approach, a formal lognormality test can be performed on the basis of the regression model:

$$(4A.4) \quad E_{20j}^{it} = \alpha + \beta Q_{20j}^{it} + v_j^{it},$$

where $j = 1,2,3,4$ denotes the income quintile; $i = 1,2,\ldots,N$ is a country index, and $t = 1,2,\ldots T_i$ denotes the date of each income (or expenditure) survey available for country i. In general T_i will differ across countries, resulting in an unbalanced sample. In equation 4A.4, the theoretical quintiles Q_{20j}^{it} are constructed on the basis of the observed Gini coefficients G^{it}, as implied by equations 4A.1–4A.3:

$$(4A.5) \quad Q_{20j}^{it} = \Phi\left(\Phi^{-1}(0.2j) - \sqrt{2}\,\Phi^{-1}\left(\frac{1+G^{it}}{2}\right)\right)$$
$$- \Phi\left(\Phi^{-1}(0.2(j-1)) - \sqrt{2}\,\Phi^{-1}\left(\frac{1+G^{it}}{2}\right)\right).$$

Testing for lognormality in model 4A.4 is equivalent to testing the joint null hypothesis: $\alpha = 0$; $\beta = 1$.

What are the results of formally testing that hypothesis? The table below presents the results of the estimation of

Annex table:

	Nested error component model-based lognormality tests					
Observed quintile	All	Income	Expenditure	Gross	Net	Net income
β	0.980	1.007	0.894*	1.009	0.960*	1.009
	(0.015)	(0.016)	(0.012)	(0.023)	(0.016)	(0.017)
α	0.002	−0.001	0.013**	−0.001	0.005**	−0.001
	(0.002)	(0.002)	(0.002)	(0.003)	(0.002)	(0.002)
Number of observations	3176	2420	756	1472	1484	892
Number of countries	130	98	65	75	97	55
σ_ε	0.0100	0.0124	0.0073	0.0141	0.0259	0.0086
σ_η	0.0000	0.0000	0.0000	0.0000	0.0000	0.0000
σ_μ	0.0027	0.0034	0.0021	0.0052	0.0019	0.0019
Ho[a]						
$\alpha = 0; \beta = 1$	0.410	0.903	0.000	0.920	0.048	0.800
$\sigma_\eta = 0$	0.041	0.498	0.496	0.080	0.031	0.074
$\sigma_\mu = 0$	0.000	0.035	0.077	0.078	0.000	0.010

Source: Authors' calculations.
Note: Robust standard errors are reported in parentheses.
a. p-values are reported.
*Ho: β = 1 rejected at the 5 percent level.
**Ho: α = 1 rejected at the 5 percent level.

model 4A.4 with the following nested structured for the error term: $v_j^{it} = \mu_i + \eta_i^t + \varepsilon_j^{it}$.

The first thing that stands out in this table is that the regression slopes and intercepts are very close to their expected values under the null of 1 and 0, respectively. Note that in the samples including expenditure observations (the first, third, and fifth columns), the estimated slopes are slightly below 1, while they are slightly above 1 in the regressions including only income-based observations. From a statistical perspective, we can formally reject the null of unit slope in the expenditure and net subsamples (third and fifth columns). In turn, the estimated intercepts are positive in the samples including expenditure-based observations and negative in those including only income-based observations. As with the slopes, in the expenditure and net subsamples we can reject the null of zero intercept. The bottom panel of the table reports Wald tests of the null hypothesis of lognormality. Under the null, the test statistic follows a chi-square distribution with two degrees of freedom. As would be expected in light of the point estimates, the null can be rejected at the 5 percent level in the two samples in which expenditure-based observations represent a sizable share of the total number of data points. In contrast, the samples containing only income-based observations show little evidence against the null—the p-values range from 0.41 to 0.92. In the full sample, in which expenditure-based observations represent about 20 percent of the total, we also fail to reject the null, with a p-value of 0.41.

Notes

1. The exception is when per capita income levels are below the poverty line, in which case progressive distributional change leads to increasing poverty.

2. Admittedly, World Bank (2005e) presents evidence for 14 countries suggesting a strong positive correlation between growth and changes in inequality during the 1990s. In particular, a 1 percent growth rate is associated with a 0.5 percent increase in the Gini coefficient. The fact that growth and changes in inequality do not appear to be correlated does not mean that inequality will not increase in a

particular growth episode. It just means that having information on a country's growth rate does not add much to infer the possible change in inequality.

3. This, of course, need not always be the case, since many policies are likely to be both growth promoting and equality enhancing. But some empirical evidence suggests that not all policies have this feature (Barro 2000; Lundberg and Squire 2003; Lopez 2004), and some may force policy makers to face a trade-off between faster growth and increasing income inequality.

4. The short-run results are based on all possible episodes in a country; the long-run results consider only the first and last surveys for each country. In countries with only two surveys, the short- and long-run coincide.

5. According to de Ferranti & others (2004), the only other region that has inequality levels comparable to those observed in Latin America is Sub-Saharan Africa.

6. The mean income/poverty line figures have been computed using GDP per capita valued in 2000 constant US dollars PPP. The ratios roughly correspond to a poverty line of $2 a day in 2000 US dollars.

7. Admittedly, the Gini coefficients for Belize, Guyana, St. Lucia, and Trinidad and Tobago are more than 10 years old.

8. Interestingly, there seems to be a negative correlation between levels of income and levels of inequality. The correlation between per capita income/poverty line and the Gini coefficient for the 23 countries in the sample is -0.36 and significantly different from 0.

CHAPTER 5

Pro-Poor Growth in Latin America

There is no doubt that growth must be at the center of any successful poverty reduction strategy. However, are all pro-growth policies equally pro-poor? Is it possible that some policies lead to higher growth but leave poverty unchanged or, even worse, lead to higher poverty? Similarly, does the composition of growth matter, or can all sectors be considered equally pro-poor? Finally, what is the role of taxes and transfers in this context? Should policy makers focus only on improving the distribution of market incomes along with the growth process, or do they have to complement these actions with tax and transfer interventions that directly target disposable income?

CHAPTER 4 ARGUED THAT FAST POVERTY reduction in the region would require the implementation of development strategies that aim at simultaneously achieving fast sustained growth rates and more equal societies. This general advice, however, leaves unanswered several questions of critical interest for policy makers: are all pro-growth policies equally pro-poor? Is it possible that some policies lead to higher growth but leave poverty unchanged or, even worse, lead to higher poverty? Will policy makers face a trade-off between faster growth and higher inequality? Similarly, does the composition of growth matter, or can all sectors be considered equally pro-poor? If the composition of growth does matter, should policy makers aim at biasing growth toward some particular sectors? Finally, what role do taxes and transfers play in this context?

This chapter explores these issues in three complementary ways. It addresses them first from a policy perspective and reviews what is known about the effect on inequality of a number of growth-enhancing policies. In many circumstances the positive impact that a policy has on growth will be reinforced by its positive impact on the distribution of income. But it is also plausible that some pro-growth policies are associated with higher income inequality. This potential trade-off may in turn result in development strategies that may lead, on the one hand, to faster growth but, on the other hand, to no change in poverty or perhaps to even higher levels of poverty. Thus, if the objective is to reduce poverty, policies will have to be considered according to their potential impact on both growth and inequality.

The chapter then adopts a sectoral perspective and focuses on whether growth in different sectors of economic activity influences poverty in different ways. As discussed in *Beyond the City: The Rural Contribution to Development* (de Ferranti and others 2005), differences in labor intensities in the location of economic activities or in sector-related spillovers can result in growth in different sectors having different effects on poverty. To anticipate some of the empirical findings of this chapter, we find that, indeed, the sectoral composition of growth matters for poverty reduction.

Finally, we also review the extent to which policies aimed at improving the distribution of market incomes (defined as the distribution of income among households determined by market rewards to the private assets and efforts of individuals before government intervention) need to be complemented with tax and transfer interventions that directly target disposable incomes (defined as the distribution of income after taxes have been levied and transfers have been paid). Disposable incomes, after all is said and done, are the relevant distribution to consider in poverty reduction strategies. The need to resort to taxes and transfers as a poverty reduction tool will depend largely on whether the distribution of disposable income is mainly driven by changes in the distribution of market incomes or alternatively by government interventions using the tax-and-transfer instrument.

Are all pro-growth policies equally pro-poor?

If policies could be easily categorized as growth enhancers or inequality reducers, then policy makers could target a growth-inequality objective by selecting a set of policies expected to promote high growth and a second set aimed at reducing inequality. In practice, however, things are likely to be more complex not only because of the inherent difficulties of selecting appropriate policies tailored to an individual country's specific situation but also because in most cases policies are likely to affect growth and inequality simultaneously and in some circumstances even produce conflicting outcomes. Figure 5.1 illustrates this point with a simple representation of the links between policies and poverty reduction. It shows that a policy's effect on poverty reduction depends not only on its effect on income growth and the way that growth translates into poverty reduction, but also on the policy's simultaneous effect on income inequality and the way inequality changes are translated into poverty reduction.

From the discussion in chapter 4, it should be clear that policies that contribute to faster growth and lower inequality will reduce poverty. However, it is far less clear how a

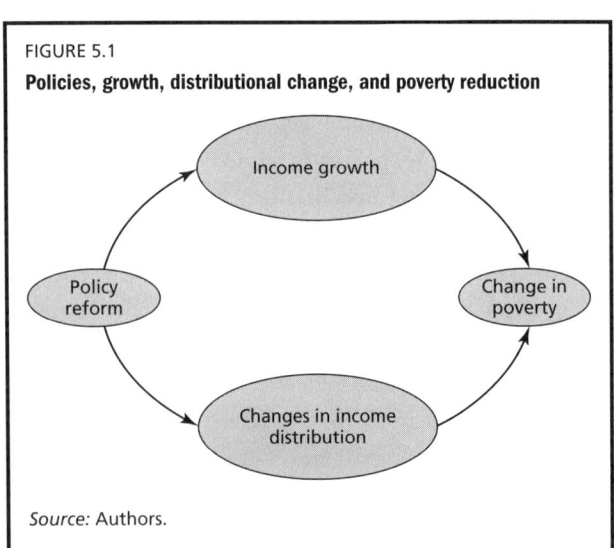

FIGURE 5.1
Policies, growth, distributional change, and poverty reduction

Source: Authors.

growth policy that has an associated increase in inequality will affect poverty. For example, if a policy or policy package leads to a significant acceleration of growth of, say, 2 percent, and simultaneously to a very slight deterioration in the distribution of income, one could possibly expect poverty to decline and hence consider the policy package an acceptable alternative even if it leads to a higher dispersion of incomes. In contrast, if a policy package leads only to modest growth but increases inequality substantially, then one would have to be wary of a potential increase in poverty associated with that package. Moreover, since growth and changes in inequality affect poverty in different ways from country to country, depending on initial incomes and inequality levels, then similar pro-growth policies can be expected to have different poverty effects in different countries.

These problems are further complicated by the dynamics and time lags involved in the adjustment processes of income levels and income inequality following the implementation of a particular policy. Those lags may generate intertemporal poverty dynamics. Consider a pro-growth policy package that has a negative impact on inequality. If the growth and inequality effects become apparent at substantially different times, then the policy intervention may increase poverty in the short run and decrease it in the long run. This would be the case if the inequality effect of the policy is felt immediately but the growth effect is not felt for some time. This section explores these issues.

The simultaneous impact of policies on growth and inequality

The past few years have witnessed an explosion of works analyzing the way different policies affect growth. According to Durlauf and Quah (1999), the number of determinants of growth considered in the literature is greater than the number of countries in the standard growth data set, and a review of all these determinants is outside the scope of this report. Instead, table 5.1 presents a partial survey of policy areas where progress is typically considered as pro-growth, the indicators typically used to assess progress, and some of the empirical works that have analyzed its relevance. For example, the existing literature largely supports the idea that countries tend to grow faster when they have a higher capital stock, a more-developed financial sector, better institutions, more trade openness, smaller governments, better public infrastructure, and good macroeconomic management.

Two disclaimers need to be made here. The first regards the unanimity of these results: in almost all of the areas

TABLE 5.1

Economic policies and growth: Review of the evidence

Policy area	Indicator category	Econometric results
I. Structural policies and institutions		
Education	Enrollment rates, years of education	[+]: Barro (1991, 2001); Mankiw, Romer, and Weil (1992); Loayza, Fajnzylber, and Calderón (2005)
	Quality of education	[+]: Barro and Lee (2001)
	Allocation of talents	[+]: Murphy, Shleifer, and Vishny (1991)
	R&D investment	[+]: Coe and Helpman (1995)
Financial development	Private domestic credit (% GDP)	[+]: Levine, Loayza, and Beck (2000); Loayza, Fajnzylber, and Calderón (2005)
	Liquid liabilities (% GDP)	[+] via total factor productivity growth: Beck, Levine, and Loayza (2000)
		[+] only for countries with well-developed financial systems: Rioja and Valev (2004).
Government burden	Distortionary taxation	[–]: Kneller, Bleaney, and Gemmell (1999) for OECD, Gupta and others (2005) for developed countries
	Corporate taxes	[–]: Lee and Gordon (2005)
	Labor income tax, marginal tax rates	[0]: Lee and Gordon (2005)
	Government consumption	[–]: Loayza, Fajnzylber, and Calderón (2005)
Infrastructure	Infrastructure stocks	[+]: Sanchez-Robles (1998); Bougheas, Demetriades, and Mamuneas (2000); Easterly (2001); Esfahani and Ramírez (2003); Calderón and Servén (2004)
	Infrastructure quality	[+]: Calderón and Servén (2004)
Governance	Institutional quality (Business Environment Risk Intelligence; International Country Risk Guide)	[+]: Knack and Keefer (1995)
	Absence of corruption	[+]: Mauro (1995)
	Kauffman et al. indicators	[+]: Dollar and Kraay (2003); Acemoglu, Johnson, and Robinson (2001, 2002); Hall and Jones (1999)
Trade openness	Exports and imports (% GDP)	[+]: Ben-David (1993); Edwards (1998); Dollar and Kraay (2003)
	Index of outward orientation / openness	[+]: Dollar (1992); Sachs and Warner (1995); Wacziarg and Welch (2003)
	Openness adjusted by geography	[+]: Frankel and Romer (1999); Loayza, Fajnzylber, and Calderón (2005)
II. Stabilization policies		
Macroeconomic stabilization	CPI inflation rate	[–]: Fischer (1993); Loayza, Fajnzylber, and Calderón (2005)
		[–] for high-inflation periods: Bruno and Easterly (1998); Fischer, Sahay, and Végh (2002)
External imbalances	Real exchange rate overvaluation	[–]: Dollar (1992); Easterly (2001); Loayza, Fajnzylber, and Calderón (2005)
		[–] and larger impact the higher the overvaluation: Collins and Razin (1999); Aguirre and Calderón (2005)
Financial turmoil	Systemic Banking Crises	[–]: Kaminsky and Reinhart (1999); Dell'Arriccia, Detragiache, and Rajan (2005); Loayza, Fajnzylber, and Calderón (2005)

Source: Authors.
Note: [+] implies a positive and significant relationship between growth and the corresponding economic policy. [–] reflects a negative and significant relationship, and [0] denotes no statistical relationship between the variables.

included in table 5.1, at least one work raises serious doubts about the robustness of the results. A classic example usually cited is the work by Levine and Renelt (1992), which examines whether the conclusions from existing growth studies are robust to small changes in the conditioning information set. They conclude that almost all results are indeed quite fragile (the exceptions are the investment rate, the ratio of international trade to GDP, and the initial level of income of the country in question).

The second disclaimer is that table 5.1 should not be construed as implying that countries trying to achieve fast, sustained growth should aim at making progress in each and all of these areas simultaneously. In fact, in World Bank (2005c), it is argued that while sustained growth depends on key elements that need to be fulfilled over time—such as the accumulation of human and physical capital, the efficient allocation of resources in the economy, the adoption of technology, and the sharing of the benefits of growth—the importance of each of these elements depends on the particular country and particular period. That is, countries should probably aim at making progress in the areas that are more relevant to their specific context and initial conditions. Progress in areas that do not have much relevance for the particular country and period may lead to disappointing results.

The literature is far less unanimous on how progress in the pro-growth areas listed in table 5.1 is expected to affect income inequality. As table 5.2 suggests, there is some consensus in some areas. For example, progress on the education, governance, infrastructure, and macroeconomic stability fronts is typically associated with declines in income inequality (see also de Ferranti and others 2004). In other words, policies supporting progress in those areas could be considered win-win policies where the inequality impact reinforces the growth impact of the policies.

However, in at least three other areas the findings are more mixed and subject to some controversy. These regard the roles played by the financial sector, international trade, and the size of the government in determining income inequality. We now pause to review in more detail what is known about the way progress in these three areas affects income distribution.

Financial development

Theoretically, the effect of financial development on inequality and poverty remains ambiguous. Theoretical models consider that financial market imperfections can perpetuate wealth inequalities in the presence of indivisible investments. Poor entrepreneurs—having no collateral, credit history, or connections—are especially affected by asymmetries of information, transaction costs, and contract enforcements costs, as well as other imperfections in the capital markets. These capital market imperfections may hinder the allocation of capital to poor entrepreneurs with high-return projects (they may, for example, postpone investment in human capital) and further increase inequalities (Banerjee and Newman 1994; Galor and Zeira 1993). In this case, financial development would reduce poverty not only through higher growth—by improving the allocation of capital—but also through a more egalitarian distribution of income—by relaxing market imperfections and granting the poor access to credit markets. These effects appear to play a critical role in explaining the results in chapter 6 regarding the negative impact of poverty on growth.

However, it is also possible to argue that financial development may worsen income inequality (at least in the initial stages of economic development). The development of domestic financial intermediaries may benefit primarily the rich since poorer sectors of the economy rely mostly on informal banking and family connections to finance their projects. For example, Greenwood and Jovanovic (1990) have argued that the relationship between financial development and income inequality varies according to the stage of economic development. At earlier stages of development, financial development may increase inequality since only rich people have access to the financial sector. Such access requires an initial set-up cost that poor households cannot afford. As financial intermediaries develop, growth and savings increase, and the inequalities rise. At later stages, the proportion of people that have access and can profit from financial development increases. The distribution of income across agents stabilizes, and growth converges to a higher level than the initial one.

What does the empirical evidence suggest on this front? Unfortunately a quick review of table 5.2 indicates that the empirical evidence is also mixed. On the one hand, Beck, Demirguc-Kunt, and Levine (2004) evaluate the relationship between financial development, inequality, and poverty using a cross-section of countries and find that financial development raises the growth rate of income of the poor more than proportionately, thus exerting an impact beyond the effect of financial development on average income growth—that is, approximately half of the

TABLE 5.2

Economic policies and income inequality: Review of the evidence

Policy area	Indicator category	Evidence
I. Structural policies and institutions		
Education	Education levels Educational inequality	[–] for schooling levels and [+] for schooling inequality: Adelman and Morris (1973); Ahluwalia (1976); De Gregorio and Lee (2002)
Financial development	Private domestic credit (% GDP)	[–]: Beck, Demirguc-Kunt, and Levine (2004); Li, Squire, and Zou (1998) [–] by reducing child labor: Dehejia and Gatti (2005) [+] Bonfiglioli (2004) [+]: Bourguignon (2001)
	Stock market liberalization	[0/+] in countries with larger nonagricultural sectors: Clarke, Xu, and Zou (2003) [+]: Das and Mohapatra (2003)
Government burden	Public employment Transfers (% GDP) Targeted spending Progressive tax sytems Government consumption	[–]: Milanovic (2000) [–]: Milanovic (2000) [–]: Kakwani and Pernia (2000); Iradian (2005) [–]: Iradian (2005) [–]: Li and Zou (2002) [+]: Dollar and Kraay (2002) [0]: Kraay (2005)
Infrastructure	Infrastructure stocks	[–]: Estache and Fay (1995); Gannon and Liu (1997); Smith and others (2001); Leipziger and others (2003); Galiani, Gertler, and Schargrodsky (2005)
	Infrastructure quality	[–]: Calderón and Servén (2004)
Governance	Institutional quality (Business Enviromental Risk Intelligence; International Country Risk Guide)	[+] at earlier stages and [–] at later stages of development: Chong and Calderón (2000); Li, Xu, and Zou (2000)
Trade openness	Exports and imports (% GDP)	[+]: Barro (2000), Lundberg and Squire (2003) [+] in countries with abundant skilled labor: Spilimbergo, Londoño, and Székely (1999) [0]: Dollar and Kraay (2002, 2004)
	Tariffs	[0]: Edwards (1997); Milanovic and Squire (2005) [+]: Milanovic (2005)
	Trade liberalization	[+]: Morley (2000); [+] on wage differentials: Behrman, Birdsall, and Székely (2003)
II. Stabilization policies		
Macroeconomic stabilization	CPI inflation rate	[+] and more detrimental for countries with high or hyperinflation: Easterly and Fischer (2001), Bulir (2001), Li and Zou (2002)
Financial turmoil	Systemic banking crises	[+]: Baldacci, De Mello, and Inchauste Comboni (2002); Honohan (2004)

Source: Authors.
Note: [+] implies a positive and significant relationship between inequality and the corresponding economic policy, [–] reflects a negative and significant relationship, and [0] denotes no statistical relationship between the variables.

overall impact of financial development on the growth rate of income of the poor is not explained by the impact of financial development on average growth. Not only are their estimates significant but they also suggest a large economic impact.

This positive influence of financial development on inequality and poverty at the aggregate level is consistent with country-case studies that show persistent poverty levels among households that lack access to credit markets. Jacoby (1994) and Jacoby and Skoufias (1997) find that in the presence of adverse shocks, households in Peru and India tend to reduce human capital investments in their children. Similarly, Dehejia and Gatti (2005) indicate that child labor rates are higher in countries with underdeveloped financial systems.[1] Specifically, they find that child labor is inversely related to financial development and is particularly sizable among low-income countries.

A second strand of the empirical literature argues that since the less-favored sectors of the population hold only a small fraction of the country's assets, financial development may not affect income inequality and poverty. In general, a disproportionate concentration of financial institutions and services in the main metropolitan areas of a country, more specifically in its capital, is observed in many Latin American countries. This fact may lead some to think that the link between poverty and access to credit at the regional level may be different from the evidence obtained from cross-country studies. Even from aggregate results, there is evidence that the impact of financial development on poverty may be different across activities or regional groups. An interesting aggregate result from Clarke, Xu, and Zou (2003) claims that financial development may reduce income inequality, with the impact being larger (in absolute value) if financial development guarantees access to people working in agriculture. They argue that giving access to credit to the poorest of the poor—typically poor people in rural areas—will improve the distribution of income and reduce poverty.

Bonfiglioli (2004), argues that financial development may affect inequality in different ways. First, it improves risk sharing, thereby reducing income volatility for a given size of the risky sector. Second, it raises the share of population that is exposed to earnings risk. The first effect tends to reduce inequality, while the second boosts it. When Bonfiglioli empirically validates the model, she finds a result in line with the Greenwood and Jovanovic (1990) predictions. Inequality rises with the level of financial development until it reaches a certain level and then it declines.

Openness to international trade

Trade liberalization and openness to trade are usually viewed as key elements of successful growth strategies. However, trade policy may induce countervailing forces on income distribution and poverty alleviation. On one hand, in a two-sector economy with different skill intensities, the Heckscher-Ohlin model of international trade predicts that trade reform in a skill-abundant country will increase the relative price of goods produced in the skill-intensive sector. The accompanying Stolper-Samuelson theorem predicts that this change in product prices will be translated into an increase in the wages of workers in the skill-intensive sector of the economy. Liberalization should then reduce wage differentials if product market changes shift production toward a country's comparative advantage, which within the assumptions of the classical framework would seem to benefit less-schooled workers relative to more-schooled workers in most developing countries.

On the other hand, a number of possible countereffects could result in higher wage dispersion. For example, the preliberalization framework might have protected unskilled workers who find themselves unemployed following the implementation of the liberalization agenda. Capital goods may become cheaper, allowing entrepreneurs to substitute capital for labor. Moreover, since workers with more schooling tend to complement physical capital, the demand for skills could increase and eventually lead to skill-biased technological change. For example, de Ferranti and others (2003) argue that the observed increases in the wage of skilled workers in Latin America were probably transmitted through trade, foreign direct investment, and licensing from the United States and other OECD countries.

Thus it is possible to find sensible theoretical arguments suggesting that inequality can move in one or the other direction with trade opening. So, what does the empirical evidence say in this regard? Once again, the empirical evidence is quite segmented. In one of the first studies at the aggregate level for developing economies, Edwards (1997) evaluates whether income inequalities are higher in open economies and whether trade liberalization leads to a less egalitarian distribution of income. Using data on tariffs and nontariff barriers, he finds that inequality is higher in countries with more distortions in their external sector and that trade reforms do not appear to have a significant impact on the distribution of income. Similarly, Dollar and Kraay (2003) find no evidence that trade affects inequality.

A different picture emerges from Milanovic and Squire (2005), who provide a critical review on the issues of whether trade liberalization increases wage inequality and from Lundberg and Squire (2003) and Barro (2000) who estimate the impact of trade on the Gini coefficient. Most of the studies in this strand of the literature find that trade reforms have a negative, although modest, effect on the distribution of income. Milanovic and Squire also examine the effects of tariff reductions on inequality among occupations and find that a 1 point decrease in the average tariff rate is associated with an annual increase of 5.7 percent in interoccupational inequality (thus implying an annual increase of 1.2 points in the Gini coefficient for a country with an average interoccupational Gini of approximately 24).

Similarly, Milanovic (2005) evaluates the impact of trade liberalization on the distribution of income and finds that increased trade openness reduces the income share of the bottom eight deciles and raises the income share of the top two deciles (in other words, poor and middle-income groups seem to be hit harder the more their country's economy is integrated into world goods markets). Only when the level of income reaches a certain threshold (which Milanovic estimates at about $8,000 in purchasing power parity) does openness appear to benefit the poor and the middle class. Milanovic illustrates the economic significance of his results by considering the impact on income distribution of a 0.2 increase in the trade-to-GDP ratio, from 0.7 to 0.9, which was the world average increase between 1985 and 2000. In a country with a mean income of $2,000 where the second decile's mean income is $800, higher trade openness would reduce the income share of that decile of the population by 3.8 percent, to a mean income of $760 (Milanovic, 2005, 33).

Beyond income poverty, trade openness may have additional impacts on poverty, broadly construed through channels touched upon in chapter 2. First, international trade may affect poverty through its influence on the *rate of mortality*. Improved health programs in developing countries may be explained by the transmission of health technologies from industrial economies. The idea behind this argument is that the health sector in the developing countries becomes more productive by implementing new technologies embodied in their imports of capital goods. For instance, Papageorgiou, Savvides, and Zachariadis (2005) find that higher imports from countries responsible for medical research and development in the world are related to lower mortality rates.

Soares (2005) argues that although the diffusion of productive technologies may partly explain the process of the diffusion of health technologies, there are some crucial aspects that are specific to the sector. First, some aspects of health (such as personal hygiene, food preparation and handling, and water treatment, among others) are outcomes of the household production process. Absorption of health technologies, in this case, may depend on the accumulation of knowledge of households. In addition, to the extent that health improvements do not depend on specific medical interventions, the role that embodied technological change plays is negligible. Second, health technologies, to some extent, have features corresponding to public goods. Inefficient private provision may lead to the implementation of several public health programs. This implies that diffusion of health technologies goes beyond the embodiment of new technologies.

Second, a recent strand of the literature evaluates the impact of international trade openness on poverty through its impact on *income risk*. Trade reforms may affect individual risk by reallocating capital and labor across firms and sectors, thus raising short-run individual labor risk, and by increasing the elasticity of goods and the derived labor demand functions. If shocks create larger fluctuations in wages and employment because of higher demand elasticity, tariff reductions may lead to increased individual income risk. Conversely, greater openness may reduce income risk by reducing the volatility of goods prices that an autarkic economy may face relative to an economy integrated into the world economy. In sum, economic theory does not provide a clear indication of the nature of the relationship between openness and income risk, and the empirical work is ambiguous. On the one hand, Fajnzylber and Maloney (2005d) find no evidence that increased openness increases labor demand elasticities in Colombia and Chile and weak evidence for Mexico. On the other hand, Krebs, Krishna, and Maloney (2005) find that trade policy affects permanent income risk and argue that the welfare magnitudes are significant (see box 5.1).

Size of the government

A third area of possible conflict between the growth and inequality objectives derives from the way the government uses fiscal policy in the fight against poverty; a more specific issue is the relationship between inequality and the size of the government. Despite the significant role that governments can play in the provision of public goods and services, governments may also be a drain on private activity. This is likely to be the case if governments impose high taxes, assume roles more appropriate for the private sector, and maintain ineffective public programs and a bloated bureaucracy. Thus in principle, larger governments are likely to harm growth prospects. On this aspect, it can be said that the empirical growth literature shows a certain degree of consensus.

The effect of the size of the government on inequality is less clear, however. One factor influencing that effect is the structure of spending. For example, whether the bulk of

BOX 5.1
Trade policy and income risk

Although a large body of literature deals with the impact of trade liberalization on levels of wages or income, Krebs, Krishna, and Maloney offer the first attempt to estimate empirically the effects of trade policy on individual income risk, as well as the welfare consequences of changes in income risk induced by trade policy changes. Using household surveys and manufacturing data for Mexico during 1987–98, the authors find that tariff levels do not affect income risk but that tariff changes do. Individual income risk may increase more than 30 percent in the event of a 5 percent reduction in tariffs. In addition, the authors find that the impact of other macroeconomic shocks on income risk is affected by trade policy. For instance, a 10 percent appreciation of the real exchange rate (RER) would raise income risk by 35 percent if tariffs were 10 percent, and by 60 percent if tariffs were 5 percent. In contrast, a decline of 5 percent in GDP growth would raise income risk by 25 percent if the tariff is 10 percent, and by 60 percent if the tariff is 5 percent. In sum, trade reforms increase the sensitivity of income risk to macroeconomic shocks. This result is consistent with the prediction of Newberry and Stiglitz (1984) that negative productivity shocks would have smaller equilibrium effects on output and employment in a closed economy than in an open economy.

Krebs, Krishna, and Maloney then calculate the welfare effects using a simple dynamic general equilibrium model. The direct impact of tariff reduction is an increase in individual income risk of 0.005 (from a mean level of 0.008 to 0.013), and the corresponding welfare cost is 0.98 percent of permanent consumption if the coefficient of relative risk aversion (CRAA) is equal to 1 (under logarithmic preferences). For higher levels of risk aversion (a coefficient equal to 2), the welfare cost of higher income risk would increase to 1.96 percent of lifetime consumption. A 10 percent real appreciation would raise the income risk from 0.008 to 0.011 with a 10 percent tariff, and the welfare costs are 0.59 and 1.18 percent of lifetime consumption if the coefficient of risk aversion is equal to 1 and 2, respectively. For lower tariffs (5 percent), individual income risk increases to 0.014, and the corresponding welfare costs are 1.18 and 2.36 percent for the different levels of risk aversion. A drop in output of 5 percent would lead to higher income risk (from 0.008 to 0.01) with welfare costs of 0.39 percent of lifetime consumption if the coefficient of relative risk aversion is equal to 1, and 0.78 percent if it is equal to 2. If tariffs were lowered to 5 percent, income risk rises to 0.013, and the welfare costs are higher—0.98 and 1.96 percent of lifetime consumption. In sum, the impact on individual income risk of trade reforms through their direct and indirect effects in amplifying the impact of macroeconomic shocks are economically significant.

Welfare effects of trade reform

Simulation	Changes in individual income risk	Welfare change CRRA = 1	Welfare change CRRA = 2
Trade reform			
Tariff reduction of 5 percent	0.005	0.98	1.96
	(0.002)	(0.39)	(0.79)
Macroeconomic factors			
Tariff level of 10 percent			
GDP growth lower by 5 percent	0.002	0.39	0.78
	(0.001)	(0.20)	(0.40)
RER appreciation of 10 percent	0.003	0.59	1.18
	(0.001)	(0.20)	(0.39)
Tariff level of 10 percent			
GDP growth lower by 5 percent	0.005	0.98	1.95
	(0.001)	(0.29)	(0.59)
RER appreciation of 10 percent	0.006	1.18	2.36
	(0.002)	(0.40)	(0.80)

Source: Krebs, Krishna, and Maloney (2005d).
Note: Numbers in parentheses are standard errors.

public spending is devoted to the social sectors and other programs, such as infrastructure, from which the poor are likely to benefit has an impact on the evolution of inequality. Moreover, the structure of spending within social sectors also matters. For example, figure 5.2 shows absolute incidence curves of several public spending programs in the Latin American region. Each curve has been computed as the average of country-specific incidence curves; upward-sloping lines indicate that richer quintiles benefit more than poorer quintiles. Downward-sloping curves indicate progressive spending.

This figure indicates that while public spending on health, primary education, and cash transfer programs benefits people in the lower part of the distribution more than people in the higher part, other types of social spending, such as on tertiary education, pensions, unemployment insurance, and electricity subsidies, are highly regressive. In particular, the first quintile of the population does not seem to benefit at all from public spending on tertiary education and pensions, whereas more than half of all spending in these two areas benefits the top quintile. Clearly, similar levels of aggregate social spending may have dramatically different impacts on income inequality depending on the social programs being implemented; substantial gains in reducing inequality could be achieved by simply reallocating resources within a given budget envelope.

At the same time, it is also possible to argue that if public spending is a burden for the economy and growth, then the government is likely to be more predatory than benevolent. And a predatory government may be motivated by a desire to direct rents to specific groups, which typically are not the poor. Even where governments are benevolent in character, a retrenchment of the public sector can lead to cuts in programs that benefit the poor. And if public employment plays a safety-net role (by overstaffing public units, perhaps to gain the support of particular groups), then retrenchment may lead to increasing inequalities. Furthermore, there is some evidence indicating that in general governments tend to pay premium salaries (above market rates) to unskilled workers at the expense of higher-grade employers' salaries. Clearly, this policy is not likely to lead to efficiency gains by any standard, but it admittedly has an income distribution component.

On the empirical front, the literature is again quite divided, with results for all possible tastes. Some empirical evidence suggests that larger governments—measured either by a higher share of workers in the public sector or by a higher level of transfers as a ratio to GDP—tend to be associated with lower inequality (Milanovic 2000). Similarly, Li and Zou (2002) also find that higher government spending is usually associated with lower inequality. But Dollar and Kraay (2002) find that the incomes of the poor decline with greater government spending even after controlling for average income levels (that is, the size of the government is associated with increases in income inequality). Kraay (2005) finds that government spending does not have a significant effect on the Gini coefficient.

Pro-growth, pro-poor: Is there a trade-off?

On the whole, the previous discussion indicates that in a number of policy areas, progress is likely to be a win-win situation in that it will lead to faster growth and lower inequality (and hence lower poverty). Yet there are some areas where a potential conflict can appear. The three areas reviewed above that potentially lead to growth-inequality trade-offs are especially important for Latin America. Further financial deepening appears as a critical ingredient of sustained development in Latin America. Trade issues have received significant attention given ongoing liberalization efforts in the region. Similarly, as argued below, the size of Latin American governments is smaller than one would expect, even controlling for level of development.

Unfortunately, just knowing that progress in a particular policy area may create some growth-inequality trade-offs is of limited use in inferring the impact on poverty. Moreover, studies that estimate the simultaneous impact of policies on growth and inequality, so that one can compare outcomes associated with the same inputs more or less accurately, are very rare (Li and Zou 2002; Lundberg and Squire 2003), and none of them consider the joint impact on poverty reduction. To begin to address these shortcomings, we now build on a recent study of the World Bank's Latin American region by Norman Loayza, Pablo Fajnzylber, and Cesar Calderón, *Economic Growth in Latin America and the Caribbean: Stylized Facts, Explanations, and Forecasts* (2005).

Before proceeding, however, we would like to make a clarification. Dealing with these issues is extremely complex. Indeed, as some development practitioners argue, if the economics and the development professions more generally still do not have a completely clear picture of what works and what does not work for economic growth, it might seem pretentious to address not only how a policy affects the growth rate but also how that policy affects the

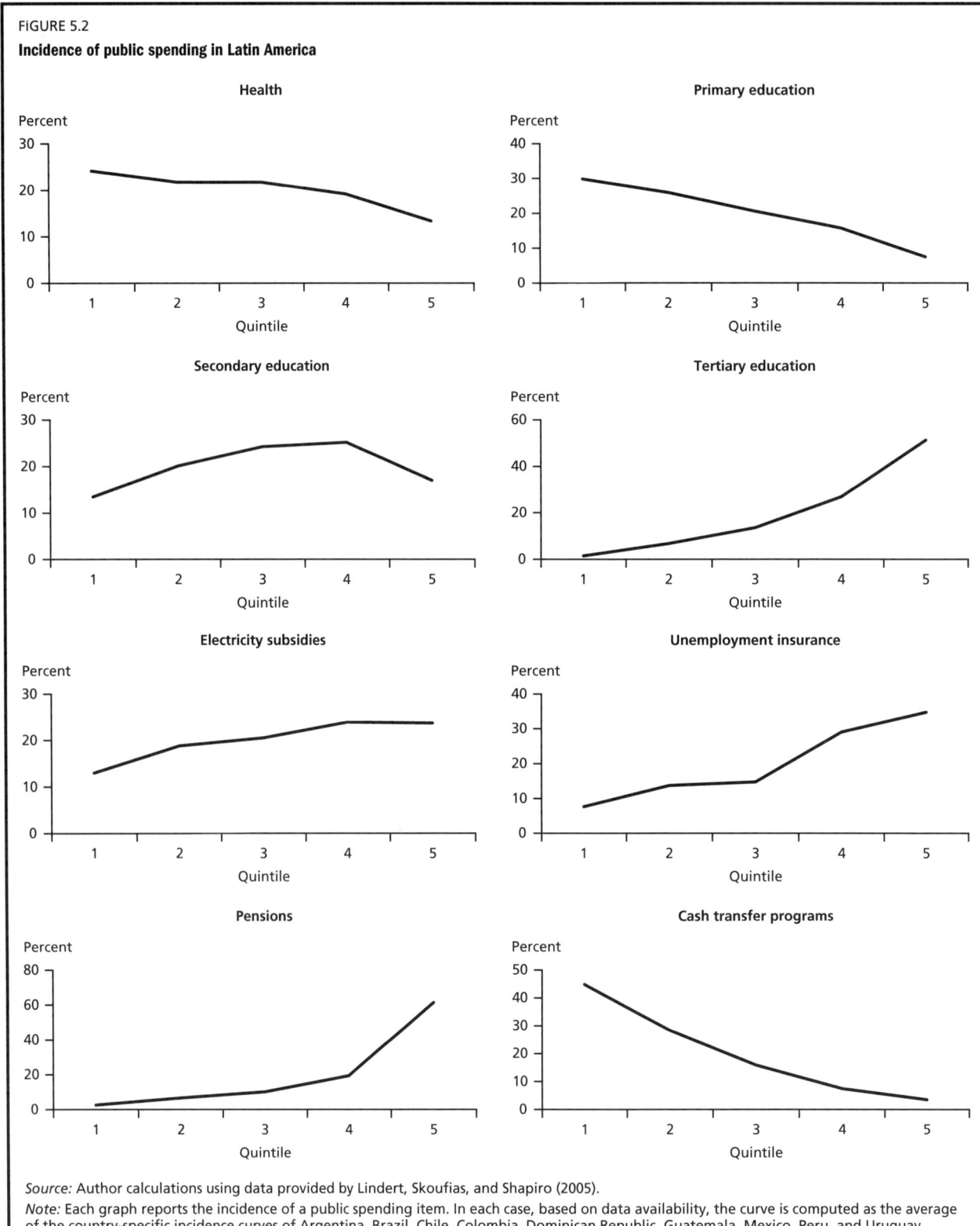

FIGURE 5.2
Incidence of public spending in Latin America

Source: Author calculations using data provided by Lindert, Skoufias, and Shapiro (2005).
Note: Each graph reports the incidence of a public spending item. In each case, based on data availability, the curve is computed as the average of the country-specific incidence curves of Argentina, Brazil, Chile, Colombia, Dominican Republic, Guatemala, Mexico, Peru, and Uruguay.

TABLE 5.3
Growth and inequality regressions

Variable	Growth	Change in logged Gini
Lagged inequality		−0.242
		(13.32)
Initial GDP per capita	−0.018	
	(3.80)	
Initial output gap	−0.237	
	(8.52)	
Education	0.017	−0.022
	(6.7)	(2.77)
Financial depth	0.006	0.014
	(4.28)	(2.83)
Trade openness	0.01	0.024
	(3.14)	(3.04)
Government burden	−0.015	−0.018
	(3.18)	(2.71)
Public infrastructure	0.007	−0.016
	(2.71)	(3.32)
Governance	−0.001	0.005
	(0.68)	(1.74)
Price stability	−0.005	0.008
	(1.89)	(2.16)
Cyclical volatility	−0.277	0.112
	(3.76)	(1.41)
External imbalances	−0.006	−0.002
	(3.90)	(0.32)
Banking crisis	−0.029	−0.021
	(7.42)	(4.02)
External conditions	0.072	0.051
	(4.98)	(1.87)

Source: Loayza, Fajnzylber, and Calderón (2005); Lopez (2004).
Note: Numbers in parentheses are *t*-statistics.

patterns of growth. We stress that we are not aiming to set any particular debate on how specific policies may affect poverty. Our purpose here is simply to explore the practical relevance of potential trade-offs between economic growth and inequality when poverty reduction is the overarching policy objective.

To be more specific on the way these simulations have been performed, we build on Loayza, Fajnzylber, and Calderón, who relate cross-national growth rates to the policy areas in tables 5.1 and 5.2, plus other controls such as transitional convergence, cyclical reversion, and external conditions (see also annex 5A). The first column of table 5.3 reports the results that are obtained from their empirical regression model. It suggests that countries that have shown progress on the variables described above as growth determinants have tended to grow more.

The second step in this exercise is reestimating a similar model that now relates changes in inequality (as measured by the Gini index) to the same set of policy determinants, excluding those aimed at capturing income convergence and cyclical reversion and including lagged inequality to capture the possibilities of inequality convergence and a dynamic adjustment. The second column of table 5.3 reports the results of estimating this second model. This combined exercise now allows us to explore the simultaneous impact on growth and inequality of progress on the different policies.

The estimates in table 5.3 indicate that consistent with the earlier discussion, several policy areas may present growth-inequality trade-offs. More specifically, while a more developed financial sector, an economy more open to international trade, and a smaller government may all be associated with faster growth, they also seem to be associated with higher levels of income inequality.

How do these results feed into poverty changes? To explore whether there is a growth-poverty trade-off associated with the potential growth-inequality trade-off of these policies, we use the results of table 5.3 with growth and inequality elasticities estimated under the assumption of lognormality for income levels (see chapter 4). Recall that under lognormality, the impact on poverty of changes in growth and inequality depends on the country's initial per capita income and inequality levels. Thus, table 5.4 presents the result of the simulation for different values of the Gini index and different levels of per capita income relative to the poverty line. This table also differentiates between the short-run and the long-run impact of the policies on poverty, something that may generate poverty dynamics when the speeds of adjustment of per capita income levels and inequality are different.

Several messages emerge from this exercise. First, the policies have a distinctly different impact on poverty over the long run than they do in the short run. Over the long run, progress in the three policy areas is estimated to contribute to poverty reduction, but in the short run there is the possibility of a growth-poverty trade-off (that is, growth accompanied by higher poverty caused by the parallel deterioration of income distribution). The table also shows that the estimated orders of magnitude of the short-run impacts are much smaller than the orders of magnitude of the long-run impacts, something that should give perspective to the short-run costs and long-run benefits of the different policies. That said, however, we do not want to minimize the potential negative impact, even if it is only temporary, that some policies can

TABLE 5.4

Net growth elasticities of poverty to selected policies

| | Short-run impacts | | | | Long-run impacts | | | |
| | Gini coefficient | | | | Gini coefficient | | | |
PL/pc income	0.3	0.4	0.5	0.6	0.3	0.4	0.5	0.6
Financial sector development								
0.16	0.14	0.09	0.06	0.05	−1.32	−0.65	−0.36	−0.17
0.33	0.05	0.03	0.03	0.02	−1.03	−0.54	−0.29	−0.18
0.5	0.02	0.01	0.01	0.01	−0.79	−0.43	−0.25	−0.16
0.66	0.00	0.01	0.01	0.01	−0.63	−0.35	−0.22	−0.12
0.9	0.00	0.00	0.00	0.00	−0.44	−0.28	−0.18	−0.11
1.1	0.00	0.00	0.00	0.00	−0.33	−0.23	−0.16	−0.12
Trade liberalization								
0.16	0.25	0.15	0.11	0.08	−2.17	−1.07	−0.59	−0.27
0.33	0.08	0.06	0.04	0.04	−1.71	−0.89	−0.48	−0.30
0.5	0.03	0.02	0.02	0.02	−1.31	−0.72	−0.42	−0.27
0.66	0.01	0.01	0.01	0.01	−1.05	−0.58	−0.37	−0.20
0.9	0.00	0.00	0.00	0.01	−0.74	−0.46	−0.29	−0.18
1.1	0.00	0.00	0.00	0.00	−0.55	−0.38	−0.26	−0.19
Government burden								
0.16	−0.14	−0.09	−0.07	−0.05	4.21	2.18	1.27	0.70
0.33	−0.03	−0.03	−0.02	−0.02	2.95	1.59	0.90	0.60
0.5	0.00	−0.01	−0.01	−0.01	2.15	1.21	0.73	0.49
0.66	0.01	0.00	0.00	−0.01	1.66	0.93	0.61	0.36
0.9	0.01	0.01	0.00	0.00	1.14	0.72	0.47	0.30
1.1	0.01	0.01	0.00	0.00	0.83	0.58	0.40	0.31

Source: Lopez (2004).
Note: PL/pc income is the ratio of the poverty line to per capita GDP. The tables is computed under the assumption that income follows a lognormal distribution.

have on poverty, especially when *temporary* may mean several years.

Second, different countries may react to the same policy in different ways. Table 5.4 indicates that even if the same policy had the same effect on growth and inequality, its impact on poverty reduction would be different depending on the country. As discussed in chapter 4, poverty in richer and more unequal countries is relatively more reactive to changes in inequality than to changes in mean income. At the same time, poverty in poorer and more equal countries is relatively more reactive to growth than to changes in income inequality. This finding implies that in the absence of compensatory mechanisms or complementary policies, policy makers may be better placed to implement policies involving growth-inequality trade-offs in poorer and more equal countries. In richer and more unequal countries, policy makers may need to consider implementing adequate compensatory mechanisms along with policies that have a growth-inequality trade-off effect.

Complementarities and nonlinearities in the development process

Do these findings imply that poverty reduction strategies should tend to avoid policies that involve potential growth-inequality trade-offs? The answer to this question is unequivocally no. There is now some evidence (Gallego and Loayza 2002; Calderón and Fuentes 2005; Loayza, Oviedo, and Servén 2005) that from an economic development point of view not only does the "quantity" of an implemented policy matter but so does the overall policy mix, something that the models used in the simulation exercise cannot capture. In fact, one important limitation of our simulations is that they are based on simple linear relationships that implicitly assume that policy makers can obtain a desired outcome on the growth or inequality fronts by making progress in a single policy area without addressing other potential constraints on the economy.

In practice, however, it seems foolhardy to assume that a poverty reduction strategy can be uniquely based on win-win types of policies without addressing bottlenecks in other areas such as the financial sector or external trade distortions, especially if progress in those areas can potentially lead to higher income inequality. Consider, for example, a country that liberalizes capital flows but does not show any respect for property rights. It would be surprising if that country managed to realize the benefits of potential foreign direct investment, and it is perhaps more likely that domestic capital would flee the country.

Simple linear models cannot account for complementarities, understood as the interactions that take place among and between policies and existing conditions of the country, region, or individual, but they can nonetheless be extremely important. For example, Gallego and Loayza (2002) estimate the "extra bonus" enjoyed by good performers that jointly implement a series of growth-promoting measures and eliminate bottlenecks in different areas at more than 1 percentage point of their growth rate.

At a more practical level, Lederman, Maloney, and Servén (2005) argue that the effects of NAFTA varied widely among different types of workers, firms, and regions in Mexico. Workers with higher skills and education seem to have benefited more than workers with lower skills. Large firms also seem to have benefited more than small and medium-size ones, probably because of the greater availability of credit to larger firms after the financial crisis of 1994. Similarly, commercial agricultural producers with access to irrigated land seem to have experienced significant productivity gains, whereas smaller producers experienced no effect. Finally, states with higher initial levels of education, better infrastructure, and better local institutions accelerated their income convergence toward the United States, but there was little or no movement toward convergence among Mexico's poorer southern states.

Are some policy complementarities more critical to successful poverty reduction than others? Several attempts have been made in the literature to assess the relevance of policy complementarity for growth, although most of these studies have focused on the possible complementarity between just two policies or growth determinants. Among those that have received significant attention are education and institutions.

Policy complementarities and education

The role of education as an important policy complement in the growth process is clear: education is not only an input in the production process, it can also determine the rate of technological innovation and facilitate the absorption of technologies. For example, de Ferranti and others (2003) argue that the interaction between technology and skill is critical in determining growth, productivity, and the distribution of earnings across individuals. That report also points to evidence suggesting that low levels of skill can constrain the acquisition of technology through trade and foreign direct investment.

The academic literature has also devoted significant attention to the topic. For example, Levin and Raut (1997) show the high degree of complementarity that exists between human capital and growth in the export sector for a sample of semi-industrial countries. They note that the export sector is likely to be able to use human capital more efficiently than can the rest of the economy. This would be the case, for example, where educated workers are able to adapt more quickly to the sophisticated technology and rapid production changes required for competitiveness in world markets. Similarly, Borensztein, De Gregorio, and Lee (1998) present evidence of complementarity between foreign direct investment and human capital. They argue that foreign direct investment contributes to higher productivity and higher economic growth only when the host country has a sufficient capability to absorb the advanced technologies.

This education complementarity to growth is important for Latin America. For although the region's record on net primary enrollment rates is quite encouraging, most Latin American countries have massive deficits in net enrollments in secondary education (figure 5.3). These educational deficits are apparent even after controlling for income levels. Controlling for per capita income levels, the secondary enrollment deficit for the region is estimated at about 19 percent. For tertiary education, the estimated deficit is lower but still above 10 percent.

Thus not only is the low stock of skilled human capital in Latin America limiting the possibility of technology

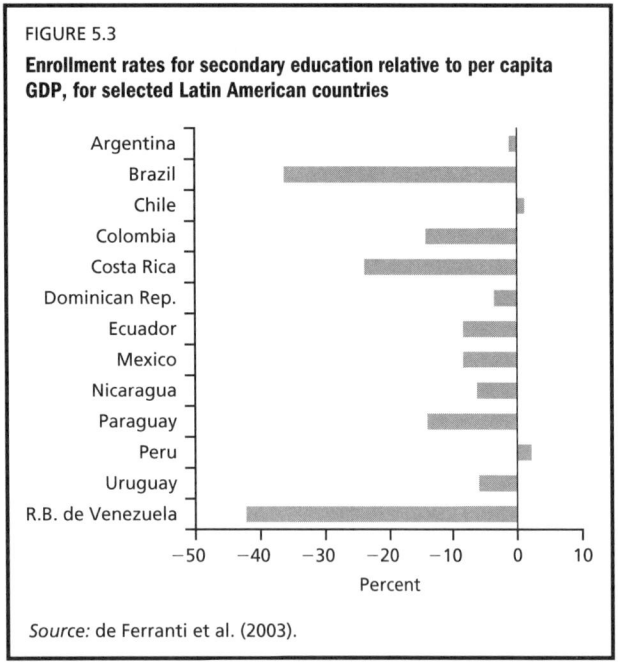

FIGURE 5.3
Enrollment rates for secondary education relative to per capita GDP, for selected Latin American countries

Source: de Ferranti et al. (2003).

adoption, but it may also be affecting the way other policies such as trade or capital account liberalization influence the growth process.

Policy complementarities and institutions

A second area that has received significant attention as a potential policy complement is institutional quality. Institutions, understood as the rules and norms constraining human behavior (North 1990), basically establish the rules of the game for a society. The importance of institutions in the process of development has long been understood—going back at least to the writings of Adam Smith. More recently, it has been argued that growth-enhancing policies, including in the areas of human capital accumulation and trade openness, are less likely to be effective where political and other institutions are weak. As a result, these arguments continue, the adverse effects of weak institutions on economic performance are reinforced by their interaction with other policies.

For example, World Bank (2005c) notes that the effectiveness of financial liberalization on growth depends to a large extent on the underlying institutions: intermediaries; markets; and the informational, regulatory, legal, and judicial framework. When supervision and financial regulation are weak, liberalization may encourage domestic financial institutions to build up excessive risk by borrowing excessively and expanding lending to overly risky activities. As a result, financial resources may end up allocated to activities that are not the most productive. In those cases, it should be no surprise if financial sector liberalization fails to meet expectations (and even results in a crisis).

At the academic level, Calderón and Fuentes (2005) have explored whether the empirical evidence supports this view and conclude that institutional quality seems to play a significant role in understanding the impact on growth of both financial sector liberalization and openness to trade. Moreover, not only do these policies have a greater impact on growth impact when institutions are good, but in countries with low institutional quality, the impact on growth may actually be negative. One example is a financial sector liberalization that ends in crisis through lack of oversight. Similarly, Loayza, Oviedo, and Servén (2005) estimate that high levels of regulation are associated with higher macroeconomic volatility, lower growth, and more informality in labor markets. However, this effect is observed mainly in countries with low institutional quality. As the quality of institutions improves, the negative impact of regulation on macroeconomic performance and growth disappears.

Is this type of policy complementarity relevant in the Latin American context? Figure 5.4 plots the average for the six indexes contained in the Kaufman, Kraay, and Mastruzzi (2004) database of institutional quality measured against the log per capita income level of each country. The figure indicates that a very close association between per capita

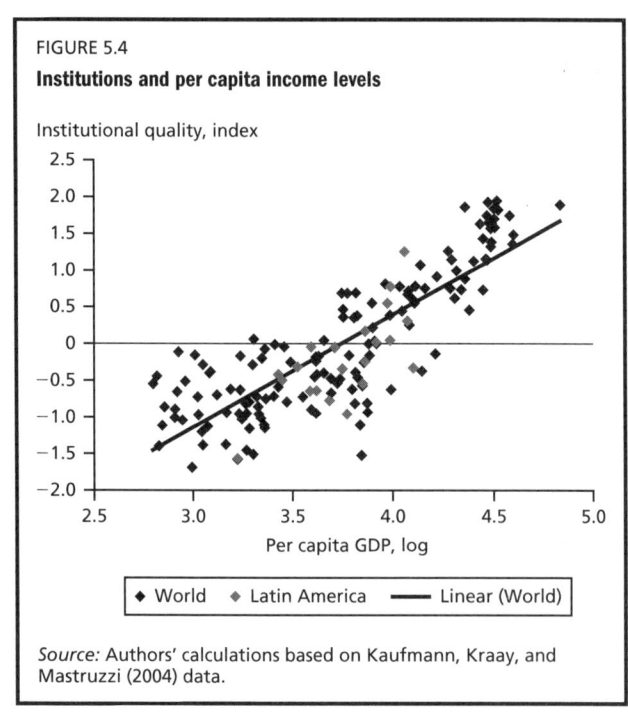

FIGURE 5.4
Institutions and per capita income levels

Source: Authors' calculations based on Kaufmann, Kraay, and Mastruzzi (2004) data.

TABLE 5.5
Institutional quality in Latin America

Country	Institutional quality	Country	Institutional quality
Argentina	−0.34	Honduras	−0.51
Bolivia	−0.43	Jamaica	−0.05
Brazil	0.01	Mexico	0.04
Chile	1.25	Nicaragua	−0.32
Colombia	−0.55	Panama	0.16
Costa Rica	0.77	Paraguay	−0.78
Dominican Republic	−0.25	Peru	−0.35
Ecuador	−0.66	Trinidad and Tobago	0.3
El Salvador	−0.06	Uruguay	0.54
Guatemala	−0.65	Venezuela, R. B. de	−0.97
Haiti	−1.59	**Median**	**−0.32**

Source: Authors' calculations using data from Kaufman, Kraay, and Mastruzzi (2004).

income levels and institutional quality, something that in turn suggests that a comparison of institutional quality based on absolute indicators may be misleading. To address this issue in part, table 5.5 tabulates the relative performance of countries in the region controlling for income levels. More specifically, the table reports the difference between the observed institutional index and its expected value.

Table 5.5 indicates that two-thirds of the countries in the sample have a negative sign, indicating institutional underperformance. The countries with a clear positive sign are Chile, Costa Rica, Panama, Trinidad and Tobago, and Uruguay. Brazil, El Salvador, and Mexico are clustered around the regression line, and the rest are well below it. Haiti, Paraguay, and República Bolivariana de Venezuela have the strongest negative signs. Clearly, as in education, many Latin American countries may be limiting the effectiveness of some of their poverty reduction policies by not improving the effectiveness of their institutions.

Does the composition of growth matter?

In the previous section we addressed several policy issues related to pro-poor growth. Determining the effects of growth on poverty can also be addressed from a sectoral point of view. Beyond accounting issues related to the relative size of the sector in question, there are a number of reasons why growth in some sectors may alleviate poverty more than growth in other sectors.[2] One reason is the relationship between the geographic location of a sector's production and the incidence of poverty in the area. According to this argument, in the absence of spatial mobility, growth

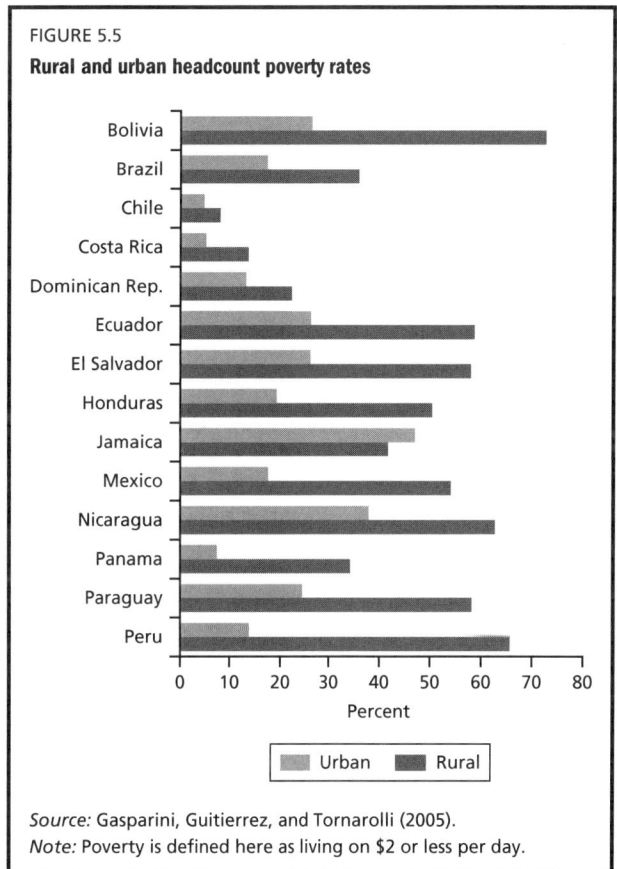

FIGURE 5.5
Rural and urban headcount poverty rates

Source: Gasparini, Guitierrez, and Tornarolli (2005).
Note: Poverty is defined here as living on $2 or less per day.

in sectors located where the poor live would likely have a large impact on poverty alleviation (see chapter 7 for a discussion of spatial mobility, poverty, and growth).

The existing empirical evidence seems to give some support to this view. Figure 5.5 illustrates the different poverty rates of urban and rural areas in a selected number of Latin American countries. The figure reveals that rural poverty rates tend to be much higher than urban poverty rates. In Peru, for example, about two-thirds of the rural population is poor, compared with 4 percent in urban areas. The median rural poverty rate for the 14 countries in the figure is 52 percent; the median urban poverty rate is 19 percent. Thus is growth in the agricultural sector more propoor than growth in the nonagricultural sector? In *Beyond the City: The Rural Contribution to Development,* de Ferranti and others (2005) found that, on average, the expansion of agricultural activities in Latin America would contribute less to overall poverty reduction than the expansion of the nonagricultural sector. To a large extent, however, this result was a consequence of the agricultural sector's smaller size. In fact, relative to its size, agricultural growth in Latin America tends to be more pro-poor than overall growth in nonagricultural sectors.

A second explanation for why some sectors have a larger impact on poverty reduction than others is related to the potential spillovers between sectors. If one sector acts as a locomotive for other sectors, then growth in the locomotive sector would be expected to have a larger impact on poverty. Figure 5.6 illustrates this issue for a two-sector economy (rural and nonrural) using results from Bravo-Ortega and Lederman (2005). More specifically, panel A of figure 5.6 shows the estimated percent increase in the nonrural sector associated with a 1 percent increase in rural GDP for Latin America, other developing countries excluding Latin America, and high-income developed countries. This panel shows that developing countries, including Latin America, experienced positive effects emanating from growth in the rural sector. On average, a 1 percent increase in rural activities would translate into a 0.12 percent increase in nonrural activities.

Conversely, panel B of this figure shows that growth in the nonrural sector would have a very modest (and statistically insignificant) impact on Latin American rural growth. In other developing countries and in high-income developed countries, growth in the nonrural sector is associated with a shrinking of rural output, something known as the "pull effect." Generally speaking, one effect of this asymmetry is that different sectors lead to different rates of poverty reduction even if they have similar shares of GDP and a similar impact on poverty, controlling for growth.

The labor intensity of growth may also explain why growth in different sectors seems to have different effects on poverty. Loayza and Raddatz (2005) stress that differences in the relative labor intensities of various sectors help explain why their effects on poverty alleviation are not the same. How different, then, is relative labor intensity across sectors and across countries? Is the pattern of sectoral growth elasticities of poverty consistent with relative labor intensities?

Figure 5.7 presents box-plots for the cross-country distribution of relative labor intensities corresponding to six economic sectors. Agriculture is clearly the most labor-intensive sector: the ratio of median labor intensity to

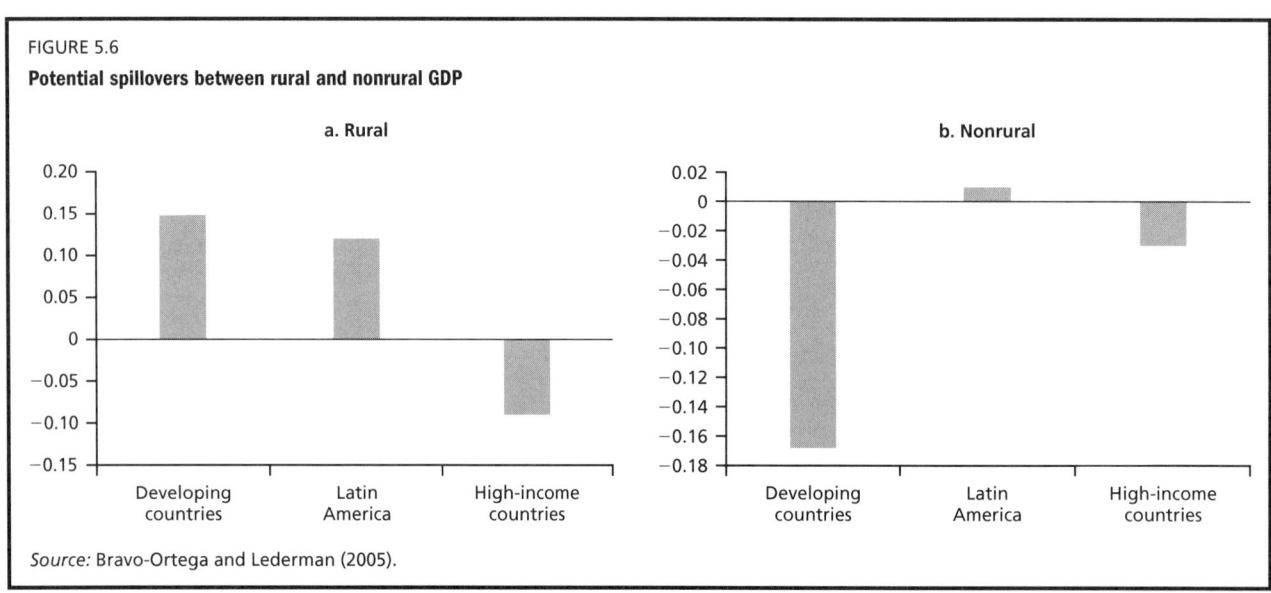

FIGURE 5.6
Potential spillovers between rural and nonrural GDP

Source: Bravo-Ortega and Lederman (2005).

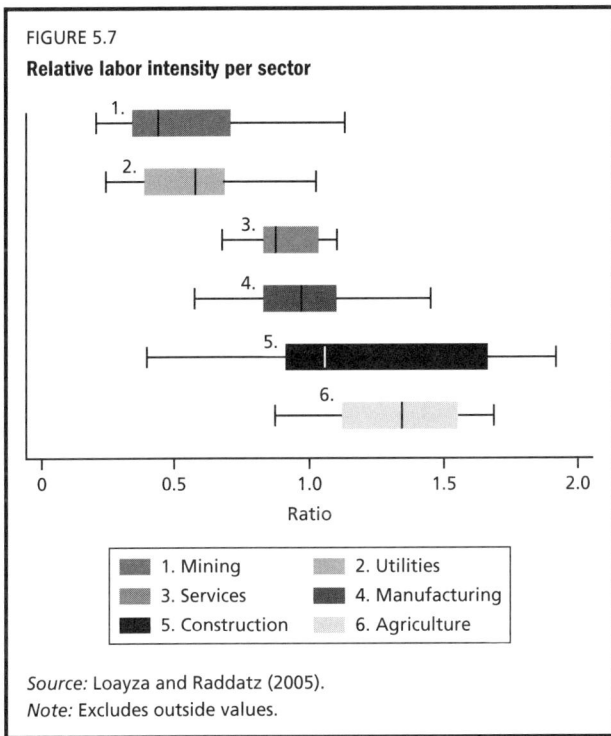

FIGURE 5.7
Relative labor intensity per sector

1. Mining
2. Utilities
3. Services
4. Manufacturing
5. Construction
6. Agriculture

Source: Loayza and Raddatz (2005).
Note: Excludes outside values.

TABLE 5.6
Poverty reduction and sectoral growth

Sector growth	Unconstrained	Partially constrained	Partially constrained, robust
Agriculture growth	−15.228	−15.952	−13.08
	(−1.80)	(−2.37)	(−2.03)
Mining growth	4.575	4.521	4.256
	(1.17)	(1.39)	(1.40)
Manufacturing growth	−2.051	−1.235	−1.241
	(−1.42)	(−1.64)	(−1.68)
Utilities growth	5.463	4.521	4.256
	(0.86)	(1.39)	(1.40)
Construction growth	−1.477	−1.235	−1.241
	(−0.33)	(−1.64)	(−1.68)
Services growth	−0.480	−1.235	−1.241
	(−0.19)	(−1.64)	(−1.68)

Source: Loayza and Raddatz (2005).
Note: The dependent variable is the change in headcount poverty. *t*-statistics are in parentheses. Growth rates are share weighted.

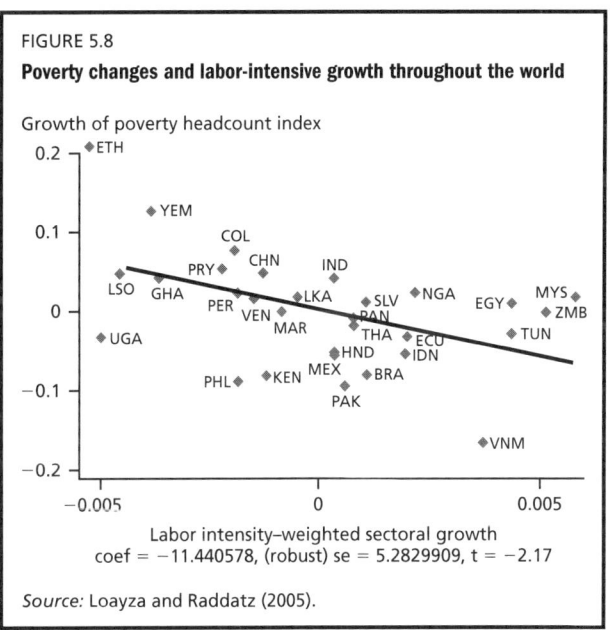

FIGURE 5.8
Poverty changes and labor-intensive growth throughout the world

coef = −11.440578, (robust) se = 5.2829909, t = −2.17

Source: Loayza and Raddatz (2005).

sector size is nearly 1.4 and most corresponding country values are larger than 1. Construction, manufacturing, and services can be grouped in another category of labor intensity, with median ratios surrounding 1. The construction sector is notable in that its cross-country distribution of relative labor intensities is quite dispersed around the mean. Mining and utilities are the least labor-intensive sectors, with median ratios around 0.5 and moderately concentrated distributions.

The notion that relative labor intensity determines a sector's influence on poverty alleviation is consistent with the pattern of coefficients on sectoral growth in table 5.6. This table presents the results of regressing changes in headcount poverty on sectoral growth interacted with the share of the sector in total value added. Given the somewhat small sample size available and relatively large dispersion across countries, three different specifications are used. The first is a fully unrestricted specification. The second pulls together sectors that appear to have similar effects on poverty. The third also controls for the impact of extreme observations or outliers.

The table indicates that growth in agriculture appears to have a clear, significant poverty-reducing effect. Growth in manufacturing, construction, and services also appears to have a poverty-reducing effect, which is statistically significant at marginal levels. In contrast, growth in mining and utilities does not seem to help reduce poverty, once growth in other sectors is controlled for. Thus agriculture, the most labor intensive-sector, presents the largest growth elasticity of poverty, while mining and utilities carry the lowest elasticities for poverty reduction. Manufacturing, services, and construction can be found in the middle of *both* labor intensity and poverty reduction effects.

The relevance of sectoral labor intensity is also apparent from figure 5.8, which shows a partial-regression plot linking the change in poverty to sectoral growth weighted by labor intensity. This figure confirms a negative pattern that is well established by most observations in the sample. Thus, it appears that in addition to the size of growth, the degree of labor intensity in that growth is statistically and economically relevant for explaining poverty reduction.

We emphasize, however, that these results should not be used as a rationale for adopting industrial policies that bias the sectoral composition of growth toward some sectors in the name of a higher growth elasticity of poverty. Such policies may result in the country moving away from its comparative advantages because policy makers may face a trade-off between a higher growth elasticity of poverty and a lower growth rate for the economy as a whole.

Removing bias, especially against the agricultural sector, and overcoming underinvestment in public goods (such as education and infrastructure) in rural areas are completely different issues, however. According to de Ferranti and others (2005), overall public expenditures in Latin America are allocated with an apparent pro-urban bias. Similarly, the results discussed in this section also support the removal of biases against labor, whether policy induced or not, so that effective opportunities can be created for the poor in growing economic activities.

The role of taxes and transfers in reducing income inequality

So far we have focused on the impact that different policies and sectors have on poverty reduction through their effect on market incomes. In practice, however, the relevant distribution for poverty purposes is that of disposable income, which takes into account the redistributive role of the government through taxes and transfers. Thus, what is the role of the government budget and, more specifically, of taxes and transfers in explaining the distribution of disposable income in Latin America? And what are the possibilities of making progress on this front?

In a recent paper Lindert, Skoufias, and Shapiro (2005) present estimates of the Gini coefficient of eight Latin American countries before and after transfers. Their findings indicate that in seven of the countries, public transfers (defined as social assistance plus social insurance) help modestly to lower levels of income inequality. In Peru transfers have the opposite effect and contribute to higher inequality (see figure 5.9) The average change in the Gini coefficient of household income as a result of public transfers for the eight countries in figure 5.9 is around 1 percentage point.

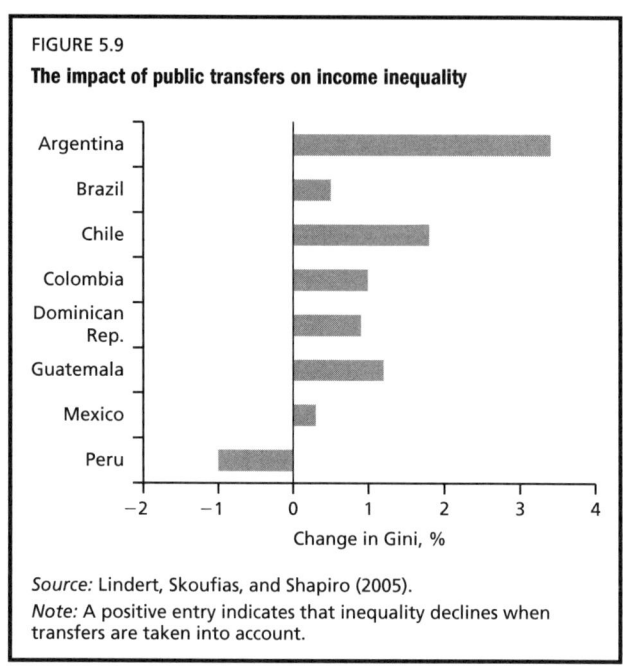

FIGURE 5.9
The impact of public transfers on income inequality

Source: Lindert, Skoufias, and Shapiro (2005).
Note: A positive entry indicates that inequality declines when transfers are taken into account.

Similarly, according to World Bank (2005d), income inequality is unaltered in El Salvador regardless of whether it is estimated before or after government transfers. Finally, analysis undertaken for this report indicates that public transfers would contribute to declines in the Gini coefficient of about 4 points in Bolivia; 2–3 points in Costa Rica; 1–2 points in Ecuador, Nicaragua, Uruguay, Paraguay, and República Bolivariana de Venezuela; and 1 point or less in Honduras.

As for the impact of taxation on the distribution of income, Engle, Galetoviv, and Raddatz (1998) estimate that in 1996 the after-tax Gini coefficient for Chile was 0.496, compared with the before-tax Gini of 0.488—this despite the fact that Chile's tax system is the most effective in Latin America, collects the most from personal income taxes, and has the highest marginal rates. Moreover, these researchers estimate that even if tax allowances were eliminated from the personal income tax and underreported income was taxed, the improvement in the Gini index would be only marginal, and they argue that the more unequal the distribution of market incomes, the less the redistributive effect of progressive taxation. Although the evidence that emerges from these studies is clearly very limited, it indicates that in most Latin American countries, market income inequality does not likely differ much from disposable income inequality.

In contrast, the role played by the tax and transfer instrument in developed countries is apparently much more significant. For example, according to Atkinson (2003), the Gini coefficient of market income in the United Kingdom is around 0.53 whereas the Gini coefficient of disposable income is much lower: around 0.35. That is, taxes and transfers reduce income inequality in the United Kingdom by 18 percentage points as measured by the Gini coefficient. Atkinson makes similar estimates for Canada, Finland, Germany, and Sweden. He does not provide the elements to compare the role of taxes and transfer in the United States, but according to the U.S. Census Bureau, the Gini coefficient of income before taxes and transfers is 0.47, whereas the OECD estimates a Gini of 0.34 for disposable income in the United States.

A similar picture emerges from data provided by EUROMOD, a source of harmonized microdata on the different income components before and after redistribution through the tax-benefit system for 15 members of the European Union (EU).[3] As can be observed in panel A of figure 5.10, the EUROMOD data provide estimates of the Gini coefficient that are virtually identical to those provided by Atkinson (2003) for the countries where there is overlap; the exception is the market income Gini for Sweden, where the estimate is now 0.45.

Panel A also indicates that the Gini coefficient of market incomes for the United Kingdom and Ireland are similar: a high 0.53 and 0.52, respectively. Surprisingly, even the Nordic countries of the EU15, which are traditionally praised for their levels of equality, also show very high inequality in market incomes. The Gini indexes for Denmark, Finland, and Sweden are 0.49, 0.49, and 0.45, respectively. The most equal countries in terms of market incomes are Austria and Netherlands with Gini coefficients of 0.38 and 0.39, respectively. According to the EUROMOD data, the population-weighted average Gini of the EU15 countries before taxes and transfers is 0.47.

After taxes and transfers, however, the Gini coefficient is substantially lower in all the countries.[4] For the EU15 as a whole it is 0.33. That is, in the EU15 taxes and transfers lower the Gini coefficient by 14 points. This decline is even larger in Denmark and Ireland where taxes and transfers lower the Gini by 20 and 19 points, respectively. Even the countries that distribute the least through the tax-benefit system (Greece, Italy, and Portugal) still manage to lower their Gini index by more than 10 points. One final point: even though there may be some comparability issues, the EU15 as a whole and the United States have basically the same levels of inequality both before and after taxes and transfers.

A natural question that emerges from this discussion is of great relevance for fiscal policy, namely, from a redistributive point of view, is the role played by taxes more important or less important than the role played by transfers in the EU countries? To address this issue, panel B reports the Gini coefficient of market income before and after taxes and social security contributions. This panel suggests that the coefficient does not change much for the EU15 overall, falling just 2 points after taxes; in some countries—Denmark, Finland, and Sweden, it even increases. The reason for this is apparent from panel C, which indicates that the Gini coefficient of taxes is very similar to the Gini coefficient of market incomes across the different European countries. If taxes are a constant proportion of income at all points in the distribution (that is, if it is a flat tax), the Gini coefficient will not change at all after taxes.

However, the story from panel D, which compares the Gini coefficients of transfers and market incomes, is radically different. For the EU15 overall, the Gini of transfers is a low 0.04, indicating an almost perfectly equal allocation of transfers along the income distribution. Thus, to a large extent most of the redistribution observed in the EU countries comes from the transfer component rather than from the tax component. This is not to say that taxes are not important. In fact, since they finance the transfers, they are critical. However, the relevance of taxes for reducing income inequality would appear to be more related to the tax level than to the structure (in fact, the correlation coefficient between redistribution and tax level as a percentage of GDP is 0.41).

What can we learn from this? First, the evidence presented above indicates that redistribution takes place largely through transfers rather than through taxes. Taking into account the potential negative impact of taxes on economic efficiency, this finding suggests that policy makers interested in the use of the tax-benefit instrument to address income inequality and poverty concerns should first address the composition and structure of existing transfer programs, and when in need of additional resources use taxes to increase collections while minimizing economic distortions.

Second, the data also suggest that this is an area where Latin America can make progress. Even if one assumes that the Latin American market income Gini coefficient is 4 percentage points above the disposable income Gini (which on

FIGURE 5.10
Gini coefficient in selected countries before and after taxes and transfers

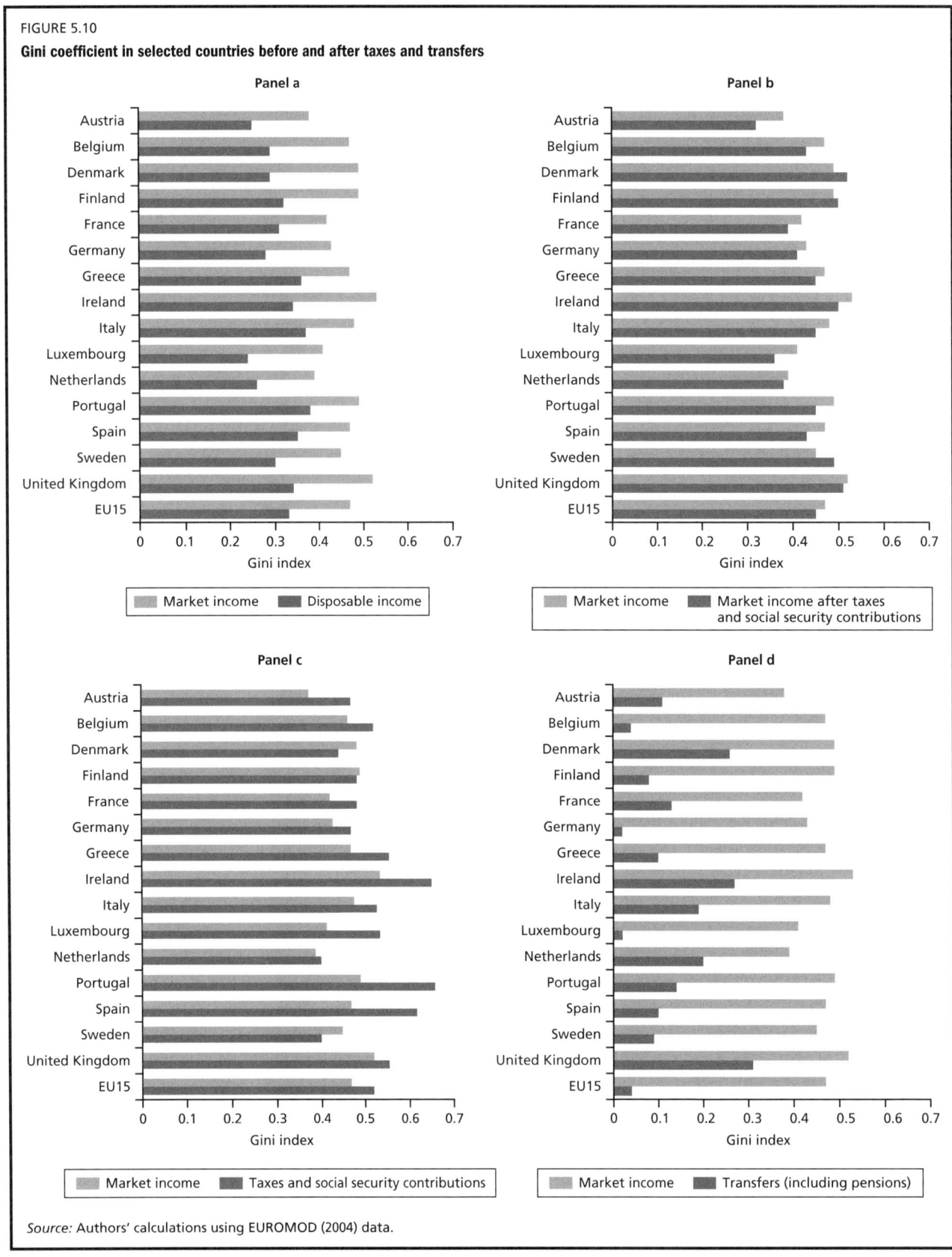

Source: Authors' calculations using EUROMOD (2004) data.

the basis of the evidence presented above would seem a high estimate), fully half of the differences in disposable income inequality between Latin America and Europe (or the United States) are attributable to the different effectiveness of tax and transfer systems.[5]

However, several caveats are in order when moving from this stylized fact to the design of policy. First, these calculations do not include in-kind transfers such as those pertaining to public health, education, or housing, the bias of which we have not examined in this report. Second, the level of taxes and transfers may itself affect the observed level of market income inequality, an effect that is difficult to follow without careful modeling. Finally, at this point we cannot separate transfers from the well-off to the poor from pensions, which are intertemporal transfers from the well-off now to themselves (or others like them) during retirement when incomes are low. Thus, it is possible that our analysis overestimates the magnitude of the redistribution effect of transfers.

Why do Latin America's taxes and transfers have such a low redistributive impact?

Several reasons may explain why taxes and transfers have such a low redistributive impact in Latin America. First, total tax revenues as a percentage of GDP are generally low. This is so whether one measures revenue in absolute terms (in 2000, Latin American countries were collecting, on average, half as much as industrial countries were) or as the level of per capita GDP of the individual countries. Figure 5.11 indicates that only three Latin American countries have tax revenues above the regression line (Honduras, Nicaragua, and Uruguay), while only one (Brazil) has revenue on the regression line. The rest of the region is collecting less than would be expected given their level of development—dramatically less in some cases—notably, Argentina, at 12 percent of GDP, and Colombia, El Salvador, and Paraguay, at 8 percent of GDP.

This regional underperformance is particularly relevant because even though the structure of the taxes may not be the most relevant factor from a redistributive point of view, the quantity of taxes does matter both as a factor that mitigates fluctuation in market incomes (see box 5.2) and as a determinant of the overall budget envelope available for use on the spending side.

A natural question is whether the poor performance of the region on the revenue front is generated by the poor performance of one particular tax category or whether it is caused by problems common to the overall taxation framework.

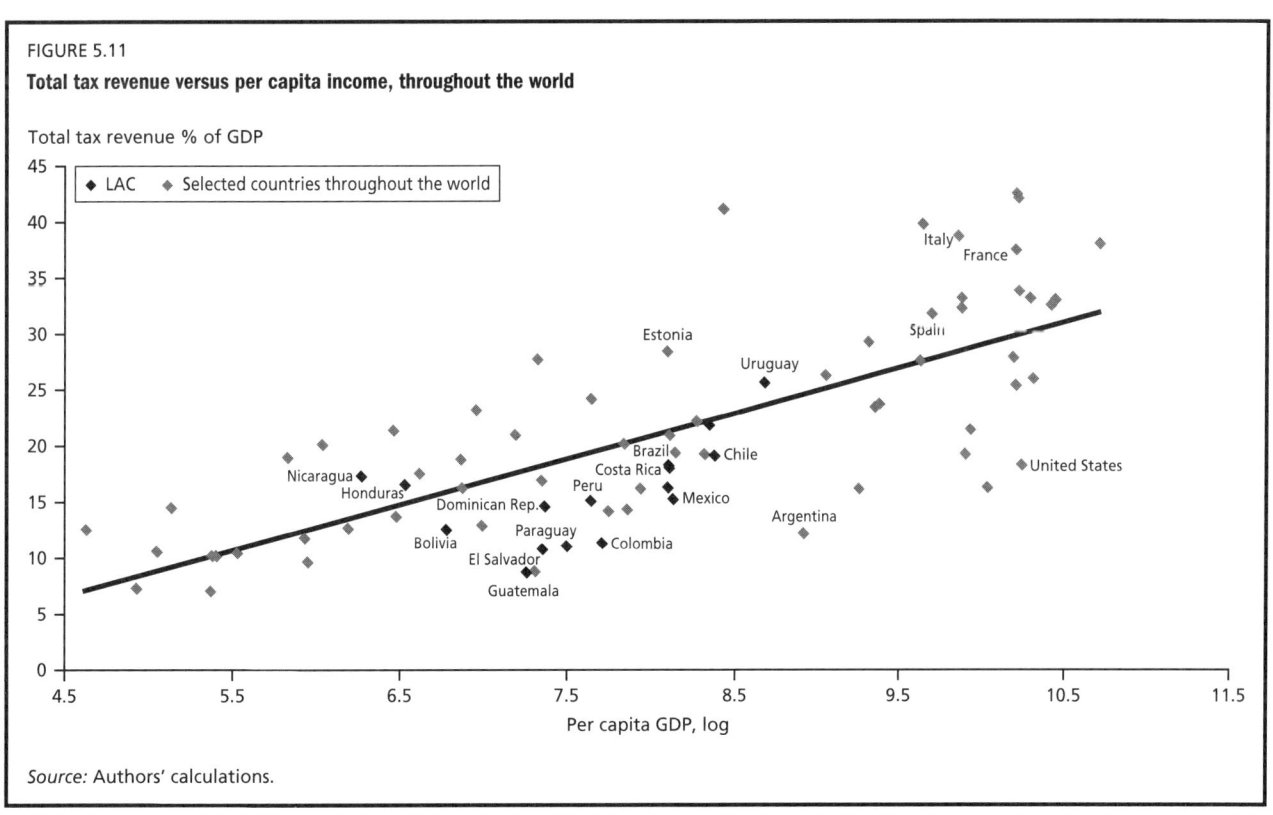

FIGURE 5.11
Total tax revenue versus per capita income, throughout the world

Source: Authors' calculations.

> **BOX 5.2**
> **Taxes, transfers, and inequality**
>
> The overall impact of the government budget depends on the combined effect of taxes and expenditure. A progressive transfer system financed by a proportional tax is progressive overall. Moreover, personal taxation may dampen disequalizing changes in the market distribution, even where the tax system is purely proportional. A simple example may help to illustrate this point. Suppose there is a group, referred to for convenience as the poor, that makes up a proportion p of the population and has zero market income. The poor receive a state transfer, b, financed by a proportional tax at rate t on the income of the rest, $1-p$, of the population. The transfer is revenue neutral in that the sum of market incomes is equal to the sum of net incomes after taxes and transfers.
>
> Suppose now that inequality increases in the market incomes of the nonpoor population, leaving the mean unaffected, so that the same tax t finances the same transfer. A given increase in the Gini coefficient for market income translates into an increase in the inequality of disposable income of $1-t$ as much. With a tax rate of 50 percent, an increase of market inequality of 5 percentage points corresponds to an increase of 2.5 points in disposable income inequality. Thus countries with low taxation levels will find a close mapping from changes in market income inequality and disposable income inequality, whereas this association will be much lower in countries with higher tax levels.
>
> *Source:* Based on Atkinson (2004).

TABLE 5.7

How much is Latin America undercollecting?
(percent of GDP)

Country	Total	Corporate	Personal	Goods and services	International trade	Property
Argentina	−12.3	−1.2	−4.4	−3.4	−1.1	−0.3
Bolivia	−3.6	−1.5	−1.5	1.5	−2.7	1.1
Brazil	−0.7	−1.3	−3.7	−0.8	−1.9	−0.5
Chile	−3.6	−2.4	−4.0	2.9	−0.4	−0.5
Colombia	−8.6	1.6	−2.7	−1.7	−1.7	−0.3
Costa Rica	−3.3	−1.0	−3.0	0.0	−0.1	−0.4
Dominican Republic	−4.0	−1.2	−1.1	−1.6	2.9	−0.3
El Salvador	−7.7	−1.1	−1.5	−0.5	−1.6	−0.3
Guatemala	−9.4	−1.0	−2.0	−1.5	−1.8	−0.3
Honduras	1.4	—	—	—	—	—
Mexico	−5.2	−2.4	−3.6	1.0	−1.9	−0.5
Nicaragua	3.2	−2.3	−0.7	4.5	−2.4	−0.2
Panama	−3.5	−1.0	−3.4	−3.2	0.4	−0.1
Paraguay	−8.0	−0.6	−2.6	−1.5	−1.0	−0.1
Peru	−4.6	−0.7	−2.0	1.4	−1.4	−0.2
Uruguay	1.8	−0.7	−3.4	1.9	−0.8	0.8
Venezuela, R.B. de	−6.4	6.0	−3.5	−3.4	−0.9	−0.1
Median	−4.0	−1.0	−2.9	−0.6	−1.2	−0.3

Source: Authors' calculations.
Note: — = not available. A negative entry indicates that the country is collecting less than it should, taking into account its per capita income level.

To address this issue, table 5.7 reports how much each of several Latin American countries is undercollecting, controlling for per capita income levels (defined as the difference between the actual tax revenue collection in each country and its predicted value once differences in income levels are taken into account). The table clearly shows that the median country in the region is collecting 4 percentage points of GDP less than one would expect, with Argentina, Colombia, El Salvador, Guatemala, and Paraguay showing collection levels that are 7.5 percentage points below the predicted value.

The table shows that the region is undercollecting no matter whether the tax is on personal income, property, corporate income, goods and services, or trade. It is noteworthy that in the case of the personal income tax, not a single country is collecting above or in line with expectations. In effect, the only tax that Latin America seems to be collecting more or less in accordance with the international experience is the goods and services tax.[6]

Moving to the spending side, the first aspect to mention is that not all transfers are the same. In fact, given the differences in incidence and unit values, we have divided "social protection transfers" into two broad categories:

- *Social insurance (SI)*: transfers for which beneficiaries make contributions that involve some degree of "risk pooling," but the benefit they receive is not necessarily directly proportional to what they contribute; and
- *Social assistance (SA)*: transfers for which beneficiaries do not make a direct "risk-pooling" contribution.

Within this second group particularly attractive vehicles are the conditional cash transfer (CCT) programs such as *Bolsa Escola* in Brazil, the *Subsidio Unico Familiar* (SUF) and *Solidiario* programs in Chile, *Familias en Acción* in Colombia (see box 5.3), *Programa de Asignación Familiar* in Honduras, and *Oportunidades*, previously known as *Progresa*, in Mexico. Under these programs, the receipt of the transfers is conditioned on the household investing in the education and health status of their members. This type of program has the benefit of contributing to an immediate reduction in inequality and poverty through the cash transfer component and to a sustained decrease in poverty over the medium-to-long run through the associated accumulation of human capital by the beneficiaries. In that sense these transfers are not a trade-off between growth and redistribution, as could be argued with more traditional pure cash transfers.

The low impact of transfers on income inequality occurs even though Latin American social assistance programs, and in particular conditional cash transfer programs, tend to be well targeted. The problem is that their unit values are small (figure 5.12), which considerably limits their ability to redistribute income. In Peru, for example, the unit value of social insurance transfers (pensions) is about 10 times higher than the value of food-based social assistance programs.

In some cases, social insurance programs, such as pensions and unemployment insurance, have much larger unit values, but these programs tend to be regressive, mainly because they are accessible only through employment in the formal labor market.[7] Since poor households tend to work in the informal labor market, they do not have access to these benefits. Nonetheless, these programs constitute a significant portion of total public spending, much of which is financed by general taxation (due to deficits in contributions). In most cases, even the net subsidies to social insurance (those financed by general taxation, net of contributions) are still several times higher than spending on targeted social assistance programs (figure 5.13).

Thus, there is scope for both fiscal savings and improvements in equity by reducing pensions deficits and improving accessibility by poor and informal workers. The redistributive and poverty impacts of well-targeted programs, such as conditional cash transfers, could be enhanced through broader coverage and higher unit transfers, provided that these reallocations are accompanied by design incentives to promote work efforts and link beneficiaries to complementary services to help them get beyond cash assistance.

Simulating redistributive packages

In the previous sections we discussed the structure of taxation in Latin America and reviewed the situation regarding public transfers, but so far we have not addressed the required fiscal effort the region should make to reduce poverty through the tax and transfer instrument. The answer to this question is critical for assessing both the practical possibilities of achieving fast poverty reduction through redistribution over the short run and the potential for improvement on this front over the long run.

This section takes a first pass at this issue with the purpose of illustrating the order of magnitude of the required efforts. It presents the results of simulating the incremental tax rates associated with reducing poverty by 25, 50, and 75 percent over a 10-year horizon under a simple tax and transfer scenario. The redistributive policy we consider would tax all income at the same rate and allocate the revenues in equal amounts per capita. Here, the resulting decline in the Gini coefficient is similar to the tax rate. This simple redistributive policy, although not targeted to the poor, is not far from the actual fiscal system of several countries (including those of the EU15 reviewed above), where taxes are approximately proportional and per capita

BOX 5.3
Conditional cash transfers in Colombia

The *Familias en Acción* program is a conditional cash transfer program that has successfully increased human capital accumulation in low-density, high-poverty regions of Colombia. The program was initiated in 2001 amid high unemployment, slow economic growth, increasing armed conflict, and increased poverty rates. Although impact evaluations from Mexico's *Oportunidades* suggested that this program design could be effective, the Colombian doubters argued that *Familias en Acción* would create a culture of dependency and crowd out adult labor, that the cash would be diverted to adult consumption, that fertility rates would increase, and that the human capital impacts observed in Mexico were an anomaly that could not be replicated in Colombia. A well-designed and implemented program, coupled with carefully designed impact evaluations, showed not only that the critics were wrong but also that such a program had potential in poor, rural zones. The objectives of the *Familias en Acción* program were to complement the income of extremely poor families with children under age 18 by

- Reducing the nonattendance and desertion rates of students
- Improving health outcomes of children under age 7
- Improving health care practices for children, including improving nutrition and early stimulation and curbing family violence.

Familias en Acción was implemented in 631 municipalities, covering 58 percent of all low-density areas, and benefited nearly 1 million children in 340,000 families. Before the program began, the target population had monthly household expenditures below US$30 per capita, 10 percent of the children were severely malnourished, nearly 50 percent of the children under age 6 were ill, and 9 percent of primary school children and 37 percent of secondary school children were not attending school.

Eligible families were those who were indigent poor and living in the target municipality. Families with children younger than age 7 were eligible for a bimonthly transfer equivalent to US$17 if they complied with the growth and development control appointments for their children over the two-month period. Mothers of school-age children received the equivalent of US$5.50 monthly for each child who met the primary school attendance requirements and US$10 monthly for each child who met the secondary enrollment requirements.

An impact evaluation using a randomized sample design showed that after two years, the *Familias en Acción* program had significant impacts on health:

- Food consumption, especially of proteins and dairy, increased;
- Vaccinations increased by 7–12 percentage points;
- Children's height increased by 0.62–0.75 centimeters, and their weight increased by 0.32–0.48 kilograms;
- Illness dropped by 11 percentage points;

and on education:

- Secondary school attendance increased by 4.6–10.1 percentage points; and
- Primary school attendance increased by 3 percentage points.

The program did not generate the adverse incentive effects that were feared. The evaluations showed:

- Child labor declined by an average of 80 hours a month;
- Adult labor increased by 3.6–6.5 percentage points;
- Participants were 2.5 percentage points less likely to migrate;
- Birth rates declined by 9–13 percentage points; and
- Alcohol, tobacco, and other adult consumption did not increase.

Given these positive results, the future of the program looks bright. The government has implemented the program in pilot urban areas to determine its effectiveness in high-density, high-poverty zones and, depending on the results from future impact evaluations, plans to expand coverage to the entire poor population by the year 2019. On a larger scale, the *Familias en Acción* program shows that successful conditional cash transfer programs, such as Mexico's *Oportunidades* and Brazil's *Bolsa Escola* program, can be replicated elsewhere. Careful evaluation has provided a new data point that supports the human capital accumulation power of conditional cash transfers, with few of the efficiency losses predicted.

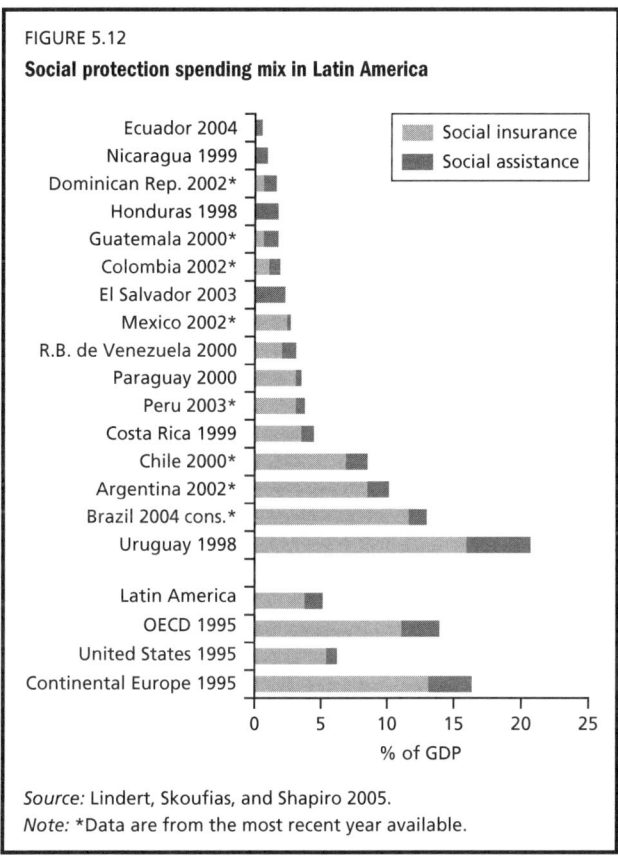

FIGURE 5.12
Social protection spending mix in Latin America

Source: Lindert, Skoufias, and Shapiro 2005.
Note: *Data are from the most recent year available.

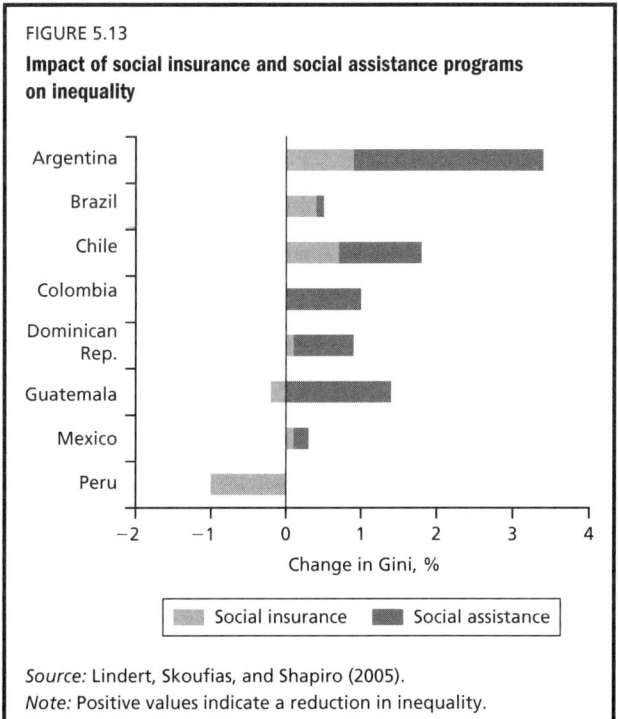

FIGURE 5.13
Impact of social insurance and social assistance programs on inequality

Source: Lindert, Skoufias, and Shapiro (2005).
Note: Positive values indicate a reduction in inequality.

public expenditures do not vary substantially with income. Our simulations assume that there are no efficiency costs (that is, the increase in taxes and transfers does not affect growth), something that admittedly may be unrealistic given the typical inefficiency costs associated with taxation.

For comparison purposes, we also estimate the growth rates that would be required to achieve the same poverty reduction objectives when growth is not accompanied by any distributional change, as well as the required tax increases needed when growth averages 3 percent a year over the 10-year horizon. Table 5.8 reports the results of the first two simulations, and figure 5.14 shows the incremental tax rate associated with the third simulation.

For example, according to table 5.8, Costa Rica has to grow at an annual rate of 2.6 percent for the next decade to reduce poverty by 25 percent, assuming no changes in inequality. The corresponding growth rates for the targets of reducing poverty by 50 and 75 percent are 6.1 percent and 14.2 percent, respectively. Notice that even though fast poverty reduction in the region requires a significant acceleration in observed growth rates, the estimates in table 5.8 are not completely unrealistic. The median per capita growth rate of the estimates associated with reducing poverty by 25 percent is 2.4 percent, whereas that of the second target is 5.5 percent. The third target—reducing poverty by 75 percent—would require a less realistic growth rate of about 10 percent.

Looking now at the incremental tax rates required to reduce poverty through redistribution alone, the estimates in table 5.8 indicate that if the objective is cutting poverty in half over a 10-year period, the tax rates of the region should increase by between 5 percent (Chile) and 33 percent (Nicaragua). The median values associated with the three poverty reduction targets in our simulations are 11, 20, and 29 percent. Over a 10-year period, these incremental tax rates would produce the same poverty reduction as would the neutral growth rates we estimate in the first simulation.

Needless to say, such high tax increases seem unrealistic from a practical point of view. Moreover, with these incremental tax rates, it would be very difficult to maintain our assumption of no efficiency costs associated with the tax and transfer policy—in practice if one allowed for some negative impact on income growth, one would expect the necessity for an even higher incremental tax rate.

Obviously, the two simulations shown in table 5.8 are extreme cases. Figure 5.14 attempts to illustrate the benefits

TABLE 5.8

Results of simulations of income-neutral growth rate and incremental tax rate

| | Neutral growth | | | Redistribution | | |
| | Income growth rate | | | Incremental tax rate | | |
Country	25%	50%	75%	25%	50%	75%
Argentina (2004)	2.2	5.0	10.2	5.6	10.5	15.8
Bolivia (2002)	3.5	8.6	20.8	19.0	31.4	40.9
Brazil (2003)	2.4	5.4	12.8	5.3	9.9	15.9
Chile (2003)	1.4	3.4	8.1	2.3	4.8	8.7
Colombia (2004)	3.1	9.9	17.3	8.2	17.0	25.1
Costa Rica (2003)	2.6	6.1	14.2	4.5	8.5	13.3
Dominican Republic (2004)	1.5	3.4	6.3	4.4	8.7	13.2
Ecuador (2003)	2.3	5.4	10.5	14.5	25.2	34.3
El Salvador (2003)	2.7	6.4	13.9	19.0	31.8	42.2
Honduras (2003)	2.3	5.6	9.8	12.8	22.9	30.1
Mexico (2002)	2.6	7.2	25.9	10.9	21.4	32.8
Nicaragua (2001)	2.5	5.5	9.8	20.9	33.2	42.0
Panama (2002)	2.2	5.3	10.1	4.4	8.8	12.9
Paraguay (2002)	3.7	9.5	27.2	16.8	28.0	37.3
Peru (2002)	2.4	5.5	10.2	11.1	19.6	26.9
Uruguay (2003)	1.2	2.6	5.4	2.7	5.5	9.5
Venezuela R. B. de (2000)	2.1	4.8	9.2	14.4	25.3	34.8

Source: Gasparini, Gutierrez, and Tornarolli (2005).

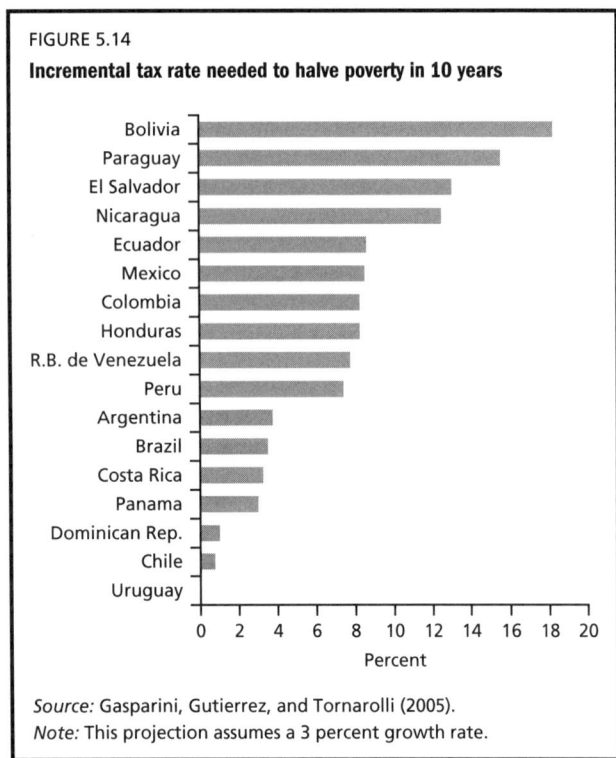

FIGURE 5.14
Incremental tax rate needed to halve poverty in 10 years

Source: Gasparini, Gutierrez, and Tornarolli (2005).
Note: This projection assumes a 3 percent growth rate.

that would appear from strategies based both on growth and on improvements in the distribution of income through taxes and transfers. The figure reports the estimated incremental tax rates that would be needed to cut poverty in half over a 10-year period with a per capita growth rate of 3 percent a year. Even if the tax increases are much lower than those reported in table 5.8, they are still quite significant and in most cases above the tax level for each country given its per capita income level. For example, Bolivia, El Salvador, Nicaragua, and Paraguay would need tax increases in excess of 12 percent.

On the whole, one message that emerges from this analysis is that even though taxes and transfers can complement growth in Latin American development strategies, assuming that this instrument can substitute for growth to reduce poverty in the medium run seems unrealistic. Thus policies that address the evolution of market income in terms of growth and its distribution will have to be central to the development strategies of the region.

Concluding remarks

In this chapter we have explored a number of issues of particular interest for policy makers preparing poverty reduction strategies. First, we have argued that there are several pro-growth areas where Latin America needs to make progress and where there may be potential trade-offs with inequality and even with poverty reduction goals in the short run. For example, several studies have found that trade openness (an area of particular relevance given ongoing liberalization efforts in the region) may lead to higher inequality through greater divergence of wage incomes. To a large extent this result may be related to the very desirable adoption of technologies that tend to be skill biased, thus enhancing the returns to and the demand for education, a phenomenon found globally. Nonetheless, the poor and poor regions might be left behind in the short run. In the long run, however, the evidence presented in this chapter suggests that all pro-growth policies will lead to lower poverty regardless of their impact on inequality.

We also argued that these results indicate that governments may need to adopt complementary policies behind the border—facilitating access to education, expanding infrastructure to lagging areas with the potential to tap into the benefits of liberalization, and offering conditional transfers for poor peasants who may lose out in the transition. These complementary policies can significantly mitigate the inequality effects while considerably enhancing the growth effects, permitting the country to take full advantage of the opportunities brought about by trade opening. A parallel argument could be made based on concerns that greater trade openness will increase the risk that workers face. Although little evidence has emerged to suggest that this is true, were it the case, income support programs could mitigate the impact on poverty and the disincentive effects on human capital accumulation.

Another question explored in the chapter is whether differences in sectoral growth affect the impact that growth has on poverty reduction. We concluded that the composition of growth does matter for poverty reduction, and we stressed that policies that induce a sectoral bias in growth may conflict in the long run with pursuit of a country's natural comparative advantage, leading to growth-impeding inefficiencies. That is, policy makers aiming at biasing growth toward sectors with a high growth elasticity of poverty may have to face a trade-off between a high growth elasticity of poverty and higher growth.

Another matter is to make sure that policy biases and inefficiencies against, for example, rural development are lifted and that growth opportunities are enhanced by the efficient provision of public goods and national and sectoral "innovation" policies. Incomes of the poor, including those from agriculture and off-farm activities, thrive with higher trade openness, when rural expenditures focus on the provision of public goods (rural roads, health and education, research and development, extension services), and when policy biases against labor mobility (fiscal generosity for capital-intensive activities, stiff labor markets) are removed.

Finally, the chapter explored the extent to which policies aimed at reducing poverty through market incomes must be complemented with taxes and transfers. It concluded that achieving a more redistributive and efficient pattern of public expenditures along OECD patterns would significantly reduce poverty and inequality. Given the centrality of growth to the goal of poverty reduction, however, policy makers may wish to ensure that efforts on that front have impacts favorable to growth. That would imply dealing first with some of the shortcomings in public spending, including the regressive nature of some big-ticket items such as tertiary education, subsidies to electricity, and pensions. It is worth stressing once more that the highest level of targeting toward the poor comes from social assistance programs, especially conditional cash transfer programs, which in addition to ranking among the most progressive in Latin America, combine a transfer with the condition of engaging in the accrual of human capital. Finally, on the tax front, first items in the agenda would be strengthening anti-tax evasion programs and addressing the existing high level of exemptions.

Annex 5A

Simulating the impact of pro-growth policies on poverty

The empirical models used to asses the impact of pro-growth policies on poverty take the following form: $y_{it} - y_{it-1} = \delta y_{it-1} + \omega' x_{it} + \nu_i + \tau_t + \upsilon_{it}$, and $g_{it} - g_{it-1} = \alpha g_{it-1} + \beta' x_{it} + \mu_i + \eta_t + \varepsilon_{it}$, where y is the log of per capita income, g is the log of the Gini coefficient, x represents the set of explanatory variables other than the lagged measure of income or inequality, ν and μ are unobserved country-specific effects, τ and η are time-specific effects, and υ and ε are the error terms. The subscripts i and t represent country and time period.

Beyond expressing the impact that the coefficients of the different policies may have on growth and inequality, these models can be employed to obtain estimates of how poverty changes would be associated with a change of x in policy j. The presence of dynamics allows us to differentiate between the immediate impact that a change in a given policy has on both income and inequality and the long-run impact that results from the dynamic feedback. For example, changes to policy j will lead in the short run to:

$$(5A.1) \qquad \frac{dp}{dx_j} = \omega_j \times \gamma + \beta_j \times \phi,$$

where p is the log of the poverty measure.[8] In the long run these changes will lead to:[9]

$$(5A.2) \qquad \frac{dp_{LR}}{dx_j} = -\frac{\omega_j}{\delta} \times \gamma - \frac{\beta_j}{\alpha} \times \phi.$$

Clearly, if the dynamics in the original models are similar (that is, if δ is similar to α), then equation 5A.1 reduces to 5A.2 scaled up to $\delta = \alpha$. But if one of the variables adjusts much faster than the other, one should also expect to find dynamics in poverty. In 5A.1 and 5A.2, γ and ϕ are the growth and inequality elasticities of poverty that can be obtained from assuming that income follows a lognormal distribution.

Notes

1. There are several mechanisms through which the development of credit markets might affect child labor. At the household level, credit constraints can prevent households from optimally trading off a child's contribution to current household income against future returns from her schooling. In particular, households may resort to child labor to smooth transitory income shocks. Credit markets also potentially affect the demand for child labor through their impact on firms' development.

2. From an accounting point of view, it is likely that growth in bigger sectors of economic activity has a larger impact on poverty reduction than growth in smaller sectors. Intuitively, if a sector accounts for a small share of economic activity, then it is likely that few people (both poor and nonpoor) benefit from growth in that sector and that the sector thus contributes only slightly to poverty reduction.

3. http://www.econ.cam.ac.uk/dae/mu/emodstats/index.htm

4. Excluding the social security contributions does not change much the results.

5. As noted in the text, the Gini coefficient of disposable income for the EU15 is 0.33 (about 20 percentage points lower than that of Latin America). In contrast, the Gini coefficient of market incomes is 0.47 (about 10 percentage points lower than that in Latin America when we assume that the Gini of market income inequality is cut by 4 percentage points through taxes and transfers). Thus overall, of the 20-percentage-point difference in the Ginis of disposable income, 10 percentage points are attributable to higher market income inequality and the rest to the role of the government interventions. Clearly, estimates of market income Gini coefficients that are less than 4 percentage points above disposable income Ginis for Latin America would imply an even higher relevance of taxes and transfers. For example, if, for the region as a whole, taxes and transfer lowered the Gini only 1.3 percentage points (the average for the countries in figure 9), then taxes and transfers would account for about two-thirds of the differences in disposable income inequality levels between Europe and Latin America.

6. Although the deviation from the predicted value is smaller in the case of the property tax, the volume of the property tax tends to be much smaller than the volume of the goods and services tax.

7. The evidence in Lindert, Skoufias, and Shapiro (2005) indicates that the richest quintiles of the population tend to receive a higher share of total social insurance spending, whereas in general the poorest quintiles receive a higher share of social assistance.

8. Strictly speaking, one should also consider an error term emerging from using a discrete approximation to an infinitesimal interval.

9. This assumes that $\delta \neq 0$ and $\alpha \neq 0$. If the parameter controlling the dynamics is 0, all the adjustment would take place immediately.

CHAPTER 6

Does Poverty Matter for Growth?

There is ample evidence that growth reduces poverty. This justifies having a pro-growth package at the heart of any poverty reduction strategy. However, is it also the case that poverty reduction is good for growth? Is there a possibility of entering a virtuous circle by which growth lowers poverty and in turn lower poverty results in faster growth?

THE PREVIOUS CHAPTERS HAVE EXPLORED the link between growth and poverty by focusing on the poverty-reducing effect of growth and the factors that shape it. It was argued that in poorer and more equal countries, development strategies aimed at poverty reduction should emphasize growth. As countries become richer or more unequal, however, policy makers should try to balance growth and distribution concerns because in those circumstances poverty may be much more sensitive to changes in relative incomes than to changes in mean income.[1] We also addressed whether the pattern of growth associated with specific policies and sectors is more pro-poor in some circumstances than in others. We concluded that even though over long-run horizons most pro-growth policies will also be pro-poor (in the sense that the poor receive some benefit from the particular policy), in principle one can expect that growth will have differing effects on poverty in the short run depending on the policies with which it is associated.

A debate on the pro-poorness of a particular pattern of growth can be very appealing from an intellectual viewpoint but of little practical relevance if there is no growth—of any type—to start with or if growth is too low to make a dent in poverty. This in fact may be the root problem because as some development practitioners argue, existing global poverty levels are probably more related to the insufficient growth experienced by developing countries over the past decades than to particularly anomalous patterns of growth. Today the annual median per capita income in developing countries is $3,000, a figure that indicates only modest progress since 1975, when the median income level was about $2,500. Over this same time period, median per capita income in developed countries increased from about $15,000 to more than $25,000.

Against this background and given that the achievement of growth—any type of growth—is a big challenge in itself, should a discussion on growth and poverty reduction, or pro-poor growth, focus first on how to achieve growth and only then consider how to ensure that its pattern is pro-poor? This chapter argues that, on the contrary, the disappointing growth performance of developing countries makes the growth-poverty link even more critical. Not only does low growth mean that even small deteriorations in income inequality may lead to higher poverty (see Cord, Lopez, and Page 2005 for a discussion). It also means that poverty per se may be a barrier to growth, as suggested by several theoretical models developed in the economics

---

This chapter relies heavily on the background paper "Too Poor to Grow," prepared for this report by H. Lopez and L. Servén (2005b).

literature. In other words, countries do not grow fast because they are too poor to grow. This direction of causality from poverty to growth in turn opens the door to the existence of poverty traps, in which poverty and growth interact in a vicious circle where high poverty leads to low growth and low growth in turns leads to high poverty.

The theoretical appeal of poverty-traps models is clear: these models explain a number of stylized facts on the growth-poverty link (such as the disappointing growth performance of developing countries relative to the developed world or the existence of convergence clubs[2]) for which the traditional neoclassical growth model is inappropriate. Beyond the theoretical appeal, however, several aspects related to the poverty-traps view of the development process are likely to have important policy implications. First, at a strategic level, the existence of poverty traps should mitigate the debate on whether development strategies should rely more on pro-growth or pro-poor policies, because strategies that do not take into account the bidirectional relation between poverty and growth will likely lead to disappointing results: poverty will not decline without growth, but growth will be difficult unless the constraints affecting the poor are also addressed. Second, if a country is trapped in a bad equilibrium, then market policies may not be enough to break the vicious circle between poverty and growth, and policies that change the state of development may be needed. In this regard, country-specific analytical work that blends growth and poverty analyses into a single entity and tries to uncover the potential complex set of interactions operating in a given country would be a first step toward determining exactly which policies are needed to break the poverty trap. Third, at a more operational level, one implication of the potential existence of poverty traps is that the biggest payoff to growth (and hence to poverty reduction) would likely result from policies that not only promote growth but also exert an independent, direct impact on poverty—thereby reducing the drag of poverty on growth.

This chapter elaborates on these issues. It motivates the discussion by briefly reviewing arguments put forward in the literature suggesting how poverty can become self-reinforcing and potentially lead to multiple equilibriums. The chapter then examines the empirical evidence on the dynamics of per capita income. First, it reviews the recent growth experience in the developed and developing worlds, concluding that the developing world has underperformed systematically relative to the developed countries. In fact, the evidence presented here suggests a bimodal income distribution, with countries showing a tendency to cluster around either a high-level efficient equilibrium or a low-level inefficient equilibrium. This clustering is consistent with one of the predictions of poverty-traps models.

Of particular interest here are the findings for the cross-country distribution of incomes in the Latin American region. In contrast to the global data, this distribution appears to be roughly unimodal, implying that most Latin American countries belong to the same convergence club and thus share the same dynamics of the development process in the region. When we also ask to which country cluster the region belongs—the rich or the poor—the results are mixed. On the one hand, it is difficult to argue that the region is stuck in the low, inefficient equilibrium (although admittedly some weak evidence suggests that a few countries in the region—namely, Bolivia, Honduras, and Nicaragua—could be trapped in the poor-countries club).[3] On the other hand, the region does not seem to belong to the rich-countries club either. On the whole, the region would be better described as in an intermediate state somewhere between the very poor and the very rich.

Finally, the chapter presents new empirical evidence suggesting that poverty deters investment and growth, especially where the degree of financial development is limited. This result appears consistent with stylized theoretical models in which financial market imperfections prevent the poor from taking advantage of their investment opportunities, and it suggests a particular mechanism through which poverty affects growth. Admittedly, this mechanism is not necessarily exclusive; moreover, there are other channels, such as education, health, and innovation, through which high poverty can potentially feed back into lower growth rates. In any case, we emphasize here that this chapter, and more generally this report, does not aim at setting the debate on the existence of poverty traps (defined as the existence of multiple steady states); admittedly the empirical evidence on this question is mixed at best. Instead, its main concern is whether the empirical evidence supports a weaker version of the predictions derived from poverty-traps models, namely, that poverty tends to hold back growth.

A poverty-traps view of the development process

The past few years have witnessed the emergence of a booming theoretical literature aimed at explaining why poverty may be self-reinforcing and therefore why countries that start out being poor continue to be persistently

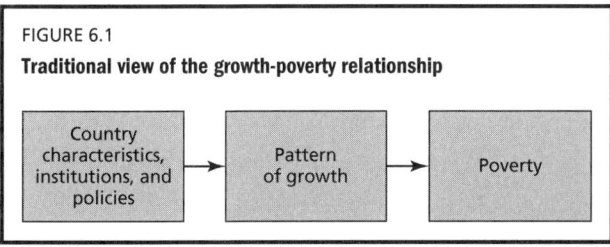

FIGURE 6.1
Traditional view of the growth-poverty relationship

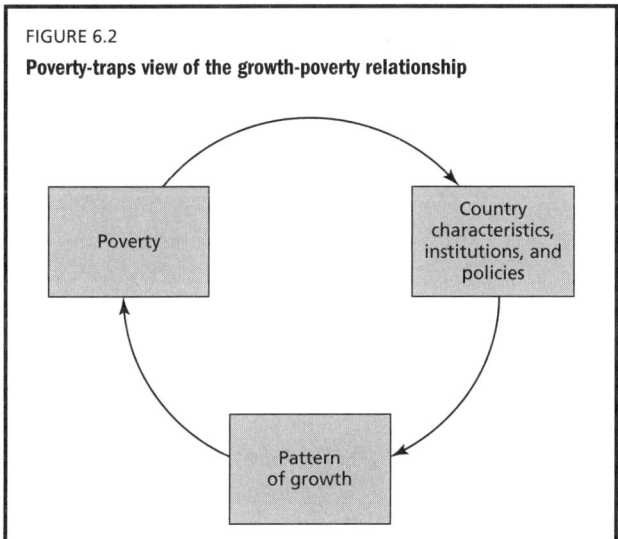

FIGURE 6.2
Poverty-traps view of the growth-poverty relationship

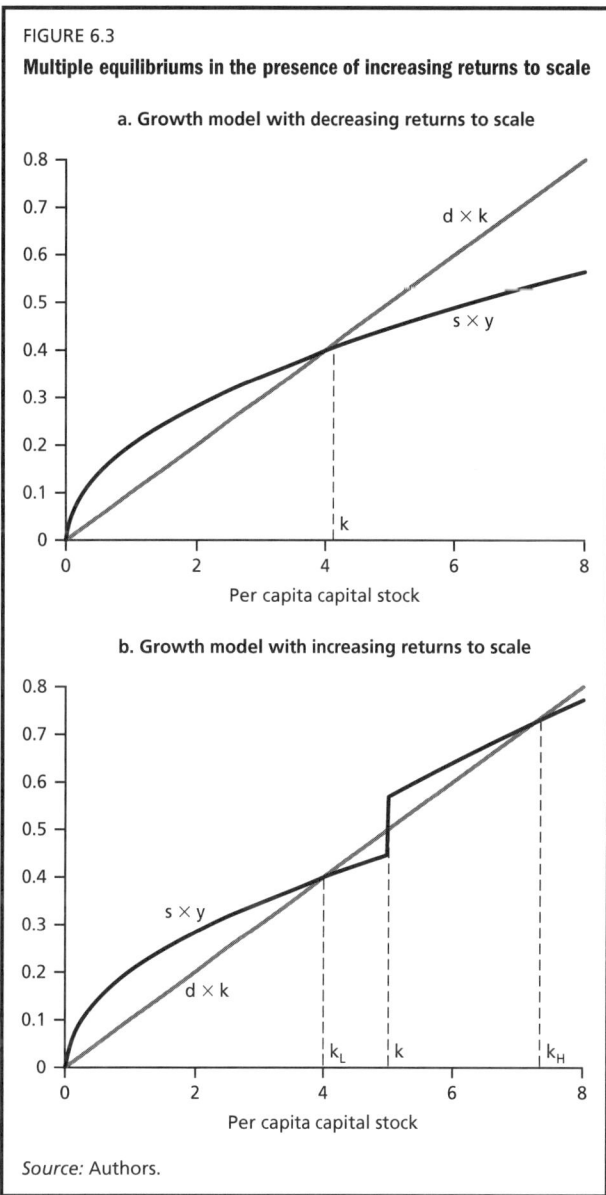

FIGURE 6.3
Multiple equilibriums in the presence of increasing returns to scale

Source: Authors.

poor over the long run (see Azariadis and Stachurski 2005 for a survey). In the traditional view of development (presented schematically in figure 6.1), country constraints (institutions, policies, internal and external shocks, and the like) are considered to be largely exogenous (that is, they are not determined within the system). In contrast, the poverty-traps literature stresses the possibility that poverty has feedback effects on growth, a dynamic that has the potential to create poverty traps and that results in a very different picture of the development process (figure 6.2).

One critical difference between the two development views is that in the poverty-traps view, different equilibriums may exist that are stable and self-reinforcing so that the initially poor may stay poor and the initially rich stay rich. Figure 6.3 illustrates this point, comparing the results of the standard neoclassical growth model with decreasing returns to scale (panel A) with a model that exhibits increasing returns to scale (panel B). In the case of the standard neoclassical growth model, the equilibrium is uniquely determined by the intersection of per capita savings and investment ($s \times y$) with the rate of depreciation of the per capita capital stock ($d \times k$). If, however, the production function experiences a technological jump (discussed in more detail later), there would be two steady states, and countries would tend toward one or the other equilibrium depending on their initial position. The lower equilibrium could be thought of as a poverty trap. Countries with capital below k_L would initially grow and converge toward the steady-state k_L. Countries between k_H and k would converge toward k_H. Thus initially poor countries would converge toward the low, inefficient equilibrium whereas initially rich countries would tend toward the high, efficient equilibrium, producing a bimodal cross-country distribution of income.

In these circumstances policies aimed at eliminating market distortions that prevent the economy from moving toward its equilibrium may be highly effective at achieving their objective. The problem is that the economy may be headed toward an inefficient equilibrium. Thus poverty-traps models have the ability to explain both why poor economies may have a tendency to underperform richer economies and why the benefits of good policies fail to materialize. What are the mechanisms that lead to this type of feedback from poverty to growth? Several channels, typically in the form of departures from the basic neoclassical model, have been explored in the literature.[4] We briefly discuss three of those channels here.

Increasing returns to scale and poverty traps

As suggested earlier, one mechanism that may potentially lead to poverty traps is the existence of increasing returns to scale (this is the issue illustrated in panel B of figure 6.3). Increasing returns may appear when the adoption of newer and more efficient technologies has an associated fixed cost. For example, Murphy, Shleifer, and Vishny (1989) argue that even if modern technologies are freely available to poor countries, when the size of the domestic market is small relative to the fixed costs required to adopt the new, more efficient technology, firms may not have the right incentive to do so. As a result, initially richer economies may enter a virtuous circle, whereas initially poorer economies may end up stuck with less-efficient technologies and lower income levels. Increasing returns may also appear in the presence of complementary production processes that act as an incentive for firms to match workers of similar skills, in which case the incentive to educate increases as the initial pool of skilled workers increases (Kremer 1993).

Market failures and poverty traps

A second mechanism that may generate poverty traps is related to the existence of potential market imperfections in credit and insurance markets. With perfect capital markets, investment decisions in physical or human capital depend on the expected returns (probably adjusted by risk) of the investment and on the associated cost. When the returns are higher than the cost of capital, an individual would have the same incentive to invest regardless of his or her initial income level: theoretically, poor people could always borrow the capital they need to make the investment and then repay the loan out of the returns of the investment.

However, in real life—and especially in developing countries—capital and financial markets are plagued with imperfections. In many economies large segments of the population may not have access to credit at all. In some cases, access to credit is denied because the poor do not have the necessary collateral. In other cases, financial operators may find it difficult to enforce contracts, and an individual's access to credit will likely be constrained by his or her initial wealth; those with low or no initial wealth may be excluded from capital markets. Moreover, even those with access to credit may encounter significant constraints. Since deposit rates tend to be much lower than borrowing rates (figure 6.4), the opportunity cost of capital is lower for those who need to borrow less. For example, the average interest rate spread (lending minus deposit) for 2003 in the

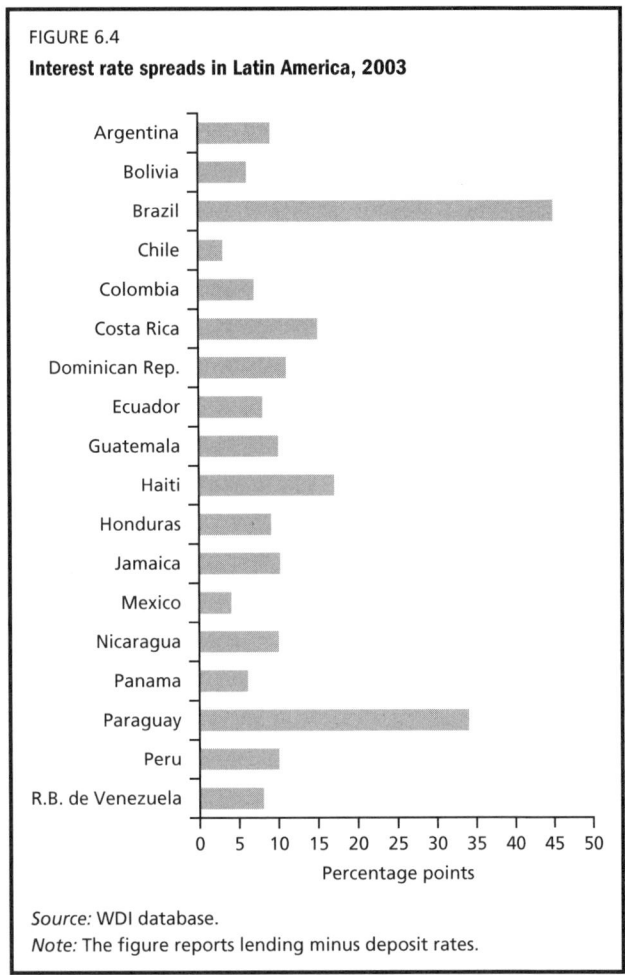

FIGURE 6.4
Interest rate spreads in Latin America, 2003

Source: WDI database.
Note: The figure reports lending minus deposit rates.

sample of Latin American countries included in figure 6.4 is about 10 percentage points, but in specific countries (Brazil and Paraguay), it is more than 30 points. Thus, if both a rich and a poor person face a similar rate of return on a project, it is likely that the rich person will invest much more than the poor person. In other words, the opportunities and costs of borrowing can be very different for rich and poor people and play against the latter group.

Imperfect capital markets coupled with fixed costs imply that important segments of the population are excluded from investment opportunities. For example, Banerjee and Newman (1994) stress the effect that an individual's initial wealth has on the level of physical investment when there are credit constraints. Thus high poverty rates might result in low investment rates and hence in lower growth.

Galor and Zeira (1993) make a similar argument. They note that people at the bottom of the income distribution may not be able to cover the expense of education or access the financial sector to borrow for that purpose. In this case high poverty rates result in low educational outcomes because poor individuals likely opt out of the education sector and work at unskilled, low-return labor. Note that this effect goes beyond the lower supply of education possibilities in poorer countries and focuses on the demand side. As argued in de Ferranti and others (2003), education levels are a vital complement for technological advance and are thus a critical element in understanding growth rates (box 6.1).

Institutional mechanisms and poverty traps

The theoretical literature also stresses the role played by the institutional framework in generating poverty traps. For example, Engerman and Sokoloff (forthcoming) argue that institutions that place economic opportunities beyond the reach of broad segments of society are likely to result in reduced growth rates because modern economies require broad participation in entrepreneurship and innovation. In addition, a natural tendency for those who hold power to try to perpetuate that power results in path dependence and persistence for the institutional framework. These two elements together help explain the tendency for poverty and bad institutional arrangements to coexist and persist over time.

Similarly, Mauro (2002) considers low economic growth in countries with persistent corruption and notes that some countries appear to be stuck in a bad equilibrium characterized by pervasive corruption with no sign of improvement. He argues that one reason why rooting out widespread corruption is so difficult may be that it just does not make sense for individuals to attempt to fight it, even if everybody would be better off if corruption were to be eliminated. For example, if corruption is widespread in an administration, civil servants might find it difficult to decline bribes in exchange for favors because their superiors may expect a portion of the bribe for themselves. In contrast, in bureaucracies that are generally honest, a real threat of punishment deters individual civil servants from behaving dishonestly. This is an example of a strategic complementarity, whereby if one agent does something it becomes more profitable for another agent to do the same thing. The tendency of corruption to persist, together with the negative impact of corruption on growth (Mauro 1995), would then explain why some countries may be caught in inefficient equilibriums.

BOX 6.1
Education and technology

Productivity differences between countries and between firms within countries are profoundly affected by differences in skills and technology. It is therefore no surprise that the East Asian tigers—Hong Kong (China), Republic of Korea, Singapore, and Taiwan (China)—which exhibit well-above-average rates of total factor productivity growth, also outperform Latin America on measures of technology and skills. The same is true for some of the successful natural resource–based economies. Within Latin America, the best-performing country, Chile, concurrently had positive increases in productivity, substantial skill upgrading, and increases in all indicators associated with technology transfer and innovation.

Source: de Ferranti and others 2003.

In summary, a variety of mechanisms that typically do not fit the assumptions underlying the neoclassical model may both cause poverty and perpetuate it over the long run. Moreover, many of these mechanisms may well interact with and reinforce each other. For example, corruption may exacerbate credit access problems if the public sector subsidizes or guarantees credit to some privileged groups in society at the expense of poorer segments of the population. Similarly, institutional frameworks with weak enforcement of the rule of law may discourage investment in sectors where intellectual property rights have a high value for the firm. That in turn can lower the demand for skilled workers and hence the incentives for individual workers to invest in skill acquisition. The next section reviews some existing empirical evidence on the practical relevance of these models.

Empirical evidence on poverty traps

Over the last decades, the world has become increasingly divided into two clubs—one of rich countries, the other of poor countries. Figure 6.5 plots median per capita growth rates for industrial and developing countries between 1963 and 2003.[5] It also plots median per capita growth rates for Latin America. The figure indicates that, apart from one short period in the second half of the 1970s and another in the early 2000s, the typical developing country has experienced lower growth rates than the typical rich country.

Over the 1963–2003 period, median per capita growth in industrial countries has outpaced median growth in developing countries by an average of more than 1 percent a year.[6] Moreover, there are two extended periods of time—the 1960s and early 1970s, and the mid- to late 1980s—where the differences are consistently in the range of 2 percent a year.

Latin America does not seem to be an exception among developing countries; the growth performance of the region over the 40-year period was fairly consistent with the performance observed in other developing countries. The differences between Latin America and all developing countries were notable for three periods: the early 1980s, when Latin America was badly hit by the debt crisis and recorded median growth rates below −1 percent; the early 1990s, when the region did much better than the rest of the developing countries; and the late 1990s, when once again Latin America experienced a significant deceleration following the financial crises in East Asia in 1997 and in Russia in 1998.

The underperformance of the developing world relative to the developed world appears even more dramatic when one looks at the evolution of median per capita income levels over time (figure 6.6). Because developing countries have been experiencing lower growth rates for prolonged periods of time, the gap between the per capita income levels of rich and poor countries has been steadily increasing. In the early 1960s, the income level of the median

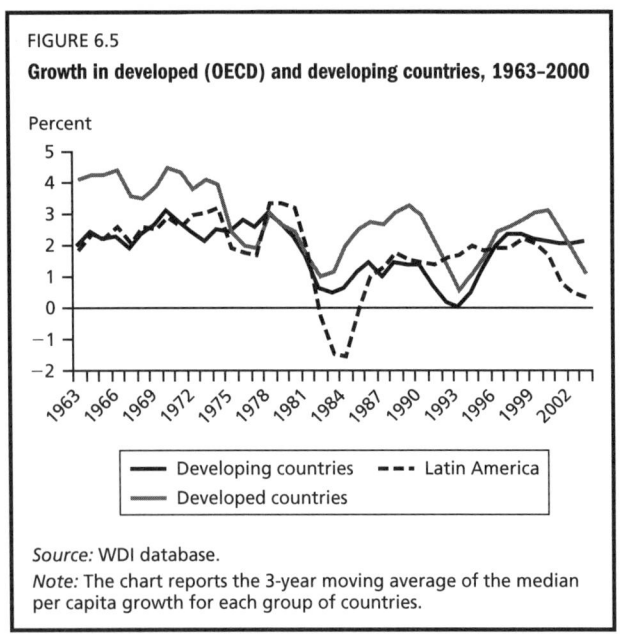

FIGURE 6.5
Growth in developed (OECD) and developing countries, 1963-2000

Source: WDI database.
Note: The chart reports the 3-year moving average of the median per capita growth for each group of countries.

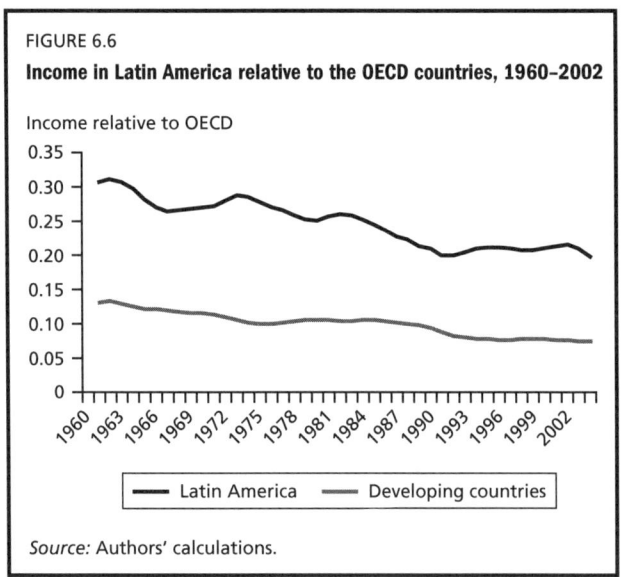

FIGURE 6.6
Income in Latin America relative to the OECD countries, 1960-2002

Source: Authors' calculations.

developed country was six times greater than the income level of the median developing country; today income in the median developed country is close to nine times greater (representing a 50 percent increase in the gap). More dramatically, in 1960 the income of the richest country at the time, Switzerland, was about 50 times the income of the poorest country, Malawi. Today, the richest country is Luxembourg, which has a per capita income level that in purchasing power parity is almost 120 times that of Sierra Leone, now the poorest country.

The use of the median as a summary statistic is somewhat limited because it does not show the significant heterogeneity that exists at the country level. Yet, even if we focus on the evolution of income on a country-by-country basis (table 6.1), the majority of the Latin American countries (the exception is the Dominican Republic) have income levels today that are lower than they were in 1960 relative to the income of OECD countries. Not only have the majority of Latin American countries lost ground over the past 25 years but in some cases the decline has been very significant. Take the case of Argentina, the richest country of the region in 1960 with a per capita income level that was close to the level of industrial countries (85 percent). Forty years later Argentina's relative income has declined to 43 percent of the industrial countries' level. Similarly, the relative per capita income of Nicaragua has declined from 49 percent in 1960 to about 12 percent in 2000. Today three countries in Latin America (Bolivia, Haiti, and Honduras) have PPP-adjusted per capita GDP levels that are less than 10 percent of the income of the developed countries. In 1960 no country in the region had a relative income level below 20 percent.

On the whole, this evidence is at odds with the convergence predictions of the simple neoclassical model and instead is more consistent with what World Bank economist Lant Pritchett (1997) refers to as "divergence big time": "Whichever way the debate about whether there has been some 'conditional' convergence in the recent period is settled, the fact remains that one overwhelming feature of the period of modern economic growth is massive

TABLE 6.1

Median income in Latin America and the Caribbean relative to the industrial countries

Country	1960	1970	1980	1990	1998	2003
Argentina	0.85	0.72	0.64	0.40	0.52	0.43
Bolivia	0.22	0.15	0.14	0.10	0.10	0.09
Brazil	0.30	0.28	0.38	0.29	0.29	0.27
Chile	0.37	0.30	0.26	0.26	0.36	0.36
Colombia	0.32	0.27	0.27	0.27	0.25	0.24
Costa Rica	0.46	0.37	0.38	0.29	0.32	0.34
Dominican Republic	0.21	0.18	0.22	0.19	0.22	0.24
Ecuador	0.22	0.16	0.19	0.16	0.14	0.13
El Salvador	0.38	0.32	0.24	0.17	0.18	0.17
Guatemala	0.26	0.22	0.23	0.16	0.15	0.15
Guyana	0.30	0.23	0.20	0.16	0.17	0.15
Haiti	0.31	0.18	0.18	0.11	0.07	0.06
Honduras	0.20	0.15	0.15	0.11	0.10	0.09
Jamaica	0.29	0.28	0.19	0.18	0.15	0.14
Mexico	0.42	0.39	0.44	0.34	0.33	0.32
Nicaragua	0.49	0.46	0.26	0.13	0.12	0.12
Panama	0.26	0.28	0.29	0.21	0.24	0.24
Paraguay	0.25	0.21	0.27	0.21	0.19	0.17
Peru	0.41	0.35	0.30	0.18	0.19	0.19
Trinidad and Tobago	0.49	0.46	0.53	0.32	0.32	0.38
Uruguay	0.62	0.43	0.43	0.33	0.37	0.29
Venezuela, R.B. de	0.69	0.54	0.38	0.26	0.25	0.17
Latin America	0.31	0.28	0.26	0.19	0.21	0.19

Source: Authors' calculations using GDP per capita ($2,000 PPP) from the *World Development Indicators* for various years. Data before 1975 has been computed using available per capita growth rates for the period 1960–75 and the per capita GDP level of 1975.

divergence of absolute and relative incomes across countries, a fact which must be grappled with in a fully satisfactory model of economic growth and development."

Convergence clubs

What explains this apparent divergence between developed and developing countries? Could it be attributable to the existence of multiple states of development toward which different countries converge, creating convergence clubs? If so, where is the Latin American region in this picture? Are there also regional convergence clubs that will result in regional clusters of development or, instead, can the region be viewed as a single entity? We now address these questions in turn.

Convergence clubs in absolute income levels

The first question concerns the dynamics of cross-national per capita income levels and the existence of convergence clubs. Panel a of figure 6.7 presents the histograms of per capita income for 1960 and 1999 computed for 102 countries using data from the Penn World Table (PWT6.1). The histograms suggest that whereas in the early 1960s the distribution of income appeared to be unimodal in the early 1960s, by the late 1990s it had become trimodal,

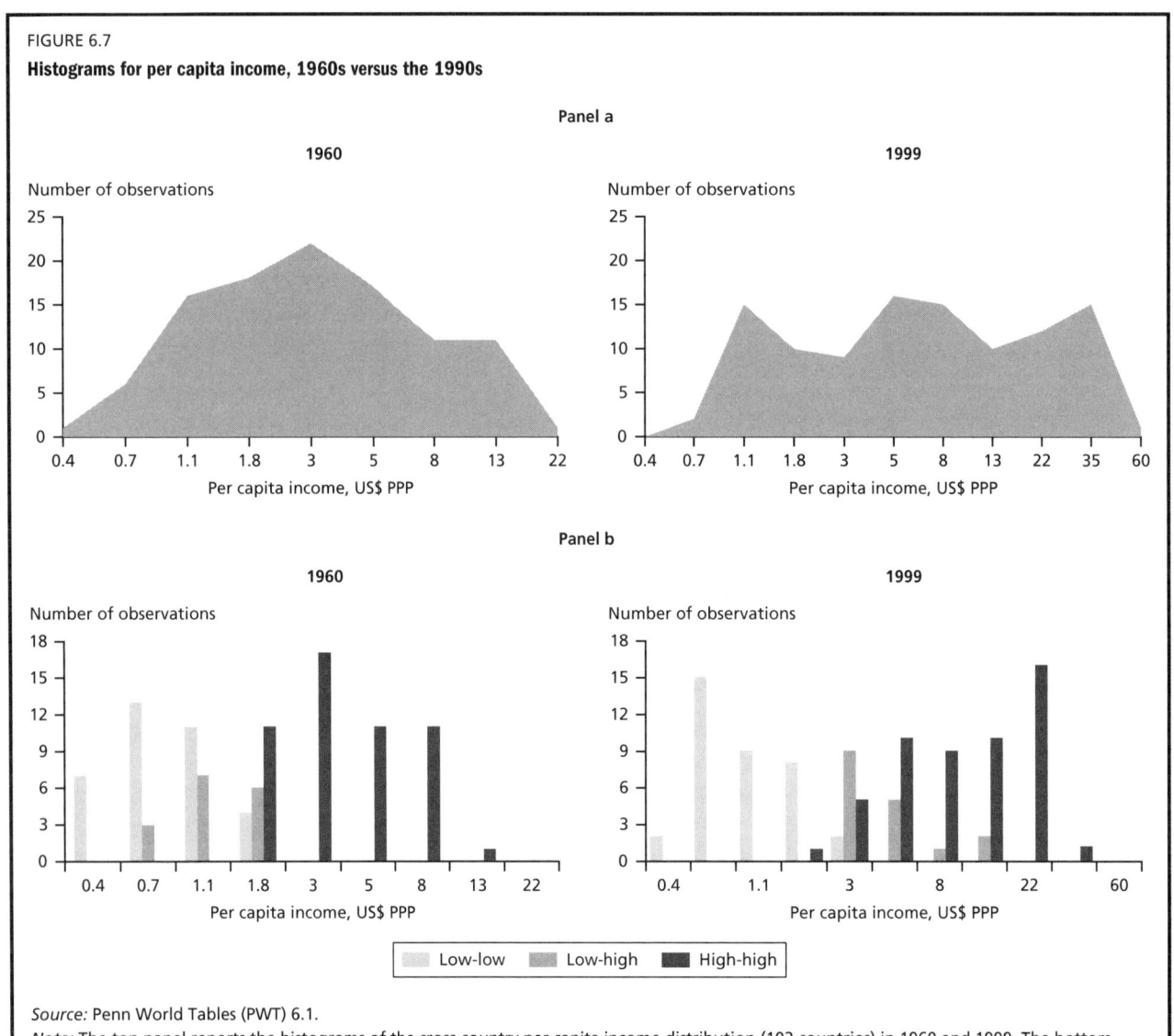

FIGURE 6.7
Histograms for per capita income, 1960s versus the 1990s

Source: Penn World Tables (PWT) 6.1.
Note: The top panel reports the histograms of the cross country per capita income distribution (102 countries) in 1960 and 1999. The bottom panel presents the transitions of three groups of countries: low-low shows countries that in both 1960 and 1999 had per capita income levels below $3,400; high-high shows countries that in both 1960 and in 1999 had per capita income levels above $3,400; low-high shows countries that in 1960 were below $3,400 and in 1999 were above $3,400.

with a low peak at $1,100; a second peak between $5,000 and $8,000, and a third peak around $35,000.[7]

In panel b we attempt to discriminate between convergence clubs and present the histograms for three groups of countries. Here we follow an approach similar to the one used by Mayer-Foulkes (2003) in his study of convergence clubs in life expectancy and divide the sample into four groups. The first group includes those countries whose per capita income levels were below $3,400 in both 1960 and 1999. This is the per capita income level of the poorest industrial country in 1960 (Portugal) and is very close to the observed peak in 1960. We refer to that group as low-low. The second group includes countries with per capita income levels above $3,400 in both 1960 and 1999. This is the high-high group. The third group (low-high) comprises countries with per capita income levels below $3,400 in 1960 and above $3,400 in 1999. No country falls in the fourth group, which notionally corresponds to a high-low group, and the numbers of countries in each of the other three groups are quite balanced.

Panel b shows three markedly different behaviors. The initially rich countries present the highest per capita growth rates. The median income of the high-high club increased from about $7,500 in 1960 to about $22,000 in 1999 (table 6.2). The transition countries (the low-high group) also show considerable growth (from a median income of about $2,400 in 1960 to about $5,400 in 1999), but the average annual growth rate is lower than in the high-high group by almost 0.7 percentage point. Finally, the low-low group shows very low growth. The median income for the 37 countries in this group increased from about $1,050 in 1960 to just $1,300 in 1999, which implies an average annual increase of about half a percent.

Clearly, the peaks in the histogram for 1999 may not correspond to the equilibriums for the different groups, especially if the groups are in a transition toward a steady state. Where, then, is each of these groups heading? The annex to this chapter discusses a simple procedure that can be used to estimate the steady state for each group. Implementation of this procedure suggests convergence but to three dramatically different steady states. For the low-low group, the estimated equilibrium for per capita income is around $1,700. For the low-high group, the equilibrium is around $11,000, and for the high-high group, the point estimates suggest an equilibrium well above current levels.

How does the Latin American region fare in this context? Is the apparent bi- or trimodality of the world distribution also observed in the region, or do all the countries in the region belong to a single cluster? To answer these questions, figure 6.7 plots a histogram similar to the one in panel A of figure 6.6 but restricts the sample to Latin American countries. In contrast to the full sample, the estimated cross-country distributions of per capita income for Latin America appear to be unimodal for both the early 1960s and the late 1990s. The peak in 1960 is around $3,000, which is fully consistent with the global data. The peak in 1999 is around $8,000, which implies average annual growth in the 2.5 percent range, approximately halfway between the growth rates for the global high-high and low-high groups.

How do we interpret these results? Well, it depends on whether we see the glass as half full or half empty. As a half-full glass, it seems difficult to argue that the region is stuck in the low, inefficient equilibrium (the one corresponding to the equilibrium around $1,700). More likely, taking into account the initial starting point and the evolution of income levels over the 1960–99 period, the region is better characterized as belonging to the low-high transition group (for which the estimated equilibrium for income per capita is in the $11,000 range). As a half-empty glass, the region does not seem to belong to the high-high equilibrium either. On the whole, the region would be better described by an intermediate state somewhere in between the very poor and the very rich.

One issue needs to be highlighted before we continue, however. Careful observation of figure 6.8 indicates that the dispersion of regional income in 1999 is significantly higher than it was in 1960. This results from the relatively good performance of some of the economies that were richer to begin with (Chile, Mexico, and Uruguay) and the modest performance of some of the poorer economies (Bolivia, Honduras, and Nicaragua), which initially

TABLE 6.2
Median income of convergence clubs

Club	Countries	Median income 1960	Median income 1999	Annual increase (%)
Low-low	37	1,046	1,277	0.51
Low-high	33	2,395	5,442	2.13
High-high	32	7,417	21,632	2.78

Source: Authors' calculations.

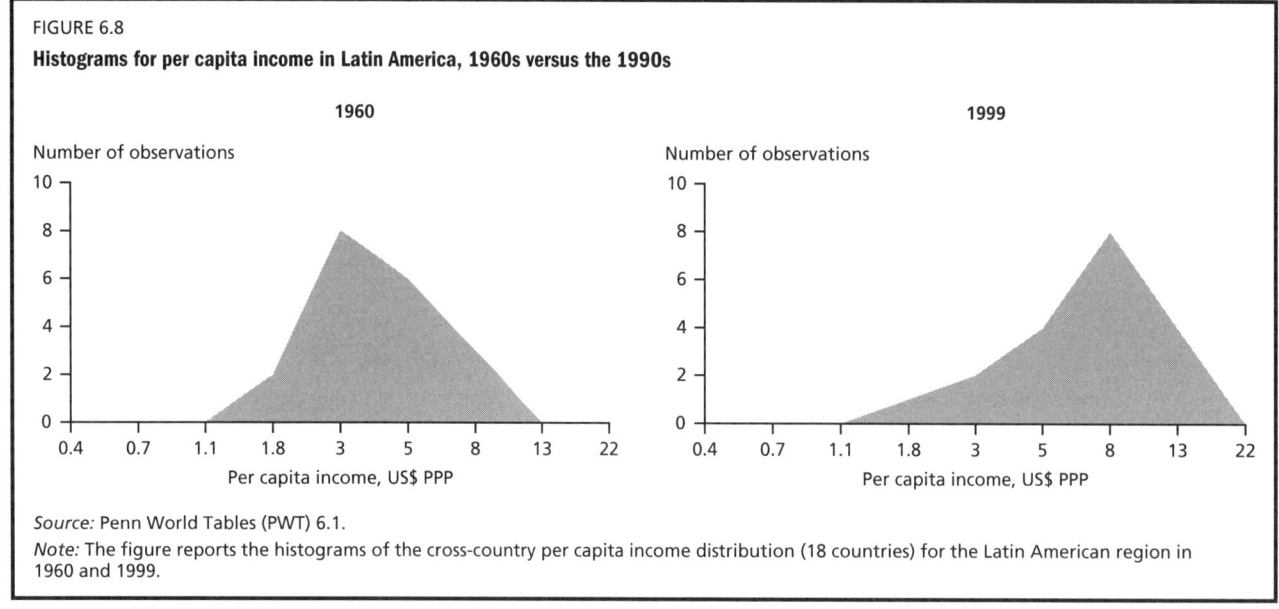

FIGURE 6.8
Histograms for per capita income in Latin America, 1960s versus the 1990s

Source: Penn World Tables (PWT) 6.1.
Note: The figure reports the histograms of the cross-country per capita income distribution (18 countries) for the Latin American region in 1960 and 1999.

experienced average annual growth rates below 0.5 percent (Nicaragua's average annual growth rate was in negative territory). At least three countries in the region appear to have a performance that is more consistent with that observed for the low-low group in figure 6.7, and these countries could potentially be trapped in the low equilibrium. In other words, behind figure 6.8 there could be a bimodal distribution, with a second steady state toward the lower end of the distribution that is not apparent because the associated probability mass is very low (that is, because only a few countries belong to that group).

Convergence clubs in relative incomes

An alternative way to look at the cross-national distribution of income is based on an analysis of relative income levels and on the probability that a country moves between states of development. In the technical annex to this chapter, we review some methodological details and present some empirical results that can be used to estimate equilibrium values for the distribution of income. Figure 6.9 reports results for five states of relative development. In state 1 are the poorest countries of the world: those with per capita income levels below 25 percent of average world per capita income. In state 2 is a group of richer but still relatively poor countries: those with per capita income levels between 25 and 50 percent of average world per capita income. State 3 includes economies that have income levels between 50 percent and the world average. States 4 and 5 cover the richest countries: those with per capita incomes

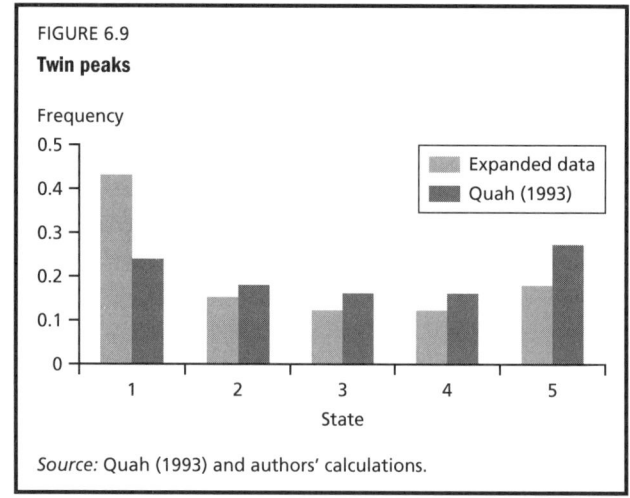

FIGURE 6.9
Twin peaks

Source: Quah (1993) and authors' calculations.

between the world average and twice the average, and those with incomes above twice the average, respectively.

Figure 6.9 plots the equilibrium as computed by Quah (1993) on the basis of data spanning 1962–84, and it also plots the equilibrium that results when the analysis is based on an expanded sample covering 1960–99. A number of interesting points are revealed in this figure. First, both samples suggest the presence of convergence clubs at either end of the income distribution: there is a cluster of poor countries around a low per capita income equilibrium and a second cluster around the high per capita income equilibrium (that is, the poor tend to stay poor and the rich tend to stay rich). However, while the 1962–84 sample results in a picture of the world that is divided almost

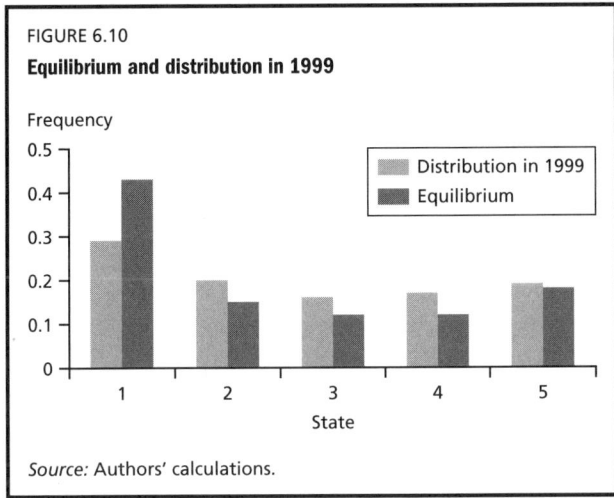

FIGURE 6.10
Equilibrium and distribution in 1999

Source: Authors' calculations.

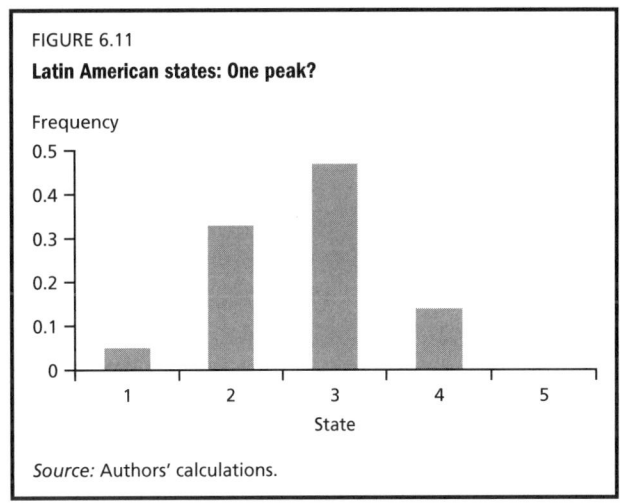

FIGURE 6.11
Latin American states: One peak?

Source: Authors' calculations.

symmetrically, the 1960–99 sample produces a distribution that is clearly skewed toward the lower equilibrium (that is, the cluster of poor countries has more members).

In other words, while evidence of some type of bimodality still exists, the expected long-run frequency of countries in the first state increases by almost 20 percentage points (from 0.24 to 0.43) by expanding the sample. This finding implies that the updated estimates predict more countries falling behind (at least relative to the world average). This is further explored in figure 6.10, which compares the distribution in 1999 to the estimated equilibrium. The figure suggests that unless there are changes in the transitional dynamics of the growth process, the number of countries in the first state can be expected to increase.

Unlike our previous analysis where the empirical evidence pointed toward a three-club characterization, this body of evidence is more consistent with the existence of two convergence clubs. One is composed of very poor countries, apparently with loose rules of admission; on the basis of the data to 1999, more than 40 percent of the countries belong to this club. The second club—the rich-countries club—is much more exclusive, and our estimates suggest that only about 20 percent of the countries belong to it. (The remaining 40 percent of the countries lie somewhere in between these two convergence clubs.)

The difference between having two or three clubs is key for Latin America, given our earlier conclusion that the region fell somewhere between the low and the high equilibrium. To explore this issue, we replicate the previous exercise but use data only for Latin America. The results suggest that there are important differences in the estimated long equilibrium (figure 6.11). As in figure 6.8, the obtained results for the region do not show evidence of bimodality. Instead, there seems to be a long-run equilibrium around state 3. The cross-country distribution of income, however, is not symmetrical, and long-run equilibrium computed on the basis of the estimated transition matrix places 80 percent of Latin American countries in states 2 and 3; these are countries whose relative income ranges from 25 percent of the world average to the world average.

These results are largely consistent with those of the previous analysis and show the region on an equilibrium that is well below the world average. The estimates also show a disturbing tendency for Latin American countries to cluster around the lower tail of the equilibrium. Here the only thing we can do is to speculate that a relatively small group of countries in the region do not belong to the state 3 equilibrium and instead converge around state 2.

Convergence clubs in other dimensions of poverty

So far we have focused on the cross-national distribution of per capita income. However, there is no reason to constrain the analysis to the income dimension of welfare. Convergence clubs may also involve specific health phenomena. For example, the theory of efficiency wages in Dasgupta and Ray (1986) implies the possibility of a low-productivity, low-nutrition trap. Mayer-Foulkes (2003) argues that the existence of convergence clubs is also apparent in life-expectancy dynamics. Figure 6.12 presents cross-national life-expectancy histograms for 1960 and 2002. These histograms indicate the presence of a two-peaked pattern in

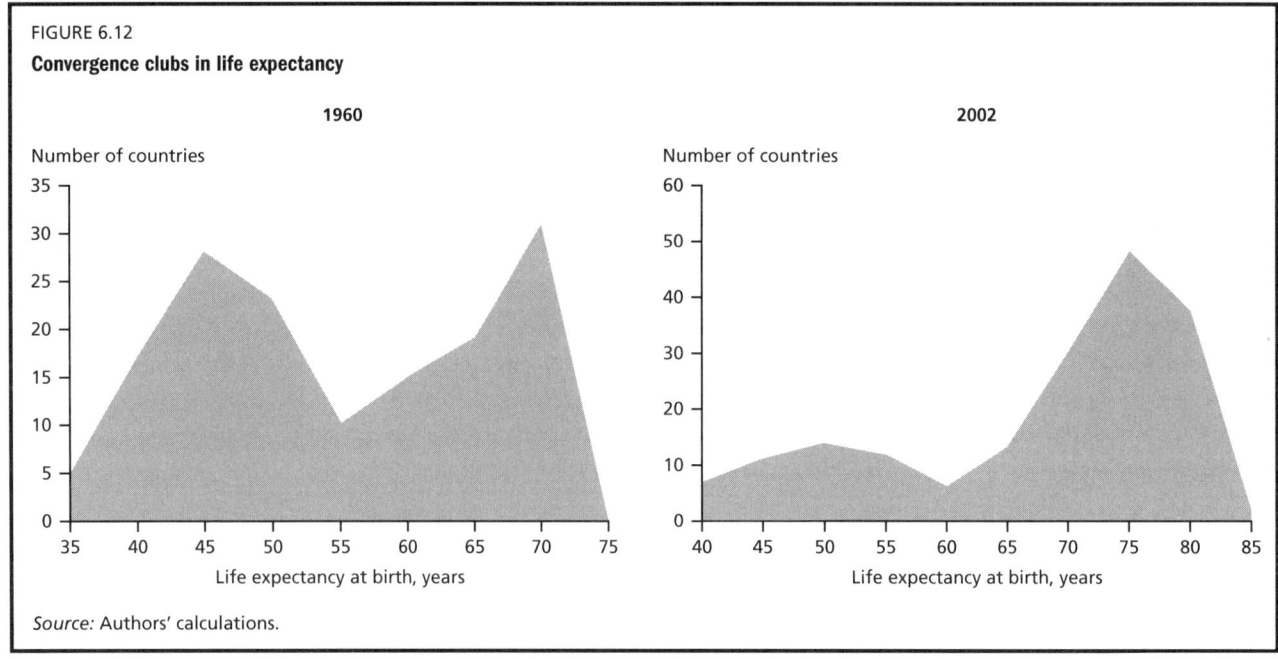

FIGURE 6.12
Convergence clubs in life expectancy

Source: Authors' calculations.

both periods. It is also evident that the mass of the low peak declines between 1960 and 2002, whereas the mass of the high peak increases. These figures are basically a replica of those in Mayer-Foulkes (2003) and indicate that the cross-country data on life expectancy are consistent with the presence of three convergence clubs (with a different number of members): one for the low equilibrium, one for the high equilibrium, and one for a third transitional group.

Formal tests of the poverty-traps hypothesis

The empirical evidence discussed here is supportive of a multimodal distribution in cross-national per capita income levels, which is consistent with the predictions of poverty-traps models. However, as Azariadis and Stachurski (2006) argue, one has to be extremely careful to avoid taking these empirical findings as evidence of poverty-traps phenomena. In fact, in a recent study, Bloom, Canning, and Sevilla (2003) stress that a multimodal distribution in cross-country income levels is also consistent with the existence of fundamental differences between countries that result in different but unique equilibriums for each country. Thus, in principle one has to be able to determine whether bimodality results from two "similar" countries having completely "different" states of development (that is, poverty traps) or from fundamental differences between the two countries.

With these ideas in mind, Bloom, Canning, and Sevilla (2003) move beyond the pure description of the cross-national income distribution and find that the existence of twin peaks in the data is more likely attributable to multiple equilibriums than to fundamental forces. This, in turn, supports the hypothesis that poverty traps with low and high equilibriums underlie the dynamics of per capita income.

An alternative way to determine the existence of poverty traps is to investigate specific sources of multiple equilibriums. One such approach is the calibration of models consistent with the poverty-trap hypothesis. Once a model has been calibrated, its empirical relevance can be assessed. For example, Graham and Temple (2004) calibrate a two-sector general equilibrium model and then explore the extent to which this model is able to explain the real data. The model considers a traditional agricultural sector with diminishing returns and a nonagricultural sector with increasing returns (in the vein of our earlier discussion about poverty traps in the presence of increasing returns to scale). As it turns out, the degree of increasing returns is one of the key parameters underlying the simulations, and depending on its assumed value, the model can explain between 15 and 60 percent of the variance of incomes. The Graham and Temple analysis has the same limitations in the Latin American context, however. In particular, as the authors recognize, the model appears to explain the existing income differences between the low- and middle-income countries better than it explains the differences between middle-income and developed countries. Thus while the results they obtain offer some ideas of why African countries are so poor, they have much less to say about the current positions of Latin America relative to the industrial countries.

Kraay and Raddatz (2005) also calibrate simple aggregate models capable of generating poverty traps through low savings or low technology at low levels of development.[8] The basic idea behind these models is that if either the saving rate or productivity increases above a certain threshold of development, it would then be possible to find poverty-trap-like features in the data. To assess the empirical relevance of these models, Kraay and Raddatz explore whether saving rates exhibit the sort of nonlinear relationship implied by the model for the existence of poverty traps, and whether scale effects on productivity are of a magnitude consistent with the theoretical model. Unlike Graham and Temple's findings, their results do not lend much support to the existence of poverty traps based on these mechanisms. In particular, their technology-based model suggests that for a poverty trap to exist, the estimated returns to scale would have to be in the 1.4 to 2.5 range. This interval is much higher than is typically found in the literature, where most studies report constant to moderate increasing returns.

Another strand of the empirical poverty-traps literature has explored the existence of nonconvexities by exploiting existing microeconometric evidence. For example, McKenzie and Woodruff (2004) examine the empirical relevance of the assumptions that minimum start-up costs are high relative to wealth and that returns to capital are low at low investment levels (see Banerjee and Newman 1993). Using microenterprise data for Mexico, McKenzie and Woodruff show that the median investment levels of new firms in some sectors are very low (about US$100, or less than half of the monthly earnings of even a low-wage worker). They also show that the marginal return to capital is quite high even for low levels of invested capital (in the $200 range), concluding that the Mexican evidence does not support this particular mechanism as a candidate to justify the existence of poverty traps.

Similarly, Lokshin and Ravallion (2004) test for the existence of a threshold effect in household incomes using data for Russia and Hungary. They find no evidence to support the poverty-traps hypothesis (although they do find that the adjustment of income to shocks is nonlinear). Their results indicate that households tend to bounce back from transient shocks, although the adjustment process is slower for poorer individuals. Jalan and Ravallion (2002) use household panel data from China, however, and find that aggregate physical and human capital endowments play a significant role in household consumption growth, a finding that they argue is consistent with the existence of regional poverty traps.

On the whole, it must be acknowledged that the empirical evidence on the existence of poverty traps is, at best, mixed. How then do we explain the existence of convergence clubs alongside the relative lack of evidence on the existence of poverty traps? One possibility is that poverty traps do exist and that the econometric models used to test such hypotheses are unable to capture the dynamics behind the data. An alternative possibility is that poverty traps do not exist in the strict theoretical sense (multiple equilibriums created, for example, by increasing returns to scale or any other mechanism), but that poverty is still a barrier to growth by which poorer countries find it more difficult to grow than richer countries. In this regard, Azariadis and Stachurski (2006) use a much more general definition and classify any self-reinforcing mechanism that causes poverty to persist as a poverty trap. Note that with this alternative definition in mind, the important question is not whether the development process is characterized by the existence of multiple equilibriums but rather how persistent and self-reinforcing the mechanisms are that lock in poverty over time frames that matter from a policy perspective. But is there any empirical evidence suggesting that poverty may represent a barrier to growth? The next sections explore this issue.

What is the empirical evidence on poverty's impact on growth?

The past few years have witnessed a renewed interest in both the theoretical and the empirical relationship between inequality and growth. At the theoretical level, two main types of arguments have been put forward: sociopolitical economy arguments and credit constraint–factor accumulation arguments.

The sociopolitical economy arguments stress the role that high inequality may play in the decisions of various agents and how these decisions may influence growth. For example, Alesina and Rodrik (1994) suggest that high inequality may lead to lower growth if the level of taxation has a negative impact on capital accumulation, if taxes are proportional to income but the benefits of public expenditure accrue equally to all individuals (implying that an individual's preferred levels of taxation and expenditure are inversely related to her income), and if the tax rate selected by the government is the one preferred by the median voter. Similarly, Alesina and Perotti (1996) argue that highly unequal societies create incentives for individuals to engage in activities, such as crime, that are outside normal markets and that sociopolitical instability discourages accumulation because of current disruptions and future uncertainty. In both cases, high levels of inequality may lead to lower future growth.

The credit constraint–factor accumulation argument emphasizes the possibility that some individuals will be excluded from the economic process because they have neither the resources nor the means to borrow them to engage in potentially profitable economic activities. For example, as discussed earlier, Galor and Zeira (1993) argue that the process of development is characterized by complementarity between physical and human capital so that growth increases as investment in human capital increases. However, credit constraints may prevent poorer individuals from investing in education and thus affect growth prospects by reducing the number of individuals who are able to invest in human capital. Similarly Aghion, Caroli, and García-Peñalosa (1999) show that if there are decreasing returns to individual capital investments and if credit imperfections mean that individual investments are an increased function of initial endowments, then the concentration of investment in fewer richer people will negatively affect growth.

Admittedly for a given level of income, higher inequality will lead to higher poverty. But note that the credit constraint–factor accumulation argument is more a poverty argument than an inequality argument. Yet, to the best of our knowledge, the hypothesis that countries suffering from higher levels of poverty grow less rapidly than those countries with less poverty has remained untested. To fill that gap, in a background paper for this report, Lopez and Servén (2005b) make a first attempt to provide a direct empirical assessment of the impact of poverty on growth (see the technical appendix).

The main results of that work are the following:

- Poverty has a consistently negative impact on growth that is significant both statistically and economically.
- This negative growth effect seems to work through investment in the sense that high poverty deters investment, which in turn lowers growth.
- The data suggest that this mechanism operates only at low levels of financial development, consistent with the predictions of theoretical models that underscore financial market imperfections as a key mechanism of poverty traps.

We now review each of these findings in some detail.

Poverty is bad for growth

Lopez and Servén (2005b) begin with the observation that if poverty hampers growth, then countries with higher initial poverty should grow less rapidly than comparable countries with lower initial poverty, all else being equal. This hypothesis is a weaker version of the predictions derived from the analytical models on poverty traps, in that to support it one does not need to find evidence of multiple equilibriums but simply empirical proof that poverty tends to hold back growth. Using a standard growth model augmented to include a suitable poverty measure among the explanatory variables, the authors find that after controlling for other factors, poverty has a negative and strongly significant impact on growth, which is also economically significant. On average, a 10 percent increase in poverty reduces annual growth by 1 percentage point. This finding is robust to a number of basic departures from the basic specification in Lopez and Servén (2005b),[9] including:

- *The use of alternative poverty lines.* The estimated impact on growth of a change in headcount poverty is very similar regardless of the poverty line ($2, $3, or $4 a day) used in the computation of the poverty index. Changes to the poverty line have an impact on the estimated coefficient of poverty of around 0.01.
- *The use of different sets of control variables.* Changing controls seems to have only a moderate effect on the estimated negative impact of poverty on growth. Depending on the control set used, a 10 percent increase in headcount poverty reduces growth prospects by between 0.7 and 1.3 percent.

- *The use of different poverty measures (headcount, poverty gap, squared poverty gap).* Changing the definition of poverty does affect the estimated coefficients of poverty, which are not comparable across definitions. However, the coefficients continue to be negative and statistically significant; in absolute value, the coefficients of the poverty gap and square poverty gap tend to be larger than the coefficient corresponding to the headcount definition.
- *The use of alternative estimation methods.* One of the problems dealing with highly persistent endogenous data is that the standard GMM estimation method based on internal instruments may not fully eliminate the potential reverse causality bias. To control for this problem, Lopez and Servén (2005b) also present results based on cross-sections that should not suffer from reverse causality (although admittedly they may suffer from fixed-effects bias). The results also confirm the negative impact of poverty on growth.
- *Adding inequality to the regression models.* When inequality is added to the empirical models, the sign, significance, and magnitude of the poverty effect decline somewhat in absolute value, and the estimate is less accurate. It remains highly significant, however, suggesting that the poverty variable does capture a true poverty effect rather than an inequality effect. This result is also robust to adding inequality and squared inequality to control for the likely nonlinear relation between poverty and inequality.

In principle, the finding that poverty lowers growth does not necessarily rule out the convergence of cross-national incomes (conditional convergence in this case) predicted by the neoclassical model, but the empirical estimates in Lopez and Servén (2005b) do imply the existence of a threshold poverty level beyond which divergence would occur. For example, with the baseline estimates in Lopez and Servén, there would be divergence for levels of the poverty headcount (with a $2-per-day poverty line) above 10 percent.

BOX 6.2

Is Latin America different?

Although the Lopez and Servén (2005b) results do not explicitly consider whether the impact of poverty on growth varies by geographic region, extending the model to test this possibility is relatively simple. In fact, we have reestimated their basic models to allow Latin American poverty levels to have an impact on growth that is different from the average for the group (that is, we are allowing the Latin American region to be "different"). The table below reports the results of this exercise.

This table suggests that Latin America may indeed be different. In particular, the estimates of the coefficients for Latin America are always negative and significant (in other words, poverty would reduce growth more in Latin America than in the typical country of the world). The magnitude of the Latin American dummy declines significantly in absolute value as the poverty line used in the computation of headcount poverty increases, from −0.23 under a $2-a-day poverty line to about −0.10 under a $4-a-day poverty line (although admittedly the standard error in the former case is also much larger than in the latter).

Poverty and growth: Is Latin America different?

	Poverty line					
	$2 a day		$3 a day		$4 a day	
	All	LAC dummy	All	LAC dummy	All	LAC dummy
Parameter	−0.114 (0.02)	−0.237 (0.08)	−0.128 (0.02)	−0.165 (0.05)	−0.140 (0.02)	−0.098 (0.03)

Source: Authors' calculations.

Transmissions channels from poverty to growth

What are the channels through which poverty might influence growth? A quick review of the theoretical literature suggests a number of potential channels including investment, human capital (both education and health), innovation and mobility, and risk.

Poverty and investment

Several theoretical models on poverty traps exploit the result that high poverty levels (typically coupled with credit constraints) are likely to affect the investment rate negatively. But what do we actually know about the relationship between poverty and investment? Although the literature has paid significant attention to the impact of income levels on the investment rate (see, for example, Ben-David, 1995), little is known about the impact of poverty on investment. As a first pass at the issue, we ranked 99 countries for which we have income, poverty, and investment data according to their per capita income in the mid-1990s.[10] Then we partitioned these countries into 10 groups of 10 countries each (the last group has only 9 countries). The poorest countries in the sample are in the first group, the next poorest 10 countries are in the second group, and so on; thus the 9 richest countries form the tenth group.

For each group, figure 6.13 plots median (log) income in panel A, poverty ($2 poverty line) in panel B, and gross fixed capital formation relative to GDP in panel C.[11] Inspection of this figure reveals a clear nonlinear pattern in the relationship between income, poverty, and investment. For example, headcount poverty falls dramatically between the first and fourth groups—from about 66 percent to less than 8 percent, but after that it declines much more modestly as one moves up the income-group classification. Similarly, investment increases from 14 to about 22 percent of GDP between the first and fourth groups, and then remains virtually constant between the fourth and tenth groups. Note that these nonlinearities are not driven by the underlying income data (panel A), whose association with investment seems to be well described by a linear pattern.

The figure suggests a closer association between poverty and investment than between income levels and investment. In fact, the correlation coefficient between the income series in panel A and the investment series in panel C is about 0.55 (that is, investment tends to be higher in richer countries), whereas the correlation coefficient

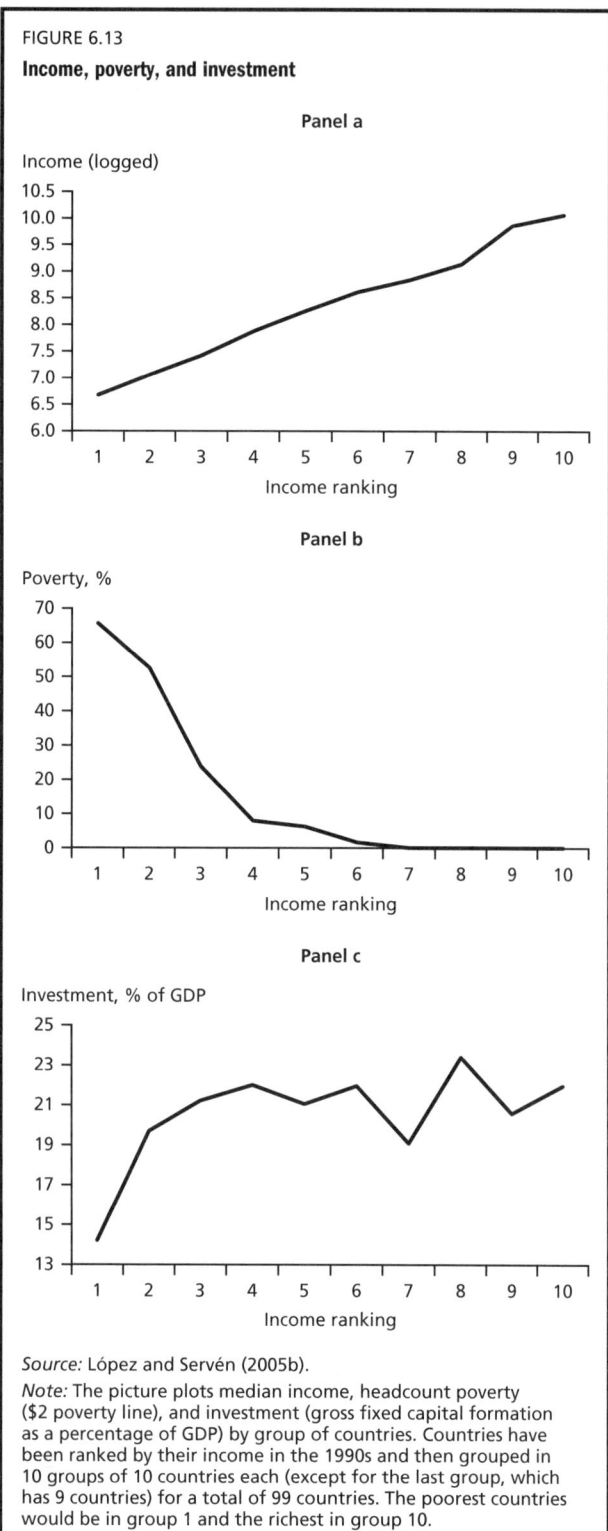

FIGURE 6.13
Income, poverty, and investment

Source: López and Servén (2005b).
Note: The picture plots median income, headcount poverty ($2 poverty line), and investment (gross fixed capital formation as a percentage of GDP) by group of countries. Countries have been ranked by their income in the 1990s and then grouped in 10 groups of 10 countries each (except for the last group, which has 9 countries) for a total of 99 countries. The poorest countries would be in group 1 and the richest in group 10.

between the investment series and the poverty series shown in panel B is −0.77.

Does this apparent close association between poverty and investment withstand econometric scrutiny? Apparently yes. Lopez and Servén (2005b) estimate the impact of poverty on investment using a simple accelerator model and find that, all else being equal, a 10 percent increase in poverty is likely to be associated with a decline in investment of about 6–8 percentage points. This result is robust to the use of different poverty lines and alternative measures of investment.

This finding suggests a potential explanation for poverty's negative effect on growth: a higher poverty rate leads to a lower investment rate, which leads to lower growth. In fact, when one econometrically explores the impact of poverty on growth controlling for investment, the investment rate turns out to belong to the growth equation, but poverty does not enter significantly in the various specifications (that is, the impact of poverty on growth is captured by the investment variable).[12]

The role of the financial sector

As noted above, theoretical models on poverty traps tend to exploit the joint impact of high poverty and credit constraints on growth. The basic idea is that poverty is likely to have a greater effect on investment when financial sector development is limited. Thus, one would expect to find that the impact of poverty on investment is affected by the degree of financial sector development.

Table 6.3 reports the results of estimating an empirical investment equation (based on the simple accelerator model) augmented with two variables aimed at capturing any potential difference in the effect of poverty on investment in countries with a highly developed financial sector ($Poverty^{HFD}$) and in those with a less developed financial sector ($Poverty^{LFD}$).[13] The results of this exercise indicate that, as expected, investment rates tend to be highly persistent, to

TABLE 6.3

Does financial sector development play a role in the poverty-investment interaction?

Variable	GFCF			GCF		
	(1)	(2)	(3)	(4)	(5)	(6)
Investment ($t-1$)	0.721	0.716	0.735	0.653	0.656	0.674
	(0.04)	(0.04)	(0.05)	(0.03)	(0.03)	(0.03)
Income (in logs) ($t-1$)	−0.005	−0.011	−0.010	−0.005	−0.006	−0.002
	(0.00)	(0.00)	(0.01)	(0.00)	(0.00)	(0.01)
Growth (t)	0.524	0.507	0.498	0.620	0.616	0.612
	(0.04)	(0.04)	(0.04)	(0.04)	(0.05)	(0.05)
PPP ($t-1$)	−0.004	0.001	−0.001	0.000	0.000	−0.001
	(0.00)	(0.00)	(0.00)	(0.01)	(0.01)	(0.01)
Terms of Trade (t)	0.079	0.089	0.100	0.071	0.078	0.079
	(0.02)	(0.02)	(0.02)	(0.02)	(0.02)	(0.03)
$Poverty^{HFD}$ ($\$2$) ($t-1$)	0.031			0.016		
	(0.03)			(0.03)		
$Poverty^{LFD}$ ($\$2$) ($t-1$)	0.055			−0.057		
	(0.03)			(0.02)		
$Poverty^{HFD}$ ($\$3$) ($t-1$)		−0.002			0.011	
		(0.03)			(0.03)	
$Poverty^{LFD}$ ($\$3$) ($t-1$)		−0.059			−0.038	
		(0.02)			(0.02)	
$Poverty^{HFD}$ ($\$4$) ($t-1$)			0.003			0.025
			(0.03)			(0.03)
$Poverty^{LFD}$ ($\$4$) ($t-1$)			−0.039			−0.010
			(0.03)			(0.03)

Source: Lopez and Servén (2005b), table 9.
Note: Numbers in parentheses are standard errors. The table reports the results of regressing investment on the variables in the first column. In columns 1, 2, and 3, we use the ratio of gross fixed capital formation (GFCF) to GDP as the measure of investment. In columns 4, 5, and 6, we use the ratio of gross capital formation (GCF) to GDP. PPP is a measure of the price of capital goods, and $Poverty^{LFD}$ and $Poverty^{HFD}$ are the poverty headcounts of countries with low and high financial sector development, respectively. The poverty line used for each variable is given in US$.

be procyclical, and to negatively depend on the cost of capital goods. Moreover, the impact of poverty on investment is more adverse in countries with less developed financial sectors. In fact, poverty does not seem to affect investment at high levels of financial sector development when credit constraints for the poor may not be so relevant.

These findings are consistent with those in Giuliano and Ruiz-Arranz (2005) who analyze the impact on investment and growth of foreign workers' remittances. Giuliano and Ruiz-Arranz find that remittances typically have a positive impact on investment but that this impact declines with the level of financial sector development. In other words, remittances seem to alleviate the credit constraints on the poor and through that channel contribute to capital accumulation and growth.

Poverty and education

There is a clear relationship between education and poverty reduction. Education has a very strong impact on earning potential, expands labor mobility, promotes the health of parents and children, and reduces fertility and child mortality. For example, the World Bank's 2005 poverty assessment for El Salvador (World Bank 2005) estimated that the per capita income of a household whose head had a primary education was 13 percent higher, on average, than that of a household with an uneducated head. The gain from a household head with a secondary school education was about 26 percent relative to a head with a primary school education, whereas the average gain from a household head having a university education was about 38 percent.

Similarly, the Bank's poverty assessment for Honduras in 2001 (World Bank 2001a) reported that in urban areas during the 1990s, workers with 7 years of school increased their labor income by 9 percent over workers with 6 years of school, whereas an increase from 15 to 16 years resulted in additional income of 14 percent. The income gains in rural areas from comparable improvements in schooling were estimated at 11 and 18 percent, respectively.

Education is also crucial to achieve sustained economic growth and hence sustained poverty reduction. As noted in chapter 5, human capital plays a central role in long-run growth. Education directly contributes to worker productivity and to more rapid technological adaptation and innovation. This point is particularly relevant for growth in Latin America because most Latin American countries have massive deficits in secondary enrollment (de Ferranti and others 2003). For the region the deficit is estimated at about 19 percent, but in some countries it is much higher. In Brazil, for example, the secondary school enrollment deficit is estimated at 36 percent and in República Bolivariana de Venezuela at 42 percent.

However, as discussed in detail in chapter 9, poverty may also affect education levels so that the relationship between poverty reduction and education is one of double causality. In table 6.4 we present the results of estimating a simple econometric model for the years of secondary schooling using cross-country data.[14] In addition to the lagged dependent variable, it includes among the explanatory variables the following indicators: per capita income to control for the country's level of development, the pupil-to-teacher ratio to capture quantity and quality efforts at the country level, and poverty (as measured by the headcount index using the $2-, $3-, and $4-a day poverty lines).

Table 6.4 shows that, as expected, secondary education is highly persistent. It also indicates that richer countries (as measured by per capita income levels) have more-educated populations, and that a lower quality of education (as measured by a higher pupil-to-teacher ratio) is associated with less-educated populations. Finally, higher poverty levels typically result in lower average years of secondary education.

On the whole, this discussion highlights the possibility that poverty and growth interact through the education

TABLE 6.4

Does poverty lead to lower secondary education?

Dependent variable is average years of secondary education			
Secondary education ($t-1$)	0.95	0.94	0.94
	(0.00)	(0.00)	(0.00)
Income	0.12	0.11	0.08
	(0.01)	(0.01)	(0.01)
Pupil/teacher ratio	−0.01	−0.01	−0.01
	(0.00)	(0.00)	(0.01)
Poverty ($2 a day)	−0.08		
	(0.04)		
Poverty ($3 a day)		−0.09	
		(0.03)	
Poverty ($4 a day)			−0.16
			(0.03)

Source: Authors' calculations.
Note: Numbers in parentheses are standard errors. The table reports the results of regressing the average years of secondary education on the variables. Although not reported here, the standard specification tests do not indicate any particular problem with the estimated model or the instruments used.

channel. As the literatures on both growth and microeconomic determinants of poverty stress, higher education levels result in higher growth and higher household income levels and therefore in lower poverty. At the same time, lower poverty levels feed back into the system and result in higher education, creating the potential for a virtuous circle between growth and poverty.

Poverty and health

Poorer countries have much worse health indicators than richer countries, most likely because of the bidirectional causality between income and health. On the one hand, empirical evidence indicates that higher income levels lead to better health indicators For example, Pritchett and Summers (1996) estimate that the long-run income elasticity of infant and child mortality in developing countries lies between 0.2 and 0.4. On the basis of those estimates, they calculate that more than 500,000 child deaths in the developing world in 1990 alone could be attributed to the poor economic performance in the 1980s.

On the other hand, there are a number of channels through which health can affect growth and income levels.

- *Productive efficiency.* Healthier workers are more productive. When health improves, more output can be produced with any given combination of skills, physical capital, and technological knowledge. One way to think about this effect is to take health as another component of human capital, analogous to the skill component.
- *Learning capacity.* Health plays an important role in determining the rate of return to education. Children who are well nourished and alert gain more from a given amount of education.
- *Creativity.* Just as a healthier person is more efficient in producing goods and services, so is the person likely to be more efficient in producing new ideas and hence in his or her ability to innovate (see also below).
- *Life expectancy.* Increases in life expectancy have a direct effect on the average skill level of the population. This is a consequence of two forces. When the probability of dying young is high, the discount rate is also high, making it optimal for people to start working early in their life and not to stay at school too long. Similarly, when life expectancy is short, the depreciation rate of human capital is high, making its accumulation less profitable.

For example, Fogel (1994) argues that nutrition and health have a significant influence on labor productivity and estimates that when labor is adjusted for intensity (measured by calories), improved gross nutrition explains about one-third of economic growth in the United Kingdom since 1800. Similarly, Boucekkine, de la Croix, and Licandro (2003) estimate that the observed improvements in adult mortality since the 18th century account for 70 percent of the growth acceleration that occurred before the industrial age. They argue that exogenous improvements in adult mortality between 1600 and 1800 increased individual incentives to build human capital and, as a consequence, investment in education rose, which in turn exerted a positive effect on economic growth.

Mayer-Foulkes (2001) has studied the long-term impact of health on economic growth in Latin America. Although he is unable to disentangle the relative contribution of such factors as nutrition and adult mortality, his results indicate that typical health improvements for adults may be associated with a permanent incremental increase in annual growth of between 0.8 and 1.5 percent. Thus poverty can also affect growth through the health channel. High poverty may result in worse health, which feeds back into lower growth, creating the possibility of a vicious circle.

Poverty and innovation

The discussion so far has suggested that poverty can hamper economic growth by choking an economy's ability to accumulate various forms of productive capital. Another potential link between poverty and growth exists, however, one that concerns an economy's ability to innovate and thus improve the productivity or efficiency of capital, labor, and other factors of production. Moreover, poverty's negative effect on capital accumulation can itself hamper innovation when capital investments are required to cover the costs of innovation. For instance, introducing new export products can require investments to understand market regulations and product standards, or simply to experiment with various business plans to achieve an efficient production process. Similarly, more sophisticated innovations with commercial value can be achieved only through investments in research and development. And both types of innovations can require at least a minimum amount of education. Consequently poverty, which is associated with low levels of human and physical capital, can be associated with lower levels of innovation at the national level (for a given level of national income per capita). In other words, poverty can effectively limit the number of potential innovators, not because community members are not talented, but because poverty prevents them from undertaking the necessary investments to bring about economically meaningful innovations.

While the links between poverty and innovation remain understudied, and our understanding of the drivers of innovation and technical progress in general is quite modest, recent research by Klinger and Lederman (2005) sheds some light on this important issue. These authors studied the determinants of two types of innovations, namely, the introduction of new export products and patenting activity across countries and over time. This study reports the so-called marginal effects of population and poverty, and their interaction on the number of new products exported by a sample of 70 countries during 1994–2003. It also presents the same marginal effects, but for patenting activity during the 1980s and the 1990s. It is worth highlighting that these analyses controlled for numerous other variables that might also affect innovative activity.[15]

In any case, Klinger and Lederman find that the median (or typical) effect of poverty on export "discoveries" is about −0.02; for patenting activity, it is about −0.06. In other words, for each 1 percent increase in a country's poverty rate, the number of export innovations falls by 0.02 percent and the number of patents falls by 0.06 percent. Since the monetary value of exports and patents can be quite high, the economic consequences of poverty through these innovation channels should be worrisome. Perhaps more interesting, the empirical evidence also suggests that poverty affects innovation by affecting the number of potential innovators within a country. For both export discoveries and patenting, the effect of population size on innovation activity declines with poverty. A plausible explanation for this result is that poverty reduces the number of people with sufficient human and physical capital needed to produce innovation.

Poverty, mobility, and risk

According to de Ferranti and others (2000), volatility is considerably higher in all developing regions than in industrial economies. The less-diversified economies in lower-income countries, as well as limited access to external financing, expose these countries to higher risk and thus greater volatility. This then translates into higher volatility in aggregate wage measures and unemployment rates. Thus poverty seems to lead to higher risk.

At the same time, mobility through the income distribution may have impacts that promote growth. Hart (1981, 9), for example, argues that "it is mobility which provides the sticks for those who do not wish to move down the distribution and the carrots for those who wish to move up." More generally, the accumulation of human capital that is so critical to intergenerational mobility has effects on growth; a greater possibility for moving up the income ladder stimulates greater investment, which in turns leads to higher growth.

Mobility is also seen as an indicator of efficiency: high levels of income fluctuations may be seen as evidence that individuals are moving fluidly from one position to another, responding to changes in supply and demand for labor. Labor legislation that leads to segmented labor markets where certain classes of workers are therefore rationed out of good jobs, liquidity constraints that prevent individuals from migrating to more prosperous regions, or deficient financial markets that deny good entrepreneurs the resources they need to grow both restrict mobility and lead to poor allocation of resources. They can also be elements of poverty traps, which are explicitly about the inability of low-income groups to move up in the distribution.

However, chapter 2 argued that the unpredictable element of mobility constitutes risk that adversely affects welfare. For this reason, advanced societies have developed insurance and other mechanisms to reduce the risk that individuals and families face. Simulations that measure how risk-averse people are suggest that these welfare effects are large. In addition, a recent strand of the literature (Krebs 2003) argues that risk also has negative impacts on growth. As chapter 9 discusses, individuals' decisions to invest in education are strongly dependent on the perceived long-run gains in income. But like any other investment, the riskier the expected return, the less attractive it becomes. Cunha, Heckman, and Navarro (2005) argue that college attendance is lower than expected given the relatively high average return to education because roughly 40 percent of the observed variability in postcollege incomes is unpredictable: if individuals could make their decisions based on their actual incomes, 25 percent of high school graduates would rather be college graduates and 31 percent of college graduates would have stopped at high school. Hence, "uncertainty about future outcomes greatly affects schooling choices, and there is plenty of scope for ex-post regret," the three write (54). In countries where workers face large shocks to their labor incomes, because of either frequent bouts of unemployment or high earnings volatility caused, perhaps, by inflation, or where frequent illness prevents working, the incentive to invest in education may fall even more. The resulting lower levels of education in turn dampen growth.

Here, then, is another example where two dimensions of poverty—health and risk—undercut growth, and the magnitudes appear large. Krebs, Krishna, and Maloney (2005) make an attempt to assess empirically the effect on human capital accumulation and growth of declines in the level of income risk of Argentina and Mexico to the U.S. levels. Their findings indicate that if Mexico could lower its labor market risk to Argentine levels, it could potentially increase its growth rate permanently by almost half a percentage point (table 6.5). The amount that growth would have to increase to increase the total welfare measure by an equivalent amount has two components. The first is the direct loss that is attributable to workers' and families' dislike of risk; this effect is worth the equivalent of a 0.59 percent permanent loss in yearly growth. The second component is the additional effect that arises because risk also makes workers and their families invest less in human capital; this has a direct impact on welfare of 0.48 percent. On the whole, the effect of lowering Mexico's risk to Argentine levels is equivalent to increasing growth by slightly more than 1 percent, a huge amount in a country where growth rates hover around 2 percent. If Argentina could reduce its risk to U.S. levels the effect would be less dramatic—growth would increase only about 0.2 percent—but still important over the long run.

These are only ballpark estimates. Clearly, the Mexican and Argentine economies are not identical to the U.S.

TABLE 6.5
The impact of risk on growth

Factor	United States	Argentina	Mexico
Income risk	0.15	0.18	0.21
Growth rate (%)	2.00	1.81	1.33
In education (%)	28.12	25.8	21.8
Direct loss due to risk (%)			0.59
Loss due to lower growth (%)			0.48
Total welfare loss (%)			1.07

Source: Krebs, Krishna, and Maloney (2005b) for Argentina and Mexico; Meghir and Pistaferri (2004) for United States.

economy, and, more fundamentally, simple algebraic models cannot capture all the very subtle effects. Nonetheless, the exercise suggests that the magnitudes of effects arising from the presence of high risk in Latin America are large and that risk thus needs to be treated as an important dimension of an effective poverty reduction and growth strategy. Not only are policies to ameliorate risk beneficial from a pure vulnerability point of view, they may also be central to growth.

Concluding remarks

This chapter explored the possible existence of links between growth and poverty reduction by which growth lowers poverty and lower poverty in turn contributes to faster growth. We reviewed several possible theoretical arguments that support the existence of such links. Among the most prominent are those arguments in the poverty-traps literature that suggest that the countries of the world are increasingly divided into two convergence clubs—the rich and the poor. Membership in the poor club is considered a huge handicap for growth and hence for poverty reduction.

The chapter then assessed the empirical evidence on this front and found mixed results. On the one hand, we presented evidence of convergence clubs in both absolute and relative income levels: richer countries converging toward the rich-club equilibrium, and poorer countries toward the poor-club equilibrium. By these measures, Latin America seems to be a homogeneous entity that is converging toward an equilibrium somewhere between the rich and the poor clubs. On the other hand, we also reviewed several empirical works that have formally tested whether the bimodality in the cross-national distribution of income is driven by poverty traps. In this regard, most, although not all, of the studies tend to reject the poverty-traps hypothesis.

Finally, we posed one simple question. Even if there is no evidence of poverty traps in the strict sense, is it still possible that poverty is a barrier to growth? We addressed this question from two different directions. First, we reviewed the empirical evidence contained in a background paper for this report, which found that countries with higher poverty levels tend to grow less than countries with lower poverty levels. The estimates presented in this chapter suggest that an additional 10 percentage points in the headcount poverty index cut growth prospects by about 1 percentage point. Second, we explored a number of potential channels through which poverty might lead to lower growth. This evidence indicated that in countries with higher poverty rates, accumulation of both physical and human capital (education and health) is lower. Evidence also suggests that countries with higher poverty levels have lower rates of innovation (a critical contributor to growth) and higher risk.

It must be noted that in many of these channels the financial sector may play a very significant role, either by imposing a binding financial constraint on the poor that may prevent them from undertaking investments in human and physical capital or by preventing them from hedging against risk. Thus, the development and operation of the financial sector also appear to matter for the potential feedback effect from poverty to growth.

Overall, the results of this chapter suggest two main messages. First, the focus of the growth-poverty discussion needs to be shifted from the possible effects of growth on the poor (on which ample evidence has already been collected) to the relationships between growth and poverty. That shift in focus should mitigate the debate on whether development strategies should rely more on pro-growth or pro-poor policies, because strategies that do not take into account the bidirectional relation between poverty and growth will likely lead to disappointing results: poverty will not decline without growth, but growth will be difficult unless the constraints affecting the poor are also addressed. Second, at a more operational level, considering poverty and growth as part of the same problem suggests that the biggest payoff to growth (and hence to poverty reduction) is likely to result from policies that not only promote growth, but also exert an independent, direct impact on poverty—hence reducing the drag of poverty on growth.

Annex 6A

Convergence clubs and long-run equilibriums

One way to estimate the long-run per capita income equilibrium for each convergence club is based on the concept of β-convergence (see Barro and Sala-i-Martin 1995). This concept relies on the estimation of the following simple model:

$$(6A.1) \quad [\ln(Y_{1999}) - \ln(Y_{1960})]/39 = \mu + \beta \ln(Y_{1960}),$$

where Y denotes per capita income and the subscript refers to the year in question. Values of $\beta < 0$ would indicate convergence (β-convergence, to be more precise), and one

could expect the countries in the group to cluster around the equilibrium values over the long run. In contrast, values of $\beta > 0$ would indicate divergence, and one would expect to observe that the dispersion in the cross-country distribution of per capita income increases as time goes by. Finally, for $\beta = 0$ there is neither convergence nor divergence. This simple model can be used to estimate the expected value of income over time when $\beta < 0$, which is given by $-\mu/\beta$.

The table below reports the results of estimating the previous model for the full sample of countries and for the three clubs discussed in the text (low-low, low-high, and high-high). The first noteworthy point is that, not surprisingly, in view of figure 6.7, the full sample presents divergence ($\beta > 0$). However, when we reestimate the model for each of the three clubs we obtain convergence, the point estimates of β are always negative (although admittedly for the high-high group, the estimate is not significant, which in turn may suggest that although there is no divergence, there may not be convergence either).

Convergence clubs

Club	Parameter β	Parameter μ	Equilibrium US$
All	0.0033* (0.0017)	−0.007 (0.014)	Divergence
Low-low	−0.0117* (0.003)	0.087* (0.024)	1,717
Low-high	−0.0178* (0.0069)	0.165* (0.053)	10,600
High-high	−0.006 (0.004)	0.07* (0.036)	120,000

Source: Authors' calculations.
*Significant at the 5 percent level.

Convergence clubs and country transitions

To explore the distribution of income levels across countries, Quah (1993) takes each country's income level relative to the world average; allocates each observation to one of five states: 0–0.25, 0.25–0.5, 0.5–1, 1–2, and 2 and above (that is, the first state includes the poorest countries and the fifth state the richest); computes a transition matrix measuring the probability that a country in one state changes state by averaging the observed one-year transitions over every year from 1962 to 1984; and evaluates the long equilibrium consistent with the stationary distribution.

When we replicate all these calculations but use data for 1960–99, we obtain the following transition matrix:

$$M = \begin{Bmatrix} 0.987 & 0.013 & 0 & 0 & 0 \\ 0.038 & 0.935 & 0.026 & 0 & 0 \\ 0 & 0.033 & 0.936 & 0.031 & 0 \\ 0 & 0 & 0.032 & 0.954 & 0.014 \\ 0 & 0 & 0 & 0.009 & 0.991 \end{Bmatrix},$$

where a typical element m_{ij} measures the probability that a country in state i shifts to state j. So, for example, the probability that a country in the first state remains in its state is almost 99 percent, whereas the probability that it moves to the second state is about 1 percent. Similarly, the probabilities that a country in the second state remains in the same state, progresses to the third, and returns to the first state are 93 percent, 2.6 percent, and 3.8 percent, respectively; thus suggesting that the probability that an economy in state 2 falls behind is slightly larger than the probability of the same economy going ahead. This type of asymmetric behavior also applies to countries in state 3 and more markedly to those in state 4 where the probability of falling behind is more than double the probability of advancing.

Using the transition matrix M, it is now possible to compute the associated long-run equilibrium for the distribution of income levels by allowing the time horizon of the iterations to expand. This exercise results in the following equilibrium values for each of the five states under consideration: 0.43, 0.15, 0.12, 0.12, and 0.18.

Convergence clubs and country transitions in Latin America

The previous exercise can be replicated using data only for Latin America. The resulting transition matrix in this case is as follows:

$$M_{LAC} = \begin{Bmatrix} 0.875 & 0.125 & 0 & 0 & 0 \\ 0.02 & 0.928 & 0.052 & 0 & 0 \\ 0 & 0.036 & 0.948 & 0.016 & 0 \\ 0 & 0 & 0.055 & 0.945 & 0 \\ 0 & 0 & 0 & 0.154 & 0.846 \end{Bmatrix}.$$

There are at least two important differences between M_{LAC} and M. First, M displays more persistency in the first and fifth states than M_{LAC} does (the estimated persistency of states 2, 3, and 4 is very similar in both cases). Whereas the estimated probability that an economy in either state 1 or state 5 of the global sample continues in the same state is about 99 percent, the same probability for Latin America is estimated at 87 percent and 85 percent, respectively. Thus the Latin American region seems to display more mobility at the extremes of the distribution than does the global distribution: both getting out of extreme poverty and getting out of extreme richness seems easier in Latin America than in the rest of the world.

The second difference regards the probability of moving ahead for a Latin American country in state 3 or 4; that probability appears to be lower than it is in the rest of the world. In particular, a Latin American country in state 3 has about half the probability of moving to state 4 as do state 3 countries in the global sample (1.6 percent and 3.1 percent, respectively). More dramatically, the estimated probability of moving from state 4 to state 5 is nil in Latin America. These differences would result in a regional equilibrium given by 0.052, 0.33, 0.47, 0.14, and 0.

Estimating the impact of poverty on growth

The empirical strategy that Lopez and Servén (2005b) use to explore the links between poverty and growth in the data is based on the addition of a suitable measure of poverty to an otherwise standard empirical cross-nation growth regression:

(6A.2) $(y_{it} - y_{it-1}) = \delta y_{it-1} + \omega' x_{it} + \beta p_{it-1} + v_i + \upsilon_{it}$,

where y is the log of per capita income, p is a measure of poverty, x represents a set of control variables other than lagged income (discussed shortly), v_i is a country-specific effect, and υ_{it} is an i.i.d. (independent and identically distributed) error term. However, several aspects of this empirical strategy require attention.

Estimation issues

Estimation of the previous equation poses two main challenges, namely, the presence of country-specific effects and the possible simultaneity of some of the explanatory variables with growth. These problems are addressed by using a GMM estimator (Arellano and Bover 1995 system estimator) that relies on internal instruments. Admittedly, with highly persistent instruments, that estimation method may not fully eliminate the potential bias related to reverse causality. To control for this problem, Lopez and Servén (2005b) also present results based on cross-sections, which should not suffer from reverse causality. In this regard, changing the estimation method does not dramatically affect the results.

Control variables

The empirical growth literature has experimented with so many alternative sets of explanatory variables that according to Durlauf and Quah (1999), by 1998 the number of individual regressors that had been considered as potential explanatory variables in growth regressions exceeded the number of countries in the standard growth data set. Rather than adding to the already huge variety of growth models, Lopez and Servén (2005b) use a baseline specification that relies on the controls used by Perotti (1996), Forbes (2000), Banerjee and Duflo (2003), and Knowles (2005). However, Lopez and Servén also experiment with two alternative sets to check whether the results are sensitive to changes in the controls. The basic finding is that changing controls does not significantly affect the estimated impact of poverty on growth.

Missing variables

The problem of missing variables is quite standard in this type of analysis. However, one variable in this context—inequality—needs particular attention. A relatively extensive literature already relates inequality and growth. For example, Alesina and Rodrik (1994) and Perotti (1996) find a negative relationship between inequality and growth on the basis of cross-section data, but Li and Zou (1998) and Forbes (2000) obtain the opposite result using aggregate panel data. Barro (2000) finds that inequality may affect growth in different directions depending on the country's level of income, while Banerjee and Duflo (2003) conclude that the response of growth to inequality changes has an inverted U-shape. Given the relation between inequality and poverty, excluding inequality from the equation could lead to the poverty variable capturing a pure inequality effect rather than a poverty effect. The empirical findings in this regard confirm that the estimated impact of poverty on growth does not result from poverty acting as a proxy for inequality either in a linear or in a nonlinear fashion.

Notes

1. Clearly, given the aversion of societies to high income inequality levels (see de Ferranti and others 2004), one could also justify the need to pay attention to distributional issues on the basis of political economy arguments.

2. By convergence club, we refer to a tendency of countries to converge to different equilibriums for per capita income levels. For example, Quah (1993), among others, finds evidence suggesting that the cross-country distribution of income may be well characterized by a twin-peak structure with poor and rich countries clustering around two different equilibriums.

3. Although not included in the sample, it is likely that Haiti also belongs to this group.

4. See Azariadis and Stachurski (2005) for a complete survey, and Lustig, Arias, and Rigolini (2003) for a nontechnical review.

5. For the purposes of this report, the industrial, or developed, countries group covers the OECD economies that are not eligible for lending from the International Bank for Reconstruction and Development. Figure 6.5 was constructed as follows. First, for each year we compute the median growth rate for all the countries in the relevant group for which the annual *World Development Indicators* report data. Then we apply a three-year, backward-moving average filter to smooth the series.

6. Admittedly, if the analysis were to take into account population weights, the story for the 1990s would be different: per capita growth would be approximately the same in both the developing and developed worlds. China and India account for much of this evening out, not only because they had almost 40 percent of the world's population during the 1990s, but also because India and especially China had excellent growth records. These differences are a reflection of the different ways in which economic performance can be measured. If individuals are the preferred unit of analysis, then weighted averages are probably more useful. If, instead, the unit of analysis is the country (as is the case when one focuses on country policies and country performance), then medians seem more appropriate.

7. Admittedly, it would be possible to argue that the 1960s distribution has two peaks: one around $3,000 and the other around $13,000.

8. For savings, Kraay and Radatz (2005) use a representative agent framework, something that rules out the possibility of credit market failure. In the Solow framework they use, the roles of jumps in saving and jumps in technology are more or less interchangeable.

9. Overall the results are backed by almost 90 robustness checks.

10. This approach is similar to that of Ben-David (1995) who focuses on the impact of income levels on investment. We pick the 1990s because it is the period over which more poverty observations are available.

11. The results remain virtually unchanged if one uses gross capital formation (GFC) as the investment measure.

12. This result is robust to the use of different measures of the investment rate.

13. Poverty^{HFD} is equal to the poverty headcount when the stock of credit to the private sector in the country/year in question is larger than the sample median and zero otherwise. Poverty^{LFD} equals the poverty headcount when the stock of credit to the private sector in the country/year in question is smaller than the sample median and 0 otherwise. Clearly, Poverty^{HFD} + Poverty^{LFD} = Poverty.

14. Estimation is performed using the GMM system estimator with internal instruments. This estimator therefore controls for unobserved fixed effects and potential endogeneity of the explanatory variables. The data are the same as in Lopez and Servén (2005b), except for the pupil-to-teacher ratio and expenditure in education, which come from the *World Development Indicators*.

15. Klinger and Lederman (2005) control for GDP per capita, export growth, population size, the sectoral concentration of innovation, past innovation activity, expenditures in research and development (in the case of patents granted by the U.S. Patent and Trademark Office), and exports to the United States (in the case of patents granted by the U.S. Patent and Trademark Office). These authors obtained similar results when using the share of the population with less than a high school education, but they were unable to differentiate between the effects of poverty on both human capital and physical capital reducing the effective share of the population capable of undertaking productive innovations.

CHAPTER 7

Subnational Dimensions of Growth and Poverty

Poverty rates within Latin American countries differ as much as those across countries. Moreover, some groups of subnational units seem to behave as convergence clubs, suggesting the existence of regional poverty traps. The presence of agglomeration externalities and relatively weak equilibrating mechanisms, especially through migration, creates important trade-offs in policies toward lagging regions.

CHAPTER 6 EXPLORED HOW THE REGION fares in the overall distribution of world income and concluded that, with some important exceptions, the region is situated in an intermediate position between the high-income countries and the really poor. However, comparing regions within countries reveals differences in prosperity that are staggering and of the magnitudes seen internationally. For example, in 2000, income per capita in the poorest municipality in Brazil was barely 10 percent of that in the richest; in Mexico, per capita income in Chiapas was only 18 percent of that in the capital. The mobility of subnational units across the income distribution has been studied as much as the movement of countries and individuals across the global income distribution. There is also a similar concern with the existence of poverty traps, although with some policy twists particular to the geographical level of analysis.

The 2005 World Bank regional flagship report for Latin America, *Beyond the City: The Rural Contribution to Development* (de Ferranti and others 2005) provided compelling evidence that the quantity and quality of jobs are highly influenced by regional characteristics and argued that there was scope for a territorially targeted development policy. Building on that work, we first focus on the evidence for geographic inequality, spatial concentration, and regional mobility in Latin America. We focus primarily on Brazil, Chile, and Mexico, which have generated the most careful data and analytical work to date. For Brazil and Mexico, we also consider regional convergence of nonincome measures of well-being. We then turn to some possible explanations for the existence of regional convergence clubs, the failure of intranational income-equilibrating mechanisms, and finally to selected policy issues.

What is spatial inequality, how is it measured, and what are the regional trends?

To capture the relevance of geography, traditional indexes of income inequality can be decomposed along the spatial dimension and poverty rates calculated for each of the spatial units.[1] Compared with a time series in which the ordering of data points is given naturally, the definition of the relevant spatial unit—the state, department, province, municipality, or perhaps even finer disaggregations—is more arbitrary. As Shorrocks and Wan (2005) show, looking across several countries, the component of inequality due to differences *between* geographical regions averages around 12 percent of overall inequality, with a maximum of 51 percent depending on the subdivisions of the data used. This is broadly consistent with Kanbur and Venables' (2005) conclusion that the available empirical evidence suggests that spatial inequality may account, at most, for one-third of

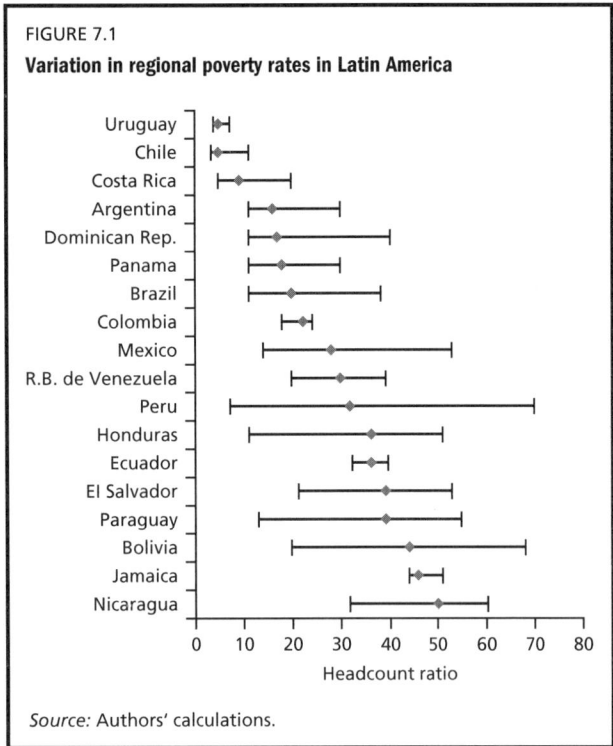

FIGURE 7.1
Variation in regional poverty rates in Latin America

Source: Authors' calculations.

total interpersonal inequality (that is, inequality between individuals); in other words, the majority of inequality occurs *within* spatial units.

A similar pattern is sound in Gasparini, Gutierrez, and Tornarolli (2005) for Latin America and the Caribbean. Regional differences account for more than 20 percent of inequality in Paraguay and Peru and for more than 10 percent in the Dominican Republic and República Bolivariana de Venezuela. For most of Latin America, the regional differences appear to contribute substantially less. However, this finding seems to say much more about how very large the idiosyncratic differences are between people than about how small differences in well-being are across spatial units. Figure 7.1 shows that variation of the poverty rate across regions is very large for many Latin American countries. In Bolivia, Honduras, Mexico, Paraguay, and Peru, the difference in poverty counts among regions is more than 40 percentage points. The fact that some regions of Peru have counts of under 10 percent while others hover above 70 percent speaks for itself about the importance of integrating spatial considerations into poverty analysis.

Identifying spatial concentration

Beyond knowing that poverty is concentrated in particular geographic units, we would also like to know if these units are contiguous, perhaps forming regional clusters, or whether poor municipalities or states are randomly distributed among rich ones. We also would like to know whether such spatial patterns are persistent—are we dealing with regions "spatially" trapped in a vicious circle of low growth–low investment–low growth, as explained in chapter 6? An emerging spatial econometrics literature provides the tools and indicators to begin to analyze these questions (box 7.1), and recent studies have measured the spatial distribution of incomes and how it has evolved over time in Brazil, Chile, and Mexico. Ideally, we would examine average household incomes or poverty rates rather than per capita state incomes, but the long spans of data required are not available for these variables, so we work primarily with state-level GDP per capita.

For each of the three countries, we present a set of comparable figures and statistics (see box 7.1) to assess the degree of spatial clustering, as well as the mobility patterns of states within the national income distribution. The upper panel in each of the figures 7.2, 7.4, and 7.5 presents the standard deviation that is used in the literature to capture "sigma" convergence among log incomes per capita of the subnational units together with Moran's *I*, which captures the spatial concentration (clustering) of that income. The middle panel shows the Moran scatter plots that offer a visual presentation of whether states are clustered in "neighborhoods" with similar levels of income—high- or low-level convergence clubs—or whether they are more or less randomly distributed for the beginning and end of the sample period. Finally, the bottom panel presents the "stochastic kernels," or three-dimensional mobility plots, introduced by Quah (1997) to study income dynamics.[2] The advantage of these kernels over simple plots of income distribution is precisely that one can see changes of position that might be hidden by identical "snapshot" distributions. Each kernel presents state income relative to the country ("country-relative") in time *t* on the Y axis and in time $t + 5$ or $t + 10$ on the X axis. Information on each state's position within the country's income distribution across many different multi-year periods is integrated to form each kernel. If there is no movement at all among states, the kernels would consist of a single vertical plane along the 45-degree line shown. The fact that there is some mobility—states do change relative position—gives the kernel its volume. Were there are a lot of mobility but no convergence (in other words, if states were just switching places), one would see an inverted bowl or half sphere. Slicing the volume parallel to the

> **BOX 7.1**
> **Tools to detect spatial association**
>
> In the spatial statistics literature, a number of methods and indicators have been proposed to capture the interrelatedness of geographical areas (Anselin 1988, 1995; Griffith 1996). The extent of spatial dependence of a given variable among a set of spatially distributed units, such as regional per capita income for the Brazilian states, can be assessed by computing a global spatial dependence statistic such as Moran's I, which reads as follows:
>
> $$I = \frac{N}{S} \frac{\sum_{ij}^{N} w_{ij} z_i z_j}{\sum_{i=1}^{N} z_i^2},$$
>
> where N is the number of regions, w_{ij} are the elements of a $(N \times N)$ binary contiguity matrix W (taking the value 1 if regions i and j share a common border and 0 if they do not), S is the sum of the elements of W, and z_i and z_j are normalized vectors of the log of per capita income of each state. Positive values of Moran's I indicate positive spatial dependence, which indicates a clustering of similar attribute values, whereas negative values are associated with clustering of dissimilar values. To further explore the spatial pattern of the data, it is important to investigate not only whether the overall regional income distribution of a country is spatially concentrated but also in which specific states this concentration occurs and whether high- or low-income values are clustered. We focus our analysis on local indicators of spatial association (LISA), as developed by Anselin (1995), and on the interpretation of the Moran scatter plot (Anselin 1993).
>
> Two properties of LISA are important to note. First, the value of a local statistic for each observation indicates the extent of (significant) spatial clustering of similar values around that observation. This means that the local indicator Li enables us to infer the statistical significance of the pattern of spatial association at that location. Second, the sum of the local indicators of spatial association for all observations is proportional to the global indicator of spatial association (Anselin 1995)
>
> $$I_i = \frac{N z_i \sum_j^N w_{ij} z_j}{\sum_{i=1}^{N} z_i^2}.$$
>
> Extra help with the interpretation of the local statistics is provided by the Moran scatter plot, which is a graphical complement to LISA that can be used to visualize local (in)stability. The Moran scatter plot shows the values of Wzi versus zi, where W is the row-standardized (that is, rows sum to 1), first-order contiguity matrix, and zi are the standardized values of per capita income. In the current context, we plot the standardized log of per capita income of a state against its spatial lag (standardized as well), which corresponds to the weighted average income (per capita and logarithmic) of a state's neighbors. The Moran scatter plot divides the x-y space into four distinct areas, corresponding to four types of possible local spatial associations between a state and its neighbors. In quadrant I rich states coincide with rich neighbors; in quadrant II poor states have rich neighbors; in quadrant III poor states are surrounded by poor neighbors; and in quadrant IV rich states have poor neighbors. States located in quadrants I and III represent the association of similar values (positive spatial correlation), whereas states located in quadrants II and IV show the association of opposite values (negative spatial correlation). The concentration of states in quadrants I and III is to be expected in a scenario in which rich and poor states cluster separately, generating differentiated areas of high and low income. If states were located randomly, occupying the four quadrants without a discernible pattern, spatial dependence would be nonexistent. Notwithstanding an identifiable clustering, local instabilities may still be found for individual observations.

X axis reveals the distribution of states at each initial income ten (or in the case of Mexico, five) years later. Significant income convergence would result in a rotation of the kernel toward the Y axis: states with lower incomes in t would have higher *relative* incomes in $t + 5$, and vice versa. Divergence would lead to the reverse.

Brazil: Slow overall convergence and clear signs of spatial polarization

Brazil presents a case where there has been an overall decrease of the standard deviation of state per capita incomes, implying a process of convergence (see figure 7.2). At the same time, the evidence (Moran's I) strongly rejects

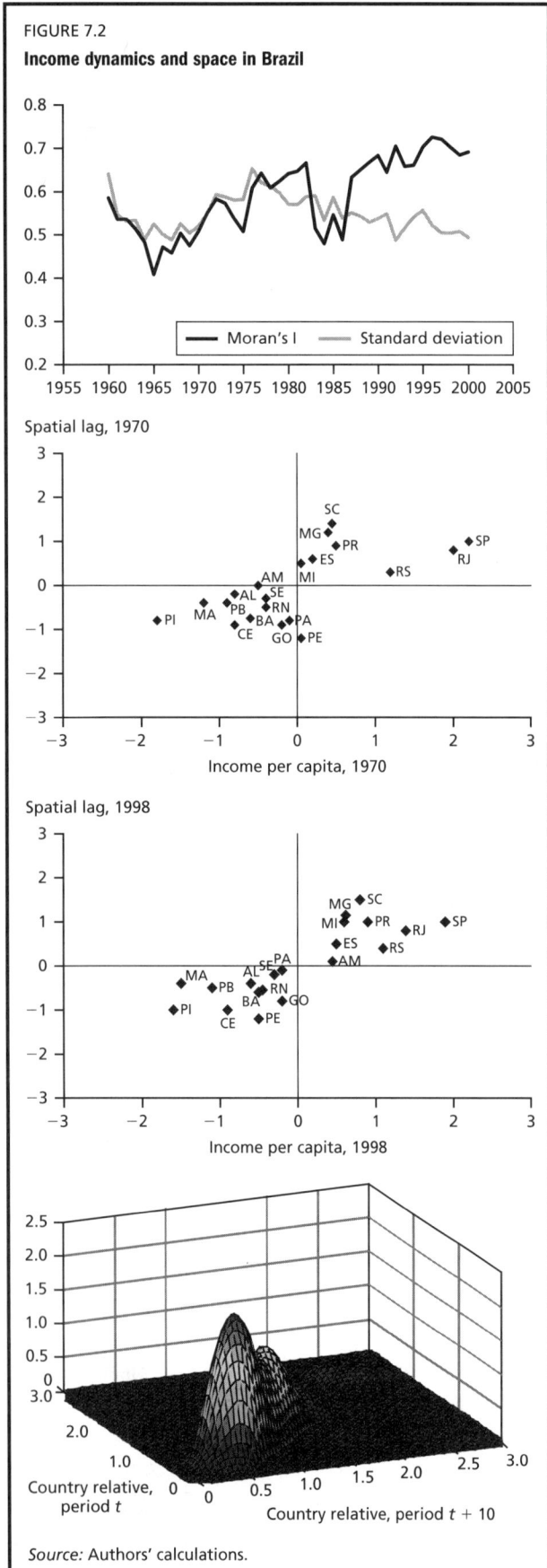

FIGURE 7.2
Income dynamics and space in Brazil

Source: Authors' calculations.

the idea that incomes are randomly distributed across states. The scatter plots confirm this by showing that most states are found in quadrants I and III: rich states are found in rich neighborhoods (their spatial lag), and poor among poor. The local Moran statistics that offer a parametric measure of the spatial relationship of a state to its immediate neighborhood show that income is concentrated in two well-defined spatial clusters: the low-income northeast region—Piauí (PI), Ceará (CE), Rio Grande do Norte (RN), Paraíba (PB), Pernambuco (PE), and Bahia (BA)—and the more prosperous southeast region comprised of Rio de Janeiro (RJ), São Paulo (SP), Paraná (PR), and Minas Gerais (MG).

Looking across time reveals two important findings. First, a comparison of the 1970 and 2000 scatter plots shows a clear, substantial persistence in the relative positions of states; these patterns are found, in slightly weaker form, as far back as the data allow us to look—1939. Second, at the same time that state incomes appear to be converging in Brazil, the data suggest, somewhat counterintuitively, that spatial clustering has increased across the same period. The kernel further clarifies what is occurring. The relatively modest convergence in incomes does not impart any noticeable rotation off the diagonal of the cluster, and the overall narrowness of the kernel suggests relatively little mobility among states. Further, there are two-well defined humps, suggesting convergence clubs similar to the "twin peaks" pattern detected by Quah (1997) for the world distribution of incomes (along with a very rich outlying minipeak around 2.5 times average national incomes) that Moran's *I* suggests is growing more defined with time.[3]

More disaggregated data at the municipality level allow an even clearer definition of this pattern. The left panel of figure 7.6 shows that the bell-shaped 1970 income distribution has given way to a bimodal, or "two-humped," distribution in 2000. The scatter plots of the municipal data (figure 7.3) suggest that there were fewer outliers in 2000 than in 1970, and hence a lower overall dispersion. But the diagonal concentration has split into two distinct groups, with the richer municipalities and neighborhoods pulling away from the poorer municipalities in poor neighborhoods. This is less clearly seen in the state-level scatter plots: São Paulo and Rio are less extreme than before as other states have caught up, but the cluster of moderate-income states in the middle is missing. That the action is at the state level is confirmed by other evidence, however: In 1970, 60 percent of the inequality among municipalities was attributable to differences among states that they are

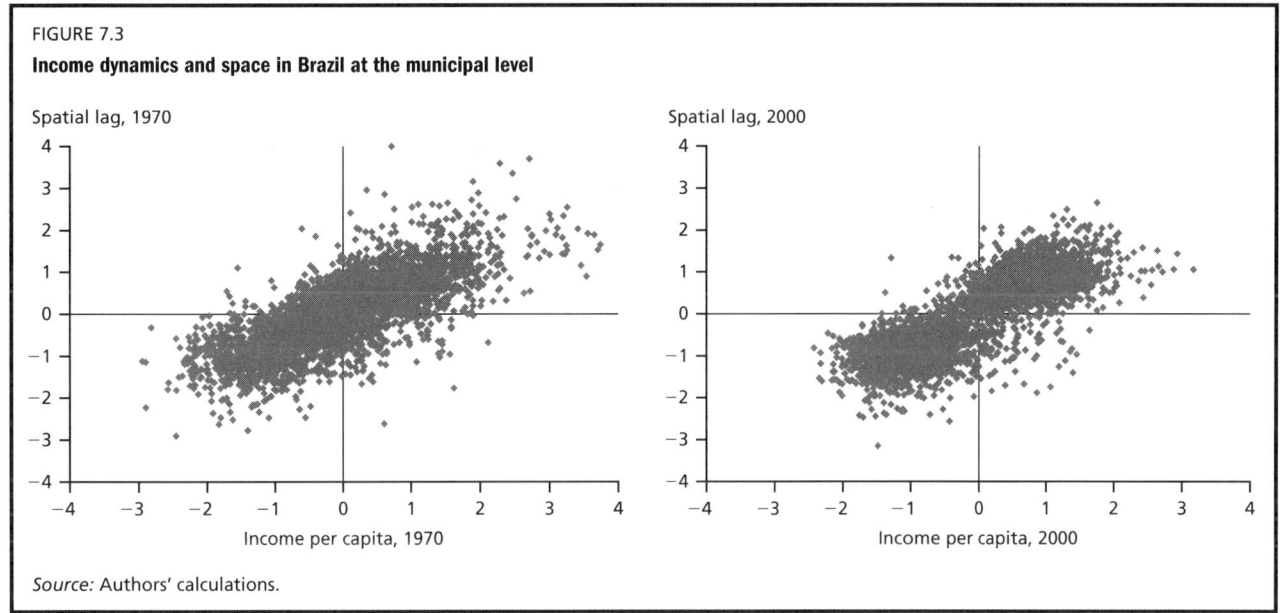

FIGURE 7.3
Income dynamics and space in Brazil at the municipal level

Source: Authors' calculations.

part of; in 2000 that figure had risen to 72 percent. The dramatic decrease in inequality between 1970 and 2000 has been almost entirely (98 percent) due to decreases in within-states inequality.

Chile: Divergence and spatial concentration

Aroca and Bosch (2000) find similar strong evidence of spatial clustering in Chile (figure 7.4). In particular they find a low-income cluster comprising the southern regions VIII, IX, and X that was also evident in the 1960s. Again, there is overall convergence in regional incomes at the same time that one sees evidence of more spatial concentration in the 1990s, a period of rapid overall growth of the Chilean economy. The impressive increase in the overall indicator of spatial dependence was caused by the emergence of a cluster of high income per capita in the north of the country, especially around regions I, II, and III, although the economic forces driving each state do not seem closely related. However, this time the kernel does not show such a clear convergence-club story, partly because the relatively few observations do not permit clear definition of the kernel. But overall, there appears to be a one-hump (unimodal) distribution with some outliers. Again, the lining up of the kernel along the 45-degree axis and its overall narrowness suggests relatively little movement among states. In sum, Chile until 1995 was another case of income convergence with increased spatial concentration. Recently, however, both forces are moving in the same direction—toward divergence.

Mexico: Openness, divergence, and spatial concentration

Mexico shows a case of increasing income disparities across states combined with increased spatial clustering—the reversal of a process of convergence and declustering that began around the period of unilateral liberalization (1987) and continued through the signing of the NAFTA treaty (1995). As in Brazil and Chile, there is clear evidence in the various Moran statistics of convergence clubs and polarization in Mexico; again, the kernel suggests little mobility among states and the emergence of another case of twin peaks (figure 7.5). Aroca, Bosch, and Maloney (2005) show that much of the increase in both dispersion and spatial concentration is explained by the adjoining states of Oaxaca, Guerrero, and Chiapas, which have fallen behind and been unable to take advantage of new economic opportunities, thus consolidating a longstanding low-income cluster in the far south.

The increased dispersion in per capita incomes does not seem to be driven by the emergence of a strong northern region in Mexico: the frontier states have benefited from their proximity to the United States, but beyond these frontier states, there appears to be little evidence of a steepening gradient in state incomes, and there is almost a random distribution of incomes and growth rates in the middle of the country. To the degree that there is an emerging cluster, it appears to be forming among a group of states closer to Mexico City. Nor is it obvious that distance from the United States should condemn the southern states

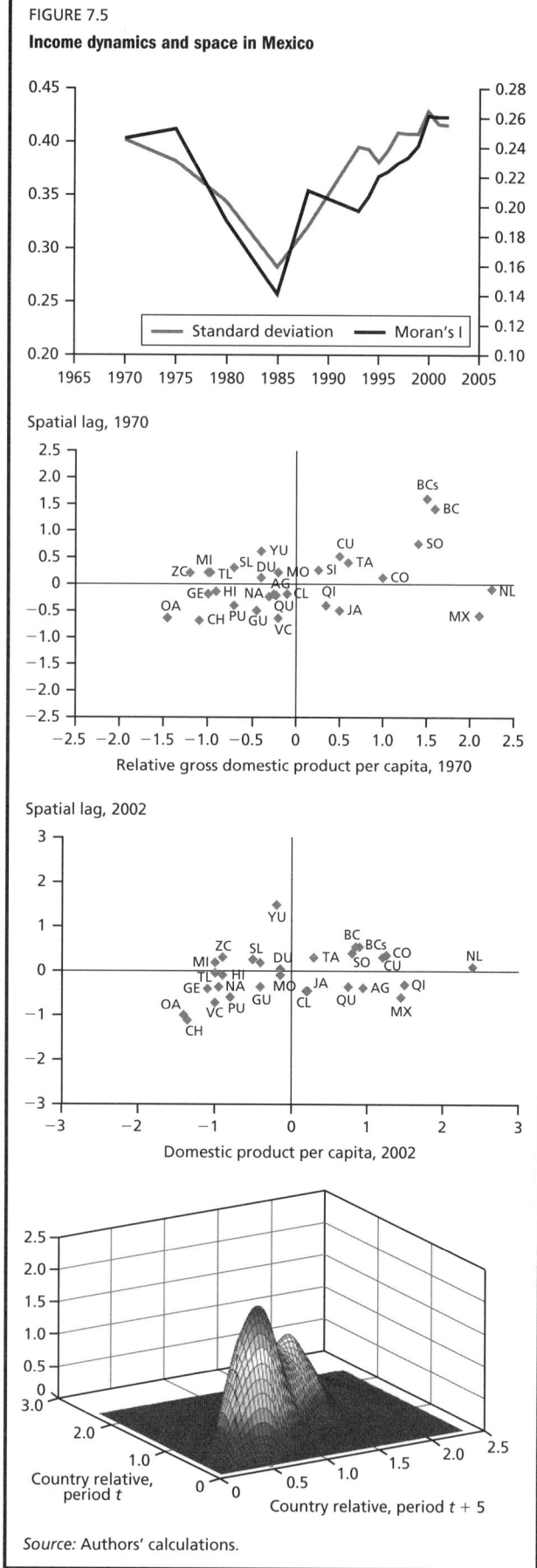

FIGURE 7.4

Income dynamics and space in Chile

Source: Authors' calculations.

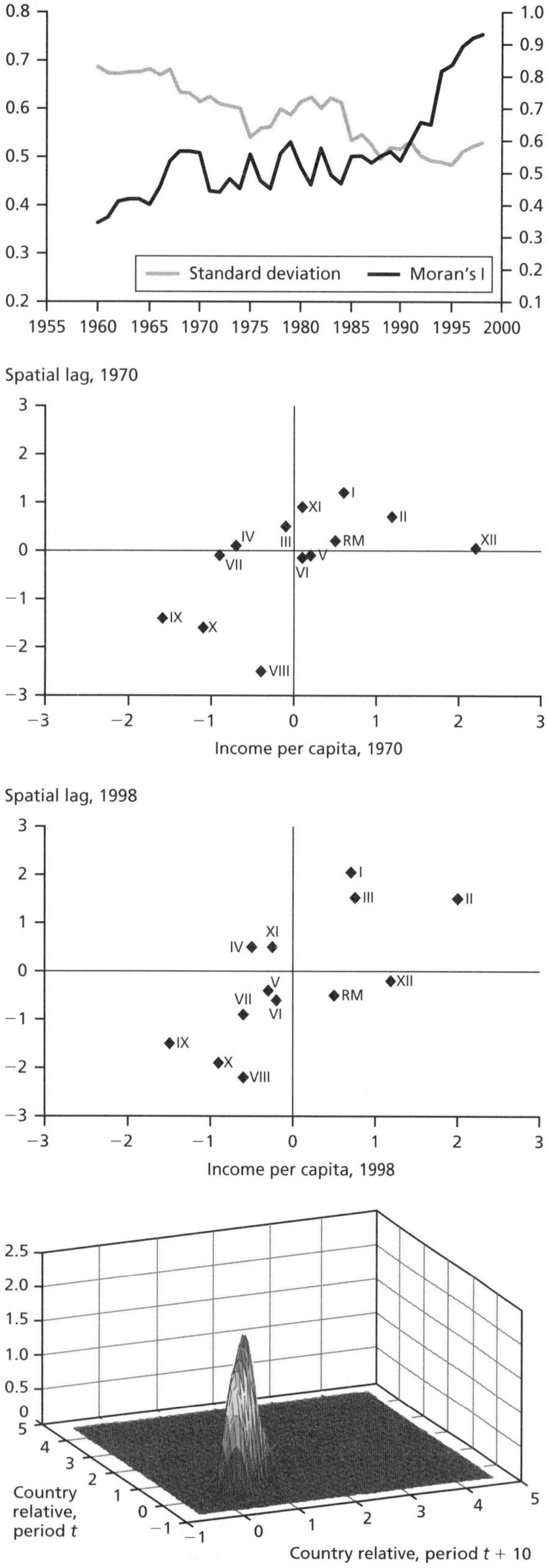

FIGURE 7.5

Income dynamics and space in Mexico

Source: Authors' calculations.

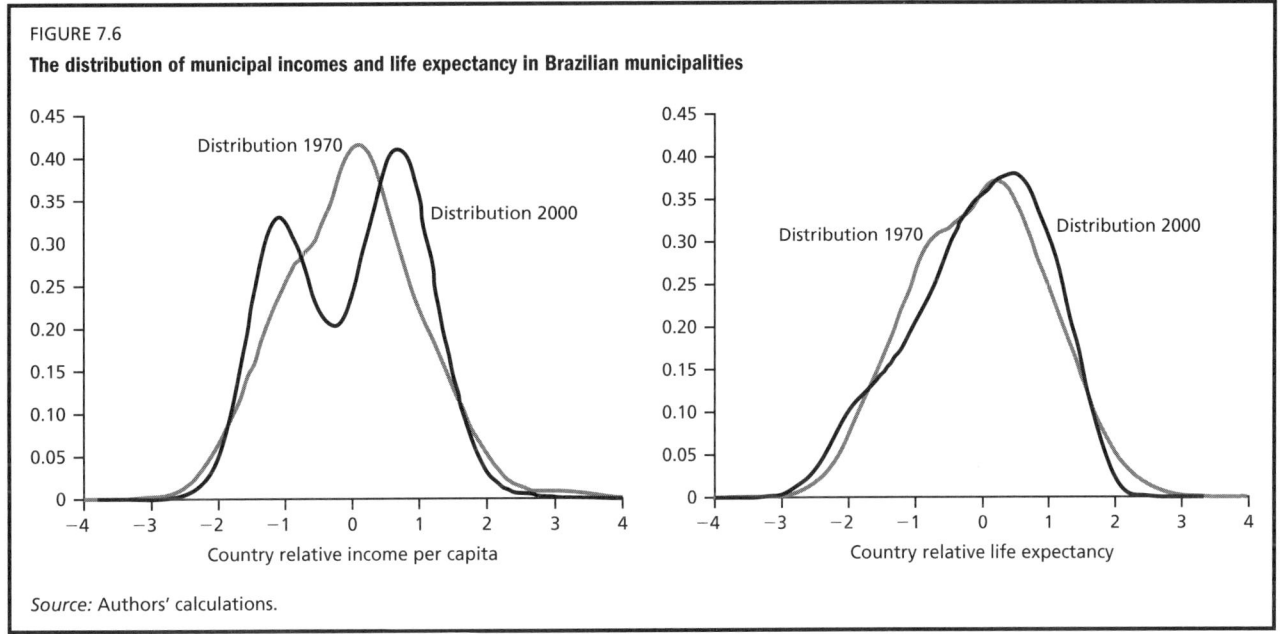

FIGURE 7.6
The distribution of municipal incomes and life expectancy in Brazilian municipalities

Source: Authors' calculations.

to their traditional position at the bottom of the distribution, given the proximity of the southeast coast to the port of Miami and the substantial rail links throughout southern Mexico to the port of Veracruz; all other things equal, the southern states should have been well positioned to enjoy a boom from trade liberalization (box 7.2).

Nonincome welfare measures

That said, as chapter 2 suggested, income is only one dimension of welfare, and focusing on it excessively may obscure the evolution of welfare more fully considered. Figure 7.6 shows that the distribution of life expectancy in Brazilian municipalities does not follow the same pattern of increasing bimodality that is found in incomes. A similar finding emerges for Mexico, as shown in figure 7.7. The dispersion of rates of infant mortality, mortality, literacy, and school attendance shows a steady decreasing trend across the last 30 years, despite the convergence and then divergence of incomes. Both cases suggest, first, that distribution trends in regional welfare may be improving. Second, they suggest an important role for policies that fight poverty independent of those dedicated to growth per se.

Why do we observe regional convergence clubs?

Chapter 6 reviewed the literature on why convergence clubs emerge among countries, and much of the same logic applies to regions as well. Two views receive particular attention in the literature. First, the New Economic Geography literature focuses on the interplay of agglomeration externalities resulting from the availability of specialized labor or intermediate inputs and technology spillovers, on the one hand, and transportation costs on the other (see Krugman 1991, 1993a; and Fujita, Krugman, and Venables 1999). Once agglomeration has started in a particular place, for whatever reason, even a historical accident as Krugman (1993a) points out, reinforcing forces are at play that perpetuate the situation. Lack of agglomeration effects

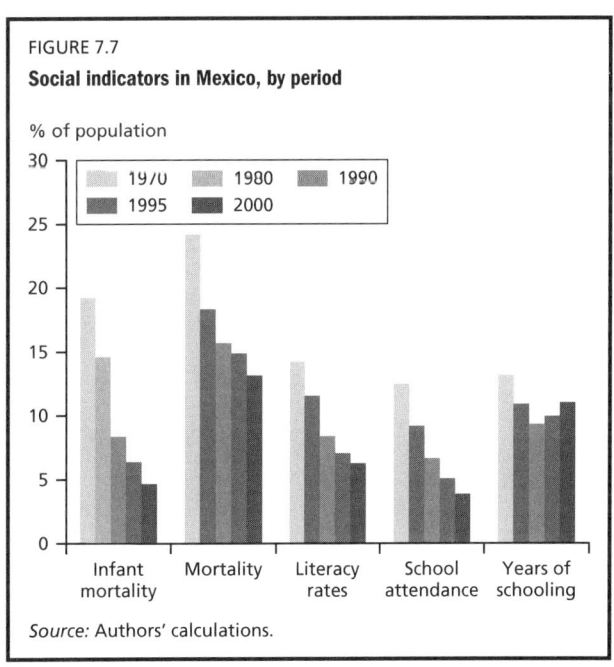

FIGURE 7.7
Social indicators in Mexico, by period

Source: Authors' calculations.

> BOX 7.2
> **Will trade liberalization increase regional disparities? NAFTA and Mexico**
>
> Much of the work that analyzed the impacts of trade reform and that predicted the impact of NAFTA on Mexico examined the potential response of specific industries, but was silent on how their location might be affected. In one possible scenario, Hanson (1997) suggested, along the lines of the new economic geography, that firms might choose to locate nearer the U.S. market, on the border, and shift away from the traditional Mexico City agglomeration centrally positioned to serve the domestic market. The benefits of proximity to the border would likely dissipate with distance and, as some have argued, lead to increased dispersion of welfare between north and south.
>
> But there are other elements to consider as well. To begin, the new economic geography is not without theoretical ambiguity: Behrens and Gaigne (2003), for example, suggest that the finding that trade liberalization increases geographic polarization depends critically on the specific modeling of internal transport costs. Second, Krugman and others (see Head and Mayer, forthcoming, for a review) have noted the remarkable persistence of patterns of industry distribution over very long periods of time and large changes in economic environment. This persistence may arise from the power of accumulated agglomeration externalities sparked initially by often trivial historical accident, in Krugman's view, or perhaps, the importance after all of natural advantages that anchor industries to their existing locales. In both the new economic geography and Heckscher-Ohlin-Vanek (HOV)-based views, it is not clear whether the sudden increase in demand from abroad, and an increase in supply of cheaper and better quality inputs, may lead to the displacement of existing nonborder growth poles, or to their reenergizing.
>
> In Mexico, these types of considerations suggest that the postintegration geographical patterns of economic performance may be more subtle and hard to predict. The higher costs of exporting from established central industrial locales, such as Queretaro, Aguascalientes, or Guadalajara, might be offset by their well-trained workforces and lower levels of congestion. Domestic and potential foreign firms in these areas serving the Mexican market may be further energized by the increased access to cheaper and higher-quality inputs from abroad and the lowered risk implied by, especially, the NAFTA agreement. Further, the location of some potential growth industries is clearly driven by immobile endowments not necessarily concentrated on the border. NAFTA potentially has a stimulative impact on nonborder areas with natural endowments with its elimination of import restrictions to the United States on mangos (produced in Guerrero and Michoacan), pineapples (Veracruz, Oaxaca, Tabasco), and grapes in 1994 and as it phases out restrictions on tomatoes (Jalisco) and avocados (Michoacan) by 2008. Both agricultural production and exports made large gains in the post-NAFTA period.
>
> Further, other forms of nonroad transport may offer low-cost transport to the U.S. market for nonborder regions. The two largest airports after Mexico City are found in Jalisco (center-south) and Yucatan (south). Airlift capacity, along with its high level of human capital and good governance, was critical to Intel's plant location in Costa Rica, south of Mexico. Yucatan also benefits from the shallow water port of Progreso that offers easy access to U.S. ports in the Gulf of Mexico as well as those in Central and South America and the Caribbean. It is perhaps not surprising that in 2003, Yucatan had the second-highest concentration of *maquila* employment of a nonborder state, exceeded only by Jalisco. The port of Veracruz, the entry point for Mexico's first globalizing influence in the 16th century, remains the country's most important, with extensive road and rail networks that connect the central and southern states, again to the Gulf of Mexico ports. Given this ready water access, *all other endowments equal,* it seems as plausible to find a southern pole or a southeastern corridor enjoying the same benefits of proximity as it would to see the region being left behind. In fact, to date, there is very little evidence that either the 1985 unilateral trade liberalization or NAFTA has led to a correlation of growth with distance from the border.
>
> *Source:* Aroca, Bosch, and Maloney (2005).

also drives the reverse pattern: remote indigenous communities may have few workers to attract industry, a small local market to produce for, and hence few economies of scale. In between can be found the smaller islands of the Caribbean where there are few economies of scale in infrastructure, governance, or even diversification against adverse shocks and where the small pool of qualified labor can make these countries less attractive to foreign investors.[4]

Second, natural advantages anchor industries to their existing locales. Davis and others (1997) argue that traditional endowment-based trade theories such as the HOV framework, perform so well as a theory of the location of production in Japanese regions that the New Economic Geography literature actually adds little to our understanding. Ellison and Glaeser (1999) find that only 21 percent of U.S. industries exhibit levels of geographical concentration significantly higher than those predicted by natural advantages such as weather or natural resources. Redding and Vera-Martin (2004) show that both theoretically and in 45 regions of Europe, factor endowments are important in determining the location of production.[5]

Both views can contribute to explaining the very high persistence of patterns of concentration of economic activity documented above and in prominent cities of the region. Medellin, Colombia, São Paulo, Brazil, and Monterrey, Mexico, all grew around a natural resource industry, usually mining, but the cities later diversified, often to very different industries. Both views also may help explain differences in what Jalan and Ravallion (2002) term "geographic capital," which may determine whether households enjoy a rising or stagnating standard of living. The elements of this capital include roads, technological spillovers from advanced producers to those less so, and health care. The evidence on the importance of these factors is mixed for Latin America and the Caribbean. Duarte, Ferreira, and Salvato (2003) argue that income differences among regions in Brazil largely reflect different levels of human capital, more than differing returns that might arise from complementarities with other regional endowments such as roads; they estimate that if the northeast states had the same educational endowment as those in the southeast, the average income gap would almost completely close. On the other hand, in Peru, Escobal and Torero (2005) find strong complementarities between private assets (human capital) and public assets (transport, telephones, sewerage): the increase in expenditures by families in response to a cluster of interventions to build public assets often multiplied the effects of the private assets. Whether one believes that being asset-poor in this fashion constitutes a poverty trap strictly defined, the logic of Lopez and Servén (2005b), described in chapter 6, that poverty in these dimensions and others hinders growth resonates here as well.

Although evidence to date is limited, these asset deficits may also dampen the transmission of growth impulses from dynamic areas to poorer ones. The dampening effect can work through numerous channels (De Vreyer and Spielvogel 2005): producers establish supply links with firms in other regions; growing markets in the dynamic hub create new market opportunities for firms in neighboring localities; new technologies or ideas are copied or otherwise disseminated.[6] These spillovers are the subject of an emerging literature on "spatial externalities," which are captured by a measure of the degree of spillover, called the "spatial multiplier" (Anselin 2003). Current estimates of average multipliers are fairly small. For Mexico, Bosch (2003) finds that a 10 percent increase in growth in one state leads to a 1.5–6.5 percent increase in growth in the neighboring states.[7] For Brazil, De Vreyer and Spielvogel (2005) find that a 10 percent increase in the average income per capita of a Brazilian municipality raises the growth rate of the neighboring municipalities by 2.6 percent; a finding consistent with Bosch, Aroca, Fernandez, and Azzoni (2003).[8] These are average measures that may overstate spillovers to poorer regions; moreover, they suggest that growth impulses from Mexico City or São Paulo are unlikely to have much stimulative effect on the peripheral regions of their countries.

That a positive growth shock to one state rapidly dissipates is consistent with the observation of areas of high and low economic activity in the same country. What is less clear is why earnings and hence levels of poverty differ across regions where movement of capital, labor, and technology should, in theory, equalize earnings and hence poverty rates. Lucas (1990) offered an explanation for why capital does not flow to poor countries based on differences in levels of human capital, and a similar logic holds within countries. For example, evidence from rudimentary data for Mexico suggests that foreign direct investment tends to pass over areas with low levels of literacy such as Mexico's southern states (Aroca and Maloney 2002). A World Bank report on Mexico's southern states (World Bank 2003) points to additional missing complements to foreign investment, including a lack of proper infrastructure, weak financial systems, unclear property rights, and an atmosphere of conflict. Knowledge flows, stressed as critical to growth and prosperity in *Closing the Gap in Education and Technology* (de Ferranti and others 2003), are strongly related to capital and educational accumulation, and require an even more sensitive set of conditions to foster (Maloney and Rodriguez-Clare 2005). Given that the capital cities of the region lag in the effectiveness of their national innovation systems, even less can be expected from the lagging regions.

Does migration work as an equilibrating mechanism?

Perhaps more surprising is that migration from region to region appears relatively limited as an equilibrating mechanism. Generally, migration is thought to be induced through the labor market, which makes state-level wages, rather than GDP per capita differences, the more relevant measure. Although wages show somewhat less variance than GDP per capita in Mexico, persistent gaps exist, and the southern states remain at the bottom of the distribution, with their wages only 50 percent of those of the states with the highest average wages. Overall in Latin America, these wage gaps often range between 15 and 40 percent after controlling for worker characteristics, but they can be even higher in countries with sharp geographical differences.[9] Much of the migration is, in fact, rural to urban, and data for Bolivia, Brazil, Colombia, and Peru reveal that the urban wages are often two to three times higher than rural wages in these countries.

Migration flows have been less than what might be expected given these wage differentials.[10] In Mexico net migration from the impoverished Chiapas, Guerrero, and Oaxaca states amounts to 2–2.5 percent of the population over a period of five years; similar rates are found in the lagging regions VIII, IX, and X in Chile. A quick comparison indicates that this dearth of migration may have an impact on wage gaps: In the Dominican Republic, where the earnings gap between some rural and urban areas is less than 10 percent, migrants make up 44 percent of the urban labor force; in Bolivia, where the regional earnings gap is 50 percent, migrants make up less than 10 percent of urban workers.

Trying to understand the determinants of these flows, Aroca and Hewings (2002) and Aroca and Maloney (forthcoming) find that the determinants of interregional migration flows for Chile and Mexico, respectively, are broadly in line with the mainstream literature on migration. Labor market variables such as wages, unemployment levels, and transport costs affect migration in predictable ways. However, the responsiveness to wage differentials is not large enough to equalize differentials.[11] In seeking to explain low elasticities and low mobility generally, a long literature identifies liquidity constraints—the inability to borrow against the gains that would occur if a family migrated—and there is clear evidence of this effect in Mexico.[12] Both liquidity constraints and the risks associated with moving can be mitigated to some degree by the existence of networks of established migrants in the destination; a now-expansive literature documents that migrants to the United States tend to come from areas that have long been sources of migration. There can also be crowding of urban labor markets and an expansion of poverty pockets in near-urban areas (Lucas 1988). Further impediments may include poorly defined property rights in the sending region and language or cultural barriers.

Another provocative explanation is put forward by Aroca (2005b), who notes that in Chile from 1993 to 2003, there was essentially no correlation between unemployment and growth at the subnational level, while there was a clear and significant negative relationship at the national level. This could partly be explained by the fact that the percentage of individuals who live in one region but work in another i.e., commuters is roughly double the percentage of migrants on an annual basis. Further, commuting to a destination seems closely related to inflows of foreign direct investment to the destination region and negatively related to housing costs in that area. Thus, it may be that in terms of real income net of local costs, commuting is actually preferred to migration and constitutes a significant but heretofore understudied equalization mechanism.

Finally, consistent with our argument in favor of multidimensional approaches to welfare and the discussion of converging social indicators above, it may be that money isn't everything after all. Arias and Sosa-Escudero (2004) find that, after controlling for socioeconomic characteristics and access to basic services, rural residents in Bolivia no longer considered themselves poorer than the urban population despite remaining more likely to be income-poor. Although Chuquisaca, a region with a very high fraction of indigenous population, is the second poorest region as measured by income, its residents rated themselves *the least poor* in the country. Thus, geographical and cultural attractions may offset income poverty and prevent further arbitraging of spatial earnings differentials.[13] Further, life at the "destination" may be less attractive than incomes suggest. As mentioned in chapter 2, residents of the province of Buenos Aires, the second richest province in Argentina, rated themselves as poorer than virtually every other region of the country. This self-rating may reflect negative agglomeration (congestion) effects of living in big urban areas, or a greater awareness of relative poverty in the presence of stark income differentials.

The link back to growth and policy issues

What do these persistent inequalities in spatial income (if less obviously welfare) and the lack of labor mobility imply for growth and policy? The growth issue is, in fact, less straightforward than it appears at first sight, and that, in turn, complicates the policy debate. At the level of the subnational unit, all the arguments outlined in chapter 6 showing that poverty-related factors may slow growth hold, and a case can be made for policies to ameliorate them. In addition, Kanbur and Venables (2005), among others, have stressed that regional inequalities correlated to ethnic, linguistic, or religious divisions provide fertile ground for internal conflict that can undermine economy-wide growth.[14]

Yet in the world of the new economic geography, the case for reorienting resources to disadvantaged zones becomes less clear, and the literature to date has been very circumspect on policy prescriptions. Fundamentally, this literature argues that if existing externalities mean that the current agglomerations actually show the highest potential for growth, then focusing on poor regions will actually decrease national growth. The goal must be to find a way to move people and resources to the existing rich centers. Box 7.3 suggests that such a trade-off between equity and growth appears to have been important in Spain. Unfortunately, more generally the literature offers little guidance on whether it is the externalities relative to agglomeration or those leading to dispersion of activity that are more important, so we do not know whether existing agglomerations are too big or too small. As an example of the reigning agnosticism, Krugman (1999, 160) remarks: "One may have opinions—I am quite sure in my gut, and even more so in my lungs, that Mexico City is too big—but gut feelings are not a sound basis for policy."

Poverty rates vs. poverty density

Chomitz (2005), however, argues that a more subtle use of spatial information can attenuate these potential trade-offs to some measure. Figure 7.8 displays two maps of Brazil, one showing poverty rates and the other showing poverty densities, or the number of poor people. The maps clearly show that the more rural northern states have the highest poverty rates, while the big cities, both north and south, show the highest concentrations of poor people. The same is true of Bolivia, where the border regions with Argentina and Chile have the highest proportions of poor people but not very many of them, while the developed regions with high growth potential—La Paz, Cochabamba, and Santa Cruz—have the highest numbers of poor people. Therefore, provided that existing agglomerations are not already too large, the theoretical trade-offs may be less important than we initially thought—in other words, a large chunk of the poor are, in fact, in areas with potentially higher growth. Chomitz's observation allows us to define four different spatial categories (table 7.1) that imply distinct policies, some of which allow investment in potential high-growth areas with large numbers of poor people.

Areas with high poverty rates and low poverty density capture the essence of Chomitz's trade-off. In areas of low population density, the cost of infrastructure per person is higher, or, alternatively, the returns to investment are low relative to areas of greater density, which can reap economies of scale. The high-poverty-rate, low-poverty-density area is unlikely to develop substantial economic dynamism, and policies thus need to focus more on direct poverty alleviation and on programs that will impart skills useful in other, more dynamic regions. Conditional cash transfer programs or other education and health initiatives or, perhaps, agricultural research and development would be most appropriate in these circumstances.

In areas with low poverty rates and high poverty density, often urban or relatively dense rural areas where agglomeration forces have already taken place, policies aimed at fostering growth have good chances of reaching the poor and translating into important poverty reductions. The major problem is to ensure that wealthy groups do not capture the flow of resources. For this reason, self-targeting mechanisms, such as those envisaged in the Argentine and Colombian workfare programs, are particularly appropriate. That said, conditional cash transfer schemes, such as *Familias en Acción* in Colombia or *Oportunidades* in Mexico, where targeting is quite good, have been used in this type of situation.[15]

Areas with high poverty rates and high poverty density have the potential to take advantage of projects with

BOX 7.3
Trade-offs in regional policy: The Spanish experience

De la Fuente (2002) estimates that the European cohesion funds meant to remedy regional inequalities within the EU contributed significantly to the growth of poorer regions of Spain and to the reduction of regional disparities. However, he also points out that there has been an opportunity cost in terms of overall efficiency for the country. This is suggested in the figure below, which presents the return to (marginal product of) infrastructure in the Spanish regions in 1995. Objective 1 regions are those poorer regions that were targeted by the cohesion funds, virtually all of which show below average returns. It is clear that the highest returns are found in Madrid, Catalonia, and Balearic Islands that were not objective 1 regions and, in fact, are the richest. In other words, a much higher return for the country as a whole would have occurred had the funds gone toward the most developed regions.

De la Fuente (2003) further simulates the convergence of Spain toward the European mean of incomes and the convergence of the Objective 1 regions toward the Spanish mean income under three possible scenarios: the actual relative incomes (BASE); the resulting relative incomes in the absence of cohesion funds (SIN); and the result of distributing the funds efficiently among all the Spanish regions according to the marginal returns to infrastructures. The results again suggest that cohesion funds helped the targeted regions converge toward the national mean, as well as Spain's convergence toward the European income level. In reality, the income gap between Spain and the EU15 closed by 2.9 points between 1993 and 2000 and the gap in relative incomes between Objective 1 regions and the rest of Spain decreased 2.2 points. In the second scenario, the convergence toward the European mean was only 1 point and the gap between Objective 1 regions and the others rose 5.6 points. Finally, had the cohesion funds been distributed efficiently among all the regions, the overall growth of the Spanish economy would have caught up quicker with the other members of the European Union (closing the gap by 3.9 points). However, the gap between the Objective I regions and the rest of Spain would have increased by 7.4 points, even more than the gap would have been in the absence of the European funds.

How the European cohesion funds benefited the different Spanish regions, 1995

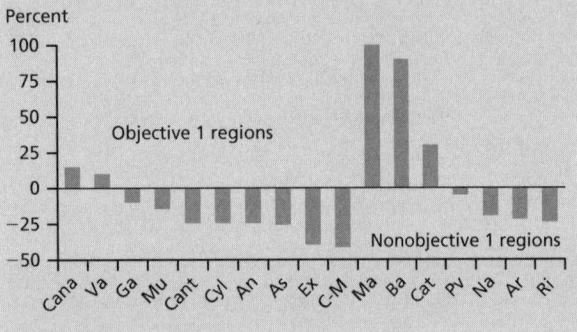

Source: De la Fuente (2002).
Note: Percentage deviations from the national average.

TABLE 7.1
Typology of appropriate actions according to poverty rate and density

	Type of area	
Type of project	Low poverty density	High poverty density
Low poverty rate	No special programs needed	Investments that boost labor demand Self-targeting antipoverty projects
High poverty rate	Investments with no scale economies Agricultural research and development Education Cash transfers	Rural roads, other infrastructure

Source: Chomitz (2005).

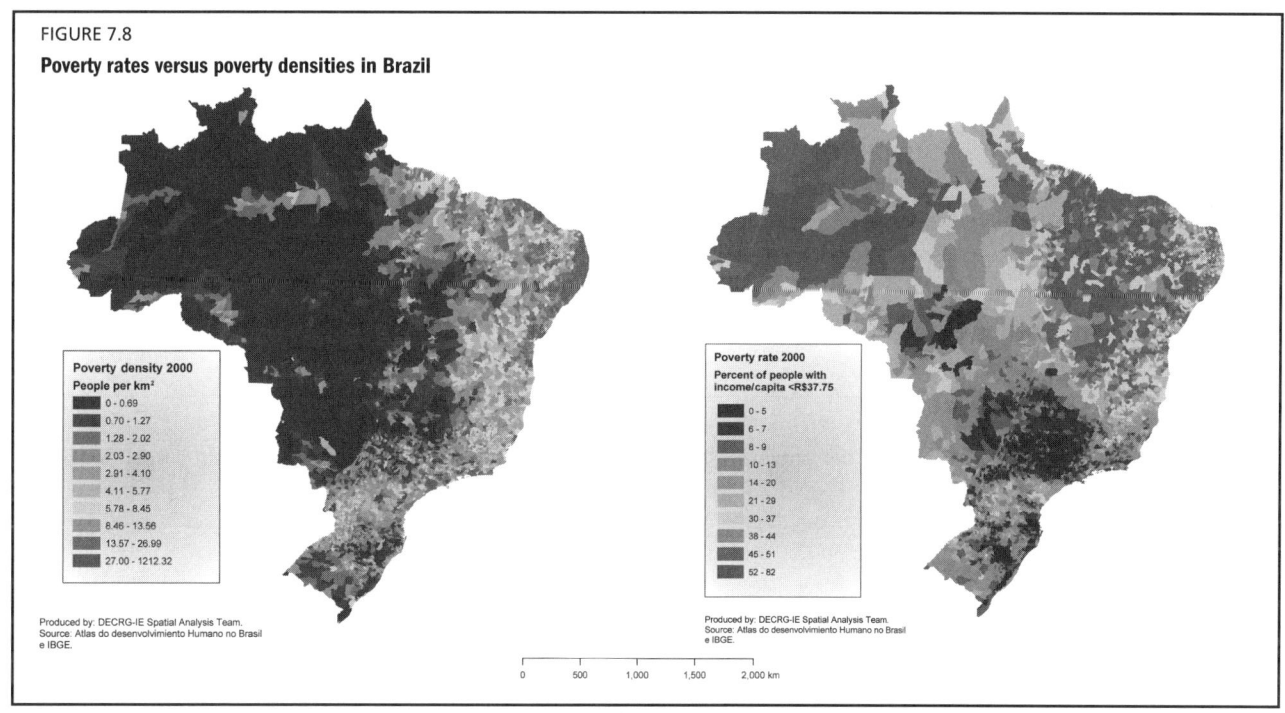

FIGURE 7.8
Poverty rates versus poverty densities in Brazil

BOX 7.4
Rural roads and poverty reduction in El Salvador

El Salvador has a high-density population in rural areas that corresponds with the high-poverty-rate, high-poverty-density category in table 7.1. The country increased its rate of investment from 1 percent of GDP in 1998–99 to 1.9 percent of GDP in 2002–3. The increase was mostly concentrated in the rehabilitation of the primary road network after the 2001 earthquake, paving of main sand roads, and maintenance. Roughly 26 percent of the 2,200 cantons around the country directly benefited from the improvements.

Rural roads are thought to contribute to poverty reduction through access to education and health, and expansion of markets for agricultural products. To measure the improvement in access, Yepes (2004) estimated two indicators using a rural panel of households: the average distance from households to paved roads, and the distance to the market place in rural areas. Both indicators are closely linked to the poverty level. The poorest households live almost double the distance to a paved road, and have 25 percent longer travel time to market, as do nonpoor households. Over the 1999–2001 period, significant improvements in both indicators were reported for extremely poor households: travel time was reduced from 53 to 46 minutes, roughly the level of moderately poor households. A systematic study of the impact on poverty of these improvements suggests that extreme poverty fell 8.8 percent in the control group, while in the cantons where roads improved, poverty fell 13.9 percent. The net contribution of better rural roads to extreme poverty of 5 percent seems remarkable for such a short period of time.

Source: Yepes (2004).

economies of scale and be subject to low levels of leakage of resources to the nonpoor. Infrastructure investments such as rural roads may be a good example of successful projects for these areas (box 7.4).

From a practical point of view, the increasing use of detailed poverty maps to identify poor groups and then targeting poverty policies yields dividends. Elbers and others (2004) showed that in Cambodia, Ecuador, and Madagascar, allocating funds to geographically defined subgroups of the population according to their relative poverty status could achieve the same degree of poverty reduction with 40 percent fewer resources than traditional methods require.

TABLE 7.2

Public investment effects in Mexico, 1970–2000

Public investment	Growth GDP per capita	Infant mortality	Years of schooling
Productive Activities			
Industry	0.0068		
Agriculture	0.0302		
Infrastructure and Communications	0.0394	−0.0224	
Social Investment			
Education	0.0043	−0.0870	0.0052
Health	0.0018	−0.0211	0.0022

Source: Bosch and Cobacho (2005).
Note: All coefficients are significant at the 5 percent level. The GDP coefficient includes both direct effects and indirect effects through the other two variables.

And if Mexico City is, in fact, too big?

History suggests, however, that policy makers often judge that present agglomerations are too big, or that other considerations lead them to resist abandoning entire regions to low levels of economic activity and extensive conditional cash transfer programs. In fact, as *Beyond the City* and other recent World Bank reports have noted, Latin America has substantial experience with ambitious regional development programs that have met with mixed success, and this report will not attempt a comprehensive survey of the literature.[16] The now-vast OECD literature on the effects of public investment policies generally finds a positive impact on growth and sometimes inequality although, again, as the Spanish case suggests, these policies do not necessarily maximize national growth.[17] The evidence for Latin America and the Caribbean is thinner but generally concurs.[18] What does merit emphasis, however, is that traditional regional policy has, to some degree, neglected discussion about the role of human capital, knowledge transmission, innovation, and improving economic environments—the very factors that emerge consistently as correlated with regional income differences (see chapter 6).

In an attempt to capture the development impact of a broader set of interventions, Bosch and Cobacho (2005) model the direct and indirect effects of five types of Mexican regional federal investment (industry, agriculture, infrastructure and communication, education, and health) not only on GDP growth, but also on broader measures of welfare such as infant mortality and education; working in a simultaneous equations framework allows them to model the cross-effects of the different types of investment.[19] Table 7.2 shows that investment in productive activities (industry and agriculture) positively affects growth. Consistent with Calderón and Servén (2004), public spending in infrastructure and communications do so as well, but part of the effect comes through a channel of reducing infant mortality by improving access to the water supply. Social investment in education and health increases the years of schooling and lowers infant mortality, and these effects also feed back through the overall increase in growth. The estimates also suggest that these policies have been responsible for the observed convergence in nonincome measures of poverty at a time when per capita state incomes were diverging.[20]

Conclusions

To sum up, regional disparities in poverty and income are large and persistent. In two of the three countries studied, overall dispersion in per capita state incomes is falling, while in all three cases, the spatial distribution moves the other way toward becoming more concentrated. Generally, the natural equilibrating flows of factors, especially migration, do not operate with enough vigor to equalize incomes, so policy makers need to articulate region-based policies. The trade-off posed by the new economic geography between investing in those agglomerations with high rates of return versus those poorer areas that would yield less aggregate growth needs to be kept in mind as a particular policy wrinkle specific to the regional level of analysis. But whether policy chooses to focus on already advanced areas with well-designed antipoverty programs for areas of low-density poverty, or to attempt a comprehensive strategy for developing such low-density areas, the lessons from chapter 6 pertain: a comprehensive approach that keeps in mind the feedbacks directly back to growth that accrue from attacking poverty across a broad front is likely to have more success than more traditional approaches focusing on narrow incentives to production.

Notes

1. See Shorrocks and Wan (2005). To measure the contribution to inequality, we simply partition the sample into a set of geographical regions and then calculate the two components of aggregate inequality; a weighted average of regional inequality (within-group component) and the between-group component term, which captures the inequality attributable to variations in average incomes across regions.

2. For a detailed description on how to compute and interpret the kernels, see Quah (1997).

3. Laurini, Andrade, and Valls Periera (2004) confirm these twin humps at the municipal level.

4. For a thorough treatment of the challenges facing the Caribbean, see World Bank (2005f).

5. Theoretically they show this should be the case regardless of the degree of factor mobility. Working in a similar tradition, Bernstein and Weinstein (2002) reintroduce the importance of transport costs as a means of anchoring the indeterminacy intrinsic to HOV when the number of goods exceeds the number of factors.

6. See Bottazi and Peri (2003) for a study of regional spillovers in Italy.

7. But after allowing for growth effects of neighboring states to work through these variables, particularly literacy, the spillover impact is reduced to only 0.6 percent.

8. The spatial effect of explanatory variables is consistent with Chomitz (2005), who shows what appear to be positive spillover effects on wages and employment from income growth in nearby regions. His estimates for nonmetropolitan areas show that a 10 percent income increase in close neighborhood regions is associated with a 7 percent increase in a region's wages and a 2 percent increase in employment.

9. See background studies summarized in the next section and World Bank poverty assessments for other countries.

10. In fact, countries differ in ways that we poorly understand. In Bolivia and the Dominican Republic, for example, interurban migration dominates (especially to larger cities), although seasonal and temporary migration to the rural sector in Bolivia is on the order of migration to the city in the first place. The idea that migration is a one-way flow thus seems seriously incomplete. In both countries, earnings were improved by migration. That is, despite a potential lack of contacts and urban know-how, migrants got competitive urban jobs for their skills. Thus, migration likely reduces poverty directly and possibly indirectly through remittances. See Tannuri-Pianto, Pianto, and Arias (2004). For Mexico, see Taylor (2001) and Taylor, Yúnez-Naude, and Cerón (2004).

11. Following the technique developed by Gabriel, Shack-Marquez, and Wascher (1993) for examining the same question in the United States, Aroca and Hewings (2002) and Aroca (2005a) conclude that, for plausible values of the local labor demand and supply elasticities, only a proportion of the shock in wages is arbitraged by migration.

12. See Aroca and Maloney (forthcoming). Traditional specifications have entered the wage of both the destination and origin wages with the latter generally entering insignificantly. However, if wages are entered as both a relative wage, wj/wi, and a free-standing initial wage term capturing liquidity constraints, both variables enter very significantly and are of expected sign.

13. Urban migrants often initially settle in ethnically similar neighborhoods, which suggests that networks lower the effective cost of moving and that a minimum agglomeration may be needed to elicit larger-scale migration.

14. An emerging empirical growth literature has documented the impact of fragmentation indexes and polarization on growth. See Easterly and Levine (1997), Rodrik (1999) and Brock and Durlauf (2001), Alesina and others (2003).

15. See Gertler, Martinez and Rubio (2005). They show that in Mexico, CCTs led to long-term rises in living standards that persisted after the termination of the program and that the return on investment was quite high and that households are both liquidity and credit constrained.

16. As an example, Brazil's high-profile programs of fiscal incentives for regional development have generally been thought disappointing for a variety of reasons, including inefficiencies and poor management. These efforts also have been dwarfed by lending, for instance, by the Brazilian Development Bank (BNDES), based on nonregional criteria such as export promotion. Recent studies suggest that regional subsidies to the north and northeast represent only 12 percent of total subsidies for export promotion and industrialization, which tend to favor the industrialized regions of the south. See Calmon (2003) and World Bank (2005a).

17. Easterly and Rebelo (1993) find a positive relationship between public investment in transportation and communications and overall growth using a sample of 100 countries. Knight, Loayza, and Villanueva (1993) also find positive effects on investment on growth for OECD countries. As noted above, De la Fuente (2002) shows that in Europe the structural and cohesion funds have played an important role in reducing or at least maintaining disparities within countries but also warns of the possible dangers of inefficiently allocating scarce resources. More recently, Calderon and Servén (2004) show how public infrastructure has been a determinant factor in promoting growth and reducing inequality. Foster and Araujo (2001) find positive effects of improvements in basic services infrastructure (electricity, water supply, telecommunications) for poverty reduction in Guatemala.

18. Ramirez and Nazmi (2003), using a cross-section of Latin American countries, find positive effects of public investment on

growth. Rodriguez-Oreggia and Rodriguez-Pose (2004), using a cross-section of Mexican regions, find a significant effect across 1970–85 that disappears in the period 1985–2000.

19. There are three main equations in the model. Growth in GDP per capita is determined by education, infant mortality, the different kinds of investments, and a number of control variables. Similarly, years of education depend directly on investments in education, infrastructure, and other controls. Finally, infant mortality is affected by years of education and investments in health and infrastructure. Therefore, public expenditure in education has a direct effect on education and an indirect effect on growth and infant mortality. Infrastructure may affect growth directly and through its effects on the social variables.

20. Further, as suggested by World Bank (2003), a multipronged approach that attacked health and education directly probably would also have growth dividends.

CHAPTER 8

Microdeterminants of Incomes: Labor Markets, Poverty, and Traps?

The preceding chapters focused on the cross-national and spatial aspects of the coexistence of high and persistent poverty and low rates of economic growth in Latin America. The next two chapters amplify that analysis through the lens of households and individuals. This chapter examines the role that labor and other assets and their market returns play in generating persistent low earnings and inequality in the region. It concludes that public investments and policies to foster the poor's accumulation of assets (including equitable returns to their investments) would facilitate their mobility and would exploit complementarities in the generation of income that are essential for ensuring that the poor benefit from and participate in the growth process.

THE PERSISTENCE OF POVERTY ARISES FROM the inability of certain population groups to increase their long-term income generation potential. Addressing this situation requires an understanding of the factors that prevent poor families from moving out of low-productivity economic activities. The poverty-traps literature emphasizes that the main determinants of the poor's inability to take advantage of growth opportunities are insufficient asset holdings, thresholds in the returns to those assets, fixed or switching costs of productive transitions, and limited access to credit or insurance.[1] Of particular importance is the ability of the poor to use their labor (their most abundant asset) in wage jobs, self-employment, or their own microenterprises. Labor earnings often account for more than two-thirds of total household income of the Latin American poor.[2] The pricing of labor reflects productivity differentials across workers and jobs, sector and regional supply-demand imbalances, and nonmarket factors. Low-earnings traps can result from deficiencies in the endowments that enhance the productivity (quality) of labor assets (such as human capital or infrastructure) as well as from earnings differentials that arise from barriers to mobility in the labor market (such as discrimination or impediments to migration) and that are unrelated to skills.

This chapter examines some of the mechanisms that may prevent the Latin American poor from participating in the growth process, thus keeping them in persistent poverty. Unfortunately, little long-span panel data has been collected for the region, which prevents in-depth analyses of the duration of poverty and its main determinants throughout the region.[3] The chapter instead relies on the limited, though highly consistent, evidence that is available on these issues. Drawing from cross-section survey data, the chapter discusses the variation in the level and growth path of labor earnings across individuals of different skills, demographics, and job characteristics, with

---

This chapter draws from the studies by Arias and Diaz (2004), Gasparini, Gutierrez, and Tornarolli (2005), Sosa-Escudero and Lucchetti (2004), and Sosa-Escudero and Cicowiez (2005), and from background analyses for this report by Bustelo (2005), Tannuri-Pianto, Pianto, and Arias (2005) and Sosa-Escudero, Marchionni, and Arias (2005).

attention to the quantitative importance of potential barriers to mobility (segmentation across sectors, occupations, or locations) as a source of low earnings and poverty traps. The chapter then analyzes the main determinants of income growth and poverty persistence, drawing primarily on analytical work from a unique panel household survey in rural El Salvador and evidence from other countries. The chapter pays special attention to complementarities (threshold or "bundling" effects) between publicly provided assets and household characteristics (observed and unobserved) as drivers of family income growth.

The chapter reaches two main conclusions. First, labor market segmentation is a second-order source of low earnings in the region relative to low levels of productivity. Most low earnings and thus poverty are not generated directly by the labor market, but largely reflect differences in workers' productive endowments (chiefly education) and overall productivity levels in the countries of the region. The reduction of earnings disparities specifically associated with gender, ethnicity and race, the informal economy, occupation, sector of employment, or geographic location would have a larger immediate impact on inequality than on poverty, particularly in the poorest countries in the region. The feedback effects of inequality in the pricing of labor on human capital accumulation (discussed in chapter 9) and the unequalizing role of unmeasured worker characteristics (such as education quality, labor market ability, and family connections) deserve greater attention as potential sources of poverty traps.

Second, a detailed analysis of rural El Salvador and consistent evidence from other countries suggest that household-level poverty traps are a phenomenon of practical relevance in Latin America and the Caribbean. Not everyone benefits equally from growth: often individuals and families with bundles of favorable characteristics (observed and unobserved) reap faster-than-average income growth—this is especially true of the more mobile. Important complementarities between public investments and household characteristics mean that poor families often lack the minimum level of private and public assets required to exploit growth opportunities fully. While lack of family endowments is the main driver behind persistent low incomes and poverty, high volatility and the inability to ensure against shocks are also important sources of variation in incomes, much more so than in developed countries.

Policies to improve the functioning of labor markets, including sound regulations and institutions, should facilitate productivity growth while guarding equity in the labor market. The poor are generally disadvantaged in several dimensions. Public investments and policies in one area (such as credit or roads construction) may have heterogeneous impacts depending on the level of assets and other initial conditions affecting the poor. A minimum coordination of public interventions in poor areas can help exploit synergies and overcome the associated potential poverty traps that may affect households with a bundling of unfavorable characteristics.

The distribution of earnings: The role of worker endowments and labor markets

There are two distinct perspectives on how labor markets affect poverty and inequality (Fields 2004). In one view, earnings are mainly determined by the interplay of the supply and demand of labor in competitive, frictionless labor markets. Differences in wages arise from differences in marginal labor productivity and workers' preferences, which in turn depend on individual characteristics either observed (such as education and work experience) or unobserved (such as unmeasured skills or industriousness) and the quality of the economic and institutional environment that determines overall productivity levels. In this view, low labor productivity—resulting, for example, from low human capital or technological innovations—is the main reason for persistent low earnings. A number of researchers adhere to an alternative view of labor pricing in developing countries that is best characterized by segmented, dualistic markets where earnings differences between workers of similar skills result from discrimination (ethnicity or gender) or barriers to mobility across occupations (such as informal/formal jobs), sectors (subsistence agriculture/off-farm jobs), and locations (rural/urban areas). These barriers can be related to labor market institutions such as unionization, minimum wages, and other labor regulations, and to labor market connections and geographic mobility costs. In this second view, labor markets per se generate unequal advantage and low-earnings traps.

While analytically useful, this distinction is artificial. Inequality in the pricing of skills has feedback effects to the incentives to invest in skills and innovation. As discussed in chapter 9, lower returns to schooling associated with exclusion can help sustain low-education poverty traps. Recent studies find that the process of job reallocation contributes

15 to 50 percent of productivity growth in an economy (IDB 2004). For instance, informality can trap significant resources in low-productivity activities. Lacking access to capital, many micro- and small enterprises cannot capitalize productivity gains through scale economies and innovation and may be trapped in a bad equilibrium: because of low productivity, they cannot afford the costs of participating in formal institutions, but informality in turn limits the potential for productivity growth. Hence, A fluid labor market is important for sustainable increases in productivity in the region.

Considerable evidence indicates that unobserved heterogeneity among individuals with the same human capital, sector of work, and demographic characteristics is very important in explaining earnings levels and earnings differentials in Latin America and the Caribbean. A large portion (around 40–60 percent) of earnings inequality in the region remains "unexplained" by measured worker characteristics.[4] Factors unobserved by the analyst such as the quality of education, family background, labor market connections, and individual industriousness are distributed unevenly across workers. These characteristics may grant an advantage in access to high-paying jobs, affecting the returns to skills and the price of labor in the labor market. Workers from poor families may be disproportionately disadvantaged in these unobserved earnings determinants. With these issues in mind, this chapter review what is known about the main sources of the level and differences in earnings in the region, and the links to poverty and overall income inequality.[5]

Earnings and productivity: Education and the quality of the economic environment

A key factor behind the persistent low levels of earnings in the region is low and stagnant productivity. Real wages moved one-for-one with labor productivity between the mid-1980s and early 2000s (IDB 2004), but labor productivity stagnated during this period, with half of the countries exhibiting a decline. Thus, the scope for sustained earnings gains has been limited, a reflection in part of the region's sluggish skills accumulation and overall productivity trends.

Education is the single most important individual determinant of earnings, accounting for about one-third of overall earnings inequality in the region. One study found that disparities in educational endowments and in returns to education as one of the main factors driving differences in poverty and income inequality between Brazil, Mexico, and the United States (Bourguignon, Ferreira, and Leite 2002). High levels of education are needed to escape from poverty in most countries in Latin America. As discussed in detail in chapter 9, on average, Latin American workers with a university diploma earn one and a half to three times as much as uneducated workers, while those with a secondary degree earn up to one and a half times as much. Moreover, returns to schooling tend to be higher (often by 2 to 4 percentage points) for workers located higher up in the earnings distribution given observed characteristics, so the payoff to education may depend on a worker's endowment of unobserved characteristics.

Earnings also depend on demand factors and, more generally, a country's economic and institutional environment. Labor productivity trends mimic the region's lukewarm overall productivity growth, measured by total factor productivity, which was negative in the 1980s and meager in the 1990s. In contrast, East Asia experienced a sustained increase in productivity and labor earnings during this period. Achieving significant poverty reduction is harder in countries with a low earnings base (where unskilled workers earn very little), a point illustrated in figure 8.1. The figure

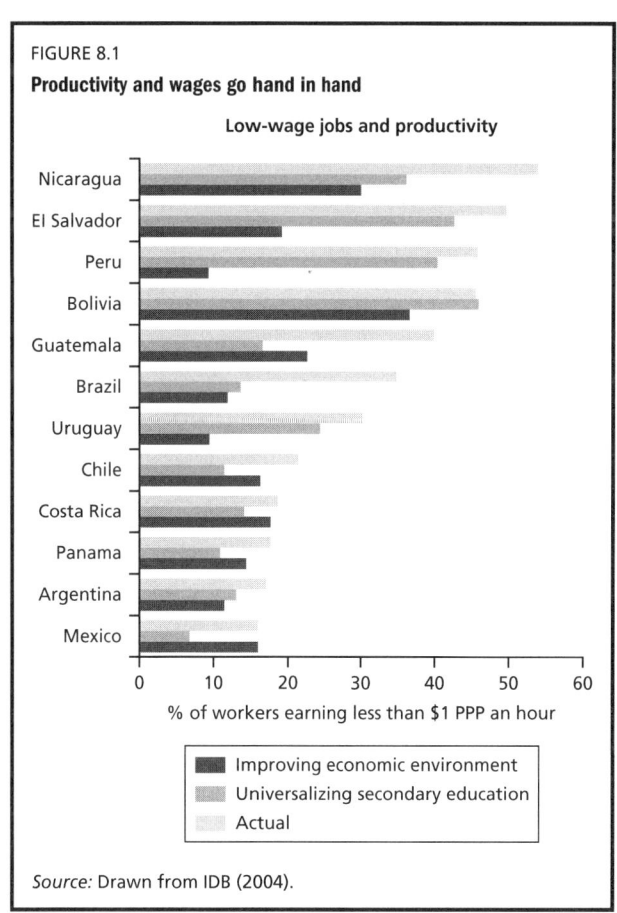

FIGURE 8.1
Productivity and wages go hand in hand

Source: Drawn from IDB (2004).

reports hypothetical simulations for a sample of 12 countries where earnings of unskilled workers are made to match those of analogue Mexican workers—the country with the largest unskilled hourly wages (as measured in purchasing power parity dollars) in this particular sample of countries. In the poorest countries, the fraction of low-wage jobs would fall by more or at least as much in this scenario as in a scenario where the labor force had universal secondary education at prevailing earnings levels. While highly artificial, these results highlight that addressing low overall productivity through improvements in the economic and institutional environment (for example, with policies to foster private investment and technological change) can go a long way in lowering poverty rates in the region.[6]

Earnings disparities unrelated to skills

Differentials in earnings adjusted for human capital are quantitatively important in the region. Earnings disparities associated with gender and ethnic or racial background are often attributed to labor market discrimination. Sectoral, occupational, and location earnings inequality may reflect segmentation that impedes labor mobility to higher-paying jobs or earnings differentials related to fringe or nonmonetary characteristics of jobs.

While women likely experience some degree of discrimination in the labor market, it does not seem to be of first order. The gender gap in average earnings (adjusting for education and potential experience) ranges from 12 percent in Mexico to 47 percent in Brazil, and improved during the 1990s to almost match the gender gap in the United States, which nevertheless is still wider than the gender gap in most other OECD countries. The gender gap in Latin America also reflects the effect of women's role in the household on their labor force participation and occupational choice.[7] Moreover, women do not generally face a disadvantage in the returns to investments in schooling.

Race and ethnicity are a more significant source of earnings disadvantage.[8] The indigenous population in the region on average earns 46 to 60 percent of the earnings of the nonindigenous population, while *pardos* (mixed race) and *pretos* (blacks) in Brazil earn just over half of average earnings for whites. Poverty rates are also higher for indigenous populations in Bolivia, Guatemala, and Peru and among African descendants in Brazil. The limited evidence suggests that these higher poverty rates arise largely from the disadvantage nonwhites face in human capital (quantity and quality) and its returns.[9] In Brazil, after racial earnings gaps are adjusted for workers' schooling, parental education, and school quality, a typical nonwhite worker with a secondary education faces a 16 percent lifetime average-earnings disadvantage; while significant, this is far short of the 50 percent unadjusted earnings gap. Contrary to findings for gender, differences in returns to schooling across ethnic and racial groups are significant (often 1 to 3 points). Whether they reflect gaps in school quality or labor market discrimination, these unequal returns may discourage skills accumulation by the nonwhite population (see chapter 9).

Evidence indicates there may be greater pay discrimination at higher-salary jobs for any given skill level.[10] For instance, the earnings of the best-paid *pardos* in Brazil are similar to those of the best-paid white workers, but when comparing workers at the bottom of the salary scale *pardos* and *pretos* face the same earnings disadvantage relative to *whites*. Thus the gradient of skin color affects mobility opportunities, so that the saying in Brazil "money whitens" applies only to *pardos*. In Chile, the gender wage gap increases from 10 percent to about 40 percent as women move up the earnings distribution. The returns to experience are similar for women and men in the lower part of the earnings distribution, but are significantly lower in the top of the distribution. Thus, labor market discrimination seems more likely to occur when workers cannot be denied the higher-paying jobs within occupations on the basis of their observed productive attributes (Darity and Mason 1998).

The poor are often employed in agriculture, construction, retail-trade sectors, and informal occupations, and they tend to live in laggard areas, all of which cause their wages to be lower regardless of skills.[11] As noted in chapter 7, regional earnings gaps within Latin America are also quantitatively important given that poorer regions lack natural resources as well as agglomeration externalities in skills, infrastructure, and other factors of production.

Of particular interest are earnings gaps between formal and informal jobs. Salaried workers in the informal economy and the self-employed account for 25 to 70 percent of employment across countries in the region. The average earnings gap between workers in small firms (a proxy for informal wage employment) and those in large enterprises is about 30 percent (similar to the gap in the United States) and ranges from 17 to 51 percent across countries (IDB 2004). Average earnings for the self-employed (most of whom are also informal) are typically far less than those of formal salaried workers. The informal-formal earnings gaps primarily stem from low skill endowments despite unequal rewards to skills. Around two-thirds of the informal-formal average earnings gap is explained by differences in worker skill endowments, and the rest by a lower remuneration to these endowments in the informal sector.[12]

Moreover, the pattern of informal-formal remuneration gaps along the earnings scale is consistent with a two-tier informal sector. This is illustrated in figure 8.2 for Bolivia. It decomposes the informal-formal earnings gap into a portion attributable to differences in measured characteristics across workers in each sector and a component attributable to differences in how each sector rewards such characteristics for workers in the 10th, median, and 90th earnings percentiles in each sector. The latter component is often taken, although not without question, as a measure of segmentation. The results suggest that segmentation might exist for informal salaried workers in low- to average-paying jobs and for the self-employed at low-paying jobs for their skills set. At the best-paid jobs for any skill level, the returns to skills are similar between sectors so that these workers can move between sectors with little wage penalties. Similar patterns are found in Argentina, Brazil, and the Dominican Republic.

Overall, the evidence summarized above suggests that earnings differentials unrelated to skills are a second-order source of low earnings relative to differences in workers' productive endowments. While debate continues about the policy significance of these earnings differentials, it is clear that facilitating labor mobility is key if the poor are to escape their condition. This issue is discussed next.

Market segmentation and mobility

The applied literature on what makes growth more pro-poor has focused on how the pattern of growth affects poverty. As noted in chapter 5, studies have shown that growth brings about more poverty reduction when it extends to the geographical areas or sectors where the poor are concentrated so as to make more intensive use of unskilled labor. This report does not deal with the complex issues—such as the sources of growth or the political economy of government intervention—surrounding "industrial" (or selective) policies to induce a sectoral bias in growth. In any event, the evidence provided here and in the 2005 regional flagship report *Beyond the City: The Rural Contribution to Development* (de Ferranti and others 2005) points in another direction. The

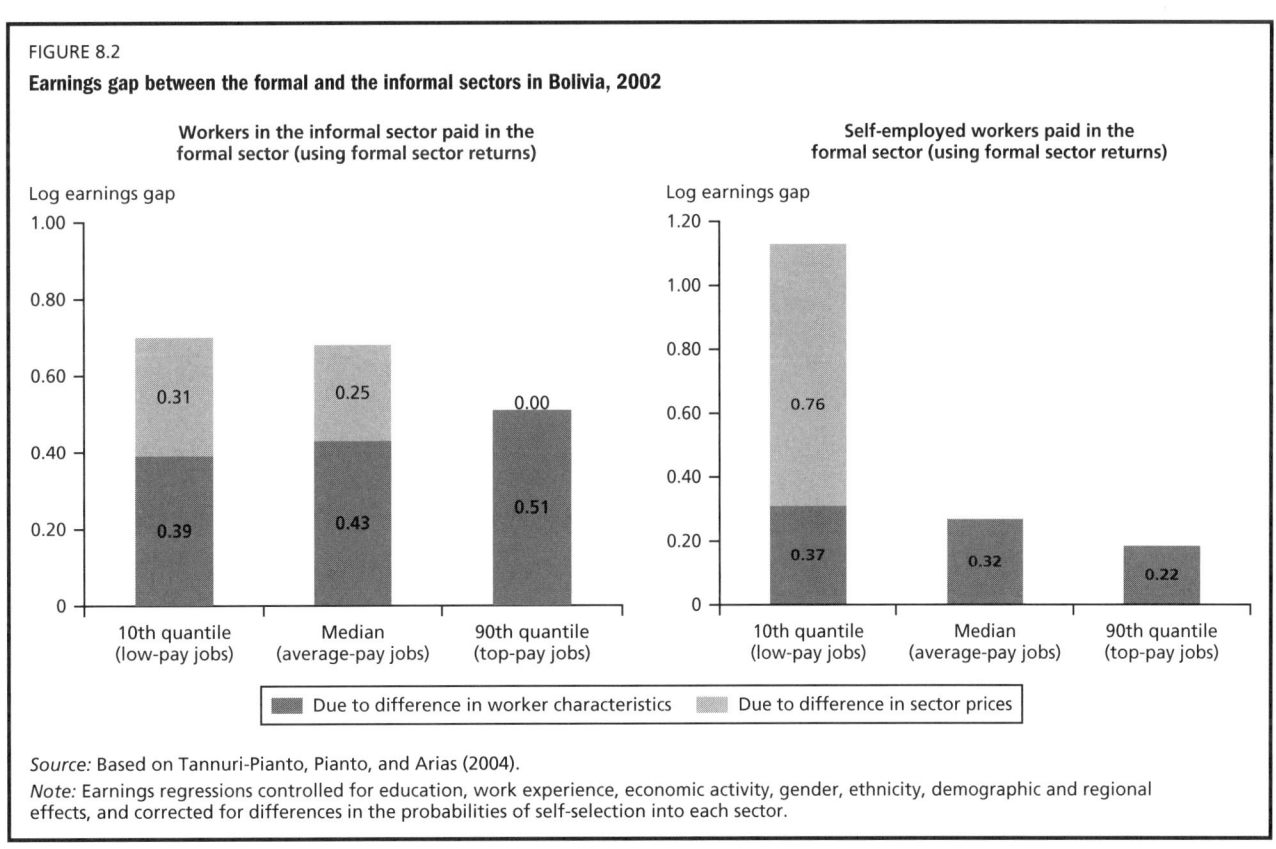

FIGURE 8.2

Earnings gap between the formal and the informal sectors in Bolivia, 2002

Source: Based on Tannuri-Pianto, Pianto, and Arias (2004).
Note: Earnings regressions controlled for education, work experience, economic activity, gender, ethnicity, demographic and regional effects, and corrected for differences in the probabilities of self-selection into each sector.

incomes of the poor thrive when the poor are able to diversify to more viable economic activities.

Since development involves a shrinking agricultural sector and increasing urbanization, longer-term poverty reduction depends crucially on the ability of the poor to engage in dynamic (competitive) economic activities. In some cases market segmentation may prevent mobility because workers in low-earnings sectors, occupations, and regions face high costs or barriers to mobility. In others, differences in nonmonetary benefits of jobs mean that observed mobility may be lower than one would expect given observed earnings differentials.

One important issue concerns movements out of subsistence agriculture to higher-yield crops or to nonfarm rural activities. As stressed in the 2005 flagship report, evidence from country studies underscores the critical importance for poor households of a minimum bundle of asset holdings (chiefly, human capital and rural roads) and risk protection (such as remittances and safety nets) so that they can undertake productive diversification strategies. For instance, using panel data for El Salvador, Tannuri-Pianto, Pianto, and Arias (2005) find that more-educated households and those with other asset holdings such as stable access to electricity and proximity to a paved road are more likely to rely heavily on off-farm activities for their income generation. Moreover, these effects are multiplicative. Closer proximity to rural roads increases the chances that individuals with more initial asset holdings will shift from agriculture to nonfarm employment compared with individuals with fewer assets. Remittances reinforce the impact of education on the probability of leaving agriculture. This means that families lacking a minimum bundle of assets and risk mitigation capacity are less likely to benefit directly from off-farm employment opportunities induced by rural investments.

In urban areas, a key question is the extent to which informal and formal sector participation reflects segmentation or voluntary choice. The conventional view of the inferiority of informal jobs has been questioned (Maloney 2004). An alternative view points out that many informal salaried and self-employed workers (especially youth, married women, and the unskilled) may voluntarily choose this sector as an entry point to the labor force and to enjoy nonmonetary benefits such as greater flexibility, the ability to exploit entrepreneurial skills to improve mobility, and avoidance of burdensome regulations. In studying patterns of transitions across employment states (including those who are unemployed and those out of the labor force) in Argentina, Brazil, and Mexico, Bosch and Maloney (2005) find significant evidence supporting the latter view. Figure 8.3 illustrates this for Mexico. Patterns of movements across sectors are consistent with the sectors showing a fair degree of integration and transitions not solely driven by earnings differentials, although informal jobs take on more slack during downturns.

However, as noted earlier, a nonnegligible fraction of informal workers face earnings penalties that are too large and that are not offset by nonmonetary benefits; these earnings penalties may be related to low-productivity traps resulting from lack of skills or credit constraints. Moreover, since access to social protection (such as health care or pensions) in most of the region remains tied to a formal employment contract and since informal workers face higher unemployment risk, they may be disinclined to upgrade their skills and diversify to more promising occupations (both formal and informal).

Recognizing the considerable heterogeneity in the informal sector, researchers are beginning to agree that the informal sector has two distinct components: workers who choose this sector voluntarily and conform more closely to entrepreneurship motives, and those who use this sector as employment of last resort. The relative size of each tier depends on country-specific contexts, particularly on the level of productivity in the formal sector, the demographic and skills composition of the labor force, and the incentives resulting from tax and labor regulations.

Finally, as discussed in chapter 7, the spatial pattern of economic growth can influence the effect that poverty reduction has on a given growth rate, especially if transportation and market connectivity are low and migration costs are high. That chapter highlighted some of the issues related to geography and cultural factors that may contribute to persistent spatial earnings differentials and thus be a source of poverty traps. Country case studies of household determinants of migration indicate that the young, moderately educated (secondary or primary), women, and smaller families are more likely to migrate to urban localities, but that individuals from the poorest locations and the indigenous are more prone to rural-to-rural migration (Tannuri-Pianto, Pianto, and Arias 2004; de Ferranti and others 2005; see also Taylor, Yúnez-Naude, and Cerón 2004, and Taylor 2001 for Mexico). The persistence of regional earnings gaps and small migration flows should receive more attention in the region's policy agenda.

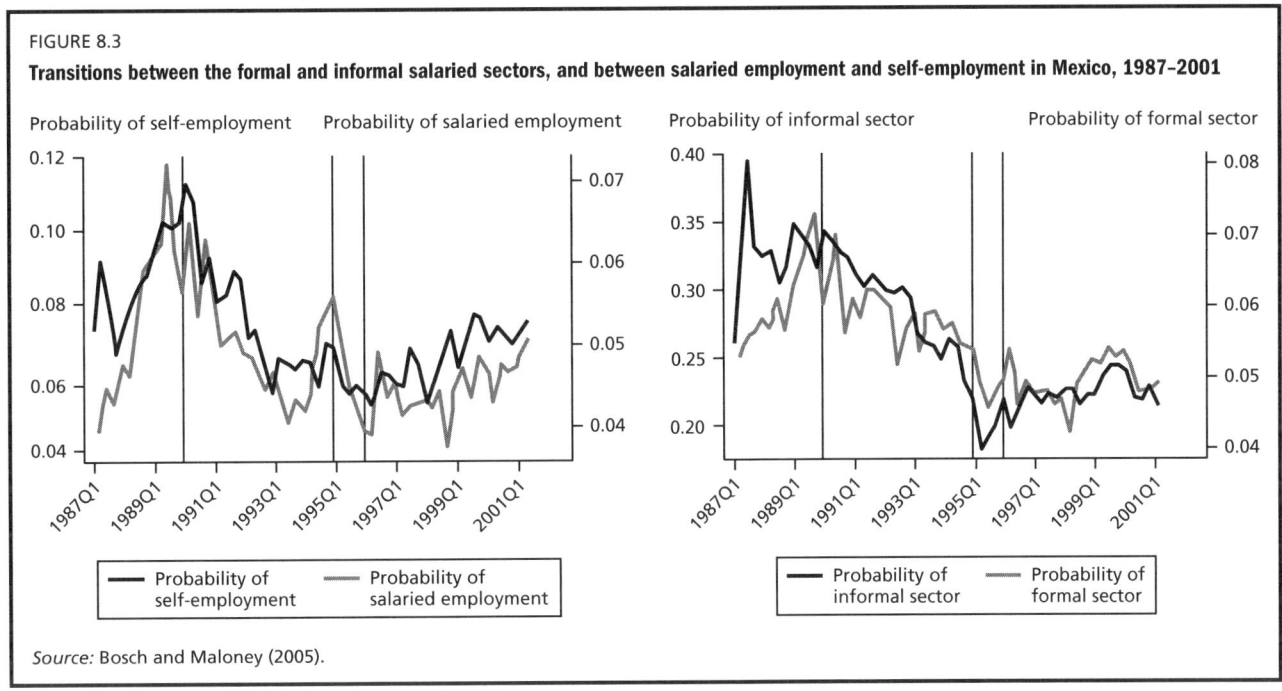

FIGURE 8.3
Transitions between the formal and informal salaried sectors, and between salaried employment and self-employment in Mexico, 1987–2001

Source: Bosch and Maloney (2005).

Microdrivers of changes in the income distribution

In this section, we ascertain the quantitative importance of the numerous earnings determinants in driving the growth path of earnings for individuals with different characteristics. We do this by isolating the quantitative contribution of the different factors to past changes in the income distribution. This exercise also helps illustrate the profile of workers who have been benefiting from growth as well as the profile of those who have been left behind. We look particularly at changes in poverty and inequality in a few selected countries. Recent studies for Argentina (1992–2001), Bolivia (1993–2002), the Dominican Republic (1997–2002), and Peru (1997–2002) used fairly comparable microsimulations of counterfactual income distributions that allow unobserved worker skills to affect the returns to the worker's characteristics.[13] The analysis here extends the simple growth-redistribution decompositions in chapter 4. The main goal is to find answers to the question: what would the level of poverty (inequality) have been in the country if factor X (such as education or its returns) had not changed? The question is answered by simulating the distribution of income that results from changes in the relevant factor while all others are kept unchanged, that is, by estimating a counterfactual distribution (see annex 8A).

The selected countries reflect a variety of trends in poverty and inequality in the region. Argentina suffered a dramatic increase in income poverty and inequality during the 1990s. Peru also saw a significant increase in both variables between 1997 and 2002. Bolivia experienced a modest reduction in urban poverty during the first half of the 1990s, followed by an increase during 1997–2002. The Dominican Republic saw little change in poverty during this period, and a large increase in the inequality of labor incomes. Tables 8.1 and 8.2 illustrate the main results for Argentina and Peru.

Overall, changes in poverty and income inequality in the region during recent episodes of economic growth and downturn reflect several microforces, some reinforcing, others counteracting each other. Forces that lead to unequalizing income growth have dominated and explain the disconnect between the performance of the overall economy and incomes of families at the lower end of the distribution in several countries.

Particular note should be taken of two common forces. First, the unequalizing effect of a moderate upgrading of the educational level of the workforce is fairly visible and accentuated by the rise in the returns to higher education. Unskilled earnings, primarily in agriculture, tend to lag behind and prevent many rural families from benefiting from growth and escaping poverty. Second, researchers are

TABLE 8.1

Decompositions of poverty and inequality changes in Argentina, 1992–2001

Effect	Inequality Gini[a]	Poverty FGT(0)	Poverty FGT(2)
Observed change in hours of work	8.0	17.3	17.3
1. All the coefficients	2.9	7.5	2.1
Returns to education	0.8	–1.2	–0.3
Gender gap	0.1	–0.8	–0.2
Returns to regions	–0.1	–0.4	–0.1
Number of children	–0.1	1.0	0.4
2. Structure education	–0.3	–0.4	–0.2
3. Structure children	–0.1	–0.1	–0.1
Observed change in earnings	7.5	7.6	7.6
1. All the coefficients	1.6	1.1	0.7
Returns to education	–0.4	–1.1	–0.4
Gender gap	0.7	0.4	0.1
Returns to regions	–0.1	0.0	0.0
Returns to sectors	0.7	0.4	0.1
2. Structure education	0.8	–0.9	–0.2

Source: Based on Bustelo (2005).
a. Based on equivalent household income.
F.G.T. = Foster, Greer, Thorbecke indicator

TABLE 8.2

Decompositions of poverty and inequality changes in Peru, 1997–2002

Effects	Inequality Gini[a]	Poverty FGT(0)	Poverty FGT(2)
Observed 1997–2002	3.5	6.3	2.7
Returns to education	1.0	0.3	0.2
Gender wage gap	–1.3	–1.1	–0.9
Returns to experience	6.5	–8.3	–4.1
Education	1.0	–0.2	–0.1
Regions	1.5	–0.1	0.3
Sectors	–0.7	–0.9	–0.2

Source: Based on Sosa-Escudero and Lucchetti (2004).
a. Based on equivalized household income.

increasingly recognizing the importance of unmeasured worker skills for labor market performance; these skills include school quality, labor market connections, and unmeasured individual ability (such as spunk or industriousness). The effect on income inequality of changes in education returns is magnified by the uneven change in the returns across workers at different points of the adjusted earnings distribution (except in Argentina). This finding may suggest that among well-educated workers, those from better-quality schools or with better connections have been able to cling to the better-paid jobs.

Furthermore, the generally small contribution of individual factors to changes in poverty and inequality points to the inadequacy of single explanations for the sources of distributional change. Individuals with some bundling of favorable characteristics are more likely to take advantage of better employment opportunities throughout the growth process. Evidence on this is presented in the next section.

Determinants of income dynamics: Lessons from rural El Salvador

Our previous discussion of the main sources of labor earnings differences in the region and their evolution over time relied on cross-section data; this approach presumes that the growth path of earnings (and its determinants) for any given individual and his relative position in the earnings distribution is well represented by the growth path of average earnings and the rank of a typical individual with similar characteristics. For example, the change in average earnings of a typical college-educated worker is taken as a proxy for the increase in earnings experienced by all workers with a college education.

As discussed in chapter 2, this approach may not provide adequate answers to questions such as whether poverty is transitory or permanent. Nor does it reveal the factors that make poverty transitory for some individuals and permanent for others. Answering these questions requires longitudinal data sets that are rarely available in Latin America. In the following discussion, we examine in some detail the empirical relevance of some of the mechanisms that may lead to poverty traps by using a unique panel data set of close to 500 rural households in El Salvador (FUSADES–Ohio State University, hereafter dubbed BASIS) continuously followed during a six-year period (1995–2001; see the annex 8A). Although six years is not a great time span, it is a major improvement over the one-to two-year panels that have been used to study mobility in Latin America. This data set also allows more careful analysis of the confluence of unfavorable characteristics that may conspire to generate persistent poverty and inequality. We rely on existing studies using these data and new analysis of the main microdeterminants of growth in incomes, accounting for the role of unobserved heterogeneity of households and individuals in rural El Salvador.[14]

In addition to the availability of better-quality data, El Salvador offers a promising context in which to study these issues. The country achieved considerable improvements in poverty and other indicators of living conditions during the 1990s. Rural poverty fell by 20 points according to the national household survey and by 28 points using the BASIS data, which provide information on rural incomes in greater detail and probably greater precision (see World Bank 2005e). Much of the progress in rural areas is related to a significant economic diversification away from traditional agriculture such as basic grains, coffee, and sugar to off-farm productive activities; important investments in rural infrastructure that improved access to markets; and an important inflow of international remittances. Yet half of Salvadorans in rural areas remain poor, and a quarter live in mere subsistence. While the findings of one country study clearly cannot be directly extrapolated to the entire region, they do offer important insights into the mechanics of income and poverty dynamics in a context of significant poverty reduction driven by private strategies and public investments. We first discuss the findings on the determinants of income growth and the importance of complementarities between income determinants (observed and unobserved).

The BASIS data confirm that determinants of income growth are fairly similar to those entering cross-sectional earnings functions. Numerous analyses with this data set indicate that assets endowments (land, education), access to markets and infrastructure (road, credit), household risk-coping strategies (productive diversification, microenterprise development, remittances), and household demographics (size, composition, gender) all affect family income growth. Tables 8.3 and 8.4 present the results of random effects (RE) and fixed effects (FE) regressions of individual wages and per capita household incomes on relevant socioeconomic characteristics (Tannuri-Pianto, Pianto, and Arias 2005).[15] The FE results are presented for three quantiles of the earnings-income distribution to investigate whether the returns to observed characteristics depend on unobserved (unmeasured) income determinants. More detailed results are discussed in the next section.

The main overall findings are:

- Nonfarm jobs carry a large wage premium, which varies with gender and a worker's initial education level.[16] Switching to a nonfarm activity increases

TABLE 8.3

Determinants of rural individual wages, El Salvador

	Individual earnings equations				
	Mean regressions		Quantile fixed effects regressions		
	Fixed effects	Random effects	25th	50th	75th
Effect on log hourly wages, in 2001 colones	Coefficients		Coefficients		
Education	0.011	0.021***	0.008	0.013	0.014*
Experience	0.028**	0.014***	0.018	0.018	0.022
Experience^2	−0.033	−0.021**	−0.002	−0.005	−0.013
Head household		0.114**			
Female		−0.018			
Nonfarm main sector	0.135*	0.205***	0.156*	0.252*	0.316*
Distance from bus stop (km)	−0.047***	−0.045***	−0.031*	−0.039*	−0.038*
Distance from bus stop^2	0.0017*	0.0023***	0.0003	0.0012	0.0017
Distance from bus stop * education	0.002	−0.001	0.003*	0.001	0.000
Nonfarm * Female	−0.236*	−0.153**	−0.118	−0.157	−0.228*
Nonfarm * Education	0.023*	0.043***	0.013	0.008	0.009
Constant	1.203***	1.144***	1.150*	1.230*	1.220*
Regional and year dummies	Yes	Yes	Yes	Yes	Yes

Source: Based on Tannuri-Pianto and others (2005).
*Significant at 10 percent.
**Significant at 5 percent.
***Significant at 1 percent.

TABLE 8.4

Determinants of rural per capita family incomes, El Salvador

Effect on log yearly per capita income, in 2001 colones	Household income equations				
	Mean regressions		Quantile fixed effects regressions		
	Fixed effects	Random effects	25th	50th	75th
	Coefficients		Coefficients		
Average education workers	0.011*	0.026***	0.004	0.007	0.012*
Log number of workers in household	0.118***	0.131***	0.075*	0.086*	0.108*
Log number of children and elderly	−0.052**	−0.073***	−0.036*	−0.042*	−0.084*
Distance to paved road	−0.005	−0.006*	−0.001	−0.002	−0.006*
Distance to paved road^2	0.0002	0.0002**	0.0000	0.0000	0.0002*
Electricity	−0.058	0.023	−0.029*	−0.020	−0.021
Formal credit	0.153***	0.110**	−0.008	0.008	0.040
Other credit	−0.005	−0.007	−0.030	−0.022	−0.023
Remittances (*10,000)	−0.0122	−0.0115	−19.3000	−9.2500	9.1500
Subsidies (*1,000)	0.0012	−0.0010	0.8320	2.6000	3.9300
Activity diversification index	0.001	0.000	0.001	0.001*	0.000
Number of Microenterprises	0.076***	0.084***	0.077*	0.062*	0.089*
Non traditional farm sector	0.013	0.046	−0.006	0.019	0.034
Non farm sector	0.163***	0.185***	0.145*	0.147*	0.156*
Constant	9.367***	9.301***	9.210*	9.300*	9.450*
Regional and year dummies	Yes	Yes	Yes	Yes	Yes

Source: Based on Tannuri-Pianto and others (2005).
*Significant at 10 percent.
**Significant at 5 percent.
***Significant at 1 percent.

average wages for males by 14 percent. Meanwhile, only well-educated females benefit from joining the nonagriculture sector, those women with below-average education (three and five years in the traditional agriculture and nonfarm sectors, respectively) can even experience wage losses.

- Households that engage more intensively in nonagriculture activities accrue a 17 percent income gain. Surprisingly, there is no significant income difference between traditional and nontraditional agricultural households, suggesting that partial diversification to nontraditional crops fails to boost agricultural incomes once one controls for household characteristics and idiosyncratic effects that affect activity choice.
- Returns to education are seemingly low in the agricultural sector and at least twice as large in nonfarm employment, as identified through workers who switch sectors. Changes in education do not correlate significantly with mean earnings, likely as a consequence of very little real variation in educational levels over the panel. The income gains from education for a household that remains predominantly on the farm are lower (1.1 percent) than if they had switched to nonfarm activities, although again this finding may be downward biased (the effect is twice as large in the random effects regression). Workers that are closer to markets earn higher wages, perhaps because they incur lower transaction costs (in time and money) associated with engaging in the market economy. Earnings decrease with distance from the market, declining by about 4 percent a kilometer and reaching a maximum penalty of 27 percent for workers at about 10 kilometers from a bus stop (more than 80 percent of workers are at least that far away). Similarly, households that get closer to a paved road also derive higher per capita incomes, the effects being very similar to those on labor earnings.
- Having or gaining access to formal credit positively affects incomes by 15 percent, while informal credit has no discernible effect on average family incomes.

- Families' capacity to diversify risks has a mixed impact on family incomes. Income diversification (measured by the Simpson Diversification Index), remittances, and subsidies do not affect average family per capita income.[17] However, opening a microenterprise increases income by about 8 percent.

These results offer some comfort that the conclusions derived from cross-section income differentials are a good approximation of the drivers of income growth. Next we focus on the role of complementarities between public investments and household characteristics (observed and unobserved) that lead to lower income growth for many poor families. These effects can rarely be isolated with cross-section data given the high colinearity between socioeconomic characteristics (such as the high confluence of unfavorable characteristics among the poor), a problem that is overcome by the time variation in a panel context.

When it rains it pours: complementarities and initial conditions matter

One of the main mechanisms behind poverty traps is the existence of minimum thresholds and strategic complementarities caused by externalities or coordination failures in production or income generation. These can arise under limited capacity to face catastrophic shocks, credit market restrictions (resulting from imperfect credit information and low collateral), and fixed costs of carrying an investment that households cannot amortize in the short term. Households may be unable to borrow or save the minimum amount necessary to go beyond the fixed cost or the outlay required for an investment to be profitable, be it the adoption of a more modern cropping technique or investments in higher education. In other words, convex or lower initial returns to investments may prevent making investments that become profitable only beyond a given investment threshold. Strategic complementarities occur when individual decisions or private rates of return to investments depend on a family's initial assets and the broad capital stock. For example, whether a household benefits from the paving of rural roads may depend on its level of assets and human capital and on its access to credit. This interdependency can give rise to coordination failures that prevent entire regions or population groups from diversifying to economic activities with higher returns. Minimum coordination of investments at the national, regional, or group level may be needed for potentially profitable investments and income diversification to materialize.

These issues can be examined in two ways: first, by including nonlinear terms and interactions between relevant observed characteristics in the income (labor earnings) regressions shown in tables 8.3 and 8.4; and, second, by allowing the returns to observed characteristics to depend on the conditional income or earnings quantile of the household or worker, that is, on its rank in the income (earnings) distributions that would obtain if all workers had the same measured characteristics (for methodological details, see the annex 8A).[18] The conditional quantile of a household or worker depends on unobserved characteristics such as school quality, or work ethic, or differences in household productivity, such as differences in cropping methods or soil yield. Coefficients that increase (decline) significantly over the quantiles indicate that unobserved income determinants operate as complements to (substitutes for) the relevant measured characteristic. For example, households with idiosyncratically low productivity may benefit less from having access to credit or being closer to markets, in which case the returns to credit and rural roads will be lower at the bottom quantiles of the conditional income distribution.

The results indicate that complementerities play an important role in determining which rural families share fully in income growth opportunities (Tannuri-Pianto, Pianto, and Arias 2005). Individuals and households with bundles of favorable characteristics observed or unobserved reap faster income growth, especially those moving out of agriculture. Some of these findings are illustrated in figure 8.4. The main conclusions are summarized here:

- Often a minimum level of education (an average of six years among family members) is needed for households to fully exploit the income gains from improvements in access to roads and credit and to leverage remittances.
- The impact of road proximity and human capital on income growth depends on unobserved income determinants. Closer road proximity does not affect incomes of households at the bottom 25 percent of the income distribution given their observed characteristics, while those in the top 25 percent reap the highest income gains.
- Higher remittances correlate with increases in labor income only among households with more education

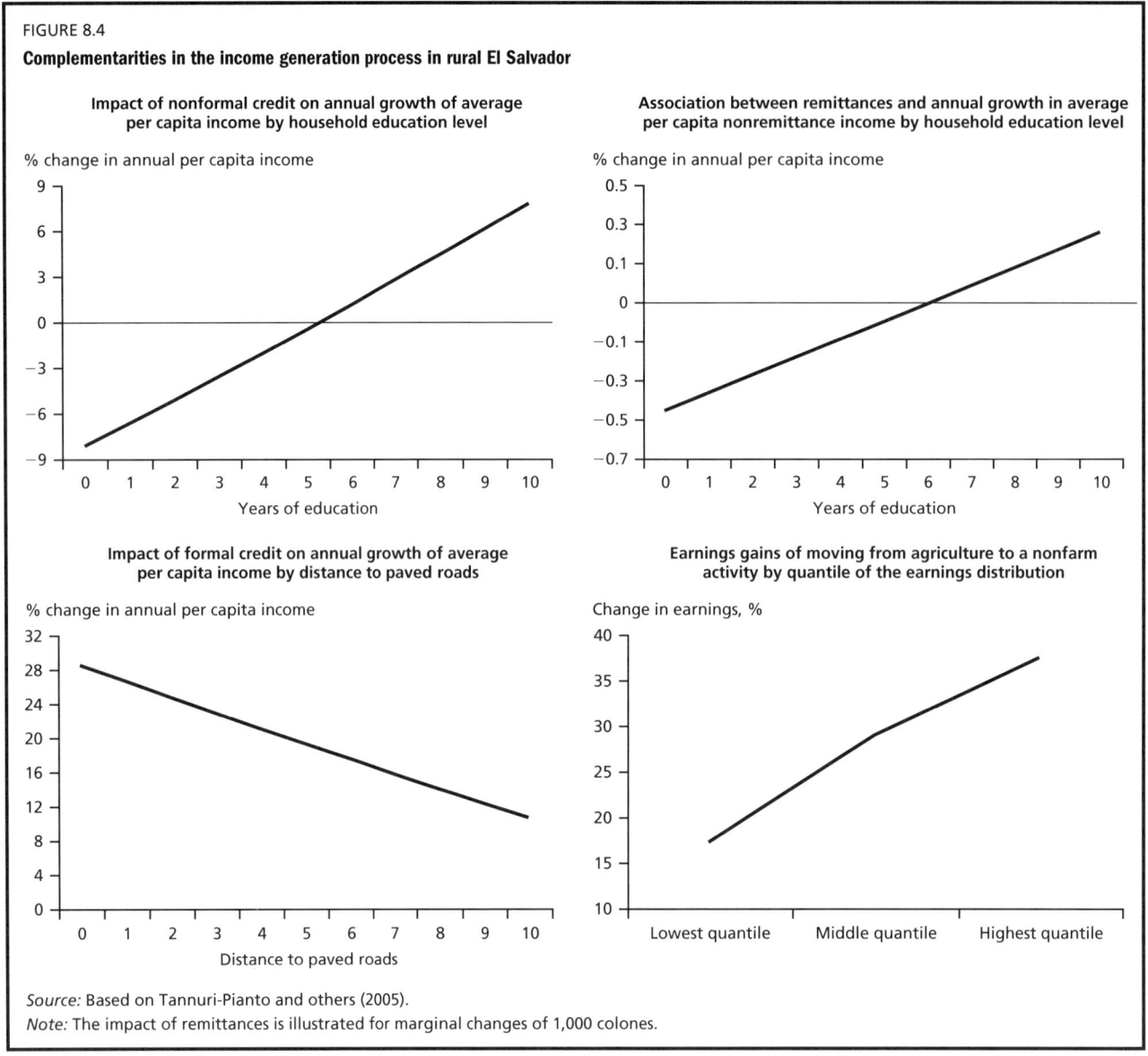

FIGURE 8.4

Complementarities in the income generation process in rural El Salvador

Source: Based on Tannuri-Pianto and others (2005).
Note: The impact of remittances is illustrated for marginal changes of 1,000 colones.

and higher idiosyncratic productivity. For the less educated, the regression correlation is negative, which may suggest that remittances serve as a safety net (they smooth negative income shocks) or that they may induce negative labor supply effects (by increasing the reservation wage at which individuals accept work).

These results uncover evidence of threshold and interaction (bundling) effects that prevent the poor from benefiting fully from rural investments and their own diversification strategies and may also discourage them from undertaking potentially profitable investments. Individuals with largely unfavorable characteristics are more likely to sink in low-wage farm and off-farm jobs. Informal credit, remittances, and unobserved income determinants all complement a household's human capital in generating income. In many cases, a minimum of primary education appears to be necessary for households to fully exploit the benefits from credit and remittances. Moreover, road access partially substitutes for lack of education (and vice versa) so that rural transportation investments have a greater benefit for more-isolated and less-educated households, which are more likely to be poor. Similar results were found in studies for Peru (Saavedra and Torero 2004) and for other countries in Central America (World Bank 2004c). A minimum coordination of public interventions in rural areas is needed to exploit these synergies and overcome the associated threshold effects that constrain the incomes of households with a bundling of unfavorable characteristics.

Now that we have established the main microdeterminants of income growth and found that they usually interact in reinforcing or offsetting ways, it is natural to ask whether the dynamics of the income generation process are such that low-income status and thus poverty tend to persist over time. That is, what are the chances that low-income families in El Salvador in 1995 will still be low-income families in 2001? How much of this persistent poverty hinges on idiosyncratic and transitory characteristics of families (measured and unmeasured), and how much on external shocks or fortune? We turn to these questions next.

Income and poverty persistence: Shocks, observed and unobserved endowments

Income dynamics are best understood under the "permanent-transitory income hypothesis" of Friedman and Kuznets (1954), which assumes two components in the determination of incomes over time. One is a permanent component that reflects an individual or family long-term income potential related to productive characteristics such as human capital, other assets, and unmeasured skills. The second is a transitory component that captures external factors, such as economic swings, individual-specific shocks, or plain measurement error, that cause incomes to depart from their permanent level.

In subsequent empirical work, the issue of income and poverty persistence has been studied from the perspective of intergenerational income mobility and more recently of poverty vulnerability. In essence both views ask how likely it is that a household of given characteristics will find itself in poverty at a given future time. The answer ultimately depends on the household's long-term consumption prospects and the consumption volatility it faces. In theory a household can be continuously poor because its endowments yield only low-income potential or because it is systematically affected by income shocks that it is unable to smooth. Each of these factors depends on the state and evolution of household characteristics (observed and unobserved) and on the aggregate environment. The literature on intergenerational income mobility has emphasized the first aspect. Starting with the classic work in the United States by Lillard and Willis (1978) and MaCurdy (1982) and continuing more recently with work by Geweke and Keane (2000), this literature has focused on developed countries where relatively longer panel data allow examination of long-term income persistence. The second strand is more common in developing countries and regions like Latin America where short panels or cross-section data have been used to examine the link between poverty and the inability to insure risks (see, for example, Chaudhuri, Jalan, and Suryahadi (2002); Chaudhuri (2000); Pritchett, Suryahadi, and Sumarto (2000); Jalan and Ravallion (1999); and Ravallion and Chaudhuri (1997). Vulnerability arising from high volatility requires interventions to reduce and insure risks, while vulnerability arising from low endowments calls for policies to support the accumulation of endowments and long-term income potential.

Table 8.5 illustrates the transitory (vulnerability) and permanent (persistence) aspects of rural poverty in El Salvador. The BASIS data reveal the considerable income volatility faced by rural Salvadorans.[19] In any given year, the results show, the poverty rate hides continuous movements in and out of poverty of different individuals. Around 6 out of 10 rural households fell into poverty temporarily during 1995–2001, although more than half of these had an income stream above the poverty line for most of the period. In addition to the inherent risk attached to rural incomes, this volatility reflects a series of aggregate shocks including two earthquakes and the impact of declining world coffee prices on coffee producers. At the same time, almost 4 out of 10 households never

TABLE 8.5

Permanent and transitory poverty in rural El Salvador, 1995–2001

States	Percent of households	Percent with average per capita incomes over the period *below* the poverty line	Percent with average per capita incomes over the period *above* the poverty line
Permanent poor (all 4 periods)	25.1	25.1	n.a.
Transient poor	61.9	27.9	33.9
3 of 4 periods	24.8	21.1	3.8
2 of 4 periods	19.7	6.0	13.8
1 of 4 periods	17.2	0.9	16.4
Nonpoor	13.1	n.a.	13.1
Percent of households	100	53.0	47.0

Source: Based on Beneke de Sanfelíu and Shi (2004).
Note: n.a. = not applicable.

crossed the poverty mark: one-quarter of all households remained poor the entire period, while 13 percent always stayed above the poverty threshold. This finding points to the significance of the structural determinants of poverty in rural El Salvador.

Which factors make poverty transitory for some individuals and permanent for others? What is the role of "uncontrollable" factors such as economic shocks or unexploited externalities such as a lack of public goods? Recent studies with the El Salvador data point to some valuable answers, illustrated in figure 8.5. With respect to poverty vulnerability, human capital of the family, its proximity to markets, and its reliance on subsistence agriculture (proxy of risk aversion or the inability to self-insure from risk) all increase the probability that a rural Salvadoran household remained permanently poor during 1995–2001. The level of human capital was a particularly strong factor in determining whether families were likely to sink into poverty or become highly vulnerable to falling into poverty.

In a study using the El Salvador data, Rodriguez-Meza and Gonzalez-Vega (2004) found evidence that the risks faced by households to materialize its future consumption prospects given its current characteristics (observed and unobserved) are a possible cause of poverty traps. Their study showed that recovery from an income shock is quick for the relatively rich in rural areas but much lengthier for the poor. This result, however, might be somewhat sensitive to estimation methods since they use a short time span to identify highly nonlinear income dynamics.

In a background study for this report, Sosa-Escudero, Marchionni, and Arias (2005) used a different approach that focuses on the sources of income persistency. Their evidence shows that transitory income shocks are the major source of variation in incomes across rural families in El Salvador, much more so than in developed countries.[20] However, the correlation of bad shocks is relatively low (0.24) in these data. Over a lifetime, good shocks and bad shocks cancel each other out so that transitory shocks are not as important in determining whether an individual's or a household's income stays the same as are endowments, including unobserved income determinants. Indeed, about two-thirds of the persistency in low- and high-income states is attributable to idiosyncratic differences between families, including unobserved heterogeneity. Observed income determinants, chiefly education, account for about half of this income persistence. Consequently, low income potential is a strong predictors of low

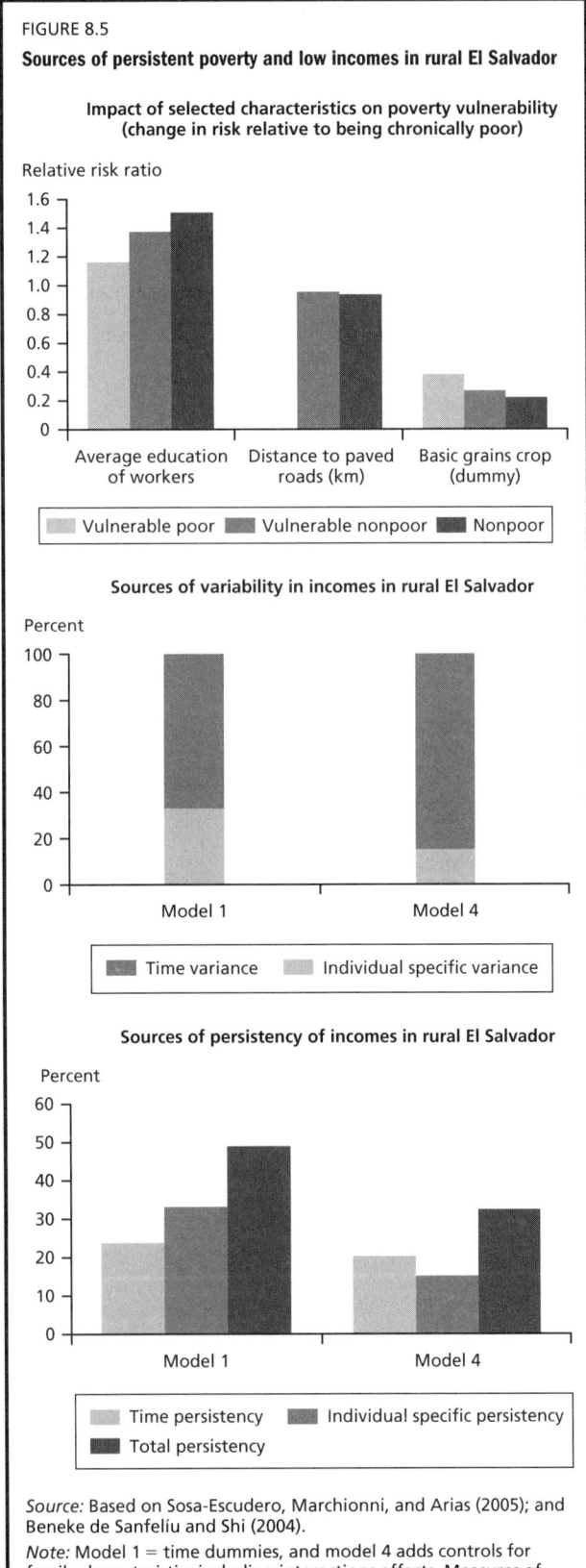

FIGURE 8.5

Sources of persistent poverty and low incomes in rural El Salvador

Source: Based on Sosa-Escudero, Marchionni, and Arias (2005); and Beneke de Sanfeliú and Shi (2004).

Note: Model 1 = time dummies, and model 4 adds controls for family characteristics including interactions effects. Measures of time and individual persistency do not add up to total persistency and should not be compared. The relevant comparison is the change in each component moving from model 1 to model 4.

incomes later in life. In other words, while a large proportion of total cross-section inequality (as measured by the variance of logarithmic incomes) is explained by income instability, life-cycle inequality results largely from the permanent income component, particularly from the relatively time-invariant productive characteristics of families and their members.

Being persistently poor in rural El Salvador thus seems more likely to result from the lack of endowments needed to escape a lifetime of low income than from the inability to ensure against income shocks. Many of these endowments can be influenced by policy interventions, although not always in the short term; in particular, it takes one to two decades for a family to accumulate levels of human capital sufficient to escape poverty.

Implications for policies

The findings reviewed in this chapter suggest several policy approaches that could improve the prospects for more equitable growth and poverty reduction:

- Most of the earnings differentials, and thus poverty and income inequality in Latin America and the Caribbean, are not generated by earnings differentials in the labor market; instead, these differentials reveal what firms and workers bring to the market. Many of the poverty and earnings disparities in the region reflect the level of productivity of firms and differences in workers' productive endowments; distortions in the allocation of workers and jobs are of second-order importance. What is important are the feedback effects to human capital accumulation the labor market creates through the pricing of labor (earnings returns). There is a need to reverse the unequalizing role of unmeasured worker characteristics (such as deficiencies in early-childhood development, education quality, and labor market connections) in commanding higher wages. This is discussed in more detail in chapter 9.
- Labor markets do not seem to operate with pervasive segmentation. The reduction of residual earnings disparities associated with gender, ethnicity and race, informality, occupation, sector of employment, and geographic location would have a larger impact on reducing overall inequality than on reducing poverty levels, a finding that is symptomatic of overall low labor productivity. Although of second-order importance, reducing the portion of these earnings gaps associated with discrimination and labor market frictions can boost the incentives for disadvantaged groups to invest in skills acquisition and facilitate the mobility of workers.
- Bridging the gaps in education (both quantity and quality) and other productive characteristics of workers can go a long way toward reducing the wide earnings disparities in the region. But it will not be enough to reduce poverty significantly. In most countries, low levels of labor productivity are a chief constraint to earnings potential. Thus policies that promote an economic and institutional environment conducive to productivity growth are important for reducing the incidence of low-paid jobs and making investments in skills more attractive.
- Labor market interventions, including changes in labor legislation and its application, should focus on achieving a better balance between protecting workers and unleashing the potential for productivity growth in the region. This calls for actions aimed at reducing discriminatory practices or location-specific biases and facilitating the mobility of workers such as more effective enforcement of equal pay and merit promotion regulations, labor market intermediation services, more flexible work schedules, and establishment of child care centers.
- The evidence from rural El Salvador indicates that despite considerable persistence in individuals' and households' sectors of specialization, there is room for public policies to encourage mobility. Education and access to services (such as electricity and water) and markets (roads) affect the probabilities of transitioning from the farm to the nonfarm sector and vice versa.
- The poor are generally disadvantaged in several dimensions. We find significant evidence of important complementarities between rural investments and rural household characteristics (observed and unobserved) in determining the probability of sector participation and the returns to their income-deriving endowments. Public investments and policies in one area (such as credit access or road construction) may have heterogeneous impacts depending on the initial conditions affecting the poor, particularly their observed and unobserved productive endowments.

- Access to markets can be increased through investments in basic infrastructure, which contribute to a household's ability to attain the minimum level of wealth, educational skills, or credentials needed to move to modern occupations. Rural development could be made more effective with some minimum coordination of rural investments and programs—such as education, road construction, and the establishment of microcredit schemes—so that they benefit the more-isolated and poorest families.
- Policy interventions that generate synergies and break the mutually reinforcing mechanisms that lead to poverty traps could ignite a virtuous cycle between growth and broad poverty reduction. National development policies need to maintain a long-term perspective to give the investments needed to break low incomes and poverty persistence (for example, in human capital formation) time to mature and translate into significant improvements in family incomes.

Annex 8A

Data and methodological details

Data

Most of the new analysis for this chapter relies on the rural panel survey conducted by the Fundación Salvadoreña para el Desarrollo Económico y Social (FUSADES) in El Salvador and the Rural Finance Program at Ohio State University, in Columbus Ohio. The survey investigates demographic, occupational, and physical assets (such as infrastructure, land, and housing) among other characteristics that affect the income dynamics of rural households and their strategies for coping with risk. The panel data set is composed of four biennial observations for the years 1995, 1997, 1999, and 2001. The main sample used in our analysis is 449 households that were observed in all four years. The attrition rate (individuals dropping from the panel) is about 30 percent and largely occurred from the first to the second wave when it was decided the survey would be continued as a panel. The evidence from previous studies indicates that attrition does not appear to have a significant effect on either the sample composition or the validity of statistical inference from this sample (see Rodriguez-Mesa and Gonzalez-Vega 2004 for more details).

Estimation methods

A primer on quantile regressions

The technique of quantile regression (Koenker and Bassett 1978) is used extensively in the background studies for this chapter and chapter 9 because it provides a rich characterization of the effect of the explanatory variables on the conditional distribution of the dependent variable (such as the distribution of earnings). When there is sizable unobserved heterogeneity in the data, mean linear regression models provide only a limited characterization of this distribution and of the role of explanatory factors. Quantile incomes regression analysis is useful given the income inequality in Latin America and the Caribbean, as well as the limitations of existing surveys in collecting all relevant earnings determinants.

For example, we can estimate regression lines for various percentiles of the adjusted (conditional) wage distribution, that is, the distribution of earnings that results if all workers have the same observable characteristics. For instance, median regression (the 50th quantile) splits the sample in half (half of the residuals above and half below the regression line) and gives the same results as Ordinary Least Squares (OLS, mean regression) when the wage distribution is symmetric. This allows unobserved wage determinants to interact with measures of observed skills. This interaction is captured by regression coefficients that vary across percentiles of the adjusted wage distribution. This way we can recover different impacts of the explanatory variables throughout the entire distribution without imposing any prior assumptions such as normality or constant variance of regression errors. Results are also robust to outliers in wage data.

Suppose that X is a dummy variable for gender (women = 1). The quantile regression coefficient measures the gender wage gap between a woman and a man with similar education and experience at the same conditional quantile of the wage distribution. For example, the coefficient in the 90th percentile yields the wage disadvantage faced by women in the top 10 percent of best-paid jobs for any given level of observed skills while the 10th percentile coefficient yields the gap for women in the bottom 10 percent of jobs on the earnings scale. Now suppose that X consists of years of formal education. OLS provides a single estimate of the returns to education, the average for the whole population. Individual returns to education, however, may depend on some unobservable factors, like quality of education, unmeasured skills, or labor market

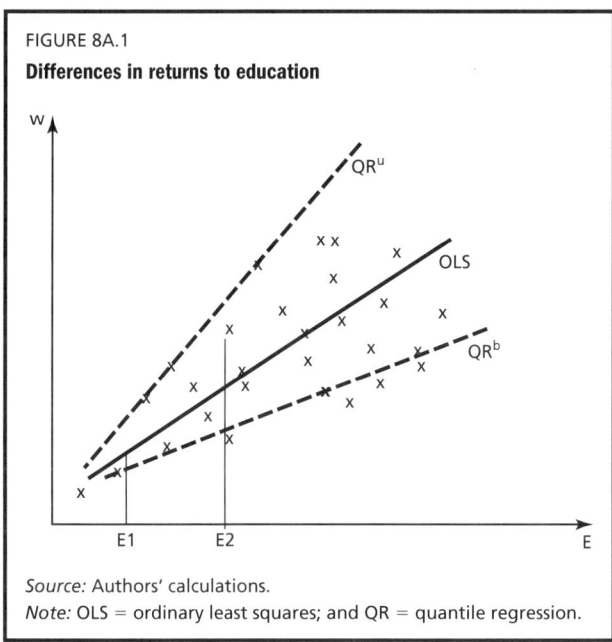

FIGURE 8A.1
Differences in returns to education

Source: Authors' calculations.
Note: OLS = ordinary least squares; and QR = quantile regression.

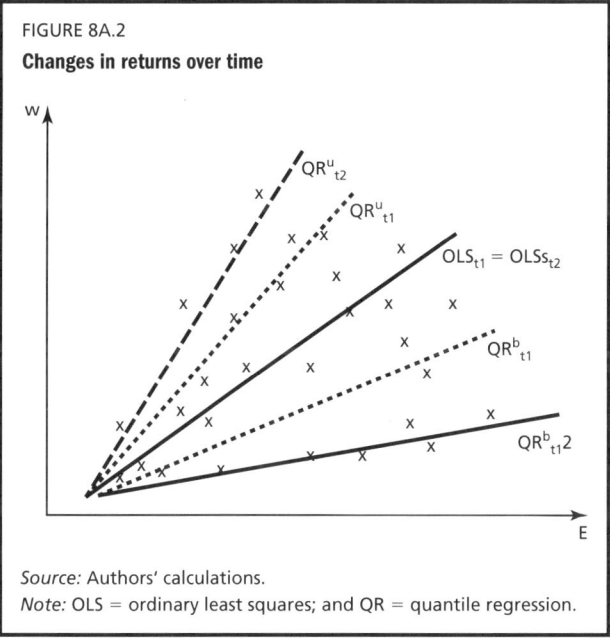

FIGURE 8A.2
Changes in returns over time

Source: Authors' calculations.
Note: OLS = ordinary least squares; and QR = quantile regression.

Explaining changes in income distribution

Microeconometric simulations of counterfactual distributions are helpful to characterize past distributional changes and to simulate the distributional impact of changes in economic factors and public policies. The idea is to simulate the distribution of labor income at time t as a function of individual observable characteristics affecting wages and employment, the parameters that determine the effects of these characteristics on market hourly wages and employment outcomes (participation and hours of work), and unobservable characteristics. A counterfactual distribution in time t_1 is generated by taking some of its determinants (parameters or distribution of characteristics) as if they were those of time t_2 and then comparing this counterfactual distribution to the actual distribution observed in t_1. The difference between the two distributions can be attributed to the change in the selected determinants between t_1 and t_2. This method isolates the contribution of changes in observed household characteristics (endowments), the returns to those characteristics, and unobserved heterogeneity in the returns.

Four studies—Gasparini and others (2004) for Bolivia; Sosa-Escudero and Lucchetti (2004) for Peru; Sosa-Escudero and Cicowiez (2005) for the Dominican Republic; and Bustelo (2005) for Argentina—use these methods to estimate regressions for a reduced form of a labor supply model with two equations, one for the number of hours of work and one for wages. The explanatory variables include the typical measures of workers' human capital (education and experience, proxied by age and its square), demographic characteristics such as gender and ethnicity, job characteristics (sector of activity and labor-informality indicators), and geographical location. The earnings equations are estimated separately for household heads and nonheads, both in rural (except in Argentina) and urban areas. The decompositions are carried out for one or two periods in the 1990s and early 2000s using national household survey data.

The decomposition analysis is enriched with estimates of quantile earnings equations that are used to generate counterfactual distributions when the whole family of returns to education (varying across quantiles) changes or for changes in each of the return quantile coefficients. This procedure, used throughout the report, may provide a richer characterization of past and predicted changes in the income distribution generated by economic and social changes or policy interventions. Particularly, when investigating changes in

connections, and hence may differ across workers (figure A8.1). In fact, recent studies for several countries suggest that returns are higher for workers at the top of the distribution. Moreover, it is possible for the returns to education to increase for workers in the upper quantiles of the wage distribution and decline for those in the bottom quantiles, leaving the average return unchanged (figure 8A.2). Quantile regressions allow an assessment of these important potential differences.

educational structure, we can simulate the new individual wage from upgrading education according to the wage-education profile of the particular percentile to which the individual belongs. See each study for details.

Quantile regression for panel data

Tannuri-Pianto, Pianto, and Arias (2005) estimate recent extensions of quantile regressions to longitudinal data allowing individual specific effects. The analogue in least squares regression is a fixed effects model estimated for a balanced panel of households. Koenker (2004) considers the following model for the conditional quantile functions of the response of the jth observation on the ith individual y_{ij}

$$(8.A1) \quad Q_{y_{ij}}(\tau \mid x_{ij}) = \alpha_{ij} + x'_{ij}\beta(\tau) \quad \begin{array}{l} j = 1, \ldots, m_i, \\ i = 1, \ldots, n. \end{array}$$

In this formulation the αs have a pure location shift effect on the conditional quantiles of the response. The effects of the covariates, x_{ij} are permitted to depend upon the quantile, τ, of interest, but the αs do not. With least squares methods, one can transform y and X to deviations from individual means, and then compute $\hat{\beta}$ from the transformed data. This decomposition of projections is not available for quantile regression, and we are required to deal directly with the full problem and the computational complexities associated with it. For this we use the algorithm proposed by Koenker (2004) and rely on the bootstrap (300 replications) to obtain standard errors for the regression quantile coefficient estimates.

Analysis of income persistency

In their study of income persistency in rural El Salvador, Sosa-Escudero, Marchionni, and Arias (2005) applied the linear panel model with first-order serial correlation of the classic work of Lillard and Willis (1978). This is a linear dynamic model for household income with first-order autocorrelation:

$$(8A.2) \quad y_{it} = x_{it}\beta + \mu_i + v_{it}.$$
$$(8A.3) \quad v_{it} = \varphi v_{i,t-1} + \varepsilon_{it}, \; |\varphi| < 1,$$

where $\mu_i \sim iid\,(0, \sigma^2_\mu)$, $\varepsilon_{it} \sim iid\,(0, \sigma^2_\varepsilon)$, independent of each other and of x_{it}. In this specification the potential sources of persistence are x_{it}, μ_i and the presence of serial correlation in the observation-specific error process. μ_i represents individual-specific "unobserved heterogeneity," and the serially correlated structure in the error term represents "state dependence" of the shocks. Consistent estimation of all the parameters is done relying on the method of moments as in Baltagi (2001, 82–83).

The empirical strategy consists of the following:

- Implement the Bera, Sosa-Escudero, and Yoon (2001) robust test for the presence of unobserved heterogeneity, state dependence, or both, based on a "null" model of no persistency (plain pooled OLS).
- Estimate the dynamic model using instrumental variables to obtain some relevant parameters and corroborate the validity of the Lillard-Willis specification.
- Implement the Lillard-Willis approach: estimate a base model to measure overall persistency (only $y_{i,t-1}$ as regressor); control for $x_{i,t}$ and $x_{i,t-1}$; and control for u_i and then for the presence of $x_{i,t}$ and $x_{i,t-1}$ under serially correlated errors. Four model specifications are considered: model 1 is only time dummies; model 2 adds basic educational and demographic characteristics and geographic controls; model 3 adds credit, market access, and other economic characteristics; and model 4 adds interactions between the latter characteristics. See Sosa-Escudero, Marchionni, and Arias (2005) for more details.

Notes

1. For studies based on an asset-based approach to poverty persistence, see Carter and Barrett (2005), and Attanasio and Székely (2002) for Latin America.

2. See De Ferranti and others (2004) and World Bank country poverty assessments available at www.worldbank.org/lac\poverty.

3. For recent studies for Africa, see Barrett Carter, and Little (forthcoming).

4. The R^2 of earnings regressions controlling for all of these characteristics are typically 0.4 to 0.6 (in Brazil).

5. For far more comprehensive surveys of earnings studies in the region, see de Ferranti and others (2003, 2004) and IDB (2004).

6. See IDB (2004), de Ferrranti and others (2003), and recent World Bank poverty assessments for Bolivia, Brazil, Dominican Republic, Ecuador, and Peru, for example, for country-specific studies of the importance of productivity for escaping poverty and low earnings.

7. Females tend to have more intermittent labor force participation (rates in the region average 48 percent compared with 52 percent in East Asia and 70 percent in the United States). Women's actual labor market experience is lower than men's for a number of reasons, particularly child bearing. Married women often participate in informal sector jobs that grant more time flexibility, so their lower pay may partly reflect a flexibility premium. See Kim and Polachek (1994), Cox Edwards, Duryea, and Ureta (2001), and Cunningham (2001).

8. See, for example, the studies in Hall and Patrinos (2005) and Arias, Yamada, and Tejerina (2004).

9. Differences in schooling and other characteristics account for over 70 percent of ethnic earnings gaps in Bolivia; Guatemala, and Ecuador and about 50 percent in Peru.

10. For ethnicity and race, see Arias, Yamada, and Tejerina (2004) for Brazil; Gasparini and others (2004) for Bolivia; and Sosa-Escudero and Lucchetti (2004) for Peru. For gender in Chile, see Montenegro (2001).

11. Sector earnings differentials average 10 to 15 percent in the region (after falling with economic restructuring), not unlike those in the United States; some differentials reach more than 40 percent in some sectors and countries, however (IDB 2004).

12. See Tannuri-Pianto, Pianto, and Arias (2004a) for Bolivia; Carneiro and Henley (2002) for Brazil; World Bank (2005b) for the Dominican Republic; and Bustelo (2005) for Argentina (although Bustelo does not correct for self-selection into the informal and formal sectors).

13. The studies are Gasparini and others (2004) for Bolivia, Sosa-Escudero and Lucchetti (2004) for Peru, Sosa-Escudero and Cicowiez (2005) for the Dominican Republic, and extensions of the analyses by Bustelo (2005) for Argentina. See Bourguignon, Ferreira, and Lustig (2005) for similar microsimulation studies.

14. We rely on Tannuri-Pianto and others (2005); the background paper for this report by Sosa-Escudero, Marchionni, and Arias (2005); Beneke de Sanfeliu and Shi (2004); Rodriguez-Mesa and Gonzalez-Vega (2004); Lanjouw (2001); and other references therein.

15. The latter are robust to omitted variable biases since the effects are identified from the within-period covariation between socioeconomic variables (such as workers who switch sectors or changes in distance to roads) and incomes or wages. However, the FE results for variables with little time variability such as education (a small fraction of workers remain in school) may be biased downward (because of higher signal-to-noise ratios). In this case RE are preferred, since they reflect both cross-section and within-period variation.

16. The sectoral classification of individuals and households—traditional and nontraditional agriculture and nonfarm—is based on primary occupation and the number of hours spent in each sector. See Tannuri-Pianto, Pianto, and Arias (2005) for details.

17. The diversification index is created by counting each different source of income weighted by its contribution to total household income; it captures the ability of households to diversify the economic activities (such as crops cultivated, variety of microenterprises) in which their members engage.

18. This approach relies on recent developments in quantile regression for longitudinal data (Koenker 2004). See the annex.

19. Beneke de Sanfeliu and Shi (2004) report that about 80–85 percent of households moved at least one decile upward or downward and 30–45 percent moved two deciles or more from period to period.

20. Using a similar methodology, Freije and Souza (2002) report similar results for Venezuela.

CHAPTER 9

Breaking the Cycle of Underinvestment in Human Capital in Latin America

Human capital is essential for enhancing the productivity of the Latin American poor and accelerating growth and poverty reduction. Why are the Latin American poor not accumulating enough human capital? What main policies can ensure they get the minimum level of skills required to break the cycle of poverty and low human capital? This chapter finds that an educational divide keeps the poorly educated in persistent poverty. That divide is caused by a combination of liquidity constraints and lumpy and uneven returns to schooling.

HUMAN CAPITAL, IN ITS BROADEST sense, encompasses the levels of education, health, and nutrition of the population. Despite some uncertainty surrounding the results from cross-country empirical studies, human capital (proxied by education or health levels) is generally considered one of the key determinants of growth. In a previous report in this series, for example, de Ferranti and others (2003) described how educational investments are crucial for increased productivity, rapid technological adaptation, and innovation, all essential for sustained growth. Chapter 8 illustrated how sufficient levels of education are critical if poor Latin American families are to benefit fully from growth opportunities and to reduce earnings inequality in the longer term. Chapter 7 pointed to cross-country empirical evidence showing that poverty may affect education levels, thus opening the possibility of a two-way causality in this relationship.

This chapter investigates the mechanisms that could support this double causality and their bearing on the disappointing level of skills upgrading and persistent poverty of the region. In particular, it aims to improve the understanding of the main barriers to and opportunities for significantly boosting the pace of educational progress and poverty reduction in Latin America and the Caribbean.

The chapter begins with a well-known fact: families with less than secondary schooling tend to be poor, and they tend not to invest enough in education for their children to escape poverty. Several questions then become central: Is this situation perpetuating across generations? Can market forces be expected to break down this poverty–low-education cycle, say, with sustained economic growth? Or are there self-reinforcing mechanisms that tend to reproduce the cycle? If so, what are they, and what sorts of public policy interventions are needed to address them?

- The chapter shows that Latin America is divided between individuals who are highly educated and those who have little education, and this divide is simultaneously a source and a result of subsistence incomes across generations. Since parental education and income are strongly correlated with children's educational attainment, the educational divide is also

This chapter is based on background analyses for this report by O. Arias, A. M. Diaz, and V. Fazio.

self-reinforcing across generations. The dominant mechanism in most countries is a function of a vicious investment dynamic: returns to schooling are low when it is cheaper to invest and become attractive when the costs of schooling are hard to afford.

We corroborate these findings in ten countries, showing that:

- Returns to schooling are essentially flat when students are in primary and secondary school and increase only with and after completion of secondary education. This pattern is consistent with a skill bias in labor demand from technological change in the region (de Ferranti and others 2003).
- Opportunity costs (forgone family income from children's potential earnings) and direct costs are larger for poor families with children in their final high school years and at the tertiary level, thus making liquidity constraints more binding.
- In some cases the full return to educational investments materializes only around completion of secondary or tertiary education.
- In most countries, poor families face below-average returns to tertiary (and sometimes secondary) education, perhaps because of disadvantages in family factors needed for skills development at home (such as family background or attitudes toward schooling) and lack of access to quality schools or high-pay jobs.

These findings suggest that the value options of a secondary or university diploma alone cannot be expected to break Latin America's educational divide. Poor families have to juggle current subsistence needs against investments in schooling that carry a remote and uncertain payoff. The end result: they invest in climbing the educational ladder while it is cheap, but stop when it becomes more costly and when the full return to the investment cannot be realized because of the children's poor academic performance or the inability to buy higher-quality education. Of course, families are guided by other strong nonmonetary considerations when investing in their children's education. But the harsh economic reality of poverty too often becomes preponderant.

Comprehensive policies are needed to break the vicious cycle of poverty and low educational attainment in the region. These policies must move beyond typical narrow educational policies to encompass integrated strategies for developing long-term skills that correct deficiencies in early-childhood development of poor children, strengthen grade transitions and degree completion, upgrade education quality for the poor, and improve the operation of labor markets.

The educational transition in the region: Slow and unbalanced progress

As a starting point, we illustrate two relevant findings of the 2003 flagship report on education and technology (de Ferranti and others 2003). First, skills upgrading through formal education, the so-called educational transition, has been much slower in Latin America and the Caribbean than in East Asia, although both regions started with similar educational attainment in 1960 (figure 9.1). Second, the transition in most Latin American countries has followed a

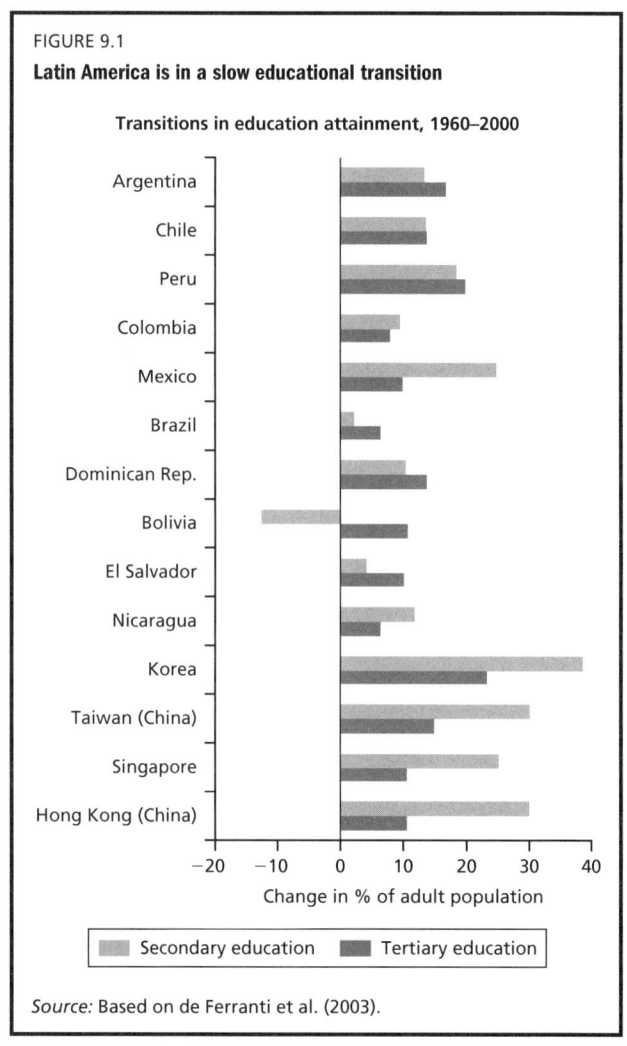

FIGURE 9.1
Latin America is in a slow educational transition

Transitions in education attainment, 1960–2000

Source: Based on de Ferranti et al. (2003).

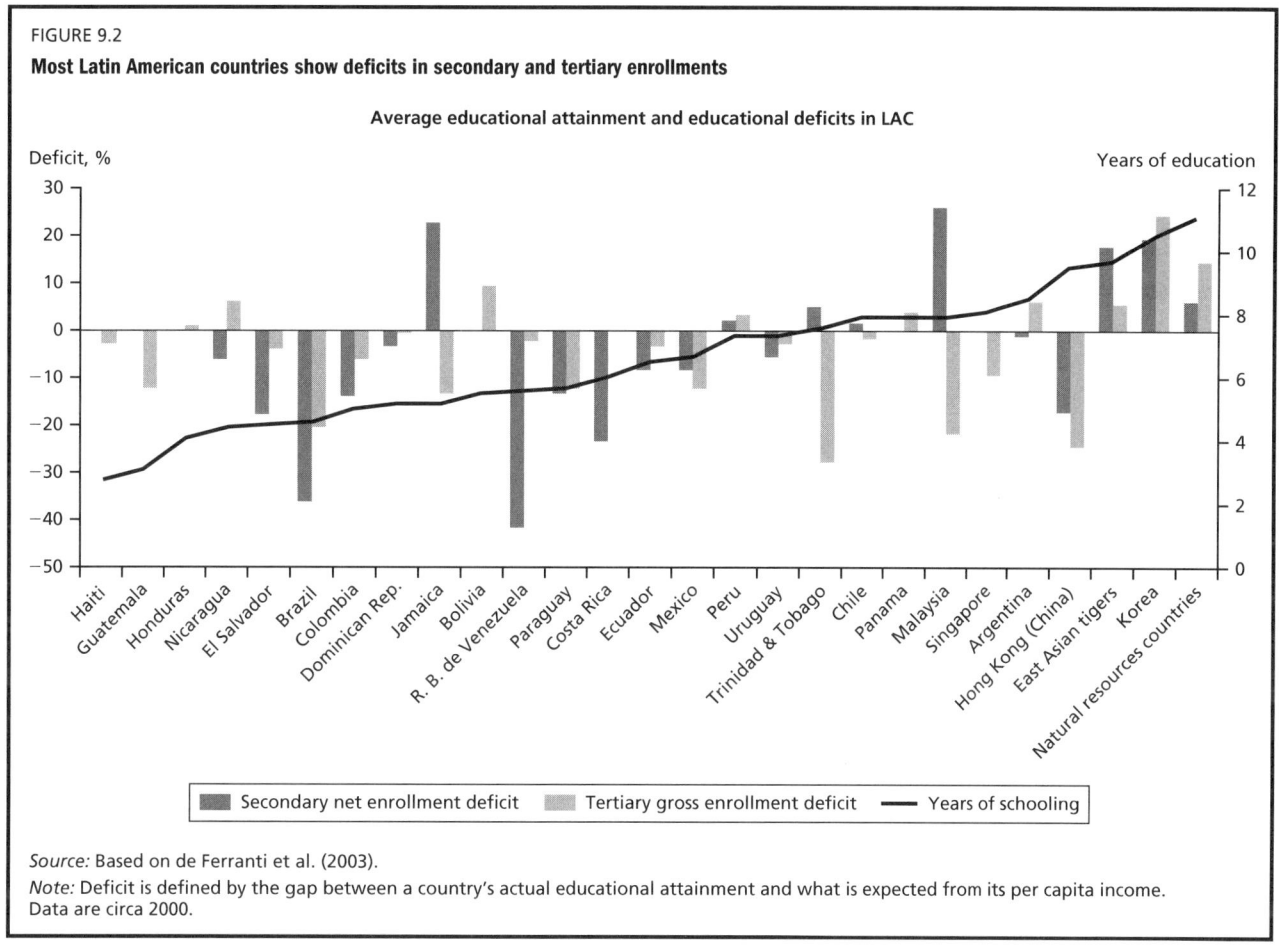

FIGURE 9.2
Most Latin American countries show deficits in secondary and tertiary enrollments

Average educational attainment and educational deficits in LAC

■ Secondary net enrollment deficit ■ Tertiary gross enrollment deficit — Years of schooling

Source: Based on de Ferranti et al. (2003).
Note: Deficit is defined by the gap between a country's actual educational attainment and what is expected from its per capita income. Data are circa 2000.

pyramid distribution, with smaller numbers of people with secondary education than with primary education. In contrast, East Asia moved to a distribution with higher numbers of secondary-educated workers than of those with primary or tertiary education. Some Latin American countries, such as the Dominican Republic and El Salvador, even funded tertiary schools at the expense of secondary schools and so developed an even larger "missing middle" of secondary education. As a result, most of the region has significant deficits in secondary and tertiary schooling (figure 9.2) and a lower accumulation of average years of education, a first-pass measure of skills.

The 2003 flagship report and the recent regional companion to the *World Development Report: Making Services Work for the Poor* (World Bank 2004d) analyzed institutional factors affecting educational markets and the provision of education in the region. In this chapter we focus on the specific links between education and poverty and its intergenerational transmission.

Poverty and human capital: A two-way relationship

Poverty can be related to the accumulation of human capital as both cause and effect. That higher educational attainment during youth leads to higher incomes later in life is probably the most documented finding in empirical microeconomics.[1] At the same time, poverty leads to lower human capital formation through various mechanisms discussed below. Figures 9.3 and 9.4 illustrate the two-way relationship between poverty and schooling for our sample of Latin American and Caribbean countries, ranked by their overall educational development (see annex 9A).

Figure 9.3 shows that in all countries the fraction of poor individuals falls systematically as the education level of the head of family rises.[2] In fact, a typical family head requires at least a high school diploma to make a significant dent in poverty. Poverty rates are 25 to 40 percentage points lower among families headed by high school graduates compared with those whose head has not completed

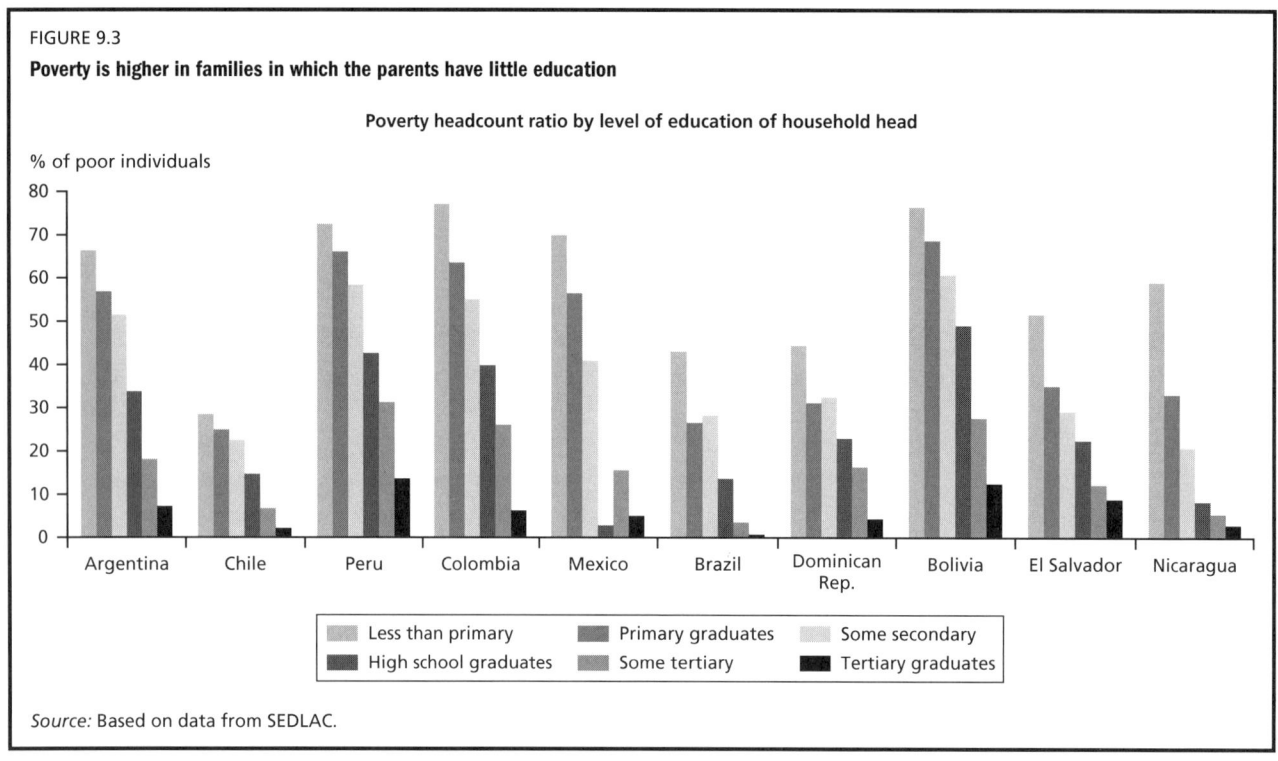

FIGURE 9.3

Poverty is higher in families in which the parents have little education

Poverty headcount ratio by level of education of household head

Source: Based on data from SEDLAC.

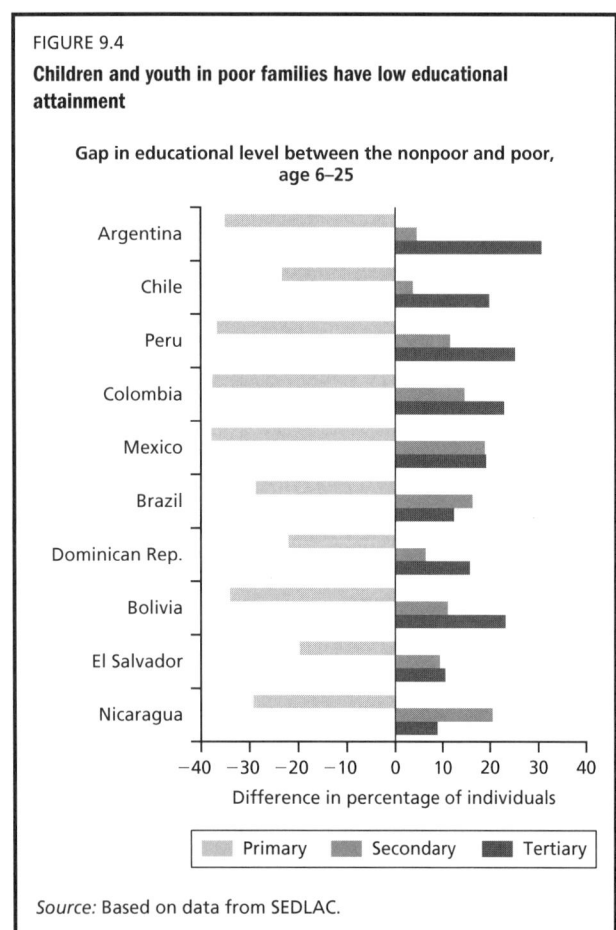

FIGURE 9.4

Children and youth in poor families have low educational attainment

Gap in educational level between the nonpoor and poor, age 6–25

Source: Based on data from SEDLAC.

primary education. Only a college education secures an income level that makes ends meet: in almost all countries less than 10 percent of individuals are in poverty when the family is headed by a college graduate. Income poverty regressions in numerous World Bank country poverty assessments corroborate that households with main earners (heads and spouses) who have secondary education and above are typically two to three times less likely to be poor.[3]

Figure 9.4 illustrates the reversed stream of the cycle: poor families invest much less in human capital of their offspring. A much lower proportion of Latin American children and youth from poor families reach secondary and tertiary education than do children of richer families. The fraction with only primary education is 20 to 30 points higher among the poor; the college education gap reaches 20 percentage points or more among countries like Argentina, Bolivia, Chile, Colombia, and Peru. The achievement gap between the poor and nonpoor is much smaller at the secondary level, although it still ranges from 15 to 20 percentage points in Brazil, Mexico, and Nicaragua. The relatively more egalitarian distribution of high school students reflects the already noted failure to expand secondary education massively in the region.

Thus, the acceleration of educational development in the region requires filling in the missing middle of the educational pyramid through a more egalitarian skills upgrading. History indicates that under current national progression rates, it may take two to four decades to erase the schooling gaps between the poor and nonpoor in these countries.[4] Several self-reinforcing mechanisms could prevent this catch-up from happening and lead to persistent underinvestment or a slowing down in human capital formation and to poverty traps. These are discussed below.

Human capital formation: Sources of underinvestment traps

Human capital formation is a synergistic process that starts very early in life. A large body of literature documents the importance of adequate health and nutrition for developing cognitive capacity, readiness to learn at school, and greater productivity in adult life.[5] With the acquisition of formal schooling and training from childhood to adulthood, these early investments crystallize in the development of marketable skills (Heckman 1997, 2000). The number of years of education are therefore only a first-pass measure of the skills embodied in individuals. The productivity content of an individual's educational level depends on the quality of family and school formation during infancy, childhood, and adolescent years.

The determinants of human capital investments are captured in the well-known Becker (1967, 1975) model of human capital and household behavior. Parents make schooling decisions for their children to maximize the welfare of all household members by allocating family resources (including time in the home) among consumption, work, schooling, and leisure. Education is an investment with associated costs made in exchange for future benefits, that is, on the basis of net expected returns. The costs include direct outlays such as school fees and other related expenditures and the indirect opportunity cost of time (including forgone earnings from work), as well as any nonmonetary costs related to aptitude and readiness to learn. Private benefits from higher levels of education are generally future higher earnings in the labor market but also include increased capabilities to function in a modern society.

The costs and benefits of schooling are influenced by supply and demand factors related to household characteristics, public investments, and the functioning of labor and education markets. Among chief supply factors, low accessibility of schools offering required grades and deficiencies in the educational system can limit the school progression of children and youth. On the demand side, family income or wealth, parental education, the number of offspring, and unequal access to higher-paying jobs can affect access to higher-quality schools, attitudes and family time devoted to schooling, and ultimately child scholastic performance and the returns to schooling. The poverty-traps literature points to several self-reinforcing mechanisms that can lead to sluggish school transitions coupled with persistent poverty in entire economies or certain population groups (Azariadis and Stachurski 2005; Bowles, Durlauf, and Hoff 2004; and Mayer-Foulkes 2004). These mechanisms and their empirical implications are described below.

Credit constraints and increasing, lumpy returns: Too poor to afford schooling

The inability to afford education is the most recognized inhibitor of human capital formation. Credit restrictions and indivisibilities in human capital investments can lead to self-sustaining underinvestment and poverty traps even if the returns to education are high (Galor and Zeira 1993; Ljungqvist 1993). This can happen especially when families must invest in their children's schooling for a span of many years before education becomes a profitable endeavor.

Educational investments are the prime example where adverse selection, moral hazard, and the lack of acceptable collateral can lead to suboptimal investment by the poor. Several studies show that the main cost factor making schooling investments unattractive to very poor families is the opportunity cost of the children and young people who can work at home or receive pay in the labor market (Basu 1999; Strauss and Thomas 1995). This situation is aggravated in families with many small children (Behrman, Pollak, and Taubman 1989; Haveman and Wolfe 1995) and in rural or periurban areas with remote public schools and a deficient basic infrastructure. Direct costs, such as school fees, become relatively more binding on poor families at the postsecondary level. Liquidity constraints and the inability to borrow against future higher earnings lead to underinvestment.

Moreover, many poor families may underinvest in schooling because the full benefits of the investment are too remote. The probability of getting to the tertiary level is lower for children of poor families, so they may face both a lower expected return and more uncertainty in realizing income gains from schooling. This can happen when the returns to education increase markedly with the level of education, as has been widely documented in Latin America (de Ferranti and others 2003; IDB 2004; Bourguignon, Ferreira, and Lustig 2005). There also may be a diploma, or "sheepskin" effects, whereby much of the schooling earnings premium accrues to those who have completed a high school or hold a university degree.[6] In this case the option value of completing secondary school and going to the university is the main incentive to attend school in the first place. For a poor family the rate of return to education may compensate for the cost of delaying present consumption (their discount rate) only when children can complete a minimum level of education (such as primary or secondary school). Hence, poor children are more likely to drop out of school once or before they reach education levels where liquidity constraints become more binding, as is the case in the transition from secondary to university education. We next discuss some mechanisms that may lower the returns to schooling for the poor.

Intergenerational and agglomeration effects: Too poor to benefit from more schooling

Multiple failures in the skills development process can inhibit the development of the scholastic and labor market abilities of poor children and youth and thus lower both their educational attainment and returns to schooling. Human capital formation is a long-term process subject to important intergenerational and agglomeration externalities. Families and community environments have a key role to play in the early development of cognitive and noncognitive skills critical to the schooling process. Failures in developing these skills either at home or in the first grades of school accumulate and hinder a child's readiness to learn. The quality of schools is, of course, central to developing basic cognitive and problem-solving skills that complement education and readily translate into higher productivity in the labor market. These multiple skills crystallize in an individual's "scholastic ability" (readiness to learn at school) and "labor market ability" (capacity for on-the-job acquisition of skills).

While scholastic and labor market abilities are correlated, they can lead to different schooling and labor market outcomes. Scholastic abilities are reflected in academic scores and lead to higher educational attainment (including its quality content), while labor market abilities refer to the skills needed to learn and adapt to different tasks and problem-solving environments. The lay terms for these abilities are "book smarts" and "street smarts." In the labor market these abilities result in higher returns to whatever level of education an individual acquires.[7]

Children born into disadvantaged families are at higher risk of experiencing malnutrition, illnesses, and home environments less conducive to learning, and they tend to receive a lower quality of schooling. They therefore tend to develop less motivation and readiness to learn, as well as to have lower levels of the noncognitive skills complementary to education. It is difficult to remedy fully the impact that these deficiencies in a child's early years can have on the development of skills during youth and adulthood through formal schooling or training.[8] Poor children therefore can face important long-term learning constraints even in the absence of short-term liquidity constraints to attending school. These deficiencies can lead to more grade repetition, delayed progression, lower expected returns to schooling as adults, and ultimately little transition to higher education grades.

Social exclusion caused by overt discrimination or biases in public investment allocations can prevent poor families from taking advantage of human capital production externalities (such as spatial or labor market spillovers). Residential segregation can lead to dismal funding for schools in poor communities and to negative sociological factors such as the absence of role models and externalities for learning ("peer group" effects), trapping children of poor families in low levels of education.[9] Lack of labor market connections or discrimination may hinder their access to the higher-paying jobs available for their level of schooling. Although discriminatory practices can hurt the efficiency of profit-maximizing firms, there is evidence that the effects of exclusion on human capital formation and socioeconomic status can persist for generations, impervious to competitive market pressures (Borjas 1992; Heckman 1997).

There are also externalities in human capital formation related to interdependencies between private investments in skill and broader capital formation, particularly skills agglomeration and technological innovation. Countries or regions lacking a minimum skill level (typically workers with some secondary schooling) are less likely to attract more technology and domestic or foreign investments in technology and areas that require research and development (R&D) skills.[10] Lack of technology investments holds back the growth in the demand for skills and thus the ability to maintain attractive private returns to higher levels of education under a massive educational expansion. The ensuing slowing down in the transitions to higher educational grades in turn continues to hinder technology upgrading and reinforces the low-skill, low-innovation cycle.

The upshot of all the mechanisms described here is to alter the poor's expectations of the likely returns to long-term schooling investments. Even if average returns to education are high, at any education level, there may be considerable variation in returns to schooling for new entrants to the labor market. While the evidence points to a pro-cyclical relationship between macroeconomic crises and educational enrollment in the region (since the lowering of opportunity costs dominates liquidity constraints), less is known about the impact of the region's ever-present volatility on long-term investments in secondary and college attendance.[11] This and other sources of uncertainty in returns can trap the poor in suboptimal education levels despite decisive public efforts to expand their access to schooling by removing infrastructure and credit constraints.

Identifying human capital underinvestment traps: In search of the smoking guns

How can we examine the empirical relevance of these mechanisms for explaining the slow educational transitions of many Latin American countries? The data requirements for conducting proper empirical tests of the relevant hypotheses are prohibitive—namely, a long panel data set covering a representative sample of families, including clean indicators of nutrition, health, and cognitive and noncognitive abilities of children and adults, along with standard socioeconomic characteristics. In a recent detailed study for Mexico, Mayer-Foulkes (2004) relied on evidence from a specialized health household survey and income and expenditure cross-section surveys to examine mechanisms generating human development traps. Building on his analysis, we uncover the supporting evidence for the following empirical regularities in the ten countries we are focusing upon:

- A multipeaked education distribution (grade clustering) that shows a persistent divide between those with low levels of education and those with high levels. The evidence also shows persistent delayed transitions to higher grades, closely related to family income and exclusion.
- Increasing and heterogeneous returns to education. Particularly notable are returns that become significantly more attractive at higher levels of education; show significant spikes for graduation grades (sheepskin effects); and are lower for individuals from poor, lower-ability, and disadvantaged families and regions.
- Strong intergenerational effects in human capital formation, chiefly, strong effects of liquidity constraints (such as low family income and high family size) and long-term family-limiting factors (such as low parental education and family effects on education returns) on the educational progression of children and youth.

In examining these hypotheses, we rely on recent living conditions household surveys to estimate for each country a full set of Mincerian returns to education. These measure variation across education levels and workers' observed and unobserved characteristics (see annex 9A). They also track microdeterminants of grade progression for individuals in the 6–25 age range, with a focus on the effect of family factors on grade-to-grade transition probabilities while accounting for the sequential nature of schooling investment decisions (see annex 9A).

Evidence supporting a combination of these elements would make a stronger case for the existence of human capital underinvestment traps. For example, underinvestment traps are more likely at play when educational attainment is low despite high returns to schooling (at all levels of education and for all workers) and when liquidity constraints affect progression to higher education grades. Poverty traps may also arise when the low- and high-education divide occurs at a level of education insufficient to make ends meet. For each country we take a hard look at the evidence to draw conclusions about the quantitative importance of the underlying mechanisms.

The educational ladder in Latin America: A persisting educational divide

Educational transitions can be thought of as climbing a ladder, where at each step, or grade, individuals and their families decide whether to move up to the next step. If educational attainment were determined solely by an individual's liking for schooling, the percentage of people at each step would not vary significantly by income or other demographics. Figures 9.5, 9.6, and 9.7 show the distributions of the educational attainment of the working-age population (ages 15–65) across income groups, location, and cohorts for four countries chosen to represent the variety of observed educational progressions. These depict the percentage of individuals at each step of the educational ladder.[12]

Figure 9.5 starts with the national distributions for Bolivia, Chile, Mexico, and Nicaragua. These help visualize the overall clustering of individuals around specific grades (taller bars) and also offer grand summaries of the

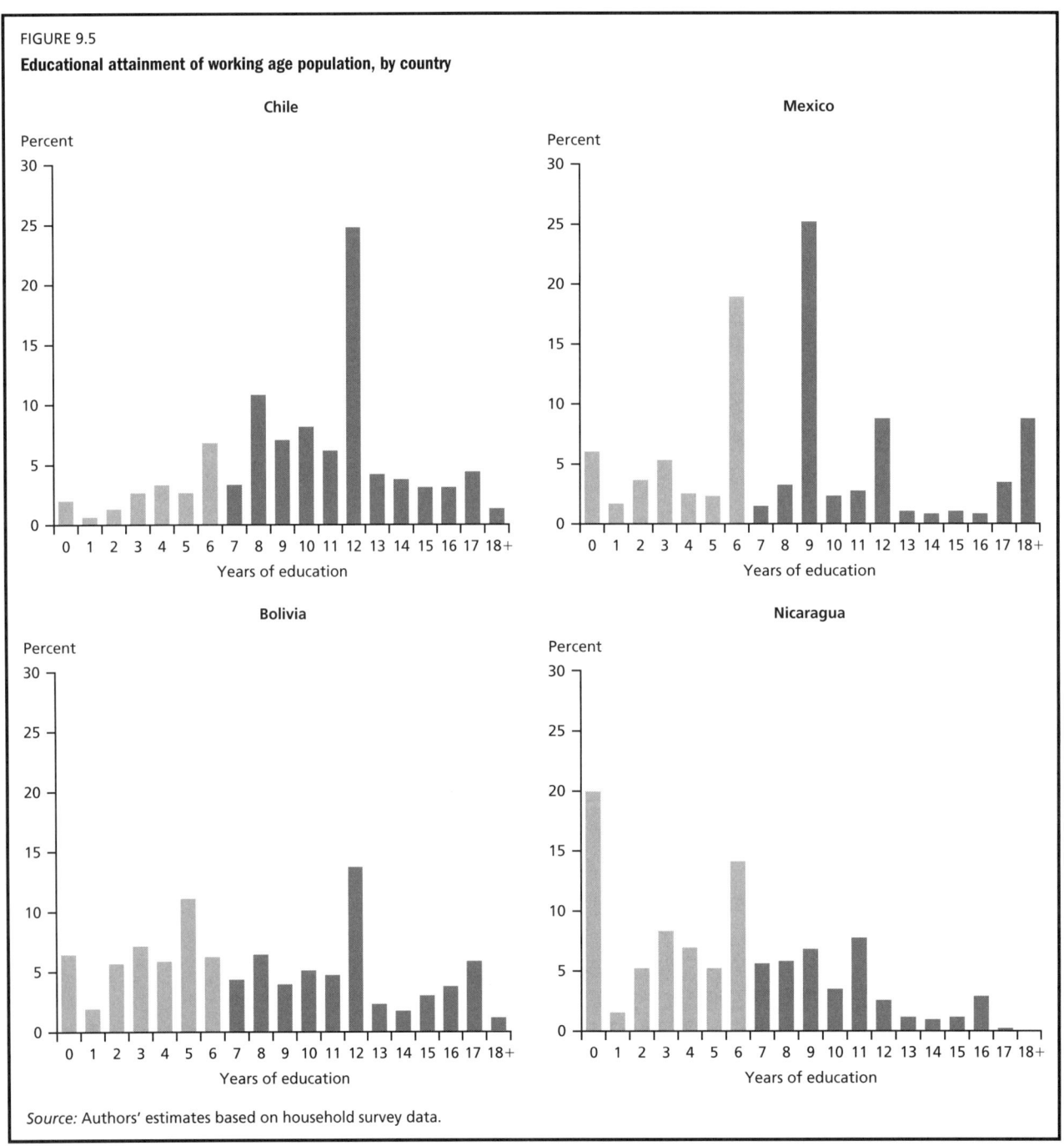

FIGURE 9.5
Educational attainment of working age population, by country

Source: Authors' estimates based on household survey data.

skills-matching possibilities faced by firms. Two different grade clusters stand out in Chile (those completing basic education and high school graduates) and Mexico (those with complete primary and those reaching up to lower secondary). A third, much smaller cluster in these countries is apparent for those completing tertiary schooling and beyond. The distribution of skills is more diluted in Bolivia and Nicaragua (with peaks centered at very low grades), a sign of failures in completing diploma-granting grades and of delayed grade transitions (overage students). The grade clustering in Argentina, Brazil, and Colombia mimics that in Mexico, with one of the peaks at secondary completion and with higher dispersion in Argentina and Brazil. Peru closely resembles the Chilean grade distribution, but with a higher density of university graduates; while the Dominican Republic and El Salvador mimic the grade distribution in Bolivia and Nicaragua. It would be harder for firms in the latter four countries to match workers to more technology-intensive investments.

The clustering of educational achievement crystallizes in an educational divide of the population strongly related to income class and area of residence. Figure 9.6 presents the educational distributions for the poorest 30 percent and the richest 30 percent in the representative cases of Argentina, Brazil, El Salvador, and Mexico. The two educational grade groupings noted for Chile and the modest clustering in tertiary education are strongly reinforced across income classes in Argentina as well as in Mexico, except that completion of lower secondary education is not an income-schooling divide for Mexicans. High school completion is the sharp dividing line between the poorest and richest in Brazil, while few of the very poor working-age Salvadorans have finished primary education. The income–school grade groupings in Chile, Colombia, and Peru are similar to Brazil's, although with varying degrees and more visible college graduate clusters. Nicaragua and, to a lesser degree, Bolivia and the Dominican Republic mimic El Salvador's groupings. The richest Latin Americans do not stand out as university-goers. The best performers are in Argentina, Colombia, and Mexico, where around one-third of individuals from the richest families obtain a university degree, compared with more than half of all adults in the United States and Canada.

The slicing of educational groupings for urban and rural workforces is even more startling (figure 9.7). In Brazil, Bolivia, El Salvador, and Nicaragua, the bulk of the rural workforce has not gone beyond primary education, and roughly 20 to 30 percent of workers have no schooling. Barely 15 percent reach lower high school in Mexico, and only about 10 percent finish a full course of secondary school in Chile, Colombia, and Peru.[13] Hence, poor rural families unable to migrate to urban centers can hardly count on education as a means of mobility to better jobs.

Except for the more educationally developed countries, the educational divide of the population seems to be sustained over time, with prolonged and unequal educational transitions still the norm among younger individuals. Figure 9.8 illustrates the typology of education transitions for three birth cohorts (ages 15–25, 26–40, and 41–65) that attended school during the last 60 years (each spanning roughly two decades) in Argentina, Colombia, El Salvador, and Mexico.[14] Despite steady progress in educational attainment, clustering at grades below secondary completion is still prominent in many countries.

In the less educationally developed countries, progress in educational attainment is not yet strongly visible in the younger labor force, and attainment of higher grades remains sparse. For example, 20 percent of the young Salvadoran workforce still has no schooling whatsoever, only slightly less than older cohorts there. Colombia has a balanced transition with a single peak at secondary completion, while postsecondary education is still rare for the two younger cohorts. That is, they show signs of moving toward a diamond-shaped educational distribution. Chile and Peru show a similar pattern. The schooling ladder in Mexico remains largely twin-peaked for the youngest cohort, with clustering at lower secondary completion becoming more pronounced (30 percent of the youth). Argentina is the only case where the youth appear to be in a balanced educational transition that breaks the postsecondary education barrier and points to an inverted-pyramid-shaped education distribution. However, about 20 percent of prime-age Argentines and 30 percent of the older cohort hold only a basic education degree.

The data for children and youth currently in school indicate that these patterns of educational transitions are being reinforced. Figure 9.9 presents net enrollment rates of individuals in the 6–18 age range for most countries in the region. The demand for schooling, signaled by almost universal enrollment rates, is strong up to age 13, which corresponds to the completion of primary education in most countries. Net enrollment rates begin falling fast beyond this age, with the exception of Argentina, Chile, and Jamaica, where dropout rates accelerate only after the first

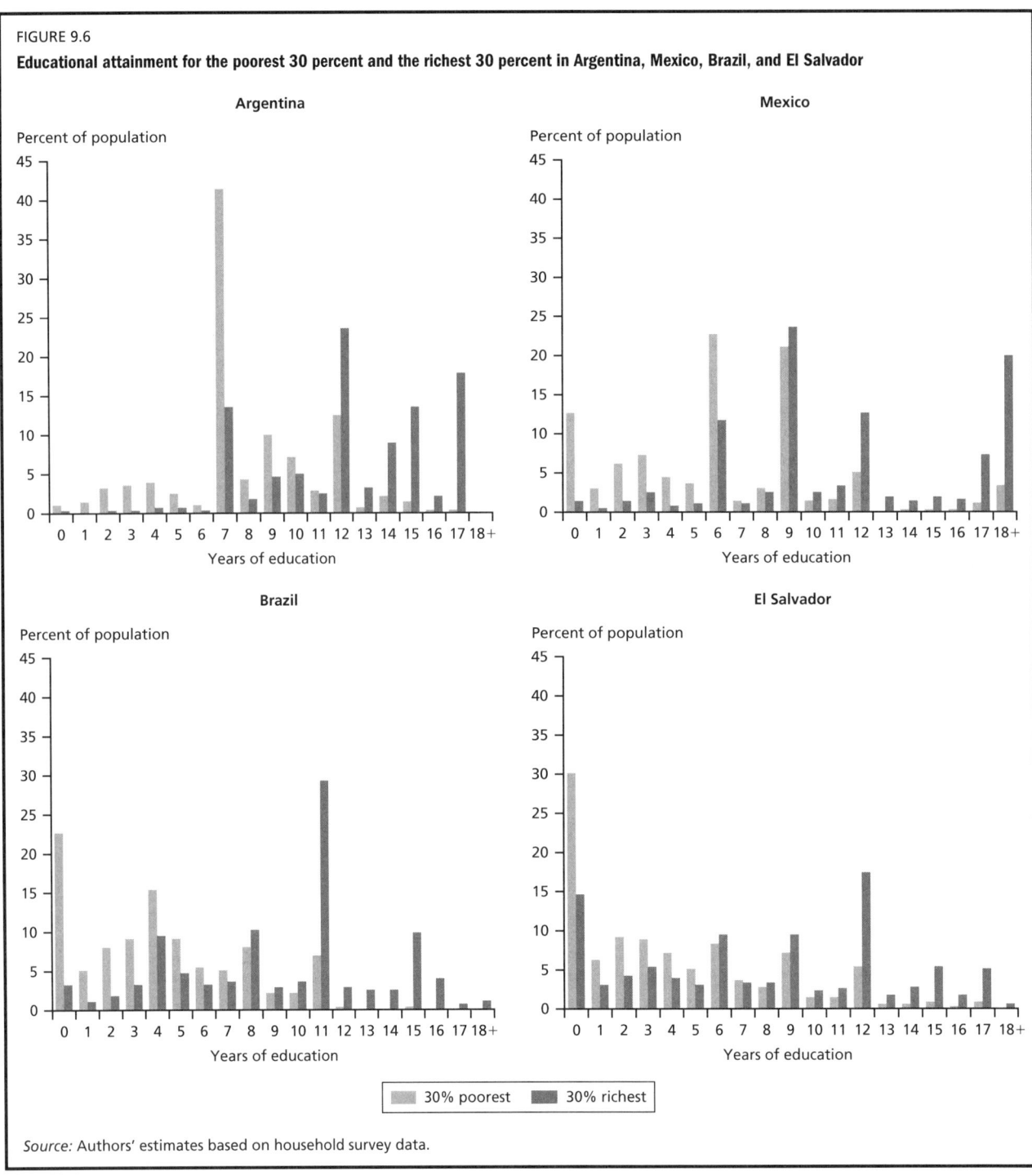

FIGURE 9.6

Educational attainment for the poorest 30 percent and the richest 30 percent in Argentina, Mexico, Brazil, and El Salvador

Source: Authors' estimates based on household survey data.

years of high school (15–18 age range). Further analysis of these data in numerous country studies shows that the drop in enrollment rates is generally more marked among children and youth from poor families.[15] The smooth decline in enrollments during the secondary cycle in most countries suggests that lack of secondary school facilities is not the main driving factor.

One common reason for the sharp decline in enrollment is that Latin American children experience delayed transitions mainly due to grade repetition. Figure 9.9 also shows the dismal performance of the region in ensuring high rates of on-time progression to the next grade. This low on-time progression to the next grade, combined with high enrollment, results in substantial numbers of children who

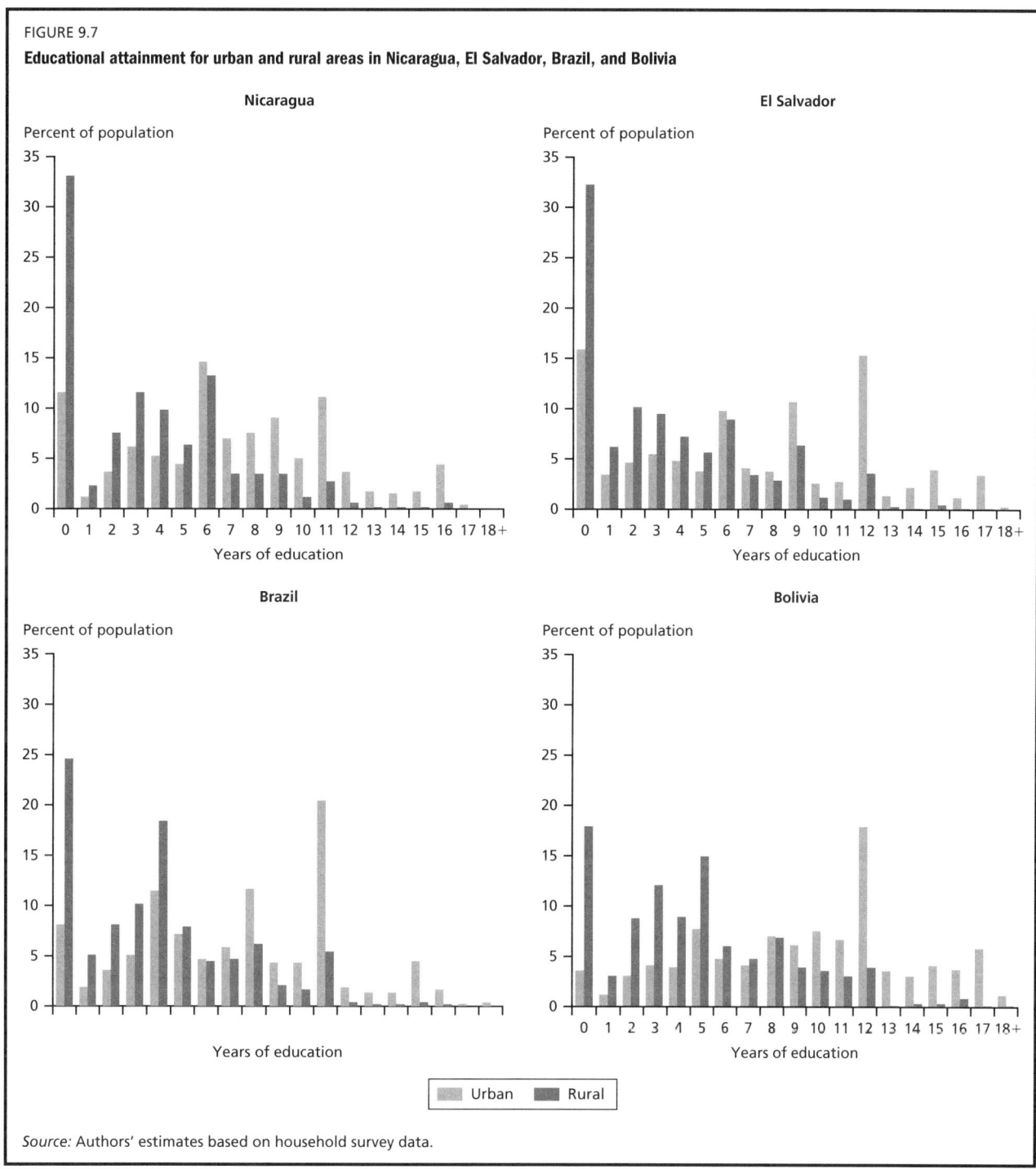

FIGURE 9.7
Educational attainment for urban and rural areas in Nicaragua, El Salvador, Brazil, and Bolivia

Source: Authors' estimates based on household survey data.

are overage for the grade they are in. For example, in many Central American countries, 40 to 50 percent of children are two or more years overage when they reach secondary education (World Bank 2005b).

Table 9.1 illustrates the poor record of most countries in the region in turning children's and youth's contact with the educational system into years of schooling. For each country it compares a measure of average years spent in school (the "1–12" educational system, 6–18 age range, proposed by Urquiola and Calderón 2004) with the actual number of grades that children have completed, on average. The first column captures the expected number of years that a child will spend in school given the country's current enrollment patterns. It provides a convenient

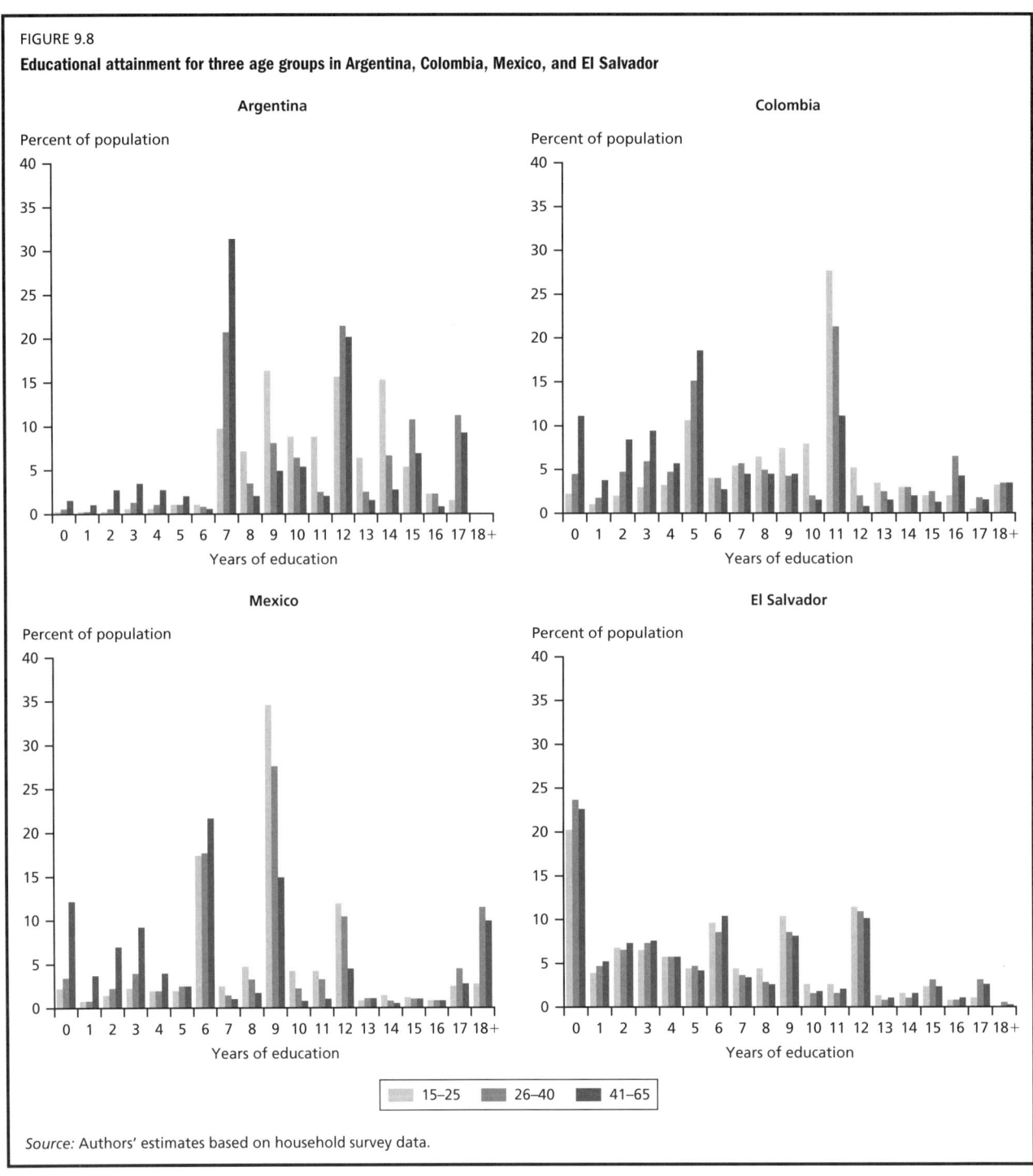

summary of the resources (in a time scale) spent by countries to keep children in school.[16] The gap with respect to the actual grades completed (third column) indicates how effectively educational systems turn average years in school into average number of grades completed.

Latin American children stay, on average, two to four extra years in school than needed to complete a full course of secondary education. The countries with lower educational attainment—Belize, Brazil, and Nicaragua, for example— tend to be among the worst performers on this indicator.

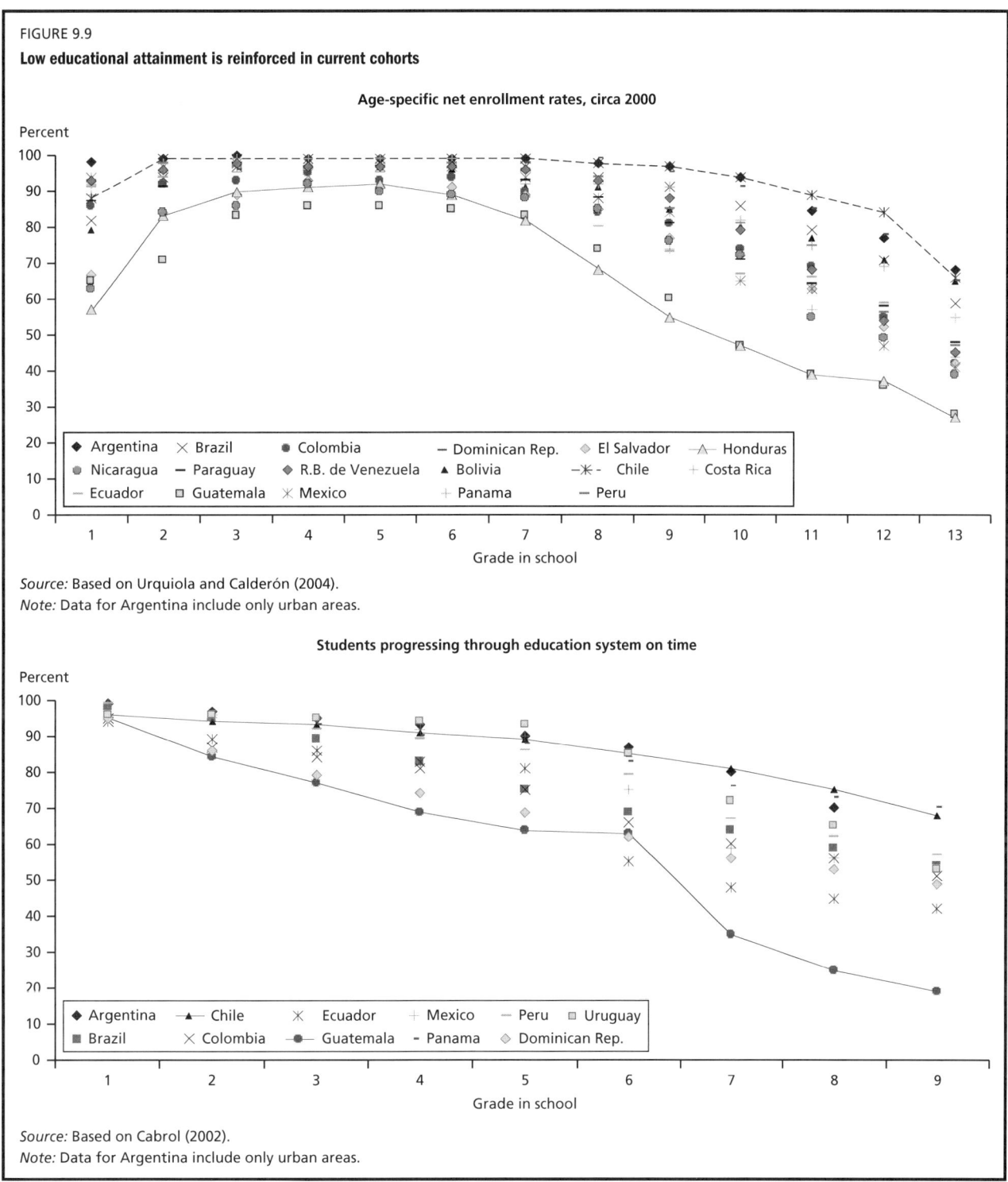

FIGURE 9.9
Low educational attainment is reinforced in current cohorts

However, countries like the Dominican Republic, Jamaica, and Uruguay, which stand out in keeping children in school, are fairly inefficient in the production of years of schooling. This low on-time progression slows down the accumulation of skills, lowers the returns to education (by delaying full entry into the labor market), and likely increases the risk of eventually dropping out.

To summarize, Latin America's success in improving average educational levels, with close to universal primary enrollment, has not been sufficient to reverse the persisting

TABLE 9.1

Average years of schooling in the "1-12" educational system and excess years spent in school, 6-18 age range, circa 2000

Country	Average years spent in school	Average number of grades completed	Average excess years spent in school
Chile	12.1	10.4	1.7
Argentina[a]	12.1	9.8	2.3
Panama	11.5	9.5	2.0
Peru	11.1	9.0	2.1
Bolivia	11.2	8.9	2.3
Jamaica	11.7	8.8	2.9
Ecuador	10.4	8.7	1.7
Mexico	10.6	8.7	1.9
Uruguay[a]	11.4	8.7	2.7
R. B. de Venezuela	11.0	8.6	2.4
Colombia	10.5	8.4	2.1
Paraguay	10.7	8.4	2.3
Dominican Republic	11.8	8.3	3.5
El Salvador	10.0	8.0	2.0
Costa Rica	10.5	7.8	2.7
Brazil	11.4	7.3	4.1
Belize	10.6	6.6	4.0
Honduras	8.6	6.2	2.4
Haiti[a]	8.8	5.9	2.9
Nicaragua	9.7	5.9	3.8
Guatemala	8.2	5.5	2.7

Source: Based on Urquiola and Calderón (2004).
a. Data for urban areas only.

educational divide in the population except in the more educationally advanced countries. Only Chile, Colombia, and Peru show signs of moving fast toward a diamond-shaped educational distribution. Argentina appears to be moving toward this pattern as well, although on a somewhat longer horizon, while Brazil shows delayed but steady progress. The population in the other countries sorts into two groups, one of individuals with low schooling (typically less than secondary education) and the other with more-educated individuals (secondary and above). These patterns of educational attainment emerge strongly across income and regional lines, with rural residents and the poorest families predominantly trapped in the low-education group. Patterns of school progression of current student cohorts indicate that this educational divide repeats itself as a result of high repetition and dropout rates. Since completion of at least a secondary education is needed for typical poor families to have a real chance of escaping subsistence levels, this educational divide might be self-reinforcing and induce persistent poverty across family generations.

Why aren't poor families leading their offspring to a level of education sufficient to better their chances of escaping this potential intergenerational poverty cycle? As noted before, liquidity constraints, deficient infrastructure, and low returns to education may be to blame. These are in turn linked to both short-term (income, for example) and long-term family factors.

Liquidity constraints, family factors, and educational investments: A sneak preview

The reasons Latin American children and youth reveal for being out of school consistently point to a combination of high opportunity costs, perceived low benefits, and access constraints.[17] Figure 9.10 illustrates how the relative emphases on each factor vary by age, gender, and poverty levels in four selected countries. The following patterns emerge:

- Work-related reasons (opportunity and direct costs) tend to be the most pressing in all countries, especially among boys, youth of postsecondary school age, and the poor.
- Low benefits are more important among the poor, boys, and children of primary and secondary school age, particularly in Bolivia and El Salvador.
- Other reasons, including pregnancy, family problems, or other idiosyncrasies, are more prevalent among girls, at younger ages, and among the rich, particularly in Chile and Colombia.
- Limited physical access appears to be a less-pressing factor overall, but is evident mostly among primary-school-age children, particularly in Chile, Colombia, the Dominican Republic, and Nicaragua.

Figure 9.11 shows that the relationship between educational investments and proxies of some of the above factors are largely consistent with self-assessments. The cost of schooling appears to be pressing largely for youth of postsecondary school age. The top panel in the figure shows that the opportunity cost, proxied by the contribution of youth's earnings to total family incomes, of sending young children to school is negligible in most countries. While the forgone income increases for adolescents of secondary education age, it still represents less than 10 percent of family incomes.

The greater concern of poor families for present rather than future consumption (that is, a higher discount rate) is very likely to make liquidity constraints binding in the transition from secondary to tertiary school. The income

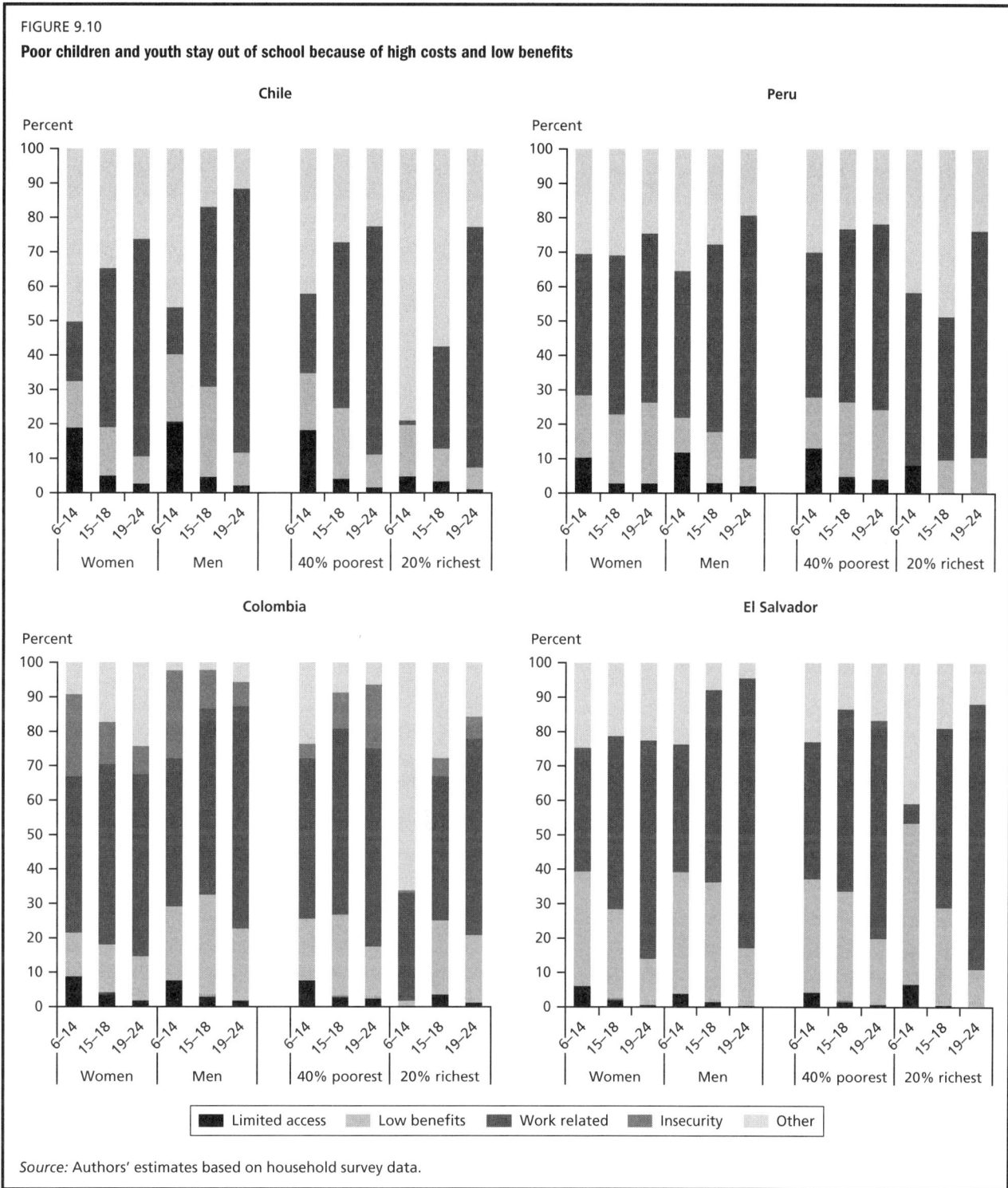

FIGURE 9.10
Poor children and youth stay out of school because of high costs and low benefits

Source: Authors' estimates based on household survey data.

loss for poor families that invest in postsecondary schooling is more significant than for the relatively rich, ranging from 10 to 17 percent for very poor youth and from 14 to 22 percent for the moderately poor (except in the Dominican Republic). The income loss is in addition to the high tuition costs of higher-quality private secondary schools and universities and should be weighted against the promise of high returns to postsecondary schooling.[18] Even for poor youth with access to free public schools, the high dependence of their families on their earnings to make ends meet almost

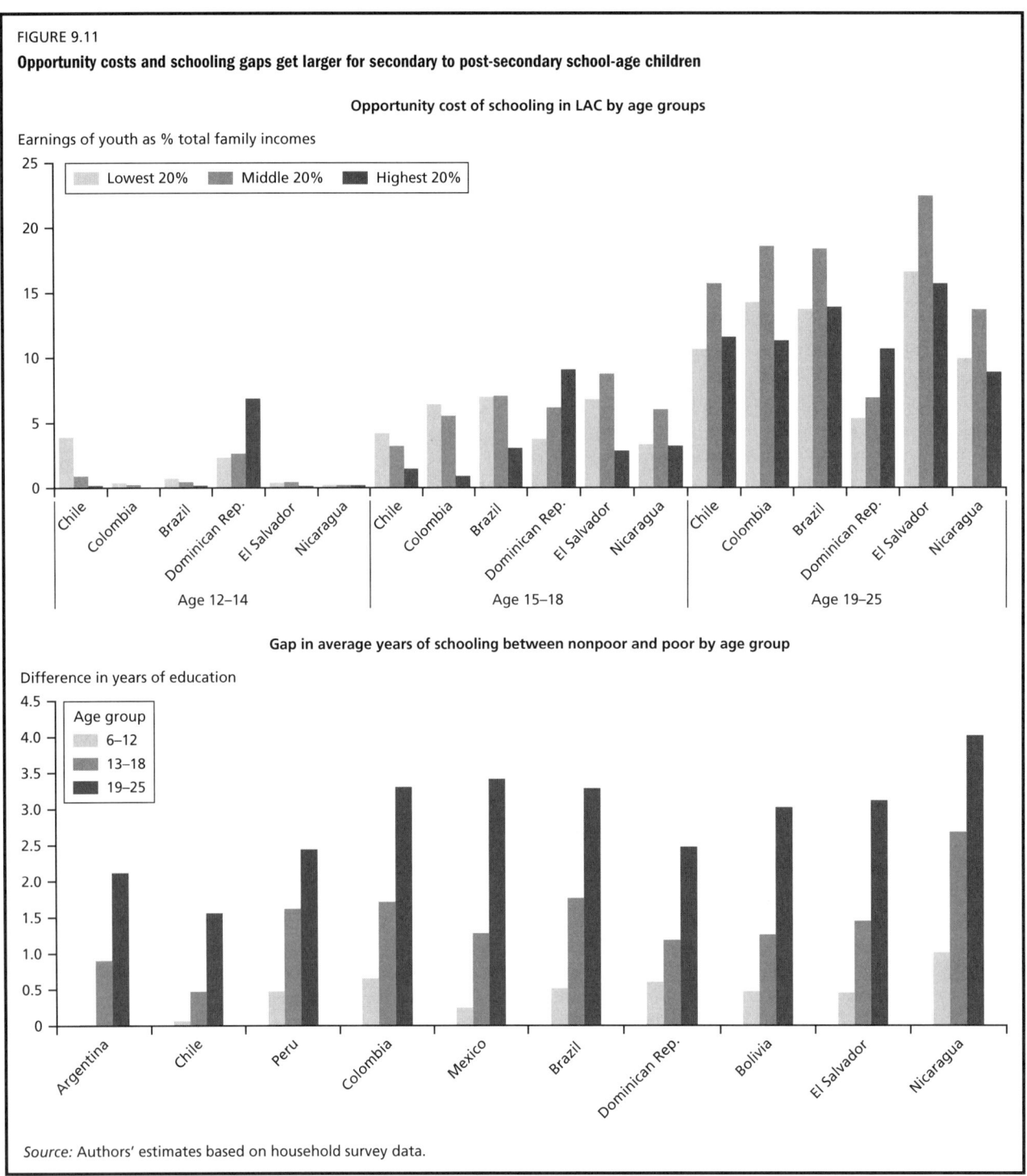

FIGURE 9.11

Opportunity costs and schooling gaps get larger for secondary to post-secondary school-age children

Source: Authors' estimates based on household survey data.

certainly deters transitions to higher education grades. No wonder poor Latin American children start to fall significantly behind the nonpoor in average years of schooling in their teenage and young adult years (bottom panel).

Finally, as noted in chapter 2, well-educated parents tend to have better-educated children. Figure 9.12 portrays this for Brazil, Colombia, and the Dominican Republic, illustrating the strong correlation between parental education and educational attainment and how this is mediated by income levels, school access (proxied by area), and race. Parental education compensates for low incomes and lack of access in Colombia and the Dominican Republic. In Brazil,

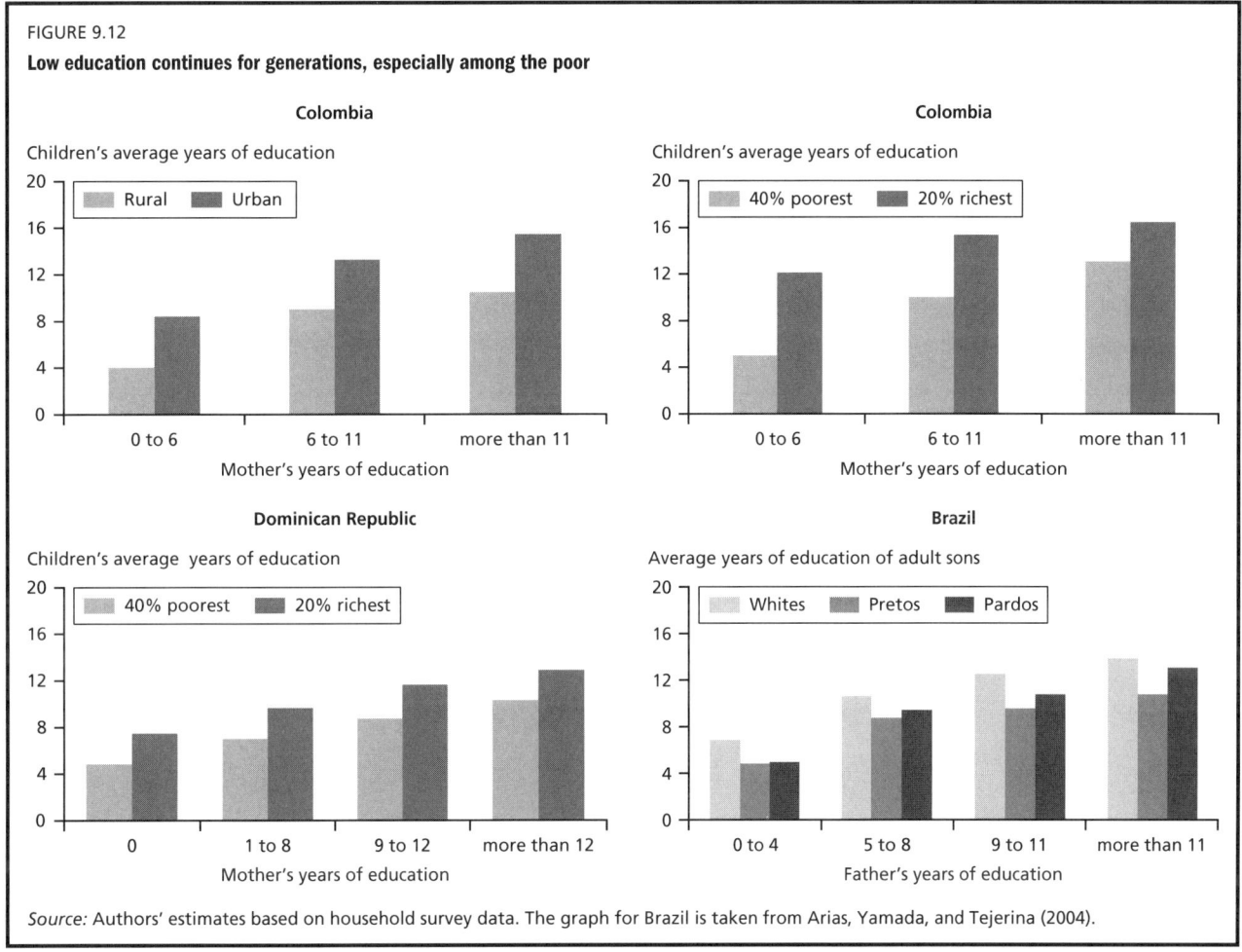

FIGURE 9.12
Low education continues for generations, especially among the poor

Source: Authors' estimates based on household survey data. The graph for Brazil is taken from Arias, Yamada, and Tejerina (2004).

pretos (blacks) are caught in an intergenerational low-education trap. Differences in returns to schooling may be behind this unequal educational mobility. We turn to these differences next.

The private value of schooling: How much does it pay? To whom?

The numerous studies estimating returns to education in Latin America and the Caribbean point to several stylized facts:

- Overall, average returns are relatively high compared with other regions of the world, but there is significant variation in returns across countries in the region (Psacharopoulos and Patrinos 2004).
- Education contributes significantly to rising earnings inequality: the average return to tertiary education rose, while returns to those completing secondary and primary education remained sluggish or declined over the 1990s in most countries (de Ferranti and others 2003, 2004; IDB 2004; Bourguignon, Ferreira, and Lustig 2005).
- The trends in returns to schooling are largely attributed, although not indisputably, to relative demand shifts—caused by trade liberalization and parallel technical change—that favor more skilled workers (Bourguignon, Ferreira, and Lustig 2005; de Ferranti and others 2003, 2004; IDB 2004).

If the returns to tertiary education are high and increasing, why do we not see many more Latin American children (including more of the rich) moving up to the top of the education ladder? A detailed analysis of returns to schooling in our sample of ten countries suggests that the pattern of returns may be an important part of the story behind the persisting educational divide in several of these countries. There are two main findings. First, returns to education are lumpy, and diplomas often matter a great deal—in many cases education seems attractive only when the long-term investments needed to complete at least a full course of secondary and some tertiary education can be realized. Second, in most countries the high average returns to tertiary education are not available to everyone alike; in particular, poor families tend to accrue returns to their investments in higher levels of education that are significantly below the average market return.

Figure 9.13 presents a snapshot of various measures of the average returns to education in the ten countries. These indicators answer distinct questions about the education investment process. The top left panel shows the evolution of the average earnings premium for schooling as individuals move up each step of the education ladder from no schooling to university completion, while the top right panel simply presents the per year returns that result from dividing this by the number of grades completed. The two panels are informative of the *cumulative* increase

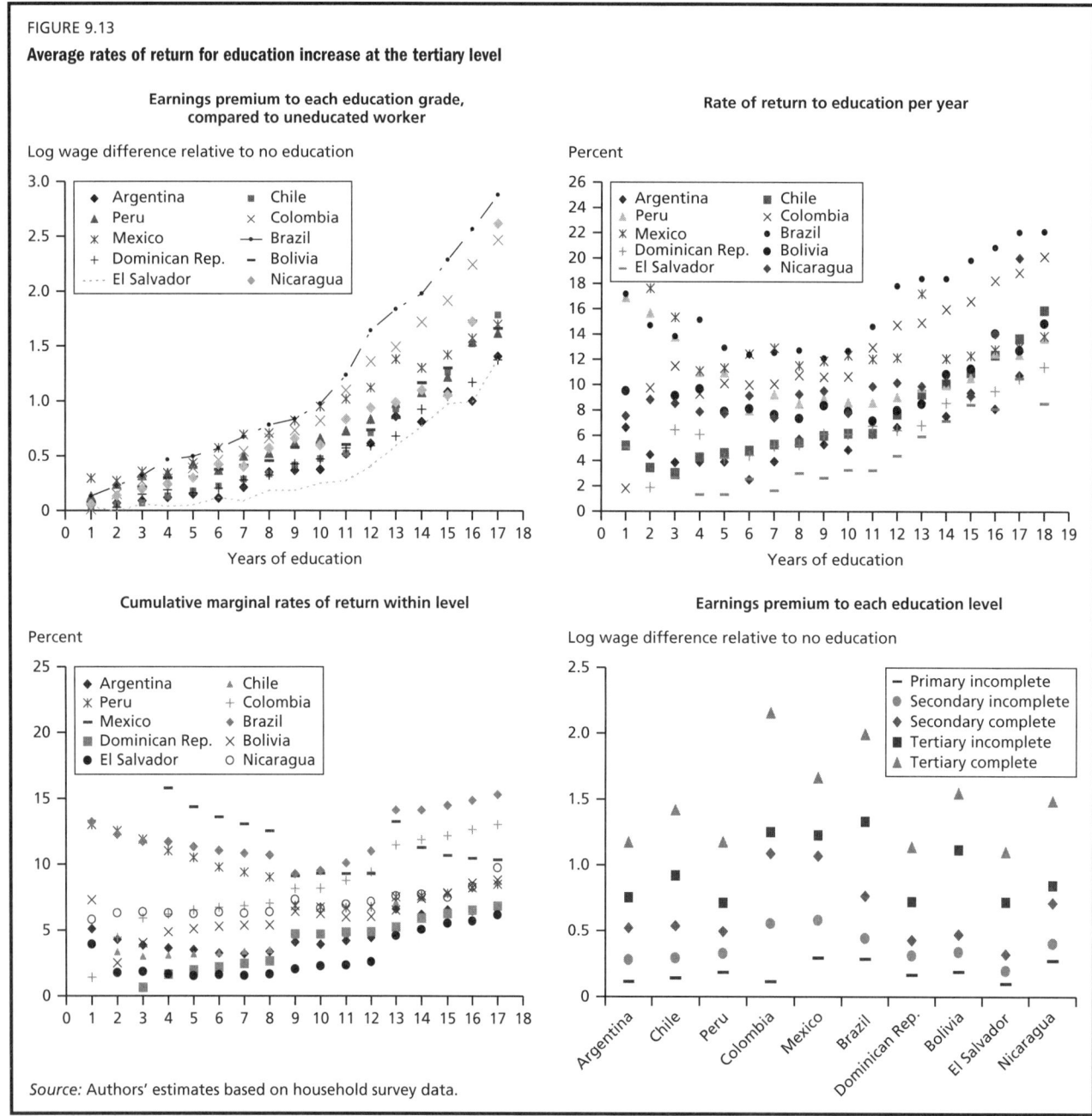

FIGURE 9.13
Average rates of return for education increase at the tertiary level

Source: Authors' estimates based on household survey data.

in average earnings of a successful school progression. In other words, for the family of a child just starting school, it answers the question, "On average, how much will she make if she reaches grade A (total and per year completed)?"

The bottom left panel shows the cumulative change in the *marginal* annual returns *within* each education level, computed as a moving average of the grade-to-grade difference in the return coefficients shown in the top right panel. These reveal the *additional* average earnings gains from completing each subsequent grade of primary, secondary, and tertiary education and may be the relevant indicators for the family in deciding whether or not their child should continue in school for an additional year given that she has reached grade A. Finally, the bottom right panel depicts the average earnings premium for each level of education defined according to the educational system of each country. The vertical distance between the points gives the *marginal* mean returns to each education level. These returns reflect the actual average value ascribed by local labor markets to a degree and thus capture any labor market signaling effect of degree completion.[19] For the child just starting school, the underlying marginal returns answer the question: "On average, how much more will she make if she reaches/completes education level X?" Cross-country comparisons of the data in this panel should be treated with caution due to variations in the structures of educational systems.

As one moves up the education ladder, average returns to schooling increase fairly similarly across countries, although the differences widen considerably at higher grades. The average of annual returns in the ten countries studied is about 6 percent for completion of eight years of basic education, 7.5 percent for secondary school graduates, and 11 percent for university graduates.[20] The lowest and highest returns in the sample are consistently observed in Brazil and El Salvador, ranging from 2.3 percent a year in El Salvador to 9.8 percent in Brazil for an eight-year course of basic education, from 3.4 to 11.8 percent for a secondary degree, and from 8 to 16.9 percent for a five-year course of tertiary education.

Several telling patterns are noticeable. The marginal returns to each subsequent grade stay constant or decline for the first eight years of basic education, increase in the first years of secondary education, and soar with and beyond completion of secondary education.[21] Except for Brazil, Mexico, and Peru, the annual average returns to investment in the basic education cycle are below 10 percent. Argentina, Chile, the Dominican Republic, and El Salvador have notably low average returns to basic education, ranging from 2 to 4 percent a year. Marginal returns are generally higher for those obtaining some or completing tertiary education (bottom panels), while the average returns to completing a full course of secondary schooling are more meaningful in Brazil, Colombia, and Mexico and negligible in Bolivia, the Dominican Republic, and El Salvador. In Argentina, Brazil, El Salvador, and Nicaragua, the full value of a college education accrues only after getting a diploma or completing a full four- to five-year course at a university. Those planning to work and study to finance college have a harder time doing so in these countries.

A key conclusion is that, barring liquidity and access constraints, the value option of getting a secondary or university diploma may be the strongest incentive for poor Latin American youth to break the educational divide. The low and flat returns to basic education in all countries and to high school education in the less-advanced countries suggest that workers who do not finish these cycles, say, workers with four to eight or nine to twelve years of schooling, are highly substitutable in the labor market. It is the completion of successive higher grades that makes earlier school investments more rewarding. Unless the prospects of reaching higher education grades are good, poor youth have few incentives to continue beyond basic education.

Yet do these average returns to education give a fair indication of the incentives to invest in education for everyone? There are two reasons why the answer might be no. First, returns to education can vary across workers according to gender, race and ethnicity, residential location, and other unobserved (unmeasured) characteristics such as quality of education, family background factors, and individual spunk.[22] Second, to the extent that individuals and families act on the expected returns to education in making their schooling decisions, estimates of average returns to education may not accurately represent the actual return to those not currently in school. For example, the returns to tertiary education could reflect the average quality (ability) of those who already have a college education. We now explore the empirical relevance of these issues (except for gender, which is less correlated with poverty and access constraints to schooling).

Variations in returns to schooling: Rural and racial dimensions

Earning incentives for rural workers are similar to—in some countries even higher than—those for urban workers. Figure 9.14 illustrates that there are few differences in the returns to education in urban and rural labor markets, and when the differences are more visible, they favor rural workers.

In Brazil, Chile, and Nicaragua, education returns, particularly to secondary education, are mildly larger in urban areas, but in Bolivia, Mexico, and Peru, they are much higher for rural workers over the whole range of levels of education. Other countries, including Colombia, show no gaps between urban and rural workers. These results reflect the growing importance of nonfarm occupations in rural economies. The majority of uneducated rural workers throughout Latin America are employed in agriculture, where education is less productive, while the more skilled hold nonfarm jobs. Since incomes in rural areas start from a lower base, workers in nonfarm jobs get a larger earnings

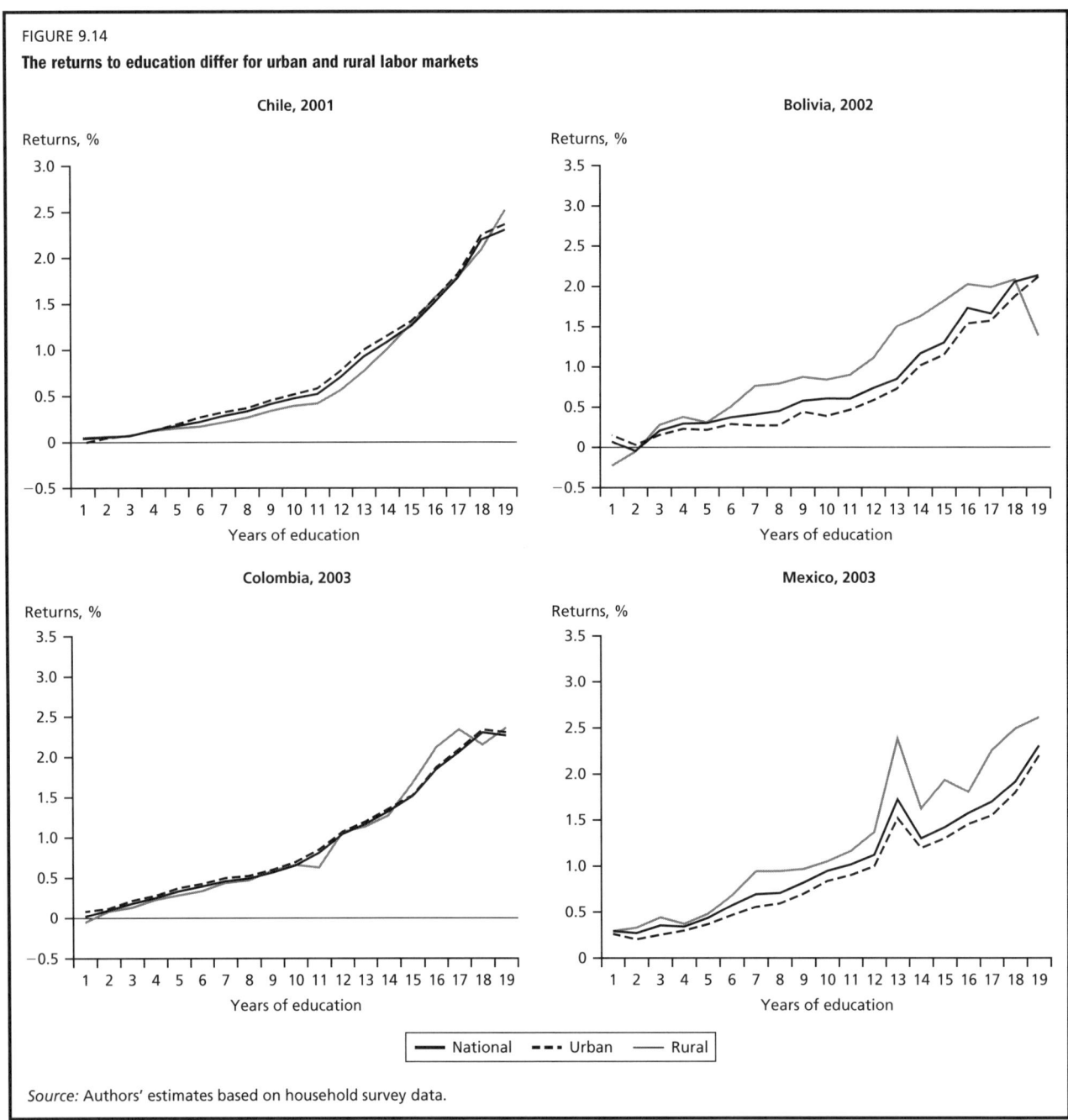

FIGURE 9.14
The returns to education differ for urban and rural labor markets

Source: Authors' estimates based on household survey data.

kick from education than do comparable workers in urban areas. Hence, a lack of earnings dividends from schooling should not be a first-order deterrent for rural families to invest in education except for those unable to engage in growing rural economic activities.

The influence of racial inequality on returns to education is stronger, although labor market discrimination may not be the main culprit. Several studies find that indigenous and Afro-descendant populations are restricted in access to the better-paying jobs. In Bolivia, Brazil, Guatemala, and Peru, these populations have average returns to schooling that are 1 to 3 percentage points lower than whites.[23] That compounds a disadvantage in educational attainment that ranges from an average of two to three full years of schooling.

There is evidence that differences in other components of human capital have a significant bearing on these results. Studies for Bolivia and Brazil (Mercado, Andersen, and Muriel 2003; Arias, Yamada, and Tejerina 2004) show that the lower education quality and parental education of nonwhites can explain more of the gap in returns than labor market discrimination. Differences in the formal education of parents in Brazil account for 1 percentage point of the edge in average returns of white men relative to *pretos* and 0.5 percentage point of the gap relative to *pardos* (mixed-race Brazilians) (figure 9.15). The fact that whites attend school in states with relatively better-quality education further accounts for half of their remaining lead in the returns to education. Overall, after factoring in racial differences in the quantity and quality of individual education and family background, the average earnings gap between white and nonwhite Brazilian workers falls from 46 percent to a 16 percent earnings disadvantage unrelated to workers' productive potential.

However, labor market inequality related to skin color imposes larger earnings penalties on blacks in the higher-paying jobs of any given skills. As shown in figure 9.15, while *pretos* and *pardos* located at the bottom of the salary scale enjoy a similar payoff to education, the best-paid quintile of *pardos* have a schooling return advantage of about 1 percentage point over the best-paid quintile of *pretos* with similar observed skills. This finding is consistent with studies showing that labor market discrimination is more likely when nonwhite workers cannot be denied access to the higher-paying jobs within occupations on the basis of their observed productive attributes (Darity and Mason 1998). While further research is needed to ascertain

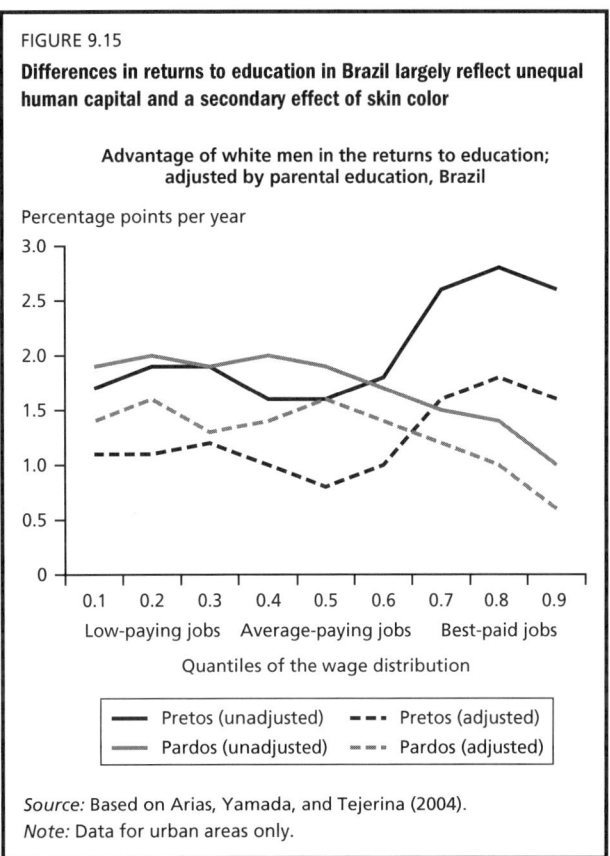

FIGURE 9.15

Differences in returns to education in Brazil largely reflect unequal human capital and a secondary effect of skin color

Source: Based on Arias, Yamada, and Tejerina (2004).
Note: Data for urban areas only.

the sources of ethnic and racial earnings inequality in the region, these populations do face lower incentives to invest in schooling that should be addressed by human capital and labor market policy interventions.

Unobserved abilities and the returns to the marginal labor market entrant

A flurry of studies shows that returns to education can vary among individuals with the same race, gender, labor market experience, or sector of employment because of the complementarity between education and unobserved earnings determinants.[24] The latter are related to the multiple skills that constitute an individual's scholastic and labor market abilities that may create more channels for acquiring higher levels of education as well as the higher-paying jobs for any given level of education. Data on the quality of schools, family background, labor market connections, and characteristics of communities in early childhood can serve as proxies for these abilities but are often absent in household surveys. Nonetheless, it is important to factor in these and other sources of variation in the costs and benefits of schooling across families and individuals.

Average returns to education can misrepresent the actual incentives faced by less-schooled individuals to move up the education ladder. Two distinct possibilities are relevant (Carneiro and Heckman 2003; and Card 2001). First, there may be "cream skimming," in which the best-quality students (those with higher abilities or higher returns) are more likely to get a university (or secondary) education, while the less talented (low returns) are more prone to join the pool of the less educated. In this case the returns for individuals with low propensity to attend university (the less talented) will be lower than the average return for the already college educated. Second, faced with binding liquidity constraints, many talented high school dropouts may be unable to attend university despite high expected earnings gains. That is particularly true for those in the best-paid unskilled jobs who face higher forgone earnings if they opt to continue their schooling. Thus, many marginal entrants to college may actually have returns above the average return to current college graduates. Which effects predominate depends on the strength of the correlation between schooling costs and benefits along income lines and education levels. In either case the average returns to secondary or university education are insufficient to assess the schooling investment incentives for youth randomly selected from the population or for those from disadvantaged families.

How does this issue bear on the question of underinvestment in human capital and poverty? The second case above is a clear-cut example of schooling underinvestment caused by credit constraints that may be addressed through conditional cash transfers or student loan programs. In the first case more evidence is needed on the role of long-term family factors or other externalities in generating low returns to education to assess the case for underinvestment. For example, if returns are low in general because of a deficient school system or unsound economic policies, then from a private perspective, families' schooling investments may be "just right" for existing returns.[25] The most appropriate policies to promote more education need not bear a direct link with poverty.

Differences in empirical measures of schooling returns across income groups can be informative about whether short-term liquidity constraints or long-term family effects are more significant. Since very poor families should face more binding liquidity constraints, their measured returns to education could be higher because at the margin only the more talented (with very high expected returns) become more schooled. However, returns would be higher for more affluent families to the extent they have an edge in producing higher scholastic aptitude and labor market skills. While there are bright and industrious individuals in both poor and rich families, the factors affecting a child's readiness to learn, quality of schooling, and labor market connections tend to lower the returns to educational investments of poor families. These disadvantaging effects should be compounded and thus be more visible at higher education levels.

To examine the importance of these issues, we estimate a series of returns to education and assess whether returns are lower for poor families. We fitted earnings functions through 10 different percentiles of the conditional wage distribution in each country, that is, for workers located at the bottom to the top of the salary scale adjusted by their demographics and skill levels. Figure 9.16 illustrates the returns to each level of education for workers in the 20th, 50th and 80th wage percentiles in selected countries, which represent the schooling returns to the low- average- and best-paid workers at jobs of any skill level.[26] Taking the position of workers in the adjusted salary scale as a proxy of their unobserved ability, differences in returns along the salary scale reflect variations in their unmeasured skills.

In most countries returns to schooling, particularly at the tertiary level, are higher for workers who have the best-paid jobs for their skills. The differences are quite large in Chile, El Salvador, and Nicaragua, where the top-rank (high ability) college workers enjoy returns to tertiary education that are 30 to 40 percent larger than the returns for the college-educated in jobs with lower pay. Returns for basic and secondary education are similar to the average return except in Brazil and Chile, where returns to completion of secondary education are 30 to 40 percent larger for the best-paid workers. Only in the Dominican Republic and Peru are the returns roughly similar throughout the earnings scale.

There is further evidence that the poor tend to benefit less from higher education. Figure 9.17 illustrates the results of following a procedure that maps the schooling returns of workers (implicitly reflecting rankings of unmeasured human capital) to the rankings of per capita incomes of their families (see annex 9A). Returns to a university education (complete or incomplete) tend to be higher for the richest families in all countries where we observed significant differences. The gaps in returns between the rich and the poor are somewhat muted (20 percent in Chile and 40 percent in Nicaragua, for example), reflecting the fact

FIGURE 9.16

Returns to each level of education for the three tiers of the earnings distribution

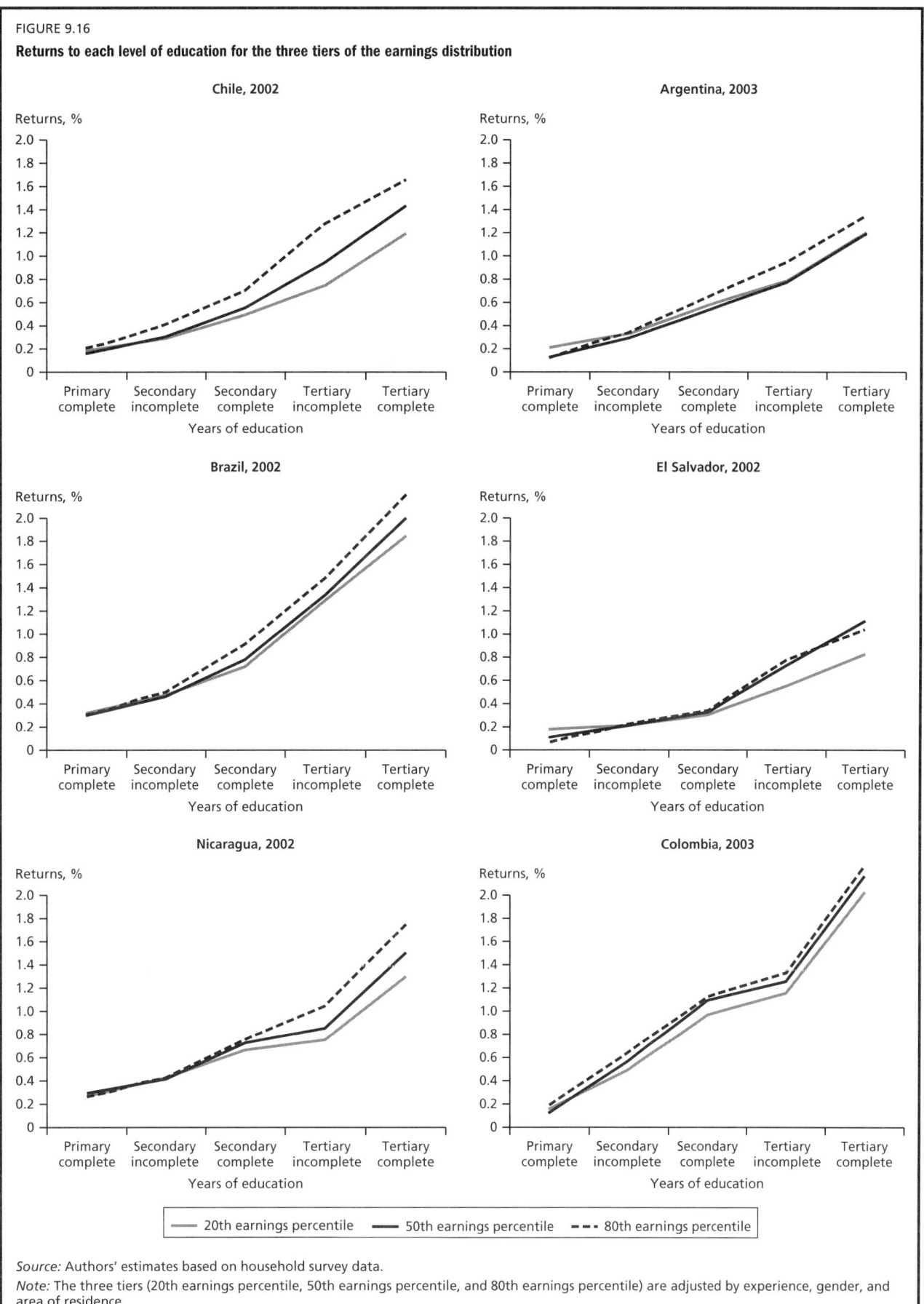

Source: Authors' estimates based on household survey data.
Note: The three tiers (20th earnings percentile, 50th earnings percentile, and 80th earnings percentile) are adjusted by experience, gender, and area of residence.

FIGURE 9.17
Correlation between returns to each level of education and poverty

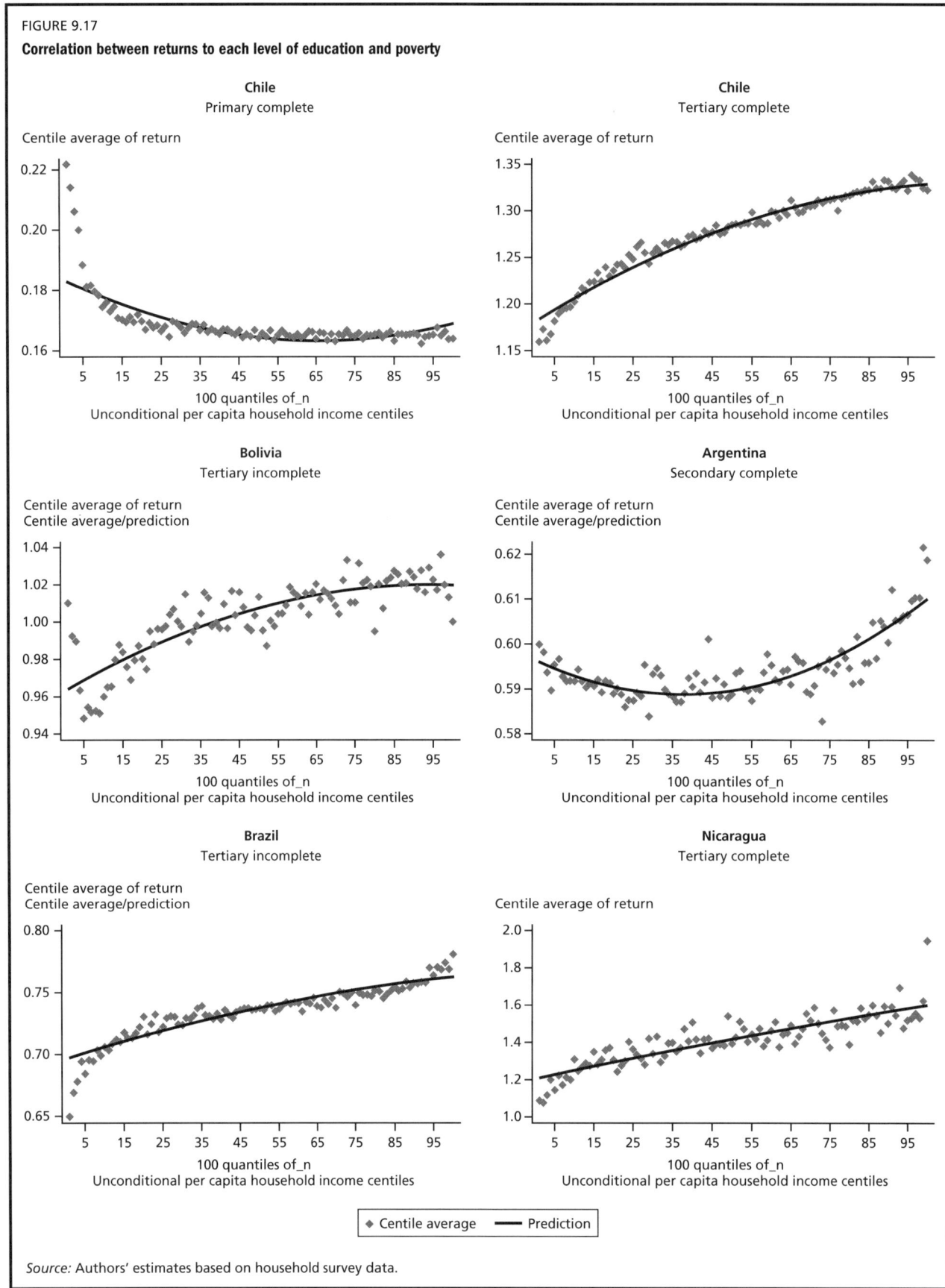

Source: Authors' estimates based on household survey data.

that some workers from poor families also benefit from unobserved labor market abilities that are complementary to schooling. However, the poor face lower returns to tertiary education returns, since they tend to have a disproportionate disadvantage in the production of skills at home and school. Note that returns to basic and secondary education are fairly constant along family income lines and, in some countries like Argentina, Colombia, and El Salvador, may slightly favor the poor. The low and flat returns to lower levels of education offer similar investment disincentives to the poor and the rich.

Figure 9.18 shows that differences in schooling returns blur the incentives to make additional investments in secondary and higher education for workers that rank low in the adjusted salary scale (those with lower unmeasured skills). For example, in Bolivia and Chile the marginal earnings gains from having some tertiary education are close to 80 percent for the best-paid workers, but only 30 to 40 percent for those who end up in the less-well-paid jobs. The differential returns are less staggering in other countries like El Salvador and Nicaragua but are still significant and add up to overall low marginal returns to tertiary education.

Bolivia is one of the few countries in the sample where marginal schooling returns are higher for workers at the bottom of the job ladder; this happens in the transition from primary to secondary school and for completion of tertiary education. Recall that marginal returns to having some tertiary education are lower for the low-ranking Bolivian workers. That is, the few low-ranking Bolivian workers who reach tertiary education enjoy a relatively larger boost in earnings along the way but end up with similar returns to the investment once they get a university diploma. The latter is highly suggestive that liquidity constraints hinder transitions to higher grades in Bolivia.

What lies behind these differences in the returns to schooling? As noted earlier, education and incomes may be highly correlated across generations. The poor are also constrained by longer-term family factors that affect both educational achievement and adult earnings, such as home schooling, family wealth (which buys quality schooling), and family connections. Family background and school quality—information rarely collected in survey data—remain unaccounted for in the analysis, which may cause us to misrepresent the returns to education, as well as the impact of short-term liquidity constraints in educational attainment.

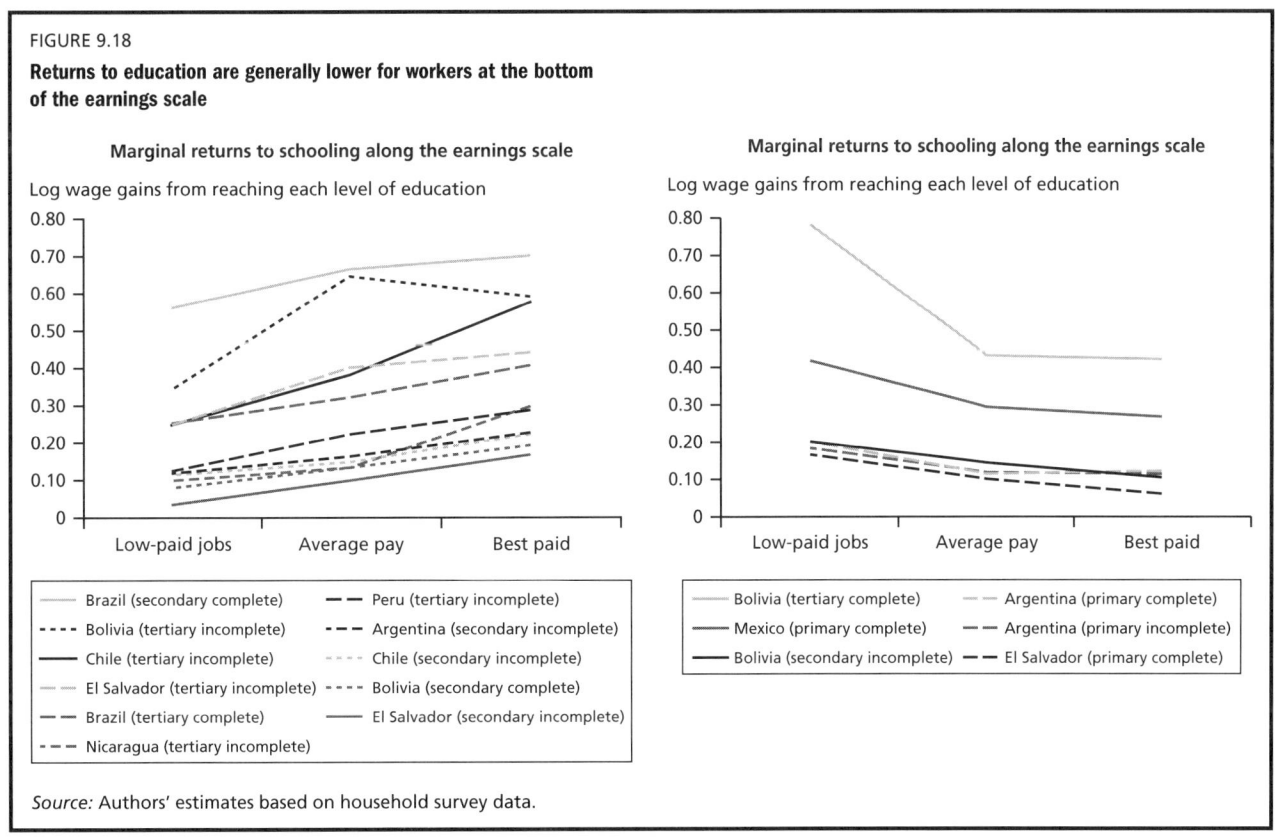

FIGURE 9.18

Returns to education are generally lower for workers at the bottom of the earnings scale

Source: Authors' estimates based on household survey data.

An examination of the data in Colombia and the Dominican Republic, the only two countries with reliable parental education data in recent household surveys, indicates that the offspring of more-educated parents do enjoy higher earnings, but returns to education are not vastly overstated as a result. Failing to purge parental effects on the earnings of their offspring overstates education returns by only 3–7 percent, except for the returns to primary education for low-paid workers and to tertiary education for the best-paid workers, which are overstated by 40 percent and 11 percent, respectively. Similarly, as shown in figure 9.18, Arias, Yamada, and Tejerina (2004) found that the returns to education in Brazil are about 10 percent overstated due to the joint impact of family background on the education of children and youth and their earnings as adults. While still sparse, this evidence is remarkably consistent with the consensus of the literature that estimates returns to education in the United States to be slightly overstated by about 10 percent. This suggests that the estimated returns to education shown here are not severely misrepresenting the earnings-schooling relationship.[27]

In addition to the well-known positive effect on children's educational attainment, the education of parents boosts the earnings of sons and daughters. In Colombia and the Dominican Republic, children's earnings are increased by 20–35 percent (7–15 percent) for each parent with a college (high school) education compared with a parent with primary education. This could reflect an impact on returns to education that is difficult to isolate with cross-section data. Using longitudinal data, Altonji and Dunn (1996) found that returns to schooling are higher for children of more-educated parents. In Brazil, Arias, Yamada, and Tejerina (2004) found substantial earnings payoffs to higher levels of parental education that vary across race groups. Father's education generates more significant earnings gains for whites, while mother's schooling was more important to boost the earnings of nonwhites. The authors interpret these as suggestive that father's education plausibly proxies wealth and thus school quality and family connections in the labor market. Meanwhile mother's schooling more closely captures differences in the home production of skills in light of the low female labor force participation at the time workers were schooled. This means that effects of parental education need to be accounted for before interpreting a correlation between low family incomes and low educational attainment as evidence of short-term liquidity constraints.

The spare evidence on the impact of school quality in Latin America suggests that it is a significant source of variation in the returns to education. The Arias, Yamada, and Tejerina (2004) study for Brazil measured the impact of education quality on schooling returns from cross-state and intercohort variations in pupil-teacher ratios—proxies for education quality. Figure 9.19 illustrates its main finding: workers educated in states with a lower pupil-teacher ratio (say, by 10 students) have higher average returns to education (by 0.9 percentage point for each year of schooling). Large class sizes are not uncommon for Latin American poor children, especially those in marginal urban schools. The pupil-teacher ratio is also correlated with other key inputs of the educational process, such as instructional time, educational materials, and teachers' education and experience. In another study for Brazil, Albernaz, Ferreira, and Franco (2002) found that other indicators of school quality, such as teachers' educational level and school infrastructure, have significant effects on children's educational performance. Mizala and Romaguera (2002) summarize the evidence for other countries in the region. Therefore, differences in education quality could plausibly account for an important portion of the gaps in returns to education between the poor and nonpoor in the region. This highlights the critical importance of enhancing the quality of the educational supply for the poor.

To summarize, the high value ascribed to a university education in Latin America is not available to everyone. College-educated workers with lower unmeasured human capital, particularly the poor, do not receive the same returns to their education as do other workers with college education. Long-term family factors, particularly education quality and parental education, appear to be important determinants of the productivity of schooling investments and earnings as adults. While the total returns to tertiary education for the poor are still significant, even mild liquidity constraints could quickly take children and youth from disadvantaged families off the path to reaching higher education grades. In the next section we weigh the evidence on the relative contribution of short-term and long-term poverty factors to Latin America's persistent educational divide.

Short-term or long-term poverty: Which is more pressing for schooling investments?

We discern the relative importance of liquidity constraints and long-term family factors in preventing Latin American children from getting sufficient schooling to escape

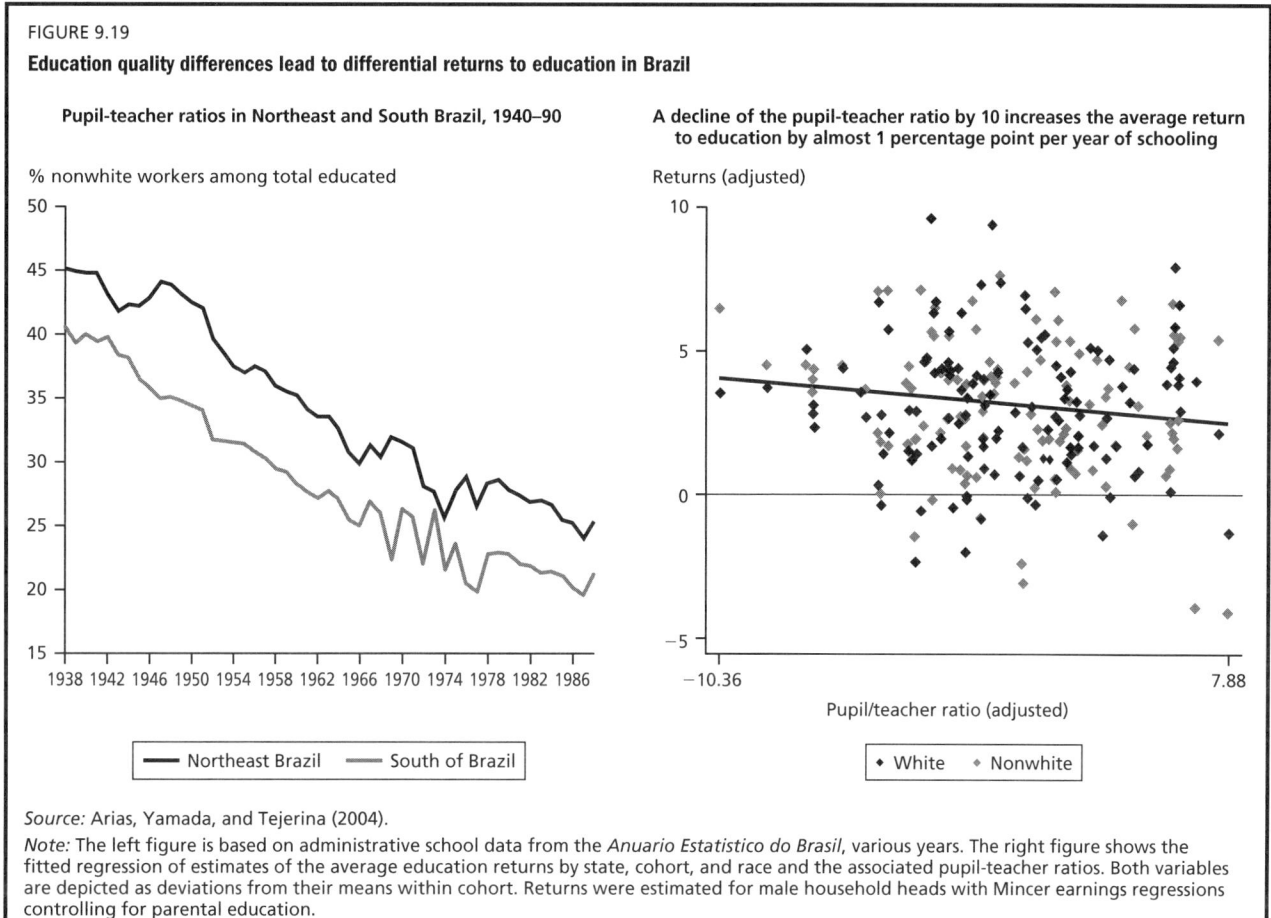

FIGURE 9.19

Education quality differences lead to differential returns to education in Brazil

Source: Arias, Yamada, and Tejerina (2004).
Note: The left figure is based on administrative school data from the *Anuario Estatistico do Brasil*, various years. The right figure shows the fitted regression of estimates of the average education returns by state, cohort, and race and the associated pupil-teacher ratios. Both variables are depicted as deviations from their means within cohort. Returns were estimated for male household heads with Mincer earnings regressions controlling for parental education.

poverty by means of survival (hazard) regressions (see annex 9A). This analysis is common in clinical studies of the effect of a new drug treatment on patients' chances of "survival" from a disease after a certain time has elapsed. We examine how child and family characteristics affect the risk that children and adolescents (6–25 age range) fail to enroll in school (primary, secondary, or tertiary) at a given grade (a proxy of school dropout) given the number of grades already completed, thus capturing the sequence of the entire schooling investment process.[28] Incomes, proxies of physical access, returns to education, and family demographics could be considered "treatments" to the extent they can be manipulated by specific policy interventions. School variables that affect the learning and schooling process are not explicitly part of the analysis due to lack of data, so their effect is captured by family socioeconomic characteristics that influence the capacity to access better-quality schools. The analysis is conducted for Brazil, Chile, Colombia, the Dominican Republic, El Salvador, and Nicaragua to illustrate the effects along the region's gradient of educational development. Figure 9.20 illustrates the main results. The findings are summarized below.

• *Family effects do matter a great deal*. Compared with having a college-educated mother, having a mother with only primary education increases the risk of school dropout by as much as 160 percent in Chile and 60 percent in El Salvador. A father with low education *additionally* increases the risks of school failure by up to 140 percent in Chile and 40 percent in the Dominican Republic. These are substantial impacts given the high degree of assortative mating in the region. These risks are cut by one-half or two-thirds when the parents have a secondary education; children of Central American fathers with high school education have the same chance as children of college-educated fathers to move up the educational ladder. In Colombia, having *grandparents* with little education increases the risk of school failure of children and youth even when parental education, incomes, and other family characteristics are accounted for. That is, low educational attainment in Colombia tends to persist

FIGURE 9.20

Factors that have an impact on moving up the educational ladder

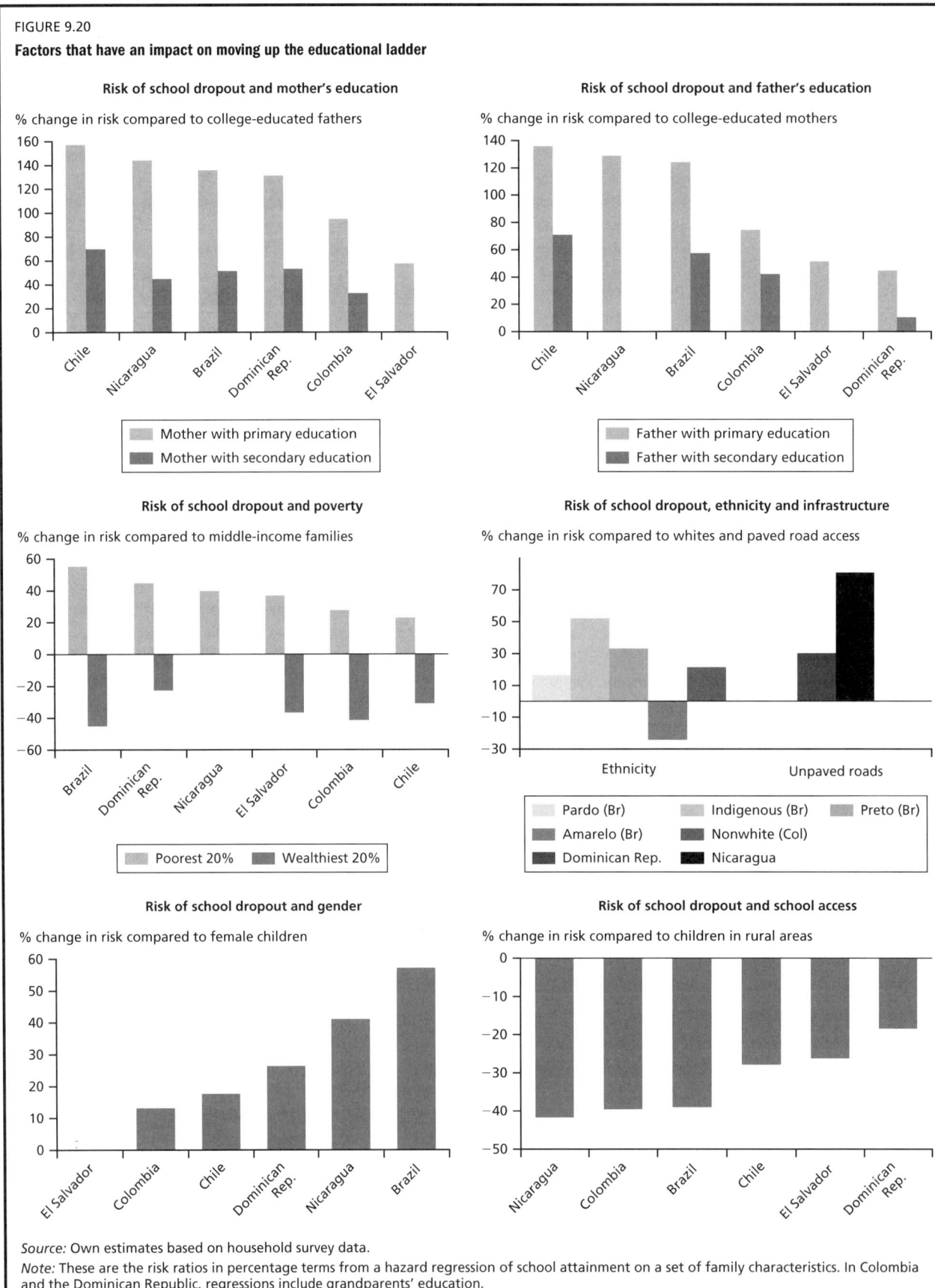

Source: Own estimates based on household survey data.
Note: These are the risk ratios in percentage terms from a hazard regression of school attainment on a set of family characteristics. In Colombia and the Dominican Republic, regressions include grandparents' education.

strongly across three family generations. The effects of the education of the mother and grandmother are remarkably similar but are lower for grandfather's than for father's education (see figure 9.19). It seems plausible that simultaneous conditioning on current income and parental and grandparents' education yields cleaner measurements of liquidity constraints and the quality of skills development at home and schools. Thus the results affirm that both short-term and long-term family factors (family background, liquidity constraints) and the quality of schools are central to accelerate human capital formation in the region.

There is further evidence that higher expected returns to education (at higher grades) and a better-quality home environment correlate with more stable school progressions. Children from nonwhite families face a higher risk of leaving school early: 20 percent in Colombia and Nicaragua, and 17 to 52 percent for *pardos*, *pretos*, and indigenous people in Brazil. Moreover, children and youth in female-headed households face a three to four times bigger risk of dropping out of school in Brazil, Chile, and the Dominican Republic, although school dropout is not affected by whether the mother is a salaried employee or self-employed. Since we are purging income and family background factors, the latter effects plausibly reflect the lower expected returns to education for nonwhites, as well as the constraints on single parents in providing quality school supervision of children (such as doing homework) and role models. Although the effects are small, some evidence shows that the expectation of higher returns to education at higher grades also encourages more-even school progressions. Using a proxy, albeit imperfect, of the differential schooling return that children might face due to abilities inherent to their families, we find that those with higher family returns for secondary completion (Brazil and Nicaragua) and college education (Chile and Nicaragua) are less likely to drop out of school.[29] Altogether, these findings further reaffirm the role of long-term family factors in enhancing the productivity and incentives for schooling investments.

• *Liquidity constraints play a relatively smaller but significant role.* Children and youth from the poorest 20 percent of families face a higher risk of school failure compared with those from middle-class families: the difference ranges from 55 percent in Brazil to 20 percent in Chile. This risk is half as large for families in the second quintile and then tapers off the richer a family becomes, suggesting that being below a subsistence threshold interferes with school progression. For example, in Nicaragua only children from the poorest 40 percent of families face a higher risk of school failure than the richest families. In El Salvador and Nicaragua, international remittances—which in this context are a relatively more exogenous income source—lower the risk of school failure, although modestly. Boys, irrespective of whether they are rich or poor, face a much higher risk of dropout than do girls in Brazil, the Dominican Republic, and Nicaragua (40–60 percent), and a modestly higher risk in Chile and Colombia (13–17 percent). Moreover, each additional young sibling (age 6–12) increases the risk of school failure for any one of the siblings (by 4 to 22 percent across countries), while more children of secondary school age actually lower the risk in Brazil, the Dominican Republic, and El Salvador (by 5 to 22 percent). All of these effects were obtained controlling for parental education and proxies of family returns to education and are thus highly suggestive that liquidity constraints are binding, to different degree, in all of the countries.

• *Physical access constraints remain operative, binding most when returns are higher.* The risk of school failure is 40 percent higher in the rural areas of Brazil, Colombia, and Nicaragua (all countries with higher returns to education) and 20–30 percent higher in the rural areas of the Dominican Republic and El Salvador (with the lowest returns). Deficient infrastructure (proxied by unpaved roads) increases the risk of school dropout by 80 percent in Nicaragua and by 30 percent in the Dominican Republic. The poorest regions in Brazil, Chile, and Colombia, where basic infrastructure is generally more deficient, show higher risks of school failure, but these become weaker or even reverse signs after adjusting for family socioeconomic characteristics. Migrants are at higher risk for dropping out of school in Colombia (15 percent, in part perhaps capturing violence-related displacement), Nicaragua (45 percent), and the Dominican Republic (70 percent); only in Brazil do they face lower risk (5 percent). However, school supply does not seem the most prevalent consideration for migration. For instance, only 14 percent of Dominicans age 3–22 who migrated in the past five years stated school-related reasons; a similar fraction sought income opportunities.

What conclusions can we draw from these results and the preceding analyses? The main lesson is that long-term family factors, liquidity, and school access constraints conspire, in different degrees, to generate human capital underinvestment traps that hinder sustained and balanced educational progression in the region. The two main elements interacting in the resulting vicious cycle are a pattern of schooling returns that makes it unattractive for many poor families to invest in education, namely, returns that are low and flat in the eight-year basic education cycle, rise significantly at the tertiary level but are lower for poor families and only occasionally mature fully when a degree is completed; and liquidity constraints stemming from subsistence incomes and borrowing constraints.

The extent of underinvestment traps and the relative weight of the intervening factors varies across countries. A few patterns can be identified that are likely responsible for reinforcing educational divides within countries:

- Chile, Colombia, and Peru are the countries relatively better positioned in our sample to experience a faster transition toward a diamond-shape (broad secondary base) educational distribution; these three countries are favored by relatively high and smoother returns to schooling and a relatively lower fraction of the prime-age population with very low education (less so in Colombia). Potential limiting factors are unequal schooling returns (especially in Chile) and liquidity and learning constraints related to family educational and wealth endowments and ethnicity, which result in home and school quality gaps for the poor's offspring.
- Bolivia's unequal educational transition and Nicaragua's very low educational attainment result from a similar set of limiting factors, with a strong role played by liquidity constraints exacerbated by relatively high returns that materialize fully only near or upon degree completion and by larger gaps in secondary school infrastructure. The low levels of skills in these two countries pose a high risk that they will fall into a self-reinforcing cycle of low technology, low demand for skills, and low innovation and skills investments.
- In Argentina, a high fraction of poor families with low parental education, low returns to the primary and secondary education cycle, uncertain tertiary returns (maturing with degree completion), and high discounting of the future may be preventing poor children from sharing in the fast transition of recent age cohorts to largely free secondary and tertiary public education.[30]

- Brazil's low schooling attainment and high educational inequality likely arise from the interplay of multiple sources: high but very unequal returns (which are lower for the poor) to secondary and tertiary education, persistent intergenerational family effects, pressing liquidity constraints, and localized supply bottlenecks. Mexico's sharp educational divide reflects a similar though less marked situation, as Mayer-Foulkes (2004) has more fully documented.
- Finally, the acceleration of educational transitions in the Dominican Republic and El Salvador is constrained mainly by exceedingly low returns to education on top of already low overall earnings, largely related to poor readiness to learn (a result itself of low parental schooling) and particularly deficient education quality.[31] Thus, liquidity constraints in these countries do not appear to be as important as increasing the incentives of families to make sustained investments in education.

These are not intended as exhaustive explanations of the low educational attainment in these countries, but as important links to poverty and its intergenerational transmission. Similar patterns may be operative in other Latin American countries where poor children and youth do not succeed in completing higher grades. Each merits detailed examination in specific country studies incorporating institutional analyses of the educational systems.

Implications for human capital formation policies

This chapter examined how Latin America's educational divide between two groups of low and highly educated individuals is simultaneously a source and a result of subsistence incomes across generations. As for any investment, the confluence of opportunity (attractive returns) and possibility (liquidity, quality schools, and home environments) is essential to human capital accumulation. Poor Latin American families lack elements from both in different degrees. The main overall implication of the results discussed here is the need for integrated, long-term strategies for skills development that exploit the synergies in the lifecycle human capital accumulation process in which both families and schools play a central role. Specific implications for human capital formation policies (nutrition and health, education, and training) are:

- *Leveling the initial playing field for children at risk.* It is imperative to address the unequalizing impact of deficiencies in early-childhood development and deficient parenting on the educational attainment of poor children and their capacity to command higher returns to education as adults. Although nutritional failures are very hard to remedy after the child's first two years, almost half of Latin American and Caribbean countries are not on track to meet the UN Millennium Development Goal of halving malnutrition by 2015.

Well-targeted interventions to strengthen the capacities of families to create early human capital should be prioritized. For example, conditional cash transfer programs can be used to induce parents to devote more attention to children's health and nutrition by conditioning transfers on maternal and infant health care. The experience with the Head Start program in the United States and similar interventions elsewhere in the world can serve as a guide for more systematically targeting infants at long-term risk. Although costly, these interventions are very likely to pass rigorous cost-benefit assessments because of their demonstrated long-term impacts on children's readiness to learn and socioeconomic success as adults.

- *Strengthening the full option value of education for the poor.* Since families factor in the promise of the payoff to higher education in their investment decisions, educational policies should adopt a systemic view. Fragmentary educational policies, focused solely on ensuring narrow objectives such as primary completion or coverage goals, are no longer as effective in the global economy where a minimum of secondary education is needed to compete for above-subsistence wages. While scarce resources and political capital require setting spending and reform priorities, removing binding supply and demand constraints at all levels of the education system, even on a small scale, is crucial to signal low-income families that their educational investments have better chances of maturing with improved access to higher grades.

Where education returns are high and basic infrastructure is deficient, public investments in the construction and upgrading of schools and roads are essential. The development of multigrade schools, learning from best practices such as the Colombian *Escuela Nueva* and the Chilean MECE Rural, can address supply constraints cost effectively. Public-private partnerships to exploit good-quality private urban secondary schools with excess capacity and other modalities such as distance education can be considered when the preconditions for their success exist.

Liquidity constraints have been the main motivation for cash transfers to the poor tied to school attendance, as in the *Oportunidades* program in Mexico, *Bolsa Escola* in Brazil, and similar programs in Central America and the Andean region. The opportunity cost of children's school attendance does not seem very binding until the child completes primary school or reaches the lower secondary grades. Schemes that encourage investments throughout full courses of basic education or lower secondary education (for example, a lump-sum grant for those graduating from high school) may hold substantial promise for reducing dropouts and inducing poor parents to invest more time helping their children succeed in school.

Well-designed (means-tested and merit-based) university student loan programs and scholarships also have a role in facilitating access for low-income and high-performing students. These should build in features to ensure their sustainability, such as delegation of loan processing and recovery to private banks with partial government guarantees on the repayment. These loan programs may be more feasible with the gradual development of individual credit registries that increase the long-term costs of a default. Moreover, a strategic partnership with the private sector (including private universities) and civil society is needed to fund and operate these programs through competitive biddings. Needed also are policies to promote the development of the tertiary education market, such as those discussed in de Ferranti and others (2003).

- *Making education count for the poor.* The take-up rate on student loans—or for that matter enrollment in free public universities—may be low because eligible persons perceive that their expected returns to tertiary education do not compensate for the forgone earnings. Gaps in enrollment in secondary schools and above persist in Argentina, Brazil, and Mexico, where public university is largely free. Thus, policies are needed to increase the returns to education for the poor to encourage them to move up the education ladder.

The main challenge is to gain a better understanding of how to reduce grade repetition among the poor. The role of automatic promotion policies in the early grades, learning deficiencies due to poor learning environments at home, and failures in the instruction process, including inadequate teaching and large class sizes, should be analyzed with data on schools, children, and family characteristics through vigorous impact analyses.

Possible policies include decentralizing school management to get parents more involved and committed to their children's school progress, offering incentives to encourage qualified teachers and principals to work in disadvantaged schools, adapting innovations to improve learning environments in disadvantaged schools and communities, upgrading textbooks and school aids, providing teacher training, and expanding computer education in secondary schools. The consistent application of international standardized tests to assess performance progress should become common practice. Unfortunately, there is not a well-tested recipe to follow, but rather a host of international experiences, both failures and successes to learn from.

Some targeted and performance-based increases in public expenditures, particularly at the secondary level, might be needed in some countries. While overall education expenditures in most countries in the region are not low and increases in spending do not always translate into better outcomes, there might be limits to what can be achieved with pure efficiency gains unless expenditures in education are increased. Countries such as the Dominican Republic and others in Central America have clear expenditures deficits and are already relatively output efficient, so a sustainable increase in education expenditures is needed.

Other policies to improve access to jobs may include enacting and enforcing antidiscrimination laws and establishing intermediation services that help well-educated ethnic and racial populations obtain greater access to better-quality jobs. Where returns to education are too low, the best medium-term policies lie in promoting technology-intensive investments that demand skills. This is actually a precondition to ensuring a country's ability to maintain attractive private returns to higher levels of education under a massive educational expansion.

• *Interventions to fill minimum instructional gaps of the adult population.* Given the strong family effects we have shown here, especially of parental education, there is a role for programs targeted at improving the educational level and skills of the adult population. Recent experiences in Chile and Mexico in support of lifelong learning hold some promise. For instance, the national *Chile Califica* program is designed primarily to strengthen the link between what is taught in the latter years of secondary schools and what the labor market demands.

Investing now: The demographic window of opportunity

Demographic forces offer many countries in the region a unique opportunity to translate the human capital accumulation of young cohorts into a more productive labor force and a faster reduction in poverty. Most countries are in the midst of a demographic transition where the "dependency ratio" (the fraction of the population that is too young or too old to work) is declining. This is illustrated in figure 9.21 for Bolivia; Bolivia and Haiti are the only Latin American countries just beginning the first stage of demographic transition. As countries go through this transition, labor force participation is expected to rise. Because the share of younger cohorts in the working-age population will rise faster, older and poorly educated workers can be replaced with younger workers at a fast pace. Most Central American countries just recently started this process and can still reap most of these benefits, while the rest of the region is much more advanced but still has a decade or so to take advantage of the transition.

As the bottom panel of figure 9.21 shows, changes in fertility in most of the region are favorable to human capital accumulation. In almost every Latin American country today, fertility rates are falling, families are having fewer children, and women are increasingly joining the labor market. This means more resources to invest in quality education for children as well as lower costs of making the investments. But patience is required. This is a gradual transition, and it will take more than a decade for skill investments to translate into a more productive labor force and improvements in national and family incomes.

Human capital formation, including schooling, is an extremely time-dependent process. For families unable to do it at the right time, the opportunity is gone. In Argentina, 30 percent of workers ages 41–65 and 20 percent of prime-age workers are stuck with a basic education that puts those heading families at high risk of poverty. These families have to wait a decade or more before any schooling bequests to their young children can lift family incomes significantly. Further taking into account the positive spillovers of a labor force with rising minimum levels of education on technology adoption, productivity, and growth, it is hard to overstate the critical importance of pushing the "education for all" agenda. In many countries, the demographic window of opportunity is closing; the time to invest is now.

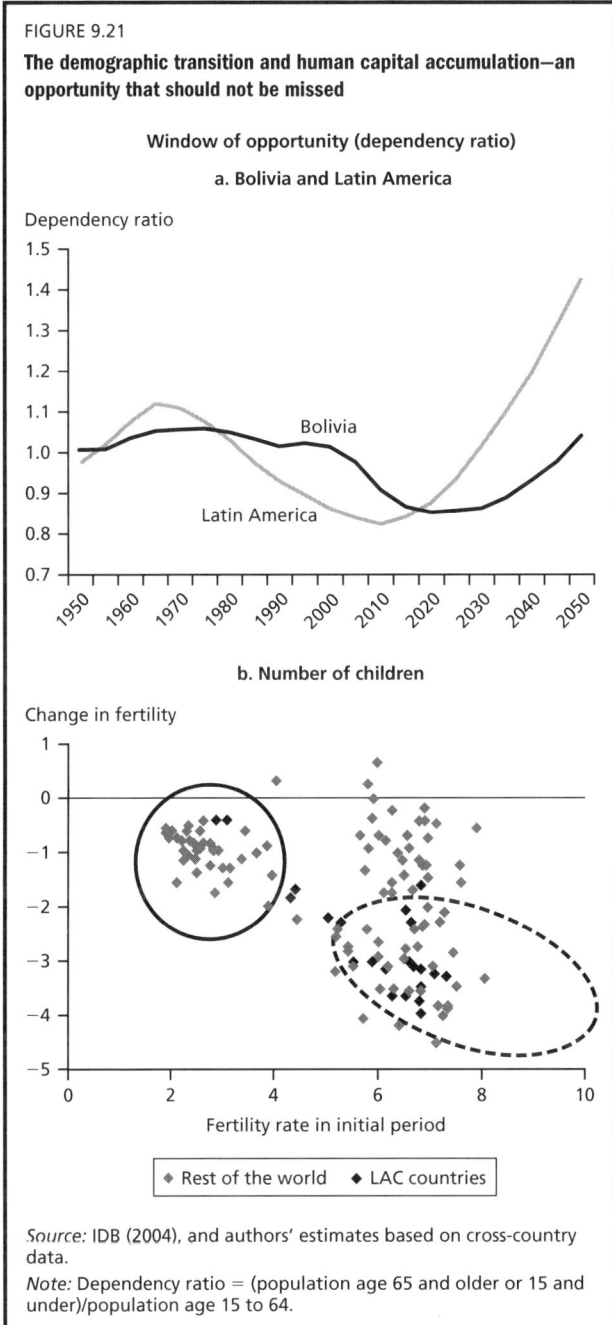

FIGURE 9.21
The demographic transition and human capital accumulation—an opportunity that should not be missed

Source: IDB (2004), and authors' estimates based on cross-country data.
Note: Dependency ratio = (population age 65 and older or 15 and under)/population age 15 to 64.

The best policies, in terms of a social cost-benefit calculation, may not be the most palatable for short political horizons or for political economy reasons. Such is the case with early-childhood interventions and major reforms of the educational system. Overcoming political failures that prevent consensus around the need to address the large achievement gaps between poor and nonpoor children is critical to the region's long-term human capital accumulation and prospects for sustained growth.

Annex 9A

Data and methodological details

Data

We employ household living conditions and labor force surveys for 10 countries chosen to represent the different levels of educational development in the region. Below are the countries, the national household survey data sets used in the report, and their educational ranking:

Andean Countries: Bolivia, ECH-MECOVI 2002; Colombia, ECV 2003; Peru, ENAHO 2002.

Central America and the Caribbean: El Salvador, EHPM 2002; Mexico, ENIGH 2000; Nicaragua, EMNV 2001; Dominican Republic, ENCOVI 2004.

South America: Argentina, EPH 2003; Brazil, PNAD 2002; Chile, CASEN 2001.

Estimation of returns to education

We rely on Mincer earnings functions: $\ln W_{ij} = a_j + b_j educ_{ij} + q_j X_{ij} + e_{ij}$, with j = quantile of the earnings distribution. We are primarily interested in the b_j (returns to education), controlling for some demographic characteristics

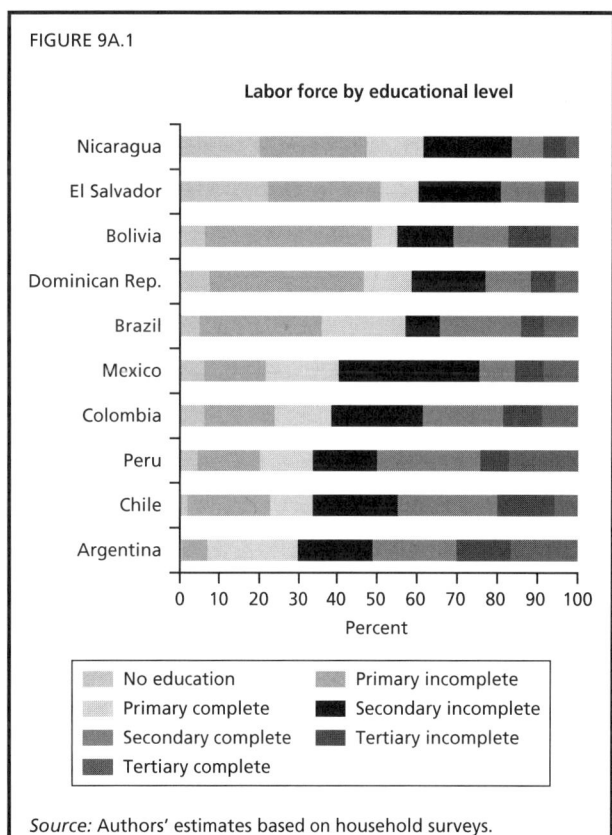

FIGURE 9A.1
Labor force by educational level

Source: Authors' estimates based on household surveys.

(X_{ij} = gender, urban/rural). Education is specified as a set of year dummies for the last grade completed (a total of 18) and as 6 dummies for the maximum level of education (incomplete and complete). Marginal returns to education are derived from the difference in log wages between two consecutive grades or education levels. We estimate these equations for 20 percentiles of the earnings distribution using quantile regression to assess the consistency of the behavior of returns along the distribution and report results for selected quantiles.

Linking returns to education to poverty

To map the quantile returns to education to the per capita family income distribution, we employ the following methodology, used by (Arias (2004) and Tannuri-Pianto, Pianto, and Arias (2005).

Quantile regression allows us to measure heterogeneity in the returns to education that is not related to measured worker characteristics. The ranking of workers in the conditional earnings distribution can be taken as a proxy of their level of "ability," or unmeasured earnings determinants. We would like to link these conditional returns to workers' positions in the (unconditional) per capita household income distribution.

To do this, we first identify the conditional quantile of each worker in the wage distribution. We perform quantile regressions for 20 quantiles and then identify the quantile to which each worker belongs as the quantile for which the worker is predicted to have the smallest wage residual (in absolute value). That is, the conditional quantile of worker i given by θ_i is determined as $\theta_i = \arg\min_\tau(\varepsilon_{\tau,i})$, where $\tau = 0.05, 0.2, \ldots, 0.95$. We assign to each worker the estimated education coefficient for his or her level of education and given quantile β_{θ_i}.

Next we compute household-specific returns for each level of education by averaging the return coefficients across workers who belong to the same household. This implicitly averages the level of "ability" of working members to obtain the family return to education. We then regress the household-specific returns for each education level on the (unconditional) household's percentile, C_i, in the per capita household income distribution. The samples in these second-stage regressions are composed of households with positive returns. We consider two specifications, the first including only dummies for the five quintiles and the second, the unconditional percentile and its square. To properly gauge the statistical significance of the results, the second-stage regressions are weighted to account for the standard errors of the estimates of quantile return coefficients from the first stage Mincerian equations.

Estimation of hazard "schooling-progression" functions

To ascertain the role of factors affecting the cost and expected benefits from continuing schooling, we employ Cox hazard regression methods (see Cox Edwards and Ureta 2003 for a first application to school attainment).

Hazard (risk) analysis is synonymous with time-to-event analysis, which studies a variable that measures the duration between a particular starting time (entrance to school) and a particular end time of interest (school dropout), and a set of independent variables thought to be related to the end-time variable (school dropout). In general, censored observations arise whenever the dependent variable represents a time to event, and the duration of the study is limited in time. In this case, the time to event is the time between completion of a one-year study period and the time the child drops out of school. Subjects that are not enrolled at the time of the survey and did not complete a full education course (primary to college) are assumed to have dropped out. The individuals who are enrolled represent censored observations, since they have not yet completed their entire education spells. The method of analysis takes the censoring into account and correctly uses the censored observations as well as the uncensored observations.

Assuming away reentry after a temporary absence from school, schooling attainment is the last grade completed before the failure to enroll, that is, the years of completed schooling. The event that schooling attainment G takes the value g is equivalent to the event that the child drops out of school after achieving g grades. Thus, the probability of failing to enroll in $g + 1$ matches the probability of attaining g years of schooling, conditional on past enrollment decisions. From this we can derive the risk, or hazard rate, of dropping out of school after completion of grade g and before the completion of grade $g + 1$, given that the child has continuously been in school up to the $g + 1$ enrollment time. A "failure" event here is to drop out after grade g, which exactly corresponds to the failure of enrolling in $g + 1$ at the beginning of the school year.

The hazard rate in this case is the probability that an individual will drop out of school at a certain point in time (at risk of dropping out), that is, the rate at which dropouts occur. The aim of the analysis is to determine how the independent variables (covariates) described below affect the school dropout rate. For example, if a child has a hazard rate of 1.2 at six years of education and a second child has a hazard rate of 2.4 at the same time, then the second child's risk of dropping out would be two times greater at six years of education.

We use the Cox's Proportional Hazard model, which assumes that independent variables exert a proportional effect on the baseline hazard rate of school failure. Cox's regression model is a semi-parametric technique that models:

(9A.1) $\quad h[(t), (z_1, z_2, \ldots, z_n)] = h_0(t) e^{(b_1 z_1 + \cdots + b_m z_m)}$,

where $h[(t), (z_1, z_2, \ldots, z_n)]$ denotes the hazard ratio, given the values of the covariates. The term $h_0(t)$ is known as the baseline hazard, that is, the hazard for the respective individual when all independent variable values are equal to zero. This can be estimated through a linear model of the form:

(9A.2) $\quad \log \left\{ \dfrac{h[(t), (z_1, z_2, \ldots, z_n)]}{h_0(t)} \right\} = b_1 z_1 + \cdots + b_m z_m$

The estimated coefficients can be interpreted as relative risk ratios. The baseline survival curve is shifted up or down by each of the covariates. The proportional hazard technique estimates a coefficient for each independent variable that indicates the direction and degree of flexing that the predictor has on the survival curve. A coefficient equal to 0 (relative risk ratio of 1) means that a variable has no effect on the baseline hazard; a positive coefficient (risk ratio greater than 1) implies that larger values of the variable are associated with a greater risk of school dropout; and a negative coefficient (risk ratio less than 1) means a lower risk.

The hazard regressions include a full set of family characteristics: gender of the child, area of residence, family per capita income, international remittances when available, the number of children ages 6–12 and the number ages 13–17, education of the father and mother (for the sample that still live with their parents), whether the household is headed by a female, whether the mother and father work as salaried workers or are self-employed, some interactions of these variables, and regional control dummies.

Two important features of the analysis are examinations of the effect on enrollment of liquidity constraints and of the unobserved component of the family return to education. For the first we use two specifications, one controlling for the log of income per capita, and another including a set of dummies for the family's income quintile. The latter is useful since liquidity constraints are consistent with non-linear income effects; in other words, the poorest households (first income quintile) should be relatively more constrained than, say, the not-so-poor or the middle-class households, especially for sending their children to private schools. For the second issue, we use the average return to education of each family computed from all working household members (ages 26–65) and their rank in the conditional wage distribution (that is, the return at the percentile at which they fall in the distribution), as explained above. The latter is a proxy, albeit imperfect, of the expected differential return that a child or youth might face from each level of education due to the abilities inherited from his or her family. These returns for each level of education (primary to college completion), adjusted by their estimated standard errors, are included in some of the hazard regression specifications.

School variables are missing from the schooling regression analysis. This means that family background variables, that is, parental education, also capture family wealth effects that allow access to better-quality schools. Also missing are variables capturing the scholastic ability of children. In an uneasy truce with available data, we hope any biases are ameliorated by the controls for family background variables (especially in Colombia and the Dominican Republic, where grandparents' education is included) and by imputed measures of family earnings abilities.

Notes

1. Card (1999), Lemieux (2004), and Heckman and Todd (2004) offer a comprehensive review of the literature. Psacharopoulos and Patrinos (2004) provide a large set of cross-country empirical results.

2. The poverty rates are based on national poverty lines and therefore should not be used to make comparisons or rankings across countries.

3. The most recent reports can be found in www.worldbank.org\lac\poverty.

4. As reported in de Ferranti and others (2003), high-performing countries in East Asia increased their average schooling by just under five years between 1960 and 2000, while most countries in Latin America and the Caribbean increased theirs by two to three years. during this period.

5. See Mayer-Foulkes (2004) for a review of numerous studies, and also the 2005 *World Development Report*.

6. This happens when employers regard these workers as more talented (more productive) so that a diploma acts as a signal of their productivity, as illustrated in the job market signaling model of Nobel Prize winner Mike Spence.

7. This important distinction is present in the various studies of Heckman and coauthors on human capital accumulation and heterogeneous returns to schooling. See, for example, his Nobel Prize lecture (2000).

8. See Mayer-Foulkes (2004) and Heckman (2000) for empirical evidence from numerous studies.

9. When parents cannot set a higher educational bar by example, children and youth could turn to relatives, peers, or mentors. Durlauf (1996), Bénabou (1994), Manski (2000), Akerlof and Kranton (2002), and sources in Bowles, Durlauf, and Hoff (2004) show how these mechanisms can generate low human capital formation and poverty traps. Lalive and Cattaneo (2004) present evidence of the impact of social interactions on schooling decisions.

10. See, for example, Lucas (1988), Azariadis and Drazen (1990), Kremer (1993), and Acemoglu (1997) for growth and poverty-traps models of skill agglomerations, and De Ferranti and others (2003) for empirical evidence on the correlation between technological and skills investments in Latin America and the Caribbean.

11. Behrman, Duryea, and Székely (1999) conclude that 80 percent of the slowdown in educational progress in the region in the 1980s and 1990s was associated with macroeconomic volatility. Carneiro, Hansen, and Heckman (2003) find supporting evidence of a negative effect of variation (uncertainty) in the returns on college attendance in the United States.

12. The patterns tend to persist between families given the high degree of assortative mating on the basis of education (de Ferranti and others 2004). Distributions by gender reveal that girls and boys have about the same level of school attainment in most countries.

13. Only the Dominican Republic shows a relatively equal, flat distribution of schooling for both the rural and urban labor force. Argentina's household survey does not collect data for rural areas.

14. The cohorts cover those individuals born in 1980–90, 1965–79, and 1940–64.

15. See, for example, World Bank (2004a) for Central America as well as recent country poverty assessments. In a few countries, such as the Dominican Republic, the income-enrollment gaps are modest (World Bank 2005b).

16. It is obtained by cumulatively adding age-specific net enrollment rates. For example, if the net enrollment rate in a given country is 86 percent at age 6 and 93 percent at age 7, the average 7-year-old in the country has spent 1.79 years in school. See Urquiola and Calderón (2004) for more details.

17. Some examples of answers in each category are: (1) Work related: need to work, economic difficulties, and help at home; (2) low benefits: not interested, low grades, and too old; (3) limited access: remote school, difficult to get to, and lack of slots; (4) other: sickness, pregnancy/maternity, military service, and miscellaneous. In Colombia, insecurity includes those reporting they stay home because of insecure streets and being displaced.

18. The private sector accounts for more than half of the university market in Brazil and Colombia, close to 40 percent in Chile and Peru, and 20–30 percent in Mexico. Annual tuition costs are almost equivalent to per capita income in Brazil and Colombia and 30 to 50 percent of per capita income in Argentina and Chile (de Ferranti and others 2003).

19. The surveys in Chile, Colombia, the Dominican Republic, Mexico, and Nicaragua contain information to distinguish individuals with a tertiary (university) diploma. In the other countries, tertiary completion was assigned to those with five years of tertiary education or more.

20. The estimates of returns are comparable to those reported in de Ferranti and others (2003), being within 2 percentage points difference in some countries, but differ from those reported in IDB (2004), which are generally much larger. The difference stems from surveys, samples (IDB 2004 is restricted to prime-age men), and measurement methodology (treatment of incomplete and complete degrees). We impose fewer restrictions on the sample and estimating equations.

21. The high school graduation effects are weaker in the Dominican Republic, Mexico, and Peru. In Brazil and Colombia, returns jump in the 11th grade, the last year of secondary school in these countries.

22. Education alone accounts for up to one-third of overall earnings differentials in Latin America and the Caribbean. The fraction of the variance in earnings explained by education, gender, and region of residence is as high as 0.48 in Brazil and Colombia and as low as 0.05–0.10 in rural areas of El Salvador and Nicaragua (given that there is little variance in earnings differentials in rural areas). Other factors, including differences in education returns, contribute to earnings inequality in the region.

23. See Hall and Patrinos (2004) and Jiménez and Landa (2004) for Bolivia; Trivelli (2004) for Peru; Larrea and Montenegro (2004) for Ecuador; Arias, Yamada, and Tejerina (2004) for Brazil.

24. This strand of studies is growing exponentially. See, for example, Carneiro, Heckman and Vytlacil (2001); Carneiro (2003); Carneiro, Hansen, and Heckman (2001, 2003); Carneiro and Heckman (2003); and Arias, Sosa-Escudero, and Hallock (2001) for the United States. See Blundell, Dearden, and Sianesi (2005) for European countries. For numerous Latin America countries, see World Bank (2004); Arias, Yamada, and Tejerina (2004); Arabsheibani, Carneiro, and Henley (2002); Lopez-Acevedo (2001); Montenegro (2001); and Saavedra and Maruyama (1999).

25. From a social standpoint, there could still be a case for public intervention to address underinvestment given the positive externalities of education in the form of lower fertility, crime, and the like.

26. The grade-specific return profiles are similar to those in the top left panel of figure 9.12, that is, returns are relatively constant in the transitions between education levels.

27. Card (1999). Other, somewhat dated, studies for Brazil (Lam and Schoeni 1993), Panama (Heckman and Hotz 1986), and Peru (Behrman and Wolfe 1984) report higher upward biases in education returns after purging the effects of parental education and other family variables on earnings and educational attainment. Their findings might suggest this effect may depend on the stage of educational development of the country. Another issue is that controls for variables highly correlated with own schooling such as parental

education may exacerbate a downward bias in the estimated returns to education when people misreport their education.

28. Cox Edwards and Ureta (2003) first applied these methods to study school transitions in El Salvador; Raymond and Sadoulet (2003) recently used it to study impacts of the Mexican *Oportunidades* program.

29. The effects are small given the little range of variation in imputed returns. An average return to each education level is imputed to each family using the education returns at the percentile where all working members (ages 26 to 65) fall in the conditional individual earnings distribution (that is, their ranking in unobserved earnings determinants).

30. Herrán and Van Uythem (2001) show that students who drop out often belong to families where the parents have no more than a primary education, while parents of those staying at school have completed more than nine years of education.

31. World Bank (2005b).

Bibliography

Acemoglu, D. 1997. "Training and Innovation in an Imperfect Labor Market." *Review of Economic Studies* 64 (3): 445–64.

Acemoglu, D., S. Johnson, and J. Robinson. 2001. "The Colonial Origins of Comparative Development: An Empirical Investigation." *American Economic Review* 91: 1369–1401.

———. 2002. "Reversal of Fortune: Geography and Institutions in the Making of the Modern World Income Distribution." *The Quarterly Journal of Economics* 117 (4): 1231–94.

Acemoglu, D., and J. Robinson. 2002. "The Political Economy of Kuznets Curve." *Review of Development Economics* 6 (2): 183–203.

Adelman, I., and C. Morris. 1973. "Economic Growth and Social Equity in Developing Countries." Stanford, CA: Stanford University Press.

Agence Française de Développement, Bundesministerium für Wirtschaftliche Zusammenarbeit und Entwicklung, U.K. Department for International Development, and World Bank. 2005. *Pro-Poor Growth in the 1990s: Lessons and Insights from 14 Countries.* Operationalizing Pro-Poor Growth Research Program. Washington, DC: World Bank.

Aghion, P., E. Caroli, and C. García-Peñalosa. 1999. "Inequality and Economic Growth: The Perspective of the New Growth Theories." *Journal of Economic Literature* 37: 1615–60.

Aguirre, A., and C. Calderón. 2005. "Real Exchange Rate Misalignment and Economic Performance." Working Paper 315, Central Bank of Chile, Santiago, April.

Ahluwalia, M. 1976. "Income Distribution and Development: Some Stylized Facts." *American Economic Review* 66: 128–35.

Aitchison, J., and J. Brown. 1966. "The Lognormal Distribution." Cambridge: Cambridge University Press.

Akerlof, G., and R. Kranton. 2002. "Identity and Schooling: Some Lessons for the Economics of Education." *Journal of Economic Literature* 40 (4): 1167–1201.

Albernaz, A., F. Ferreira, and C. Franco. 2002. "Qualidade e equidade no ensino fundamental brasileiro." *Pesquisa e Planeamiento Econômico* 32 (3): 453–76.

Alesina, A., A. Devleeschauwer, W. Easterly, and S. Kurlat. 2003. "Fractionalization." *Journal of Economic Growth* 8 (2): 155–94.

Alesina, A., and D. Perotti. 1996. "Income Distribution, Political Instability, and Investment." *European Economic Review* 40 (6): 1203–28.

Alesina, A., and D. Rodrick. 1994. "Distributive Politics and Economic Growth." *Quarterly Journal of Economics* 109: 465–90.

Altimir, O. 1987. "Income Distribution Statistics in Latin America and their Reliability." *Review of Income and Wealth* 33 (2): 111–55.

Altonji, J., and T. Dunn. 1996. "The Effects of Family Characteristics on the Return to Education." *Review of Economics and Statistics* 78 (40): 692–704.

Andersen, L. 2001. "Social Mobility in Latin America: Links with Adolescent Schooling." Washington, DC: Inter-American Development Bank.

Anderson, G., I. Crawford, and A. Liecester. 2005. "Statistical Tests for Multidimensional Poverty Analysis." Paper presented at the International Conference on the Many Dimensions of Poverty, Brasilia, August 29–31.

Andrade, E., F. Veloso, R. Madalozzo, and S. Ferreira. 2003. "Do Borrowing Constraints Decrease Intergenerational Mobility in Brazil? A Test Using Quantile Regression." IBMEC Working Paper 2003-3, Brazil.

Anselin, L. 1988. *Spatial Econometrics: Methods and Models*. Dordrecht, Netherlands: Kluwer Academic Publishers.

———. 1993. "The Moran Scatterplot as an ESDA Tool to Assess Local Instability in Spatial Association." Paper presented at the GISDATA Specialist Meeting on GIS and Spatial Analysis, Amsterdam, December.

———. 1995. "Local Indicators of Spatial Association: LISA," *Geographical Analysis* 27: 93–115.

———. 2003. "Spatial Externalities, Spatial Multipliers and Spatial Econometrics." *International Regional Science Review* 26: 153–66.

Antman, F., and D. McKenzie. 2005. "Poverty Traps and Nonlinear Income Dynamics with Measurement Error and Individual Heterogeneity." Unpublished paper, Stanford University and World Bank.

Arabsheibani, G., F. Carneiro, and A. Henley. 2002. "Human Capital and Earning Inequality in Brazil 1988–1998: Quantile Regression Evidence." Policy Research Working Paper 3147, World Bank, Washington, DC.

Arellano, M., and O. Bover. 1995. "Another Look at the Instrumental Variable Estimation of Error-Components Models." *Journal of Econometrics* 68: 29–52.

Arias, O. 2004. "Poverty in El Salvador during the 1990s: Evolution and Characteristics." Background chapter for the 2004 World Bank Poverty Assessment of El Salvador, Washington, DC.

Arias, O., and J. Diaz. 2004. "Earnings Differentials in Latin America and the Caribbean: Determinants, Trends and Links to Poverty and Inequality." Background paper for the World Bank Labor Stocktaking in the Latin American and Caribbean Region, Washington, DC.

Arias, O., and W. Sosa-Escudero. 2004. "Subjective and Objective Poverty in Bolivia." Background paper for the 2005 World Bank Bolivia Poverty Assessment, Washington, DC.

Arias, O., W. Sosa-Escudero, and K. Hallock. 2001. "Individual Heterogeneity in the Returns to Schooling: Instrumental Variables Quantile Regression Using Twins Data." *Empirical Economics* 26 (1): 7–40.

Arias, O., G. Yamada, and L. Tejerina. 2004. "Education, Family Background, and Racial Earnings Inequality in Brazil." *International Journal of Manpower* 25 (3–4): 355–74.

Aroca, P. 2005a. "The Effect of Interstate Migration on Wage Inequality among Mexican States." Unpublished paper, Universidad Catolica del Norte, Chile.

———. 2005b. "Regional Labor Markets, Migration and Commuting." Unpublished paper, Universidad Catolica del Norte, Chile.

Aroca, P., and M. Bosch. 2000. "Crecimiento, Convergencia y Espacio en las Regiones Chilenas: 1960–1998." *Estudios de Economía* 27 (2): 199–224.

Aroca, P., M. Bosch, and W. Maloney. 2005. "Spatial Dimensions of Trade Liberalization and Economic Divergence: Mexico 1985–2002." World Bank, Washington, DC.

Aroca, P., and G. Hewings. 2002. "Labor Market Adjustment and Regional Growth in Chile, 1982–1992." *Annals of Regional Science* 36: 197–218.

Aroca, P., and W. Maloney. Forthcoming. "Migration, Trade, and Foreign Direct Investment in Mexico." *World Bank Economic Review*.

Atkinson, A. 2003. "Top Incomes in the United Kingdom over the Twentieth Century." Nuffield College, University of Oxford, U.K.

———. 2004. "Increased Income Inequality in OECD Countries and the Redistributive Impact of the Government Budget." In *Inequality, Growth and Poverty in an Era of Liberalization and Globalization*, ed. G. Cornia. Oxford: Oxford University Press.

Atkinson, A., and F. Bourguignon. 1982. "The Comparison of Multi-Dimensional Distributions of Economic Status." In *Social Justice and Public Policy*. London: Harvester Wheatsheaf.

Atkinson, A., F. Bourguignon, and C. Morrison. 1992. *Empirical Studies of Earnings Mobility*. Chur, Switzerland: Harwood Academic Publishers.

Attanasio, O., and M. Székely. 2002. "Wage Shocks and Consumption Variability in Mexico during the 1990s." RES Working Paper Series 451, Research Department, Inter-American Development Bank, Washington, DC.

Azariadis, C., and A. Drazen. 1990. "Threshold Externalities in Economic Development." *Quarterly Journal of Economics* 105 (2): 501–26.

Azariadis, C., and J. Stachurski. 2005. "Poverty Traps." In *Handbook of Economic Growth*, ed. P. Aghion and S. Durlauf. North Holland.

Baldacci, E., L. De Mello Jr., and M. Inchauste Comboni. 2002. "Financial Crises, Poverty, and Income Distribution." IMF Working Paper 02/4, International Monetary Fund, Washington, DC.

Baltagi, B. 2001. *A Companion to Theoretical Econometrics*. Oxford, U.K.: Blackwell.

Banerjee, A., and E. Duflo. 2003. "Inequality and Growth: What Can the Data Say?" *Journal of Economic Growth* 8: 267–99.

Banerjee, A., and A. Newman. 1993. "Occupational Choice and the Process of Development." *Journal of Political Economy* 101: 274–98.

———. 1994. "Poverty, Incentives, and Development." *American Economic Review* 84 (2): 211–15.

Barrett, C., and B. Swallow. 2005. "Fractal Poverty Traps." SAGA Working Paper, Cornell University, Ithaca, NY.

Barrett, C., M. Carter, and P. Little. Forthcoming. "Understanding and Reducing Persistent Poverty in Africa." *Journal of Development Studies*.

Barro, R. 1991. "Economic Growth in a Cross-Section of Countries." *Quarterly Journal of Economics* 106: 407–43.

———. 2000. "Inequality and Growth in a Panel of Countries." *Journal of Economic Growth* 5: 5–32.

———. 2001. "Human Capital and Growth." *American Economic Review* 91: 12–17.

Barro, R., and J. Lee. 2001. "Schooling Quality in a Cross-Section of Countries." *Economica* 68 (272): 465–88.

Barro, R., and X. Sala-i-Martin. 1995. *Economic Growth*. New York: McGraw Hill.

Basu, K. 1997. *Analytical Development Economics*. Cambridge, MA: MIT Press.

Basu, S. 1999. "Procyclical Productivity: Increasing Returns or Cyclical Utilization?" Working Paper 5336, National Bureau of Economic Research, Cambridge, MA.

Beck, M. 2003. "Spatial Growth Multiplier in Mexico." Unpublished paper, World Bank, Washington, DC.

Beck, T., A. Demirguc-Kunt, and R. Levine. 2004. "Finance, Inequality, and Poverty: Cross-Country Evidence." NBER Working Paper 10979, National Bureau of Economic Research, Cambridge, MA.

Beck, T., R. Levine, and N. Loayza. 2000. "Finance and Sources of Growth." *Journal of Financial Economics*, 261–300.

Becker, G. 1967. "Human Capital and the Personal Distribution of Income: An Analytical Approach." Woytinsky Lecture 1. Ann Arbor: University of Michigan, Institute of Public Administration.

———. 1975. "Human Capital: A Theoretical and Empirical Analysis." New York: Columbia University Press for the National Bureau of Economic Research.

Becker, G., T. Philipson, and R. Soares. 2005. "The Quantity and Quality of Life and the Evolution of World Inequality." *American Economic Review* 95 (1): 277–91.

Becker, G., and N. Tomes. 1979. "An Equilibrium Theory of the Distribution of Income and Intergenerational Mobility." *Journal of Political Economy* 6: 1153–89.

Behrens, K., and C. Gaigne. 2003. "Interregional and International Trade: Seventy Years after Ohlin." CEPR Discussion Paper 4065, Center for Economic Policy Research, London.

Behrman, J., N. Birdsall, and M. Székely. 1999. "Intergenerational Mobility in Latin America: Deeper Markets and Better Schools Make a Difference." In *New Markets, New Opportunities?* ed. N. Birdsall and C. Graham. Washington, DC: Brookings Institution Press.

———. 2003. "Economic Policy and Wage Differentials in Latin America." Working Paper 29, Center for Global Development, Washington, DC.

Behrman, J., S. Duryea, and M. Székely. 1999. "Schooling Investments and Macroeconomic Conditions: A Micro-Macro Investigation for Latin America and the Caribbean." Working Paper 407, Inter-American Development Bank, Washington, DC.

Behrman, J., A. Gaviria, and M. Székely. 2001. "Intergenerational Mobility in Latin America." Inter-American Development Bank, Washington, DC.

Behrman, J., R. Pollak. and P. Taubman. 1989. "Family Resources, Family Size, and Access to Financing for College Education." *Journal of Political Economy* 97 (2): 398–419.

Behrman, J., and B. Wolfe. 1984. "The Socioeconomic Impact of Schooling in a Developing Country." *Review of Economics and Statistics* 66 (2): 296–303.

Bénabou, R. 1994. "Human Capital, Inequality, and Growth: A Local Perspective." *European Economic Review* 38: 817–26.

Benabou, R., and E. Ok. 2001. "Mobility as Progressivity: Ranking Income Processes According to Equality and Opportunity." NBER Working Paper 8431, National Bureau of Economic Research, Cambridge, MA.

Ben-David, D. 1993. "Equalizing Exchange: Trade Liberalization and Income Convergence." *Quarterly Journal of Economics* 108: 653–79.

———. 1995. "Convergence Clubs and Diverging Economies." Working Paper 40/95, Foerder Institute for Economic Research, Tel Aviv University, Tel Aviv.

Beneke de Sanfeliu, M., and M. Shi. 2004. "Dinámica del Ingreso en El Salvador." Serie de Investigación 2. Antiguo Cuscatlán: Departamento de Estudios Económicos y Sociales (DEES)/FUSADES.

Bera, A., W. Sosa-Escudero, and M. Yoon. 2001. "Tests for the Error Component Model in the Presence of Local Misspecification." *Journal of Econometrics* 101 (1): 1–23.

Bernstein, J., and D. Weinstein. 2002. "Do Endowments Predict the Location of Production? Evidence from National and International Data." *Journal of International Economics* 56: 55–76.

Bértola, L. 1998. "El PBI de Uruguay 1870–1936 y otras estimaciones." Documento de Trabajo 43, Unidad Multidisciplinaria, Facultad de Ciencias Sociales, Universidad de la República, Montevideo.

———. 2005. "A 50 años de la curva de Kuznets, una reivindicación sustantiva: distribución del ingreso y crecimiento económico en Uruguay y otros países de nuevo asentamiento desde 1870." Instituto Laureano Figuerola de Historia Económica, Working Paper Series No. 05-04, Universidad Carlos III de Madrid.

Bértola, L., and J. G. Williamson. 2003. "Globalization in Latin America before 1940." NBER Working Paper 9687, National Bureau of Economic Research, Cambridge, MA.

Birdsall, N., and C. Graham. 1998. "New Ways of Looking at Old Inequities: Market Reforms, Social Mobility, and Sustainable Growth (Latin America in Comparative Context)." Working paper, Brookings Institution and the Inter-American Development Bank, Washington, DC.

Bloom, D. E., D. Canning, and J. Sevilla. 2003. "Geography and Poverty Traps." *Journal of Economic Growth* 8: 355–78.

Blundell, R., L. Dearden, and B. Sianesi. 2005. "Evaluating the Effect of Education on Earnings: Models, Methods and Results from the National Child Development Survey." *Journal of the Royal Statistical Society. Series A (Statistics in Society)* 168 (3): 473–512.

Bonfiglioli, A. 2004. "Equities and Inequality." Unpublished paper, HES, Stockholm University, Stockholm.

Borensztein, E., J. De Gregorio, and J.-W. Lee. 1998. "How Does Foreign Direct Investment Affect Economic Growth?" *Journal of International Economics* 45 (1): 115–35.

Borjas, G. 1992. "The Intergenerational Mobility of Immigrants." NBER Working Paper 3972, National Bureau of Economic Research, Cambridge, MA.

Bosch, M., P. Aroca, I. Fernandez, and C. Azzoni. 2003. "Growth Dynamics and Space in Brazil." *International Regional Science Review* 26 (3): 393–418.

Bosch, M., and B. Cobacho. 2005. "Effects of Federal Public Investment in Mexico, 1970–2000." Unpublished paper, World Bank, Washington, DC, and Universidad Politecnica de Cartagena, Mexico.

Bosch, M., and W. Maloney. 2005. "Labor Market Dynamics in Developing Countries: Comparative Analysis Using Continuous Time Markov Processes." World Bank, Washington, DC.

Bottazi, L., and G. Peri. 2003. "Innovation and Spillovers in Regions: Evidence from European Patent Data." *European Economic Review* 47: 687–710.

Boucekkine, R., D. de la Croix, and O. Licandro. 2003. "Early Mortality Declines at the Dawn of Modern Growth." *Scandinavian Journal of Economics* 105: 401–18.

Bougheas, S., P. Demetriades, and T. Mamuneas. 2000. "Infrastructure, Specialization, and Economic Growth." *Canadian Journal of Economics* 33: 506–22.

Bourguignon, F. 2001. "Crime As a Social Cost of Poverty and Inequality: A Review Focusing on Developing Countries." In *Facets of Globalization International and Local Dimensions of Development*, ed. S. Yusuf, S. Evenett, and W. Wui, 171–92. Discussion paper series WDP 415, World Bank, Washington, DC.

———. 2003. "The Growth Elasticity of Poverty Reduction; Explaining Heterogeneity across Countries and Time Periods." In *Inequality and Growth: Theory and Policy Implications,* ed. T. Eicher and S. Turnovsky. Cambridge, MA: MIT Press.

———. 2004. "The Poverty-Growth-Inequality Triangle." Unpublished paper, World Bank, Washington, DC.

Bourguignon, F., and S. Chakravarty. 2003. "The Measurement of Multi-Dimensional Inequality." *Journal of Economic Inequality* 1 (1): 25–49.

Bourguignon, F., F. Ferreira, and P. Leite. 2002. "Beyond Oaxaca-Blinder: Accounting for Differences in Household Income

Distributions across Countries." Policy Research Working Paper 2828, World Bank, Washington, DC.

Bourguignon, F., F. Ferreira, and N. Lustig. 2005. *The Microeconomics of Income Distribution Dynamics in East Asia and Latin America*. Washington, DC: World Bank.

Bourguignon, F., F. Ferreira, and M. Menendez. 2003. "Inequality of Outcomes and Inequality of Opportunities in Brazil." Texto para discussao 48, Departmento de Economia, Pontifícia Universidade Católica do Rio de Janeiro (PUC-Rio).

Bourguignon, F., and C. Morrisson. 2002. "Inequality among World Citizens." *American Economic Review* 92 (4): 727–44.

Bowles, S., S. Durlauf, and K. Hoff. 2004. *Poverty Traps*. Princeton, NJ: Princeton University Press.

Bravo-Ortega, C., and D. Lederman. 2005. "Agricultural and National Welfare around the World: Causality and International Heterogeneity since 1960." Policy Research Working Paper 3499, World Bank, Washington, DC.

Brock, W., and S. Durlauf. 2001. "Discrete Choice with Social Interactions." *Review of Economic Studies* 68 (2): 235–60.

Browning, M., L. Hansen, and J. Heckman. 1999. "Micro Data and General Equilibrium Models." In *Handbook of Macroeconomics*, ed. J. Taylor and M. Woodford. Vol. 1, 543–636. Amsterdam, New York, and Oxford: Elsevier Science.

Bruno, M., and W. Easterly. 1998. "Inflation Crises and Long-Run Growth." *Journal of Monetary Economics* 41: 3–26.

Buchinsky, M. 1994. "Changes in the U.S. Wage Structure 1963–1987: An Application of Quantile Regression." *Econometrica* 62 (2): 405–58.

Bulir, A. 2001. "Income Inequality: Does Inflation Matter?" IMF Staff Paper 48, 139–59, International Monetary Fund, Washington, DC.

Bustelo, M. 2005. "Tracing Out the Changes in Inequality and Poverty in Argentina Using Micro Econometric Decompositions Techniques (1992–2001)." CEDLAS Working Paper 13, available at www.depeco.econo.unlp.edu.ar/cedlas/.

Cabrol, M. 2002. "Los Desafíos de la Educación Secundaria. ¿Qué nos Dice el Análisis de Flujos?" Economic and Sectorial Studies Series RE-02-004, Inter-American Development Bank, Washington, DC.

Calderón, C., and R. Fuentes. 2005. "Cuanto Explican las Reformas y la Calidad de las Instituciones el Crecimiento Chileno? Una Comparación Internacional." Working Paper 314, Central Bank of Chile, Santiago.

Calderón, C., and L. Servén. 2004. "The Effects of Infrastructure Development on Growth and Income Distribution." Policy Research Working Paper 3400, World Bank, Washington, DC.

Calmon, P. 2003. "Evaluation of Subsidies in Brazil, and Overview." Unpublished paper, Universidad de Brasilia, Barasdilia.

Calvo, E., J. Torre, and M. Szwarcberg. 2002. *The New Welfare Alliance*. Buenos Aires: Universidad di Tella, Department of Political Science.

Card, D. 1999. "The Casual Effect of Education on Earnings." *Handbook of Labor Economics*. Vol. 3, 1801–63. Amsterdam: Elsevier Science, North-Holland.

———. 2001. "Estimating the Return to Schooling: Progress on Some Persistent Econometric Problems." *Econometrica* 69 (5): 1127–60.

Carneiro, F., and A. Henley. 2002. "Long Run Determinants and Short Term Dynamics of Aggregate Wages in Brazil." Discussion Paper 9610, Department of Economics, University of Wales, Aberystwyth.

Carneiro, P. 2003. "Evaluating Education Policies When the Rate of Return Varies Across Individuals." *Cuadernos de Economia* 40 (121): 516–29.

Carneiro, P., K. Hansen, and J. Heckman. 2001. "Educational Attainment and Labor Market Outcomes: Estimating Distributions of the Returns to Educational Interventions." Paper presented as Klein Lecture, University of Pennsylvania, Philadelphia.

———. 2003. "Estimating Distributions of Treatment Effects with an Application to the Returns to Schooling and Measurement of the Effects of Uncertainty on College." Working Paper 2003: 9, Institute for Labour Market Policy Evaluation (IFAU). Uppsala, Sweden.

Carneiro, P., and J. Heckman. 2002. "The Evidence on Credit Constraints in Post-Secondary Schooling." *Economic Journal* 112: 989–1018.

———. 2003. "Human Capital Policy." IZA Discussion Paper 821, Institute for the Study of Labor (IZA), Bonn, Germany.

Carneiro, P., J. Heckman, and S. Lee. 2004. "Comparative Advantage and Schooling." Working paper, University College, London.

Carneiro, P., J. Heckman, and E. Vytlacil. 2001. "Estimating the Rate of Return to Education When It Varies among Individuals." Paper presented as the Economic Journal Lecture at the Royal Economic Society meeting, Durham, England, and as the Review of Economics and Statistics Lecture, Harvard University, Cambridge, MA.

Carter, M. R., and C. B. Barrett. 2005. "The Economics of Poverty Traps and Persistent Poverty: An Asset-Based Approach." Working paper, University of Wisconsin, Madison.

Chaudhuri, S. 2000. "Empirical Methods for Assessing Household Vulnerability to Poverty." School of International and Public Affairs, Columbia University, New York.

Chaudhuri, S., J. Jalan, and A. Suryahadi. 2002. "Assessing Household Vulnerability to Poverty: A Methodology and Estimates for Indonesia." Department of Economics Discussion Paper 0102-52, Columbia University, New York.

Checchi, D., and V. Dardanoni. 2002. "Mobility Comparisons: Does Using Different Measures Matter?" Working Paper 15.2002. Dipartimento di Economia Politica e Aziendale, Università degli Studi di Milano.

Chen, S., and M. Ravallion. 1997. "What Can New Survey Data Tell Us about Recent Changes in Distribution and Poverty?" *World Bank Economic Review* 11 (2): 357–82.

———. 2001. "How Did the World's Poorest Fare in the 1990s?" World Bank, Washington, DC.

Chiquiar, C. Forthcoming. "Why Mexico's Regional Income Convergence Broke Down." *Journal of Development Economics*.

Chomitz, K. 2005. "Development Policy for a Heterogeneous Space." In *Estratégias para o Nordeste e a Amazônia,* coord. João

Paulo dos Reis Velloso (Cadernos Fórum Nacional 2). Instituto Nacional de Altos Estudos, Rio de Janeiro.

Chong, A., and C. Calderón. 2000. "Institutional Quality and Income Distribution." *Economic Development and Cultural Change* 48: 761–86.

Clarke, G., L. Xu, and H. Zou. 2003. "Finance and Income Inequality: Test of Alternative Theories." Policy Research Working Paper 2984, World Bank, Washington, DC.

Coatsworth, J. 1998. "Economic and Institutional Trajectories in Nineteenth-Century Latin America." In *Latin America and the World Economy Since 1800*, ed. J. H. Coatsworth and A. M. Taylor, 23–54. Cambridge, MA: Harvard University Press.

Coe, D., and E. Helpman. 1995. "International R&D Spillovers." *European Economic Review* 39: 859–87.

Collins, S., and O. Razin. 1999. "Real-Exchange-Rate Misalignments and Growth." In *The Economics of Globalization: Policy Perspectives from Public Economics,* 59–81. Cambridge: Cambridge University Press.

Contreras, D., R. Cooper, and J. Heman. 2004. "Dinámica de la Pobreza y Movilidad Social: Chile 1996–2001." University of Chile.

Cord, L., H. Lopez, and J. Page. 2005. "'When I Use a Word' Pro-Poor Growth and Poverty Reduction." In *Attacking Poverty: What Makes Growth Pro-Poor?* ed. M. Krakowski. Hamburg: Nomos Verlagsgesellschaft.

Cortés Conde, R. 1997. *La economía argentina en el largo plazo (Siglos XIX y XX).* Buenos Aires: Editorial Sudamericana-Universidad de San Andrés.

Cortés Conde, R., with M. Harriague. 1994. "El PBI argentino, 1875–1935." Unpublished paper. Universidad de San Andrés, Buenos Aires.

Cox Edwards, A., S. Duryea. and M. Ureta. 2001. "Women in the LAC Labor Market: The Remarkable 1990's." Working Paper Series 500, William Davidson Institute, University of Michigan, Ann Arbor, Michigan.

Cox Edwards, A., and M. Ureta. 2003. "International Migration, Remittances, and Schooling: Evidence from El Salvador." *Journal of Development Economics* 72 (2): 429–61.

Cunha, F., J. Heckman, and S. Navarro. 2005. "Separating Uncertainty from Heterogeneity in Life Cycle Earnings." *Oxford Economic Papers* 57: 191–261.

Cunningham, W. 2001. "Breadwinner Versus Caregiver: Labor Force Participation and Sectoral Choice Over the Mexican Business Cycle." In *The Economics of Gender in Mexico,* ed. E. Katz and M. Correia. Washington, DC: World Bank.

Dahan, M., and A. Gaviria. 1999. "Sibling Correlations and Social Mobility in Latin America." Inter-American Development Bank, Washington, DC.

Darity, W., and P. Mason. 1998. "Evidence on Discrimination in Employment: Codes of Color, Codes of Gender." *Journal of Economic Perspectives* 12: 63–90.

Das, M., and S. Mohapatra. 2003. "Income Inequality: The Aftermath of Stock Market Liberalization in Emerging Markets." *Journal of Empirical Finance* 10: 217–48.

Dasgupta, R., and D. Ray. 1986. "Inequality as a Determinant of Malnutrition and Unemployment: Theory." *Economic Journal* 96 (384): 1011–34.

Davis, D., D. Weinstein, S. Bradford, and K. Shimpo. 1997. "Using International and Japanese Regional Data to Determine When the Factor Abundance Theory of Trade Works." *American Economic Review* 87 (3): 421–46.

Deaton, A. 1985. "Panel Data from Time Series of Cross-Sections." *Journal of Econometrics* 30:109–26.

———. 1997. "The Analysis of Households Surveys: A Microeconomic Approach to Development Policy." Washington, DC, World Bank.

———. 2005. "Measuring Poverty in a Growing World (or Measuring Growth in a Poor World)." *Review of Economics and Statistics* 87 (1, February): 1–25.

Deaton, A., and C. Paxton. 1994. "Intertemporal Choice and Inequality." *Journal of Political Economy* 102 (3): 437–67.

———. 2001. "Mortality, Income and Income Inequality over Time in Britain and the United States." NBER Working Paper 8534, National Bureau of Economic Research, Cambridge, MA.

de Ferranti, D., G. Perry, F. Ferreira, and M. Walton. 2004. *Inequality in Latin America and the Caribbean: Breaking with History?* Washington, DC: World Bank.

de Ferranti, D., G. Perry, I. Gill, J. Guasch, W. Maloney, C. Sánchez-Páramo, and N. Schady. 2003. *Closing the Gap in Education and Technology.* Washington, DC: World Bank.

de Ferranti, D., G. Perry, I. Gill, and L. Servén, with F. Ferreira, N. Ilahi, W. Maloney, and M. Rama. 2000. *Securing Our Future in a Global Economy.* Washington, DC: World Bank.

de Ferranti, D., G. Perry, D. Lederman, and W. Maloney. 2002. *From Natural Resources to the Knowledge Economy.* Washington, DC: World Bank.

de Ferranti, D., G. Perry, D. Lederman, A. Valdes, and W. Foster. 2005. *Beyond the City: The Rural Contribution to Development.* Washington, DC: World Bank.

De Gregorio, J., and J. Lee. 2002. "Education and Income Inequality: New Evidence from Cross-Country Data." *Review of Income and Wealth* 48: 395–416.

Dehejia, R., and R. Gatti. 2005. "Child Labor: The Role of Financial Development and Income Variability across Countries." *Economic Development and Cultural Change* 53: 913–32.

Deininger, K., and L. Squire. 1996. "A New Data Set Measuring Income Inequality." *World Bank Economic Review* 10: 565–91.

De la Fuente, A. 2002. "The Effect of Structural Fund Spending on the Spanish Regions: An Assessment of the 1994–99 Objective 1 CSF." UFAE and IAE Working Papers 538.02, Unitat de Fonaments de l'Anàlisi Econòmica (UAB) and Institut d'Anàlisi Econòmica (CSIC).

———. 2003. "El impacto de los Fondos Estructurales: Convergencia real y cohesión interna." UFAE and IAE Working Papers 572.03, Unitat de Fonaments de l'Anàlisi Econòmica (UAB) and Institut d'Anàlisi Econòmica (CSIC), Barcelona, Spain.

Della Paolera, G., A. M. Taylor, and G. Bózoli. 2003. "Historical Statistics." In *A New Economic History of Argentina*, ed. G. Della

Paolera and A. M. Taylor, 376–85, plus a CD-ROM. New York: Cambridge University Press.

Dell'Ariccia, G., E. Detragiache, and R. Rajan. 2005. "The Real Effect of Banking Crises." IMF Working Paper WP/05/63, International Monetary Fund, Washington, DC.

Deutsch, J., and J. Silber. 2005. "The Order of Acquisition of Durable Goods and the Multidimensional Measurement of Poverty." Paper presented at the International Conference on "The Many Dimensions of Poverty," Brasilia, August 29–31.

De Vreyer, P., and G. Spielvogel. 2005. "Spatial Externalities between Brazilian Municipios and their Neighbors." Working paper 2005/11, Développement Institutions et Analyses de Long Terme (DIAL), University of Lille, France.

Díaz, J., R. Lüders, and G. Wagner. 1998. "Economía chilena 1810–1995: evolución cuantitativa del producto total y sectorial." Documento de Trabajo 186, Pontificia Universidad Católica de Chile, Santiago.

Dollar, D. 1992. "Outward-Oriented Developing Economies Really Do Grow More Rapidly: Evidence from 95 LDCs, 1976–85." *Economic Development and Cultural Change* 40: 523–44.

Dollar, D., and A. Kraay. 2002. "Growth Is Good for the Poor." *Journal of Economic Growth* 7: 195–225.

———. 2003. "Institutions, Trade, and Growth." *Journal of Monetary Economics* 50: 133–62.

———. 2004. "Trade, Growth, and Poverty." *Economic Journal* 114 (493): 22–49.

Duarte, A., P. Ferreira, and M. Salvato. 2003. "Regional or Educational Disparities? A Counterfactual Exercise." Ensayos Economicos 532, Fundacao Getulio Vargas, Rio de Janeiro.

Duclos, J., D. Sahn, and S. Younger. 2005. "Robust Multidimensional Poverty Comparisons." Paper presented at the International Conference on "The Many Dimensions of Poverty," Brasilia, August 29–31.

Dunn, C. 2003. "Assortative Matching and Intergenerational Mobility in Family Earnings: Evidence from Brazil." Unpublished paper, University of Michigan, Ann Arbor, Michigan.

Durlauf, S. N. 1996. "A Theory of Persistent Income Inequality." *Journal of Economic Growth* 1: 75–93.

Durlauf, S., and D. Quah. 1999. "The New Empirics of Economic Growth." In *Handbook of Macroeconomics*, ed. J. Taylor and M. Woodford. Amsterdam: North-Holland.

Easterly, W. 1999. "Life during Growth." *Journal of Economic Growth* 4: 239–76.

———. 2001. "The Lost Decades: Developing Countries' Stagnation in Spite of Policy Reform 1980–1998." *Journal of Economic Growth* 6 (2): 135–57.

Easterly, W., and S. Fischer. 2001. "Inflation and the Poor." *Journal of Money, Credit and Banking* 33:160–78.

Easterly, W., and R. Levine. 1997. "Africa's Growth Tragedy: Policies and Ethnic Divisions." *Quarterly Journal of Economics* 111 (4): 1203–50.

Easterly, W., and S. Rebelo. 1993. "Fiscal Policy and Economic Growth: An Empirical Investigation." *Journal of Monetary Economics* 32: 417–58.

Easterly, W., and L. Servén. 2003. *The Limits of Stabilization: Infrastructure, Public Deficits, and Growth in Latin America*. Washington, DC: World Bank.

Edwards, S. 1997. "Trade Policy, Growth, and Income Distribution." *American Economic Review* 87: 205–10.

———. 1998. "Openness, Productivity and Growth: What Do We Really Know?" *Economic Journal* 108: 383–98.

Egset, W., and P. Sletten. 2004. "La pauvreté en Haïti. Un profil de la pauvreté en Haïti à partir des données de l'enquête ECVH." Fafo Institute for Applied International Studies, Oslo.

Elbers, C., T. Fujii, P. Lanjouw, B. Ozler, and W. Yin. 2004. "How Much Does Disaggregation Help?" World Bank, Washington, DC.

Ellison, G., and E. Glaeser. 1999. "The Determinants of Geographic Concentration." *American Economic Review* 89 (2): 311–16.

Engerman, S., and K. Sokoloff. 2004. "Factor Endowments, Institutions, and Differential Paths of Growth among New World Economies: A View from Economic Historians of the United States." NBER Working Paper H0066, National Bureau of Economic Research, Cambridge, MA.

———. Forthcoming. "The Persistence of Poverty in the Americas: The Role of Institutions." In *Poverty Traps*, ed. S. Bowless, S. Durlauf, and K. Hoff.

Engle, E., A. Galetoviv, and C. Raddatz. 1998. "Taxation and Income Distribution in Chile: Some Unpleasant Redistributive Arithmetic." NBER Working Paper 6828. National Bureau of Economic Research, Cambridge, MA.

Escobal, J., and M. Torero. 2005. "Adverse Geography and Differences in Welfare in Peru." In *Spatial Inequality and Development*, ed. R. Kanbur and A. Venables. Oxford: Oxford University Press.

Esfahani, H., and M. Ramírez. 2003. "Institutions, Infrastructure and Economic Growth." *Journal of Development Economics* 70: 443–77.

Esquivel, G. 2000. "Geografia y Desarrollo Eeconomico en Mexico." Latin American Research Network Working Paper 389, Research Department, Inter-American Development Bank, Washington, DC.

Estache, A., and M. Fay. 1995. "Regional Growth in Argentina and Brazil: Determinants and Policy Options." Unpublished paper, World Bank, Washington, DC.

Euromod. 2004. http://www.econ.cam.ac.uk/dae/mu/emod.htm.

Fajnzylber, P., and W. Maloney. 2005. "Labor Demand and Trade Reform in Latin America." *Journal of International Economics* 66: 423–46.

Fajnzylber, P., W. Maloney, and G. Montes. 2005. "LDC Micro-Firm Dynamics: How Similar Are They to Those in the Industrialized World? Evidence from Mexico." Unpublished paper, World Bank, Washington, DC.

Ferreira, S., and F. Veloso. 2003. "Intergenerational Mobility of Earnings in Brazil." Brazilian Development Bank (BNDES) and Universidade Candido Mendes (UCAM), Brazil.

Fields, G. 2004. "A Guide to Multisector Labor Markets." Paper prepared for the World Bank Labor Market Conference, November 18–19, Washington, DC.

Fields, G., R. Duval, S. Freije, and M. Puerta. 2005. "Earnings Mobility in Argentina, Mexico, and Venezuela: Testing the Divergence of Earnings and the Symmetry of Mobility Hypotheses." Unpublished paper, Cornell University, Ithaca, NY.

Fields, G., and E. Ok. 1996. "The Meaning and Measurement of Income Mobility." *Journal of Economic Theory*.

Fischer, S. 1993. "The Role of Macroeconomic Factors in Growth." *Journal of Monetary Economics* 32: 485–511.

Fischer, S., R. Sahay, and C. Végh. 2002. "Modern Hyper- and High Inflations." *Journal of Economic Literature* 60: 837–80.

Flug, K., A. Spilimbergo, and E. Wachtenheim. 1998. "Investment in Education: Do Economic Volatility and Credit Constraints Matter?" *Journal of Development Economics* 55 (2): 465–81.

Fogel, R. 1994. "Economic Growth, Population Theory, and Physiology: The Bearing of Long-Term Processes on the Making of Economic Policy." *American Economic Review* 84 (3): 369–95.

Forbes, K. 2000. "A Reassessment of the Relationship between Inequality and Growth." *American Economic Review* 90 (4): 869–87.

Foster, J., J. Greer, and E. Thorbecke. 1984. "A Class of Decomposable Poverty Measures." *Econometrica* 52: 761–66.

Foster, V., and C. Araujo. 2001. "Does Infrastructure Reform Work for the Poor? A Case Study from Guatemala." World Bank, Latin America and the Caribbean Region, Finance, Private Sector, and Infrastructure Department, Washington, DC.

Frankel, J., and D. Romer. 1999. "Does Trade Cause Growth?" *American Economic Review* 89: 379–99.

Freije, S., and A. Souza. 2002. "Earnings Dynamics and Inequality in Venezuela: 1995–1997." Working Paper 0211, Vanderbilt University, Department of Economics, Nashville, TN.

Friedman, M. 1962. "Capitalism and Freedom." Princeton, NJ: Princeton University.

Friedman, M., and S. Kuznets. 1954. "Income from Independent Professional Practice." National Bureau of Economic Research, New York.

Fujita, M., P. Krugman, and A. Venables. 1999. *The Spatial Economy: Cities, Regions and International Trade*. Cambridge, MA: MIT Press.

Gabriel, S., J. Shack-Marquez, and W. Wascher. 1993. "Does Migration Arbitrage Regional Labor Market Differentials." *Regional Science and Urban Economics* 23: 211–33.

Galiani, S., P. Gertler, and E. Schargrodsky. 2005. "Water for Life: The Impact of the Privatization of Water Services on Child Mortality." *Journal of Political Economy* 113 (1): 83–120.

Gallego, F., and N. Loayza. 2002. "The Golden Period for Growth in Chile: Explanations and Forecasts." Series on Central Banking, Analysis, and Economic Policies, 6, Central Bank of Chile, Santiago.

Gallup, J., A. Gaviria, and E. Lora. 2003. "Is Geography Destiny?: Lessons from Latin America." Stanford University Press.

Galor, O., and J. Zeira. 1993. "Income Distribution and Macroeconomics." *Review of Economic Studies* 60 (1): 35–52.

Gamanou, G., and J. Morduch. 2002. "Measuring Vulnerability to Poverty." Discussion Paper 2002/58, United Nations University (WIDER), Helsinki.

Gannon, C., and Z. Liu. 1997. "Poverty and Transport." Unpublished paper, World Bank, Washington, DC.

Gasparini, L., M. Cicowiez, F. Gutiérrez, and M. Marchionni. 2004. "Simulating Income Distribution Changes in Bolivia: A Microeconometric Approach." Background paper for the 2005 World Bank Bolivia Poverty Assessment, Washington, DC.

Gasparini, L., F. Gutierrez, and L. Tornarolli. 2005. "Growth and Income Poverty in Latin America and the Caribbean: Evidence from Household Surveys." World Bank, Washington, DC.

Gertler, P., S. Martinez, and M. Rubio. 2005. "Investing Cash Transfers to Raise Long Term Living Standards." Unpublished paper, University of California at Berkeley.

Getis, A., and K. Ord. 1992. "The Analysis of Spatial Association by Use of Distance Statistics." *Geographical Analysis* 24: 189–206.

Geweke, J., and M. Keane. 2000. "An Empirical Analysis of Income Dynamics among Men in the PSID: 1968–1989." *Journal of Econometrics* 96: 293–356.

Gibrat, R. 1931. *Les inégalités économiques*. Paris: Sirey.

Giuliano P., and M. Ruiz-Arranz. 2005. "Remittances, Financial Development and Growth." Working Paper, International Monetary Fund, Washington, DC.

Glewwe, P. 2004. "How Much of Observed Economic Mobility Is Measurement Error? A Method to Remove Measurement Error, with an Application to Vietnam." Unpublished paper, World Bank, Washington, DC.

Glewwe, P., and G. Hall. 1998. "Are Some Groups More Vulnerable to Macroeconomic Shocks than Others? Hypothesis Tests Based on Panel Data from Peru." *Journal of Development Economics* 56: 181–206.

Goni, E., H. Lopez, and L. Servén. 2005. "Getting Real about Inequality." Unpublished paper, World Bank, Washington, DC.

Gottschalk, P., and E. Spolaore. 2002. "On the Evaluation of Economic Mobility." *Review of Economic Studies* 69 (1): 191–208.

Graham, B., and J. Temple. 2004. "Rich Nations, Poor Nations: How Much Can Multiple Equilibria Explain?" IIIS Discussion Paper 17, Institute for International Integration Studies, The University of Dublin, Ireland.

Grawe, N. 2002. "Quantile Measures of Mobility in the US and Abroad." In *Generational Income Mobility in North America and Europe*, ed. Miles Corak. Cambridge: Cambridge University Press.

GRECO (Grupo de Estudios de Crecimiento Económico). 2002. *El crecimiento económico colombiano en el siglo XX*. Bogotá: Banco de la República-Fondo de Cultura Económica.

Greenwood, J., and B. Jovanovic. 1990. "Financial Development, Growth and the Distribution of Income." *Journal of Political Economy* 98: 1076–1107.

Griffith, D. A. 1996. *Practical Handbook of Spatial Statistics*." Boca Raton, FL: CRC Press.

Guimarães, S., and F. Veloso. 2003. "Intergenerational Mobility of Earnings in Brazil." Brazilian Development Bank (BNDES) and Instituto Brasileiro de Mercado de Capitais (IBMEC), Brazil.

Gupta, S., B. Clements, E. Baldacci, and C. Mulas-Granados. 2005. "Fiscal Policy, Expenditure Composition, and Growth in Low-Income Countries." *Journal of International Money and Finance* 24: 441–63.

Haber, S. H. 1997. "Introduction." In *How Latin America Fell Behind. Essays on the Economic Histories of Brazil and Mexico, 1800–1914*, ed. S. Haber. Stanford, CA: Stanford University Press.

Hall, G., and H. A. Patrinos, eds. 2004. *Indigenous People, Poverty, and Human Development in Latin America: 1994–2004.* New York: Palgrave Macmillan.

Hall, R., and C. Jones. 1999. "Why Do Some Countries Produce So Much More Output per Worker than Others?" *Quarterly Journal of Economics* 114: 83–116.

Hanson, G. 1997. "Increasing Returns, Trade, and the Regional Structure of Wages." *Economic Journal* 107: 113–33.

———. 2001. "Scale Economies and the Geographic Concentration of Industry." *Journal of Economic Geography* 1: 255–76.

Hart, P. 1981. "The Statics and Dynamics of Income Distributions: A Survey." In *The Statics and Dynamics of Income,* ed. N. A. Klevmarken and J. A. Lybeck. Clevedon: Tieto.

Haveman, R., and B. Wolfe. 1995. "The Determinants of Children's Attainments: A Review of Methods and Findings." *Journal of Economic Literature* 33 (4): 1829–78.

Head, K., and T. Mayer. Forthcoming. "The Empirics of Agglomeration and Trade." In *Handbook of Regional and Urban Economics,* vol 4. Amsterdam: Elsevier Science, North Holand.

Heckman, J. 1997. "The Value of Quantitative Evidence on the Effect of the Past on the Present." *American Economic Review* 87 (2): 404–8.

———. 2000. "Policies to Foster Human Capital." *Research in Economics* 54 (1): 3–56.

Heckman, J., and J. Hotz. 1986. "An Investigation of the Labor Market Earnings of Panamanian Males: Evaluating the Sources of Inequality." *Journal of Human Resources* 21(4): 507–42.

Herrán, C., and B. Van Uythem. 2001. "Why Do Youngsters Drop Out of School in Argentina and What Can Be Done about It?" Inter-American Development Bank, Washington, DC.

Hirschman, A. 1981. "The Changing Tolerance for Income Inequality in the Course of Economic Development." In *Essays in Trespassing, Economics to Politics and Beyond.* New York: Cambridge University Press.

Hobjin, B., and D. Lagakos. 2003. "Inflation Inequality in the United States." Staff Report 173, Federal Reserve Bank of New York, New York.

Honohan, P. 2004. "Financial Development, Growth and Poverty: How Close Are the Links?" Policy Research Working Paper 3203, World Bank, Washington, DC.

IDB (Inter-American Development Bank). 2004. *Good Jobs Wanted: Labor Markets in Latin America.* Economic and Social Progress Report. Washington, DC.

Iradian, G. 2005. "Inequality, Poverty, and Growth." IMF Working Paper WP/05/28, International Monetary Fund, Washington, DC, February.

Jacoby, H. 1994. "Borrowing Constraints and Progress through School: Evidence from Peru." *Review of Economics and Statistics* 76 (1): 151–60.

Jacoby, H., and E. Skoufias. 1997. "Risk, Financial Markets, and Human Capital in a Developing Country." *Review of Economic Studies* 64 (3): 311–35.

Jalan, J., and M. Ravallion. 1999. "Income Gains to the Poor from Workfare: Estimates for Argentina's Trabajar Program." Policy Research Working Paper 2149, World Bank, Washington, DC.

———. 2002. "Geographic Poverty Traps? A Micro Model of Consumption Growth in Rural China." *Journal of Applied Econometrics* 17: 329–46.

Jaramillo, C., and D. Lederman, with A. Mason, D. Gould, M. Bussolo, R. Tejada, and N. Fiess. 2005. *DR-CAFTA: Challenges and Opportunities for Central America.* Washington, DC: World Bank.

Jiménez, W., and F. Landa. 2004. "Poverty and Indigenous Peoples in Bolivia, 1989–2002." Background paper for the report *Indigenous People, Poverty and Human Development 1994–2004.* World Bank, Washington, DC.

Kakwani, N., and E. Pernia. 2000. "What Is Pro-Poor Growth?" *Asian Development Review* 18: 1–16.

Kakwani, N., and H. Son. 2003. "Pro-Poor Growth: Concept, Measurement, and Application." Unpublished paper, University of New South Wales, Australia.

Kalecki, M. 1945. "On the Gibrat Distribution." *Econometrica* 13: 161–70.

Kaminsky, G., and C. Reinhart. 1999. "The Twin Crises: The Causes of Banking and Balance of Payments Problems." *American Economic Review* 89: 473–500.

Kanbur, R., and A. Venables. 2005. "Spatial Inequality and Development: Overview of UNU-WIDER Project." Cornell University, Ithaca, NY, and University of London.

Kaufmann, D., A. Kraay, and M. Mastruzzi. 2004. "Governance Matters III: Governance Indicators for 1996, 1998, 2000, and 2002." *World Bank Economic Review* 18 (2): 253–87.

Kim, M., and S. Polachek. 1994. "Panel Estimates of Male-Female Earnings Functions." *Journal of Human Resources* 29: 406–28.

Klinger, B., and D. Lederman. 2005. "Sectoral Concentration in the Search for Innovations and Export Booms." Unpublished paper, World Bank, Washington, DC.

Knack, S., and P. Keefer. 1995. "Institutions and Economic Performance: Cross-Country Tests Using Alternative Institutional Measures." *Economics and Politics* 7: 207–27.

Kneller, R., M. Bleaney, and N. Gemmell. 1999. "Fiscal Policy and Growth: Evidence from OECD Countries." *Journal of Public Economics* 74 (2): 171–90.

Knight, M., N. Loayza, and D. Villanueva. 1993. "Testing the Neoclassical Theory of Economic Growth: A Panel Data Approach." IMF Staff Paper 40 (3), International Monetary Fund, Washington, DC.

Knowles, S. 2005. "Inequality and Economic Growth: The Empirical Relationship Reconsidered in the Light of Comparable Data." *Journal of Development Studies* 41 (1): 135–59.

Koenker, R. 2004. "Quantile Regression for Longitudinal Data." *Journal of Multivariate Analysis* 91: 74–89.

Koenker, R., and G. Bassett. 1978. "Regression Quantiles." *Econometrica* 46 (1): 33–50.

Kraay, A. 2004. "When Is Growth Pro-Poor? Cross-Country Evidence." IMF Working Paper 4-47, International Monetary Fund, Washington, DC.

———. 2005. "When Is Growth Pro-Poor? Evidence from a Panel of Countries." *Journal of Development Economics.*

Kraay, A., and C. Raddatz. 2005. "Poverty Traps, Aid, and Growth." Policy Research Working Paper 3631, World Bank, Washington, DC.

Krebs, T. 2002. "Growth and Welfare Effects of Business Cycles in Economies with Idiosyncratic Human Capital Risk." Working Paper 2002-31, Brown University, Department of Economics, Providence, RI.

———. 2003. "Human Capital Risk and Economic Growth." *Quarterly Journal of Economics* 118 (2): 709–43.

Krebs, T., P. Krishna, and W. Maloney. 2004. "Trade Policy, Income Risk, and Welfare." NBER Working Paper 11255, National Bureau of Economic Research, Cambridge, MA.

———. 2005a. "Income Dynamics and Welfare." Unpublished paper, World Bank, Washington, DC.

———. 2005b. "Income Risk and Human Capital in LDCs." Unpublished paper, World Bank, Washington, DC.

———. 2005c. "Labor Market Risk and Human Capital Investment in Developing Countries." Unpublished paper, World Bank, Washington, DC.

———. 2005d. "Trade Policy, Income Risk, and Welfare." Policy Research Working Paper 3622, World Bank, Washington, DC.

Kremer, M. 1993. "The O-Ring Theory of Economic Development." *Quarterly Journal of Economics* 108 (3): 551–75.

Krugman, P. 1991. "Increasing Returns and Economic Geography." *Journal of Political Economy* 99 (3): 483–99.

Krugman, P. R. 1993a. "First Nature, Second Nature and Metropolitan Location." *Journal of Regional Science* 33: 129–44.

———. 1993b. "On the Number and Location of Cities." *European Economic Review* 37 (1): 293–98.

———. 1993c. "On the Relationship between Trade Theory and Location Theory." *Review of International Economics* 1:102–22.

———. 1999. "The Role of Geography in Development." *International Regional Science Review* 22 (2): 142–61.

Kuznets, S. 1955. "Economic Growth and Income Inequality." *American Economic Review* 45 (1): 1–28.

Lalive, R., and A. Cattaneo. 2004. "Social Interactions and Schooling Decisions." University of Zurich, Switzerland.

Lam, D., and R. Schoeni. 1993. "Effects of Family Background on Earnings and Returns to Schooling: Evidence from Brazil." *Journal of Political Economy* 101 (4): 710–40.

Lanjouw, P. 2001. "Nonfarm Employment and Poverty in Rural El Salvador." *World Development* 29 (3): 529–47.

Larrea, C., and F. Montenegro. 2004. "Indigenous People and Poverty in Ecuador." Background paper for the report *Indigenous People, Poverty and Human Development 1994–2004*, World Bank, Washington, DC.

Laurini, M., E. Andrade, and P. Valls Pereira. 2004. "Income Convergence Clubs for Brazilian Municipalities: A Non-Parametric Analysis (English version of WPE-6/2003)." Working Paper WPE 41, Business School, São Paulo.

Lederman, D., W. Maloney, and L. Servén. 2005. *Lessons from NAFTA for Latin America and the Caribbean.* Stanford, CA: Stanford University Press.

Lee, Y., and R. Gordon. 2005. "Tax Structure and Economic Growth." *Journal of Public Economics* 89 (5–6): 1027–43.

Leipziger, D., M. Fay, Q. Wodon, and T. Yepes. 2003. "Achieving the Millennium Development Goals: The Role of Infrastructure." Policy Research Working Paper 3163, World Bank, Washington, DC, November.

Lemieux, T., and K. Milligan. 2004. "Incentive Effects of Social Assistance: A Regression Discontinuity Approach." NBER Working Paper 10541, National Bureau of Economic Research, Cambridge, MA.

Levin, A., and L. Raut. 1997. "Complementarities between Exports and Human Capital in Economic Growth: Evidence from the Semi-industrialized Countries." *Economic Development and Cultural Change* 46 (1): 155–74.

Levine, R., N. Loayza, and T. Beck. 2000. "Financial Intermediation and Growth: Causality and Causes." *Journal of Monetary Economics* 46 (1): 31–77.

Levine, R., and D. Renelt. 1992. "A Sensitivity Analysis of Cross-Country Growth Regressions." *American Economic Review* 82 (4): 942–63.

Levy, S., and S. Van Wijnbergen. 1995. "Transition Problems in Economic Reform: Agriculture in the North American Free Trade Agreement." *American Economic Review* 85 (4): 738–54.

Li, H., L. Squire, and H. Zou. 1998. "Explaining International and Intertemporal Variations in Income Inequality." *Economic Journal* 108 (446): 26–43.

Li, H., L. Xu, and H. Zou. 2000. "Corruption, Income Distribution, and Growth." *Economics and Politics* 12 (2): 155–82.

Li, H., and H. Zou. 1998. "Income Inequality Is Not Harmful for Growth: Theory and Evidence." *Review of Development Economics* 2 (3): 318–34.

———. 2002. "Inflation, Growth, and Income Distribution: A Cross-Country Study." *Annals of Economics and Finance* 3: 85–101.

Ligon, E., and L. Schechter. 2002. "Measuring Vulnerability." Discussion Paper 2002/86, United Nations University (WIDER), Helsinki.

Lillard, L. 1977. "Inequality: Earnings vs. Human Wealth." *American Economic Review* 67 (2): 42–53.

Lilliard, L., and R. Willis. 1978. "Dynamic Aspects of Earnings Mobility." *Econometrica* 46 (5): 985–1012.

Lindert, K., E. Skoufias, and J. Shapiro. 2005. "How Effectively Do Public Transfers in Latin America Redistribute Income?" LACEA Working paper, World Bank, Washington, DC.

Ljungqvist, L. 1993. "Economic Underdevelopment: The Case of a Missing Market for Human Capital." *Journal of Development Economics* 40 (2): 219–39.

Loayza, N., P. Fajnzylber, and C. Calderon. 2002. "Economic Growth in Latin America and the Caribbean: Stylized Facts, Explanations and Forecasts." Unpublished paper, World Bank, Washington, DC.

———. 2005. *Economic Growth in Latin America and the Caribbean.* Washington, DC: World Bank.

Loayza, N., A. Oviedo, and L. Servén. 2005. "Regulation and Macroeconomic Performance." Policy Research Working Paper 3469, World Bank, Washington, DC.

Loayza, N., and C. Raddatz. 2005. "The Composition of Growth Matters for Poverty Alleviation." Unpublished paper, World Bank, Washington, DC.

Lokshin, M., and M. Ravallion. 2004. "Household Income Dynamics in Two Transition Economies." *Studies in Nonlinear Dynamics and Econometrics* 8 (3).

Londoño, J. L. 1995. "Distribución del Ingreso y Desarrollo Económico: Colombia en el Siglo XX." Bogotá: TM Editores.

Londoño, J. L., and R. Guerrero. 2000. "Violencia en America Latina: epidemologia y costos." In *Asalto al desarrollo: Violencia en America Latina*, ed. R. Guerrero, A. Gaviria, and J. L. Londoño. Washington, DC: Inter-American Development Bank.

Londoño, J. L., and M. Székely. 2000. "Persistent Poverty and Excess Inequality: Latin America, 1970–1995." *Journal of Applied Economics* 3 (1): 93–134.

Lopez, H. 2004. "Pro-Poor-Pro-Growth: Is There a Trade Off?" Policy Research Working Paper 3378, World Bank, Washington, DC.

Lopez, H., and L. Servén. 2005a. "A Normal Relationship? Poverty, Growth and Inequality." World Bank, Washington, DC.

———. 2005b. "Too Poor to Grow." World Bank, Washington, DC.

Lopez-Acevedo, G. 2001. "Evolution of Earnings and Rates of Returns to Education in Mexico." Policy Research Working Paper 2691, World Bank, Washington, DC.

Lucas, R. E. 1988. "On the Mechanics of Economic Development." *Journal of Monetary Economics* 22 (1): 3–42.

———. 1990. "Why Doesn't Capital Flow from Rich to Poor Countries?" *American Economic Review* 80 (2): 92–6.

Lucchetti, L. 2005. "Pobreza Subjetiva en la Argentina." Unpublished paper, World Bank, Washington, DC.

Lundberg M., and L. Squire. 2003. "The Simultaneous Evolution of Growth and Inequality." *Economic Journal* 113 (487): 326–44.

Lustig, N., O. Arias, and J. Rigolini. 2003. "Poverty Reduction and Economic Growth: Two-Way Causality." Inter-American Development Bank, Washington, DC.

Lustig, N., B. Bosworth, and R. Lawrence, eds. 1992. *Assessing the Impact of North American Free Trade*. Washington, DC: Brookings Institution.

Luttmer, E. 2002. "Measuring Economic Mobility and Inequality: Disentangling Real Events from Noisy Data." Unpublished paper, University of Chicago, Chicago.

MaCurdy, T. 1982. "The Use of Time Series Processes to Model the Error Structure of Earnings in a Longitudinal Data Analysis." *Journal of Econometrics* 18 (1): 83–114.

Maddison, A. 2005. "Measuring and Interpreting World Economic Performance 1500–2001." *Review of Income and Wealth* 51 (1): 1–35.

Maloney, W. 2000. "Self-Employment and Labor Turnover in Developing Countries: Cross Country Evidence." In *World Bank Economists' Forum*, ed. S. Devarajan, F. Rogers, and L. Squire. Washington, DC: World Bank.

———. 2003. "Informality Revisited." World Bank, Washington, DC.

———. 2004. "Informality Revisited." *World Development* 32 (7): 1159–78.

Maloney, W., and R. Azevedo. 1995. "Trade Reform, Uncertainty and Export Promotion." *Journal of Development Economics* 48 (1): 67–89.

Maloney, W., W. Cunningham, and M. Bosch. 2004. "Who Suffers Income Shocks during Crises? An Application of Quantile Analysis to Mexico: 1992–95." *World Bank Economic Review* 18 (2): 155–74.

Maloney, W., and A. Rodriguez-Clare. 2005. "Innovation Shortfalls." Unpublished paper, World Bank and Inter-American Development Bank, Washington, DC.

Maloney, W., and Q. Wodon. 1999. "Self-Employment as an Explanation for Latin Income Inequality." Unpublished paper, World Bank, Washington, DC.

Mankiw, N., D. Romer, and D. Weil. 1992. "A Contribution to the Empirics of Economic Growth." *Quarterly Journal of Economics* 107 (2): 407–37.

Manski, C. 2000. "Economic Analysis of Social Interactions." NBER Working Paper 7580, National Bureau of Economic Research, Cambridge, MA.

Martins, P. S., and P. T. Pereira. 2004. "Does Education Reduce Wage Inequality? Quantile Regressions Evidence from Fifteen Countries." *Labour Economics* 11 (3): 355–71.

Mauro, P. 1995. "Corruption and Growth." *Quarterly Journal of Economics* 110 (3): 681–712.

———. 2002. "The Persistence of Corruption and Slow Economic Growth." IMF Working Paper 02/213, International Monetary Fund, Washington, DC.

Mayer-Foulkes, D. 2001. "The Long-Term Impact of Health on Economic Growth in Latin America." *World Development* 29 (6): 1025–33.

———. 2003. "Convergence Clubs in Cross-Country Life Expectancy Dynamics." In *Perspectives on Growth and Poverty*, ed. R. van der Hoeven and A. Shorrocks, 144–71. Tokyo: United Nations University Press.

———. 2004. "The Human Development Trap in Mexico." Centro de Investigacion y Docencia Economicas (CIDE), Economic Division, Mexico.

McKenzie, D., and C. Woodruff. 2004. "Do Entry Costs Provide an Empirical Basis for Poverty Traps? Evidence from Mexican Microenterprises." Unpublished paper, Stanford University, Stanford, CA.

Meghir, C., and L. Pistaferri. 2004. "Income Variance Dynamics and Heterogeneity." *Econometrica* 72 (1): 1–32.

Mehlum, H., K. Moene, and R. Torvik. 2005. "Crime-Induced Poverty Traps," *Journal of Development Economics* 77 (2): 325–40.

Mercader-Prats, M., and H. Levy. 2004. "The Role of Tax and Transfers in Reducing Personal Income Inequality in Europe's Regions: Evidence from EUROMOD." EUROMOD Working Paper EM9/04, EUROMOD, University of Essex, Colchester, Essex, U.K.

Mercado, A., L. Andersen, and B. Muriel. 2005. "Discriminación étnica en el sistema educativo y el mercado de trabajo de Bolivia." *Latin American Journal of Economic Development*.

Metcalf, C. 1969. "The Size Distribution of Personal Income during the Business Cycle." *American Economic Review* 59 (4): 657–68.

Milanovic, B. 2000. "Determinants of Cross-Country Income Inequality: An 'Augmented' Kuznets Hypothesis." In *Equality,*

Participation, Transition, ed. V. Franicevic and M. Uvalic. New York: St. Martin's Press.

———. 2005. *Worlds Apart: Measuring International and Global Inequality.* Princeton, NJ: Princeton University Press.

Milanovic, B., and L. Squire. 2005. "Does Tariff Liberalization Increase Wage Inequality? Some Empirical Evidence." NBER Working Paper 11046, National Bureau of Economic Research, Cambridge, MA.

Mirrlees, J. 1975. "A Pure Theory of Underdeveloped Economies." In *Agriculture in Development Theory*, ed. L. Reynolds. New Haven, CT: Yale University Press.

Mizala, A., and P. Romaguera. 2002. "Equity and Educational Performance." *Journal of the Latin American and Caribbean Economic Association* 2 (2): 219–62.

Montenegro, C. 2001. "Wage Distribution in Chile: Does Gender Matter? A Quantile Regression Approach." Policy Research Report on Gender and Development, Working Paper 20, World Bank, Washington, DC.

Morley, S. 2000. "The Effects of Growth and Economic Reform on Income Distribution in Latin America." *CEPAL Review* 71: 23–40.

Murphy, K., A. Shleifer, and R. Vishny. 1989. "Industrialisation and the Big Push." *Journal of Political Economy* 97 (5): 1003–26.

———. 1991. "The Allocation of Talent: Implications for Growth." *Quarterly Journal of Economics* 106 (2): 503–30.

Murphy, K., and R. Topel. 2003. "The Economic Value of Medical Research." In *Measuring the Gains from Medical Research: An Economic Approach,* ed. K. Murphy and R. Topel. Chicago: University of Chicago Press.

Nelson, R. 1956. "A Theory of the Low-Level Equilibrium Trap in Underdeveloped Economies." *American Economic Review* 46 (5): 894–908.

Newberry, D., and J. Stiglitz. 1984. "Pareto Inferior Trade." *Review of Economic Studies* 51 (1): 1–12.

North, D. 1990. *Institutions, Institutional Change, and Economic Performance.* New York: Cambridge University Press.

Nurkse, R. 1953. *Problems of Capital Formation in Developing Countries.* New York: Oxford University Press.

Openshaw, S., C. Brundson, and M. Charlton. 1991. "A Spatial Analysis Toolkit for GIS." *Proceedings of the Second European Conference on Geographical Information Systems* (EGIS), 788–96. Utrecht: EGIS Foundation.

Openshaw, S., A. Cross, and M. Charlton. 1990. "Building a Prototype Geographical Correlates Exploration Machine." *International Journal of Geographical Information Systems* 4: 297–311.

Paglin, M. 1975. "The Measurement and Trend of Inequality: A Basic Revision." *American Economic Review* 65 (4): 598–609.

Papageorgiou, C., A. Savvides, and M. Zachariadis. 2005. "International Medical Technology Diffusion." Department of Economics, Louisiana State University, Baton Rouge; Oklahoma State University, and University of Cyprus, Nicosia.

Pareto, W. 1897. *Cours d'Economie Politique 2*. Lausanne: F. Rouge.

Perotti, R. 1996. "Growth, Income Distribution and Democracy." *Journal of Economic Growth* 1 (2): 149–87.

Plotnick, B., E. Smolensky, E. Evenhouse, and S. Reilly. 1996. "The Twentieth-Century Record of Inequality and Poverty in the United States." In *The Cambridge Economic History of the United States*, Vol. II, ed. S. Engerman and R. Gallman. Cambridge, U.K.: Cambridge University Press.

Prados de la Escosura, L. 2005. "Growth, Inequality, and Poverty in Latin America: Historical Evidence, Controlled Conjectures." Economics History and Institutions Working Papers wh 054104, Universidad Carlos III, Departamento de Historia Económica e Instituciones, Madrid.

Pritchett, L. 1997. "Divergence, Big Time." *Journal of Economic Perspectives* 11 (3): 3–17.

Pritchett, L., and L. Summers. 1996. "Wealthier Is Healthier." *Journal of Human Resources* 31 (4): 841–68.

Pritchett, L., A. Suryahadi, and S. Sumarto. 2000. "Quantifying Vulnerability to Poverty. A Proposed Measure Applied to Indonesia." Policy Research Working Paper 2437, World Bank, Washington, DC.

Psacharopoulos, G., and H. Patrinos. 2004. "Returns to Investment in Education: A Further Update." *Education Economics* 12 (2): 111–34.

Quah, D. 1993. "Empirical Cross-Section Dynamics in Economic Growth." *European Economic Review* 37 (2–3): 426–34.

———. 1997. "Empirics for Growth and Distribution: Stratification, Polarization and Convergence Clubs." *Journal of Economic Growth* 2 (1): 27–59.

Ramirez, M., and N. Nazmi. 2003. "Public Investment and Economic Growth in Latin America: An Empirical Test." *Review of Development Economics* 7 (1): 115–26.

Ravallion, M. 1997. "Can High Inequality Development Countries Escape Absolute Poverty?" *Economics Letters* 56 (1): 51–7.

———. 1998. "Poverty Lines in Theory and Practice." LSMS Working Paper 133, World Bank, Washington, DC.

———. 2004. "Pro-Poor Growth: A Primer." Policy Research Working Paper 3242, World Bank, Washington, DC.

Ravallion, M., and B. Bidani. 1994. "How Robust Is a Poverty Profile?" *World Bank Economic Review* 8 (1): 75–102.

Ravallion, M., and S. Chaudhuri. 1997. "Risk and Insurance in Village India: A Comment." *Econometrica* 65 (1): 171–84.

Ravallion, M., G. Datt, and D. van de Walle. 1991. "Quantifying Absolute Poverty in the Developing World." *Review of Income and Wealth* 37 (4): 345–61.

Raymond, M., and E. Sadoulet. 2003. "Educational Grants Closing the Gap in Schooling Attainment between Poor and Non-Poor." Economic Studies and Policy Analysis Division of the Department of Finance, Ottawa, Canada; and Department of Agricultural and Resource Economics, University of California at Berkeley.

Redding, S., and M. Vera-Martin. 2004. "Factor Endowments and Production in European Regions." CEPR Discussion Paper 3755. Centre for Economic Policy Research, London.

Rioja, F., and N. Valev. 2004. "Does One Size Fit All? A Reexamination of the Finance and Growth Relationship." *Journal of Development Economics* 74 (2): 429–47.

Rodriguez-Clare, A. 2001. "Costa Rica's Development Strategy Based on Human Capital and Technology: How It Got There, the Impact of INTEL, and Lessons for Other Countries." Paper written for the Human Development Report 2001, San Jose, Costa Rica.

Rodriguez-Mesa, J., and C. Gonzalez-Vega. 2004. "Household Income Dynamics and Poverty Traps in El Salvador." Paper written for AAEA (American Agriculture Economists Association) annual meeting, Ohio State University, Columbus.

Rodriguez-Oreggia, E., and A. Rodriguez-Pose. 2004. "The Regional Returns of Public Investment Policies in Mexico." *World Development* 32 (9): 1545–62.

Rodriguez-Pose, A., and J. Sanchez-Reaza. 2004. "Economic Polarization through Trade: Trade Liberalization and Regional Growth in Mexico." In *Spatial Inequality and Development*, ed. R. Kanbur and A. J. Venables. Oxford: Oxford University Press.

Rodrik, D. 1997. "Globalization, Social Conflict. and Economic Growth," The 1997 Raul Prebisch lecture delivered at the UN Conference on Trade and Development (published in *World Economy*, March 1998).

———. 1999. "Where Did All the Growth Go? External Shocks, Social Conflict, and Growth Collapses." *Journal of Economic Growth* 4 (4): 385–412.

Roemer, J. E. 1998. *Equality of Opportunity*. Cambridge, MA: Harvard University Press.

———. 2005. "Intergenerational Justice and Sustainability under the Leximin Ethic." Cowles Foundation Discussion Papers 1512, Cowles Foundation, Yale University, New Haven, CT.

Rosenstein-Rodin, P. 1943. "Problems of Industrialization in Eastern and South Eastern Europe." *Economic Journal* 53: 202–11.

Ruiz-Castillo J., E. Ley, and M. Izquierdo. 2002. "Distributional Aspects of the Quality Change Bias in the CPI: Evidence from Spain." *Economic Letters* 76 (1): 137–44.

Rutherford, R. S. G. 1955. "Income Distributions: A New Model." *Econometrica* 23 (3): 277–94.

Saavedra, J., and J. Diaz. 1999. "Distribución del Ingreso y del Gasto Antes y Después de las Reformas Estructurales (Perú)." ECLAC Economic Reform Series 34. European Commission for Latin America and the Caribbean.

Saavedra, J., and E. Maruyama. 1999. "Los Retornos a la Educación y a la Experiencia en el Perú, 1985–1997." In *Pobreza y Economía Social: Análisis de una Encuesta ENNIV-1997*, ed. Richard Webb and Moisés Ventocilla. Lima, Peru: Instituto Cuánto.

Saavedra, J., and M. Torero. 2004. "Labor Market Reforms and Their Impact over Formal Labor Demand and Job Market Turnover: The Case of Peru." In *Law and Employment: Lessons from Latin America and the Caribbean*, NBER Conference Report series. Chicago: University of Chicago Press.

Sachs, J., and A. Warner. 1995. "Economic Reform and the Process of Global Integration." *Brookings Papers on Economic Activity 1995* (1): 1–118.

Sanchez-Robles, B. 1998. "Infrastructure Investment and Growth: Some Empirical Evidence." *Contemporary Economic Policy* 16 (1): 98–108.

Sen, A. 1972. "Control Areas and Accounting Prices: An Approach to Economic Evaluation." *Economic Journal* 82 (325): 486–501.

———. 1985. *Commodities and Capabilities*. Amsterdam: North Holland.

———. 1999. *Development as Freedom*. Oxford: Oxford University Press.

Shorrocks, A. 1981. "Income Stability in the United States." In *The Statics and Dynamics of Income,* ed. N. A. Klevmarken and J. A. Lybeck, 175–94. Clevedon: Tieto.

———. 1993. "On the Hart Measure of Income Mobility." In *Industrial Concentration and Economic Inequality*, ed. M. Casson and J. Creedy. Cheltenham, UK: Edward Elgar.

Shorrocks, A., and G. Wan. 2005. "Spatial Decomposition of Inequality." *Journal of Economic Geography* 5 (1): 59–81.

Singh, S., and G. Maddala. 1976. "A Function for Size Distribution of Incomes." *Econometrica* 44 (5): 963–70.

Smith, D., A. Gordon, K. Meadows, and K. Zwick. 2001. "Livelihood Diversification in Uganda: Patterns and Determinants of Change across Two Rural Districts." *Food Policy* 26: 421–35.

Soares, R. 2004. "The Welfare Costs of Violence." Unpublished paper, University of Maryland, College Park.

———. 2005. "Health and Inequality in Latin America and the Caribbean." Unpublished paper, University of Maryland, College Park.

Solon, G. 2002. "Cross-Country Differences in Intergenerational Earnings Mobility." *Journal of Economic Perspectives* 16 (3): 59–67.

———. 2004. "A Model of Intergenerational Mobility Variation over Time and Place." In *Generational Income Mobility in North America and Europe*, ed. M. Corak, 38–47. Cambridge: Cambridge University Press.

Sosa-Escudero, W., and M. Cicowiez. 2005. "Exploring the Determinants of Poverty and Income Distribution in the Dominican Republic." Unpublished paper, Centro de Estudios Distributivos, Laborales y Sociales (CEDLAS), Universidad Nacional de La Plata, La Plata, Argentina.

Sosa-Escudero, W., and L. Lucchetti. 2004. "Exploring the Determinants of Poverty and Income Distribution in Peru: A Microeconometric Approach." Unpublished paper, World Bank, Washington, DC.

Sosa-Escudero, W., M. Marchionni, and O. Arias. 2005. "Exploring Sources of Income Persistency in Rural El Salvador." Unpublished paper, World Bank, Washington, DC.

Spilimbergo, A., J. Londoño, and M. Székely. 1999. "Income Distribution, Factor Endowments, and Trade Openness." *Journal of Development Economics* 59 (1): 77–101.

Stiglitz, J. 1976. "The Efficiency Wage Hypothesis, Surplus Labor and the Distribution of Income in LDCs." *Oxford Economic Papers* 28 (2): 185–207.

Strauss, J., and D. Thomas. 1995. "Empirical Modeling of Household and Family Decisions." Paper 95-12, Reprint Series, RAND, Santa Monica, California.

Tannuri-Pianto, M., D. Pianto, and O. Arias. 2004a. "Informal Employment in Bolivia. A Lost Proposition?" Paper 149, Econometric Society, New York.

———. 2004b. "Rural-Urban Migration in Bolivia: An Escape Boat?" Background paper for the 2005 World Bank Bolivia Poverty Assessment, Washington, DC.

Tannuri-Pianto, M., D. Pianto, O. Arias, and M. Beneke de Sanfeliu. 2005. "Determinants and Returns to Productive Diversification in Rural El Salvador." Background paper for the *Beyond the City:*

The Rural Contribution to Development, World Bank, Washington, DC.

Taylor, J. E. 2001. "Microeconomics of Globalization: Evidence from Mexico, China, El Salvador, and the Galapagos Islands." Report to the Latin America and Caribbean Regional Office, World Bank, Washington, DC.

Taylor, J. E., A. Yuñez-Naude, and H. Cerón. 2004. "The Effects of Rural Mexico Household Assets on Rural Activity Selection, Incomes, and Technology Adoption." World Bank, Washington, DC.

Taylor, J. E., A. Yunez-Naude, and C. Hazael. 2004. "The Effects of Mexico Household Assets on Rural-Non-Rural Activity Selection, on Incomes and Technology Adoption." World Bank, Washington, DC, and PRECESAM, El Colegio de México.

Thisse, J-F., and M. Fujita. 2000. "Economics of Agglomeration." In *The Economics of Cities*, ed. J.-M. Huriot and J.-F. Thisse. Cambridge, UK: Cambridge University Press.

Thorbecke, E. 2005. "Multi-Dimensional Poverty: Conceptual and Measurement Issues." Paper presented at the international conference on "The Many Dimensions of Poverty," Brasilia, August 29–31.

Trivelli, C. 2004. "Indigenous Poverty in Peru: An Empirical Analysis." Unpublished paper, Instituto de Estudios Peruanos (IEP). Lima, Peru.

Urquiola, M., and V. Calderón. 2004. "Apples and Oranges: Educational Enrollment and Attainment across Countries in Latin America and the Caribbean." Unpublished paper, Columbia University, New York.

Velez, C., and J. Nunez. 2005. "Multidimensional Poverty in Colombia: Explaining Improved Well-Being Despite Economic Recession and Violence." Unpublished paper. Inter-American Development Bank, Washington, DC, and Universidad de Los Andes, Bogotá, Colombia.

Wacziarg, R., and K. Welch. 2003. "Trade Liberalization and Growth: New Evidence." NBER Working Paper 10152, National Bureau of Economic Research, Cambridge, MA, December.

Williamson, J. G. 1999. "Real Wage Inequality and Globalization in Latin America before 1940." *Revista de Historia Económica* 17 (special issue): 101–42.

———. 2002. "Land, Labor, and Globalization in the Third World, 1870–1940." *Journal of Economic History* 62 (1): 55–85.

Wodon, Q., R. Ayres, M. Barenstein, N. Hicks, K. Lee, W. Maloney, P. Peeters, C. Siaens, and S. Yitzhaki. 2000. "Poverty and Policy in Latin America and the Caribbean." Technical Paper 467, World Bank, Washington, DC.

World Bank. 1990. *World Development Report 1990: Poverty.* Washington, DC: World Bank.

———. 2001a. "Honduras Poverty Assessment." Report 20531-HD. World Bank, Washington, DC.

———. 2001b. *World Development Report: Attacking Poverty.* Washington, DC: World Bank.

———. 2003. "Mexico Southern States Development Strategy." Washington, DC: World Bank.

———. 2004a. *Central America: Education Strategy Paper.* Vol. 1. Washington, DC: World Bank.

———. 2004b. "Drivers of Sustainable Rural Growth and Poverty Reduction in Central America." Report 31191, Washington, DC: World Bank.

———. 2004c. *Education Strategy Paper for Central America.* Green Cover Report. Washington, DC: World Bank.

———. 2004d. *World Development Report: Making Services Work for the Poor.* Washington, DC: World Bank.

———. 2005a. "Brazil Regional Economic Development—(Some) Lessons from Experience." Finance, Private Sector and Infrastructure Management Unit, Latin American and Caribbean Region, World Bank, Washington, DC.

———. 2005b. *Dominican Republic Poverty Assessment: Achieving More Pro-Poor Growth.* Report 32422-DO. Washington, DC: World Bank.

———. 2005c. *DR-CAFTA: Challenges and Opportunities for Central America,* Vol. 1. Working paper 32953, World Bank, Washington, DC.

———. 2005d. *Economic Growth in the 1990s: Learning from a Decade of Reforms.* Washington, DC: World Bank.

———. 2005e. "El Salvador Poverty Assessment: Strengthening Social Policy." Report 29594-SV. World Bank, Washington, DC.

———. 2005f. *A Time to Choose: Caribbean Development in the 21st Century.* Washington, DC: World Bank.

———. 2005g. *World Development Indicators.* Washington, DC: World Bank.

———. 2005h. *Pro-Poor Growth in the 1990s: Lessons and Insights from 14 Countries.* Washington, DC: World Bank.

———. 2006. *World Development Report: Equity and Development.* Washington, DC: World Bank.

———. Forthcoming. *The Redistributive Impact of Transfers in Latin America and the Caribbean.* Washington, DC: World Bank.

Yepes, T. 2004. "Infrastructure and Poverty Reduction in Rural El Salvador." Unpublished paper, Poverty Reduction and Economic Management and Human Development Sector Management Units, Latin America and the Caribbean Region, World Bank, Washington, DC.

Index

Argentina
   development gap, 45, 47, 48, 54
   education and human capital in, 168, 173, 174f, 176f, 183, 187f, 188f, 189, 194, 195
   effects of poverty on growth, 109
   indicators of poverty in, 22, 23b, 29, 31, 33, 36–37, 36t, 38
   labor and earnings differentials, 149, 150, 151, 152t
   poverty reduction, economic growth, and progressive distribution, 70
   subnational dimensions of growth and poverty, 139
   transfers and income inequality, 95, 96

Becker model of human capital and household behavior, 169
Belize, 69, 70, 176
Bolivia
   country income—level of, 104
   education and human capital in, 168, 172f, 173, 175f, 183, 188f, 189, 194, 196
   effects of poverty on growth, 109, 111
   indicators of poverty in, 22, 23b, 28, 29–31, 30f, 35b
   labor and earnings differentials, 148, 149, 151
   poverty reduction, economic growth, and progressive distribution, 62, 70
   subnational dimensions of growth and poverty, 130, 138, 139
Brazil
   development gap, 46, 47, 48, 50, 54
   education and human capital in, 168, 173, 174f, 175f, 176, 180, 181f, 183, 186, 187f, 190, 191, 193, 194, 195
   effects of poverty on growth, 107
   indicators of poverty in, 22, 26b, 27b, 28, 38
   labor and earnings differentials, 148, 149, 150
   poverty reduction, economic growth, and progressive distribution, 62, 63, 69, 70
   subnational dimensions of growth and poverty, 9t, 129, 130, 131–133, 132f, 133f, 135f, 137, 138, 139, 141f
   transfer programs in, 5
   transfers and income inequality, 97

Chile
   development gap, 47, 48, 50, 54
   education and human capital in, 168, 172f, 173, 178, 179f, 183, 186, 187f, 188f, 189, 191, 193, 194, 195, 196
   effects of poverty on growth, 107b, 111
   indicators of poverty in, 22, 23b, 24, 38
   labor and earnings differentials, 148
   poverty reduction, economic growth, and progressive distribution, 62, 63, 70
   subnational dimensions of growth and poverty, 129, 130, 133, 134f, 138, 139
   transfers and income inequality, 92, 97, 99
Colombia
   development gap, 47, 48
   education and human capital in, 168, 173, 176f, 178, 180, 181f, 183, 189, 190, 191, 193, 194, 195
   indicators of poverty in, 22, 23b, 26b, 27b, 28, 38t
   subnational dimensions of growth and poverty, 137, 138, 139
   transfer programs in, 5
   transfers and income inequality, 95, 96, 97, 98b
consumption levels as indicator of poverty, 20–27
convergence hypothesis
   absolute income levels, 110–112, 110f, 112f
   development gap in Latin America/Caribbean and, 48f, 49f
   global convergence clubs, evidence contradicting, 6–7, 7f
   long-run equilibriums for convergence clubs, 124
   nonincome welfare measures, applicability to, 113–114, 114f
   poverty-traps view of development process and, 110–114, 110f, 111t, 112–114f, 124–125
   regional/subnational convergence clubs. See subnational dimensions of growth and poverty
   relative income levels, 112–113f
   transitions of countries between convergence clubs, 124–125
Costa Rica
   indicators of poverty in, 22, 23b, 33, 35b, 35t, 38
   poverty reduction, economic growth, and progressive distribution, 62
   transfers and income inequality, 99
Cox hazard regression methods, 198–199
credit constraint—factor accumulation argument for effects of poverty on growth, 116
Cuba, 21

de Ferranti, David, editor, World Bank Latin American region flagship publications. See under World Bank
decomposition. See variance decomposition approach
decomposition of effects of economic growth, and progressive distribution on poverty reduction, 60b, 60f, 61t
demographics
   education and human capital, 196–197, 197f
   income inequalities and, 33, 35b, 35t
development gap in Latin America/Caribbean, 45–56
   colonial period, historical origins in, 45–46
   global comparisons
      income inequalities, 55f
      per capita income, 50–53, 50t, 51–53f
   income inequalities, 53–56, 54t, 55f
   per capita income, 46–53
      convergence hypothesis, 48f, 49f
      global comparisons, 50–53, 50t, 51–53f
      historical estimates, 46–48, 47t
      long-run trends, 49–50, 49f, 49t

development process. *See* economic growth
discrimination
    in education, 170, 184–185, 185*f*
    labor and earnings differentials due to, 148
distribution of income. *See* income inequalities; transfers
divergent mobility, poverty traps as, 32–33, 32*b*, 32*t*
Dominican Republic
    education and human capital in, 167, 173, 177, 179, 180, 181*f*, 183, 186, 190, 191, 193, 194
    effects of poverty on growth, 109
    indicators of poverty in, 21, 24, 25*b*, 29, 31
    labor and earnings differentials, 149, 151
    poverty reduction, economic growth, and progressive distribution, 62, 70
    subnational dimensions of growth and poverty, 130

earnings. *See* labor and earnings differentials
East Asia, Latin America/Caribbean relative to
    development gap, 50–53
    education and human capital, 166–167
    effects of poverty on growth, 107*b*
    indicators of poverty, 29*t*
    labor and earnings differentials, 147
    poverty reduction, economic growth, and progressive distribution, 57
    vicious circle of high poverty/low economic growth, 1, 2*f*, 14
East Asian financial crisis of 1997, 24, 48, 108
Economic Commission for Latin America and the Caribbean (ECLAC), poverty indicators used by, 23*b*
economic crises
    East Asia, 1997, 24, 48, 108
    Mexico, 1994, 87
    Russia, 1998, 24, 48, 108
economic growth
    effects of poverty on. *See* effects of poverty on growth
    income inequality and, 4*t*, 57–58, 58*f*, 69*t*
    low growth's relationship to poverty. *See* vicious circle of high poverty/low economic growth
    nexus between transfers, growth, and poverty reduction. *See* poverty reduction, economic growth, and progressive distribution
    poverty-traps view of development and. *See under* effects of poverty of growth
    pro-poor forms of. *See* pro-poor economic growth policies
    rates in Latin America/Caribbean, 24*t*, 25*b*
    subnational dimensions. *See* subnational dimensions of growth and poverty
Ecuador
    indicators of poverty in, 22, 23*b*, 38

poverty reduction, economic growth, and progressive distribution, 62, 70
subnational dimensions of growth and poverty, 141
education, 165–201
    data and methodologies, 197–199, 197*f*
    demographic factors, 196–197, 197*f*
    discrimination in, 170, 184–185, 185*f*
    effects of poverty on growth, 120–121, 120*t*
    gender affecting, 193
    human capital, failure of poor to accumulate, 165–166
    human capital underinvestment traps and, 169–171
    inability to afford, 159–170
    labor and earnings differentials
        effects of level of education on, 147–148, 151, 154, 155, 159
        unmeasured skills, effects of, 185–190, 187–189*f*
    liquidity constraints affecting, 178–181, 179–180*f*, 193
    parents' level of education affecting children's, 180, 181*f*, 190, 191–193, 192*f*
    persistent patterns and clusters in educational transitions, 171–178, 172*f*, 174–177*f*, 178*t*
    physical access constraints, 193
    policy implications, 194–196
    pro-poor economic growth policies, 87–88, 88*f*
    productivity differentials and, 107*b*
    quality of education, effects of differences in, 190, 191*f*
    reasons for low attainment levels, 178–181, 179–181*f*
    relationship of poverty and low levels of, 167–169, 168*f*
    relative importance of different constraints on achievement of, 190–194, 192*f*
    returns on, 181–190, 182*f*
        data and methodologies, 198
        quality of education, effects of differences in, 190, 191*f*
        racial and rural variations, 184–185*f*
        unmeasured labor market skills, effects of, 185–190, 187–189*f*
    skills crucial to success in schooling, problems in development of, 170–171
    slow pace of educational transition in region, 166–167, 166*f*, 167*f*
    unmeasured skills, effects of, 185–190, 187–189*f*
    vicious circle of high poverty/low economic growth and, 3*f*, 10–11, 10*f*, 16–17
effects of poverty on growth, 103–127
    convergence hypothesis, 110–114, 110*f*, 111*t*, 112–114*f*, 124–125
    credit constraint—factor accumulation argument for, 116

education, 120–121, 120*t*
empirical evidence of, 115–116
estimating, 125–126
financial sector development, 119–120, 119*t*, 124
formal tests of, 116–117
health, 121
innovation, 121–122
investment rates, 118–119, 118*f*
mobility and risk/security factors, 122–123, 123*t*
poverty-traps view of development and, 104–115
    convergence hypothesis, 110–114, 110*f*, 111*t*, 112–114*f*, 124–125
    empirical evidence of, 108–110, 108*f*, 109*t*
    formal testing for, 114–115
    increasing returns to scale, 105*f*, 106
    institutional mechanisms, 107–108
    investment rates, 118
    market factors, 106–107, 106*f*, 107*b*
    traditional view of development vs., 105
special regional effects of, 117*b*, 117*t*
transmission channels for, 118–123
El Salvador
    development gap, 54
    education and human capital in, 167, 173, 174*f*, 175*f*, 176*f*, 183, 186, 187*f*, 189, 191, 193
    indicators of poverty in, 22, 23*b*, 28, 38
    labor and earnings differentials, 146, 152–159, 153–154*t*, 156*f*, 157*t*, 158*f*
    poverty reduction, economic growth, and progressive distribution, 62, 70
    subnational dimensions of growth and poverty, 141*b*
    transfers and income inequality, 92, 95, 96
elasticities of poverty
    poverty reduction, economic growth, and progressive distribution, 65–66, 65*b*, 66*t*
    pro-poor economic growth policies, 86*t*
Engel/Orshansky ratio of food expenditures, 23*b*
ethnicity and race
    education, variation in returns on, 184–185, 185*f*
    labor and earnings differentials, 148
EUROMOD, 93
Europe. *See* OECD countries, Latin America/Caribbean relative to; Spain and peripheral Europe, Latin America/Caribbean relative to

financial crises
    East Asia, 1997, 24, 48, 108
    Mexico, 1994, 87
    Russia, 1998, 24, 48, 108
financial sector development
    effects of poverty on growth, 119–120, 119*t*, 124

poverty and income inequalities affected by,
78–80, 79t
formal vs. informal labor markets, earnings differentials in, 148–149, 149f
funding as means of reversing vicious circle of high poverty/low economic growth, 18–19, 18f

gender
education affected by, 193
labor and earnings differentials affected by, 148
Guatemala
indicators of poverty in, 22, 35b, 38
labor and earnings differentials, 148
poverty reduction, economic growth, and progressive distribution, 69, 70
transfers and income inequality, 96
Guyana, 69, 70

Haiti, 22, 109, 196
health and effects of poverty on growth, 121. See also life expectancy
Honduras
country income—level of, 104
development gap, 54
effects of poverty on growth, 109, 111
indicators of poverty in, 22, 23b, 28, 35b
poverty reduction, economic growth, and progressive distribution, 62, 70
subnational dimensions of growth and poverty, 130
transfers and income inequality, 97
household surveys data as indicator of poverty/economic growth, 25b, 25t
human capital
educational divide perpetuating poor's failure to accumulate, 165–166. See also education
policy implications, 194–196
relationship of poverty and accumulation of, 167–169, 168f
underinvestment traps, 169–171
vicious circle of high poverty/low economic growth and, 10–11, 16
Hungary, Latin America/Caribbean compared to, 33, 115

income as indicator of poverty, 20–27
income inequalities
convergence hypothesis, evidence contradicting, 6–7, 7f
demographics and, 33, 35b, 35t
development gap and, 53–56, 54t, 55f
economic growth and, 4t, 57–58, 58f, 69t
heterogeneity between Latin American/Caribbean countries regarding, 54
indicators of, 24–25, 25f
inflation inequality, 26–27b, 26t
in Latin America/Caribbean, 1950–2000, 1, 2f

lognormal function used to measure and express, 64–65, 64b, 64f, 71–72, 72t
mapping Latin American/Caribbean countries in income inequality space, 69t
pro-growth policies and. See pro-poor economic growth policies
reasons for persistence of, 4
spatial/geographic, 129–130, 130f
transfers to address, 4–5, 5f
income risk. See risk/security factors
income transfers. See transfers
indicators of poverty, 20–44
income/consumption levels, 20–27
inflation inequality, 26–27b, 26t
life expectancy, 28, 29t, 41
mobility, 31–33
NA (national accounts) and household surveys-based data, 25b, 25t
nonincome measures, 27–28
risk/security factors, 33–37, 34b, 41–42
self-assessments of, 9, 29–31, 30f
single-moment vs. long-term measures, 31
vicious circle of high poverty/low economic growth formed by, 41
inflation inequality, 26–27b, 26t
informal vs. formal labor markets, earnings differentials in, 148–149, 149f
innovation, poverty as limiting, 121–122
institutional quality
as poverty trap, 107–108
as pro-poor economic growth policy, 88–89, 88f, 89t
intergenerational mobility, 37–40, 38f, 38t, 39f, 42, 157–159
isometric poverty curves, 68f

Jamaica, 21, 22, 23b, 62, 177

Kuznets, Simon, 21, 31, 33, 34b, 35b, 37, 40, 157

labor and earnings differentials, 145–163
complementarities and initial conditions, relevance of, 155–157, 156f
data and methodologies, 152, 160–162
differentials in, different perspectives on mechanisms behind, 146–147
driving factors in, 151–152, 152t
education
effects of level of, 147–148, 151, 154, 155, 159
unmeasured skills, effects of, 185–190, 187–189f
El Salvador case study, 152–159, 153–154t, 156f, 157t, 158f
formal vs. informal labor markets, 148–149, 149f
gender gap, 148
mobility, 149–150, 151f

policy implications, 159–160
productivity and earnings, relationship between, 147f
race and ethnicity, 148
regional variations, 148, 150
segmentation theory, 146, 159
unmeasured worker skills, effects of, 152, 185–190, 187–189f
vulnerability to and persistence of poverty over time, 157–159, 157t, 158f
liberalization of trade. See trade liberalization
life expectancy
convergence hypothesis applied to, 113–114, 114f
effects of poverty on growth, 121
as indicator of poverty, 28, 29t, 41
subnational dimensions of growth and poverty, 132, 135f
local indicators of spatial association (LISA), 131b
lognormal function used to measure and express income inequalities, 64–65, 64b, 64f, 71–72, 72t
longevity. See life expectancy

market differentials. See labor and earnings differentials
market factors and poverty traps, 106–107, 106f, 107b
measures of poverty. See indicators of poverty
Mexico
development gap, 46, 47, 48, 50, 54
education and human capital in, 168, 171, 172f, 173, 174f, 176f, 183, 194, 195, 196
effects of poverty on growth, 111
financial crisis of 1994, 87
indicators of poverty in, 21, 22, 23b, 26b, 27, 27b, 33, 36–37, 36t, 38
labor and earnings differentials, 148, 150, 151f
NAFTA, effects of, 27, 87, 136
poverty reduction, economic growth, and progressive distribution, 62
subnational dimensions of growth and poverty, 129, 130, 133–135, 134f, 135f, 136, 137, 138, 139, 142t
transfers in, 5, 97
microdeterminants
education. See education
human capital. See human capital
labor and earnings. See labor and earnings differentials
vicious circle of high poverty/low economic growth at household level
poverty traps, 3f, 9–11, 10f
reversal strategies, 16–18
migration as equilibrating mechanism on subnational inequalities, 138–139, 150

Millennium Development Goals, 16, 23b, 28, 195
Mirrlees, efficiency wage hypothesis of, 32b
mobility
    indicators of poverty, 31–33
    intergenerational, 37–40, 38f, 38t, 39f, 42, 157–159
    labor and earnings differentials, 149–150, 151f
    poverty traps and, 32–33, 32b, 32t
    risk/security factors, 33–37, 41–42, 122–123, 123t
mortality. *See* life expectancy

NAFTA (North American Free Trade Agreement), 27, 87, 136
national accounts (NA) data as indicator of poverty/economic growth, 25b
New Economic Geography literature, 8, 15, 135, 136b, 137, 142
Nicaragua
    country income—level of, 104
    education and human capital in, 168, 172f, 173, 175f, 176, 183, 186, 189, 191, 193
    effects of poverty on growth, 109, 111
    indicators of poverty in, 22, 23b, 35b, 38
    poverty reduction, economic growth, and progressive distribution, 62, 63, 70
    transfers and income inequality, 99
nonincome welfare measures
    convergence hypothesis applicable to, 113–114, 114f
    as indicators of poverty, 27–28
    of subnational dimensions of growth and poverty, 132, 135f
North American Free Trade Agreement (NAFTA), 27, 87, 136

OECD countries, Latin America/Caribbean relative to
    development gap, 45–46
    effects of poverty on growth, 108f, 109
    labor and earnings differentials, 148
    poverty reduction, economic growth, and progressive distribution, 50–53, 55f, 56
    pro-poor economic growth policies, 93–95, 94t, 95f
    public investment policies and subnational dimensions of growth and poverty, 142
    vicious circle of high poverty/low economic growth, 1, 2f, 4, 5f, 18f

Panama, 62, 70
Paraguay
    effects of poverty on growth, 107
    indicators of poverty in, 23b, 25b, 38
    poverty reduction, economic growth, and progressive distribution, 62, 70
    subnational dimensions of growth and poverty, 130
    transfers and income inequality, 95, 96

parametric analysis of poverty reduction, economic growth, and progressive distribution, 59, 63–64, 68
permanent-transitory income hypothesis, 157
Peru
    development gap, 47, 48
    education and human capital in, 168, 173, 178, 179f, 183, 186, 194
    indicators of poverty in, 22, 23b, 26b, 27b, 28, 38
    labor and earnings differentials, 148, 151, 152t
    poverty reduction, economic growth, and progressive distribution, 62, 70
    pro-poor economic growth policies, 80
    subnational dimensions of growth and poverty, 130, 137, 138
    transfers and income inequality, 97
policy implications
    education and human capital, 194–196
    growth policies aimed at poverty reduction. *See* pro-poor economic growth policies
    labor and earnings differentials, 159–160
    public investment, 142
    subnational dimensions of growth and poverty, 139–142
    trade liberalization. *See* trade liberalization
    vicious circle of high poverty/low economic growth, 13–15
poverty
    defining, 23b
    density vs. rates, 139–141, 140t, 141f
    education/human capital accumulation and, 167–169, 168f
    effects on growth. *See* effects of poverty on growth
    elasticities of
        poverty reduction, economic growth, and progressive distribution, 65–66, 65b, 66t
        pro-poor economic growth policies, 86t
    indicators of. *See* indicators of poverty
    low economic growth and. *See* vicious circle of high poverty/low economic growth
    multidimensional aspects, 1–2
    rates in Latin America/Caribbean, 1950–2000, 1, 2f, 20–24, 21f, 21t, 24f
    subnational dimensions. *See* subnational dimensions of growth and poverty
poverty line, 23b, 63
poverty reduction, economic growth, and progressive distribution, 57–73
    alternative growth scenarios, 68–69, 68t
    choice of poverty line, significance of, 63
    country-specific considerations, 63–70
    elasticities of poverty, 65–66, 65b, 66t
    empirical and theoretical quintiles, 66–68, 67f
    importance of economic growth, 57, 58f
    importance of redistribution measures, 57, 58f
    income inequality reduction not strongly linked to economic growth, 57–58, 58f

    isometric poverty curves, 68f
    lognormal function used to measure and express income inequalities, 64–65, 64b, 64f, 71–72, 72t
    mapping Latin American/Caribbean countries in income inequality space, 69t
    parametric analysis, use of, 59, 63–64, 68
    relative importance of growth vs. redistribution, 58–63, 62f, 63f
    variance decomposition approach, 60b, 60f, 61t
poverty traps
    convergence clubs and, 110–114, 110f, 111t, 112–114f
    development process from point of view of, 104–106, 105f
    as divergent mobility, 32–33, 32b, 32t
    dynamics leading to, 32b, 32t
    empirical evidence of, 108–110, 108f, 109t
    formal testing for, 114–115
    at household level, 3f, 9–11, 10f
    human capital underinvestment, 169–171
    increasing returns to scale, 105f, 106
    institutional mechanisms and, 107–108
    investment rates and, 118
    market factors, 106–107, 106f, 107b
PPP (Purchasing Power Parity), 21, 23b
pro-poor economic growth policies, 75–102
    complementarities and nonlinearities between growth and poverty, 86–89
    conflicts and trade-offs between growth and poverty, 83–86, 85t, 86t, 139
    education, 87–88, 88f
    financial development, effects of, 78–80, 79t
    institutional quality, 88–89, 88f, 89t
    pro-growth policies that fail to reduce, or increase, poverty, 75–76, 76f
    sectoral distinctions, 89–92, 89f, 90f, 91f, 91t
    simulating impact of, 100–102
    simultaneous impact of policies on growth and income inequalities, 76–78, 77t
    size of government and public spending, 81–83, 84f
    trade liberalization, 80–81
    transfers, role of, 92–100
        low impact of current Latin American/Caribbean regimes, 95–97, 95f, 96b, 96t, 99f
        simulating effective redistributive packages, 97–102, 100f, 100t
progressive distributional changes. *See* transfers
public spending and size of government, effects of, 81–83, 84f
Purchasing Power Parity (PPP), 21, 23b

race and ethnicity
    education, variation in returns on, 184–185, 185f
    labor and earnings differentials, 148
redistribution of income. *See* transfers

regional dimensions of growth and poverty. *See*
    subnational dimensions of growth and
    poverty
República Bolivariana de Venezuela. *See*
    Venezuela, República Bolivariana de
risk/security factors
    effects of poverty on growth, 122–123, 123*t*
    mobility and, 33–37, 41–42, 122–123, 123*t*
    poverty measures and, 33–37, 34*b*, 41–42
    trade policy and, 82*b*, 82*t*
rural areas
    education, variation in returns on, 184–185, 184*f*
    mobility, labor, and earnings differentials, 150
    pro-poor economic growth policies, sectoral
        factors in, 89–92, 89*f*, 90*f*
    subnational dimensions of growth and poverty,
        141*b*
Russia, Latin America/Caribbean compared to,
    24, 33, 48, 108.115
Russian financial crisis of 1998, 24, 48, 108

sectoral distinctions in pro-poor economic growth
    policies, 89–92, 89*f*, 90*f*, 91*f*, 91*t*
security. *See* risk/security factors
segmentation of labor market, 146, 159. *See also*
    labor and earnings differentials
self-assessments of poverty, 9, 29–31, 30*f*
Sen, Amartya, 21, 27, 29, 31
size of government and public spending, effects
    of, 81–83, 84*f*
social indicators. *See* nonincome welfare measures
social security systems. *See* transfers
Spain and peripheral Europe, Latin
    America/Caribbean relative to
    development gap, 46
    poverty reduction, economic growth, and pro-
        gressive distribution, 50–53, 55*f*
    pro-poor economic growth policies, 93, 94*t*
    subnational dimensions of growth and poverty,
        139, 140*b*
    vicious circle of high poverty/low economic
        growth, 1, 2*f*, 4, 5*f*
St. Lucia, 69, 70
Stiglitz, efficiency wage hypothesis of, 32*b*
subnational dimensions of growth and poverty,
    129–144
    Brazil case study, 131–133, 132*f*, 133*f*, 135*f*
    Chile case study, 133, 134*f*
    conflicts and trade-offs between growth and
        poverty, 139
    evidence for, 8–9, 9*f*
    identifying spatial concentrations, 130–131,
        131*b*

labor and earnings differentials, 148, 150
Mexico case study, 133–135, 134*f*, 135*f*
migration as equilibrating mechanism,
    138–139
nonincome welfare measures, 132, 135*f*
policy implications of, 139–142
poverty rates vs. poverty density, 139–141,
    140*t*, 141*f*
public investment policies, 142*t*
reasons for, 135–138
special/geographic inequalities, 129–130, 130*f*
trade liberalization, effects of, 136

taxes, redistributive. *See* transfers
Theil index, 34*b*
trade liberalization
    effect on poor of, 27
    as pro-poor economic growth policy, 80–81
    risk factors, 82*b*, 82*t*
    subnational inequalities and, 136
transfers
    income inequalities addressed via, 4–5, 5*f*
    low impact of Latin American/Caribbean
        regimes, 95–97, 95*f*, 96*b*, 96*t*, 99*f*
    as poverty reduction strategy. *See* poverty
        reduction, economic growth, and
        progressive distribution
    pro-poor economic growth policies and,
        92–100
    role in reducing income inequality, 92–95, 92*f*
    simulating effective redistributive packages,
        97–102, 100*f*, 100*t*
    subnational areas with low poverty rates and
        high poverty densities, 139
Trinidad and Tobago, 69, 70

United Nations Millennium Development Goals,
    16, 23*b*, 28, 195
United States. *See* OECD countries, Latin
    America/Caribbean relative to
urban areas
    education, variation in returns on, 184–185,
        184*f*
    mobility, labor, and earnings differentials, 150
    pro-poor economic growth policies, sectoral
        factors in, 89–92, 89*f*, 90*f*
Uruguay
    development gap, 47, 48, 54
    education and human capital in, 177
    effects of poverty on growth, 111
    indicators of poverty in, 22, 38
    poverty reduction, economic growth, and pro-
        gressive distribution, 63, 69, 70

variance decomposition approach
    indicators of poverty, 34*f*, 42
    labor and earnings differentials, 149, 151,
        152*t*, 161, 162
    poverty reduction, economic growth, and
        progressive distribution, 59–63, 60*b*,
        60*f*, 61*t*
    spatial inequality and subnational dimensions
        of growth and poverty, 129
Venezuela, República Bolivariana de
    development gap, 47, 48, 50, 54
    indicators of poverty in, 22, 33
    poverty reduction, economic growth, and pro-
        gressive distribution, 62, 69, 70
    subnational dimensions of growth and
        poverty, 130
vicious circle of high poverty/low economic
    growth, 1–19
    convergence
        global convergence clubs, evidence contra-
            dicting, 6–7, 7*f*
        regional convergence clubs, evidence of,
            8–9, 9*f*
    education and, 3*f*, 10–11, 10*f*, 16–17
    effects of growth on poverty levels, 4–5
    effects of poverty levels on growth, 5–6
    evidence of, 7–8, 8*f*
    funding reversal mechanisms, 18–19, 18*f*
    at household level
        poverty traps, 3*f*, 9–11, 10*f*
        reversal strategies, 16–18
    human capital and, 10–11, 16
    indicators of poverty forming, 41
    multidimensional aspects of poverty, 1–2
    policy implications of, 13–15
    pro-growth poverty reduction to transform,
        15–19
    reasons for persistence of, 2–4
    spatial concerns and reversal strategies, 15–16
    strategic implications of, 11–13
    transfers addressing, 4–5, 5*f*

welfare payments. *See* transfers
World Bank
    Latin American region flagship publications
        (de Ferranti and others)
        2000, 2, 33, 122
        2002, 13
        2003, 10, 17, 80, 87, 88, 107, 120, 138,
            165, 166, 167, 170, 181, 195
        2004, 3, 13, 24, 45, 53, 78, 126
        2005, 13, 14, 15, 75, 90, 92, 129, 149, 150
    poverty line used by, 23*b*